Accounting
Text and Cases

The Financial Accounting Chapters
Thirteenth Edition

Accounting
Text and Cases

The Financial Accounting Chapters
Thirteenth Edition

Robert N. Anthony
Ross G. Walker Professor Emeritus
Graduate School of Business Administration Harvard University

David F. Hawkins
Lovett-Learned Professor of Business Administration
Graduate School of Business Administration Harvard University

Kenneth A. Merchant
Deloitte & Touche LLP Chair of Accountancy Leventhal School of Accounting
University of Southern California

Prakash Singh
Professor
IIM, Lucknow

McGraw Hill Education (India) Private Limited

Published by McGraw Hill Education (India) Private Limited
444/1, Sri Ekambara Naicker Industrial Estate, Alapakkam, Porur, Chennai - 600 116

Indian Adaptation done by arrangement with The McGraw-Hill Companies, Inc., New York

Accounting: Text and Cases, 13e

Print Edition:
ISBN (13): 978-93-89538-31-1
ISBN (10): 93-89538-31-9

E-Book Edition:
ISBN (13): 978-93-89538-32-8
ISBN (10): 93-89538-32-7

1 2 3 4 5 6 7 8 9   7099198   23 22 21 20 19

Printed and bound in India.

Managing Director: *Lalit Singh*

Senior Portfolio Manager: *Nikhil Wadhera*
Portfolio Manager: *Shivkant Singhal*

Senior Manager—Content Development & Production Services: *Shalini Jha*
Senior Content Developer: *Vaishali Thapliyal*

Head—Production Services: *Satinder S Baveja*
Senior Manager—Production Services: *Piyaray Pandita*

General Manager—Production: *Rajender P Ghansela*
Senior Manager—Production: *Reji Kumar*

Typeset at B2K Infotech Pvt. Ltd., No 34, 3rd Floor, AMN Towers, NSR Road, Saibaba colony, Coimbatore - 641011 and printed at Rajkamal Electric Press, Plot No. 2, Phase-IV, Kundli, Haryana.

Cover Image Source: Shutterstock/hovstik

Cover Designer: Kapil Gupta

Cover Printer: Rajkamal Electric Press

RBAYCDDTDDCLR

Visit us at: www.mheducation.co.in
Write to us at: info.india@mheducation.com
CIN: U80302TN2010PTC111532
Toll Free Number: 1800 103 5875

About the Authors

Robert N. Anthony *Harvard University*

Robert N. Anthony was the Ross Graham Walker Professor of Management Control Emeritus at Harvard Business School. Dr. Anthony joined the Harvard Business School staff in 1940 and, except for leaves of absence, was on its faculty until his retirement. From 1965 to 1968, he was Assistant Secretary of Defense, Controller, under the direction of Secretary Robert S. McNamara, responsible for preparing and defending the Department of Defense budgets. In World War II he was an officer in the Navy Supply Corps, with the final rank of Lt. Commander USNR.

He authored or co-authored of 27 books, with more than two million copies in print. These books have been translated into 13 languages. Aside from *Accounting: Text and Cases,* which was the first text and case book that discussed management accounting separately from financial accounting, his *Management Control Systems,* now in its twelfth edition (with Govindarajan), and his *Management Control in Nonprofit Organizations,* now in its seventh edition (with David Young), were the first text and case books on their respective subjects. His *Essentials of Accounting,* now in its tenth edition (with Leslie Breitner) is the most widely used programmed text on accounting. Dr. Anthony also authored a trade book called *Rethinking the Rules of Financial Accounting* and gave lectures or short courses in many American, as well as international, universities.

Dr. Anthony was a director of Warnaco, Inc., and Carborundum Company, both Fortune 500 companies, and a consultant to a number of other companies, including American Telephone & Telegraph Company; General Mills, Inc.; General Motors Corporation; and Union Pacific Railroad. He also served on committees of, or as a consultant to, many federal, state, and municipal government agencies.

For more than 25 years, he was a trustee of Colby College; he was the chairman of its budget and finance committee and its audit committee, and chairman of the Board of Trustees in 1978–1983.

Dr. Anthony was awarded honorary M.A. and L.H.D. degrees and the Marriner Distinguished Service Award from Colby College. In 1986 he was elected the 46th member of the Accounting Hall of Fame. Among his other awards were the Distinguished Accounting Educator award from the American Accounting Association, Accounting Educator of the Year Award from Beta Alpha Psi (the national accounting fraternity), Meritorious Service Award from the Executive Office of the President, Fellow of the Academy of Management, Distinguished Public Service Medal of the U.S. Department of Defense, Distinguished Leadership Award of the Federal Government Accountants Association, CINCPAC Letter of Commendation, and several awards for books and articles.

Professor Anthony also received the Institute of Management Accountants' prestigious R. Lee Brummet award. This award is given to recognize outstanding educators in the field of Management Accounting who have had a significant impact on academia and the business world.

David F. Hawkins *Harvard University*

David Hawkins has been a member of the Harvard Business School faculty since 1962. Currently, he is the Lovett-Learned Professor of Business Administration. Professor Hawkins has taught the second-year MBA courses Analysis of Corporate Financial Reports, Corporate Financial Reporting: A Global Perspective, and Managing Foreign Operations, as well as the first-year MBA course Financial Reporting and Control. He is the author of over 200 Harvard Business School cases. Professor Hawkins has acted as a consultant to numerous corporations including General Electric, Coca-Cola, Merrill Lynch, DuPont, American Express, and Honeywell. He also has been a member of the Financial Accounting Standards Advisory Committee and several Financial Accounting Standards Board Task Forces. Professor Hawkins received his Bachelor's, Master's, and doctorate degrees from Harvard University.

Professor Hawkins' research interests include the formulation of corporate financial reporting strategies, the role of earnings quality in equity security valuations, the harmonization of global financial reporting standards, and the management of corporations during periods of high inflation. For his research work, Professor Hawkins has received the *Business History Review's* Newcomen Society Award, the *California Management Review's* McKinsey Award, and the *Financial Analyst Journal's* Graham and Dodd Scroll. He has been selected as a member of the *Institutional Investor's* All American Research Team.

Professor Hawkins has published individually and with co-authors 16 books and monographs including *Computer Models for Business Case Analysis* (with Brandt Allen); *Corporate Financial Reporting: Text and Cases; Equity Valuation Models, Analysis and Valuation* (with Walter J. Campbell); *Accounting for Leases by Lessees* (with Mary Wehle); *Rating Industrial Bonds* (with Barbara A. Brown and Walter J. Campbell); *Corporate Financial Disclosure: 1900–1933; The Effectiveness of the Annual Report as a Communications Vehicle* (with Barbara A. Hawkins); and *Corporate Financial Reporting and Analysis.* In addition, he has published numerous articles and other materials directed at corporate managers, accounting standard setters, and institutional investors, and contributed to over 25 books published by others.

Kenneth A. Merchant *University of Southern California*

Kenneth A. Merchant is the current holder of the Deloitte & Touche LLP Chair of Accountancy at the University of Southern California. He teaches in USC's executive, masters, and undergraduate programs. Previously he served as Senior Associate Dean–Corporate Programs in USC's Marshall School of Business (2003–2004) and as Dean of USC's Leventhal School of Accounting (1994–2001). Professor Merchant is also a research professor (part-time) at the University of Maastricht (the Netherlands). Before joining USC in 1990, he taught at Harvard University (1978–1990) and the University of California (Berkeley) (1976–1977).

Earlier in his career, Professor Merchant was a department controller at Texas Instruments, Inc., and a senior consultant with Ernst & Ernst (now Ernst & Young). He has also worked as a freelance consultant/teacher for many organizations, including Amgen, Arco, AT&T, British Airways, Campbell Soup, Digital Equipment, IBM, McGraw-Hill, Novellus Systems, Occidental Petroleum, Philip Morris International, Tektronix, Toyota U.S.A., and World Bank. He has served on the boards of directors of four corporations.

Professor Merchant's current research projects are focused on various issues related to the design and effects of performance measurement/evaluation/incentive systems and corporate governance systems. He has published nine books and numerous journal articles and teaching cases. Professor Merchant won the American Accounting Association's (AAA's) awards for Notable Contributions to both the Behavioral Accounting (2003) and Management Accounting Literatures (1991 and 2007), the AAA Outstanding Service Award (2003), the Institute of Management Accountants' Lybrand Gold Medal Award (best paper of the year published in *Management Accounting)* (1989–90) and James Bulloch award for Innovations in Management Accounting Education (2009). He is currently a member of the editorial boards of 11 academic journals.

Professor Merchant has served as president of three AAA sections: Accounting Program Leadership Group; Management Accounting; and Accounting, Behavior and Organizations. He is a current member of the Business and Industry Executive Committee of the American Institute of Certified Public Accountants (AICPA), the Research Board of the Chartered Institute of Management Account (UK), and the Research Committee of the Financial Executive Research Foundation.

Professor Merchant is a graduate of Union College (BA), Columbia University (MBA), and the University of California–Berkeley (PhD) and is a Certified Public Accountant (Texas).

Prakash Singh *Indian Institute of Management*

Prakash Singh is a Professor of Finance and Accounting at the Indian Institute of Management, Lucknow, since 2006. He did his PhD from Birla Institute of Technology and Science, Pilani in 2004. A Mechanical Engineering graduate from HBTI, Kanpur (1993-1994), Dr. Prakash has also done his Master's in Business Administration (1997) with specialization in Finance from Department of Management Studies, Lucknow University. Besides teaching, he has also worked with Escorts Yamaha Motors Ltd., and Kotak Mahindra Primus Ltd. Put together, he has more than 20 years of work experience in industry and teaching. Dr. Prakash teaches courses related to Financial Reporting and Analysis, Management Accounting, Commercial Banking, Risk Management in Financial Institutions, Financing and Valuation of Startups at IIM Lucknow. His research and consulting interests are in the field of Corporate Restructuring, Valuation of Private Enterprises, and Funding of Startups.

Preface

An accounting text can be written with an emphasis on either of the two viewpoints: (1) what the user of accounting information needs to know about accounting or (2) what the preparer of accounting reports needs to know about accounting. This book focuses on the user of accounting information. Because such a person needs to know enough about the preparation of accounting reports to use them intelligently, this text includes the technical material needed for this purpose. The book is aimed primarily, however, at the person who wants to be a knowledgeable user of accounting information. This focus is reinforced in the book's case studies, which help the student learn that accounting is not a cut-and-dried subject with all of its "answers" clearly indicated by the application of rules.

The focus of the book makes it particularly appropriate for required core courses in accounting, in which many of the students are not planning to take further elective accounting courses. We believe that if a core course stresses the more analytical uses of accounting information by managers and outside analysts rather than the procedural details that the practicing accountant needs to know, then those students who do not take further accounting courses will be left with a positive view of the importance of accounting rather than with the negative "bean counter" stereotype. We also feel that a user orientation in the core course actually is likely to generate a greater number of accounting majors from the class than if the course is oriented more toward the person who has already decided to major in accounting. Similarly, in our experience the required accounting module in a management development program will generate little participant interest unless the module is oriented toward the nonaccountant user of accounting information. In sum, we think the book conveys the fact that accounting is interesting and fun, not dull and tedious.

Specifically, this book is used in at least the following four ways:

1. As an introductory course where most (if not all) of the students have no prior training in accounting. In many schools this introduction comprises two separate courses, one dealing with financial accounting and the other with management accounting. This book is apt for management accounting. It is used in such introductory courses both at the upper undergraduate level and in graduate programs. In addition to its widespread use in schools of business and management, it is also used in introductory accounting courses in some law schools, education schools, and schools of public health.
2. As an elective course that builds on a required introductory course in accounting—particularly where the introductory course had more of a procedural orientation and the elective is intended to be more conceptual, analytical, and user-oriented.
3. As the accounting module in a management development program where the participants represent a variety of functional and technical backgrounds.
4. As a non-technical accounting reference book for non-accountants in business and other organizations.

THE CASES

As in previous editions, the cases have been selected because of their interest and educational value as a basis for class discussion. They are not necessarily intended to illustrate either correct or incorrect handling of management problems. Skill in the management use of accounting information can be acquired, we believe, only through experience. Thinking about a case and discussing it in informal discussion groups and in the classroom require the student to do something—to analyze a problem, to weigh various factors involved in it, to make some calculations, to take a position, and so on. In class the student is required to explain her or his point of view, to defend it, to understand and appraise the arguments of colleagues, and to decide what arguments are the strongest. Practice in doing these things helps to increase skill and understanding; in fact, many educators believe that the really important parts of a subject can be learned only by experience of some sort, as opposed to merely hearing or reading about them. Thus, although the case material constitutes less than half the pages in this book, the discussion of these cases is by far the most important part of the educational process. Of course, such discussions contribute to the students' communication skills as well as to their understanding of accounting.

This edition has a total of 67 cases, 11 of which are new. It is often difficult to judge when to replace an older time-tested case (a "classic" or an "old chestnut") with which instructors are comfortable with a case of more recent vintage. Each type of case has its advantages. In making changes, we endeavored to strike a balance. We retained some of the best, and most frequently used, older cases while replacing others with some new cases. We hope that these newer cases will become the next generation of classics.

Occasionally, a student or instructor questions our use of small business settings for many of the cases. Such cases often avoid certain complexities at a point when the student is not yet prepared to deal with them. We would also note that studies have reported that small businesses (those employing fewer than 500 people) represent over 99 percent of all U.S. businesses, provide about 50 percent of all private-sector jobs, generate almost 40 percent of the GNP, and contribute two out of three newly created jobs. We therefore feel that exposure to small business cases is beneficial to students, some of whom will one day own a small business while many others will eventually work in such firms or work with them as auditors or consultants. A number of the cases included in the book are copyrighted by the President and Fellows of Harvard College. They are included by express permission. These cases, along with all of the other cases in the book, have been developed solely for class discussion and do not necessarily illustrate effective or ineffective management.

CHANGES IN THE THIRTEENTH EDITION

The adaptation is done keeping largely two things in mind:

1. Changes in Accounting Standards and difference in Indian Accounting Standards from IFRS, etc.
2. Contemporary issues which are redefining Accounting Landscape

In the first few chapters, section on Quality of Financial Reporting and Corporate Governance is added and that how markets are increasingly looking out for such factors over and above the regular financial Statements. Relevant and holistic view of looking at an organization from the view of stakeholders is also covered. Why are firms reporting extensively on CSR, Governance, and Sustainability? Firms are realizing that they can't just focus on profits and that they need to take along others also, be it society or climate and environment.

Talking about Balance Sheets and P&L, look at new generation enterprises (disruptive business models), which are becoming more and more asset light, and where the firm's valuation is driven more by intangibles (which are not even recorded on Balance Sheet). Profit may no longer be a key value driver of a firm but the kind of people you hire is definitely a value driver. Issues which have become more relevant like "treatment of discount coupons" are also included, "revisit capitalization vs expense debate", arm's length vs related party transactions, Dual class shares, Bond markets, superiority of EBITDA over PAT. Most of these topics are presented through a Caselet or through examples of real corporate events.

ACKNOWLEDGMENTS

We are grateful to many instructors and students who have made suggestions for improving this book. Included among those people are our colleagues at the Harvard Business School and the Marshall School of Business, University of Southern California, as well as the following: Russ Olive, Massachusetts Institute of Technology; Pamela Stuerke, Case Western Reserve University; Marvin Carlson, Southern Methodist University; Alan Lord, Bowling Green State University; and Marc Manalastas, Mary Victoria D. Arce, and Jon Stuart Lim-Vaña, Ateneo de Manila University, the Philippines. We extend our thanks to the reviewers who commented on the twelfth edition, as well as previous editions: Timothy Moffit, Kalamazoo College; Michael Erler and Richard Rogers, Indiana University; Laurie Pant, Suffolk University; Claude Lanfranconi, Richard Ivey School of Business; Thomas Kam and Warren Wee, Hawaii Pacific University; Len Weld, Troy State University; Mehmet Kocaculah, University of Southern Indiana; Byron K. Henry, Howard University; Jeffery Kahn, Woodbury University; Pamela Rouse, Butler University; Linda Brown, Saint Ambrose University; Ann L. Watkins, High Point University; Saad Laraqui, Embry-Riddle Aeronautical University; Noel Addy, Mississippi State University; Philip Darcy, Regis University; Frances Lynn Telavera, National University; Patricia Cummins, Troy State University; Reba Cunningham, University of Dallas; Krishagopal Menon, Boston University; Leonardo Rodriguez, Florida International University; Robert Medden, St. Francis Xavier University; William S. Hopwood, Florida Atlantic University; Andrew Felo, Pennsylvania State University; David Hurtt and Jack Ruhl, Western Michigan University; Stan Davis, Wake Forest University; Tom Hrubec, Franklin University; and Warren Wee, Hawaii Pacific University.

We also would like to thank Beth Woods, Lisa Enfinger, Helen Roybark, and Alice Sineath for their help in accuracy checking the text and Thomas Hrubec of Franklin University for creating PowerPoint® presentations to accompany the text.

Robert N. Anthony
David F. Hawkins
Kenneth A. Merchant

I am also thankful to the following reviewers for their valuable suggestions and comments:

Neerav Nagar   *Indian Institute of Management, Ahmedabad*

Sandeep Goyal   *Management Development Institute, Gurgaon*

Sowmya Subramaniam   *Indian Institute of Management, Lucknow*

S Veena Iyer   *Management Development Institute, Gurgaon*

Meena Sharma   *Vivekanand Institute of Management Studies and Research, Mumbai*

Pinky Agarwal   *ITM Business School, Mumbai*

Prakash Singh
Lucknow

Publisher's Note

McGraw Hill Education (India) invites suggestions and comments from you, all of which can be sent to ***info.india@mheducation.com*** (Kindly mention the title and author name in the subject line). **Piracy-related issues may also be reported.**

Brief Contents

Contents

Chapter 3

Basic Accounting Concepts: The Income Statement   54

Chapter 4

Accounting Records and Systems   86

Chapter 5

Revenue and Monetary Assets   114

Chapter 6

Cost of Sales and Inventories   150

Chapter 7

Long-Lived Nonmonetary Assets and Their Amortization   183

Index and Source of Cases

The cases included in this book are listed below in alphabetical order, together with their authors' names and the institution with which each author was affiliated at the time the case was written. Cases with no name shown were written by, or under the supervision of, one of the authors of this book. The copyright on all cases is indicated on the first page of each case. No case may be reproduced in any form or by any means without the permission of its copyright holder. Information on requesting permission to reproduce Harvard Business School cases is included on the copyright page of this book. We regret that we are unable to provide permission information for cases not copyrighted by Harvard.

The Nature and Purpose of Accounting

Most of the world's work is done through organizations—groups of people who work together to accomplish one or more objectives. In doing its work, an organization uses resources—labor, materials, various services, buildings, and equipment. These resources need to be financed, or paid for. To work effectively, the people in an organization need information about the amounts of these resources, the means of financing them, and the results achieved through using them. Parties outside the organization need similar information to make judgments about the organization. **Accounting** is a system that provides such information.

Organizations can be classified broadly as either for-profit or nonprofit. As these names suggest, a dominant purpose of organizations in the former category is to earn a profit, whereas organizations in the latter category have other objectives, such as governing, providing social services, and providing education. Accounting is basically similar in both types of organizations.

The Need for Information

In its details, information differs greatly among organizations of various types. But viewed broadly, the information needs of most organizations are similar. We shall out-line and illustrate these general information needs by referring to Varsity Motors, Inc., an automobile dealership.

Varsity Motors seeks to earn a profit by selling new and used automobiles and parts and accessories, and by providing repair service. It is an organization of 52 people headed by Pat Voss, its president. It owns a building that contains the showroom, service shop, a storeroom for parts and accessories, and office space. It also owns a number of new and used automobiles, which it offers for sale; an inventory of spare parts, accessories, and supplies; and cash in the bank. These are examples of the resources the company needs to conduct its business.

Illustration 1–1 depicts the different types of information that might be useful to people interested in Varsity Motors. As shown in the illustration, information can be either quantitative or nonquantitative. Quantitative information is information that is expressed in numbers. Examples of nonquantitative information are visual impressions,

**ILLUSTRATION
1–1**
**Types of
Information**

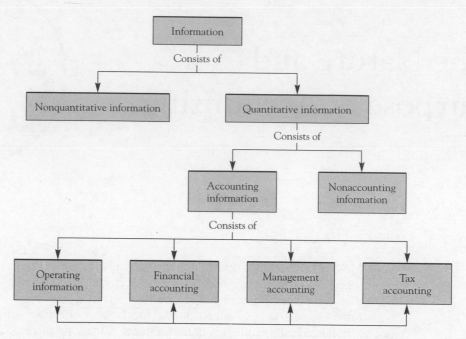

conversations, television programs, and newspaper stories. Accounting is primarily concerned with quantitative information.

Accounting is one of several types of quantitative information. Accounting information is distinguished from the other types in that it usually is expressed in *monetary* terms. Data on employees' ages and years of experience are quantitative, but they are not usually considered to be accounting information. The line here is not sharply drawn, however; nonmonetary information is often included in the notes to accounting reports when it will help the reader understand the report. For example, an accounting sales report for Varsity Motors would show not only the monetary amount of sales revenue, but also the number of automobiles sold, which is nonmonetary information.

What information is needed about the amounts and financing of the resources used in Varsity Motors and the results achieved by the use of these resources? This information can be classified into four categories: (1) operating information, (2) financial accounting information, (3) management accounting information, and (4) tax accounting information. Each is shown in the bottom section of Illustration 1–1.

Operating Information

A considerable amount of **operating information** is required to conduct an organization's day-to-day activities. For example, Varsity Motors' employees must be paid exactly the amounts owed them, and the government requires that records be maintained for each employee showing amounts earned and paid, as well as various deductions. The sales force needs to know what automobiles are available for sale and each one's cost and selling price. When an automobile is sold, a record must be made of that fact. The person in the stockroom needs to know what parts and accessories are on hand; and if the inventory of a certain part becomes depleted, this fact needs to be known so that an additional quantity can be ordered. Amounts owed by the company's customers need to be known; and if a customer does not pay a bill on time, this fact needs to be known so that appropriate action can be taken. The company needs to know the amounts it owes to others, when these amounts should be paid, and how much money it has in the bank.

Operating information constitutes by far the largest quantity of accounting information. As suggested by the arrows at the bottom of Illustration 1–1, operating information provides much of the basic data for management accounting, financial accounting, and tax accounting.

Financial Accounting Information

Financial accounting information is intended both for managers and also for the use of parties external to the organization, including shareholders (and trustees in nonprofit organizations), banks and other creditors, government agencies, investment advisers, and the general public. Shareholders who have furnished capital to Varsity Motors want information on how well the company is doing. If they should decide to sell their shares, they need information that helps them judge how much their investment is worth. Prospective buyers of these shares need similar information. If the company wants to borrow money, the lender wants information that will show that the company is sound and that there is a high probability that the loan will be repaid.

Only in rare instances can outside parties insist that an organization furnish information tailor-made to their specifications. In most cases, they must accept the information that the organization chooses to supply. They could not conceivably understand this information without knowing the ground rules that governed its preparation. Moreover, they cannot be expected to learn a new set of ground rules for each organization of interest to them, nor can they compare information about two organizations unless both sets of information are prepared according to common ground rules. These ground rules are the subject matter of financial accounting (also called **financial reporting**).

Management Accounting Information

Varsity Motors' president, vice president of sales, service manager, and other managers do not have the time to examine the details of the operating information. Instead, they rely on summaries of this information. They use these summaries, together with other information, to carry out their management responsibilities. The accounting information specifically prepared to aid managers is called **management accounting information**. This information is used in three management functions: (1) planning, (2) implementation, and (3) control.

Planning

Performed by managers at all levels, in all organizations, **planning** is the process of deciding what actions should be taken in the future. A plan may be made for any segment of the organization or for the entire organization. When Varsity Motors' service manager decides the order in which automobiles will be repaired and which mechanic will work on each of them, the service manager is engaged in planning in the same sense as, but on a smaller scale than, the president when the latter decides to build a new showroom and service facility.

An important form of planning is **budgeting**. Budgeting is the process of planning the overall activities of the organization for a specified period of time, usually a year. A primary objective of budgeting is to *coordinate* the separate plans made for various segments of the organization to ensure that these plans harmonize with one another. For example, Varsity's sales plans and service department capacity plans must be consistent. Also, budgeting helps managers determine whether the coming year's activities are likely to produce satisfactory results and, if not, what should be done. Even tiny organizations find budgeting useful; many persons prepare a budget for their household.

Planning involves making decisions. Decisions are arrived at by (1) recognizing that a problem or an opportunity exists, (2) specifying and ranking the criteria to be used to determine the best solution, (3) identifying alternative ways of addressing the problem or opportunity, (4) analyzing the consequences of each alternative, and (5) comparing these consequences to each other and the decision criteria in order to decide which alternative is best. Accounting information is useful especially in the analysis step of the decision-making process.

Implementation

Making plans does not itself ensure that managers will implement the plans. In the case of the annual budget, each manager must take actions to provide the human and other resources that will be needed to achieve the planned results. Each manager also must make more detailed implementation plans than are encompassed in the budget; specific actions to be taken on a week-to-week and even day-to-day basis must be planned in advance.

The **implementation** of these very specific plans requires supervision on the part of the manager. Although much of this activity is routine, the manager also must react to events that were not anticipated when the budget was prepared. Indeed, a key managerial responsibility is to change previous plans appropriately to adjust for new conditions. If an unexpected situation impacts more than one part of the organization, the managers affected must coordinate their responses, just as their original plans were coordinated.

Control

In Varsity Motors most automobile sales are made by salespersons and most service work is done by mechanics. It is not the responsibility of Pat Voss and the other managers to do this work themselves. Rather, it is their responsibility to see that it is done, and done properly, by the employees of the organization. The process they use to ensure that employees perform properly is called **control**. Accounting information is used in the control process as a means of communication, motivation, attention getting, and appraisal.

As a means of *communication,* accounting reports (especially budgets) can assist in informing employees about management's plans and in general about the types of action management wishes the organization to take. As a means of *motivation,* accounting reports can induce members of the organization to act in a way that is consistent with the organization's overall goals and objectives. As a means of *attention getting,* accounting information signals that problems may exist that require investigation and possibly action; this process is called **feedback**. As a means of *appraisal,* accounting helps show how well managers of the organization have performed, particularly with respect to the budgeted performance of the departments for which they are responsible. This provides a basis for a salary increase, promotion, corrective action of various kinds, or (in extreme cases) dismissal.

The relationship among the management functions of planning, implementation, and control is shown in Illustration 1–2.

Tax Accounting Information

Varsity Motors must file tax returns with the taxing authorities. As we will see later, in the United States for all companies and increasingly around the world for stock-exchange-listed companies, tax accounting rules can differ from financial accounting rules. Varsity Motors therefore must keep separate **tax accounting** records for tax purposes in those areas where it has elected to use different accounting rules for tax accounting and financial accounting.

ILLUSTRATION 1–2
Relationship of Management Functions

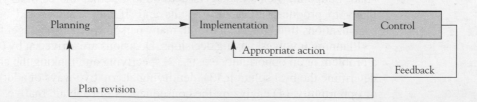

Definition of Accounting

Accounting is related to all of the activities described above, and in all of them the emphasis is on using accounting information in the process of *making decisions*. Both managers within an organization and interested outside parties use accounting information in making decisions that affect the organization. Thus, of the several available definitions of accounting, the one developed by an American Accounting Association committee is perhaps the best because of its focus on accounting as an aid to decision making. This committee defined accounting as *the process of identifying, measuring, and communicating economic information to permit informed judgments and decisions by users of the information.*

The Profession of Accounting

In most organizations the accounting group is the largest staff unit, that is, the largest group other than the "line" activities of production and marketing. The accounting group consists essentially of two types of people: (1) bookkeepers and other data-entry employees who maintain the detailed operating records and (2) staff accountants who decide how items should be reported, prepare the reports, interpret these reports, prepare special analyses, design and operate the systems through which information flows, and ensure that the information is accurate.

All publicly owned companies and many other organizations have their accounting reports audited by an independent public accounting firm. These firms also perform other services for clients. Some of these firms are very large with tens of thousands of employees and hundreds of offices around the world, with annual revenues totaling billions of dollars. They are far larger than any law firm, medical group practice, or other professional firm. At the other extreme, thousands of independent public accountants practice as individuals.

Most independent public accountants are licensed by their state and are designated as Certified Public Accountants (CPAs). The professional organization of CPAs is the American Institute of Certified Public Accountants (AICPA). Many accountants employed by industry belong to the Institute of Management Accountants (IMA). The IMA administers the Certified Management Accountant (CMA) program. Some accountants in industry also are Certified Internal Auditors (CIA). Many college and university accounting faculty members belong to the American Accounting Association (AAA).

CPAs that audit public companies are subject to the oversight of the Securities and Exchange Commission (SEC) and the Public Company Accounting Oversight Board (PCAOB). The SEC was created by the Securities Act of 1934. Its mission is to protect investors; maintain fair, orderly, and efficient securities markets; and facilitate capital formation. PCAOB is a five-person board appointed by the SEC to oversee the auditors of public companies in order to protect the interests of investor and further the public interest in the preparation of informative, fair, and independent audit reports. PCAOB has the power to set auditing standards and discipline auditors who fail to follow their standards.

Although accounting is a staff function performed by accounting professionals within an organization, the ultimate responsibility for the generation of accounting information—whether financial or managerial—rests with *management*. Management's responsibility for accounting is the reason that one of the top officers of many businesses is the **controller**. Within the division of top management's duties, the controller is the person responsible for satisfying other managers' needs for management accounting information and for complying with the requirements of financial reporting and tax accounting. To these ends the controller's office employs accounting professionals in management, financial, and tax accounting. These accountants design, install, and operate the information systems required to generate financial and managerial reports and tax returns.

Our Approach to Accounting

Accounting can be approached from either of two directions: from the viewpoint of the accountant or from the viewpoint of the user of accounting information. The former approach emphasizes the concepts and techniques that are involved in collecting, summarizing, and reporting accounting information; the latter emphasizes what the user needs to know about accounting. We focus on the latter approach. The difference between these two approaches is only one of emphasis. Accountants need to know how information is to be used because they should collect and report information in a form that is most helpful to those who use it. Users need to know what the accountant does; otherwise, they are unlikely to understand the real meaning of the information that is provided.

The approach to accounting taken here is something like that used by an airplane pilot in learning to use flight instruments. The pilot needs to know the meaning of the message conveyed by each of the instruments—for example, that a needle on a certain gauge going above a given point probably means that a certain component is not functioning properly. The word *probably* is used because, for one reason or another, an instrument may not always give the reading that it is supposed to give. As the user of the instrument, the pilot must realize this and also must understand something of the likelihood of, and the reason for, these abnormalities. On the other hand, the pilot does not need to know how to design, construct, calibrate, or repair airplane instruments. Specialists are available for these important functions.

Similarly, those who use accounting information must understand what a given accounting figure probably means, what its limitations are, and the circumstances in which it may mean something different from the apparent "signal" that it gives. They do not, however, need to know how to design, construct, operate, or check on the accuracy of an accounting system. They can rely on accountants for these important functions.

Preconceptions about Accounting

Readers of this book have already been exposed to a great deal of accounting information. Cash register or credit card receipts, checks written or (preferably) received, bank statements, merchants' and utilities' bills—all these are parts of accounting systems. Newspapers report about the profit (or losses) of a company or an industry, about dividends, or about money being spent to build new buildings; this information comes from accounting systems. Even before beginning a formal study of the subject, therefore, the reader has accumulated a number of ideas about accounting.

The trouble is that some of these ideas probably are incorrect. For example, it seems intuitively reasonable that accounting should report what a business is "worth." But accounting does not, in fact, do this, nor does it even attempt to do so. As another example, there is a general notion that the word *asset* refers to valuable things, good things to have. But the skills and abilities of an organization's employees are not assets in the accounting sense, even though they may be a key determinant of the organization's success.

Thus, as with many other subjects, students of accounting must be wary of preconceptions. They will discover that accounting *as it really is* may be different in important respects from what they had surmised it to be. They will find that there are sound reasons for these differences, and it is important that they understand these reasons. To achieve such an understanding, users need to know enough about accounting concepts and techniques to understand the nature and limitations of the accounting information. They do not, however, need the detailed knowledge that the accountant must have.

Plan of the Book

We described above four types of accounting information: operating information, financial accounting information, management accounting information, and tax accounting information. Since our viewpoint is that of the current and potential *users* (as opposed to preparers) of accounting information, we shall not describe operating and tax accounting information in any great detail. The book is therefore divided into two approximately equal parts, the first on financial accounting and the second on management accounting.

The discussion of financial accounting comes first because the structure of financial accounting underlies *all* accounting. This structure consists of a few basic principles and concepts, a set of relationships among the elements comprising the accounting system, a terminology, and a number of rules and guidelines for the application of the principles and concepts to specific situations. We shall describe the financial accounting structure in a general way in Chapters 2, 3, and 4; and we shall then go over the same ground again in more detail in Chapters 5 through 14.

The second half of the book discusses the nature and use of management accounting information. The management of an organization can establish whatever ground rules it wishes for the accounting information collected for its own use. Thus, although the principles of financial accounting are applicable to all organizations, the rules of management accounting are tailor-made to meet the needs of the management of a specific organization.

Nevertheless, a similarity exists in both financial accounting practices and management accounting practices in most organizations. There are obvious economies in using financial accounting information wherever possible for management accounting purposes rather than devising two completely different systems for the two purposes.

The Financial Accounting Framework

Suppose you were asked to keep track of what was going on in an organization in order to provide useful information for management. One way of carrying out this assignment would be to write down a narrative of important events in a log similar to that kept by the captain of a ship.

After some experience with your log, you would gradually develop a set of rules to guide your efforts. For example, since it would be impossible to write down every action of every person in the organization, you would develop rules to guide you in choosing between those events that were important enough to record and those that should be omitted. You also would find that your log would be more valuable if you standardized certain terms. People who studied it would then have a clearer understanding of what you meant. Furthermore, if you standardized terms and their definitions, you could turn the job of keeping the log over to someone else and have some assurance that this person's report of events would convey the same information that you would have conveyed had you been keeping the log yourself.

In devising these rules of keeping a log, you would necessarily be somewhat arbitrary. There might be several ways of describing a certain event, all equally good. But in order to have a common basis of understanding, you would select just one of these for use in your recordkeeping system.

All these considerations were actually involved in the development of the accounting process. Accounting has evolved over a period of many centuries, and during this time certain terminology, rules, and conventions have come to be accepted as useful. If you are to understand accounting reports—the end products of an accounting system—you must be familiar with the rules and conventions lying behind these reports.

Accounting as a Language

Accounting is aptly called the *language of business*. The task of learning accounting, very similar to the task of learning a new language, is complicated by the fact that many words used in accounting mean almost but not quite the same thing as the identical words mean in everyday nonaccounting usage. Accounting is not exactly a foreign language; the problem of learning it is more like that of an American learning to speak English as it is spoken in Great Britain. For example, the grain that Americans call *wheat* is called *corn* by the British; and the British use the word *maize* for what Americans call *corn*. Unless they are careful, Americans will fail to recognize that some words are used in Great Britain in a different sense from that used in America.

Similarly, some words are used in a different sense in accounting from their colloquial meanings. For example, accountants often use the term *net worth* to describe an amount that appears on accounting reports. The commonsense interpretation is that this amount refers to what something is worth, what its value is. However, such an interpretation is incorrect, and misunderstandings can arise if the user of an accounting statement does not understand what accountants mean by net worth. (The correct meaning, somewhat technical in nature, will be given in Chapter 2.)

Accounting also resembles a language in that some of its rules are definite, whereas others are not. There are differences of opinion among accountants about how a given event should be reported, just as grammarians differ on many matters of sentence structure, punctuation, and word choice. Nevertheless, just as many practices are clearly poor English, many practices are definitely poor accounting. In the following chapters we describe the elements of good accounting and indicate areas in which there are differences of opinion about what constitutes good practice.

Finally, languages evolve in response to the changing needs of society, and so does accounting. The rules described here are currently in use, but some of them will probably be modified to meet the changing needs of organizations and their constituencies.

Different Formats

The communication and understanding of accounting information may be further complicated by the use of different financial statement presentation formats. As far as financial reporting data are concerned, the statement user problems caused by presentational difference has been mitigated by the development and adoption of eXtensible Business Reporting Language (XBRL). XBRL is a digital business language designed to help companies communicate financial statement data internally and externally. XBRL codes every element of a set of financial statements using a simple, universal, plain-language tag. The tag allows companies to consistently communicate financial statement data originally prepared in many different forms, and it allows statement users to extract information rapidly and reliably. XBRL does not adjust data for differences in accounting principles. Its principal purpose is to adjust presentational differences. The SEC permits companies to file financial statements using XBRL.

Nature of Principles

The rules and basic concepts of accounting are commonly referred to as *principles*. The word **principle** is here used in the sense of a general law or rule that is to be used as a guide to action. This means that accounting principles do not prescribe exactly how each event occurring in an organization should be recorded. Consequently, there are many matters in accounting practice that differ from one organization to another. Most of these differences are inevitable because a single detailed set of rules could not conceivably apply to every organization. In part, the differences reflect that, within "generally accepted accounting principles," management has some latitude in which to express its own ideas about the best way of recording and reporting a specific event.

Readers should realize, therefore, that they cannot know the precise meaning of a number of the items in an accounting report unless they know which of several equally acceptable possibilities has been selected by the person who prepared the report. The meaning intended in a specific situation requires knowledge of the context.

Criteria

Accounting principles are established by humans. Unlike the principles of physics, chemistry, and the other natural sciences, accounting principles were not deduced from basic axioms, nor can they be verified by observation and experiment. Instead, they have evolved. This evolutionary process is going on constantly; accounting principles are not eternal truths.

The general acceptance of an accounting principle usually depends on how well it meets three criteria: relevance, objectivity, and feasibility. A principle has **relevance** to the extent that it results in information that is meaningful and useful to those who need to know something about a certain organization. A principle has **objectivity** to the extent that the resulting information is not influenced by the personal bias or judgment of those who furnish it. Objectivity connotes reliability, trustworthiness. It also connotes verifiability, which means that there is some way of finding out whether the information is correct. A principle has **feasibility** to the extent that it can be implemented without undue complexity or cost.

These criteria often conflict with one another. In some cases the most relevant solution may be the least objective and the least feasible. Often, in this situation a less relevant but more objective and more feasible solution may be selected.

Example

The development of a new product may have a significant effect on a company's real value—"miracle" drugs and personal computer chips being spectacular examples. Information about the value of new products is most useful to the investor; it is indeed relevant. But the best estimate of the value of a new product is likely to be that made by management, and this is a highly subjective estimate. Accounting therefore does not attempt to record such values. Accounting sacrifices relevance in the interests of objectivity.

The measure of the value of the owners' interest or equity in a biotechnology firm such as Genentech, Inc., obtained from the stock market quotations (i.e., multiplying the price per share of stock times the number of shares outstanding) is a much more accurate reflection of the true value than the amount listed as owners' equity that appears in the corporation's financial statements. The marketplace gave this value as $26.4 billion; the accounting records gave it as $6.8 billion. The difference does not indicate an error in the accounting records. It merely illustrates the fact that accounting does not attempt to report firm market values.

In developing new principles, the essential problem is to strike the right balance between relevance on the one hand and objectivity and feasibility on the other. Failure to appreciate this problem often leads to unwarranted criticism of accounting principles. It is easy to criticize accounting on the grounds that accounting information is not as relevant as it might be; but the critic often overlooks the fact that proposals to increase relevance almost always involve a sacrifice of objectivity and feasibility. On balance, such a sacrifice may not be worthwhile.

Source of Accounting Principles

The foundation of accounting consists of a set of **generally accepted accounting principles,** or **GAAP** for short. Currently, these principles are established by the Financial Accounting Standards Board (FASB). Current information about the FASB's activities can be obtained by accessing the FASB's website (http://www.fasb.org). The FASB consists of seven members with diverse accounting backgrounds who work full time on developing new or modified principles. The board is supported by a professional staff that does research and prepares a discussion memorandum on each problem that the board addresses. The board acts only after interested parties have been given an opportunity to suggest solutions to problems and to comment on proposed pronouncements. The FASB is a nongovernmental organization.[1]

It is important to note that the acronym "GAAP" when used in practice (and this text) refers to accounting standards applicable in the United States, where the acceptability of the FASB pronouncements rests on their general acceptability. In most other countries, the authority of accounting standards is based on laws enacted by the national governing bodies.

Each of the *Standards* of the FASB deals with a specific topic.[2] Collectively, they do not cover all the important topics in accounting. If an authoritative pronouncement has not been made on a given topic, accountants can treat that topic in the way they believe most fairly presents the situation.

Companies are not legally required to adhere to GAAP as established by the FASB. As a practical matter, however, there are strong pressures for them to do so. The accounting reports of most companies are audited by certified public accountants who are members of the American Institute of Certified Public Accountants (AICPA). Although the AICPA (http://www.aicpa.org) does not require its members to force companies to adhere to FASB standards, it does require that if the CPA finds that the company has not followed FASB standards, the difference must be called to public attention. Since companies usually do not like to go counter to the FASB—even though they may feel strongly that the FASB principle is not appropriate in their particular situation—they almost always conform to the FASB pronouncements.

The FASB has established a 14-member group called the Emerging Issues Task Force (EITF). As its name suggests, the EITF publishes guides, referred to as *consensuses,* on accounting issues that need to be resolved in a timely manner. Typically, these consensuses are adopted where appropriate by corporations.

Another source of pressure to conform to GAAP is the U.S. Securities and Exchange Commission (SEC). This agency, which exists to protect the interests of investors, has jurisdiction over any corporation with a class of securities listed on a national stock exchange or, if traded over the counter, with 500 or more shareholders and $10 million or more total assets. The SEC requires these companies to file accounting reports prepared in accordance with GAAP. In its *Regulation S–X,* its

---

[1] Financial accounting and reporting standards for state and local governments and government-owned entities, such as colleges and universities, are set by the Government Accounting Standards Board.

[2] Authoritative pronouncements consist of *Statements* and interpretations of the Financial Accounting Standards Board and certain pronouncements of predecessor bodies established by the AICPA. We shall refer to these earlier pronouncements as *Accounting Research Bulletins* and *Opinions.*

Financial Reporting Series Releases, and its *Staff Accounting Bulletins,* the SEC spells out acceptable accounting principles in more detail than, but generally consistent with, the pronouncements of the FASB. Legally, the Securities Exchange Act of 1934 gave the SEC the authority to promulgate GAAP; but over the years, for the most part the SEC has relied on the FASB and its predecessors for carrying out the standard-setting process.

In its past, the AICPA has issued pronouncements called *Statements of Position* (SOP) for accounting in a number of industries, including finance companies, government contractors, and real estate investment trusts. Although these pronouncements do not have the force of FASB *Standards,* organizations have followed them. Recently, the FASB has made it clear that AICPA pronouncements are not GAAP. It has asked the AICPA to cease issuing these pronouncements.

Various regulatory bodies also prescribe accounting rules for the companies they regulate. Among those subjected to such rules are banks and other financial institutions, insurance companies, and public utilities. These rules are not necessarily consistent with the principles of the FASB, although there has been a tendency in recent years for regulatory agencies to change their accounting rules so that they do conform.

The authority of the FASB and the other agencies discussed so for exists, of course, only in the United States of America. Accounting principles in other countries differ in some respects from American GAAP, but in general there is a basic similarity throughout the world. There is a major effort to codify a set of accounting principles that would apply internationally, and over 40 statements known as International Accounting Standards (IAS) have been published by the International Accounting Standards Committee (IASC)—now reorganized as the International Accounting Standards Board (IASB)—located in London, England. While retaining the name IAS for standards issued by its predecessor, standards issued by the IASB (http://www.iasb.org) are known as International Financial Reporting Standards (IFRS).

The IASB does not have the power to enforce its pronouncements. Their adoption by companies and accounting standard setters is voluntary. Nevertheless, impressed by the potential value of a global set of accounting principles, the FASB and the IASB have initiated a joint-program to converge GAAP and IFRS. This effort is supported by the SEC, which has proffered a timetable for potential mandatory adoption of IFRS for SEC registered companies beginning in 2014. Currently, over 100 countries have either adopted IFRS in whole or part or are considering IFRS adoption.

Readers of this text can assume, unless noted otherwise, the accounting for a particular transaction or event described in the text is essentially this same under both GAAP and IFRS.

A complete compilation of GAAP—FASB Accounting Standards Codification™—can be found on the FASB website. It is the single official source of authoritative, nongovernmental GAAP issued by the FASB. Guidance issued by the SEC is also incorporated in the site's materials.

Principles Vs. Rules

A major controversy in accounting is the extent to which accounting standards should be expressed in the form of broad principles versus detailed rules. IFRS tend to be stated in the form of broad principles. In contrast, much of GAAP tends to be stated in the form of bright-line rules. For example, as you will learn later, under GAAP if a term of a lease is equal to 75 percent of the economic life of the leased property, the lease will be accounted for as a capital lease.[3] On the other hand, if the lease term is

---

[3] "Accounting for Leases," *FASB Statement No. 13.*

equal to 74 or less percent of the leased property's economic life, the lease will be accounted for as an operating lease. IFRS takes a different approach. It makes the distinction between a capital and an operating lease based on which party—the lessor or the lessee—substantially bears the risks and rewards of owership.[4]

The distinction between the principle-based and rule-based accounting standards is important. Under a principle-based standards model, the accounting for transactions is more likely to reflect the substance of the transaction. Under a rule-based standards model, the accounting for a transaction is more likely to reflect the form of the transaction.

As GAAP and IFRS converge, it is anticipated that GAAP will become more principle based.

Financial Statements

The end product of the financial accounting process is a set of reports that are called **financial statements**. Generally accepted accounting principles require that three such reports be prepared: (1) a statement of financial position, which is generally referred to as a balance sheet; (2) an income statement; and (3) a statement of cash flows.[5] As we examine the details of the financial accounting process, it is important to keep in mind the objective toward which the process is aimed: the preparation of these three financial statements.

Most reports, in any field, can be classified into one of two categories: (1) **stock**, or **status, reports** and (2) **flow reports**. The amount of water in a reservoir at a given moment of time is a measure of stock, whereas the amount of water that moves through the reservoir in a day is a measure of flow. Reports of stocks are always as of a specified *instant* in time; reports of flow always cover a specified *period* of time. Reports of stocks are like snapshots; reports of flows are more like motion pictures. One of the accounting reports, the balance sheet, is a report of stocks. It shows information about the resources and obligations of an organization at a specified moment of time. The other two reports, the income statement and the cash flow statement, are reports of flows. They report activities of the organization for a period of time, such as a quarter or a year.

Companies listed on stock exchanges publish annual and quarterly financial reports. These reports can be obtained either directly from the company or from the Securities and Exchange Commission (SEC). Typically, these reports are also available directly from companies through the Internet.

For example, the Coca-Cola Company's home page (http://www.cocacola.com) contains information about Coca-Cola's products, history, and financial performance and position. (You might want to access this site to get a sense of a complete set of financial statements. After completing the financial reporting section of this book, you should be able to read and interpret these reports with confidence that you understand them.)[6]

---

[4] "Leases," *IAS No. 17.*

[5] Company financial reports also may include other financial displays, such as changes in owners' equity. This display will be explained in Chapter 10.

[6] The home pages of other well-known companies you might want to access are General Electric (http://www.ge.com), Microsoft (http://www.microsoft.com), General Motors (http://www.gm.com), Walmart (http://www.walmart.com), and IBM (http://www.ibm.com).

Listed company financial reports are also available electronically through the Securities and Exchange Commission's Electronic Data Gathering, Analysis, and Retrieval (EDGAR) system. All companies registered with the SEC use EDGAR to transmit their required filings to the SEC (http://www.sec.gov).

In this chapterwe will give a brief introduction to the balance sheet and income statement. The definitions provided should be considered as only working definitions for the purposes of this introductory chapter. The next nine chapters describe more precisely and in greater detail the balance sheet and income statement. We shall defer a description of the statement of cash flows until Chapter 11. Because this report is derived from data originally collected for the other two reports, it is inappropriate to defer the discussion of the cash flow statement until after the balance sheet and income statement have been thoroughly explained.

The Balance Sheet

Illustration 1–3 presents the December 31, 2010, balance sheet of the Holden Company. (Do not worry if you do not know what all of the account titles mean. They will be discussed in later chapters.)

The Holden balance sheet is a snapshot of the financial position of the company. It has two sides: the left, Assets, and the right, Liabilities and Owners' Equity. We will give working descriptions of each side. (More precise descriptions will be provided in Chapter 2.)

Assets

An entity needs cash, equipment, and other resources in order to operate. These resources are its assets. **Assets** are valuable resources owned by the entity. The left side of the balance sheet shows the amounts of these assets as of a certain date. For example, the amount of Cash that Holden Company owned on December 31, 2010, was $1,449,000.

Assets are resources **owned** by Holden Company. Its employees, although perhaps its most valuable resource, are not assets in accounting, because the company does not own its employees.

Liabilities and Owners' Equity

The right side of the balance sheet shows the sources that provided the entity's assets. As the heading indicates, there are two general types of sources, Liabilities and Owners' Equity.

Liabilities are obligations of the entity to outside non owner parties who have furnished resources. These parties are generally called **creditors** because they have extended credit to the entity. As Illustration 1–3 indicates, suppliers have extended credit in the amount of $5,602,000, as indicated by Accounts Payable.

Creditors have a **claim** against the assets in the amount shown as the liability. For example, a bank has loaned $1,000,000 to Holden Company, and therefore has a claim of this amount, as indicated by Bank Loan Payable.

Because an entity will use its assets to pay off its claims, those claims are against assets. They are claims against *all* the assets, not any particular assets.

The other source of the funds that an entity uses to acquire its assets is called **Owners' Equity**. There are two sources of equity funds: (1) the amount provided directly by equity investors, which is called **Total Paid-In Capital**; and (2) the amount retained from profits (or earnings), which is called **Retained Earnings**.

Creditors can sue the entity if the amounts due them are not paid. Equity investors have only a *residual claim;* that is, if the entity is dissolved, they get whatever is left

**ILLUSTRATION
1–3**
The Balance Sheet

HOLDEN COMPANY			
Balance Sheet			
As of December 31, 2010			
(000 omitted)			
Assets		**Liabilities and Owners' Equity**	
Current assets:		*Current liabilities:*	
Cash	$ 1,449	Accounts payable	$ 5,602
Marketable securities	246	Bank loan payable	1,000
Accounts receivable, net	9,944	Accrued liabilities	876
Inventories	10,623	Estimated tax liability	1,541
Prepaid expenses	389	Current portion of long-term debt	500
Total current assets	22,651	Total current liabilities	9,519
Noncurrent assets:		*Noncurrent liabilities:*	
Property, plant, equipment at cost	26,946	Long-term debt, less current portion	2,000
Less: Accumulated		Deferred income taxes	824
depreciation	13,534	Total liabilities	12,343
Property, plant, equipment—net	13,412	*Owners' equity:*	
Investments	1,110	Common stock	1,000
Patents and trademarks	403	Additional paid-in capital	11,256
Goodwill	663	Total paid-in capital	12,256
		Retained earnings	13,640
		Total owners' equity	25,896
Total assets	$38,239	Total liabilities and owners' equity	$38,239

after the liabilities have been paid, which may be nothing. Liabilities therefore are a stronger claim against the assets than equity.

We can describe the right-hand side of the balance sheet in two somewhat different ways: (1) as the amount of funds supplied by creditors and equity investors and (2) as the claims of these parties against the assets. Use whichever way is more meaningful to you.

Dual-Aspect Concept

The assets that remain after the liabilities are taken into account will be claimed by the equity investors. If an entity has assets that total $10,000 and liabilities that total $4,000, its owners' equity must be $6,000.

Because (1) any assets not claimed by creditors will be claimed by equity investors and (2) the total amount of claims (liabilities + owners' equity) cannot exceed what there is to be claimed, it follows that the total amount of assets will always be equal to the total amount of liabilities plus owners' equity.

The fact that total assets must equal, or **balance**, total liabilities plus owners' equity is why the statement is called a *balance sheet*. This equality tells nothing about the entity's financial condition; it always exists unless the accountant has made a mistake.

This fact leads to what is called the **dual-aspect concept**. The two aspects that this concept refers to are (1) assets and (2) liabilities plus owners' equity. The concept states that these two aspects are always equal. (This equality exists even if liabilities are greater than assets. For example, if assets in an unprofitable business were $100,000 and liabilities were $120,000, owners' equity would be a *negative* amount of $20,000.)

The dual-aspect concept is 1 of 11 basic accounting concepts we shall describe in Chapters 2 and 3. The dual-aspect concept can be written as an equation:

$$\text{Assets} = \text{Liabilities} + \text{Owners' equity}$$

This equation is fundamental. It governs all accounting. We can write a similar equation in a form that emphasizes the fact that owners' equity is a residual interest:

$$\text{Assets} - \text{Liabilities} = \text{Owners' equity}$$

For example, if the assets of Violet Company total $19,000 and its liabilities total $3,000, its owners' equity must total $16,000.

The term *net assets* is sometimes used instead of owners' equity. It refers to the fact that owners' equity is always the difference between assets and liabilities.

Every accounting transaction can be described in terms of its effect on this fundamental accounting equation. For example, the Violet Company spends $15,000 cash for a new car. The company's accountant would record a reduction in the asset Cash (– $15,000) and an increase in the asset Cars (+ $15,000). After recording this transaction, the fundamental equation is still in balance. Similarly, if the company had bought the car on credit rather than for cash, the equation would be in balance because the liability Accounts Payable would have increased (+ $15,000) and the asset Cars would have increased by a like amount (+ $15,000).

The amounts of an entity's assets and liabilities will change from day to day. Any balance sheet reports the amounts of assets, liabilities, and owners' equity at one point in time. The balance sheet therefore must be dated. (From here on we shall sometimes use the term *20x1* to refer to the first year, *20x2* for the next year, and so on. Thus, a balance sheet as of December 31 of the first year is dated "as of December 31, 20x1." It refers to the close of business on that day.)

Returning to Illustration 1–3, if the Holden Company prepared a balance sheet as of the beginning of business the next day, January 1, 2011, it would be the same as the one in Illustration 1–3 because nothing changes between the close of business on one day and the beginning of business on the next day.

The Income Statement

Illustration 1–4 shows the Holden Company's 2010 income statement. The amount added to Retained Earnings as a result of profitable operations during a period is the **income** of the period. An income statement explains how this income was earned. There is no standard format for an income statement. Illustration 1–4 shows one common format. (The income statement is discussed in greater detail in Chapter 3.)

The basic income statement equation is

$$\text{Revenues} - \text{Expenses} = \text{Net income}$$

The first item on this income statement is Sales Revenue, which is the amount of products (i.e., goods and services) sold or delivered to customers during the period.

The item on the second line is labeled Cost of Sales. It reports the cost of the goods or services whose revenue is reported on the first line.

The difference between sales and cost of sales is called *gross margin*. Thus,

$$\text{Gross margin} = \text{Sales revenue} - \text{Cost of sales}$$

**ILLUSTRATION
1–4**
**The Income
Statement**

HOLDEN COMPANY Income Statement For the Year 2010 (000 omitted)	
Sales revenue	$75,478
Less cost of sales	52,227
Gross margin	23,251
Less operating expenses	10,785
Income before taxes	12,466
Provision for income taxes	6,344
Net income	$ 6,122

Operating expenses are subtracted from gross margin, leaving **income before taxes**. These expenses include costs related to the current period and costs that do not benefit future periods.

The next item in Illustration 1–4, provision for income taxes, is shown separately because it is an especially important expense.

The final item (the bottom line) on an income statement is called **net income** (or **net loss**, if expenses were larger than revenues).

**"Package" of
Financial
Reports**

Illustration 1–5 is a "package" of financial reports for the Holden Company consisting of two balance sheets and an income statement. (A complete package of financial reports also would include a cash flow statement.) The illustration shows how the balance sheet, statement of retained earnings, and income statement relate to each other through the Retained Earnings account.

An income statement is a summary of certain changes in Retained Earnings that have taken place during an accounting period. In other words, an income statement reports certain changes in Retained Earnings that have taken place between two balance sheet dates.

Thus, a useful accounting "report package" consists of a balance sheet *at the beginning of* the accounting period, an income statement *for* the period, and a balance sheet *at the end of* the period.

The statement of retained earnings at the bottom of Illustration 1–5 shows that the Retained Earnings on December 31, 2009, was $13,640,000. During 2010 profitable operations resulted in net income of $6,122,000, which increased Retained Earnings by this amount. (Net income is the bottom line on the income statement.) Retained Earnings was decreased by $4,390,000, representing a distribution to the shareholders in the form of dividends. As a result, the total Retained Earnings on December 31, 2010, was $15,372,000 ($13,640,000 + $6,122,000 − $4,390,000).

Dividends are deducted from Retained Earnings because dividends are a distribution of earnings to owners. Dividends are *not* an expense.

**Financial
Statement
Objectives**

We indicated earlier that financial accounting statements, while also of use to management, are intended primarily to provide relevant information to parties external to the business. The Financial Accounting Standards Board (FASB) issued a formal statement of financial reporting objectives. The entire statement is too lengthy to describe here in detail. We will simply highlight the key objectives. (The numbering is ours, not that of the FASB.)

ILLUSTRATION 1–5

A "Package" of Accounting Reports

HOLDEN COMPANY (000 OMITTED)			
Condensed Balance Sheet As of December 31, 2009		**Condensed Balance Sheet As of December 31, 2010**	
Assets		**Assets**	
Current assets	$22,651	Current assets	$24,062
Buildings and equipment	13,412	Buildings and equipment	14,981
Other assets	2,176	Other assets	3,207
Total assets	$38,239	Total assets	$42,250
Liabilities and Owners' Equity		**Liabilities and Owners' Equity**	
Liabilities	$12,343	Liabilities	$14,622
Owners' equity:		Owners' equity:	
Paid-in capital	12,256	Paid-in capital	12,256
Retained earnings	13,640	Retained earnings	15,372
Total liabilities and owners' equity	$38,239	Total liabilities and owners' equity	$42,250

**Income Statement
For the Year 2010**

Sales revenue	$75,478
Less cost of sales	52,127
Gross margin	23,351
Less operating expenses	10,885
Income before taxes	12,466
Provision for income taxes	6,344
Net income, 2010	$ 6,122

Statement of Retained Earnings

Retained earnings, 12/31/09	$13,640
Add net income	6,122
	19,762
Less dividends	4,390
Retained earnings, 12/31/10	$15,372

Financial reporting should provide information that

1. Is useful to present and potential investors and creditors in making rational investment and credit decisions.
2. Is comprehensible to those who have a reasonable understanding of business and economic activities and are willing to study the information with reasonable diligence.
3. Is about the economic resources of an enterprise, the claims to those resources, and the effects of transactions and events that change resources and claims to those resources.
4. Is about an enterprise's financial performance during a period.
5. Helps users assess the amounts, timing, and uncertainty of prospective cash receipts from dividends or interest and the proceeds from the sale or redemption of securities or loans.

Objectives 1 and 2 apply to all financial accounting information. Note that the intended users are expected to have attained a reasonable level of sophistication in using the statements; the statements are not prepared for uninformed persons. Objective 3 is related to the balance sheet, objective 4 to the income statement, and objective 5 to the cash flow statement. As the five objectives collectively suggest, financial statements provide information about the *past* to aid users in making predictions and decisions related to the *future* financial status and flows of the business.

Sarbanes-Oxley Act

In July 2002 the U.S. president signed into law the Sarbanes-Oxley Act. It requires chief executives and chief financial officers of public companies to certify that their company's financial statements filed with the SEC are materially accurate and complete, and that in all material respects they present fairly the financial condition and results of operations of the issuer. These certifications subject the signers to potential civil and criminal liability for false certifications.

Income Tax Reporting

The Internal Revenue Service (IRS) specifies the ways in which taxable income is calculated for the purpose of assessing income taxes. Because the tax laws' purposes differ from the objectives of financial reporting, the IRS accounting regulations differ in some respects from GAAP. These differences mean that the amount of pretax income or loss shown on the taxpayer's income statement prepared according to GAAP will probably not be equal to the taxable income or loss shown on the taxpayer's income tax return.[7] How GAAP handles this difference will be covered in Chapter 10.

Thus, in the United States, financial accounting, management accounting, and income tax accounting are essentially separate processes. GAAP provides the principles for financial accounting; top management for management accounting; and the IRS and Congress for income tax accounting. The underlying operating information that is the basic data for all three processes is the same. The pieces or building blocks of operating information simply are put together in different ways for these three different processes. Though differences among the three processes do exist, in practice the similarities are greater than the differences.

Quality of Financial Reporting

The primary objective of financial reporting is to provide high-quality financial information of business entities, primarily financial in nature, which may be useful for economic decision-making (FASB, 1999; IASB, 2008). Financial reports provide a peek into the performance of a company and occupy an important position in the decisions made by investors and creditors. They are instrumental in telling a company's story to the world. These reports are also important as they positively influence capital providers and other stakeholders in making investment, credit, and similar resource allocation decisions enhancing overall market efficiency. Financial reports primarily include a balance sheet, income statement and cash flow statement. In addition to these, a financial report also consists of a self-appraisal of the company along with its functional high points. All these reasons make the importance of an accurate financial report unquestionable.

---

[7] In contrast to the United States, the governments of many countries require a company's financial accounting and tax accounting to be identical. This is changing. In many countries public companies listed on stock exchanges and, in some cases, unlisted companies are now being allowed or required to use IASB standards in reports to stockholders that differ from the local tax accounting rules.

Financial reporting in India is also set to change to Indian Accounting Standards (Ind AS), which eventually converges with IFRS. The objective of Ind AS is to ensure that an entity's Ind-AS financial statements, and its interim financial reports for the period covered by those financial statements, contain high-quality information that (a) is transparent for users and comparable over all periods presented; (b) provides a suitable starting point for accounting in accordance with Ind-AS; and (c) can be generated at a cost that does not exceed the benefits (Mca.gov.in, 2018). While corporates in India have started implementing Ind AS standards from April 1, 2016, Indian banks have been given permission to defer this transition till April 1, 2019. The eventual merger of accounting standards would provide benefits like reducing the distinctive reporting regulation between countries, reducing the cost of multinational company financial reporting, and reducing the cost of financial statement analysis (Yurisandi and Puspitasari, 2015).

In not just Indian but in a global scenario, the demand for providing clear and quality financial reports has gone up. Quality is often termed as a relational and not a physical attribute since it can't be directly measured. It can only be compared in a relationship with something else. The degree to which reported earnings capture economic reality is called earnings quality (Parsons and Krishnan, 2006). Poor earnings quality coupled with weak governance mechanisms can adversely affect the reliability of financial statements for investors, weaken the link between earnings and firm valuation, and increase transaction costs in the capital market (Sarkar, Sarkar and Sen, 2008). It is essential to provide high-quality financial reports to influence users in making investments decisions and to enhance market efficiency. It includes not just the quantifiable aspects but also the necessary non-financial aspects as well. Better the quality of financial reporting, the higher are the benefits to be achieved by users.

It includes not just the quantifiable aspects but also the necessary non-financial aspects as well.

Moreover, markets in developed economies have started putting a premium on "Quality of Financial Reporting" rather than "Quantity," which has led to increasing focus on sections in Annual Reports like "Management Discussion and Analysis" (MDA), Auditors Qualified Report, etc. It is still early in developing markets like India where market participants still largely focus on numbers like sales growth and profit margins. One of the reasons why markets have started looking at qualitative characteristics also is because of the sudden collapse of big corporates who just before the announcement of the crisis were seen as good performing businesses. What we saw recently in the case of ILFS (Infrastructure leasing and financial services) in Indian markets is a classic example of the above phenomenon. A large and highly rated NBFC suddenly reports crisis and on inquiry, the skeletons start coming out. It is being equated as India's "Lehman moment" as the NBFC has significant exposure to infrastructure projects which are largely government-sponsored.

One of the obvious challenges which "Quality" faces is the inability to quantify the measurement as any variable used to measure the "quality" will be at best a proxy variable and may have "personal biases." The variables which are commonly used to proxy "Quality of Financial Reporting" are "Relevance," "Faithful representation," "Understandability," "Comparability," and "Timeliness."

1. **Relevance:** IASB (2008) defines relevance as the capability of making a difference in decisions made by users on their capacity as capital providers. Relevance is usually operationalized in terms of predictive and confirmatory value.
2. **Faithful representation:** Faithful representation means that all information listed in the financial report must be represented faithfully, it must be complete, accurate, neutral, and free from bias and errors.

3. **Understandability:** Understandability is referred to as the process of classifying, characterizing, categorizing, then presenting the financial information clearly and concisely.

4. **Comparability:** Comparability refers to the users' ability to make comparisons over time between different financial statements of a certain entity and those of other entities (Alfredson *et al.*, 2007). This could happen by enforcing the company to use the same accounting policies and procedures, either from period to period within an entity or in a single period across entities (IASB, 2008: 39).

5. **Timeliness:** The last enhancing qualitative characteristic discussed in the IASB (2010) conceptual framework is timeliness. The framework defines timeliness as having information available to decision-makers before it loses its capacity to influence decisions (IASB, 2010). It is usually measured in terms of the number of days it takes for the auditor to sign the accounts after the book-year end.

Corporate Governance and Financial Reporting

"Corporate governance is not just corporate management, it is something much broader to include a fair, efficient and transparent administration to meet certain well-defined objectives. It is a system of structuring, operating and controlling a company with a view to achieving long-term strategic goals to satisfy shareholders, creditors, employees, customers and suppliers, and complying with the legal and regulatory requirements, apart from meeting environmental and local community needs. When it is practiced under a well-laid out system, it leads to the building of a legal, commercial and institutional framework and demarcates the boundaries within which these functions are performed." (Corporate governance: Time for a Metamorphosis' The Hindu July 9, 1997.)

Adoption of good corporate governance practices is usually done with the aim of balancing the interests of the various stakeholders a firm has. Over-emphasis on meeting the needs (or interests) of one group may jeopardize not just the interests of the other groups but also the long-term survival of the firm itself. For instance, maximization of the firm's profit at the cost of its customers and employees strips the firm of its long-term competitiveness in the market. Company management, therefore, needs to have multiple objectives as part of the company's long-term and annual plans to ensure that all the stakeholders' interests are being taken care of. There is, however, a limit on the extent to which the management can be 'true' to all the different (and often conflicting) objectives. Good corporate governance practices, e.g., having an independent board of directors, aim to instill a mechanism of control in the way the company management would work and thereby ensure that it is true to its multiple stakeholders' interests.

Market Response to Quality of Financial Reporting and Corporate Governance

Both the issues highlighted above (quality of financial reporting and corporate governance) have become more relevant in the light of recent big accounting scams or repeated misrepresentation of financial performance by the firms. It is not a phenomenon which is limited to underdeveloped markets but it is quite prevalent in developed markets too where the poor shareholder is literally taken for a ride. However, it would be worth analyzing that do investors in the capital markets look at such qualitative parameters too while making investment decisions. The obsession with quantifiable variables is not going anywhere for some reasonable time to come but sooner or later, markets will appreciate the relevance of intangible factors like quality of board structures, and the "disclosure of full and relevant information on time by firms" and many such qualitative variables. As pointed out, the lack of interest is also because of difficulties in putting a "value" to these factors and also using a proxy method of measuring them.

Summary

An organization has four types of accounting information: (1) operating information, which has to do with the details of operations; (2) management accounting information, which is used internally for planning, implementation, and control; (3) financial accounting information, which is used both by management and by external parties; and (4) tax accounting information, which is used to file tax returns with taxing authorities.

Financial accounting is governed by ground rules that in America are referred to as generally accepted accounting principles. Outside the United States, there rules are increasingly most likely to be IFRS, rather than local standards. In either case, these ground rules may be different from what the reader believes them to be, based on previous exposure to accounting information. There rules attempt to strike a balance between the criterion of relevance on the one hand and the criteria of objectivity and feasibility on the other.

The end products of the financial accounting process are three financial statements: the balance sheet, the income statement, and the cash flow statement. The balance sheet is a report of status or stocks as of a moment of time, whereas the other two statements summarize flows over a period of time.

In the United States, calculating taxable income for income tax purposes differs from the process of calculating income for the financial accounting income statement.

The basic accounting equation is

$$\text{Assets} = \text{Liabilities} + \text{Owners' equity}$$

Problems

Problem 1-1.

As of December 31, Charles Company had $12,000 in cash, held $95,000 of inventory, and owned other items that originally cost $13,000. Charles Company also had borrowed $40,000 from First City Bank. Prepare a balance sheet for Charles Company as of December 31. Be sure to label each item and each column with appropriate terms.

Problem 1-2.

Selected balance sheet items are shown for the Microtech Company. Compute the missing amounts for each of the four years. What basic accounting equation did you apply in making your calculations?

	Year 1	Year 2	Year 3	Year 4
Current assets	$113,624	$?	$ 85,124	$?
Noncurrent assets	?	198,014	162,011	151,021
Total assets	$524,600	$?	$?	$220,111
Current liabilities	$ 56,142	$ 40,220	$?	$?
Noncurrent liabilities	?	?	60,100	30,222
Paid-in capital	214,155	173,295	170,000	170,000
Retained earnings	13,785	(3,644)	1,452	2,350
Total liabilities and owners' equity	$524,600	$288,456	$?	$220,111

Problem 1-3.

Selected income statement items are shown for Astrotech Company. Compute the missing amounts for each of the four years. What basic accounting equation did you apply in making your calculations?

(*Hint:* To *estimate* the Year 4 missing numbers, compute the typical percentage each expense item is of sales for Years 1 to 3 and apply the percentage figure for each expense item to Year 4's sales.)

	Year 1	Year 2	Year 3	Year 4
Sales	$12,011	$?	$11,545	$10,000
Cost of goods sold	3,011	2,992	?	?
Gross margin	?	8,976	8,659	?
Other expenses	6,201	6,429	?	?
Profit before taxes	2,799	?	2,363	?
Tax expense	?	1,019	945	?
Net income	$ 1,679	$1,528	$ 1,418	?

Problem 1–4. An analysis of the transactions made by Acme Consulting for the month of July is shown below.

Cash	+	Accounts Receivable	+	Supplies Inventory	+	Equipment	=	Accounts Payable	+	Owners' Equity	Description of Transaction
1. +$20,000										+$20,000	Investment
2. –$ 5,000						+$7,000		+$2,000			
3. –$ 1,000				+$1,000							
4. –$ 4,500										–$ 4,500	Salaries
5. +$ 5,000		+$5,000								+$10,000	Revenues
6. –$ 1,500								–$1,500			
7. +$ 1,000		–$1,000									
8. –$ 750										–$ 750	Rent
9. –$ 500										–$ 500	Utilities
10.								+$ 200		–$ 200	Travel
11.				–$ 200						–$ 200	

Required:
a. Explain each transaction.
b. List the changes in the company's balance sheet during the month of July.
c. Prepare an income statement for the month (ignore taxes).
d. Explain the changes in the Cash account.
e. Explain why the change in the Cash account and the month's income are not the same.

Problem 1–5. During the month of June, Bon Voyage Travel recorded the following transactions:

1. Owners invested $25,000 in cash to start the business. They received common stock.
2. The month's rent of $500 was prepaid in cash.
3. Equipment costing $8,000 was bought on credit.
4. $500 was paid for office supplies.
5. Advertising costing $750 was paid for with cash.
6. Paid $3,000 employee salaries in cash.
7. Earned travel commissions of $10,000 of which $2,000 was received in cash.
8. Paid $5,000 of the $8,000 owed to the equipment supplier.

9. Used $100 of the office supplies.
10. Charged $1,000 of miscellaneous expenses on the corporate credit card.

Required:

a. Prepare an analysis of the month's transactions using the same tabular format as shown in Problem 1–4 (ignore taxes).

b. Explain how the transactions during the month changed the basic accounting equation (Assets = Liabilities + Owners' equity) for the company.

c. Prepare an income statement for the month.

d. Explain the changes in the Cash account.

e. Explain why the change in the Cash account and the month's income are not the same.

Case 1–1
Ribbons an' Bows, Inc.

In January 2010, Carmen Diaz, a recent arrival from Cuba, decided to open a small ribbon shop in the Coconut Grove section of Miami, Florida. During the month, she put together a simple business plan, which she took to several relatives whom she believed would be interested in helping her finance the new venture. Two of her cousins agreed to loan the business $10,000 for one year at a 6 percent interest rate. For her part, Carmen agreed to invest $1,000 in the equity of the business.

On March 1, 2010, with the help of an uncle who practiced law, Carmen formally incorporated her business, which she named "Ribbons an' Bows." Normally, the uncle would have charged a fee of $600 for handling the legal aspects of a simple incorporation, but, since Carmen was family, he waived the fee.

As soon as the new business was incorporated, Carmen opened a bank account and deposited the cousins' $10,000 loan and her $1,000 equity contribution. The same day, she signed an agreement to rent store space for $600 per month, paid on the last day of the month. The agreement was for an 18-month period beginning April 1. The agreement called for a prepayment of the last two months' rent, which Carmen paid out of the company bank account at the signing.

Over the next few weeks, Carmen was actively engaged in getting ready to open the store for business on April 1. Fortunately for Carmen, the previous tenant had left counters and display furniture that Carmen could use at no cost to her. In addition, the landlord agreed to repaint the store at no cost, using colors of Carmen's choice. For her part, Carmen ordered, received, and paid for the store's opening inventory of ribbons and ribbon accessories; acquired for free a simple cash register with credit-card processing capabilities from the local credit-card charge processing company after paying a refundable deposit; signed service agreements with the local phone and utility companies; ordered, received, and paid for some store supplies; and placed and paid for advertising announcing the store opening in the April 2 edition of the local paper. In addition, she bought and paid for a used desktop computer with basic business software already installed to keep track of her business transactions and correspondence.

On March 31, before opening for business the next day, Carmen reviewed the activity in the company's cash bank account. Following the deposit of the loans and equity contribution, the following payments were made.

1. Last two months' rent	$1,200
2. Opening merchandise inventory	$3,300
3. Cash register deposit	$ 250
4. Store supplies	$ 100
5. April 2 edition advertising	$ 150
6. Used computer purchase	$2,000

After reviewing her cash transaction records, Carmen prepared a list of Ribbons an' Bows assets and sources of its capital (see Exhibit 1).

EXHIBIT 1 **Carmen's March 31, 2010, Ribbons an' Bows Assets and Capital Sources List**

	Assets		Sources of Capital
Cash	$ 4,000		
Inventory	3,300		
Supplies	100		
Prepaid rent	1,200		
Prepaid advertising	150		
Computer/ software	2,000	Cousin's loan	$10,000
Cash register deposit	250	Carmen's equity	1,000
	$11,000		$11,000

Carmen eventually decided to expand her business by selling custom-designed ribbon table arrangements for weddings and other special events. This decision led to the purchase of a used commercial sewing machine for $1,800 cash on May 1.

Later, at a family Fourth of July celebration, one of Carmen's cousins reminded her that she had promised to send the cousins a financial report covering the four-month period from March 1 to June 30.

The next day, Carmen reviewed the following Ribbons an' Bows information she had gathered over the last four months.

1. Customers had paid $7,400 cash for ribbons and accessories, but she was still owed $320 for ribbon arrangements for a large wedding delivered to the customer on June 30.
2. A part-time employee had been paid $1,510 but was still owed $90 for work performed during the last week of June.
3. Rent for the three-month period had been paid in cash at the end of each month, as stipulated in the rental agreement.
4. Inventory replenishments costing $2,900 had been delivered and paid for by June 30. Carmen estimated the June 30 merchandise inventory on hand had cost $4,100.
5. The small opening office supplies inventory was nearly all gone. She estimated supplies costing $20 had not been used.

Carmen believed that the initial three months of business had been profitable, but she was puzzled by the fact that the cash in the company's June 30 bank account was $3,390, which was less than the April 1 balance of $4,000.

Carmen also was concerned about how she should reflect the following in her financial report:

1. No interest had been paid on the cousins' loan.
2. The expenditures made for the desktop computer and its related software and the commercial sewing machine. She believed these expenditures would be beneficial to the business long after June 30. At the time she purchased the commercial sewing machine, Carmen estimated that it would be used for about five years from its May 1 purchase date, when it would then have to be replaced. Similarly, on March 31, she had estimated the desktop computer and its software would have to be replaced in two years' time. Carmen believed the sewing machine and the computer along with its software would have no resale value at the end of their useful lives.
3. The free legal work performed by her uncle and the free cash register provided by the local credit-card charge processor.
4. Carmen had not paid herself a salary or dividends during the four months of operations. If cash was available, she anticipated that sometime in July she would pay herself some compensation for the four months spent working in the business. Before starting her business, Carmen had worked for $1,300 a month as a cashier in a local grocery store.

Questions

1. How would you report on the three-month operations of Ribbons an' Bows, Inc., through June 30? Was the company profitable? (Ignore income taxes.) Why did its cash in the bank decline during the three-month operating period?
2. How would you report the financial condition of the business on June 30, 2010?
3. Do you believe Carmen's first three months of operation could be characterized as "successful"? Explain your answer.

Case 1–2
Kim Fuller*

In the early fall of 2010, Kim Fuller was employed as a district sales engineer for a large chemical firm. During a routine discussion with plant chemists, Fuller learned that the company had developed a use for the recycled material, in pulverized form, made from plastic soft drink bottles. Because the state had mandatory deposits on all beverage bottles, Fuller realized that a ready supply of this material was available. All that was needed was an organization to tap that bottle supply, grind the bottles, and deliver the pulverized plastic to the chemical company. It was an opportunity Fuller had long awaited—a chance to start a business.

In November 2010, Fuller began checking into the costs involved in setting up a plastic bottle grinding business. A used truck and three trailers were acquired to pick up the empty bottles. Fuller purchased one used grinding machine but had to buy a second one new; supplies and parts necessary to run and maintain the machines also were purchased. Fuller also purchased a personal computer with the intention of using it to keep company records. These items used $65,000 of the $75,000 Fuller had saved and invested in the company.

A warehouse costing $162,000 was found in an excellent location for the business. Fuller was able to interest family members enough in this project that three of them—two sisters and a brother—invested $30,000 each. These funds gave Fuller the $50,000 down payment on the warehouse. The bank approved a mortgage for the balance on the building. In granting the mortgage, however, the bank official suggested that Fuller start from the beginning with proper accounting records. He said these records would help not only with future bank dealings but also with tax returns and general management of the company. He suggested Fuller find a good accountant to provide assistance from the start, to get things going on the right foot.

Fuller's neighbor, Marion Zimmer, was an accountant with a local firm. When they sat down to talk about the new business, Fuller explained, "I know little about keeping proper records." Zimmer suggested Fuller should buy an "off-the-shelf" accounting system software package from a local office supply retailer.

Zimmer promised to help Fuller select and install the package as well as learn how to use it. In order to select the right package for Fuller's needs, Zimmer asked Fuller to list all of the items purchased for the business, all of the debts incurred, and the information Fuller would need to manage the business. Zimmer explained that not all of this information would be captured by the accounting records and displayed in financial statements. Based on what Fuller told Zimmer, Zimmer promised to create files to accommodate accounting and nonaccounting information that Fuller could access through the company's personal computer. As Fuller's first lesson in accounting, Zimmer gave Fuller a brief lecture on the nature of the balance sheet and income statement and suggested Fuller draw up an opening balance sheet for the company.

Confident now that the venture was starting on solid ground, Kim Fuller opened the warehouse, signed contracts with two local bottling companies, and hired two grinding machine workers and a truck driver. By February 2011 the new firm was making regular deliveries to Fuller's former employer.

Questions

1. What information will Fuller need to manage the business? Classify this information in two categories: accounting information and nonaccounting information.
2. See what you can do to draw up a beginning-of-business list of the assets and liabilities of Fuller's company making any assumptions you consider useful. How should Fuller go about putting a value on the company's assets? Using your values, what is the company's opening owners' equity?
3. Now that Fuller has started to make sales, what information is needed to determine "profit and loss"? What should be the general construction of a profit and loss analysis for Fuller's business? How frequently should Fuller do such an analysis?
4. What other kinds of changes in assets, liabilities, and owners' claims will need careful recording and reporting if Fuller is to keep in control of the business?

* © Professor Robert N. Anthony.

Case 1–3

Baron Coburg*

Once upon a time many, many years ago, there lived a feudal landlord in a small province of Western Europe. The landlord, Baron Coburg, lived in a castle high on a hill. He was responsible for the well-being of many peasants who occupied the lands surrounding his castle.

Each spring, as the snow began to melt, the Baron would decide how to provide for all his peasants during the coming year.

One spring, the Baron was thinking about the wheat crop of the coming growing season. "I believe that 30 acres of my land, being worth five bushels of wheat per acre, will produce enough wheat for next winter," he mused, "but who should do the farming? I believe I'll give Ivan and Frederick the responsibility of growing the wheat." Whereupon Ivan and Frederick were summoned for an audience with Baron Coburg.

"Ivan, you will farm on the 20-acre plot of ground and Frederick will farm the 10-acre plot," the Baron began. "I will give Ivan 20 bushels of wheat for seed and 20 pounds of fertilizer. (Twenty pounds of fertilizer are worth two bushels of wheat.) Frederick will get 10 bushels of wheat for seed and 10 pounds of fertilizer. I will give each of you an ox to pull a plow, but you will have to make arrangements with Feyador the Plowmaker for a plow. The oxen, incidentally, are only three years old and have never been used for farming, so they should have a good 10 years of farming ahead of them. Take good care of them because an ox is worth 40 bushels of wheat. Come back next fall and return the oxen and the plows along with your harvest."

*Source: Academic Note "Another Implorable Occurrence," W. T. Andrews, ACCOUNTING HORIZONS, Vol. 9-No.3, April 1974, pp. 369–370. © American Accounting Association.

Ivan and Frederick genuflected and withdrew from the Great Hall, taking with them the things provided by the Baron.

The summer came and went, and after the harvest Ivan and Frederick returned to the Great Hall to account to their master for the things given them in the spring. Ivan said, "My Lord, I present you with a slightly used ox, a plow, broken beyond repair, and 223 bushels of wheat. I, unfortunately, owe Feyador the Plowmaker three bushels of wheat for the plow I got from him last spring. And, as you might expect, I used all the fertilizer and seed you gave me last spring. You will also remember, my Lord, that you took 20 bushels of my harvest for your own personal use."

Frederick spoke next. "Here, my Lord, is a partially used ox, the plow, for which I gave Feyador the Plowmaker 3 bushels of wheat from my harvest, and 105 bushels of wheat. I, too, used all my seed and fertilizer last spring. Also, my Lord, you took 30 bushels of wheat several days ago for your own table. I believe the plow is good for two more seasons."

"You did well," said the Baron. Blessed with this benediction, the two peasants departed.

After they had taken their leave, the Baron began to contemplate what had happened. "Yes," he thought, "they did well, but I wonder which one did better?"

Questions

1. For each farm, prepare balance sheets as of the beginning and end of the growing season and an income statement for the season. (Do not be concerned that you do not have much understanding of what a balance sheet and income statement are; just use your intuition as best you can.)
2. Which peasant was the better farmer?

Case 1–4

ILFS: India's Lehman moment

A week before Lehman Brothers, one of the most prestigious investment banks in the USA collapsed in the autumn of 2008, the US Treasury had stepped in to bail out Fannie Mae and Freddie Mac, big players in America's mortgage-lending market. Initially, $100 billion was the authorized bailout package that surged to $187 billion over time. And the treasury's emergency intervention was based on the premise that Washington must do its bit to reconstruct a financing ecosystem build on trust. The almost sudden collapse of the US financial system including big Banks, Credit Rating and Insurance companies has raised serious questions on the quality of disclosures as most of these companies were reporting good performance just a few quarters back. Clearly, there was a case of misrepresentation on part of the banks and the poor investors were left high and dry.

Exactly ten years later, Mumbai's policy and money-market bigwigs sat around oak-paneled boardrooms to decide the fate of a troubled financier that, although nowhere as large as the embattled leaders in US housing securitization, owns and runs arterial roads, ports, and warehouses across India. Hence, reviving IL & FS (Infrastructure Leasing and Financial Services Ltd) and designing its turnaround is as crucial to infrastructure - and capital-deficient India as was Washington's challenge to revive the mortgage securitization market. By way of federal intent and urgency, the similarities are evident. But in both cases, it was the poor taxpayer whose hard-earned money was put to bail out big corporations who were plagued by some very poor decisions made by top paid managers. In a way, it was a white-collar crime sponsored by the taxpayer.

In both the above situations, the corporations (Lehman in US and ILFS in India) has regularly released financial information duly vetted by the worlds best auditors and therefore markets never challenged or raised any doubts on these numbers. At the end of the day, investors all over the world trust financial information released by all kind of corporations because of the auditor's stamp. As a result of such incidents, confidence in the entire accounting reporting system is broken and the investors start doubting the very accounting process itself.

Last heard, the Serious Fraud Investigation Office (SFIO) has initiated investigations into a whistleblower complaint sent by a Deloitte employee and will summon its top officials for questioning to find out whether the Infrastructure Leasing & Financial Services (IL&FS) group's auditor deliberately ignored several red flags in the company's books, recommended creating complex structures, and in a quid pro quo received high fees from the bankrupt company. A few Deloitte officials have already been asked to join the inquiry, an SFIO source said, adding it was aware of the audit shortcomings and was now looking into IL&FS books of the last five years.

Questions

1. Should tax payer's money be used to bail out large institutions whose managers have taken huge risks exposures and are now staring at a collapse?
2. Discuss the role of players like Credit Rating agencies and the role of auditors in light of the above accounting scams, etc.
3. How can boards of large firms be made more effective so that such undesirable behavior of senior management can be controlled?
4. Is there a "market mechanism" which exists to prevent managers from excessive risk taking? Where will such mechanism be more effective?

Basic Accounting Concepts: The Balance Sheet

This chapter describes 5 of the 11 basic concepts from which principles of accounting are derived. Also described, in a preliminary way, are the nature of the balance sheet and the principal categories of items that appear in it. Finally, the chapter shows how amounts that appear in the balance sheet are changed to reflect events that affect an organization's resources.

The material presented here should be regarded as an overview. Each of the topics introduced will be discussed in more depth in later chapters.

Basic Concepts

Accounting principles are built on a foundation of a few basic concepts. These concepts are so basic that most accountants do not consciously think of them; they are regarded as self-evident. Nonaccountants will not find these concepts to be self-evident, however. Accounting could be constructed on a foundation of quite different concepts; indeed, some accounting theorists argue that certain of the present concepts are wrong and should be changed. Nevertheless, in order to understand accounting as it now exists, one must understand the underlying concepts currently used.

The Financial Accounting Standards Board (FASB) has adopted a number of *Statements of Financial Accounting Concepts*. These statements are intended to provide the FASB with explicit conceptual criteria to help resolve future accounting issues, rather than trying to deal with each issue on an ad hoc basis. The concept statements themselves do not establish generally accepted accounting principles (GAAP). Other groups, including the International Accounting Standards Board, have published statements of basic accounting concepts. These publications are similar in many respects to the FASB's concept statements.

The concepts we shall use in this book, while not identical to those listed by other authors or groups, reflect concepts that are widely accepted and applied in practice by accountants in the United States. These 11 concepts are as follows:

1. Money measurement
2. Entity

3. Going concern
4. Cost
5. Dual aspect
6. Accounting period
7. Conservatism
8. Realization
9. Matching
10. Consistency
11. Materiality

The first five are discussed below, and the other six are discussed in Chapter 3.

The Money Measurement Concept

In financial accounting, a record is made only of information that can be expressed in monetary terms. The advantage of such a record is that money provides a common denominator by means of which heterogeneous facts about an entity can be expressed as numbers that can be added and subtracted.

Example

Although it may be a fact that a business owns $30,000 of cash, 6,000 pounds of raw material, six trucks, 50,000 square feet of building space, and so on, these amounts cannot be added together to produce a meaningful total of what the business owns. Expressing these items in monetary terms—$30,000 of cash, $9,000 of raw material, $150,000 of trucks, and $4,000,000 of buildings—makes such an addition possible. Thus, despite the old cliché about not adding apples and oranges, it *is* easy to add them if both the apples and the oranges are expressed in terms of their respective monetary values.

Despite its advantage, the money measurement concept imposes a severe limitation on the scope of an accounting report. Accounting does not report the state of the president's health, that the sales manager is not on speaking terms with the production manager, that a strike is beginning, or that a competitor has placed a better product on the market. Accounting therefore does not give a complete account of the happenings in an organization or a full picture of its condition. It follows, then, that the reader of an accounting report should not expect to find therein all of the facts, or perhaps even the most important ones, about an organization.

Money is expressed in terms of its value at the time an event is recorded in the accounts. Subsequent changes in the purchasing power of money do not affect this amount. Thus, a machine purchased in 2010 for $200,000 and land purchased 20 years earlier for $200,000 are each listed in the 2010 accounting records at $200,000, although the purchasing power of the dollar in 2010 was much less than it was 20 years earlier. It is sometimes said that accounting assumes that money is an unvarying yardstick of value, but this statement is inaccurate. Accountants know full well that the purchasing power of the dollar changes. They do not, however, attempt to reflect such changes in the accounts.[1]

---

[1] In countries with high inflation rates, accountants initially record events in terms of their monetary value and then in subsequent periods adjust any remaining balances upward to reflect the changes in the purchasing power of the currency. For example, if the annual inflation rate is 100 percent, land bought for $10,000 at the beginning of the year would be reported at $20,000 one year later ($10,000 * 200 ÷ 100).

The Entity Concept

Accounts are kept for entities, as distinguished from the persons who are associated with these entities. An **entity** is any organization or activity for which accounting reports are prepared. Although our examples tend to be drawn from business companies, accounting entities include governments, churches, universities, and other nonbusiness organizations.

In recording events in accounting, the important question is, how do these events affect the entity? How they affect the persons who own, operate, or otherwise are associated with the entity is irrelevant. For example, suppose that the owner of a clothing store removes $100 from the store's cash register for his or her personal use. The real effect of this event on the owner as a person may be negligible; although the cash has been taken out of the business's "pocket" and put into the owner's pocket, in either pocket the cash belongs to the owner. Nevertheless, because of the entity concept, the accounting records show that the business has less cash than it had previously.

It is sometimes difficult to define with precision the entity for which a set of accounts is kept. Consider the case of a married couple who own and operate an unincorporated retail store. In *law* there is no distinction between the financial affairs of the store and those of its owners. A creditor of the store can sue and, if successful, collect from the owners' personal resources as well as from the resources of the business. In *accounting,* by contrast, a set of accounts is kept for the store as a separate business entity, and the events reflected in these accounts must be those of the store. The non-business events that affect the couple must not be included in these accounts. In accounting, the *business* owns the resources of the store, even though the resources are legally owned by the couple, and debts owed by the business are kept separate from personal debts owed by the couple. The expenses of operating the store are kept separate from the couple's personal expenses for food, clothing, housing, and the like.

The necessity for making such a distinction between the entity and its owners can create problems. Suppose, for example, that the couple lives on the same premises as the business. How much of the rent, electric bill, and property taxes associated with these premises is properly an expense of the business, and how much is personal expense of the family? Answers to questions like these are often difficult to ascertain, and are indeed somewhat arbitrary.

For a *corporation* the distinction is often quite easily made. A corporation is a legal entity, separate from the persons who own it, and the accounts of many corporations correspond exactly to the scope of the legal entity. There may be complications, however. In the case of a group of legally separate corporations that are related to one another by shareholdings, the whole group may be treated as a single entity for financial reporting purposes, giving rise to what are called *consolidated* accounting statements. Conversely, within a single corporation, a separate set of accounts may be maintained for each of its principal operating units. For example, General Electric Company maintains separate accounts for each of its many business units (appliances, lighting, aircraft engines, capital services, and others).

One entity may be part of a larger entity. Thus, a set of accounts may be maintained for an individual elementary school, another set for the whole school district, and still another set for all the schools in a particular state. There even exists a set of accounts, called the *national income accounts,* for the entire economic activity of the United States. In general, detailed accounting records are maintained for entities at the lowest level in the hierarchy, and reports for higher levels are prepared by summarizing the detailed data of these low-level entities.

The Going-Concern Concept

Unless there is good evidence to the contrary, accounting assumes that an entity is a **going concern**—that it will continue to operate for an indefinitely long period in the future. The significance of this assumption can be indicated by contrasting it with a possible alternative, namely, that the entity is about to be liquidated. Under the latter assumption, accounting would attempt to measure at all times what the entity's resources are currently worth to potential buyers. Under the going-concern concept, by contrast, there is no need to constantly measure an entity's worth to potential buyers, and it is not done. Instead, it is assumed that the resources currently available to the entity will be used in its future operations.

Example

At any given moment, a blue jeans manufacturer has jeans in various stages of the production process. If the business were liquidated today, these partially completed jeans would have little if any value. Accounting does not attempt to value these jeans at what they are currently worth. Instead, accounting assumes that the manufacturing process will be carried through to completion, and therefore that the amount for which the partially completed jeans could be sold if the company were liquidated today is irrelevant.

If, however, the accountant has good reason to believe that an entity *is* going to be liquidated, then its resources would be reported at their liquidation value. Such circumstances are uncommon.

The Cost Concept

The economic resources of an entity are called its **assets**. They consist of *nonmonetary assets*, such as land, buildings, and machinery, and other similar assets whose cash value is not fixed by contract, and *monetary assets,* such as money and marketable securities and other similar assets whose cash value is fixed by contract as will be described in Chapter 5. A fundamental concept of accounting, closely related to the going-concern concept, is that an asset is ordinarily entered initially in the accounting records at the price paid to acquire it—at its cost.[2] In the case of nonmonetary assets, the cost concept extends to their accounting subsequent to acquisition; cost continues to be the basis for all subsequent accounting for the asset. This is not true for most monetary assets. Subsequent to acquisition, they are accounted for at their fair value. *Fair value* is the amount at which an asset could be exchanged in a current transaction between willing parties, other than in a forced or liquidation sale.

While IFRS favors the cost concept for nonmonetary assets, it does permit as an acceptable alternative treatment the revaluation of land and buildings to their fair value subsequent to their initial recognition at cost.

Nonmonetary Assets

Since, for a variety of reasons, the real worth of an asset may change with the passage of time, the accounting measurement of nonmonetary assets does not necessarily—indeed, does not ordinarily—reflect what assets are worth, except at the moment they are acquired. There is therefore a considerable difference between the way in which nonmonetary assets are measured in accounting after their acquisition and the everyday, nonaccounting notion that assets are measured at what they are worth.

In accounting, all assets are initially recorded at their cost. (For emphasis, this is also referred to as an asset's *historical* cost.) In the case of nonmonetary assets, this amount is ordinarily unaffected by subsequent changes in the value of the asset. By contrast, in ordinary usage, the "value" of an asset usually means the amount for which it currently could be sold.

---

[2] APB *Opinion No. 20* requires that donated assets be recorded at their fair value at the date of receipt.

Example	If a business buys a plot of land (a nonmonetary asset), paying $250,000 for it, this asset would be recorded in the accounts of the business at the amount of $250,000. If a year later the land could be sold for $275,000, or if it could be sold for only $220,000, no change would ordinarily be made in the accounting records to reflect this fact.

Thus, the amounts at which nonmonetary assets are shown in an entity's accounts do *not* indicate the fair values of these assets. Probably the most common mistake made by uninformed persons reading accounting reports is that of believing there is a close correspondence between the amount at which a nonmonetary asset appears in these reports and the fair value of the asset. The amounts reported for land, building, equipment, and similar nonmonetary assets have no necessary relationship to what these items are currently worth. In general, it is safe to say that the longer a nonmonetary asset has been owned by an entity, the less likely it is that the amount at which the asset appears on the accounting records corresponds to its current fair value.

To emphasize the distinction between accounting's cost concept as it is applied to nonmonetary assets and the ordinary meaning of value, the term *book value* is used for historical cost amounts shown in accounting records.

Rationale for the Cost Concept

The cost concept as it is applied to nonmonetary assets provides an excellent illustration of the problem of applying the three basic criteria used to judge the acceptability of an accounting principle discussed in Chapter 1: relevance, objectivity, and feasibility. If the only criterion were relevance, then the application of the cost concept to the accounting for nonmonetary assets subsequent to their acquisition would not be defensible. Clearly, investors and other financial statement users are more interested in what the business and its individual assets are actually worth today than in what the assets cost originally.

The cost concept, by contrast, provides a relatively objective foundation for nonmonetary asset accounting. It is not purely objective, as we shall see, for judgments are necessary to apply it. It is much more objective, however, than the alternative of attempting to estimate fair values. A market value or current worth concept would be difficult and costly because it would require that the accountant attempt to keep track of the ups and downs through appraisals of the fair value of each nonmonetary asset during each accounting period. The cost concept leads to a much more feasible system of accounting for nonmonetary assets. As a result, readers of an accounting report must recognize that it is based in part on the cost concept, and they must arrive at their own estimate of current values partly by analyzing the information in the report and partly by using nonaccounting information.

The cost concept does not mean that all nonmonetary assets remain on the accounting records at their original purchase price for as long as the entity owns them. The cost of a nonmonetary asset that has a long but nevertheless limited life is systematically reduced over that life by the process called *amortization*, as discussed in Chapter 7. The purpose of the amortization process is to remove systematically the cost of the asset from the asset accounts and to show it as a cost of operations. Amortization has no necessary relationship to changes in market value or in the real worth of the asset.

In summary, adherence to the cost concept when accounting for nonmonetary assets indicates a willingness on the part of the accounting profession to sacrifice some degree of relevance in exchange for greater objectivity and greater feasibility.

Monetary Assets

Monetary assets are initially recorded at their cost and, in the case of most monetary assets, subsequently accounted for at their fair value. This practice raises an important accounting issue: How should the unrealized changes in a monetary asset's fair value be treated for accounting purposes? As will be explained in later chapters, if a monetary asset's carrying amount is changed at the end of each accounting period to reflect its current fair value, the offsetting adjustment is accounted for in several different ways, depending on the nature of the monetary asset.

Rationale for Fair Value

The use of fair value to account for most monetary assets subsequent to their acquisition satisfies the three basic criteria of relevance, objectivity, and feasibility used to judge the acceptability of an accounting principle. Clearly a monetary asset's fair value is relevant to readers of accounting reports, and the fair value of many monetary assets can readily be determined objectively and at a low cost.

Example

A company has invested surplus cash in 100,000 shares of the common stock of General Electric. On June 12, 2010, the management wants to determine the fair value of its investment. To achieve this objective, the management need only wait until the close of the New York Stock Exchange and then refer to one of several different stock price reporting services. Each of these would show that General Electric's common stock closed at $30 per share. Then by simple multiplication, the fair value of the investment could be determined to be $3.0 million.

But who knows what a business is worth today? Any estimate of current value is just that—an estimate—and informed people will disagree on what the estimate should be. For example, on the same day, some people believe that the shares of stock of a given company are overpriced and they should therefore sell the stock; others believe that the shares are underpriced and they buy. Furthermore, accounting reports are prepared by an organization's management. If these reports contained estimates of what the entity is actually worth (including its "goodwill"), these would be management's estimates. It is quite possible that such estimates would be biased.

Goodwill

It follows from the cost concept that if an entity pays *nothing* for an item it acquires (other than as a donation), this item will usually not appear on the accounting records as an asset. Thus, factors that contribute to the value of a company—such as the knowledge and skills that are built up as a business operates, the teamwork that exists within the organization, the importance of a favorable location, the good reputation a company has with its customers, and the trade names developed by the company—do not appear as assets in the accounts of the company.

On some accounting reports, the term *goodwill* appears. Reasoning from the everyday definition of the word, one might conclude that it represents the accountant's appraisal of what the company's intellectual capital, market power, name, and reputation are worth. This is not so. Goodwill appears in the accounts of a company only when the company has purchased another company—as discussed in Chapter 12, when one company buys another company and pays more than the fair value of its net assets (the sum of the fair value of individual assets less the sum of the fair value of individual liabilities). The amount by which the purchase price exceeds the fair value of the acquired company's net assets is called *goodwill,* representing the value of the name, reputation, clientele, or similar intangible resources of the purchased company. Unless a business has actually purchased such intangibles through a business acquisition, however, no item for goodwill is shown in its accounts. If the item does appear, the amount shown initially is the purchase price, even though the management may believe that the real value is considerably higher.

Example

When Philip Morris Incorporated paid $5.8 billion to acquire the General Foods Corporation, $2.8 billion of the purchase price was allocated to the purchased "goodwill," which included the value of the General Foods organization and its various brand names (e.g., Jell-O, Good Seasons, Kool-Aid, Maxwell House). This $2.8 billion was recorded in the Philip Morris accounts as goodwill. It had never been recognized as an asset by General Foods.

The Dual-Aspect Concept

The economic resources of an entity are called *assets*. The claims of various parties against these assets are called **equities**. There are two types of equities: (1) **liabilities**, which are the claims of creditors (that is, everyone other than the owners of the business), and (2) **owners' equity**, which is the claims of the owners of the business. (Owners' equity for an incorporated business is commonly called **shareholders' equity**.) Since all of the assets of a business are claimed by someone (either by its owners or by its creditors) and since the total of these claims cannot exceed the amount of assets to be claimed, it follows that

$$Assets = Equities$$

This is the **fundamental accounting equation** expressed in its general form. It is the formal expression of the dual-aspect concept. As we shall see, all accounting procedures are derived from this equation. To reflect the two types of equities, the expanded version of the equation is

$$Assets = Liabilities + Owners' equity$$

Events that affect the numbers in an entity's accounting records are called **transactions**. Although it is certainly not self-evident to a beginning accounting student, every transaction has a *dual impact* on the accounting records. Accounting systems are set up to record both of these aspects of a transaction; this is why accounting is called a **double-entry system**.

To illustrate the dual-aspect concept, suppose that Ms. Jones starts a business and that her first act is to open a bank account in which she deposits $40,000 of her own money. The dual aspect of this transaction is that the business now has an asset, cash, of $40,000, and Ms. Jones, the owner,[3] has a claim, also of $40,000, against this asset. In other words,

$$Assets (cash), \$40,000 = Equities (owner's), \$40,000$$

If, as its next transaction, the business borrowed $15,000 from a bank, the business accounting records would change in two ways: (1) They would show a $15,000 increase in cash, making the amount $55,000, and (2) they would show a new claim against the assets, the bank's claim, in the amount of $15,000. At this point, the accounting records of the business would show the following:

Cash	$55,000	Owed to bank	$15,000
		Owner's equity	40,000
Total assets	$55,000	Total equities	$55,000

---

[3] Recall from the entity concept that the accounts of the business are kept separate from those of Ms. Jones as an individual.

To repeat, every transaction recorded in the accounts affects at least two items. There is no conceivable way that a transaction can result in only a single change in the accounts.

The Balance Sheet

The financial position of an accounting entity as of a specified moment in time is shown by a **balance sheet**. Its more formal name is a **statement of financial position**. More specifically, the balance sheet reports the assets and equities (liabilities and owners' equity) of the entity at a specified moment in time.[4] Because the balance sheet is a snapshot as of an instant in time, it is a status report (rather than a flow report).

A simplified balance sheet for a corporation is shown in Illustration 2–1. Before considering its details, first examine this balance sheet in terms of the basic concepts already described. Note that the amounts are *expressed in money* and reflect only those

ILLUSTRATION 2–1

	GARSDEN CORPORATION ← Name of entity
	Balance Sheet ← Name of statement
	As of December 31, 2010 ← Moment of time

Assets			Liabilities and Shareholders' Equity		
Current assets:			*Current liabilities:*		
Cash	$ 3,448,891		Accounts payable	$ 6,301,442	
Marketable securities	246,221		Taxes payable	1,672,000	
Accounts receivable	5,954,588		Accrued expenses	640,407	
Inventories	12,623,412		Deferred revenues	205,240	
Prepaid expenses	377,960		Current portion of		
Total current assets		$22,651,072	long-term debt	300,000	
			Total current liabilities		$ 9,119,089
Property, plant, and equipment:			*Long-term debt*		3,000,000
Land		642,367	Total liabilities		$12,119,089
Buildings and equipment, at cost	$26,303,481				
Less: Accumulated depreciation	13,534,069	12,769,412	*Shareholders' equity:*		
			Paid-in capital	$ 5,000,000	
Net property, plant, and equipment		$13,411,779	Retained earnings	19,116,976	
			Total shareholders' equity		$24,116,976
Other assets:					
Investments	$ 110,000				
Intangible assets	63,214	173,214			
Total assets		$36,236,065	Total liabilities and shareholders' equity		$36,236,065

[4] A balance sheet dated December 31 is implicitly understood to mean "at the close of business on December 31."

matters that can be measured in monetary terms. The *entity* involved is the Garsden Corporation, and the balance sheet pertains to that entity rather than to any of the individuals associated with it. The statement assumes that Garsden Corporation is a *going concern.* The nonmonetary asset amounts stated are governed by the *cost concept.* Many of the monetary assets are recorded at their fair value. The *dual-aspect concept* is evident from the fact that the assets listed on the left-hand side of this balance sheet are equal in total to the liabilities and shareholders' equity listed on the right-hand side.

Because of the dual-aspect concept, the two sides of the balance sheet necessarily add up to the same total. This equality does not tell anything about the company's financial health. The label *balance sheet* can give the impression that there is something significant about the fact that the two sides balance. This is not so; the two sides always balance.

In the Garsden Corporation balance sheet, assets are listed on the left and equities on the right.[5] (Normally, the dollar amounts would be rounded to the nearest thousand dollars. We have not done this to emphasize the fact that assets equal equities precisely.)

An Overall View

The balance sheet is the fundamental accounting statement in the sense that *every* accounting transaction can be analyzed in terms of its dual impact on the balance sheet. To understand the information a balance sheet conveys and how economic events affect the balance sheet, the reader must be absolutely clear as to the meaning of its two sides. They can be interpreted in either of two ways, both of which are correct.

Resources and Claims View

One interpretation, the resources and claims view, has already been described. The items listed on the asset side are the economic resources of the entity as of the date of the balance sheet. The amounts stated for each asset are recorded in accordance with the basic concepts described above. Liabilities and owners' equity are claims against the entity as of the balance sheet date. Liabilities are the claims of outside parties—amounts that the entity owes to banks, vendors, employees, and other creditors. Owners' equity shows the claims of the owners.

However, an entity's owners do not have a claim in the same sense that the creditors do. In the Garsden Corporation illustration, it can be said with assurance that govern-mental taxing authorities had a claim of $1,672,000 as of December 31, 2010—that the corporation owed them $1,672,000, neither more nor less. It is more difficult to interpret as a claim the amount shown as shareholders' equity, $24,116,976. *If* the corporation were liquidated as of December 31, 2010, *if* the assets were sold for their book value, and *if* the creditors were paid the $12,119,089 owed them, then the shareholders would get what was left, which would be $24,116,976. However, these "if " conditions are obviously unrealistic. According to the going-concern concept, the corporation is not going to be liquidated; and according to the cost concept, the nonmonetary assets are not shown at their liquidation values.

The shareholders' equity (or owners' equity) might be worth considerably more or less than $24,116,976. The shareholders' equity of a healthy, growing company is usually worth considerably more than its "book value"—the amount shown on the balance sheet. On the other hand, if a company is not salable as a going concern and is liquidated with the assets being sold piecemeal, the owners' proceeds are often only a small fraction of the amount stated for shareholders' equity on the balance sheet.

---

[5] Outside the United States, other balance sheet formats are often used. A common format is to list assets at the top of the page and to list equities beneath them. This format is called the *report form.* The balance sheet format used by the Garsden Corporation is called the *account form.*

Often when a bankrupt company's assets are liquidated, the proceeds are inadequate to satisfy 100 percent of the creditors' claims, in which case the owners receive nothing.

The resources and claims view of the balance sheet has some shortcomings. We have already pointed out the difficulty of interpreting shareholders' equity as a claim. Also, the notion of "claiming" assets is rather legalistic, and has the most meaning if a company is being liquidated in bankruptcy—which is inconsistent with the going-concern concept. Therefore, the second way of interpreting the balance sheet has considerable merit. It is described in the next section.

Sources and Uses of Funds View

In this alternative view, the left-hand side of the balance sheet is said to show the forms in which the entity has used, or *invested,* the funds provided to it as of the balance sheet date. These investments have been made in order to help the entity achieve its objectives, which in a business organization include earning a satisfactory profit. The right-hand side shows the *sources of the funds* that are invested in the assets—it shows how the assets were *financed.* The several liability items describe how much of that financing was obtained from trade creditors (accounts payable), from lenders (long-term debt), and from other creditors. The owners' equity section shows the financing supplied by the owners. (The two ways in which the owners of a business corporation provide it with funds—paid-in capital and retained earnings—will be explained later in the chapter.)

Thus, with the sources and uses of funds view, the fundamental accounting equation, Assets = Liabilities + Owners' equity, has this interpretation: Every dollar invested in the entity's assets was supplied either by the entity's creditors or by its owners; and every dollar thus supplied is invested in some asset.

Both ways of interpreting the balance sheet are correct. In certain circumstances, the resources and claims view is easier to understand. In analyzing the balance sheet of a going concern, however, the sources and uses of funds view usually provides a more meaningful interpretation.

Account Categories

Although each individual asset or equity—each building, piece of equipment, bank loan, and so on—could conceivably be listed separately on the balance sheet, it is more practicable and more informative to summarize and group related items into classifications or **account categories**. There is no fixed pattern as to the number of such categories or the amount of detail reported. Rather, the format is governed by management's opinion about the most useful way of presenting significant information on the status of the entity.

As in any classification scheme, the categories are defined so that (1) the individual items included in a category resemble one another in significant respects and (2) the items in one category are essentially different from those in all other categories. Although the items included in a category are similar to one another, they are not identical.

Example

The category labeled *cash* usually includes money on deposit in interest-paying accounts as well as money on deposit in checking accounts. These two types of money are *similar* in that they are both in highly liquid form, but they are not *identical* because certain restrictions may apply to withdrawals from interest-paying accounts that do not apply to checking accounts.

The balance sheet in Illustration 2–1 gives a minimum amount of detail. The terms used on this balance sheet are common ones, and they are described briefly below. More detailed descriptions are given in Chapters 5 through 9.

Note that the amounts in Illustration 2–1 are rounded to the nearest dollar. Cents are rarely shown; and in a large company, the amounts are usually rounded to thousands or even millions of dollars. Although rounding is done in preparing financial statements, the underlying detailed records are maintained to the cent.

Assets

We shall now supersede the short definition of *assets* given in the preceding section by the following more exact statement: **Assets** are economic resources that are controlled by an entity and whose cost (or fair value) at the time of acquisition could be objectively measured. The four key points in this definition are (1) an asset must be acquired in a transaction, (2) an asset must be an *economic resource,* (3) the resource must be *controlled* by the entity, and (4) its cost (or fair value) at the time of acquisition must be *objectively measurable.*

A resource is an *economic* resource if it provides *future benefits* to the entity. Resources provide future benefits under any of three conditions: (1) They are cash or can be converted to cash, (2) they are goods that are expected to be sold and cash received for them, or (3) they are items expected to be used in future activities that will generate cash inflows to the entity. Thus, economic resources are either cash or items that will eventually result in cash inflows.

Example

Garsden Corporation is a manufacturing company. The cash that it has on deposit in banks is an asset because it is money that can be used to acquire other resources. Amounts owed by customers are assets that when collected will generate cash. The goods Garsden has manufactured and still has on hand are assets because they are expected to be sold. The equipment and other manufacturing facilities it owns are assets because it is expected that they will be used to produce additional goods. However, merchandise that cannot be sold because it is damaged or obsolete is not an asset, even though it is owned by the business, because it will not generate cash.

Control is an accounting concept similar to, but not quite the same as, the legal concept of ownership. When a business buys an automobile on an installment loan (e.g., it pays $575 a month for 36 months), the business may not own the car in the legal sense because title to the car does not pass to the buyer until the last installment has been paid. Nevertheless, if the business has the full use of the car, the automobile is regarded as being fully controlled by the business and is an asset. Possession or temporary control is not enough to qualify the item as an asset, however.

Example

Office space leased on an annual basis is not an asset, nor is an automobile or other piece of equipment that is leased for a relatively short time. In both cases, the entity's control over the use of the item is only temporary. On the other hand, if a business leases a building or an item of equipment for a period of time that equals or almost equals its useful life, such an item is an asset even though the entity does not own it.

The *objective measurability* test is usually clear-cut, but in some instances it is difficult to apply. If the resource was purchased for cash or for the promise to pay cash, it is an asset. If the resource was manufactured or constructed by the business, then money was paid for the costs of manufacture or construction, and it is an asset. If the resource was acquired by trading in some other asset or by issuing shares of the company's stock, it is an asset. If the resource was donated and it has future benefit, then the resource is an asset. On the other hand, as already pointed out, a valuable reputation is not an asset if it arose gradually over a period of time rather than being acquired in a transaction at an objectively measurable cost.

On most business balance sheets, assets are listed in decreasing order of their liquidity, that is, in order of the promptness with which they are expected to be converted into cash.[6]

Assets are customarily grouped into categories. Current assets are almost always reported in a separate category. All noncurrent assets may be reported together or in various groupings such as "property, plant, and equipment" and "other assets," as shown on the Garsden Corporation balance sheet.

Current Assets

Cash and other assets that are expected to be realized in cash or sold or consumed during the normal operating cycle of the entity or within one year, whichever is longer, are called **current assets**. Although the usual time limit is one year, exceptions occur in companies whose normal operating cycle is longer than one year. Tobacco companies and distilleries, for example, include their inventories as current assets even though tobacco and liquor remain in inventory for an aging process that lasts two years or more.

Cash consists of funds that are readily available for disbursement. Most of these funds are on deposit in interest-paying accounts and checking accounts in banks, and the remainder are in cash registers or petty cash boxes on the entity's premises.

Marketable securities are investments that are both readily marketable and expected to be converted into cash within a year. These investments are made in order to earn some return on cash that otherwise would be temporarily idle.

Accounts receivable are amounts owed to the entity by its customers. Accounts receivable are reported on the balance sheet as the amount owed less an allowance for that portion that probably will not be collected. (Methods of estimating this "allowance for doubtful accounts" are described in Chapter 5.) Amounts owed the entity by parties other than customers would appear under the heading **notes receivable** or **other receivables** rather than as accounts receivable. If the amounts owed to the company are evidenced by written promises to pay, they are listed as notes receivable.

Inventories are the aggregate of those items that are either (1) held for sale in the ordinary course of business, (2) in process of production for such sale, or (3) soon to be consumed in the production of goods or services that will be available for sale. Note that inventory relates to goods that will be sold in the ordinary course of business. A truck offered for sale by a truck dealer is inventory. A truck used by the dealer to make service calls is not inventory; it is an item of equipment, which is a noncurrent asset.

Prepaid expenses represent certain assets, usually of an intangible nature, whose usefulness will expire in the near future. An example is an insurance policy. A business pays for insurance protection in advance. Its right to this protection is an asset—an economic resource that will provide future benefits. Since this right will expire within a fairly short period of time, it is a current asset. The amount on the balance sheet is the amount of the unexpired cost of the future benefit.

Example

If on January 1, 2010, Garsden Corporation paid $250,000 for insurance protection for two years, the amount of prepaid insurance expense on the December 31, 2010, balance sheet would be $125,000, which is the cost of the one year of protection then remaining.

Property, Plant, and Equipment

This category consists of assets that are tangible and relatively long-lived. The term **fixed assets** is also used for this category. The entity has acquired these assets in order to use them to produce goods and services that will generate future cash inflows. If such assets are instead held for resale, they are classified as inventory, even though

---

[6] Outside the United States, on some balance sheets, the order is reversed and the least liquid assets are listed first.

in a sense they are long-lived assets. (They will be long-lived to their purchaser, but they are not expected to be held long term by their seller.)

In the balance sheet shown in Illustration 2–1, the first item of property, plant, and equipment is land, which is reported at its cost, $642,367. Land is shown separately because it is not depreciated, as are buildings and equipment. The first amount shown for buildings and equipment, $26,303,481, is the *original cost* of all the items of tangible long-lived property other than land—the amounts paid to acquire these items. The next item, accumulated depreciation, means that a portion of the original cost of the buildings and equipment, amounting to $13,534,069, has been written off, allocated as a cost of doing business. Depreciation will be discussed in detail in Chapter 7.

Other Assets

Another type of noncurrent asset is **investments**. These are securities of one company owned by another either in order to control the other company or in anticipation of earning a long-term return from the investment. They are therefore to be distinguished from marketable securities, which are a current asset reflecting the short-term use of excess cash.

Intangible assets include goodwill (briefly described earlier), patents, copyrights, trademarks, franchises, and similar valuable but nonphysical things controlled by the business. They are distinguished from prepaid expenses (intangible *current* assets) in that they have a longer life span than prepaid expenses.

Liabilities

In general, **liabilities** are obligations to transfer assets or provide services to outside parties arising from events that have already happened. (A few complicated items that may appear in the liabilities section of the balance sheet do not fit this definition; they will be discussed in later chapters.) Liability obligations exist as a result of *past* transactions or events. Thus, on December 31, wages not yet paid to an employee who worked from December 27 to December 31 are a liability; but that person's wages to be earned next week (the first week in January) are not a liability as of December 31.[7]

Liabilities are claims against the entity's assets. Unless otherwise noted, an individual liability is not a claim against any *specific* asset or group of assets. Thus, although accounts payable typically arise from the purchase of items for inventory, accounts payable are claims against the assets in general and not specifically against inventories. If a liability *is* a claim against a specific asset, its title indicates that fact, as in a *mortgage* loan or *secured* long-term debt.

With minor exceptions, a liability is reported at the amount that would be required to satisfy the obligation as of the balance sheet date.[8] For a loan, this includes the principal that is owed as well as any interest earned by the lender but unpaid as of the balance sheet date. (Often this interest payable or "accrued" interest is shown separately from the principal owed.) Thus, if the December 31 balance sheet showed $100,000 for a loan payable and $1,000 interest payable on that loan, a $101,000 payment to the lender would be required to satisfy the loan liability obligation as of December 31. Note that the total amount needed to satisfy the obligation is reported, not just the portion of that total that is due and payable as of the balance sheet date. The $100,000 loan is a liability even though there may be no principal payment due for another five years.

Current Liabilities

Liabilities that are expected to be satisfied or extinguished during the normal operating cycle or within one year, whichever is longer, are called **current liabilities**.

---

[7] Although, in a sense, employees are not outside parties, in accounting they are considered such to the extent that they are not owners of the entity. Only owners of the entity are inside parties.

[8] We shall describe an alternative interpretation of the amount of a liability in Chapter 8.

Accounts payable represent the claims of suppliers arising from their furnishing goods or services to the entity for which they have not yet been paid. (Such suppliers often are called **vendors**.) Usually these claims are unsecured. Amounts owed to financial institutions (which are suppliers of funds rather than of goods or services) are called **notes payable** or **short-term loans** (or some other name that describes the nature of the debt instrument) rather than accounts payable.

Taxes payable shows the amount that the entity owes government agencies for taxes. It is shown separately from other obligations both because of its size and because the amount owed may not be precisely known as of the date of the balance sheet. Often the liability for federal and state income taxes is shown separately from other tax liabilities, such as property taxes.

Accrued expenses represent amounts that have been earned by outside parties but have not yet been paid by the entity. Usually there is no invoice or similar document submitted by the party to whom the money is owed. Interest earned by a lender but not yet paid by the entity is an accrued expense. Another example is the wages and salaries owed to employees for work they have performed but for which they have not yet been paid. The term *accrued expenses,* although frequently used as a balance sheet category, is not as descriptive as the names used in the detailed records for specific accrued expenses, such as **interest payable** and **wages payable**.

Deferred revenues (also called **unearned revenues**) represent the liability that arises because the entity has received advance payment for a service it has agreed to render in the future. An example is unearned subscription revenues, which represent magazine subscription payments received in advance, for which the publishing company agrees to deliver issues of its magazine during some future period.

Current portion of long-term debt represents that part of a long-term loan that is due within the next 12 months. It is reported separately from the noncurrent portion so that current liabilities will give a complete picture of the entity's short-term obligations.

Other Liabilities

Those obligations that do not meet the criteria for being classified as current liabilities are simply called **other liabilities**. They are also sometimes called **noncurrent liabilities** or **long-term debt**.

Example	Garsden Corporation has a $3,300,000 loan outstanding. Of this amount, $300,000 is due within the next year and is therefore a current liability. The remaining $3 million is due in some future period (or periods) beyond the next year (i.e., after December 31, 2010) and is thus shown as long-term debt.
Owners' Equity	The **owners' equity** section of the balance sheet shows the amount the owners have invested in the entity. The terminology used in this section varies with different forms of organization. In a corporation, the ownership interest is evidenced by shares of stock, and the owners' equity section of its balance sheet is therefore usually labeled **shareholders' equity** or **stockholders' equity**.

Paid-In Capital

The shareholders' equity of the Garsden Corporation's balance sheet is divided into two main categories.[9] The first category, called **paid-in capital** or **contributed capital**, is the amount the owners have invested directly in the business by purchasing shares of stock as these shares were issued by the corporation. Paid-in capital in most

---

[9] A third section, called *other comprehensive income,* may be included in the owners' equity section of some balance sheets. It is discussed in Chapter 10.

corporations is further subdivided into **capital stock** and **additional paid-in capital**. Each share of stock has a stated or "par" value; capital stock shows this value per share times the number of shares outstanding.[10] If investors actually paid more to the corporation than the stated value (as is almost always the case) for their shares, the excess is shown separately as additional paid-in capital.

Example

Garsden Corporation has outstanding 1 million shares of common stock with a par value of $1 per share. Investors actually paid into the corporation $5 million for these shares. The balance sheet in Illustration 2–1 could be modified to show:

Paid-in capital:		
Common stock at par	$1,000,000	
Additional paid-in capital	4,000,000	
Total paid-in capital		$5,000,000

Retained Earnings

The second category of shareholders' equity is labeled *retained earnings*. The owners' equity increases through *earnings* (i.e., the results of profitable operations) and decreases when earnings are paid out in the form of dividends. **Retained earnings** is the difference between the *total* earnings of the entity *from its inception* to date and the *total* amount of dividends paid out to its shareholders *over its entire life*. That is, the difference represents that part of the total earnings that have been retained for use in—*reinvested* in—the business.[11] If the difference is negative, the item usually is labeled **deficit** rather than retained earnings.

Note that the amount of retained earnings on a given date is the *cumulative* amount that has been retained in the business from the beginning of the corporation's existence up to that date. The amount shown for Garsden Corporation means that *since the company began operations,* the total amount of its earnings reinvested in the business after paying out dividends is $19,116,976.

Note also that the amount of retained earnings does not indicate the *form* in which the retained earnings have been reinvested. They may be invested in *any* of the resources that appear on the assets side of the balance sheet. (This is true of all liabilities and items of owners' equity, not just retained earnings.) There is a common misconception that there is some connection between the amount of a company's retained earnings and the amount of cash it holds. There is no such connection. This should be apparent from the fact that the Garsden Corporation balance sheet shows over $19 million of retained earnings but only $3.4 million of cash.

Net worth is a synonym for the term *owners' equity* that is frequently used in articles and conversation. *Net worth* can be a misleading term because it implies that the amount indicates what the owners' interest is "worth," which, as has been emphasized, is erroneous. For this reason, the use of the term *net worth* in financial statements is frowned upon.

---

[10] Par value is a dollar amount printed on the face of common stock certificates. It seldom has any significance today. A stockholder who paid less to the issuing company than the par value of the common stock received could be held liable in bankruptcy for the difference between the stock's par value and the amount paid for it. To guard against this possibility, the par value is set at a nominal amount and the selling price is higher than the par value.

[11] Shareholders' equity also can be affected by events other than the issuance of common stock and the accumulation of earnings and the distribution of these earnings as dividends. Some of these events will be discussed in later chapters.

Owners' equity is also sometimes called **net assets**, since the amount shown for owners' equity is always equal to assets net of (i.e., minus) liabilities. Similarly, the Financial Accounting Standards Board defines owners' equity simply as "the residual interest in the assets of an entity that remains after deducting its liabilities."[12] The use of the word *residual* reflects the fact that in law, owners' claims rank below creditors' claims. For the same reason, common stock is sometimes referred to as a "residual security."

Unincorporated Businesses

In unincorporated businesses, different terminology is used in the owners' equity section. In a **proprietorship**—a business owned by one person—the owner's equity is customarily shown as a single number with a title such as "Lee Jones, capital," rather than making a distinction between the owner's initial investment and the accumulated earnings retained in the business.

In a **partnership**, which is an unincorporated business owned jointly by several persons, there is a capital account for each partner. For example:

Jane Davis, capital	$75,432	
Wayne Smith, capital	75,432	
Total partners' capital		$150,864

A proprietorship or partnership balance sheet also may show a reconciliation of the beginning and ending balance in each owner's capital account. An owner's capital is increased by her or his share of the entity's earnings during the period and is decreased by the owner's **drawings**. (Drawings in an unincorporated firm are analogous to a corporation's dividends.) For example, a proprietorship's 2010 year-end balance sheet might show the following:

Lee Jones, capital, as of January 1, 2010	$180,000
Add: 2010 earnings	45,000
Deduct: 2010 drawings	(40,000)
Lee Jones, capital, as of December 31, 2010	$185,000

The reader may have heard the terms *partnership accounting* and *corporation accounting* and thus may have formed the impression that different accounting systems are used for different forms of business organizations. This is not so. The treatment of assets and liabilities is generally the same in all forms of business organizations: Differences occur principally in the owners' equity (capital) section, as noted above.[13]

Having explained the two principal components of owners' equity in a corporation, we can now expand the fundamental accounting equation to read

$$\text{Assets} = \text{Liabilities} + \text{Paid-in capital} + \text{Retained earnings}$$

[12] FASB, *Statement of Financial Accounting Concepts No. 6.*
[13] Nonbusiness organizations do treat certain items differently than businesses, but these differences are beyond the scope of this book.

Ratios

In using financial statement information, it often is helpful to express certain important relationships as ratios or percentages. Some of these ratios will be introduced at appropriate places throughout the book and they will be summarized in Chapter 13. A **ratio** is simply one number expressed in terms of another. It is found by dividing one number, the base, into the other. Since Garsden Corporation (Illustration 2–1) had current assets of $22,651,072 and current liabilities of $9,119,089, the ratio of its current assets to its current liabilities is $22,651,072 ÷ $9,119,089, or 2.5 to 1.

Current Ratio

The ratio of current assets to current liabilities is called the **current ratio**. It is an important indication of an entity's ability to meet its current obligations because if current assets do not exceed current liabilities by a comfortable margin, the entity may be unable to pay its current bills. This is because most current assets are expected to be converted into cash within a year or less, whereas most current liabilities are obligations expected to use cash within a year or less. As a rough rule of thumb, a current ratio of at least 2 to 1 is believed to be desirable in a typical manufacturing company. Garsden's current ratio of 2.5 to 1 is therefore satisfactory. (The "to 1" part of the ratio is usually not explicitly stated; Garsden's current ratio is simply 2.5.)

Balance Sheet Changes

At the moment an entity begins, its financial status can be recorded on a balance sheet. From that time on, events occur that change the numbers on this first balance sheet, and the accountant records these transactions in accordance with the concepts given earlier in this chapter. Accounting systems accumulate and summarize these changes as a basis for preparing new balance sheets at prescribed intervals, such as the end of a quarter or a year. Each balance sheet shows the financial condition of the entity as of the date it was prepared, after giving effect to all of these changes.

Although in practice a balance sheet is prepared only at prescribed intervals, in learning the accounting process it is useful to consider the changes one by one. This makes it possible to study the effect of individual events without getting entangled with the mechanisms used to record these transactions. The following examples show the effects of a few transactions on the balance sheet. For simplicity, they are assumed to occur on successive days.

Original Capital Contribution

Jan. 1   John Smith starts an incorporated CD and tape store called Music Mart, Inc. He does this by depositing $25,000 of his own funds in a bank account that he has opened in the name of the business entity and taking $25,000 of stock certificates in return. He is the sole owner of the corporation. The balance sheet of Music Mart, Inc., will then be as follows:

MUSIC MART Balance Sheet As of January 1			
Assets		**Liabilities and Owner's Equity**	
Cash	$25,000	Paid-in capital	$25,000

Bank Loan

Jan. 2   Music Mart borrows $12,500 from a bank; the loan is evidenced by a legal document called a *note*. This transaction increases the asset, cash, and the business incurs a liability to the bank called *notes payable*. The balance sheet after this transaction will appear thus:

MUSIC MART Balance Sheet As of January 2			
Assets		**Liabilities and Owner's Equity**	
Cash	$37,500	Notes payable	$12,500
		Paid-in capital	25,000
Total	$37,500	Total	$37,500

Purchase of Merchandise

Jan. 3   The business buys inventory (merchandise it intends to sell) in the amount of $5,000, paying cash. This transaction decreases cash and increases another asset, inventory. The balance sheet will now be as follows:

MUSIC MART Balance Sheet As of January 3			
Assets		**Liabilities and Owner's Equity**	
Cash	$32,500	Notes payable	$12,500
Inventory	5,000	Paid-in capital	25,000
Total	$37,500	Total	$37,500

Sale of Merchandise

Jan. 4   For $750 cash, the store sells merchandise that costs $500. The effect of this transaction is to decrease inventory by $500, increase cash by $750, and increase owner's equity by the difference, or $250. The $250 is the profit on this sale. To distinguish it from the paid-in capital portion of owner's equity, it is recorded as retained earnings. The balance sheet will then look like this:

MUSIC MART Balance Sheet As of January 4			
Assets		**Liabilities and Owner's Equity**	
Cash	$33,250	Notes payable	$12,500
Inventory	4,500	Paid-in capital	25,000
		Retained earnings	250
Total	$37,750	Total	$37,750

Balance Sheet of Start Ups

There has been a paradigm shift in the way new players are doing businesses and that has resulted in an altogether different structure of Financial Statements of the firms. Over the years, the traditional items in the Balance Sheets have gone through a transformation; at least for the new businesses which are driving on major technological breakthrough almost disrupting the existing business practices. Moreover, there is a clear shift towards "asset light" businesses resulting in a very small Balance Sheet size and still attracting very large market valuations. A few years back, we couldn't have imagined a company having inventory which is almost virtual like "seats in an airline" and "hotel rooms in hotel" which are there and also not there but this is exactly what companies like Makemytrip.com and Oyohotels.com are doing. An intangible inventory which is the "value driver" of a firm and whose price is dynamically determined (based on demand and supply) could sound like really weird but that's what exactly is happening today.

When you look at the Asset side of a Balance Sheet of a typical e-commerce firm like Flipkart, it doesn't have any "Property, Plant and Equipment (typically classified as PPE generically called Fixed Assets) nor do they have much inventory of products which they sell. They, however, do sell products by calling themselves a "technology platform" and their revenue runs into billions but the products they sell don't really reflect on the Balance Sheet. A student of Accounting can't really make out anything about the nature of the firm by looking at the Balance Sheet. For the valuation of any typical firm, the starting point has always been their financial statements but with such businesses, just the balance sheet is actually not an indication of their real value.

How Same Items Mean Different Things Now

Another set of firms which are making Balance Sheet almost irrelevant are "intellectual capital driven firms" where the main "value driver" (real assets) are human resource and given that the Accounting standards don't allow the human resource to be recorded, the balance sheet of such firms (like Microsoft) don't provide any understanding of the nature of business. Actually, looking at the Balance sheet of such firms like Microsoft, one gets an impression of an "Investment bank" rather than a Software company. Financial Markets understand that the valuation of such firms is driven by the products being developed by the brilliant engineers in the firm and the firms, to keep the valuation high, keep on hiring the best talent from the best schools in the world and pay them handsomely to retain them.

If one looks at the Liability and Equity side of the Balance sheet of such firms, we see hardly any debt or borrowing in these firms which is quite understandable given the fact that they hardly have any assets to mortgage to the bank as collateral. This is the reason why these firms always fall short of funds and have to keep selling or diluting the equity to stop the "fund tap" from drying out. The new investors are always perplexed by the high valuation such firms attract despite the fact that they don't have significant assets and have almost no debt on their Balance sheets. The prospective investors need to be educated on the fact that the real assets (The Team of people) are not recorded and therefore the high valuations.

So, is the Balance Sheet no longer reflecting the true and fair valuation of the firm and that we, as investors have to look beyond just Balance Sheet to understand the valuation of a firm. The traditional valuation models relied largely on the future cash-generating capability of the tangible assets of the firm, and largely ignored the "intangible assets." In the current context, the situation has turned upside down and more and more valuations these days are driven by "intangibles" rather than "tangibles." And more so, the "intangibles" which are not recorded on the Balance Sheet especially world-class human resource.

Another item on the Balance Sheet which has become really big but sadly doesn't contribute much to the overall valuation of the firm is "Cash and Cash Equivalents." Again, firms which don't need heavy investment in Fixed Assets but generate attractive margins in their businesses don't really know what to do with that surplus earnings and therefore usually sit on huge piles of "Cash and Cash Equivalents." Of course, they would need cash to pay their "world-class human resource" handsomely and on time and also ensure the employees of job security even if chips are down. Some large MNCs like Apple have "Cash and Cash Equivalents" to the size of GDPs of many poor countries.

Concluding Comment

At this point, readers should not be alarmed if they do not yet fully understand some of the topics in this chapter. In subsequent chapters, we shall expand considerably on the concepts, categories, and terms introduced here. We shall describe modifications and qualifications to some of the basic concepts, and we shall introduce many additional terms that are used on balance sheets. We shall not, however, discard the basic structure that was introduced in this chapter; it was based on the equation Assets = Liabilities + Owners' equity. Furthermore, it is important to remember that *every* accounting transaction can be recorded in terms of its effect on the balance sheet. The reader should be able to relate all the new material to this basic structure.

Summary

The basic concepts discussed in this chapter may be briefly summarized as follows:

1. *Money measurement.* Accounting records only those facts that can be expressed in monetary terms.

2. *Entity.* Accounts are kept for entities as distinguished from the persons associated with those entities.

3. *Going concern.* Accounting assumes that an entity will continue to exist indefinitely and that it is not about to be liquidated.

4. *Cost.* Nonmonetary and monetary assets are ordinarily entered in the accounts at the amount paid to acquire them. This cost, rather than current fair value, is the basis for subsequent accounting for nonmonetary assets. Most monetary assets are accounted for at fair value following their acquisition.

5. *Dual aspect.* Every transaction affects at least two items and preserves the fundamental equation: Assets = Liabilities + Owners' equity.

The balance sheet shows the financial condition of an entity as of a specified moment in time. It consists of two sides. The assets side shows the economic resources controlled by the entity that are expected to provide future benefits to it and that were acquired at objectively measurable amounts. The equities side shows the liabilities, which are obligations of the entity, and the owners' equity, which is the amount invested by the owners. In a corporation, owners' equity is subdivided into paid-in capital and retained earnings.

Problems

Problem 2–1.

a. If assets equal $95,000 and liabilities equal $40,000, then owners' equity equals _____.

b. If assets equal $65,000 and owners' equity equals $40,000, then liabilities equal _____.

c. If current assets equal $25,000, liabilities equal $40,000, and owners' equity equals $55,000, the noncurrent assets equal _____.

d. If the current ratio is 2.2:1, current assets are $33,000, and noncurrent assets equal $55,000, then owners' equity is _____. (Assume that all liabilities are current.)

e. What is the current ratio if noncurrent assets equal $60,000, total assets equal $95,000, and owners' equity equals $70,000? (Assume that all liabilities are current.)

Problem 2–2.

Prepare a balance sheet as of June 30, for the J. L. Gregory Company, using the following data:

Accounts payable	$ 241,000	Cash	$ 89,000
Accounts receivable	505,000	Equipment (at cost)	761,000
Accrued expenses	107,000	Estimated tax liability	125,000
Accumulated depreciation on buildings	538,000	Inventories	513,000
Accumulated depreciation on equipment	386,000	Investment in the Peerless Company	320,000
		Land (at cost)	230,000
Bonds payable	700,000	Marketable securities	379,000
Buildings (at cost)	1,120,000	Notes payable	200,000
Capital stock	1,000,000	Retained earnings	?

Problem 2–3.

Indicate the net effect on assets, liabilities, and owners' equity resulting from each of the following transactions:

1. Capital stock was issued for $100,000 cash.
2. Bonds payable of $25,000 were refunded with capital stock.
3. Depreciation on plant and equipment equaled $8,500 for the year.
4. Inventory was purchased for $15,900 cash.
5. $9,400 worth of inventory was purchased on credit.
6. Inventory costing $4,500 was sold for $7,200 on credit.
7. $3,500 in cash was received for merchandise sold on credit.
8. Dividends of $3,000 were declared.
9. The declared dividends of $3,000 were paid.
10. The company declared a stock split, and replaced each outstanding share with two new shares.

Problem 2–4.

D. Carson and F. Leggatt formed a partnership on June 1 to operate a shoe store. Carson contributed $50,000 cash and Leggatt contributed $50,000 worth of shoe inventory. During the month of June, the following transactions took place:

1. Additional shoe inventory was purchased at a cost of $24,000 cash.
2. Total cash sales for the month were $31,000. The inventory that was sold had a cost of $15,500.
3. Carson withdrew $6,200 of cash drawings. Leggatt withdrew only $3,700 of cash drawings.

4. The partnership borrowed $50,000 from the Third National Bank.
5. Land and a building were purchased at a cash cost of $25,000 and $50,000, respectively.

Required:
  a. Prepare a balance sheet as of June 1.
  b. Prepare a reconciliation of the beginning and ending balances for each owner's capital account.
  c. Prepare a balance sheet as of June 30.

Problem 2–5.
The January 1 balance sheet of the Marvin Company, an unincorporated business, is as follows:

MARVIN COMPANY Balance Sheet As of January 1			
Assets		**Liabilities and Owner's Equity**	
Cash	$25,000	Notes payable	$20,000
Inventory	50,000	Capital	55,000
Total	$75,000	Total	$75,000

The following transactions took place in January:

Jan. 4   Merchandise was sold for $12,000 cash that had cost $7,000.
     6   To increase inventory, Marvin placed an order with Star Company for merchandise that would cost $7,000.
     8   Marvin received the merchandise ordered from Star and agreed to pay the $7,000 in 30 days.
   11   Merchandise costing $1,500 was sold for $2,500 in cash.
   16   Merchandise costing $2,000 was sold for $3,400 on 30-day open account.
   26   Marvin paid employees for the month $4,200 in cash.
   29   Purchased land for $20,000 in cash.
   31   Marvin purchased a two-year insurance policy for $2,800 in cash.

Required:
Describe the impact of each transaction on the balance sheet, and prepare a new balance sheet as of January 31.

Problem 2–6.
As of December 31, Brian Company had the following account balances:

Accounts payable	$5,000	Long-term investments	$1,500
Accounts receivable	7,000	Marketable securities	3,500
Bonds payable	8,000	Plant and equipment	8,500
Cash	2,000	Wages payable	1,500
Current portion of bonds payable	2,000		

Required:
  a. What was the current ratio?
  b. Explain what the current ratio measures.

CASES

Case 2–1
Maynard Company (A)*

Diane Maynard made the following request of a friend:

> My bookkeeper has quit, and I need to see the balance sheets of my company. He has left behind a book with the numbers already entered in it. Would you be willing to prepare balance sheets for me? Also, any comments you care to make about the numbers would be appreciated. The Cash account is healthy, which is a good sign, and he has told me that the net income in June was $19,635.

The book contained a detailed record of transactions, and from it the friend was able to copy off the balances at the beginning of the month and at the end of the month as shown in Exhibit 1. Diane Maynard owned all the stock of Maynard Company. At the end

* © Professor Robert N. Anthony.

of June, Diane Maynard paid herself an $11,700 dividend and used the money to repay her loan from the company.

Questions

1. Prepare balance sheets as of June 1 and as of June 30, in proper format.
2. Make comments about how the financial condition as of the end of June compared with that at the beginning of June.
3. Why do retained earnings not increase by the amount of June net income?
4. As of June 30, do you feel that Maynard Company is worth the amount in Shareholder's Equity, $619,446? Explain.

EXHIBIT 1 Account Balances

	June 1	June 30
Accounts payable	$ 8,517	$ 21,315
Accounts receivable	21,798	26,505
Accrued wages payable	1,974	2,202
Accumulated depreciation on building	156,000	157,950
Accumulated depreciation on equipment	5,304	5,928
Bank notes payable	8,385	29,250
Building	585,000	585,000
Capital stock	390,000	390,000
Cash	34,983	66,660
Equipment (at cost)	13,260	36,660
Land	89,700	89,700
Merchandise inventory	29,835	26,520
Note receivable, Diane Maynard	11,700	0
Other noncurrent assets	4,857	5,265
Other noncurrent liabilities	2,451	2,451
Prepaid insurance	3,150	2,826
Retained earnings	221,511	229,446
Supplies on hand	5,559	6,630
Taxes payable	5,700	7,224

Case 2–2
Music Mart, Inc.*

On a sheet of paper, set up in pencil the balance sheet of Music Mart, Inc., as it appears after the last transaction described in the text (January 4), leaving considerable space between each item. Record the effect, if any, of the following events on the balance sheet, either by revising existing figures (cross out, rather than erase) or by adding new items as necessary. At least one of these events does not affect the balance sheet. The basic equation, Assets = Liabilities + Owners' equity, must be preserved at all times. Errors will be minimized if you make a separate list of the balance sheet items affected by each transaction and the amount (+ or −) by which each is to be changed.

After you have recorded these events, prepare a balance sheet in proper form. Assume that all these transactions occurred in January and that there were no other transactions in January.

1. The store purchased and received merchandise for inventory for $5,000, agreeing to pay within 30 days.
2. Merchandise costing $1,500 was sold for $2,300, which was received in cash.
3. Merchandise costing $1,700 was sold for $2,620, the customers agreeing to pay $2,620 within 30 days.

* © Professor Robert N. Anthony.

4. The store purchased a three-year fire insurance policy for $1,224, paying cash.
5. The store purchased two lots of land of equal size for a total of $24,000. It paid $6,000 in cash and gave a 10-year mortgage for $18,000.
6. The store sold one of the two lots of land for $12,000. It received $3,000 cash, and in addition, the buyer assumed $9,000 of the mortgage; that is, Music Mart, Inc., became no longer responsible for this half.
7. Smith received a bona fide offer of $33,000 for the business; although his equity was then only $26,970, he rejected the offer. It was evident that the store had already acquired goodwill of $6,030.
8. Smith withdrew $1,000 cash from the store's bank account for his personal use.
9. Smith took merchandise costing $750 from the store's inventory for his personal use.
10. Smith learned that the individual who purchased the land (No. 6 above) subsequently sold it for $14,000. The lot still owned by Music Mart, Inc., was identical in value with this other plot.
11. The store paid off $6,000 of its note payable (dis-regard interest).
12. Smith sold one-third of the stock he owned in Music Mart, Inc., for $11,000 cash.
13. Merchandise costing $850 was sold for $1,310, which was received in cash.

Case 2–3
Lone Pine Cafe (A)*

On March 31, 2010, the partnership that had been organized to operate the Lone Pine Cafe was dissolved under unusual circumstances, and in connection with its dissolution, preparation of a balance sheet became necessary.

The partnership was formed by Mr. and Mrs. Henry Antoine and Mrs. Sandra Landers, who had become acquainted while working in a Portland, Oregon, restaurant. On November 1, 2009, each of the three partners

* Based on a case decided by the Supreme Court of the State of Oregon (216 P.2d 1005). © Professor Robert N. Anthony, Harvard Business School.

contributed $16,000 cash to the partnership and agreed to share in the profits proportionally to their contributed capital (i.e., one-third each). The Antoines' contribution represented practically all of their savings. Mrs. Landers' payment was the proceeds of her late husband's insurance policy.

On that day also the partnership signed a one-year lease to the Lone Pine Cafe, located in a nearby recreational area. The monthly rent on the cafe was $1,500. This facility attracted the partners in part because there were living accommodations on the floor above the restaurant. One room was occupied by the Antoines and another by Mrs. Landers.

The partners borrowed $21,000 from a local bank and used this plus $35,000 of partnership funds to buy out the previous operator of the cafe. Of this amount, $53,200 was for equipment and $2,800 was for the food and beverages then on hand. The partnership paid $1,428 for local operating licenses, good for one year beginning November 1, and paid $1,400 for a new cash register. The remainder of the $69,000 was deposited in a checking account.

Shortly after November 1, the partners opened the restaurant. Mr. Antoine was the cook, and Mrs. Antoine and Mrs. Landers waited on customers. Mrs. Antoine also ordered the food, beverages, and supplies, operated the cash register, and was responsible for the checking account.

The restaurant operated throughout the winter season of 2009–2010. It was not very successful. On the morning of March 31, 2010, Mrs. Antoine discovered that Mr. Antoine and Mrs. Landers had disappeared. Mrs. Landers had taken all her possessions, but Mr. Antoine had left behind most of his clothing, presumably because he could not remove it without warning Mrs. Antoine. The new cash register and its contents were also missing. No other partnership assets were missing. Mrs. Antoine concluded that the partnership was dissolved. (The court subsequently affirmed that the partnership was dissolved as of March 30.)

Mrs. Antoine decided to continue operating the Lone Pine Cafe. She realized that an accounting would have to be made as of March 30 and called in Donald Simpson, an acquaintance who was knowledgeable about accounting.

In response to Mr. Simpson's questions, Mrs. Antoine said that the cash register had contained $311 and that the checking account balance was $1,030. Ski instructors who were permitted to charge their meals had run up accounts totaling $870. (These accounts subsequently were paid in full.) The Lone Pine Cafe owed suppliers amounts totaling $1,583. Mr. Simpson estimated that depreciation on the assets amounted to $2,445. Food and beverages on hand were estimated to be worth $2,430. During the period of its operation, the partners drew salaries at agreed-upon amounts, and these payments were up to date. The clothing that Mr. Antoine left behind was estimated to be worth $750. The partnership had also repaid $2,100 of the bank loan.

Mr. Simpson explained that in order to account for the partners' equity, he would prepare a balance sheet. He would list the items that the partnership owned as of March 30, subtract the amounts that it owed to out-side parties, and the balance would be the equity of the three partners. Each partner would be entitled to one-third of this amount.

Questions

1. Prepare a balance sheet for the Lone Pine Cafe as of November 2, 2009.
2. Prepare a balance sheet as of March 30, 2010.
3. Disregarding the marital complications, do you suppose that the partners would have been able to receive their proportional share of the equity determined in Question 2 if the partnership was dissolved on March 30, 2010? Why?

Case 2–4
Debt Raising by Asset-Light firms

Firms all over the world use either the debt or the equity route to raise funds for growth, expansion, etc. While the equity route allows them to raise funds by selling their shares to the public at large via an IPO or through private deals where a block of shares is sold to few private investors, the debt route allows them to raise funds from a bank or a financial institution at a fixed rate of interest and for a predefined tenure. Banks were more than happy to lend the deposits, raised by them, as loans to profitable good firms (from the deposits of the depositors) and since they were acting as a custodian of public deposits, they always insisted on a collateral security which is used to recover money from the borrower just in case the business fails. Traditionally, banks have been known for lending against the assets (both long-term assets as well as current assets) in the Balance Sheet. So, when they used to lend for a longer period for let's say the purchase of machinery, the machine would also act as collateral security for the bank. When they used to lend for a shorter period, popularly called as working capital, the inventory used to be the collateral.

Today, with more and more firms going "asset-light" because of the shift in the business models as such, the scope for fundraising via the debt route is more or less non-existent for such firms. This is not only bad news for the firm but also for the banks because even if banks want to lend to these good firms, their hands are tied because of non-availability of any kind of asset of the borrowing firm which qualifies for collateral. This leads to a serious shortage of funds for many new ventures and start-ups whose success rate depends on timely availability of funds (as they burn cash very quickly). Also, lately banks are seeing another major challenge in their traditional way of lending. The banks have not been able to recover much money from the sale of collateral assets (in case of default of the borrower). So, even though, at the time of making the loans, it appeared to be fully secured (backed with a collateral asset) but when the actual default happens, banks are not able to sell the pledged assets of the borrower or sell it at a huge discount (haircuts).

Questions

1. What are the advantages/disadvantages of asset-heavy (asset-light) business models? Do they affect the market valuation too?
2. In light of businesses becoming "asset-light", how do the firms raise funds for future growth and expansion if the equity option is not feasible?
3. What do the banks/lenders need to do to overcome some of the such "real challenges"?

Basic Accounting Concepts: The Income Statement

CHAPTER 3

Chapter 1 introduced the idea of income. This chapter goes deeper into the measurement of income as used in financial accounting and describes the income statement, the financial statement that reports income and its determinants.

In the course of this discussion, we shall explain the last 6 of the 11 basic concepts listed in Chapter 2:

6. Accounting period
7. Conservatism
8. Realization
9. Matching
10. Consistency
11. Materiality

As was the case in Chapter 2, the discussion of topics in this chapter is introductory. Each will be explained in more depth in later chapters.

The Nature of Income

Chapter 2 described the balance sheet, which reports the financial condition of an entity as of one moment in time. Chapter 3 describes a second financial statement, the income statement, which summarizes the results of operations for a period of time. It is therefore a flow report, as contrasted with the balance sheet, which is a *status* report. These two financial statements illustrate the only two ways in which any entity—whether it be a business, a human body, or the universe—can be described: (1) in terms of flows through time and (2) in terms of its status or state as of one moment in time.

Flows in a business are continuous. Their essential nature, in many businesses, is indicated by the simplified diagram in Illustration 3–1. The business has a pool of cash that it has obtained from investors or from past profitable operations. It uses this

ILLUSTRATION 3–1
Basic Business Financial Flows

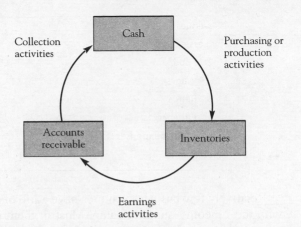

cash to acquire inventories, either by purchasing goods from others or by producing them itself. It also incurs other costs. (Accounts payable and various other assets and liability accounts may intervene between the incurrence of these costs and the cash outflow to pay for them.) It sells the goods to customers. The customers either pay cash or agree to pay later, thus creating accounts receivable. When the customer pays, the pool of cash is replenished.

For most types of businesses, the income statement focuses on the section of the flow diagram that is labeled *earnings activities*— also commonly called the business's *operating activities* or simply its *operations*. The income statement reports the nature and magnitude of these activities for a specified period of time.

Essentially, this report consists of two elements. One reports the inflows (creation) of assets—cash or accounts receivable—that result from the sale of goods and services to customers; these amounts are called **revenues**. The other reports the outflows (consumption) of resources that were required in order to generate these revenues; these amounts are called **expenses**. Profit (more formally, **income**) is the amount by which revenues exceed expenses. Since the word income is often used with various qualifying adjectives, the term **net income** is used to refer to the net excess of all the revenues over all the expenses. Some companies use the term **net earnings** rather than net income. If total expenses exceed total revenues, the difference is a **net loss**.

Basic Concepts

The Accounting Period Concept

Net income for the entire life of an organization is relatively easy to measure. It is simply the difference between the money that comes in and the money that goes out (excluding, of course, money invested by the owners or paid to the owners).

Example

Michael and Judith Lincoln operated a children's camp for one summer, renting all the necessary facilities and equipment. Before the camp opened, they invested $24,000 for food, the initial rental payment, and certain other costs. The camp received $122,400 in fees from parents. At the end of the summer, after all affairs were wound up, the Lincolns had their original $24,000 investment back and $15,237 additional. This $15,237 was the net income of the camp business. It was the difference between the revenues they received from parents and the expenses incurred for food, wages, and other costs. The income statement for the business looked like this:

Revenues		$122,400
Less expenses:		
Food	$42,756	
Wages	46,935	
Rental	12,000	
Other costs	5,472	
Total expenses		107,163
Net income		$ 15,237

Relatively few business ventures have a life of only a few months, as was the case with the Lincolns' summer camp. Most of them operate for many years. Indeed, in accordance with the going-concern concept, it is usually assumed that the life of a business is indefinitely long. Management and other interested parties are unwilling to wait until the business has ended before obtaining information on how much income has been earned. They need to know at frequent intervals how things are going.

This need leads to the **accounting period concept:** Accounting measures activities for a specified interval of time, called the accounting period. For the purpose of reporting to outsiders, one year is the usual accounting period.[1] Most corporate bylaws require an annual report to the shareholders, and income tax reporting is also on an annual basis.

In the majority of businesses, the accounting year, or **fiscal year,** corresponds to the calendar year; but many businesses use the natural business year instead of the calendar year. For example, nearly all department stores end their fiscal year on January 31, which is after the holiday season rush and its repercussions in the form of returns, clearance sales and depleted inventories.

Interim Reports

Management needs information more often than once a year. Income statements for management are therefore prepared more frequently. The most common period is a month, but the period may be as short as a week or even a day. The Securities and Exchange Commission (SEC) requires published quarterly income statements from companies over which it has jurisdiction. These reports are called **interim reports** to distinguish them from the annual reports.[2]

Businesses are living, ongoing organisms. The act of chopping the continuous stream of business events into time periods is therefore somewhat arbitrary, since business activities do not stop or change significantly as one accounting period ends and another begins. This fact makes the problem of measuring income for an accounting period the most difficult problem in accounting.

Example

If the Lincolns operated a year-round hotel instead of a summer camp, their income for a year could not be measured simply as the difference between the money taken in and the money paid out. As of the end of the year, some of the guests would not have paid their bills. Yet these unpaid bills are an asset, accounts receivable, that surely increases the "well-offness" of

[1] Pacioli, the first author of an accounting text, wrote in 1494: "Books should be closed each year, especially in a partnership, because frequent accounting makes for long friendship." Luca Pacioli, *Summa de Arithmetica Geometria Proportioni et Proportionalita*, from the translation by John B. Geijsbeck.

[2] Outside the United States, a common practice of companies listed on stock exchanges is to issue semiannual interim statements.

the business even though the cash has not yet been received. Conversely, some of the cash paid out may have been for the purchase of an asset, such as the hotel itself, that will benefit the business beyond the end of this accounting period. It would be incorrect to conclude that the hotel's income has been decreased by the amount of such payments.

Relation between Income and Owners' Equity

As explained in Chapters 1 and 2, the net income of an accounting period increases owners' equity. More specifically for a corporation, net income increases retained earnings. In order to understand the implication of this relationship, let us refer to the January 4 transaction of Music Mart, Inc. (page 45). On that day, merchandise costing $500 was sold for $750 cash. Looking first at the effect of this transaction on assets, we note that although inventory decreased by $500, cash increased by $750, so that the total assets increased by the difference, $250. From the dual-aspect concept, which states that the total of the assets must always equal the total of the liabilities and owners' equity, we know that the liabilities and owner's equity side of the Music Mart, Inc., balance sheet also must have increased by $250. Since no liabilitieswere affected, the increase must have occurred in owner's equity. In summary, because assets were sold for more than was paid for them, the owner's equity increased. Since owner's equity is made up of paid-in capital and retained earnings and since the owner did not contribute more capital, the increase must have been in retained earnings. Such net increases in retained earnings are called **income**.

In understanding how this income came about, let us consider separately two aspects of this event: the $750 received from the sale and the $500 decrease in inventory. If we look only at the $750, we see that it is an *increase* in cash and a corresponding increase in retained earnings. The $500, taken by itself, is a decrease in the asset, inventory, and a corresponding *decrease* in retained earnings. These two aspects illustrate the only two ways in which earnings activities—that is, operations— can affect retained earnings: They can increase it or they can decrease it.

Revenues and Expenses It follows that revenues and expenses also can be defined in terms of their effect on retained earnings: A revenue is an increase in retained earnings resulting from the operations of the entity, and an expense is a decrease.[3]

Restating the transactions described above in these terms, there was revenue of $750, expense of $500, and income of $250. The basic equation is

$$\text{Revenues} - \text{Expenses} = \text{Net income}$$

This equation clearly indicates that income is a *difference*. Sometimes the word *income* is used improperly as a synonym for *revenue*. This is because the approved definitions as given above are of relatively recent origin and some individuals have not kept up with the latest developments. Also, some nonprofit entities such as churches refer to their "income and outgo" or "income and expenses" rather than to revenues and expenses.

On an income statement, no misunderstanding is caused by such an error because revenues, however labeled, appear at the top and net income at the bottom. But in other contexts confusion can be created. For example, if one reads that Company X had income of $1 million, a completely false impression of the size of the company is given if the intended meaning was that Company X had revenues of $1 million.

[3] As pointed out in Chapter 2, unincorporated businesses ordinarily do not subdivide owners' equity into paid-in capital and retained earnings. Nevertheless, conceptually the distinction between changes in owners' equity related to paid-in capital and those related to retained earnings is both valid and useful in an unincorporated business.

Income Not the Same as Increase in Cash

It is extremely important to understand that the income of a period is associated with changes in *retained earnings* and that it has no necessary relation to changes in *cash* during that period. Income connotes "well-offness": Roughly speaking, the bigger the income is, the better off the owners are. An increase in cash, however, does not necessarily mean that the owners are any better off—that the retained earnings portion of their equity has increased. The increase in cash may merely be offset by a decrease in some other asset or by an increase in a liability, with no effect on retained earnings at all.

Again, reference to the transactions of Music Mart, Inc., may help to clarify this point. When Music Mart borrowed $12,500 from the bank on January 2 (page 45), its increase in cash was exactly matched by an increase in the liability to the bank. There was no change in retained earnings; no income resulted from this transaction. The $12,500 was not revenue; it was the proceeds of a borrowing transaction, whereas revenues are related to earnings transactions. Similarly, the purchase of inventory for $5,000 cash on January 3 resulted in a decrease in cash, but there was an exactly corresponding increase in another asset, inventory. Owner's equity was not changed. This was an asset purchase transaction, not an earnings transaction.

As we have already seen, the sale for $750 of inventory costing $500 *did* result in income. But note that the income was $250, whereas cash increased by $750; even here, the income is different from the amount by which the cash increased. In short, although individuals typically measure their *personal income* by the amount of money they receive, this concept of income is not correct when applied to a *business* entity.

The Conservatism Concept

Managers are human beings. Like most humans, they would like to give a favorable report on how well the entity for which they are responsible has performed. Yet, as the Financial Accounting Standards Board says, "prudent reporting based on a healthy skepticism builds confidence in the results and, in the long run, best serves all of the divergent interests [of financial statement users]."[4] This long-standing philosophy of prudent reporting leads to the **conservatism concept.**

This concept is often articulated as a preference for understatement rather than over-statement of net income and net assets when dealing with measurement uncertainties. Thus, if two estimates of some future amount are about equally likely, there is a preference for using the smaller number when measuring assets or revenues, and the larger for liabilities or expenses. For decades, the concept was stated informally as "anticipate no profits but anticipate all losses."

We state the conservatism concept's two aspects somewhat more formally:

1. Recognize *revenues* (increases in retained earnings) only when they are *reasonably certain*.
2. Recognize *expenses* (decreases in retained earnings) as soon as they are *reasonably possible*.

Example

In December 2010 Lynn Jones agrees to buy an automobile from Varsity Motors, Inc., for delivery in January 2011. Although this is good news to Varsity Motors, it is possible that something will go wrong and the sale will not be consummated. Therefore, the conservatism concept requires that the revenue not be recorded, that is, *recognized*, until the automobile is actually delivered. Thus, Varsity Motors does not recognize revenue from this transaction in 2010 because the revenue is not *reasonably certain* in 2010, even though it is *reasonably possible*. Rather, if the automobile is actually delivered in 2011, revenue is recognized in 2011.

---

[4] "Qualitative Characteristics of Accounting Information," *FASB Statement of Accounting Concepts No. 2.*

As another example, an uninsured automobile disappears from Varsity Motors' premises in December 2010. Possibly, it will be recovered; possibly, it has been stolen and is gone forever. In the latter case, Varsity Motors' retained earnings has decreased; the company has incurred an expense. Suppose that Varsity Motors is not reasonably certain that the auto is gone forever until early 2011. Nevertheless, the conservatism concept requires that the expense be recognized in 2010, the year in which it became *reasonably possible* that there was an expense, rather than in 2011, the year in which the expense became *reasonably certain*.

As a final example, consider the amount reported as inventory. If late in 2010 an entity learns that the selling price of certain goods in its inventory has declined to less than the cost of these goods, a loss (i.e., an expense) is recognized in 2010, even though in actual fact prices may rise again and the goods may be sold in 2011 at a profit. This is because it is *reasonably possible* that owners' equity has been reduced in 2010. (This "lower of cost or market" rule, probably the most well-known application of the conservatism concept, is described in Chapter 6.)

Obviously, in various situations, there are problems in deciding what is meant by such imprecise phrases as *about equally likely, reasonably certain*, and *reasonably possible*. For some specific problems, accounting principles give guidance—for example, the inventory principle just described. However, as with many accounting matters, judgment is often involved, and there is only a fine line between "prudently" reporting net income and owners' equity on the one hand and misleadingly understating them on the other.

Application to Revenue Recognition

In general, revenue from the sale of goods is recognized in the period in which goods were delivered to customers. Revenue from the performance of services is recognized in the period in which the services were performed. For many events, cash is received at the time of delivery or performance, and this is excellent evidence that the revenue has been earned. This is the case with most supermarkets and for many transactions in other retail stores and service firms. It can happen, however, that the cash is received in either an earlier period or a later period than that in which the revenue is recognized. Examples of each are given below.

Precollected Revenue   Magazine publ3ishing companies sell subscriptions that the subscriber pays for in advance; the company receives the cash *before* it renders the service of providing the magazine. Referring to Illustration 3–2, if subscription money is received this year for magazines to be delivered next year, the revenue belongs in next year. The money received is recognized as an increase in cash, not as revenue for this year, and an offsetting liability is recorded on the balance sheet as of the end of this year. The liability, **precollected** (or **unearned**) **revenue**, represents the company's obligation to provide its subscribers the future issues of the magazine for which they have already paid. Similarly, rent on property is often received in advance. When this happens, the revenue is properly recognized by the landlord in the period in which the

ILLUSTRATION 3–2

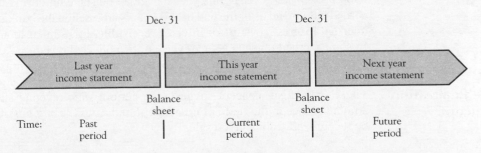

	Dec. 31	Dec. 31	
	Last year income statement	This year income statement	Next year income statement
		Balance sheet	Balance sheet
Time:	Past period	Current period	Future period

services of the rented property are provided, not the period in which the rent payment is received. In sum, precollected revenues have been *paid* to the entity but have not as yet been *earned* by the entity.

Accounts Receivable   The converse of the above situation is illustrated by sales made on credit: The customer agrees to pay for the goods or services sometime *after* the date on which they are actually received. The revenue is recognized in the period in which the sale is made. If the payment is not due until the following period, an asset— **accounts receivable**— is shown on the balance sheet as of the end of the current period. When the bill is paid by the customer (i.e., the account receivable is collected), the amount received is not revenue. Rather, it reduces the amount of accounts receivable outstanding and increases cash, leaving retained earnings unchanged. The *sale* is the earnings transaction that affects retained earnings; collection of the account receivable is the conversion of a noncash asset into cash, which is not an earnings transaction.

The distinction between revenue and receipts is illustrated in the following tabulation, which shows various types of sales transactions and classifies the effect of each on cash receipts and sales revenue for "this year":

		This Year	
	Amount	Cash Receipts	Sales Revenue
1. Cash sales made this year	$200	$200	$200
2. Credit sales made last year; cash received this year	300	300	0
3. Credit sales made this year; cash received this year	400	400	400
4. Credit sales made this year; cash received next year	100	0	100
Total		$900	$700

In this illustration, this year's total cash receipts do not equal this year's total sales revenue. The totals would be equal in a given accounting period only if (1) the company made all its sales for cash or (2) the amount of cash collected from credit customers in the accounting period happened by chance to equal the amount of credit sales made during that period.

Accrued Revenue   When a bank lends money, it is providing a service to the borrower, namely, the use of the bank's money. The bank's charge for this service is called **interest**, and the amount the bank earns is **interest revenue**. The bank earns interest revenue on each day that the borrower is permitted to use the money. For some loan transactions, the borrower does not actually pay the interest in the year in which the money was used but rather pays it next year. Even if this interest payment is not made until next year, the bank has *earned* revenue this year for a loan outstanding during the year. The amount earned but unpaid as of the end of this year is an asset on the bank's balance sheet called **accrued interest revenue** or **interest receivable**. It is similar to an account receivable. In sum, accrued revenue is the reverse of precollected revenue: Accrued revenues have been *earned by* the entity but have not as yet been *paid to* the entity.

The Realization Concept

The conservatism concept suggests the period *when* revenue should be recognized. Another concept, the **realization concept**, indicates the *amount* of revenue that should be recognized from a given sale.

Realization refers to inflows of cash or claims to cash (e.g., accounts receivable) arising from the sale of goods or services. Thus, if a customer buys $50 worth of items at a grocery store, paying cash, the store realizes $50 from the sale. If a clothing store sells a suit for $300, the purchaser agreeing to pay within 30 days, the store realizes $300 (in receivables) from the sale, *provided* that the purchaser has a good credit record so that payment is reasonably certain (conservatism concept).

The realization concept states that the amount recognized as revenue is the amount that is reasonably certain to be realized—that is, that customers are reasonably certain to pay. Of course, there is room for differences in judgment as to how certain "reasonably certain" is. However, the concept does clearly allow for the amount of revenue recognized to be less than the selling price of the goods and services sold. One obvious situation is the sale of merchandise at a discount—at an amount less than its normal selling price. In such cases, revenue is recorded at the lower amount, not the normal price.

Example

In many instances, the sale of a new car is made at a negotiated price that is lower than the manufacturer's list ("sticker") price for the automobile. In these circumstances, revenue is the amount at which the sale is made, rather than the list price. If the list price is $25,000 and the car is actually sold for $23,500, then the revenue is $23,500.

A less obvious situation arises with the sale of merchandise on credit. When a company makes a credit sale, it expects that the customer will pay the bill. Experience may indicate, however, that not all customers do pay their bills. In measuring the revenue for a period, the amount of sales made on credit should be reduced by the estimated amount of credit sales that will never be realized—that is, by the estimated amount of bad debts.

Example

If a store makes credit sales of $100,000 during a period and if experience indicates that 3 percent of credit sales will eventually become bad debts, the amount of revenue for the period is $97,000, not $100,000.

Although conceptually the estimated amount of bad debts is part of the calculation of revenue, in practice this amount is often treated as an expense. Thus, revenue is often reported as $100,000, and there is an expense—bad debt expense—of $3,000. The effect on net income is the same as if the revenue were reported as $97,000.

The Matching Concept

As noted earlier, the sale of merchandise has two aspects: (1) a revenue aspect, reflecting an increase in retained earnings equal to the amount of revenue realized, and (2) an expense aspect, reflecting the decrease in retained earnings because the merchandise (an asset) has left the business. In order to measure correctly this sale's *net* effect on retained earnings in a period, both of these aspects must be recognized in the same accounting period. This leads to the **matching concept:** When a given event affects both revenues and expenses, the effect on each should be recognized in the *same* accounting period.

Usually, the matching concept is applied by first determining the items of revenue to recognize for the period and their amounts (in accordance with the conservatism and realization concepts), and then matching items of cost to these revenues. For example, if goods costing $1,000 are sold for $1,500, it is first determined when the $1,500 is reasonably certain to be realized; then the $1,000 cost of sales is matched with those revenues as an expense, resulting in $500 income from the sale. However, as we shall see in later chapters, in some situations the applicable expenses are identified first, and then revenues are matched to them. Here we shall assume that applicable revenues of a period have been identified; the problem is to determine the costs that match with these revenues. These matched costs are expenses of the period.

Recognition of Expenses

In discussing the period in which an expense is recognized (i.e., recorded), we shall use four terms— *cost, expenditure, expense,* and *disbursement*— whose meanings must be kept clear. Although these terms tend to be used interchangeably in everyday conversation, in accounting they are not synonyms.

Terminology

Cost is a monetary measurement of the amount of resources used for some purpose. An **expenditure** is a decrease in an asset (usually cash) or an increase in a liability (often accounts payable) associated with the incurrence of a cost. The **expenditures** in an accounting period equal the cost of all the goods and services acquired in that period. An **expense** is an item of cost applicable to the current accounting period. An expense represents resources consumed by the entity's *earnings activities* during the current period. When an expenditure is made, the related cost is either an asset or an expense. If the cost benefits future periods, it is an increase in an asset. If not, it is an expense—a reduction in retained earnings—of the current period.[5] A **disbursement** is the payment of cash. A cash expenditure is a disbursement, but so is any cash payment, such as paying an account payable, repaying a loan, or paying a cash dividend to shareholders.

Example

An item of inventory costing $1,000 is received in March, the vendor is paid in April, and the item is shipped to a customer in May. In March there is a cost of $1,000 (acquisition of a good) and an expenditure of $1,000 (increase in accounts payable). In April there is a disbursement of $1,000 (cash payment). In May there is an expense of $1,000 (consumption of inventory).

Criteria for Expense Recognition

The matching concept provides one criterion for deciding what costs are expenses in an accounting period: The revenue and expense effects of a given event should be recognized in the same accounting period. There are two other related criteria: (1) Costs associated with activities of the period are expenses of the period and (2) costs that cannot be associated with revenues of future periods are expenses of the current period. An example of each criterion is given below.

Direct Matching

The association of cost of sales with revenues for the same goods or services has already been mentioned. Similarly, if a salesperson is paid a commission, the commission is reported as an expense in the same period in which the revenue arising from these sales is recognized. The period in which the commission is recognized as an expense may be different from the period in which the salesperson receives the commission in cash.

Example

Ms. A was paid $2,000 cash in 2010 as a commission on an order she booked late in 2010. However, the goods were not shipped, and thus the sales revenue was not recognized, until early 2011. Thus, the $2,000 is an expense of 2011. Mr. B was paid $1,000 cash in early 2011 as a commission on goods that were shipped in late 2010. The $1,000 is an expense of 2010. Note that, in both cases, the cash disbursement took place in a different period from the period in which the expense was recognized.

Period Costs

Some items of expense are associated with a certain accounting period, even though they cannot be traced to any specific revenue transactions occurring in that period.

[5] Financial statement users must be alert to the possibility that unscrupulous managers may inflate current profits by deliberately misclassifying expenditures as assets rather than expenses.

In general, these expenses are the costs of being in business. In a retail store, they include the costs of operating the store during the period, even though these costs cannot be traced directly to the specific merchandise sold. In a manufacturing firm, they include all of the costs that cannot be directly related to the goods being produced and sold. These expenses are called **period costs.**

Example	If a salesperson is paid a salary rather than a commission as in the previous example, the salary is reported as an expense in the period in which the employee works. The amount of the salary is not affected by the volume of sales, and hence there is no direct relationship between the salary cost and revenue. The salary is one of the costs of operating the business during the period and hence is related only in an indirect way to the revenue of the period.

Costs Not Associated with Future Revenue

Even if a cost item is not associated with the operations of a period, it is reported as an expense of that period if it cannot be associated with the revenue of some *future* period. An item of cost must be either an asset or an expense. For a cost of this period to be an asset, it must, by definition, be expected to provide an economic benefit in some future period. If it does not qualify as an asset by this test, it must be an expense of the current period. Even if the item of cost benefits the future in some general way, but there is no feasible or objective way of associating these benefits with specific future periods, the item is an expense.

Example	Employee training programs are intended to provide benefits to future periods in that the participants are expected to perform better as a result of the training. The future benefits of this training cannot be objectively measured, however. So training costs are charged as an expense of the current period, rather than being treated as an asset.

Under this general principle, many items of cost are charged as expenses in the current period even though they have no connection with the revenues of the period or even with the ongoing operations of the period. If assets are destroyed by fire or lost by theft, for example, the amount of the loss is an expense of the current period. In general, if a cost is incurred and there is no reasonable basis for classifying the cost as an asset, it is reported as an expense.

If during the period an item that once was classified as an asset is found to have a diminished value for future periods, the asset amount is restated to its new estimated recoverable value and the amount of the write-off becomes an expense of the period. This can happen, for example, when goods held in inventory are found to have deteriorated, become obsolete, or otherwise become unsalable.

Expenses and Expenditures	Expenditures take place when an entity acquires goods or services. An expenditure may be made by cash, by incurring a liability (such as an account payable), by the exchange of another asset (such as a trade-in vehicle), or by some combination of these. As already noted, these expenditures can be either assets or expenses. Over the entire life of an entity, most expenditures become expenses. (The exception would be assets that are liquidated as the business closes down its operations at the end of its life.) In any time segment *shorter* than the life of an entity, however, there is no necessary correspondence between expenses and expenditures.
Example	Late in 2010 $5,000 of fuel oil was purchased for cash. This was an *expenditure* of $5,000, which was the exchange of cash for another asset. If none of this fuel oil was consumed in 2010, there was no *expense* in 2010. Rather, the fuel oil was an asset as of the end of 2010. If the fuel oil was consumed in 2011, there was an *expense* of $5,000 in 2011.

Four types of transactions need to be considered in distinguishing between amounts that are properly considered as expenses of a given accounting period and the expenditures made in connection with these items. Focusing on "this year" in Illustration 3–2, these are as follows:

1. Expenditures made this year that are also expenses of this year.
2. Expenditures made prior to this year that become expenses during this year. These appeared as assets on the balance sheet at the beginning of this year.
3. Expenditures made this year that will become expenses in future years. These will appear as assets on the balance sheet at the end of this year.
4. Expenses of this year that will be paid for in a future year. On the balance sheet at the end of this year, these appear as liabilities.

Expenditures That Are Also Expenses

This is the simplest and most common type of transaction, and the least troublesome to account for. If an item is acquired during the year, it is an expenditure. If it is consumed during the same year, it is an expense of the year. *Consumed,* as used here, means more precisely that the item provides its intended benefit. For example, raw materials that are converted into goods intended to be sold are not considered to be consumed until the goods are sold. At that time, the raw materials cost is a part of the expense, cost of goods sold.

Beginning Assets That Become Expenses

On January 1 the balance sheet shows the entity's assets. Assets are resources that provide future benefits to the entity. The expenditures for the beginning-of-the-period assets were made in some earlier period. These expenditures were recorded as assets rather than as expenses because the future benefit test was met when the resources were acquired. During this year, some of these benefits are "released" and "used up" (i.e., some assets are consumed); hence, the expenditures are transformed into expenses. The three principal types of such assets are described below.

First, there are *inventories* of salable goods. These become expenses when the goods are sold.

Second, there are *prepaid expenses* (sometimes called *deferred charges*). These represent services or other assets (usually intangible) purchased prior to this year but whose benefits have not been fully used up when the year begins. They become expenses in the year in which the benefits are received—that is, when the services are used or the assets are consumed. Prepaid insurance protection, prepaid lawyers' retainer fees, and prepaid rent are such items.

Example

On December 31, 2010, a company purchased for $90,000 an insurance policy providing three years of protection. The $90,000 appears as an asset on the balance sheet of December 31, 2010. In 2011, $30,000 (one-third) becomes an expense and $60,000 remains as an asset on the balance sheet of December 31, 2011. In 2012, $30,000 more becomes an expense and $30,000 remains as an asset on the balance sheet of December 31, 2012. The remaining $30,000 is an expense in 2013.

The third category of assets that will become expenses is *long-lived (noncurrent) assets.* With the exception of land, assets have a limited useful life; they do not last forever. They are purchased with the expectation that they will be used in the operation of the entity in future periods, and they will become expenses in these future periods. The principle is exactly the same as that of the insurance policy previously mentioned, which also was purchased for the benefit of future periods. An important practical difference between a long-lived asset, such as a building, and an insurance policy, however, is that the life of a building is usually difficult to estimate whereas the life of an insurance policy is known precisely. Thus, estimating what portion of a building's cost is an expense of a given accounting period is a more difficult task than that of determining the insurance expense of a period. The mechanism used to convert the cost of fixed assets to expense is called **depreciation;** it is described in Chapter 7.

Expenditures That Are Not Yet Expenses

As the preceding examples show, some expenditures made to acquire assets are not expenses of this year because the assets' benefits have not yet been used up as of the year's end. These include not only the purchase of long-lived assets but also expenditures incurred in connection with the *production* of goods that are to be sold in some future year. Thus, wages and salaries earned by production personnel and all other costs associated with producing goods become part of the cost of the goods produced and remain as an asset, *inventory,* until the goods are sold. Chapter 6 discusses in more detail the distinction between production costs (also called *product costs),* which initially are added to inventory amounts, and other operating costs (period costs), which are expenses of the current period.

Expenses Not Yet Paid

Some expenses of this year are not paid for by the end of the year. The parties who furnished services during the year have a claim against the entity for the amounts owed them. These amounts are therefore liabilities (called **accrued expenses)** of the entity as of December 31. The liability for wages earned but not yet paid, **accrued wages** (or wages payable), is an example already mentioned. The cost of using borrowed money during a period is interest expense of that period. If this interest expense has not been paid, the end-of-period balance sheet will show a liability, **accrued interest expense** (or interest payable). Several other types of obligations have the same characteristic: Although services were rendered prior to the date for which the balance sheet is prepared, these services have not yet been paid for. The *recognition* of these expenses reduces retained earnings; the subsequent *payment* of the obligation (i.e., the disbursement) does not affect retained earnings.

For all obligations of this type, the transaction involved is essentially the same: The expense is recognized in the period in which the services were used, and the obligation that results from these services is shown in the liability section of the balance sheet as of the end of the period.

Example	In the final days of 2010, employee Aneel Prahalad earned $300 that was not paid him by year-end. This is an expense of $300 in 2010, and there is a corresponding liability of $300 (accrued wages) on his employer's balance sheet as of December 31, 2010. In 2011 when Prahalad is paid, the liability is eliminated and there is a $300 decrease in cash. Accrued wages liability will always occur for an entity whose last payday of the year does not fall on the last day of the year.

In this example, the basic equality, Assets = Liabilities + Owners' equity, is always maintained. The earning of wages resulted in an expense of $300, which was a decrease in owners' equity (retained earnings), and there was an equal increase in the liability, accrued wages. Thus, the total of the equities—liabilities and owners' equity—was unchanged. The payment of the $300 resulted in a decrease in cash and a decrease in the liability, accrued wages, so both assets and liabilities were reduced by $300.

Dividends	Dividends that a corporation pays to its shareholders are *not* expenses. Dividends are a *distribution* of net income rather than an item in the calculation of net income. Cash

dividends reduce the asset, cash, and reduce retained earnings by an equal amount. This is the only common transaction in business entities in which a reduction in retained earnings is not an expense. Similarly, in an unincorporated business, owners' or partners' drawings are not treated as expenses.

Summary of Expense Measurement

The proper classification of expenditures as either assets or expenses is one of the most difficult problems in accounting. As an aid in this process and as a summary of the preceding discussion, Illustration 3–3 gives a decision diagram that should be helpful. It shows that an entity starts an accounting period with certain assets and that during the period it makes expenditures. If these costs have not been paid for in cash or by an exchange of another asset, they result in liabilities on the end-of-period balance sheet. In preparing the end-of-period balance sheet and the period's income statement, the accountant must

ILLUSTRATION 3–3
Decision Diagram: Assets and Expenses

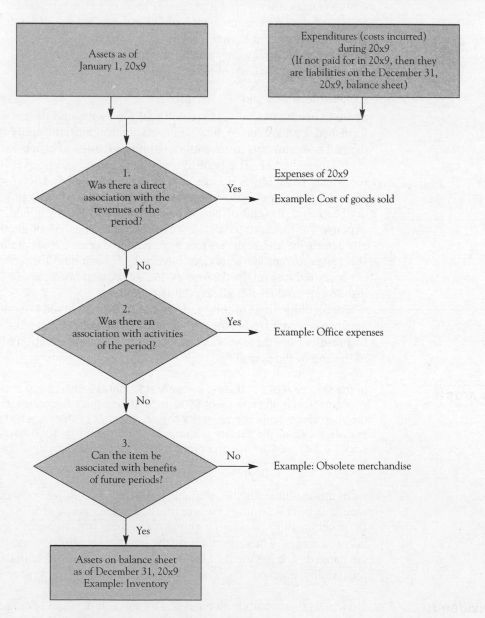

classify these assets and expenditures either as expenses, which will appear on the income statement, or as assets, which will appear on the end-of-period balance sheet. In order to do this classification, the three questions shown in the diagram must be addressed.

Gains and Losses

Throughout this chapter, revenue, which increases retained earnings, has been associated with the sale of a company's goods and services. Retained earnings can increase for other reasons. For example, if a company sells marketable securities for more than it paid for them, retained earnings has increased, but this is not sales revenue (unless the company is in the business of selling securities). Technically, such increases in retained earnings are called **gains,** to distinguish them from revenues from the sale of goods and services.

Similarly, decreases in retained earnings (except dividends) for reasons not associated with operations are referred to as **losses,** and these are sometimes distinguished from expenses. Loss of assets by fire or theft has already been mentioned. Sale of marketable securities at an amount less than was paid for them is another example.

As a practical matter, no sharp distinction is made between sales revenues and gains; they both increase retained earnings. Similarly, expenses and losses both decrease retained earnings, so again in practice no sharp distinction is made between them.

The Consistency Concept

The nine concepts that have been described so far in this and the preceding chapter are so broad that in practice there are often several different ways a given event may be recorded. For example, bad debts may be recognized either as a reduction in revenue or as an expense. The **consistency concept** states that once an entity has decided on one accounting method, it should use the *same* method for all subsequent events of the same character unless it has a sound reason to change methods. If an entity frequently changed the manner of handling a given class of events in the accounting records— for example, frequently changing between the straight-line method and an accelerated method for depreciating its building—comparison of its financial statements for one period with those of another period would be difficult.

Because of this concept, changes in the method of keeping accounts are not made lightly. If a company changes an accounting method from the method used in the preceding year, the company's outside auditors must report this in their opinion letter— the auditors' report that accompanies the annual financial statements distributed to shareholders. (Auditors' opinion letters will be described more fully in Chapter 14.)

Consistency, as used here, has a narrow meaning. It refers only to consistency *over time,* not to *logical* consistency at a given moment of time. For example, long-lived assets are recorded at cost, but inventories are recorded at the lower of their cost or market value. Some people argue that this is inconsistent. Whatever the merits of this argument may be, it does not involve the *accounting* concept of consistency. This concept does not mean that the treatment of different categories of transactions must be consistent with one another, but only that transactions in a given category must be treated consistently from one accounting period to the next.

The Materiality Concept

In law there is a doctrine called *de minimis non curat lex,* which means that the court will not consider trivial matters. Similarly, the accountant does not attempt to record events so insignificant that the work of recording them is not justified by the usefulness of the results.

Example

Conceptually, a brand-new pad of paper is an asset of the entity. Every time someone writes on a page of the pad, part of this asset is used up, and retained earnings decreases correspondingly. Theoretically, it would be possible to ascertain the number of partly used pads that are owned by the entity at the end of the accounting period and to show this amount as an asset. But the cost of such an effort would obviously be unwarranted, and no accountant would attempt to do this. Accountants take the simpler, even though less exact, course of action and treat the asset as being used up (expensed) either at the time the pads were purchased or at the time they were issued from supplies inventory to the user.

Unfortunately, there is no agreement on the exact line separating material events from immaterial events. The decision depends on judgment and common sense. It is natural for the beginning student, who does not have an appreciation of the cost of collecting accounting information, to expect an accountant to be more meticulous in recording events in the accounts than the practicing accountant actually would be.

The materiality concept is important in the process of determining the expenses and revenue for a given accounting period. Many of the expense items are necessarily estimates, and in some cases they are not very close estimates. Beyond a certain point, it is not worthwhile to attempt to refine these estimates.

Example

Telephone bills, although rendered monthly, often do not coincide with a calendar month. It would be possible to analyze each bill and classify all the toll calls according to the month in which they were made. This would be following the matching concept precisely. Few companies bother to do this, however. On the grounds that a procedure to determine the actual expense would not be justified by the accuracy gained, they simply consider the telephone bill as an expense of the month in which the bill is received. Since the amount of the bill is likely to be relatively stable from one month to another, no significant error is introduced.

Materiality is also used in another sense in accounting. The principle of **full disclosure** requires that all important information about the financial condition and activities of an entity must be disclosed in reports prepared for outside parties. In this sense, also, there is no definitive rule that separates material from immaterial information. (This topic is discussed further in Chapter 14.) In sum, the **materiality concept** states that insignificant events may be disregarded, but there must be full disclosure of all important information.

The question of what is material is important to chief executive and chief financial officers of public companies. The Sarbanes–Oxley Act became law on July 30, 2002. One of its many requirements is that chief executive officers (CEOs) and chief financial officers (CFOs) of companies registered with the Securities and Exchange Commission (SEC) must sign certifications related to the financial data contained in annual and quarterly filings with the SEC.

The certifications requires the CEO and CFO each to certify that the filings are materially accurate and complete, the financial statements and other financial information included in the filing present in all material respects the financial condition and results of operations of the company, and the issuer's internal controls do not contain any material weaknesses.

The Income Statement

The accounting report that summarizes the revenues and the expenses of an accounting period is called the **income statement** (or the **profit and loss statement, statement of earnings,** or **statement of operations).** In a technical sense, the income statement

**ILLUSTRATION
3–4**

GARSDEN CORPORATION ←	Name of entity
Income Statement ←	Name of statement
For the Year Ended December 31, 2010 ←	Time period

Net sales	$75,478,221
Cost of sales	52,227,004
Gross margin	$23,251,217
Research and development expense	2,158,677
Selling, general, and administrative expenses	8,726,696
Operating income	$12,365,844
Other revenues (expenses):	
Interest expense	(363,000)
Interest and dividend revenues	43,533
Royalty revenues	420,010
Income before income taxes	$12,466,387
Provision for income taxes	4,986,555
Net income	$ 7,479,832
Earnings per share of common stock	$ 6.82
Statement of Retained Earnings	
Retained earnings at beginning of year	$16,027,144
Add: Net income	7,479,832
Deduct: Dividends ($4 per common share)	(4,390,000)
Retained earnings at end of year	$19,116,976

is subordinate to the balance sheet. This is because it shows in some detail the items that collectively account for most of the period's net change in *only one* balance sheet item, retained earnings. ("Most" excludes dividends as well as a few relatively unusual retained earnings changes that are described in later chapters.) Nevertheless, the information on the income statement is regarded by many to be more important than information on the balance sheet. This is because the income statement reports the results of operations and indicates reasons for the entity's profitability (or lack thereof). The importance of the income statement is illustrated by this fact: In situations where accountants in recording an event must choose between a procedure that distorts the balance sheet or one that distorts the income statement, they usually choose not to distort the income statement.

In practice, there is considerable variety in the formats and degree of detail used in income statements. Illustration 3–4 shows an income statement for Garsden Corporation (whose balance sheet was shown in Illustration 2–1). It is representative of the income statements published in corporations' annual reports to their shareholders (with the exception of a few complex items that are discussed in later chapters). Income statements prepared for use by the managers of an entity usually contain more detailed information than that shown in Illustration 3–4.

The heading of the income statement must show(1) the entity to which it relates (Garsden Corporation), (2) the name of the statement (income statement), and (3) the time period covered (year ended December 31, 2009). The balance sheet in Illustration 2–1 and the income statement in Illustration 3–4 give information for only one year. To provide a basis for comparison, the SEC requires that corporate annual reports contain income statements for the most recent three years and balance sheets as of the end of the most recent two years.

Comments about the items listed on this income statement and variations often found in practice are given in the following paragraphs.

Revenues

An income statement sometimes reports several separate items in the sales revenue section, the net of which is the **net sales** (or **net sales revenue**) figure. For example, Garsden's income statement might have shown

Gross sales		$77,157,525
Less: Returns and allowances	$ 528,348	
Sales discounts	1,150,956	
Net sales		$75,478,221

Gross sales is the total invoice price of the goods shipped or services rendered during the period. It usually does not include sales taxes or excise taxes that may be charged to the customer. Such taxes are not revenues but rather represent collections that the business makes on behalf of the government. They are a liability owed to the government until paid. Similarly, postage, freight, or other items billed to the customer at cost are not revenues. These items usually do not appear in the sales figure but instead are an offset to the costs the company incurs for them. However, exceptions are made to these rules when it is not feasible to disentangle the revenue and nonrevenue portions of the items in question.

Sales returns and allowances represent the sales value of goods that were returned by customers and allowances that were made to customers because the goods were defective or for some other reason. The amount can be subtracted from the sales figure directly, without showing it as a separate item on the income statement. However, it is often considered as being important enough information to warrant reporting it separately. **Sales discounts** are the amount of discounts taken by customers for prompt payment. (These are sometimes called **cash discounts.**)

Example

Assume that a business offers a 2 percent discount to customers who pay within 10 days from the date of the invoice. The business sells $1,000 of merchandise to a customer (gross sales) who takes advantage of this discount (sales discount). The business receives only $980 cash and records the other $20 as a sales discount.

Trade discounts, which are formulas used in figuring the actual selling price from published catalogs or price lists (e.g., "list less 40 percent"), do not appear in the accounting records at all.

Other revenues are revenues earned from activities not associated with the sale of the company's goods and services. Interest and dividends earned on marketable securities owned by the company are examples. Garsden also had revenues from royalties paid by other companies that Garsden has licensed to use its patented manufacturing process. Although it is preferable to show such peripheral revenues separately from sales revenues, as in Illustration 3–4, many companies add them to net sales and report a total revenue amount.

Cost of Sales

Because of the matching concept, at the same time that income is increased by the sales value of goods or services sold, it is also decreased by the cost of those goods or services. Indeed, it would be possible to record only the net increase in retained earnings that results from a sale. However, reporting the separate amounts for sales revenue and the cost of sales provides information useful to both management and outside users of income statements.

The cost of goods or services sold is called the **cost of sales.** In manufacturing firms and retailing businesses, it is often called the **cost of goods sold**. In most businesses, the cost of sales amount is associated with a decrease in the asset inventory, which has been consumed in generating the sales revenues. (The principal exception is personal-services businesses such as barber or beauty shops, which have no significant inventories.) Procedures for measuring the cost of sales are described in Chapter 6.

Gross Margin

The difference between net sales revenue and cost of sales is the **gross margin** (or **gross profit).** It is the difference between the revenues generated from selling products (goods or services) and the related *product* costs. On most income statements, as in Illustration 3–4, this amount appears as a separate item. It does not appear separately on some companies' income statements but can be calculated as the difference between net sales and cost of sales if the company has disclosed the cost of sales amount.[6]

Expenses

The classifications given in Illustration 3–4 are a minimum. In many income statements, especially those prepared for internal use, the "selling, general, and administrative expense" category is broken down so as to show separately the principal items of which it is composed.

The separate disclosure of **research and development expense** is a requirement. Formerly, most companies included this expense as part of general and administrative expenses. Because the amount spent on research and development can provide an important clue as to how aggressive the company is in keeping its products and processes up to date, the FASB requires that this amount be reported separately if it is material.

The FASB also requires separate disclosure of the amount of **interest expense** in a period. In some instances, to be discussed in Chapter 7, the interest expense of a period is not the same as the interest cost incurred during the period.

Many companies' income statements show an amount for **operating income,** as in Illustration 3–4. To operating income are added other revenue items, and other expenses are subtracted (indicated by parentheses in Illustration 3–4); the result is **income before income taxes.** A company that shows an operating income amount wants to distinguish the income generated by its primary operating activities from its nonoperating revenues and expenses. Many companies reject this distinction. They say, for example, that interest expense reflects the cost of financing assets used in operations and therefore should not be presented in a way that suggests it is a "nonoperating" item. Nearly all companies report a pretax income amount before subtracting the **provision for income taxes** (also called **income tax expense).**

Net Income

Net income is colloquially referred to as "the bottom line" of the income statement (for obvious reasons).The bottom line must be labeled **net income or net earnings,** with no qualification or modification. (If negative, it is labeled **net loss.)** Net income also is presented on a per-share basis. The calculation of earnings per share is discussed in Chapter 9.

Statement of Retained Earnings

Strictly speaking, the income statement ends with "earnings per share." Illustration 3–4 goes beyond this to show other changes in retained earnings that have occurred during the period. This final section links the period's income statement to the beginning-of-the-period and end-of-the-period balance sheets by completing the explanation of the net

---

[6] Outside the United States, some companies do not show cost of sales as one item on the income statement. Instead, they list individual expenses by object, such as salaries and wages, usage of goods and services, and interest. In such an income statement, it is impossible to calculate the gross margin because the broad objects (e.g., salaries and wages) intermingle product costs (e.g., factory labor) with period costs (e.g., administrative salaries). The use of this format is rare in the United States. If it is used by a listed company, the SEC requires disclosure of a cost of goods sold figure and gross margin amount in the notes to the financial statements.

change in retained earnings between those two balance sheet snapshots. For Garsden, this section shows that (1) at the start of 2010, retained earnings was $16,027,144; (2) during 2010, retained earnings was increased by the amount of 2010 net income, $7,479,832, and was decreased by the amount of 2010 dividends, $4,390,000; and thus (3) at the end of 2010, retained earnings was $19,116,976. This calculation, whether shown on a separate page or included at the bottom of the income statement, is called a **statement of retained earnings** (or sometimes a **reconciliation of retained earnings**).[7]

Relation between Balance Sheet and Income Statement

The balance sheet and income statement are said to **articulate** because there is a definite relationship between them. More specifically, as shown in the statement of retained earnings, the amount of net income reported on the income statement, together with the amount of dividends, explains the change in retained earnings between the two balance sheets prepared as of the beginning and the end of the accounting period. This relationship was shown schematically in Illustration 1–5.

Income Statement Percentages

In analyzing an income statement, percentage relationships are often calculated. Usually, the net sales amount is taken as 100 percent. Each income statement item is then expressed as a percentage of net sales. The most important are the gross margin percentage and the profit margin.

The **gross margin percentage** is gross margin divided by net sales. For Garsden this is $23,251,217 ÷ $75,478,221 = 30.8 percent. It indicates the average margin obtained on products (goods or services) sold. The percentage varies widely among industries, but companies in the same industry tend to have similar gross margin percentages.

The **profit margin** is net income divided by net sales. For Garsden this is $7,479,832 ÷ $75,478,221 = 9.9 percent. Profit margins also vary widely among industries. A successful supermarket may have a profit margin of about 1.5 percent, whereas the typical profit margin in healthy manufacturing companies tends to be closer to 8 percent.

Other Concepts of Income

We have described how income is measured and reported in accordance with generally accepted accounting principles (GAAP). Not all income statements are prepared in accordance with these principles, however. Some regulatory bodies require the use of different principles by companies within their jurisdiction. Four other variations of the income concept are described below: cash-basis accounting, income tax accounting, the economic concept of income, and pro forma earnings.

Accrual versus Cash-Basis Accounting

The measurement of income described in this chapter is based on what is called *accrual accounting*. Central to accrual accounting are the realization concept and the matching concept. **Accrual accounting** measures income for a period as the difference between the revenues recognized in that period and the expenses that are matched with those revenues. As noted previously, the period's revenues generally are not the same as the period's cash receipts from customers, and the period's expenses generally are not the same as the period's cash disbursements.

---

[7] Often the statement of retained earnings is incorporated as a section of a statement of changes in owners' equity. This larger statement also includes a section showing changes in paid-in capital and a section presenting certain other changes in owners' equity.

An alternative way of measuring income is called **cash-basis accounting.** With this method, sales are not recorded until the period in which they are received in cash. Similarly, costs are subtracted from sales in the period in which they are paid for by cash disbursements. Thus, neither the realization nor matching concept applies in cash-basis accounting.

In practice, "pure" cash-basis accounting is rare. This is because a pure cash-basis approach would require treating the acquisition of inventories as a reduction in profit when the acquisition costs are paid rather than when the inventories are sold. Similarly, costs of acquiring items of plant and equipment would be treated as profit reductions when paid in cash rather than in the later periods when these long-lived items are used. Clearly, such a pure cash-basis approach would result in balance sheets and income statements that would be of limited usefulness. Thus, what is commonly called *cash-basis accounting* is actually a mixture of cash basis for some items (especially sales and period costs) and accrual basis for other items (especially product costs and long-lived assets). This mixture is also sometimes called **modified cash-basis accounting** to distinguish it from a pure cash-basis method.

Cash-basis accounting is seen most often in small firms that provide services and therefore do not have significant amounts of inventories. Examples include restaurants, beauty parlors and barber shops, and income tax preparation firms. Since most of these establishments do not extend credit to their customers, cash-basis profit may not differ dramatically from accrual-basis income. Nevertheless, cash-basis accounting is not permitted by GAAP for any type of business entity.[8]

Income Tax Accounting

Most business entities must calculate their taxable income and pay a federal tax (and in some cases, a state or local tax) based on this income. The amounts of revenues and expenses used to determine federal taxable income are usually similar to, but not identical with, amounts measured in accordance with GAAP. The differences are sufficiently significant so that it is unwise to rely on income tax regulations as a basis for solving business accounting problems, or vice versa. For example, tax regulations permit certain kinds of businesses to report income using the modified cash basis, which, as noted above, is not in accordance with GAAP.

Unless tax rates applicable to the business are expected to increase in the future, a business usually reports in its tax returns the *minimum* possible amount of taxable income in the current year, thus postponing tax payments as much as possible to future years. It does this generally by recognizing expenses as soon as legally possible, but postponing the recognition of revenue for as long as legally possible. Note that this is a process of shifting revenue and expense from one period to another. Over the long run in most businesses, there is little difference between the total expenses and revenues computed for tax purposes and the total expenses and revenues computed for financial accounting. The objective of minimizing current taxes is, as the Supreme Court has pointed out, entirely legal and ethical, provided it is done in accordance with the tax regulations. It is also legal and proper under most circumstances to calculate income one way for tax purposes and another way for financial accounting purposes (a fact that comes as a surprise to many newcomers to accounting).

---

[8] Sometimes earnings before interest, taxes, depreciation, and amortization (EBITDA) is referred to as cash earnings. This amount is, however, neither cash earnings nor accrual earnings. The earnings (E) part of EBITDA is accrual based and therefore not cash based and the exclusion of important expense items (ITDA) overstates the operating performance of the company.

Example	Income tax regulations permit the cost of most fixed assets to be charged as expenses (i.e., depreciated) over a shorter time period than the estimated useful life of these assets and at amounts in the early years that are greater than the cost of the asset benefits consumed in those years (so-called accelerated depreciation). These practices result in higher tax-deductible expenses and correspondingly lower taxable income in the early years of an asset's life, and therefore encourage businesses to invest in new fixed assets. Most businesses use these practices in calculating their taxable income, but they use different practices for financial accounting.

Although tax regulations are not described in detail in this book, references are made to accounting practices that are or are not consistent with them. The manager learns early the importance of becoming thoroughly familiar with the principal tax rules that affect the business and also the importance of consulting tax experts when unusual situations arise.

Economic Income	Economic theory is not constrained by the practical need of reporting an income amount annually to an entity's owners or other interested parties. Thus, in economic theory, *income* is defined as the difference between the value of a business at the end of an accounting period and its value at the beginning of the period, after proper adjustments for transactions with owners (i.e., additional paid-in capital and dividends). Both economists and accountants recognize that this **economic income** cannot be feasibly measured for a given accounting period. Measuring economic income would involve estimating unrealized changes in value, including changes in the value of such intangibles as a company's patents and brand names, whereas accounting income focuses on actual *transactions* that have taken place. Also, economists regard interest on all equities— both interest-bearing liabilities and owners' equity—as an element of cost. Accountants treat only the interest on borrowings as a cost on the grounds that interest on the use of owners' capital cannot be objectively measured. Consequently, accounting net income to an economist is a mixture of "true" income and the cost of using shareholders' capital. To an economist, accounting net income is an attempt to measure the income accruing to the entity's *owners*; but it is an overstatement of the income earned by the *entity itself* because the cost of using owners' funds has not been subtracted.

Pro Forma Earnings	As an alternative to GAAP-based net income, some companies report a second earnings amount known as pro forma earnings. (*Pro forma* means "As if.") This amount is net income plus certain unusual or one-time charges, such as restructuring charges and merger-related costs. The exclusion of the unusual charges in the measurement of pro forma earnings is justified on the grounds that shareholders are best served by focusing on a company's core or ongoing earnings capability. In practice, this theory often breaks down since many companies that favor pro forma earnings have recurring un-usual charges. As a result, for these companies, the so-called unusual charges are usual and should be considered part of their core earnings calculation.

Income Statement of Start ups Like Ola

We would like to continue from our discussion in the previous chapter, where we tried understanding the fact that how gradually traditional Balance Sheet structures and items are becoming increasingly irrelevant and that we need to look beyond just "tangible assets" for firm valuation. The income statement, which is the other significant financial statement released by the firm, matches the current period revenue and expenses to measure the surplus or deficit generated in the business (profitability of business). Historically, the broader understanding was to push and maximize revenues and cut down on wasteful expenses (or at least optimize the expenses) to create a viable business. Lately, this concept also appears to be little irrelevant, if not completely useless. Firms which have not generated one rupee of profit (since birth) till date are spending millions of rupees on advertising, publicity and brand promotion by hiring expensive celebrities for brand endorsement and also sponsoring mega shows and events on prime spots on the television. They continue to hire the best human resource from top colleges in the country and pay them lavishly knowing very well that they actually can't afford such expenses.

The argument which these firms and analysts in these sectors give is that these firms need to spend heavily on brand promotion for a few more years to create visibility and try and reach that critical mass of "Revenue." Post that, economies of scale will start bringing its own benefits (and then profits too will flow). When asked specifically about the time in which it will happen (how soon firms will reach critical mass?), they are completely clueless. When one sees a full-page advertisement of Flipkart in all major newspapers in the country, one is left wondering as to where is the money coming from because this firm (Flipkart) has not made any profit since they started more than 10 years ago. But then we are reminded of the fact that Walmart, the global retail giant recently bought Flipkart for more than $16 billion. Clearly, there is something of value in Flipkart, which we can't see but Walmart can.

Accounting Loss vs Market Valuation

The point therefore is the same as we discussed in the previous chapter on Balance Sheet that the traditional financial statements might have lost some of its relevance in light of the new businesses which are emerging and the markets are putting valuation on the future cash-generating capability of the "intangibles" rather than the "tangible assets." A business which is currently in losses but has the potential of wiping out the losses and turning out to be profitable in the future is a very sought after business model these days. The Income Statement of such firms appears to be miserable on account of huge expenses (most of which appear to be unwarranted) but the future potential in increasing the revenue and optimizing the expenses makes it a very attractive investment.

Another key difference in today's enterprises Income Statement is the lack of slippery items like "Depreciation Expense" of "Interest Expense." As discussed in the previous chapter, firms are becoming more and more asset-light and debt-free and therefore the above two non-operating expenses are almost negligible. That saves a lot of time and energy for equity analysts and investment bankers who then have to look through the firm's depreciation policy to add it back for calculating EBITDA (the real Cash Flows). Managers have extensively used Depreciation expense as an item to manipulate earnings to meet the market expectations and it is better if this expense is kept out of the valuation matrix.

But the lack of "slippery items" is compensated with the entry of a new item called Research and Development Expenses or Software development costs. This item also gives the same "managerial discretion" to the managers as the case was with "depreciation." Most of the new generation technology firms spent huge money on R&D and SW development which as per accounting standard could be either treated as an "expense" in P & L or an "Asset" in the Balance Sheet. The classification rule is when the R & D expenses incurred are reasonably sure to generate revenues to the firm. From that point onward, (which accountants call "technological feasibility is established"), the subsequent future expenses are capitalized as Assets. So, the biggest and the most crucial decision is to decide on that point of "technological feasibility" getting established. The recognition of this point can significantly affect the current period reported earnings as the expenses on R&D continue to be huge.

Employee Benefit expense is a significant expense category in most of the firms and this becomes a key factor in the valuation game too. Firms which have yet to make any profit keep hiring from the best campuses in the world so that the investor community gets the confidence that their firm is in "best hands" and they would soon make the firm profitable. Traditional knowledge of accounting used to guide us to "reduce the fat" and as a matter of fact, most of the companies who were in losses were advised to cut down on the "unproductive workforce" if they see any potential of turnaround. Today, what we see is actually in direct contradiction with this theory. The company knows very well that they can't actually afford such expensive employees but investors actually force them to keep hiring so that the valuation doesn't get affected (because of compromise on hiring standards).

Summary

This chapter described the remaining basic accounting concepts:

6. *Accounting period.* Accounting measures activities for a specified interval of time.

7. *Conservatism.* Revenues are recognized only when they are reasonably certain, whereas expenses are recognized as soon as they are reasonably possible.

8. *Realization.* The amount recognized as revenue is the amount that customers are reasonably certain to pay.

9. *Matching.* When a given event affects both revenues and expenses, the effect on each should be recognized in the same accounting period. Related to the matching concept are two expense recognition criteria: (1) costs associated with activities of the period are expenses of the period and (2) costs that cannot be associated with revenues of future periods are expenses of the current period (costs associated with future periods are assets).

10. *Consistency.* Once an entity has decided on a certain accounting method, it will use the same method for all subsequent transactions and events of the same character unless it has a sound reason to change methods.

11. *Materiality.* Insignificant events may be disregarded, but there must be full disclosure of all important information.

The income statement summarizes the revenues and expenses of an entity for an accounting period. The usual accounting period is one year, but many companies prepare interim income statements on a monthly or quarterly basis. The statement of retained earnings explains the change in retained earnings between the balance sheets prepared as of the beginning and the end of the period.

Only accrual-basis accounting, which employs the realization and matching concepts, is permitted under GAAP. Income tax accounting regulations differ in some important respects from GAAP, including permitting certain types of businesses to calculate taxable income using modified cash-basis accounting. Economic income is a theoretical concept rather than a practical approach to measuring income.

Problems

Problem 3–1.   N. Klein & Company had the following transactions in June. Using the matching concept, decide which of these transactions represented expenses for June.

    a. Received orders for goods with prices totaling $25,000; goods to be delivered in July.

    b. Paid office staff $9,750 for work performed in June.

    c. Products in inventory costing $1,725 were found to be obsolete.

    d. Sold goods with a cost of $25,000 in June.

    e. Paid $750 for radio advertising in June.

    f. Purchased additional inventory for $27,000.

Problem 3–2.   The Hosmer Company had June sales of $275,000. The cost of goods sold was $164,000 and other cash expenses were:

Rent	$ 3,300	Taxes	$ 1,375
Salaries	27,400	Other	50,240

Required:

What were the company's (*a*) revenues, (*b*) expenses, and (*c*) net income in June?

Problem 3–3.   What is cost of goods sold for the period, given the following information?

Purchases for the period	$78,000
Beginning inventory	27,000
Ending inventory	31,000

Problem 3–4.   Worden Corporation has the following income statement for the year:

Income Statement For the Year Ended December 31	
Sales revenues	$85,000
Expenses:	
Cost of goods sold	$45,000
Selling and administrative expenses	25,000
Income taxes	6,000
Total expenses	$76,000
Net Income	$ 9,000

Required:

    a. Calculate

       (1) Gross margin (in dollars).

       (2) Gross margin percentage.

       (3) Profit margin percentage.

    b. Interpret the results of the above calculations.

Problem 3–5. What expense items are associated with the following transactions? When and how is the income statement affected by each one?

    a. Purchased equipment for $40,000 that has a useful life of five years.

    b. Purchased land for $135,000.

    c. Purchased $7,000 worth of inventory on December 19. On December 27 sold one-half of the inventory for $6,000. On January 8, sold the remainder for $6,200. The company uses the calendar year for its fiscal year.

    d. On January 1, subscribed to a magazine for two years. The cost was $72.

Problem 3–6. The Pierson Computer Company purchased a two-year fire insurance policy, paying the $30,000 premium in October 20 × 5. The policy was dated October 1, 20 × 5, and expired on September 30, 20 × 7. With respect to this policy, what were the expenses applicable to 20 × 5, 20 × 6, and 20 × 7, and what was the asset value (prepaid insurance) as of December 31, 20 × 5, 20 × 6, and 20 × 7?

Problem 3–7. QED Electronics Company had the following transactions during April while conducting its television and stereo repair business.

    1. A new repair truck was purchased for $19,000.

    2. Parts with a cost of $1,600 were received and used during April.

    3. Service revenue for the month was $33,400, but only $20,500 was cash sales. Typically, only 95 percent of sales on account are realized.

    4. Interest expense on loans outstanding was $880.

    5. Wage costs for the month totaled $10,000; however, $1,400 of this had not yet been paid to the employees.

    6. Parts inventory from the beginning of the month was depleted by $2,100.

    7. Utility bills totaling $1,500 were paid. $700 of this amount was associated with March's operations.

    8. Depreciation expense was $2,700.

    9. Selling expenses were $1,900.

    10. A provision for income taxes was established at $2,800, of which $2,600 had been paid to the federal government.

    11. Administrative and miscellaneous expenses were recorded at $4,700.

Required:

Prepare a detailed April income statement.

Problem 3–8. Determine the amount of total assets, current assets, and noncurrent assets at the end of the period, given the following data:

Current liabilities, ending balance	$ 50,000	Purchases during the period	$40,000
Current ratio, ending	1.6:1	Inventory, ending balance	$30,000
Owners' equity, beginning		Gross margin percentage	45%
balance	$120,000	Profit margin	10%
Inventory, beginning balance	$ 35,000	Long-term debt, ending	
		balance	$40,000

CASES

Case 3–1
Maynard Company (B)*

Diane Maynard was grateful for the balance sheets that her friend prepared [see Case 2–1, Maynard Company (A)]. In going over the numbers, she remarked, "It's sort of surprising that cash increased by $31,677, but net income was only $19,635. Why was that?"

Her friend replied, "A partial answer to that question is to look at an income statement for June. I think I can find the data I need to prepare one for you."

In addition to the data given in the (A) case, her friend found a record of cash receipts and disbursements, which is summarized in Exhibit 1. She also learned that all accounts payable were to vendors for

purchase of merchandise inventory and that cost of sales was $39,345 in June.

Questions

1. Prepare an income statement for June in proper format. Explain the derivation of each item on this statement, including cost of sales.
2. Explain why the change in the cash balance was greater than the net income.
3. Explain why the following amounts are *incorrect* cost of sales amounts for June: (*a*) $14,715 and (*b*) $36,030. Under what circumstances would these amounts be correct cost of sales amounts?

EXHIBIT 1

**Cash Receipts and Disbursements
Month of June**

Cash Receipts		Cash Disbursements	
Cash sales	$44,420	Equipment purchased	$23,400
Credit customers	21,798	Other assets purchased	408
Diane Maynard	11,700	Payments on accounts payable	8,517
Bank loan	20,865	Cash purchases of merchandise	14,715
Total receipts	$98,783	Cash purchase of supplies	1,671
		Dividends	11,700
		Wages paid	5,660
		Utilities paid	900
		Miscellaneous payments	135
		Total disbursements	$67,106

Reconciliation:	
Cash balance, June 1	$ 34,983
Receipts	98,783
Subtotal	$133,766
Disbursements	67,106
Cash balance, June 30	$ 66,660

Case 3–2

Lone Pine Cafe (B)*

In addition to preparing the balance sheet described in Lone Pine Cafe (A), Mr. Simpson, the accountant, agreed to prepare an income statement. He said that such a financial statement would show Mrs. Antoine how profitable operations had been, and thus help her to judge whether it was worthwhile to continue operating the restaurant.

In addition to the information given in the (A) case, Mr. Simpson learned that cash received from customers through March 30 amounted to $43,480 and that cash payments were as follows:

Monthly payments to partners*	$23,150
Wages to part-time employees	5,480
Interest	540
Food and beverage suppliers	10,016
Telephone and electricity	3,270
Miscellaneous	255
Rent payments	7,500

* One-third to each partner.

Questions

1. Prepare an income statement for the period of the cafe's operations through March 30, 2010.
2. What does this income statement tell Mrs. Antoine?

* Copyright © Professor Robert N. Anthony.

Case 3–3

Dispensers of California, Inc.

Peter Hynes created a working model of a new and improved commercial paint spray, which he had patented. The patent had a legal life of 16 years remaining.

Hynes was eager to exploit his patent commercially, but he had no funds of his own. Several of Hynes' friends, who had used prototypes of Hynes' paint spray, offered to invest in a new corporation with a capitalization of $200,000 par value capital stock to further develop, manufacture, and market the spray and its related equipment. Before making their investment, the investors asked Hynes to prepare a profit plan projecting the company's revenues and expenses for the company's initial year of operation along with an end-of-first-year balance sheet.

Hynes agreed to prepare the requested information incorporating the following projected transactions:

1. In return for signing his patent over to the new company, which was to be called Dispensers of California, Inc., Hynes would receive 60 percent of the company's capital stock. For their part, the investors would contribute $80,000 cash for a 40 percent interest in the company.

2. Incorporation costs, $2,500.
3. Equipment to be used in assembling the paint spray dispensers, $85,000.
4. Out-of-pocket labor and development costs to re-design the paint spray dispenser to facilitate more efficient assembling, $25,000.
5. Component part purchases, $212,100.
6. Short-term loan from local bank, $30,000. (Loan to be repaid before the end of the year with $500 interest.)
7. Manufacturing payroll, $145,000.
8. Other manufacturing costs (excluding component part costs), $62,000.
9. Selling, general, and administration costs, $63,000.
10. Ending component parts inventory cost, $15,100.
11. Sales, $598,500 (all received in cash.)
12. All incorporation and product redesign costs expensed as incurred.
13. Depreciation, $8,500. (Hynes estimated the useful life of the equipment was 10 years, with no salvage value.)

14. Patent cost charged to income over a six-year period (Hynes anticipated technology developments incorporating digital flow controls would significantly reduce the current products sales in about six years' time.)
15. No inventory of unsold or partially completed dispensers at year end.
16. Cash dividends, $5,000.
17. Income tax expense, $22,500 (due to be paid during the next year).
18. All amounts due to employees, suppliers, and others, except for income taxes, paid in cash. (Hynes made this assumption because he wanted to present a "conservative" balance sheet to the investors.)

Questions

1. How might Hynes and the investors use the profit-plan in managing the business?
2. How might the projected transactions impact the company's balance sheet? (Think about each transaction in terms of its impact on both the basic accounting equation and specific accounts.)
3. Prepare a profit plan in the form of an income statement for the first year of operations.
4. Prepare a balance sheet as of the end of the first year of operations.
5. Hynes made a number of accounting decisions. Do you agree with these decisions?

Case 3–4

Pinetree Motel*

Mr. and Mrs. Ilyong Kim had purchased the Pinetree Motel in 1998 with their life savings, supplemented by a loan from a close personal friend. The motel consisted of 20 units (i.e., rentable rooms) and was located near a vacation area that was popular during both the summer and winter seasons. The Kims had entered the motel business because Mrs. Kim had long wanted to run a business of her own.

Both Mr. and Mrs. Kim felt that they had been successful. Each year saw a growth in revenue from room rentals. Furthermore, their bank balance had increased. They noted that many of their customers returned year after year. This was attributed to their location and their efforts to provide consistently clean rooms and up-to-date furnishings.

The Kims had no formal business training but felt their experience since acquiring the motel had alerted them to the management problems involved. Both Mr. and Mrs. Kim devoted their full time to operating the motel. In addition, they hired part-time help for daily room-cleaning work. They had no dining facilities but had installed vending machines to supplement room rentals. The vending machines posed no inventory or maintenance problems as the vending machine company provided servicing and maintenance.

A frequent guest at Pinetree Motel was Marcus Carter, controller of a large company. Mr. Carter visited a company branch plant near the motel several times a year. As he stayed at the motel during these trips, he became acquainted with the Kims.

In May 2006 Mrs. Kim showed Mr. Carter the current issue of a motel trade journal that contained operating data for motels with 40 or fewer units for the calendar year 2005. Mrs. Kim commented: "These figures show a profit of 21 percent. Our profit last year was $134,003 on sales of $244,461, or 55 percent. We think 2005 was our best year to date, but we can't make our figures jibe with those in the magazine, and we wonder if we really are 34 percent ahead of the industry average. Can you help us?"

Mr. Carter was interested and willing to help. He told Mrs. Kim to get the available figures for 2005 so that he could look them over that evening. The principal records the Kims kept to reflect the motel's financial transactions were a record of receipts taken from the cash register and a checkbook describing cash paid out. In addition, certain rough notations of other expenses incurred were available.

That evening Mrs. Kim showed Mr. Carter the cash summary for the year 2005, as given in Exhibit 1. Mr. Carter immediately noted that the difference between receipts and expenditures was $47,903 and asked Mrs. Kim to explain why she had stated the profit was $134,003. Mrs. Kim replied, "Oh, that's easy. Our drawings aren't expenses; after all, we are the owners. My husband and I have consistently taken only about $85,000 a year out because we want the rest of the profits to accumulate in the business. As I said, our

EXHIBIT 1 Cash Register and Checkbook Summary During 2005

Receipts	
From rooms	$236,758
From vending machines	7,703
Total	$244,461

Checks Drawn	
Owners' drawings	$ 86,100
Wages and salaries	26,305
Paid to laundry	8,800
Replacement of glasses, bed linens, and towels	1,660
Advertising	2,335
Payroll taxes	2,894
Fuel for heating	12,205
Repairs and maintenance	8,980
Cleaning and other supplies	6,820
Telephone	2,789
Electricity	5,611
Property taxes	9,870
Insurance	11,584
Interest	10,605
Total	$196,558

EXHIBIT 2 2005 Operating Data for Motels with 40 or Fewer Units (expressed as percentages of total revenues)

Revenues:	
Room rentals	98.7
Other revenue	1.3
Total revenues	100.0
Operating expenses:	
Payroll costs	22.5
Administrative and general	4.2
Direct operating expenses	5.9
Fees and commissions	3.3
Advertising and promotion	1.2
Repairs and maintenance	4.8
Utilities	7.5
Total	49.4
Fixed expenses:	
Property taxes, fees	4.4
Insurance	2.5
Depreciation	12.5
Interest	7.7
Rent	2.8
Total	29.9
Profit (pretax)	20.7

bank balance has steadily risen. Furthermore, I have a local accountant make out the annual income tax statements so I don't have to worry about them. That income tax stuff is so complicated that I avoid it."

Mr. Carter worked with the trade journal's figures (Exhibit 2) and the cash summary (Exhibit 1) that evening and quickly found he needed more information. He told Mrs. Kim that he was returning to the home office the next morning but would be back in two weeks for another visit to the branch plant. Meanwhile, he wanted Mrs. Kim to get together some additional information. Mr. Carter suggested to Mrs. Kim that an important noncash expense was depreciation. Mr. Carter also wanted to know about expenses that had been incurred in 2004 but not paid until 2005. He told Mrs. Kim to check up on wages and salaries, insurance, advertising, taxes, utilities, and any other items paid in 2005 but applicable to 2004.

In addition, Mr. Carter instructed Mrs. Kim to try to find items of expense properly chargeable to 2005 but not paid by December 31, 2005. Mrs. Kim told Mr. Carter the same types of expenses were involved, that is, wages and salaries, insurance, advertising, taxes,

EXHIBIT 3 Additional Information about the Business

Chargeable in 2004 but paid in January 2005:	
Wages and salaries	$795
Advertising	600
Payroll taxes	84
Fuel for heating	933
Telephone	105
Electricity	360
Property taxes	1,005
Insurance	2,025
Interest	687
Chargeable in 2005 but not paid by December 31, 2005:	
Wages and salaries	1,128
Advertising	996
Payroll taxes	126
Fuel for heating	840
Cleaning and other supplies	75
Telephone	153
Electricity	492
Property taxes	1,119
Interest	579

Also, 2005 depreciation charges of $30,280.

Also, 2005 cash receipts included a $1,660 payment from a company that had rented several units during December 2004 for a convention in the nearby city. There were no such uncollected rentals as of December 31, 2005.

and so forth. Also Mr. Carter inquired about income from room rentals. He asked if any of the cash receipts during 2005 related to rentals during 2004 and if therewere any rentals during 2005 that had not been collected.

During the two weeks Mr. Carter was back at the home office, Mrs. Kim checked the records and compiled the additional information requested by Mr. Carter. The evening Mr. Carter returned to the Pinetree Motel, Mrs. Kim gave him a summary of the information she had gathered (Exhibit 3). With all the additional information, Mr. Carter constructed a 2005 operating statement that matched in form the one appearing in the trade journal. He calculated both the dollar amounts and percentage composition of each expense for more useful comparison with the journal's figures.

Questions

1. Prepare a 2005 operating statement for the Pinetree Motel such as the one shown in Exhibit 2 showing dollar amounts and percentages of total revenues.
2. As Mr. Carter, what comments would you make to the Kims regarding the motel's progress to date?

Case 3–5
National Association of Accountants[1],*

Each December the incoming members of the board of directors of the National Association of Accountants (NAA) met in joint session with the outgoing board as a

EXHIBIT 1

Estimated Income Statement Year Ending December 31, 2005	
Revenues:	
Membership dues	$287,500
Journal subscriptions	31,000
Publication sales	11,900
Foundation grant	54,000
2000 annual meeting, profit	3,400
Total revenues	387,800
Expenses:	
Printing and mailing publications	92,400
Committee meeting expense	49,200
Annual meeting advance	10,800
Desktop publishing system	27,000
Administrative salaries and expenses	171,500
Miscellaneous	25,000
Total expenses	375,900
Surplus	$ 11,900

[1] Disguised name.

* © Professor Robert N. Anthony.

means of smoothing the transition from one administration to another. At the meeting in December 2005, questions were raised about whether the board had adhered to the general policies of the association. The ensuing discussion became quite heated.

NAA was a nonprofit professional association with 3,000 members. The association published two professional journals, arranged an annual meeting and several regional meetings, appointed committees that developed positions on various topics of interest to the membership, and represented the members before standards-setting bodies.

The operating activities of the association were managed by George Tremble, its executive secretary. Mr. Tremble reported to the board of directors. The board consisted of four officers and seven other members. Six members of the 2006 board (i.e., the board that assumed responsibility on January 1, 2006) were also on the 2005 board; the other five members were newly elected. The president served a one-year term.

The financial policy of the association was that each year should "stand on its own feet"; that is, expenses of the year should approximately equal the revenues of the year. If there was a deficit in 2005, this amount would normally be made up by a dues increase in 2006.

At the meeting in December 2005, Mr. Tremble presented an estimated income statement for 2005 (Exhibit 1). Although some of the December transactions were necessarily estimated, Mr. Tremble assured the board that the actual totals for the year would closely approximate the numbers shown.

Wilma Fosdick, one of the newly elected board members, raised a question about the foundation grant of $54,000. She questioned whether this item should be counted as revenue. If it were excluded, there was a deficit; and this showed that the 2005 board had, in effect, eaten into reserves and thus made it more difficult to provide the level of service that the members had a right to expect in 2006. This led to detailed questions about items on the income statement, which brought forth the following information from Mr. Tremble.

1. In 2005 NAA received a $54,000 cash grant from the Beckwith Foundation for the purpose of financing a symposium to be held in June 2006. During 2005 approximately $2,700 was spent in preliminary planning for this symposium and was included in Committee Meeting Expenses. When asked why the $54,000 had been recorded as revenue in 2005 rather than in 2006, Mr. Tremble said that the grant was obtained entirely by the initiative and persuasiveness of the 2005 president, so 2005 should be given credit for it. Further, although the grant was intended to finance the symposium, there was no legal requirement that the symposium be held; if for any reason it was not held, the money would be used for the general operations of the association.

2. In early December 2005 the association took delivery of, and paid for, a new desktop publishing system costing $27,000. This system would greatly simplify the work of preparing membership lists, correspondence, and manuscripts submitted for publication. Except for this new system, the typewriters, desks, and other equipment in the association office were quite old.

3. Ordinarily, members paid their dues during the first few months of the year. Because of the need to raise cash to finance the purchase of the desktop publishing system, the association announced in September 2005 that members who paid their 2006 dues before December 15, 2005, would receive a free copy of the book of papers presented at the special symposium to be held in June 2006. The approximate per-copy cost of publishing this book was $16, and it was expected to be sold for $18. Consequently, $32,400 of 2006 dues were received by December 15, 2005; they were included in 2005 revenue.

4. In July 2005 the association sent a membership directory to members. Its long-standing practice was to publish such a directory every two years. The cost of preparing and printing this directory was $23,200. Of the 4,000 copies printed, 3,000 were mailed to members in 2005. The remaining 1,000 were held to meet the needs of new members who would join before the next directory came out; they would receive a free copy of the directory when they joined.

5. Members received the association's journals at no extra cost, as a part of the membership privileges. Some libraries and other nonmembers also subscribed to the journals. The $31,000 reported as subscription revenue was the cash received in 2005. Of this amount, about $8,100 was for journals that would be delivered in 2006. Offsetting this was $5,400 of subscription revenue received in 2004 for journals delivered in 2005; this $5,400 had been reported as 2004 revenue.

6. The association had advanced $10,800 to the committee responsible for planning the 2005 annual meeting held in late November. This amount was used for preliminary expenses, and was included as 2005 Committee Meeting Expense. Registration fees at the annual meeting were set so as to cover all convention costs, so that it was expected that the $10,800, plus any profit, would be returned to the association after the committee had finished paying the convention bills. The 2004 convention had resulted in a $3,400 profit, but the results of the 2005 convention were not known, although the revenues and expenses were about as anticipated.

Questions

1. Did the association have an excess (revenues greater than expenses) or a deficit (expenses greater than revenues) in 2005?
2. Should the amount of surplus or deficit in 2005 affect the decision to change the annual dues for 2006?

Case 3–6
Cash Burn for better Valuations

The other day Rajiv, a retired banker was reading in the newspaper that yojini.com, an Artificial intelligence and Machine learning driven technology firm continues to hire from top engineering school campuses in the country (actually they made the largest number of offers in some top B schools too) despite reporting heavy losses. As a traditional banker, he always believed that for companies to be sustainable, they have to cut down on the expenses to remain afloat, if they are incurring losses. He has also learnt all through his career that the P&L of any business is the lifeline and if the bottom line remains in RED for a long time, it is basically the end of the story for the firm. From what he was reading about yojini.com, it seemed like a classic example of a "paradox." If the company is in losses for quite sometime now, they should hire (if at all they need to) from Tier- II colleges where the human resource would be much cheaper compared to the top college graduates.

He was further perplexed when he also read in the same article that the firm spends close to 15% of their revenue on Research and Development Expense, most of it is spent on items, the firm is not even sure whether it will bring any benefits. Being a new technology firm, they had no clue as to what is in store for them in future.

Both these two items left him so confused that he closed the newspaper and decided to go for a walk to the nearest park.

Questions

1. Why do technology firms burn cash and spend heavily on R&D expenses which should have been otherwise controlled?
2. Is the firm not worried about P&L when they continue to hire from top schools despite incurring huge losses?
3. Is P&L losing relevance for new technology start ups? If yes, why?

Accounting Records and Systems

As we emphasized in Chapter 2, each individual accounting transaction can be recorded in terms of its effect on the balance sheet. For example, the Music Mart illustration in Chapter 2 starts with the item "Cash, $25,000" on the January 1 balance sheet and then records the transaction on January 2 involving an increase of $12,500 in cash in effect by erasing the $25,000 and entering the new number, $37,500. Although this procedure was appropriate as an explanatory device, it is not a practical way of handling the many transactions that occur in the actual operations of an organization.

This chapter describes some of the accounting procedures that are used in practice. *No new accounting concepts are introduced.* The procedures described here provide the mechanical means for making it easier to record and summarize transactions. Although most organizations use computer-based accounting systems, we describe the procedures used in a manual system because the basic steps in either type of system are the same and it is easier to visualize these steps in a manual system.

Recordkeeping Fundamentals

We are not concerned here with recordkeeping procedures for the purpose of training bookkeepers. Nevertheless, some knowledge of these procedures is useful for at least two reasons. First, as is the case with many subjects, accounting is something that is best learned by doing—by solving problems. Although any accounting problem can be solved without the aid of the tools discussed in this chapter, using these tools will often speed up the problem-solving process considerably. Second, the debit-and-credit mechanism, which is the principal technique discussed here, provides an analytical framework that is similar in function to and offers the same advantages as the symbols and equations used in algebra.

In all except the smallest companies, the bookkeeping work is done on a computer. However, the computer records much detail about most transactions, and describing this detail would obscure the description of what is going on. Therefore, we focus on what is actually happening by assuming that the records are kept manually.

The Account

Assume that the item "Cash, $10,000" appears on a balance sheet. Subsequent cash transactions can affect this amount in only one of two ways: They can increase it or they can decrease it. Instead of increasing or decreasing the item by erasing the old amount and entering the new amount for each transaction, considerable effort can be saved by collecting all the increases together and all the decreases together and then periodically calculating the *net* change resulting from all of them. This can be done by adding the sum of the increases to the beginning amount and then subtracting the sum of the decreases. The difference is the new cash balance.

In accounting, the device called an **account** is used for calculating the net change. The simplest form of account, called a **T account**, looks like the account shown in Illustration 4–1. Because this account is for a brand-new entity (to be described later in this chapter), its beginning balance is zero.

The saving in effort made possible by T accounts can be seen even from this brief illustration. If the balance were changed for each of the eight items listed, four additions and four subtractions would be required. By using the account device, the new balance is obtained by only two additions (to find the 21,200 and 15,750) and one subtraction (21,200 – 15,750).

Permanent Accounts and Temporary Accounts

The accounts maintained for the various items on the balance sheet are called **permanent (or real) accounts**. At the end of each accounting period, the balance of each permanent account is determined—each account is "balanced." These balances are the numbers reported in the balance sheet as of the end of the period. The period-ending balance in a permanent account is carried forward into the next accounting period as that period's beginning balance.

Recall that revenues and expenses are respectively increases and decreases in retained earnings arising from the entity's earnings activities. Although revenue and expense transactions could be entered directly in the Retained Earnings account, this is not done in practice. Entering revenue and expense items directly to Retained Earnings would result in an intermingling of the many specific items that are required to prepare the income statement. All of these items would have to be "sorted out"—classified by income statement categories—if they were intermingled.

To avoid cluttering the Retained Earnings account, a **temporary account** is established for each revenue and expense item that will appear on the income statement. Thus, there are temporary accounts for sales revenues, cost of sales, selling expenses, and so on. Revenue and expense transactions are recorded in their respective temporary

ILLUSTRATION 4–1

Example of a T Account

Cash

(Increases)		(Decreases)	
Beginning balance	–0–		
	5,000		750
	4,000		7,200
	200		4,800
	12,000		3,000
	21,200		15,750
New balance	5,450		

accounts as the period progresses. This procedure creates a "sort as you go" routine for these transactions instead of leaving them to be sorted at the end of the period. For example, all of the entries to the Sales Revenue account can be added at the end of the period to arrive at the amount of sales for the income statement. At the end of the accounting period, all of the income statement temporary account sums are combined into one *net income* amount, which is then entered in the Retained Earnings account. Thus, in practice, Retained Earnings has *fewer* entries made to it than almost any other permanent account. (The process of combining the temporary account sums into one amount for the net change in retained earnings will be illustrated later in the chapter.)

The Ledger

A **ledger** is a group of accounts. In a manual system, it may be a bound book with the title "general ledger" printed on the cover. Inside are pages, one (or more) for each account. All the accounts of a small business could be maintained in such a book. The ledger is not necessarily a bound book, however. It may consist of a set of loose-leaf pages, or, with computers, a set of impulses on a CD or tape.

The Chart of Accounts

The accounts included in a company's system are listed in a **chart of accounts**. The list often is arranged according to the items reported on the balance sheet, that is, with Cash at the beginning and Retained Earnings at the end.

For most items, there are detailed accounts, and there may be several levels of this detail. For example, beneath the Cash account, there will be an account for each bank with which the company has deposits and, for each bank, there may be an account for each checking account, money market account, and other cash equivalents. The entries are made only to the accounts in the lowest level in this hierarchy, for example, the checking account at Bank A. In most systems, amounts are automatically added to accounts in the highest levels of the hierarchy when an entry at the lowest level is recorded. For example, a deposit of $1,000 in the checking account of Bank A would be recorded in Checking Account, Bank A; it would also add $1,000 to the Cash Bank A account, and $1,000 to the Cash account.

In developing the chart of accounts, the system designer must anticipate all the information that management might at some time want. If, for example, management wanted to know the respective level of activity of the checking account and the money market account at Bank A, and the system of accounts could not provide this information, the system would be inadequate. A code number is assigned to each account; this simplifies the task of recording. In a computer-based accounting system, an XBRL tag also may be attached to the account and its underlying components to facilitate extraction on demand and analysis of the data.

Example

Financial information related to sales revenue is often recorded in considerable detail: the item sold, the product line containing that item, the branch that made the sale, and even the responsible salesperson. Accounts are established for each of these possibilities. Consequently, many large companies have tens of thousands of accounts.

The accounts for balance sheet and income statement items are often referred to as *general ledger* accounts, a holdover from the manual system in which these accounts were recorded in a bound book called a *ledger*.

Debit and Credit

The left-hand side of any account is arbitrarily called the **debit side**, and the right-hand side is called the **credit side**. Amounts entered on the left-hand side are called **debits**, and amounts entered on the right-hand side are called **credits**. The verb *to debit* means to make an entry in the left-hand side of an account, and the verb *to credit* means to make an entry in the right-hand side of an account. *The words* debit *and* credit *have no other meaning in accounting.*

In ordinary usage, these words do have other meanings. *Credit* has a favorable connotation (such as, "she is a credit to her family") and *debit* has an unfavorable connotation (such as, "chalk up a debit against him"). In accounting these words do not imply any sort of value judgment; they mean simply "left" and "right." Debit and credit are usually abbreviated as **dr.** and **cr.**[1]

If each account were considered by itself without regard to its relationship to other accounts, it would make no difference whether increases were recorded on the debit side or on the credit side. In the 15th century, a Franciscan monk, Luca Pacioli, described a method of arranging accounts so that the *dual aspect* present in every accounting transaction would be expressed by a debit amount and an equal and offsetting credit amount.

This method made possible the following rule, to which there is absolutely no exception: *For each transaction, the debit amount* (or the sum of all the debit amounts, if there are more than one) *must equal the credit amount* (or the sum of all the credit amounts). This is why bookkeeping is called *double-entry* bookkeeping. It follows that the recording of a transaction in which debits do not equal credits is incorrect. For all the accounts combined, the sum of the debit balances must equal the sum of the credit balances; otherwise something has been done incorrectly. Thus, the debit and credit arrangement used in accounting provides a useful means of checking the accuracy with which the transactions have been recorded.

Pacioli based his procedures on the fundamental equation, Assets = Liabilities + Owners' equity. He arbitrarily decided that *asset* accounts should *increase* on the left-hand, or *debit,* side. That decision immediately led to the rule that *asset* accounts must *decrease* on the right-hand, or *credit,* side. Given those rules for asset accounts, it followed that (1) in order for debits to equal credits and (2) in order to maintain the fundamental accounting equation, then the rules for liability and owners' equity accounts had to be the opposite from those for assets. *Liability and owners' equity* accounts *increase* on the right-hand—*credit*—side, and they *decrease* on the left-hand—*debit*— side. Schematically, these rules are

Assets		=	Liabilities		+	Owners' Equity	
Debit	Credit		Debit	Credit		Debit	Credit
+	−		−	+		−	+

The rules for recording revenues and expenses are derived from the rules for owners' equity. By definition, a revenue increases owners' equity (more specifically, retained earnings in a corporation), and owners' equity increases on the credit side. It necessarily follows that *revenues are credits.* If revenues decrease, such as for a sales return, the *decrease in revenues* must therefore be a *debit.*

Expenses are the opposite of revenues in that expenses decrease owners' equity. Therefore, the rule for expenses must be the following: *Expenses are debits.* It is also commonly said that an expense account has been **charged** when it has been debited. If an expense needs to be reversed (such as when returned goods are put back into inventory, thus reversing the cost of sales entry that was made when the goods were originally sold), the *decrease in expenses* is a *credit.*

---

[1] The noun *debit* is derived from the Latin *debitur,* which means debtor. *Credit* is derived from the Latin *creditor,* which means lender. Apparently the dr. and cr. abbreviations came from the first and last letters of these Latin words. In accounting, debit and credit do *not* mean debtor and creditor.

Mastering these rules requires practice in using them rather than sheer memorization. We will therefore begin that practice by introducing you to the accounting process and first recording a simple set of transactions.

The Accounting Process

The next section of the chapter describes the accounting process. It consists of these six steps:

1. The first and most important part of the accounting process is the *analysis of transactions*. This is the process of deciding which account or accounts should be debited, which should be credited, and in what amounts, in order to reflect events in the accounting records. This requires both a knowledge of accounting concepts and judgment.
2. Next comes the purely mechanical step of *journalizing original entries*—recording the results of the transaction analysis in the journal.
3. *Posting* is the process of recording changes in the ledger accounts exactly as specified by the journal entries. This is also purely mechanical.
4. At the ending of the accounting period, judgment is involved in deciding on the *adjusting entries*. These are journalized and posted in the same way as original entries.
5. The *closing entries* are journalized and posted. This is a purely mechanical step.
6. *Financial statements* are prepared. This requires judgment as to the best arrangement and terminology, but the numbers that are used result from the judgments made in steps 1 and 4.

These six steps are taken sequentially during an accounting period and are repeated in each subsequent period. The steps are therefore commonly referred to as the **accounting cycle**. Illustration 4–2 depicts the accounting cycle schematically. Note that the ending balance sheet account balances from step 6 become the beginning balances for the next repetition of the cycle. Some accountants use a *worksheet* in the latter steps of the accounting cycle.

ILLUSTRATION 4–2
The Accounting Cycle

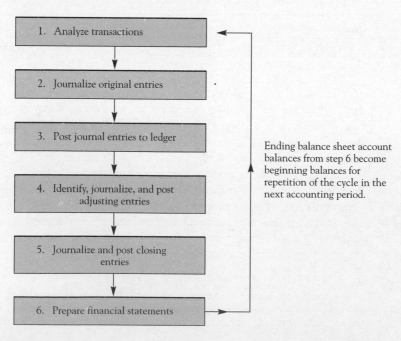

Ending balance sheet account balances from step 6 become beginning balances for repetition of the cycle in the next accounting period.

Transaction Analysis

Before it is recorded, a transaction must be analyzed to determine its dual effect on the entity's accounts. This analysis results in a decision on which account is to be debited and which is to be credited. The result of the transaction analysis must preserve the two basic identities: (1) Assets = Liabilities + Owners' equity and (2) Debits = Credits. The beginner often finds that half of the accounting entry—particularly a change in cash— is relatively obvious, but that the other half—often a change in retained earnings—is less obvious. Our advice is to first record whichever half of the entry is more obvious, whether it is the debit or the credit portion, and then figure out the less obvious half.

Example: Campus Pizzeria, Inc.

Meredith Snelson started Campus Pizzeria, Inc., on August 1. Snelson was the sole owner of the corporation. The following transactions all took place in August. Revenue and expense transactions represent *summaries* of sales and expenses for the entire month; in practice such entries could be made every day. We will present each transaction, analyze it, and show how it would be entered in the accounts. Each transaction is numbered and its number is shown parenthetically beside the entry in the account. (This is a good practice for the reader to employ when working on similar problems.)

1. On August 1, Snelson invested $5,000 in the business as owner.

Analysis: This transaction increased **Cash** (a debit). Liabilities were not affected because the $5,000 was not a loan; rather, it was contributed capital. Thus, the owner's equity account, **Paid-In Capital**, increased (a credit). This is an equity financing transaction.

Cash		
(1)	5,000	

Paid-In Capital		
	(1)	5,000

2. On August 1, the firm paid $750 rent for the month of August.

Analysis: **Cash** decreased (a credit). The rent has been paid in advance; thus, it is an asset, because the benefits of using the rented space have not yet been received. **Prepaid Expenses** is increased (a debit). This is an asset acquisition transaction: prepaid rent was acquired in exchange for cash.

Cash			
(1)	5,000	(2)	750

Prepaid Expenses		
(2)	750	

3. The firm borrowed $4,000 from a bank on a 9 percent note payable, with interest payable quarterly and the principal due in full at the end of two years.

Analysis: This was a debt financing transaction. **Cash** increased (a debit) by the $4,000 proceeds of the loan. The liability, **Notes Payable**, increased by an equal amount (a credit).

Cash			
(1)	5,000	(2)	750
(3)	4,000		

Notes Payable		
	(3)	4,000

4. Equipment costing $7,200 was purchased for cash. The expected life of the equipment was 10 years.

Analysis: **Cash** decreased by $7,200 (a credit). The equipment will provide benefits for several years, so it is an asset. The account **Equipment, at Cost**, is increased by $7,200 (a debit). This was an asset acquisition transaction: The equipment was acquired in exchange for cash.

	Cash		
(1)	5,000	(2)	750
(3)	4,000	**(4)**	**7,200**

	Equipment, at Cost	
(4)	**7,200**	

5. An initial inventory of pizza ingredients and boxes was purchased on credit for $800.

Analysis: These items will be used in the future, so they are an asset. **Inventory** is increased by $800 (a debit). The firm has not yet paid for these items but is obligated to do so at some future time. Thus, the liability, **Accounts Payable**, is increased by $800 (a credit).

	Inventory	
(5)	**800**	

	Accounts Payable	
	(5)	**800**

6. In August pizza sales were $12,000, all for cash.

Analysis: **Cash** increased by $12,000. This cash increase did not arise from a liability; nor did the owner make an additional investment. The cash was earned by selling pizzas to customers. This is an earnings transaction, which increases retained earnings. Rather than directly increasing Retained Earnings (a credit), we will increase **Sales Revenues**, a temporary account.

	Cash		
(1)	5,000	(2)	750
(3)	4,000	(4)	7,200
(6)	**12,000**		

	Sales Revenues	
	(6)	**12,000**

7. During August the pizzeria's employees were paid $3,000 in wages.[2]

Analysis: **Cash** was decreased (a credit) by $3,000. Wages represent labor resources consumed in providing the pizzeria's services to its customers. This is therefore an earnings transaction that reduces retained earnings. Rather than directly decreasing Retained Earnings (a debit), we will enter the expense in a temporary account, **Wage Expense**.

	Cash		
(1)	5,000	(2)	750
(3)	4,000	(4)	7,200
(6)	12,000	**(7)**	**3,000**

	Wage Expense	
(7)	**3,000**	

[2] Because this is an introductory example, we are disregarding certain real-world complications such as payroll taxes.

8. During the month, an additional $5,750 of ingredients and boxes was purchased on credit.

Analysis: Except for the amount, this transaction is identical to transaction 5 on page 92. Thus, **Inventory** is increased (debited) and **Accounts Payable** is increased (credited) by $5,750.	

Inventory			
(5)	800		
(8)	**5,750**		

Accounts Payable			
		(5)	800
		(8)	**5,750**

9. August sales consumed $6,000 of ingredients and boxes.

Analysis: These items have been removed from **Inventory**, so that asset account is reduced (credited). Resources consumed in generating sales revenues are expenses. Again, rather than directly reducing Retained Earnings, the $6,000 debit is made to a temporary account, **Cost of Sales**. This is an earnings transaction.

Inventory			
(5)	800	**(9)**	**6,000**
(8)	5,750		

Cost of Sales			
(9)	**6,000**		

10. At the end of the month, bills for various utilities used in August were received, totaling $450.

Analysis: The bills have not yet been paid, so **Accounts Payable** is increased by $450 (a credit). This liability is an expenditure for the utilities that were used (consumed) in August's earnings activities. These resources are thus an expense of August, and are debited to **Utilities Expense**, a temporary account.

Accounts Payable			
		(5)	800
		(4)	5,750
		(10)	**450**

Utilities Expense			
(10)	**450**		

11. During the month, $4,800 of accounts payable was paid.

Analysis: Paying bills obviously decreases **Cash** (a credit). It also reduces the obligation the entity has to its vendors, so **Accounts Payable** is also reduced (a debit).

Cash			
(1)	5,000	(2)	750
(3)	4,000	(4)	7,200
(6)	12,000	(7)	3,000
		(11)	**4,800**

Accounts Payable			
(11)	**4,800**	(5)	800
		(8)	5,750
		(10)	450

12. **On August 13, the firm catered a party for a fee of $200. Because the customer was a friend of Snelson, the customer was told that payment could be made later in the month.**

Analysis: Because services have been rendered, revenues have been earned. Thus, increase (credit) the temporary **Sales Revenues** account by $200. Since this was not a cash sale, the asset increased (debited) is **Accounts Receivable**. This is an earnings transaction.	Sales Revenues		
		(6)	12,000
		(12)	**200**
	Accounts Receivable		
	(12)	**200**	

13. **On August 29, a check was received from Snelson's friend for the party of August 13.**

Analysis: Payment (collection) of a receivable increases **Cash** (a debit). It also eliminates the receivable asset, so **Accounts Receivable** is decreased by $200 (a credit).	Cash			
	(1)	5,000	(2)	750
	(3)	4,000	(4)	7,200
	(6)	12,000	(7)	3,000
	(13)	**200**	(11)	4,800
	Accounts Payable			
	(12)	200	**(13)**	**200**

This completes—for the moment—the August transactions for Campus Pizzeria, Inc.

Balancing Accounts

The transactions we recorded above are called **original entries**. Such entries are those that obviously need to be made because a check has been written, an invoice has been received, sales have been made, and so on. After recording these original entries, a balance is taken in each account.

An asset account is balanced as illustrated earlier in the chapter for Cash: The entries on each side are added up; then the sum of the credits is subtracted from the sum of the debits to get the new balance. An asset account's balance is a debit amount. (Asset accounts are thus called **debit-balance accounts**.) The balance in Cash is $5,450. (Be-cause Cash is an asset account, it is understood that the balance is a debit amount.)

Illustration 4–3 shows the formal procedure for **ruling and balancing** an asset account. This is similar to what was shown in Illustration 4–1, except that there the line "To Balance 5,450" was omitted because we were just introducing the idea of an account. The "To Balance" entry goes with the new "Balance" entry, thus preserving the rule that no debit (here, for the new balance) is made without making an equal credit (here, "To Balance"). The double rules under the two $21,200 totals indicate that all of the information appearing above the double rules has been captured in the new balance that appears below the double rules. The procedure for ruling and balancing a liability account is completely analogous to that just described for an asset account.

The formal procedure for the temporary revenue and expense accounts differs slightly from that for the permanent accounts, as will be described below. At this point, all that is necessary is to find the sum of the credits in the Sales Revenues account and the sum of the debits in each expense account (which is trivial here because no expense account had more than one debit).

ILLUSTRATION 4–3
Balancing an Account

Cash

Beginning balance	–0–		750
	5,000		7,200
	4,000		3,000
	12,000		4,800
	200	To Balance	5,450
	21,200		21,200
Balance	5,450		

ILLUSTRATION 4–4
A Trial Balance

CAMPUS PIZZERIA, INC. Trial Balance As of August 31		
	Balance	
Account	**Debit**	**Credit**
Cash	$ 5,450	
Accounts receivable	–0–	
Inventory	550	
Prepaid expenses	750	
Equipment, at cost	7,200	
Accounts payable		$ 2,200
Notes payable		4,000
Paid-in capital		5,000
Sales revenues		12,200
Cost of sales	6,000	
Wage expense	3,000	
Utilities expense	450	
Totals	$23,400	$23,400

The Trial Balance

After determining the balance of each account, a trial balance is taken. A **trial balance** is simply a list of the account names and the balances in each account as of a given moment of time, with debit balances shown in one column and credit balances in another column. The preparation of a trial balance serves two principal purposes: (1) It shows whether the equality of debits and credits has been maintained and (2) it provides a convenient summary transcript of the ledger records as a basis for making the adjusting and closing entries (described in the next section) that precede the preparation of the period's financial statements.

Campus Pizzeria's trial balance is shown in Illustration 4–4. Because Campus Pizzeria was a new entity as of August 1, all the permanent (balance sheet) accounts had a zero beginning balance. As a result, the August 31 balances are based entirely on the 13 entries thus far recorded. In successive accounting periods, the entity's permanent accounts will have nonzero beginning balances. (We suggest that, as practice, the reader verify each amount in Illustration 4–4.)

Although the trial balance shows that total debits equal total credits and thus indicates that the integrity of the basic accounting equation has been maintained, it does not prove that errors have not been made. Entries may have been omitted entirely, or they may have been posted to the wrong account. Offsetting errors may have been made, or a transaction may have been analyzed incorrectly. For example, if the debit for the purchase of a piece of equipment were made incorrectly to an expense account rather than correctly to an asset account, the totals of the trial balance would not be affected.

The Adjusting and Closing Process

Adjusting Entries

Most entries to be made in the accounts are original entries. However, some events that affect the accounts are not evidenced by the obvious documents associated with original entries. The effects of these events are recorded at the end of the accounting period by means of **adjusting entries**. The purpose of the adjusting entries is to modify account balances so that they will fairly reflect the situation as of the end of the period.

Continuous Transactions

Most adjusting entries are made in connection with events that are, in effect, continuous transactions. Consider a tankful of fuel oil purchased for $1,000. On the day of delivery, the $1,000 of fuel oil was an asset. But each day thereafter, some fuel oil was consumed in the furnace, whereupon part of the $1,000 became an expense. Rather than record this consumption daily, a single adjusting entry is made at the end of the accounting period to show how much of the fuel oil is still an asset at that time and how much has become expense during the period. For example, if $600 was consumed and hence became an expense, $400 remains as an asset.

There are two ways of handling these events, both of which give the same result. Under one method, the $1,000 expenditure is originally recorded as an asset, Fuel Oil Inventory, as in the following entry:

Fuel Oil Inventory		Accounts Payable	
1,000			1,000

At the end of the accounting period, the Fuel Oil Inventory asset account is adjusted by subtracting the cost of fuel oil consumed, thus:

Fuel Expense		Fuel Oil Inventory	
600			600

Under the other method, the $1,000 expenditure for fuel oil is originally recorded in an expense account (instead of an inventory account). Then the fuel oil remaining at the end of the period is subtracted from expense and shown as a Fuel Oil Inventory asset, thus:

Fuel Oil Inventory		Fuel Expense	
400			400

Although neither method reflects the correct facts *within* the period (with the trivial exception that the first method does reflect the facts on the day the oil was delivered), both reflect a correct statement of the facts as of the *end* of the accounting period. Because accounting focuses on deriving the proper amounts for the statements that are prepared at the end of the accounting period, the choice between these methods depends solely on which is more convenient.

Types of Adjusting

Entries Events that require adjusting entries essentially relate to the difference between expense and expenditure and between revenue and receipts, discussed in Chapter 3. Four types of such events, together with examples of each, are given below:

1. *Recorded costs to be apportioned among two or more accounting periods.* The fuel oil transaction given above is one example. Another is a two-year insurance policy costing $1,600, originally recorded as Prepaid Insurance (an asset), $800 of which becomes an expense in the current year:

Insurance Expense		Prepaid Insurance	
800			800

When an asset is reduced, as prepaid insurance was here, it is said that there has been a **write-off** of part (or all) of the asset.

2. *Unrecorded expenses.* These expenses were incurred during the period, but no record of them has yet been made. Example: For $150 of wages earned by an employee during the period but not yet paid to the employee:

Wage Expense		Accrued Wages	
150			150

3. *Recorded revenues to be apportioned among two or more accounting periods.* As was the case with recorded costs (insurance example), these amounts were initially recorded in one account and, at the end of the accounting period, must be properly divided between a revenue account and a liability account. For example, rent collected during the period and recorded as rent revenue, $600 of which is applicable to the next period and hence is a liability at the end of the current period:

Rent Revenue		Unearned Rent Revenue	
600			600

4. *Unrecorded revenues.* These revenues were earned during the period, but no record of them has yet been made. For example, $120 of interest earned by the entity during the period but not yet received:

Accrued Interest Receivable		Interest Revenue	
120			120

Depreciation

Most long-lived assets give up their benefits to the entity in a continuous stream. Thus, the cost of these assets is continuously being converted to an expense (written off) in the same manner as the current assets—fuel oil and prepaid insurance—that were discussed previously. The item that shows the portion of such long-lived asset costs that has become expense *during an accounting period* is called **depreciation expense**. Instead of subtracting the depreciation expense for the period directly from the asset amount—instead of crediting depreciation to the account for the asset being depreciated—the credit is made to a separate account, **Accumulated Depreciation**. The adjusting entry to record the depreciation expense for a period is therefore in the following form:

Depreciation Expense		Accumulated Depreciation	
2,000			2,000

There is a reason for crediting depreciation to Accumulated Depreciation rather than directly to the asset. Generally accepted accounting principles (GAAP) require separate disclosure of (1) the original cost of the entity's depreciable assets and (2) the depreciation that has been accumulated on these assets from the time they were acquired until the date of the balance sheet. Keeping these two items separate in the accounts facilitates the necessary disclosure, which appears on the balance sheet as follows:

Equipment, at cost	$10,000	
Less: Accumulated depreciation	2,000	
Net equipment		$8,000

Accumulated depreciation is called a **contra asset account** because it is subtracted from some other asset account. Another contra asset account is Allowance for Doubtful Accounts, described below.

Other Adjustments

Accountants make a variety of other adjusting entries in order to make the accounts reflect fairly the results of the entity's operations during the period and its status as of the end of the period. An example, discussed in more detail in Chapter 5, is **bad debt expense**. This is an adjustment made in order to recognize the likelihood that not all credit customers will pay their bills, and, thus, the Accounts Receivable account may overstate the *realizable* amount of those bills. An adjusting entry that records the write-off of receivables for the estimated amount of bad debts is as follows:

Bad Debt Expense		Allowance for Doubtful Accounts	
300			300

On the balance sheet, the accumulated allowance for doubtful accounts is subtracted from accounts receivable, thus:

Accounts receivable, gross	$10,000	
Less: Allowance for doubtful accounts	300	
Net accounts receivable		$9,700

A Caution

When the student is given a problem involving the preparation of accounting statements, the precise nature of the original entries must be described, since the student has no other way of finding out about them. Information about the *adjusting* entries will not necessarily be given, however. Students, like practicing accountants, are expected to be on the lookout for situations that require adjustment.

Campus Pizzeria Adjusting Entries

A review of Campus Pizzeria's trial balance indicates three items that will generate adjusting entries: the write-off of prepaid expenses (rent), depreciation on the equipment, and accrued interest on the note payable.

14. Adjusting entry for rent expense.

Analysis: As of the end of August, the benefits from the $750 prepaid rent have all been received. Thus, the asset **Prepaid Expenses** is reduced by $750 (a credit). This rent applied to August operations, so it is an expense of August: debit **Rent Expense** for $750. This is an earnings transaction.	**Prepaid Expenses**			
	(2)	750	**(14)**	750
	Rent Expense			
	(14)	750		

15. Adjusting entry for depreciation expense.

Analysis: The equipment cost $7,200 and is expected to provide benefits for 10 years (120 months). One month's benefits have now been received, so 1/120 of the original cost, $60, is debited to **Depreciation Expense**.[3] The corresponding credit is to **Accumulated Depreciation**, a contra asset account. This is an earnings transaction.	**Depreciation Expense**			
	(15)	60		
	Accumulated Depreciation			
			(15)	60

16. Adjusting entry for accrued interest expense (interest payable).

Analysis: The bank has earned one month's interest on the note. The interest rate is 9 percent a year, so one month's interest on $4,000 will be 3/4 percent, or $30. This amount is debited to **Interest Expense**. Because the interest has not yet been paid, the credit is to the liability account, **Accrued Expenses** (or Interest Payable). This is an earnings transaction because the interest is in the nature of "rent" on the borrowed funds used this month.	**Interest Expense**			
	(16)	30		
	Accrued Expenses			
			(16)	30

Closing Entries

The temporary revenue and expense accounts are actually subdivisions of owners' equity (retained earnings). At the end of the period, the temporary accounts are *closed* to Retained Earnings in order to determine the net effect of all the revenue and expense transactions—the net income or loss. Rather than closing each temporary account

---

[3] This method of charging the cost of an asset to expense in a level stream over the asset's life is called *straight-line depreciation*. Other methods will be described in Chapter 7.

directly to Retained Earnings, however, each is first closed to an intermediate account whose purpose is to summarize the revenue and expense transactions. This account is variously called **Income Summary**, **Profit and Loss**, or **Expense and Revenue Summary**. This account reflects the net income or loss for a given accounting period. Income Summary is a *clearing* account that in turn is closed to Retained Earnings to complete the closing process.

The **closing** process consists of transferring the balance of each temporary account to the clearing account. To close a revenue account, the sum of the credits is found, and then this sum is debited to the revenue account and credited to Income Summary. This gives the revenue account a balance of zero, and transfers its former credit balance to Income Summary. The result is as though the credit balance in the revenue account were "picked up and moved" to the credit side of Income Summary without making any entry. But in an accounting system such informality is not permitted, and the transfer of the revenue balance to Income Summary must be accomplished with an equal debit and credit. For Campus Pizzeria, this is done as follows (we use letters to label the closing entries to distinguish them from the original and adjusting entries):

A. Closing the Sales Revenues account.

Explanation: The balance in **Sales Revenues** is a credit of $12,200. A debit of $12,200 will thus give the account a zero balance (i.e., close it). The corresponding credit is to **Income Summary**.		Sales Revenues		
	(A)	**12,000**	(6)	12,000
			(12)	200
			Balance	**12,200**
		Income Summary		
			(A)	**12,000**

The double rule intersecting the stem of the T account designates that it has been closed. All the information it contained is now residing, in summary form, in Income Summary. As far as preparing the financial statements is concerned, the Sales Revenue page of the ledger could now be thrown away—that is the sense in which this is a temporary account. (Of course, in practice such an accounting record would not be destroyed.)

Closing an expense account is the mirror image of closing a revenue account. There are six expense accounts to be closed (the letters continue the labeling of the closing entries): (B) Cost of Sales, (C) Wage Expense, (D) Utilities Expense, (E) Rent Expense, (F) Depreciation Expense, and (G) Interest Expense.[4] Since all of these closing entries are the same in substance, we will illustrate only one of them:

B. Closing the Cost of Sales account.

Explanation: The balance in **Cost of Sales** is a debit of $6,000; a credit of $6,000 will thus close this account. The corresponding debit is to **Income Summary**.		Cost of Sales		
	(9)	6,000	**(B)**	**6,000**
		Income Summary		
	(B)	**6,000**	(A)	12,000

---

[4] In actual accounting practice, another trial balance would be taken after the adjusting entries were made and before the closing entries commence.

At this stage, the only accounts remaining open are the permanent accounts (which are always balanced at the end of the period but are never closed) and Income Summary (which is a temporary account). Income Summary is closed in exactly the same manner as other temporary accounts, except that first the debits and credits have to be summed and netted (as in balancing a permanent account). This net amount, which is the period's *income before income taxes,* is $1,910 (explained below). It generates one more adjusting entry—the entry needed to record the estimated income tax liability arising from the period's income. Assuming that the applicable income tax rate is 20 percent, the amount of estimated tax liability is $382 ($1,910 * 0.20). This amount is debited to Income Tax Expense (a temporary account created for recording this final adjusting entry), and is credited to Income Tax Liability. Income Tax Expense is then closed to Income Summary, which completes the closing of all the expense accounts. (For simplicity, we will make the income tax expense debit directly to Income Summary so that we do not have to illustrate creating and closing another expense account that has only one entry made to it.)

To complete the closing process, Income Summary is closed. Its balance is credited (if a net profit) or debited (if a net loss) to Retained Earnings, which can then be balanced to complete the balancing of the permanent accounts.

H. Closing the Income Summary account to Retained Earnings.

		Income Summary		
Explanation: After closing all of the temporary accounts (except Income Tax Expense) to Income Summary, the sum of its debits, $10,290, is netted against the sum of its credits, $12,200. This leaves a net credit balance in the account of $1,910, which is the pretax income for August. After the income tax adjusting entry for $382 is made, **Income Summary** is closed by debiting it for $1,528; the corresponding credit is to **Retained Earnings**. Since this was a new entity as of August 1, Retained Earnings had a zero beginning balance. To complete the process, Retained Earnings is balanced in the same manner as other balance sheet accounts. Next month, any profit (or loss) for September will be added to (subtracted from) this $1,528 new beginning balance.	**(B)** 6,000 **(C)** 3,000 **(D)** 450 **(E)** 750 **(F)** 60 **(G)** 30 —— 10,290 **(17)** 382 **(H)** 1,528	**(A)** 12,200 12,200		

Income Tax Liability

	(17)	382

Retained Earnings

	Balance	–0–
To Balance 1,528	**(H)**	1,528
	Balance	1,528

Statement Preparation

After the adjusting and closing entries have been made, the period's financial statements can be prepared. The numbers for the income statement can be thought of as coming from either of two equivalent sources: (1) the balances in the temporary accounts just prior to their closing or (2) the credit (revenue) and debit (expense) entries to the Income Summary account. Amounts for the balance sheet are the balances in the permanent accounts. In most companies, the accounts reported in the financial statements are summaries of more detailed accounts in the ledger.

The August financial statements for Campus Pizzeria, Inc., are shown in Illustration 4–5. Since the accounting period was one month, these are interim statements. It is also important to remember that the August net income and the August 31 retained earnings amounts are the same in this case only because (1) this is the first accounting period for a new entity and (2) the entity did not pay any dividends in this period.

ILLUSTRATION 4–5
Financial Statements

CAMPUS PIZZERIA, INC.			
Balance Sheet			
As of August 31			
Assets*		*Liabilities and Owner's Equity*	
Cash	$ 5,450	Accounts payable	$ 2,200
Accounts receivable	0	Notes payable	4,000
Inventory	550	Accrued expenses	30
Prepaid expenses	0	Income tax liability	382
Total current assets	6,000	Total liabilities	6,612
Equipment, at cost	7,200	Paid-in capital	5,000
Less: Accumulated depreciation	60	Retained earnings	1,528
Equipment, net	7,140	Total owner's equity	6,528
Total assets	$13,140	Total liabilities and owner's equity	$13,140

Income Statement
For the Month of August

Sales revenues		$12,200
Cost of sales		6,000
Gross margin		6,200
Operating expenses:		
Wages	$ 3,000	
Rent	750	
Utilities	450	
Depreciation	60	
Interest	30	4,290
Income before income taxes		1,910
Income tax expense		382
Net income		$ 1,528

* Ordinarily, accounts with zero balances are not shown. Two are included here for completeness, since both did have entries made to them during the period.

The Journal

In the preceding illustration of the accounting process, we recorded transactions directly in T accounts. In practice, transactions are initially recorded in a journal and then T account entries are made at the end of the period based on the transactions recorded in the journal.

A **journal** is a chronological record of accounting transactions showing the names of accounts that are to be debited or credited, the amounts of the debits and credits, and any useful supplementary information about the transaction. A journal is analogous to a diary.

The traditional format for writing a **journal entry** is as follows:

dr.	Cash	5,000
cr.	Paid-In Capital	5,000

In practice, the notations dr. and cr. are not used because the accountant distinguishes debits from credits on the basis of the order (debits first) and indentation (credits indented) of the accounts. We will use the dr. and cr. in this chapter and Chapter 5 as a reminder to the reader but will follow common practice in subsequent chapters.

Illustration 4–6 shows a journal that records the first few transactions for Campus Pizzeria. With respect to format, note the following: (1) The debit entry is listed first,

ILLUSTRATION 4–6

Journal					
Date		Accounts	LF	Debit	Credit
Aug.	1	Cash	10	5,000.00	
		Paid-In Capital	30		5,000.00
	1	Prepaid Expenses	14	750.00	
		Cash	10		750.00
	1	Cash	10	4,000.00	
		Notes Payable	21		4,000.00
	2	Equipment	15	7,200.00	
		Cash	10		7,200.00
	2	Inventory	13	800.00	
		Accounts Payable	20		800.00

(2) the debit amounts appear in the left-hand money column, (3) the account to be credited appears below the debit entry and is indented, and (4) the credit amounts appear in the right-hand money column. "LF" is an abbreviation for *ledger folio,* which is the page reference to the ledger account where the entry is to be made. This reference is inserted at the time the entry is **posted** to (i.e., entered in) the appropriate T account in the ledger. Thus, the presence of numbers in the LF column indicates that the entries have been posted to the appropriate T accounts. They also provide an **audit trail**, a way of tracing the amounts in the ledger back to their sources. In some bookkeeping systems, a brief explanation is written beneath each journal entry.

The *journal* thus contains explicit instructions on the revenue and expense items to be recorded in the temporary accounts and the changes to be made to the balances in the permanent accounts. No account balance is ever changed except on the basis of a journal entry. The *ledger* is a device for *reclassifying* and *summarizing,* by accounts, information originally listed in chronological order in the journal. Entries are first made in the journal and are later posted to ledger accounts.

Accounting Systems

The simple journals and ledgers described in the preceding pages, together with the rules for using them, constitute an accounting system. But this particular system would not usually be the best system for a given organization. The optimum system is that one that best satisfies the following objectives:

1. To process the information efficiently—at low cost.
2. To obtain reports quickly.
3. To ensure a high degree of accuracy.
4. To minimize the possibility of theft or fraud.

Designing a good accounting system is a specialized job requiring a high degree of skill.

Internal Accounting Controls

Two objectives of an accounting system stated above—accuracy and protection against theft or fraud—cannot be attained absolutely without conflicting with the other two—speed and economy. An unbeatable system would be prohibitively expensive and time-consuming. A basic principle of internal accounting control, therefore, is that the system should make it *as difficult as is practical* for people to be dishonest or careless. Such a principle is based not on a cynical view of people in general but rather on the realistic assumption that a few people will be dishonest or careless if it is easy for them to do so.

Some of the devices used to ensure reasonable accuracy have been touched on already; for example, the idea of verifying one set of figures against another. The idea of divided responsibility is another important one. Whenever feasible, one person should not be responsible for recording all aspects of a transaction, nor should the custodian of assets (e.g., the storekeeper or the cashier) be permitted to do the accounting for these assets. Thus, one person's work is a check on another's. Although this does not eliminate the possibility that two people will steal through collusion, the likelihood of dis-honesty is greatly reduced.

These brief comments indicate only the nature of the problem of internal accounting control, which is a big subject. Furthermore, a book that focuses on accounting *principles,* as this one does, cannot detail the complexities involved in the *operation* of accounting systems. For example, cash transactions are very easy to analyze, whereas some textbooks on auditing contain a dozen pages of questions that should be considered in connection with the internal accounting control of the single item cash.

Computer-Based Accounting Systems

Most organizations do their accounting work by computer. In this section, we give a brief overview of computer-based accounting systems.

What a Computer-Based System Does

As noted above, some steps in the accounting cycle involve judgment, whereas others are primarily mechanical. These mechanical steps are usually referred to as **bookkeeping**. A computer-based system performs some or all of the bookkeeping steps— that is, it records and stores data, performs arithmetic operations on data, sorts and summarizes data, and prepares reports. These functions are described below as inputs, processing, and outputs.

Inputs

In some computer systems, data are entered by a data-entry clerk (using a keyboard) who copies them from a paper record such as a sales order or purchase order. In other systems, the computer accepts input data from equipment located at the point of origin. Examples are factory time records; inventory counts, when the person counting uses a handheld recording device; and receiving records, when a similar device is used.

An especially striking and familiar example of direct computer data input is the scanning device used at the supermarket or department store checkout stand. The scanner reads a bar code printed on the item (or on a tag attached to the item); this code specifically identifies the item. The computer to which the scanner is connected then uses stored information on each item's selling price to calculate an itemized list of the amount owed by the customer. A summary of sales revenue, cost of goods sold (also stored for each item in the computer), gross margin by items or categories of items, and the status of inventories is available for use by store managers at any time they desire to access the system.

The inputs to one business's computer may be the outputs of the computer of another business. For example, a factory computer may generate purchase orders for parts to be supplied by a vendor. These outputs are transmitted electronically to the vendor, where they become sales order inputs, without a paper purchase order ever being produced. Similarly, a wholesaler's salesperson may record orders placed by a retail store on a hand-held device; the information is then transmitted to a central computer by the Internet.

Processing

Once data are in machine-readable form, the chance for bookkeeping errors is reduced. The computer will not accept an entry in which debits do not equal credits. However, if a human makes an error in selecting the account, or enters the wrong number for both the debit and credit, there will be errors.

Data in machine-readable form can be used in a number of ways. For example, an airline reservation system has a record of the availability of seats in each of several fare categories for every flight the airline will operate over the next several months. Any travel agent connected to the system by a terminal can request information about flight availability and price; the computer can process hundreds of such inquiries every minute. If the agent wishes to book a seat, the computer decreases availability on the flight and sends information to the travel agency's printer, which prepares a ticket, boarding pass, itinerary, and customer invoice. Computer systems also sort data in ways that may be of interest and use to management.

Outputs

Computer-based systems can prepare reports that include either tables of numbers or graphs. These can be generated at regular intervals in a prescribed format or prepared in a form specified by an individual user. In some systems, the user produces customized reports locally by using a personal computer that can retrieve data from a central computer–based system.

Modules

Computer-based accounting systems are usually operated by several interconnected software programs, each of which is called a *module.* There may be a module for any of the following: sales orders, shipments, and the related accounts receivable (often called an *order-entry module);* manufacturing costs; purchase orders, inventory, and related accounts payable (a *purchasing module);* payroll and other personnel records; fixed asset acquisitions, location, and depreciation; income taxes; cash; and the general ledger.

Hundreds of software programs are available. Some provide a complete set of modules for a small enterprise for a few hundred dollars; for a larger company, the cost may be several thousand dollars. Some programs are designed for a specific industry (for example, time-intensive professional service businesses such as law, accounting, and architectural firms). These software programs can handle quantitative nonmonetary data as well as monetary data. Manual accounting systems, by contrast, are limited primarily to monetary data.

Problems with Computer Systems

Despite their many advantages, computer-based systems are not without their problems. Although a small company can purchase off-the-shelf software and have its system up and running in a few days, system development and installation in a larger, more complex organization may take many months and cost millions of dollars. Such systems usually require an outside consultant for their design and implementation. Moreover, technological advances make existing systems obsolete within a few years, and much time and money must be spent to update them. Nevertheless, the advantages of a computer-based system are so great that almost every organization needs one.

Unlike a manual system, a computer-based system does not leave a paper trail that can be readily audited. The system must therefore rely on the internal controls described above. In a few spectacular instances, the lack (or circumvention) of such controls has resulted in business frauds and resultant failure; but the number of such events is very small relative to the number of computer-based systems in use.

Finally, a computer-based system will not be fully effective until its developers learn to design reports that the system's users need and can understand. This job of education, for both developers and users, can be substantial. If it is not done properly, the system will spew out reports that no one uses, and the potential users will not appreciate the information that they could receive if only they knew how to ask for it.

Summary

The account is a device for collecting information about each item that is to be accounted for. It has two sides: the left-hand, or debit, side and the right-hand, or credit, side. The rules are such that asset and expense accounts increase on the debit side, whereas liabilities, owners' equity, and revenue accounts increase on the credit side. This maintains both the equation Assets = Liabilities + Owners' equity and the equation Debits = Credits.

A ledger is a group of accounts. Entries are made to ledger accounts on the basis of instructions given in a journal, which is a chronological record of transactions.

At the end of an accounting period, adjusting entries are made so that after adjustment the revenue and expense accounts will show the appropriate amounts for the period. These temporary accounts are then closed to the Income Summary account, which in turn is closed to Retained Earnings.

In manual accounting systems, special journals, subsidiary ledgers, and other devices facilitate the process of recording accounting data. A computer-based system performs the same functions more rapidly, and it can provide a variety of useful management reports if it has been designed thoughtfully and its users have been properly trained.

Problems

Problem 4–1.

Set up the following in T-account form and determine the ending balances insofar as these accounts are concerned. (Not all balance sheet accounts are shown.)

| | Beginning Balances | |
Account	Dr.	Cr.
Cash	$ 900	
Accounts receivable	3,000	
Inventory	5,700	
Accounts payable		$3,600
Note payable		950

Transactions:
1. Purchased inventory on account — $2,350
2. Sold goods on account: sales revenues — 6,350
    Cost of goods sold — 4,150
3. Paid vendors — 3,400
4. Collected from customers — 5,350
5. Paid off note payable — 950

Problem 4–2.   Write journal entries for the following transactions that occurred at Woodside Company during May and explain how each would be disclosed in Woodside's financial statements.

1. The company prepaid $14,340 rent for the period May 1–October 31.
2. Sales discounts and allowances were $34,150.
3. A loan for $3,500 at 12 percent interest continued to be owed to the company by one of its employees, who made no payments related to this loan during May.
4. Depreciation expense was $13,660.
5. Customers paid $2,730 for services they will not receive until sometime in June.
6. The company purchased $172 worth of stamps and used $100 worth of them.
7. The Allowance for Doubtful Accounts was increased by $1,350, reflecting a new estimate of uncollectible accounts.

Problem 4–3.   Luft Corporation's accounts had the following beginning balances:

Account	Dr.	Cr.
Accounts payable		$ 3,070
Accounts receivable	$ 2,160	
Accumulated depreciation		2,800
Allowance for doubtful accounts		70
Cash	1,440	
Fixed assets (at cost)	6,200	
Inventories	1,730	
Note payable (current)		600
Owners' equity		4,990
	$11,530	$11,530

During the period, the following transactions occurred:

1. Purchased inventory on account, $1,300.
2. Paid employees, $730.
3. Sold goods for cash, $1,940.
4. Sold goods on credit, $1,810.
5. Overhead and other expenses paid in cash, $900.
6. Collection of accounts receivable, $1,510.
7. Paid certain accounts payable, $1,720.
8. Received cash for revenue applicable to the *next* period, $650.
9. Increased the current note payable by $200.
10. Physical inventory showed ending balance of $1,750.
11. Depreciation expense, $300.

Required:
   a. Journalize the transactions.
   b. Set up T accounts and post beginning balances and transactions.
   c. Determine the cost of goods sold.
   d. Prepare an ending balance sheet.
   e. Prepare an income statement for the period (ignore taxes).

Problem 4–4.
The account balances in the ledger of the Dindorf Company on January 31 (the end of its fiscal year), before adjustments, were as follows:

Debit Balances		Credit Balances	
Cash and equivalents	$ 119,115	Accumulated depreciation	
Accounts receivable	162,500	on store equipment	$ 37,300
Merchandise inventory	700,680	Accounts payable	118,180
Store equipment	215,000	Notes payable	143,000
Supplies inventory	15,475	Common stock	300,000
Prepaid insurance	38,250	Retained earnings	122,375
Selling expense	24,900	Sales revenues	716,935
Sales salaries	105,750		
Miscellaneous general expenses	31,000		
Sales discounts	6,220		
Interest expense	9,300		
Social Security tax expense	9,600		
Total	$1,437,790	Total	$1,437,790

The data for the adjustments are
1. Cost of merchandise sold, $302,990.
2. Depreciation on store equipment, $12,750.
3. Supplies inventory, January 31, $5,210. (Purchases of supplies during the year were debited to the Supplies Inventory account.)
4. Expired insurance, $4,660.
5. Interest accrued on notes payable, $3,730.
6. Sales salaries earned but not paid to employees, $3,575.
7. Interest earned on savings accounts, but not recorded, $390.

Required:
a. Set up T accounts with the balances given above.
b. Journalize and post adjusting entries, adding other T accounts as necessary.
c. Journalize and post closing entries.
d. Prepare an income statement for the fiscal year and a fiscal year-end balance sheet.

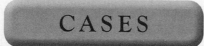

CASES

Case 4–1
PC Depot*

PC Depot was a retail store for personal computers and hand-held calculators, selling several national brands in each product line. The store was opened in early September by Barbara Thompson, a young woman previously employed in direct computer sales for a national firm specializing in business computers.

Thompson knew the importance of adequate records. One of her first decisions, therefore, was to hire Chris

* © Professor Robert N. Anthony.

Jarrard, a local accountant, to set up her bookkeeping system.

Jarrard wrote up the store's preopening financial transactions in journal form to serve as an example (Exhibit 1). Thompson agreed to write up the remainder of the store's September financial transactions for Jarrard's later review.

At the end of September, Thompson had the following items to record:

Entry Number	Account	Amount Cr.
(9)	Cash sales for September	$38,000
(10)	Credit sales for September	14,850
(11)	Cash received from credit customers	3,614
(12)	Bills paid to merchandise suppliers	96,195
(13)	New merchandise received on credit from supplier	49,940
(14)	Ms. Thompson ascertained the cost of merchandise sold was	38,140
(15)	Wages paid to assistant	688
(16)	Wages earned but unpaid at the end of September	440
(17)	Rent paid for October	1,485
(18)	Insurance bill paid for one year (September 1–August 31)	2,310
(19)	Bills received, but unpaid, from electric company	226
(20)	Purchased sign, paying $660 cash and agreeing to pay the $1,100 balance by December 31	1,760

Questions

1. Explain the events that probably gave rise to journal entries 1 through 8 of Exhibit 1.
2. Set up a ledger account (in T account form) for each account named in the general journal. Post entries 1 through 8 to these accounts, using the entry number as a cross-reference.
3. Analyze the facts listed as 9 through 20, resolving them into their debit and credit elements. Prepare journal entries and post to the ledger accounts. (Do not prepare closing entries.)
4. Consider any other transactions that should be recorded. Why are these adjusting entries required? Prepare journal entries for them and post to ledger accounts.
5. Prepare closing entries and post to ledger accounts. What new ledger accounts are required? Why?
6. Prepare an income statement for September and a balance sheet as of September 30.

EXHIBIT 1 General Journal

Entry Number	Account	Amount Dr.	Amount Cr.
(1)	Cash	165,000	
	Bank Loan Payable (15%)		100,000
	Proprietor's Capital		65,000
(2)	Rent Expense (September)	1,485	
	Cash		1,485
(3)	Merchandise Inventory	137,500	
	Accounts Payable		137,500
(4)	Furniture and Fixtures (10-year life)	15,500	
	Cash		15,500
(5)	Advertising Expense	1,320	
	Cash		1,320
(6)	Wages Expense	935	
	Cash		935
(7)	Office Supplies Expense	1,100	
	Cash		1,100
(8)	Utilities Expense	275	
	Cash		275

Case 4–2
Save-Mart*

Save-Mart was a retail store. Its account balances on February 28 (the end of its fiscal year), before adjustments, were as shown below.

Debit Balances		Credit Balances	
Cash	$ 88,860	Accumulated depreciation on store equipment	$ 11,420
Accounts receivable	127,430		
Merchandise inventory	903,130	Notes payable	88,500
Store equipment	70,970	Accounts payable	88,970
Supplies inventory	17,480	Common stock	100,000
Prepaid insurance	12,430	Retained earnings	33,500
Selling expense	10,880	Sales	988,700
Sales salaries	47,140		
Miscellaneous general expense	18,930		
Sales discounts	3,340		
Interest expense	7,100		
Social Security tax expense	3,400		
Total	$1,311,090	Total	$1,311,090

The data for the adjustments are

1. Cost of merchandise sold, $604,783.
2. Store equipment had a useful life of seven years. (All equipment was less than seven years old.)
3. Supplies inventory, February 28, $3,877. (Purchases of supplies during the year were debited to the Supplies Inventory account.)
4. Expired insurance, $7,125.
5. The note payable was at an interest rate of 9 percent, payable monthly. It had been outstanding throughout the year.
6. Sales salaries earned but not paid to employees, $2,340.

7. The statement sent by the bank, adjusted for checks outstanding, showed a balance of $88,110. The difference represented bank service charges.

Questions

1. Set up T accounts with the balances given above.
2. Journalize and post adjusting entries, adding other T accounts as necessary.
3. Journalize and post closing entries.
4. Prepare an income statement for the year and a balance sheet as of February 28.

Case 4–3
Copies Express*

Copies Express was incorporated on November 20, 2009, and began operating on January 2, 2010.

The balance sheet as of the beginning of operations is shown in Exhibit 1.

* © Professor Robert N. Anthony.

In preparing financial statements for the first year of operations, the accountant reviewed the record of cash receipts and cash disbursements for Copics Express. This information appears in Exhibit 2.

In addition, the accountant examined certain other information relative to operations. These additional items appear in Exhibit 3.

EXHIBIT 1 Copies Express, Inc.

Balance Sheet As of January 2, 2010	
Assets	
Cash	$ 2,000
Supplies	24,400
Building and equipment	300,000
Land	12,000
Total	$338,400
Liabilities and Owners' Equity	
Accounts payable	$ 10,400
Bank loan	24,000
Capital stock	304,000
Total	$338,400

EXHIBIT 2 Copies Express, Inc.

Cash Receipts and Disbursements: 2010

Cash receipts:	
Cash sales	$176,450
Collect accounts receivable	64,750
Total	$241,200

Cash disbursements:	
Wages and salaries	$ 85,750
Heat, light, power	15,000
Additional supplies	52,600
Selling and administration	28,375
Interest (Note 1)	2,880
Payment—bank loan (12/31)	12,000
Payment—accounts payable	10,400
Total	$207,005

Note 1. Interest at 12 percent per annum on the bank loan was payable June 30 and December 31 [($24,000 * .12) = $2,880]. Interest payments for 2010 were made when due.

EXHIBIT 3 Other Information Relative to Operations

1. At the end of 2010, Copies Express owed $9,875 to suppliers for the purchase of photocopy supplies for which it had not yet paid.
2. The yearly depreciation expense on the buildings and equipment was $15,000.
3. At the end of 2010, Copies Express was owed $11,000 for copying services by customers who had not yet paid. Copies Express expected that all of these customers would pay within 30 days.
4. An inventory taken of the supplies at year-end revealed that the year's cost of supplies was $60,250.
5. Income taxes for 2010 were expected to be $11,593. They were unpaid as of December 31, 2010.

Questions

1. Prepare an income statement for 2010 and a balance sheet as of December 31, 2010.
2. Be prepared to explain the derivation of each number on these financial statements.

Case 4–4

Waltham Oil and Lube Center, Inc.

On April 1 Frank Knight incorporated and capitalized with $40,000 of his savings Waltham Oil and Lube Centers, Inc. On the same day, he signed a lease and operating agreement to operate the recently constructed "Waltham Oil and Lube Center," located in Waltham, Massachusetts. The facility and name were owned by National Oil and Lube Centers, Inc., a nationwide chain of centers offering through local franchisees automobile oil change and lubrication services.

The lease and operating agreement required Knight to deposit $40,000 with National as evidence of his good faith and to pay for certain pre-operating costs incurred by National on behalf of the Waltham Center. In addition, the lease portion of the agreement called for Knight to pay beginning on May 1 and at the beginning of each month thereafter a flat lease rental payment of $1,500 per month plus $10 payable at the end of each month for every automobile Waltham Center serviced during the month. National was responsible for payment of local property taxes. Knight was responsible for maintaining the facility in good working condition and the payment for all operating expenses. The 12-month lease agreement was automatically renewed unless a 30-day notice of cancellation was given by either party. The operating portion of the agreement required Knight to purchase all of his oil and lubricating supplies and equipment from National. For its part, National agreed to provide Knight with training materials, operating consulting services, and national advertising support.

During April, Knight ordered for delivery on April 30 office furniture costing $6,000 that had a useful life of 10 years, deposited an additional $10,000 capital in the business's new checking account, and paid $1,200 for a variety of 12-month insurance coverages beginning May 1.

Knight opened the Waltham Center for business on May 1. On the same day, National deducted from Knight's $40,000 deposit $35,650 for the opening oil and grease inventory ($6,320), uniforms and other operating supplies inventory ($4,130), and an equipment purchase down payment ($25,000). The total cost of the equipment was $75,000. In addition, National also deducted the May rental ($1,500) from the deposit. The remaining $4,350 of the deposit was held by

National to apply against any future nonpayment of amounts due National.

The $75,000 worth of grease and oil guns, hydraulic jacks, and other equipment Knight bought from National was Knight's to keep. After applying the $25,200 deduction from his deposit toward this cost, Knight owed National $49,800 for the equipment. This balance was financed by giving National a noninterest-bearing note payable on the first of the month at a rate of $830 a month for 60 months.

A National sales representative told Knight the equipment was expected to have a useful life of five years. The sales representative also suggested the $75,000 equipment be depreciated on a group basis. That is, Knight would apply a single depreciation method and life to all of the equipment as if it was a single piece of equipment with no salvage value. This method, he explained, would reduce Knight's bookkeeping costs.

The business got off to a quick start. During the three-month period May through July, Knight and his staff serviced 2,340 cars. In addition to his service business, Knight was able to rent parking spaces to local citizens on a monthly basis between 7 p.m. and 7 a.m. Due to a local ordinance banning overnight street parking, these citizens were required to find off-street parking.

On August 2, Knight decided to assess how well he had done during the first three months of operations. To this end, he gathered the following information:

1. Bank account records showed deposits after March 1 of $108,600. According to notations on the checks, Knight believed $3,300 was generated by parking space rentals. The rest he assumed was oil and lubrication services revenue.
2. Bank account records showed payments for oil and grease inventory purchases from National totaling $8,230; part- and full-time employee payroll, $34,560; utilities, $1,700; miscellaneous expenses, $6,600; lease payment, $26,400; equipment payments, $2,490; and withdrawals by Knight of $4,500.
3. From personal knowledge, Knight knew that on July 31, he was owed $340 by overnight parkers and $730 from local merchants who used Waltham Center to service their delivery trucks. He was also

aware the business owed employees payroll totaling $2,100 and utility companies $350.

4. Based on a physical count, Knight had determined on July 31 that the business had inventory costing $5,290 on hand. On numerous occasions, Knight and his family had serviced their personal cars at Waltham Center.[1]

As he prepared his assessment, Knight wondered if he should make some provision for possible nonpayment of the amounts owed to his business. In addition, he had $400 in checks in his office desk drawer from parking space renters prepaying their August rentals. As of July 31, Knight had not deposited these checks in the business's bank account.

Questions

1. Prepare journal entries for the period May 1 to July 31.

2. Based on an examination of your journal entries, at the end of July, what is the balance, if any, of the following accounts:
   a. Capital
   b. Accumulated depreciation
   c. Prepaid assets
   d. Cash balance
   e. Accounts receivable
   f. Liabilities

3. Based on an examination of your journal entries, for the three-month period May 1 to July 31, what is the amount of the following:
   a. Withdrawals
   b. Cost of sales
   c. Parking revenues
   d. Lease expense
   e. Total revenues

4. How should Knight account for the $400 August parking checks? Possible bad debts? Family use of the Waltham Center's services?

[1] The retail value of these services was $450.

Revenue and Monetary Assets

This and the next four chapters discuss more thoroughly certain balance sheet and income statement items that were treated in an introductory fashion in Chapters 2 and 3. This chapter discusses the two problems in revenue recognition: (1) *When*— in which accounting period—should revenue be recognized? and (2) *How much* revenue should be recognized? A closely related matter, the measurement of monetary assets, especially accounts receivable, also is discussed.

Timing of Revenue Recognition

Presumably, most activities in a company are intended to contribute to its profit-seeking objective. These activities may include a fairly long chain of events. Illustration 5–1 depicts this sequence, called the **operating cycle,** for a typical manufacturing firm. It begins with the purchase of materials and ends with the collection of cash from customers. (The reader should consider how to modify the diagram for other types of businesses.) In accounting, revenue is recognized at a single point in this cycle. The basic reason for choosing a single point rather than attempting to measure the separate profit contribution of each part of the cycle stems from the criterion of *objectivity*. There is no objective way of measuring the amount of profit that is earned in each step of the operating cycle.

Basic Recognition Criteria

The conservatism concept and the realization concept, described in Chapter 3, suggest the following revenue recognition criteria: Revenue should be recognized in the earliest period in which (1) the entity has *substantially performed* what is required in order to earn income, (2) the amount of income can be *reliably measured,* and (3) the related assets received can readily be converted to cash or claims for cash. The FASB has combined there criteria into a revenue recognition standard that states "revenue should not be recognized until it's realized or realizable and earned."[1]

The criteria are expressed in terms of earning and measuring income rather than revenue because both the revenue and expense components of a transaction need to be

---

[1] "Recognition and Measurement in Financial Statements of Business Enterprises," *FASB Statement of Financial Accounting Concepts No. 5.*

**ILLUSTRATION
5–1**
**The Business
Operating Cycle**

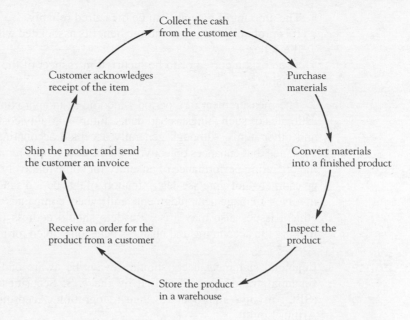

ILLUSTRATION 5–2 **Timing of Revenue Recognition**

Event	Revenue Recognition at This Time	Typical Revenue Recognition Method
1. Sales order received	No	None
2. Deposit or advance payment received	No	None
3. Goods produced	For certain long-term contracts	Percentage of completion
4. Production completed; goods stored	For precious metals and certain agricultural products	Production
5. Goods delivered or services provided	Usually	Delivery
6. Customer pays account receivable	Collection is uncertain	Installment

reliably measurable in order to recognize the revenue. Because of the matching concept, both components are recognized in the same period, and thus income is recognized. Applications of this general idea to certain types of revenues are summarized in Illustration 5–2 and discussed in more detail below.

The IFRS and GAAP basic revenue recognition standards differ in their wording and underlying theory. IFRS recognizes revenue when the "risks and rewards of ownership are transferred." In contrast, GAAP, among other requirements, recognizes revenue when it is "earned." Despite these differences, in most cases the accounting for revenue transaction will be the same under either concept.

IFRS recognizes revenue from the sale of goods when all the following conditions have been satisfied:

- The seller has transferred to the buyer the significant risks and rewards of owership of the goods.
- The seller retains neither continuing managerial involvement to the degree usually associated with ownership nor effective control over the good sold.

- The amount of revenue can be measured reliably.
- It is probable that the economic benefits associated with the transaction will flow to the seller.
- The costs incurred or to be incurred in respect of the transaction can be measured reliably.[2]

The measurement of a period's income is an approximation because it incorporates estimates of such things as bad debts, future warranty costs, useful lives of fixed assets, and other items. Although generally accepted accounting principles (GAAP) provide guidance that enhances objectivity, the fact inevitably remains that the desire to measure the operating performance of an entity for some relatively short period of time results in an estimate, not a precise determination, of that period's income. This estimate inevitably involves management judgment, and when companies are experiencing difficulties, ethical issues also may arise. Readers should address this latter consideration when making the accounting and business decisions called for in the case assignments.

SEC Response

Financial statement users should always be aware of the fact that over half of the financial fraud cases identified by the U.S. Securities and Exchange Commission (SEC) involve improper revenue recognition. According to former SEC chairman Arthur Levitt:

> Companies try to boost revenue by manipulating the recognition of revenue. Think about a bottle of fine wine. You wouldn't pop the cork on that bottle before it was ready. But some companies are doing this with their revenue—recognizing it before a sale is complete, before the product is delivered to a customer, or at a time when the customer still has options to terminate, void or delay the sale.[3]

The most common types of revenue recognition fraud are

- Recording of fictitious revenue.
- Recognizing inappropriate amount of revenue from swaps, round-tripping, or barter arrangements.
- Recognition of revenue from sales transactions billed, but not shipped ("bill and hold").
- Recognition of revenue where there are contingencies associated with the transaction that have not yet been resolved.
- Improper accounting for or failure to establish appropriate reserves for rights to refunds or exchange, liberal cancellation or refusal rights or liberal or unconditional rights of return granted through undisclosed oral or written side agreements.
- Recognition of revenue when products or services are not delivered, delivery is incomplete, or delivered without customer acceptance.[4]

Sometimes companies inflate their revenues by "channel stuffing." This is a business practice whereby a company in order to meet short-term objectives improves its revenues by loading its distribution channels with more product than they are capable of selling in the normal course of business. The inevitable result is that the following period's

---

[2] "Revenue," *IAS No. 18.*
[3] "The Numbers Game," remarks by Chairman Arthur Levitt, Securities and Exchange Commission, September 28, 1998.
[4] Ten Things about Financial Statement Fraud," Deloitte Forensic Center, 2007.

revenue growth rates decline as distribution channel attempt to realign their inventories with actual demand. Channel stuffing is not illegal as long as all of the GAAP revenue recognition requirements are met and the company discloses the channel stuffing to investor. If either of these conditions is not met, the SEC will litigate against the offending company and its management.

In accordance with Levitt's concerns, the SEC issued *Staff Accounting Bulletin No. 101 (SAB 101)*. According to *SAB 101,* the SEC generally considers revenue to be realized and earned when

1. Persuasive evidence of an order arrangement exists;
2. Delivery of the ordered goods has occurred or services have been rendered;
3. The seller's price to the buyer is fixed or determinable; and
4. Collectibility of the sale proceeds is reasonably assured.[5]

Persuasive Evidence

Purchase order and sale agreement documentation practices vary widely between customers, companies, and industries. The SEC appears to be willing to accept these practices as persuasive evidence of an agreement as long as there is some form of written or electronic evidence that a binding final customer purchase authorization, including the terms of sale, is in the hands of the seller before revenue is recognized.

Delivery

Typically, revenue is recognized when delivery has occurred and the customer has taken title and assumed the **risks and rewards of ownership** of the goods specified in the customer's purchase order or sales agreement. (It is interesting to note in this instance the SEC adopted the IASB revenue recognition standard of "risks and rewards of ownership," rather than the FASB standard "earned.") More specifically,

- Delivery is not considered to have occurred unless the product has been delivered to the customer's place of business.
- If uncertainty exists about a customer's acceptance of a product or service, revenue should not be recognized even if the product is delivered or the service performed.
- Revenue should not be recognized until the seller has substantially completed or fulfilled the terms specified in the purchase order or sales agreement.
- In licensing and similar arrangements, delivery does not occur for revenue recognition purposes until the license term begins.

Performance

In general, *SAB 101* requires substantial performance of the sales arrangement by the seller and acceptance by the customer of the product or services rendered before revenue can be recognized. *SAB 101* notes:

- A seller should substantially complete or fulfill the terms specified in the sales arrangement.
- After delivery or performance, if uncertainty exists about acceptance, revenue should not be recognized until after acceptance occurs.

[5] Securities and Exchange Commission, *Staff Accounting Bulletin No. 101.*

Consignment-Type Transactions

Products shipped pursuant to a consignment arrangement should not be recorded as revenue since the consignee has not assumed the risks and rewards of ownership. This is a long-standing rule. *SAB 101* goes further. It states that if a transaction has the characteristics of a consignment arrangement, revenue recognition is precluded even if title to the product has passed to the buyer.

Delivery Method

The typical business earns revenue by selling goods or services to customers. The business has performed substantially what is required in order to earn income when it delivers these goods or provides these services to customers. Thus, the most common approach, called the **delivery method,** is to recognize the revenue in the period in which goods are delivered or services are provided.

Revenues for goods are *not* recognized when sales orders are received. Even though in some businesses the amount of income that will be earned can be reliably estimated at that time, there has been no performance until the goods have been delivered. For services, providing the service is the act of performance. Revenues from renting hotel rooms are recognized each day the room is rented. Revenues from maintenance contracts are recognized in each month covered by the contract. Revenue from repairing an automobile is recognized when the repairs have been completed (not when the repairs are only partially completed, because the service is to provide a completed repair job).

In the usual situation, the amount of income that will be earned can be reliably estimated when goods are delivered or services provided. The test of the marketplace, a price agreed to by the customer minus the appropriate cost of sales, is usually excellent evidence of the amount of income earned. Even though some customers in the normal course of business may not pay their bills, allowances can be made for this in estimating the amount of revenue. If goods are shipped or services rendered to customers with such poor credit records that part or full collection of the related account receivables is in question, income may be recognized only when all of the costs of the sale are recovered or proportionally as collections or installment payments are received.

When goods are delivered, title usually is transferred from the seller to the buyer, but transfer of title is *not* a necessary condition for revenue recognition. When goods are sold on the installment credit basis, for example, the buyer does not have a clear title until the installment payments have been completed. (Automobile sales are a common example.) If, however, there is a reasonable certainty that these payments will be made, revenue must be recognized at the time of delivery.[6]

Consignment Shipments

In a consignment shipment, the supplier, or **consignor,** ships goods to the **consignee,** who attempts to sell them. The consignor retains title to the goods until they are sold. The consignee can return any unsold goods to the consignor. In these circumstances, performance has not been substantially completed until the goods are sold by the consignee. Thus, the consignor does not recognize revenue until that time.[7] A consignment shipment therefore represents only the movement of the supplier's asset, inventory,

---

[6] "Omnibus Opinion," *APB Opinion No. 10.*
[7] "Revenue Recognition When Right of Return Exists," *FASB Statement No. 48.* This *Statement* also describes circumstances when revenue may not be recognized even if title to the goods has passed from the consignor to the consignee.

from one place to another. The amount of merchandise out on consignment can be shown by a journal entry, at cost:

dr.	Inventory on Consignment	1,000	
cr.	Merchandise Inventory.		1,000

In the period in which these goods are sold by the consignee, the effect on the accounts of the consignor would be as in the following entries:

dr.	Cost of Goods Sold	1,000	
cr.	Inventory on Consignment		1,000
	To record the cost of consigned goods sold.		
dr.	Accounts Receivable	1,400	
cr.	Sales Revenue		1,400
	To record the consignor's sales value.		

Franchises

Some companies, called **franchisors,** sell franchises that permit the **franchisee** to use a well-known name (e.g., Taco Bell, Days Inn, Avis). The franchisor also may agree to provide advice and other services in return for the franchise fee. A franchisor recognizes revenue during the period in which it provides the services, rather than when the fee is received. In particular, a franchisor often receives a large initial fee for which it agrees to provide site selection, personnel training, advice on equipment selection, and other services. It cannot recognize revenue until these services have been provided; normally, this is after the franchisee commences operations.[8]

Percentage-of-Completion Method

High-rise buildings, bridges, aircraft, ships, space exploration hardware, and certain other items involve a design/development and construction/production period that extends over several years. Such projects are performed under contracts in which the customer provides the product specifications. The contract also stipulates either (1) predetermined amounts the customer must pay at various points during the project, called a **fixed-price contract,** or (2) some sort of formula that will determine customer payments as a function of actual project costs plus a reasonable profit, called a **cost-reimbursement contract.**

During each accounting period in which the contractor works on the contract, there has been performance. If there is reasonable assurance of the contract's profit margin and its ultimate realization, then revenue is appropriately recognized in each such period. This method of revenue recognition is called the **percentage-of-completion method** because the amount of revenue is related to the percentage of the total project work that was performed in the period.

GAAP presumes that the percentage-of-completion method will be used to account for long-term contracts. This presumption can be overcome. If the amount of income to be earned on the contract cannot be reliably estimated, then revenue must be recognized only when the project has been completed. This is the **completed-contract method.** Costs incurred on the project are held as an asset, Contract Work in Progress, until the period in which revenue is recognized.[9]

On a cost-reimbursement contract, the amount of income earned in each period often can be reliably estimated. If the owner agrees to pay cost plus 10 percent and if the

[8] "Accounting for Franchise Fee Revenue," *FASB Statement No. 45.*

[9] Long-Term Construction-Type Contracts, *ARB No. 45.* IFRS has a different approach. When the outcome of a construction contract cannot be estimated reliably, revenue should be recognized only to the extent of contract costs increased that it is probable will be recoverable. Contract costs should be expressed in the period in which they are increased. "Construction Contracts." *IAS No.11.*

ILLUSTRATION 5–3 Long-Term Contract Accounting Methods

Year	Customer Payments Received	Project Costs Incurred	Year-End Percent Complete	Completed-Contract Method			Percentage-of-Completion Method		
				Revenues	Expenses	Income	Revenues*	Expenses	Income
1	$120,000	$160,000	20	$ 0	$ 0	$ 0	$180,000	$160,000	$ 20,000
2	410,000	400,000	70	0	0	0	450,000	400,000	50,000
3	370,000	240,000	100	900,000	800,000	100,000	270,000	240,000	30,000
Total	$900,000	$800,000		$900,000	$800,000	$100,000	$900,000	$800,000	$100,000

*This amount for a year is the percent of completion *accomplished that year* times total project revenues. In this example, 20 percent, 50 percent, and 30 percent of the work was accomplished in years 1, 2, and 3, respectively.

work proceeds as planned, the revenue is 110 percent of the costs incurred in the period. A fixed-price contract usually specifies how the satisfactory completion of each phase of the project is to be determined; such points in the project are called *milestones*. If good project plans exist, the number of milestones reached enables the contractor to reliably estimate the percent complete and hence the revenue earned on the contract.

Illustration 5–3 shows the application of the two long-term contract accounting methods to a three-year project. Note that both methods report the same total project income over the entire three-year period, but only the percentage-of-completion method allocates this total to each of the three years. Also note that the customer payments (cash inflows) are irrelevant in determining the amount of revenue recognized each year under either method.[10]

Production Method

For certain grains and other crops, the government sets price supports and assures the farmer that the products can be sold for at least these prices. The minimum amount of income that will be earned therefore can be reliably measured as soon as the crops have been harvested, even though they have not been sold at that time. Furthermore, the farmer's performance has been substantially completed. In these circumstances, a case can be made for recognizing revenue at the time of harvest. This **production method** is permitted but not required by generally accepted accounting principles (GAAP). GAAP also permits revenue recognition when gold, silver, and similar precious metals have been produced from the mine, even though the metals have not yet been sold. In recent years, however, fluctuations in the sales value of these metals have been large, and the rationale for the production method is therefore weaker. Relatively few mining companies now use the production method.

Installment Method

Many retail stores sell merchandise on an installment basis, in which the customer pays a certain amount per week or per month. If the customers are good credit risks, then the payments are likely to be received and the store can reliably measure its income at the time the sale is made. In other circumstances, the amount of income that is realized cannot be reliably measured at the time the sale is made, so revenue is not recorded at that time. Instead, revenue is recognized when the installment payments are received.[11]

---

[10] For income tax accounting purposes, most long-term contracts must be accounted for under the percentage-of-completion method.

[11] "Omnibus Opinion," *APB Opinion No. 10.* This *Opinion* states that sales revenue should "ordinarily" be recognized when the sale is made and that an installment method is acceptable only when "the circumstances are such that the collection of the sales price is not reasonably assured."

In the pure **installment method,** the installment payment is counted as revenue and a proportional part of the cost of sales is counted as a cost in the same period.

In a more conservative variation, the **cost-recovery method,** cost of sales is recorded at an amount equal to the installment payment. The result is that no income is reported until the installment payments have recouped the total cost of sales.

The effect of the installment method is to postpone the recognition of revenue and income to later periods as compared with the delivery method.[12]

Example

A jeweler sells a watch in 2009 for $400, and the customer agrees to make payments totaling $200 in 2005 and $200 in 2010. (The customer would ordinarily pay interest in addition to the payments for the watch itself, but this is a separate revenue item that is disregarded here.) The watch cost the jeweler $220.

	Effect on Income Statements			
	Delivery Method		**Installment Method**	
	2009	**2010**	**2009**	**2010**
Sales revenue	$400	$ 0	$200	$200
Cost of goods sold	220	0	110	110
Gross margin	$180	$ 0	$ 90	$ 90

Real Estate Sales

Some developers sell land to customers who make a small down payment and pay the balance of the purchase price over a number of years. In some cases, the buyer later becomes disenchanted with the deal or becomes unable to continue with the payments. Because of the consequent uncertainty about the amount of income that will be realized, three conditions must be met in order for revenue to be recognized: (1) The period of cancellation of the contract with a refund to the buyer has expired; (2) the buyer has made cumulative payments equal to at least 10 percent of the purchase price; *and* (3) the seller has completed improvements (roads, utility connections, and so on) or is making progress on these improvements and is clearly capable of eventually completing them. If the improvements have been completed and the receivable from the buyer is probably collectible, then the full sales price is recognized as revenue, and appropriate costs are matched against the revenue. If the improvements are in progress, the percentage-of-completion method is used to recognize the revenue. If there is doubt as to the collectibility of the receivables, the installment method is used. If any of the three above-mentioned criteria for revenue recognition is not met, the seller records any payments received as a liability, deposits on land sales.[13]

Similar but more complex criteria govern the recognition of revenue on the sale of land for commercial use (office buildings, hotels, and other commercial property) and residential property. The required down payments range from 5 percent to 25 percent, depending on the nature of the property, and certain other requirements must be met.[14]

---

[12] Income tax regulations limit the use of the installment method.
[13] "Accounting for Sales of Real Estate," *FASB Statement No. 66.*
[14] Ibid.

Amount of Revenue Recognized

In Chapter 3 we discussed the realization concept, which states that the amount recorded as revenue is the amount that customers are reasonably certain to pay. This concept requires that certain adjustments be made to the gross sales value of the goods or services sold. These adjustments are discussed in this section.

Bad Debts

The main source of revenue in many businesses is the sale of goods or services to customers on credit, or "on account." These sales may involve a single payment or they may involve a series of payments, as in the installment sales transactions discussed above. They give rise to the sales revenue and also to the asset accounts receivable. These accounts, in turn, give rise to losses when customers do not pay the amounts they owe.

Assume that Essel Company began operations in 2010 and that the company made sales of $262,250, all on credit, during the year. In the interest of simplicity, further assume that no money had been received from customers in 2010. The records made of these transactions would result in accounts receivable of $262,250 and sales revenue of $262,250. It would be correct to report $262,250 as an asset on the balance sheet as of the end of 2010 and $262,250 as sales revenue on the income statement for 2010 if, *but only if,* it is believed that all customers eventually will pay the full amount of their obligations to Essel Company. Unfortunately, some of these customers may never pay their bills. If they do not, their accounts become **bad debts.**

Consider first the extreme case. A person makes a purchase with no intention of paying for it and in fact does not pay for it. In this case, the company has not actually made a sale at all. No revenue was actually earned, and nothing valuable was added to the asset accounts receivable as a result of this transaction. If this event were recorded as an increase in Sales Revenue and as an increase in Accounts Receivable, both of these accounts would be overstated, and income for the period and owners' equity at the end of the period also would be overstated.

In the more usual bad debt situation, the customer fully intends to pay but for one reason or another never actually makes payment. The effect is the same as that in the extreme case. Such a sale also is recorded initially by debiting Accounts Receivable and crediting Sales Revenue at the sales value of the customer's purchase. In these situations, another entry must be made to show that the amount debited to Accounts Receivable does not represent the amount of the additional asset and that shareholders' equity has not in fact increased by the amount of the sale.

Accounting Recognition of Bad Debts

When a company makes a sale, the fact that the customer will never pay the bill is, of course, not known; otherwise, the sale would not have been made. Even at the end of the accounting period, the company may not know specifically *which* of its accounts receivable will never be collected. An estimate of the amount of bad debts can nevertheless be made, and the accounting records are adjusted at the end of each accounting period to reflect this estimate.

One way of making this adjustment is by the **direct write-off method.** Accounts that are believed to be uncollectible are simply eliminated from the records by subtracting the amount of the bad debt from Accounts Receivable and showing the same amount as an expense item on the income statement. The entry to accomplish this would be as follows:

dr.	Bad Debt Expense.	200	
cr.	Accounts Receivable.		200

The direct write-off method, however, requires that the specific uncollectible accounts be identified, whereas this usually is not possible.

With an alternative procedure, the **allowance method,** the *total* amount of un-collectible accounts is estimated. This estimated amount is shown as a deduction from accounts receivable on the balance sheet and as an expense on the income statement. Instead of reducing the accounts receivable amount directly, the estimate often is shown as a separate contra asset number on the balance sheet so that the reader can observe both the total amount owed by customers and that portion of the amount that the company believes will not be collected.[15]

Accounts Involved

The balance sheet contra asset account for Accounts Receivable is called **Allowance for Doubtful** (or **Uncollectible**) **Accounts.** At one time, it was often labeled in the accounts Reserve for Bad Debts, but this caused confusion since the word *reserve* connotes to many people that a sum of money has been set aside and such is not the case. (Nevertheless, the term *bad debt reserve* is often still used in everyday conversations.) The Allowance for Doubtful Accounts is in the nature of a decrease in Accounts Receivable for specific, *but as yet unknown,* customers. The corresponding income statement account is called **Bad Debt Expense.**

Making the Estimate

In those situations in which using the direct write-off method is not feasible, any one of several methods may be used to estimate the amount of bad debt expense in an accounting period. The most common method is to estimate bad debt expense as a percentage of *credit* sales. (The percentage is applied to credit sales since, of course, cash sales do not result in bad debts.) The percentage used depends in part on past experience and in part on management's judgment as to whether past experience reflects the current situation. The allowance for doubtful accounts should be sufficient at all times to absorb the accounts that prove to be uncollectible. Because business conditions fluctuate, the amount may turn out to be too large in some periods and too small in others. In practice, because of the concept of conservatism, it is common to find that the allowance is too large rather than too small. On the other hand, there have been some cases in which the allowance for doubtful accounts turned out to be woefully inadequate.

Aging Accounts Receivable

Sometimes different percentages are applied to accounts outstanding for various lengths of time. This requires the preparation of an **aging schedule,** which is also a useful device for analyzing the quality of the asset accounts receivable. An example for Essel Company is shown in Illustration 5–4.

---

[15] Generally, income tax regulations do not permit use of the allowance method. Rather, the direct write-off method must be used for each specific account that becomes partially or totally worthless.

ILLUSTRATION 5–4 **Aging Schedule for Estimating Bad Debts**

Status as of December 31, 2010	Amount Outstanding	Estimated Percent Uncollectible	Allowance for Doubtful Accounts
Current	$207,605	1	$2,076
Overdue:			
Less than 1 month	26,003	1	260
1 up to 2 months	10,228	5	511
2 up to 3 months	7,685	10	769
3 up to 6 months	3,876	20	775
6 months and over	6,853	40	2,741
Total	$262,250		$7,132

The Adjusting Entry

Once the amount of the allowance has been determined, it is recorded as one of the adjusting entries made at the end of the accounting period. If Essel Company management estimated the allowance for doubtful accounts on the basis of the above aging schedule, the entry would be

dr.	Bad Debt Expense.	7,132
cr.	Allowance for Doubtful Accounts . . .	7,132

The accounts receivable section of the December 31, 2010, balance sheet would then appear as follows:

Accounts receivable	$262,250
Less: Allowance for doubtful accounts	7,132
Accounts receivable, net	$255,118

The 2010 income statement would show $7,132 of bad debt expense.

The contra asset account, Allowance for Doubtful Accounts, usually will have a balance even before the adjusting entry is made. In these circumstances, the amount reported as bad debt expense on the income statement will be different from the amount reported as allowance for doubtful accounts on the balance sheet. (In the Essel Company example just given, this did not occur because the company was organized in 2009, and the above entry was the first one made to Allowance for Doubtful Accounts.)

Write-Off of an Uncollectible Account

When a company decides that a specific customer is never going to pay the amount owed, Accounts Receivable is reduced by the amount owed and a corresponding reduction is made in the Allowance for Doubtful Accounts. This entry has *no effect* on Bad Debt Expense or on income of the period in which the account is written off.

Example

If sometime in 2011 the Essel Company decided that James Johnson was never going to pay his bill of $250, the following entry would be made:

dr.	Allowance for Doubtful Accounts	250
cr.	Accounts Receivable.	250

A balance sheet prepared immediately after this transaction had been recorded (assuming no other changes since December 31, 2010) would appear as follows:

Accounts receivable	$262,000
Less: Allowance for doubtful accounts	6,882
Accounts receivable, net	$255,118

Note that the *net* amount of accounts receivable is unchanged by this write-off.

Collection of a Bad Debt Written Off

If, by some unexpected stroke of good fortune, James Johnson should subsequently pay all or part of the amount he owed, Cash would be increased (i.e., debited) and a corresponding credit would be recorded, usually to add back the amount to Allowance for Doubtful Accounts on the balance sheet.

Sales Discounts

As mentioned in Chapter 3, sales revenue is recorded at not more than the sales value of the actual transaction (realization concept).

Some businesses offer a so-called **cash discount** to induce customers to pay bills quickly. For example, if a business sells goods on terms of "2/10, net/30," it permits customers to deduct 2 percent from the invoice amount if they pay within 10 days; otherwise, the full amount is due within 30 days.[16] The cash discount can be recorded in any of three ways:

1. The discount can be recorded as a reduction from gross sales.
2. The discount can be recorded as an expense of the period.
3. Sales revenue can be initially recorded at the *net* amount after deduction of the discount. Amounts received from customers who do *not* take the discount would then be recorded as additional revenue. Thus, a $1,000 sale subject to a 2 percent cash discount would be recorded at the time of sale as

dr.	Accounts Receivable	980
cr.	Sales Revenue	980

If the discount were not taken by the customer, the entry upon receipt of the customer's payment would be

dr.	Cash	1,000
cr.	Discounts Not Taken	20
	Accounts Receivable.	980

Credit Card Sales

Millions of retailers and service establishments who sell on credit have contracted with an outside agency, such as master card or visa, to handle some or all of their accounts receivable.

In these arrangements, at the point of sale, merchants send electronically the sales data and charge to a bank which next day credits the merchant's account for the sales amount. (From the bank's point of view, the entry is a credit since it increases the customer's bank balance, which is a liability of the bank.) The bank arranges to have the charges collected from the customers. So far as the merchant is concerned, this type of

---

[16] This is a powerful inducement to pay within 10 days because by forgoing the 2 percent, the customer has the use of the money only for an additional 20 days. Since there are about 18 20-day periods in a year, this amounts to an annual interest rate of 18 × 2 percent = 36 percent.

transaction is not a credit sale. No accounts receivable appear in the merchant's accounts. The original credit card swipe that is made at the time of purchase is equivalent to the customer writing a check to cover the purchase. The only difference between a credit card sale and a customer payment by check is that, in the former case, the bank deducts a fee for the service of handling the accounts receivable paperwork and assuming the risk of bad debts. This fee is in the nature of a sales discount and is recorded as such in the merchant's accounts thus:

dr.	Cash	970
	Sales Discount (Credit Cards)	30
cr.	Sales Revenue	1,000

Sales Returns and Allowances

When customers are dissatisfied with goods or services sold to them, the company may permit them to return the goods for full credit, or it may refund part or all of the sales price. In these circumstances, the amount originally recorded as revenue turns out to be an overstatement of the true amount of the sale. Sales returns and allowances are conceptually similar to bad debts.

Some companies treat sales returns and allowances in the same way that they treat bad debt expense. They estimate the percentage of revenues that will eventually result in returns and allowances and set up an account for this amount. The offsetting credit is to a liability account; thus:

dr.	Sales Returns and Allowances.	1,000
cr.	Provision for Returns and Allowances. . .	1,000

The Sales Returns and Allowances account is analogous to Bad Debt Expense. The Provision for Returns and Allowances account is analogous to Allowance for Doubtful Accounts, except the former is treated as a liability rather than as a contra asset. When goods are returned or allowances made, Provision for Returns and Allowances is debited; the credit is to the customer's account receivable or to Cash (if a refund is made).

Other companies do not attempt to estimate the amount of returns and allowances associated with sales revenue of the current period. Instead, they simply debit Sales Returns and Allowances whenever a sales return or allowance occurs, with an offsetting credit to Accounts Receivable (or to Cash, if the returned goods had already been paid for). When this practice is followed, the sales returns and allowances deducted from revenue of a period do not relate to the actual goods included in the sales revenue of that period. The justification for this apparent departure from the matching concept is that the amounts are difficult to estimate in advance, are likely to be relatively constant from one period to the next, and are relatively small. Under these circumstances, the practice is consistent with the materiality concept.

Revenue Adjustment versus Expense

The need for recognizing bad debts, sales discounts, and sales returns and allowances arises because of one aspect of the realization concept—namely, that revenues should be reported at the amount that is reasonably certain to be collected. This concept would seem to require that these amounts be subtracted from gross revenues in order to determine the net revenue of the period. The effect of some of the practices described above, however, is to report the amounts as expenses rather than as adjustments to revenues.

Whether companies report these amounts as expenses or as adjustments to revenues, the effect on income is exactly the same. The difference between the two methods is in the way they affect revenue and gross margin. The consistency concept requires that a company follow the same method from one year to the next; thus, comparisons within a company are not affected by these differences in practice. They may, however, have a significant effect when the income statements of companies that use different methods are being compared.

Example

Following are income statements for Company A, which treats the items of the type discussed in this section as adjustments to revenue, and Company B, which treats them as expenses. Otherwise, the firms are identical.

	Income Statements			
	(000s)			
	Company A		Company B	
	Amount	Percent	Amount	Percent
Gross sales	$1,000	110.0	$1,000	100.0
Less: Sales discounts	20	2.2	0	
Bad debts	40	4.5	0	
Returns	30	3.3	0	
Net sales	910	100.0	1,000	100.0
Cost of sales	600	65.9	600	60.0
Gross margin	310	34.1	400	40.0
Other expenses	210	23.1	210	21.0
Discounts, bad debts, returns	0		90	9.0
Income	$ 100	11.0	$ 100	10.0

Note the differences between the two income statements, not only in the dollar amounts of net sales and gross margin but also, more importantly, in the percentages. (In reporting percentage relationships on an income statement, net sales is customarily taken as 100 percent, and the percentages for other items are calculated by dividing each by the amount of net sales.) Various combinations of these alternatives would produce still different amounts and percentages.

Warranty Costs

Companies usually have an obligation to repair or replace defective goods. This obligation arises either because it is an explicit part of the sales contract or because there is an implicit legal doctrine that says that customers have a right to receive satisfactory products. In either case, the obligation is called a **warranty**.

If it is likely that a material amount of costs will be incurred in future periods in replacing or repairing goods sold in the current period, both the conservatism and matching concepts require that income in the current period be adjusted accord-ingly.[17] The amount of the adjustment is usually estimated as a percentage of sales revenue. This adjustment is recorded as an expense with an entry such as the following:

dr.	Estimated Warranty Expense	2,000
cr.	Allowance for Warranties	2,000

[17] Income tax regulations do not permit recognizing warranty costs until they are actually incurred.

When costs are incurred in the future in repairing or replacing the goods, Allowance for Warranties, a liability account, is debited, and Cash, Parts Inventory, or some other balance sheet account is credited. Analogous to the write-off of an uncollectible receivable, this warranty repair or replacement transaction affects neither the estimated warranty expense nor the income of the period in which it takes place.

Conceptually, Estimated Warranty Expense is an upward adjustment of Cost of Sales rather than a downward adjustment of Sales Revenue. We nevertheless have included the topic here because the accounting procedures for warranty costs are so similar to those for bad debts and sales returns and allowances. All these adjustments reduce the period's reported income.

Interest Revenue

A principal source of revenue to a bank or other lending institution is interest on the money that it lends.[18] Industrial and commercial companies also may earn interest revenue. Under the realization concept, the amount of revenue for a period is the amount the lender earned on the money the borrower had available for use during that period. Accounting for this amount depends on whether interest is paid at **maturity**— that is, when the loan is repaid—or whether it is in effect paid when the money is borrowed. In the latter case, the loan is said to be **discounted.** Examples of each are given below.

Example

Interest Paid at Maturity. On September 1, 2010, a bank loaned $10,000 for one year at 9 percent interest, the interest and principal to be paid on August 31, 2011. The bank's entry on September 1, 2010, is

| dr. | Loans Receivable.................. | 10,000 | |
| cr. | Cash.......................... | | 10,000 |

On December 31, 2010, an adjusting entry is made to record the fact that interest for one-third of a year, $300, was earned in 2010:

| dr. | Interest Receivable.................. | 300 | |
| cr. | Interest Revenue................. | | 300 |

On August 31, 2011, when the loan is repaid, the entry is

dr.	Cash.............................	10,900	
cr.	Loans Receivable.................		10,000
	Interest Receivable................		300
	Interest Revenue..................		600

Corresponding entries are made on the books of the borrower to record interest expense.

Example

Discounted Loan. On September 1, 2010, a bank loaned $10,000 for one year at 9 percent discounted. The borrower received $10,000 less the $900 prepaid interest, or $9,100.[19] On that day, the bank has a liability of $900 because it has not yet performed the service of permitting the use of the money. The bank's entry on September 1, 2010, is

dr.	Loans Receivable..................	10,000	
cr.	Cash..........................		9,100
	Unearned Interest Revenue..........		900

---

[18] In practice, this amount is often called interest *income* rather than interest *revenue*. Conceptually, it is revenue.

[19] The *effective* interest rate on this loan is more than 9 percent, since the borrower pays $900 *interest* for the use of only $9,100 for one year.

The borrower records a $9,100 increase in Cash, a $900 increase in Prepaid Interest Expense, and a $10,000 increase in Notes Payable.

On December 31, 2010, the bank makes an adjusting entry to record the fact that $300 interest (one-third of a year) was earned in 2010 and is therefore no longer a liability:

dr.	Unearned Interest Revenue	300	
cr.	Interest Revenue		300

On August 31, 2011, when the loan is repaid, the entry is

dr.	Cash	10,000	
cr.	Loans Receivable		10,000

After repayment by the borrower, an adjusting entry is also made by the bank to record the fact that $600 interest (two-thirds of a year) was earned in 2011:

dr.	Unearned Interest Revenue	600	
cr.	Interest Revenue		600

Interest Component of a Sale

When buyers purchase goods on an installment plan, they pay both for the goods themselves and for the interest that the seller charges on the amount of the unpaid balance. Revenue from the sales value of the goods should be recorded separately from interest revenue. In most sales to consumers, this separation is easy to recognize since federal regulations require that the amount of interest be specified in the sales contract. Although the goods' sales value may be recognized at the time of the sale (unless the installment method is used), the interest revenue is recognized in the period or periods in which it is earned; that is, it is spread over the life of the installment contract.

In some sales agreements, the buyer gives a note promising to pay several months or even years in the future; but the note does not explicitly indicate that an interest charge is involved. Since any rational merchant expects to receive more money for a sale that is not completed for many months in the future than for a cash sale, it is apparent that the amount of the note includes both the sales value of the goods and an interest charge. In recording the transaction, these two components must be shown separately. If the full amount of the note were recognized as revenue in the period in which the transaction took place, revenue for that period would be overstated by the amount of the interest component. The interest implicit in such a transaction is calculated by applying the going rate of interest for transactions of this general type.[20] The same principle is used for notes that state a rate of interest significantly below the going rate.

Example

On September 1, 2010, a customer purchased a piece of equipment and gave in payment a note promising to pay $10,000 one year later, with no interest stated. The going rate of interest was 8 percent. The entry on September 1, 2010, would be

dr.	Notes Receivable.	10,000	
cr.	Sales Revenue		9,259
	Unearned Interest Revenue.		741

---

[20] "Interest on Receivables and Payables," *APB Opinion No. 21*, specifies the details as to how the rate of interest is determined. The interest revenue amount is found by using present value techniques described in Chapter 8, *not* by discounting the face amount of the note.

The adjusting entry on December 31, 2010, and the entry recording payment of the note on August 31, 2011, would be similar to those given above for a discounted loan.

Transfer of Financial Assets

Companies often sell their financial assets, such as a sale of accounts receivables, to a finance company. In order for a transfer of a financial asset to be accounted for as a sale, the transferor must surrender control of those financial assets to the transferee. If the transfer does not meet this requirement, the two parties to the transaction must account for the transfer as a secured borrowing with a pledge of collateral.[21]

While the accounting outcome of a transfer of most financial assets governed by IFRS may be the same as under GAAP, the IFRS derecognition (sale) test is different. In order to qualify as a financial asset sale, *IAS No. 39* requires the transferor to transfer to the transferee substantially all the risks and rewards of ownership of the financial asset.[22]

Monetary Assets

Monetary assets are money or claims to receive fixed sums of money (e.g., accounts receivable or notes receivable). By contrast, most **nonmonetary assets** are items that will be used in the future in the production and sale of goods and services. No separate classification for monetary assets appears on the balance sheet. The traditional distinction on the balance sheet is between current assets and noncurrent assets. The reason for calling attention to the distinction between monetary and non-monetary assets is that the concepts governing the amounts at which they appear on the balance sheet subsequent to their initial recognition at cost differ for these two categories.

Difference in Reporting Monetary and Nonmonetary Assets

In general and with the notable exception of inventories (discussed in Chapter 6), *non-monetary* assets appear on the balance sheet at *unexpired cost.* When acquired, they were recorded at cost. The amount shown on the balance sheet at any time thereafter is the amount not yet written off as an expense. If a building was acquired in 1995 at a cost of $1 million and if $375,000 of its cost has been written off as depreciation expense in the intervening 15 years, the balance sheet for December 31, 2010, will report the asset amount of this building at $625,000, *regardless* of its market value at that time.

For *monetary* assets, the idea of unexpired cost is not appropriate. As we have seen above, the accounts receivable item is reported at its *estimated realizable value.* This is the effect of the adjustment for the estimated amount of bad debts included in the accounts receivable. Cash, of course, is reported at its face amount, whether on hand or deposited in banks. As indicated in Chapter 2, most other monetary assets are accounted for at their fair value.

---

[21] "Accounting for Transfers and Servicing of Financial Assets and Extinguishments of Liabilities," *FASB Statement No. 140.*
[22] "Financial Instruments: Recognition and Measurement," *IAS No. 39.*

Cash

Cash consists of funds that are immediately available for disbursement. Cash is usually held in checking accounts on which little or no interest is earned. If an entity has a temporary excess of cash, it may loan the excess to a bank and receive interest on it. The evidence of such a loan is called a **certificate of deposit.** A certificate of deposit has a maturity date, and a penalty is involved if the entity cashes it prior to that date. Therefore, these funds are not as liquid as cash in a checking account. Some companies include certificates of deposit in the amount reported for cash, whereas other companies disclose separately an amount for these certificates.

Receivables

The **accounts receivable** discussed in the preceding section were amounts due from customers. For nonfinancial institutions, these are often called **trade receivables.** As already explained, financial institutions have loans receivable and interest receivable. Also, an entity may advance funds to employees for various reasons, a principal one being to provide for travel expenses. Such receivables are reported separately from trade receivables in an account with a title such as Due from Employees.

Marketable Securities

If an entity has a temporary excess of cash, rather than—or in addition to—investing it in certificates of deposit, the entity may invest it in **marketable securities.** Marketable securities are of several types. **Commercial paper** is a colloquial name for short-term, interest-bearing promissory notes issued by large companies with high credit ratings and a temporary need for more cash. **Treasury bills** are short-term obligations of the U.S. Treasury; that is, the investor in a Treasury bill is making a short-term loan to the federal government. Stocks of companies as well as bonds of companies and government entities are also marketable securities if they are, in fact, marketable—that is, if they can be readily sold.

Most companies report marketable securities as a separate line on the balance sheet, some of them preferring the caption "temporary investments." Some companies include certificates of deposit in the marketable securities or investments total rather than as a separate item or as a part of cash. Capital stock of other companies held for the purpose of exercising some control over those companies, or stocks and bonds not traded on a securities market, are reported as **investments** rather than as marketable securities. (Investments are discussed in Chapter 12.)

Security Categories

Generally accepted accounting principles set out explicit rules for the balance sheet valuation of marketable securities.[23] Application of the rules involves classifying such securities into three categories:

1. **Held-to-maturity securities** are debt securities that the entity intends to hold to maturity. They are reported on the balance sheet at cost.
2. **Trading securities** are debt and equity securities that are held for current resale. They are reported at market value, with any unrealized gains or losses of the period

---

[23] "Accounting for Certain Investments in Debt and Equity Securities," *FASB Statement No. 115.*

included in the calculation of the period's income. The entry for an unrealized gain of $5,000 would be

| dr. | Marketable Securities . . . . | 5,000 | |
| | cr. | Gain on Marketable Securities . . . . | 5,000 |

This would increase the period's pretax income by $5,000. An analogous entry would be made for a loss, which would decrease the period's reported income.

3. **Available-for-sale securities** are debt and equity securities that do not fit either of the other two categories. They are reported at market value, and any unrealized gains (or losses) of the period are directly credited (or debited) to an owners' equity account; that is, the write-up (or write-down) does not "flow through" the income statement as it does in the case of trading securities.

Analysis of Monetary Assets

Some relationships that are helpful in analyzing a company's monetary assets are described below. They include the current ratio, the acid-test ratio, days' cash, and days' receivables. These ratios will be illustrated using the information given for Franklin Company in Illustration 5–5.

Current Ratio

As explained in Chapter 2, the current ratio is

$$\text{Current ratio} = \frac{\text{Current assets}}{\text{Current liabilities}} = \frac{\$1,245.1}{\$1,214.6} = 1.03$$

The current ratio is the most commonly used of all balance sheet ratios. It is a measure not only of the company's liquidity but also of the margin of safety that management maintains in order to allow for the inevitable unevenness in the flow of funds through the current asset and current liability accounts. If this flow were absolutely smooth and uniform (so that, for example, money coming in from customers each day exactly equaled that day's maturing obligations), the requirements for such a safety margin would be small. Since a company rarely can count on such an even flow, it needs a supply of liquid funds to be assured of being able to pay its bills when they come due. The current ratio indicates the size of this buffer.

In interpreting the current ratio, consideration of the proportion of various types of current assets is important. Even if two companies have the same current ratio, a company with a high percentage of its current assets in the form of monetary assets is more liquid than one with a high percentage in inventory. Also, the nature of the business must be considered. For example, a manufacturer that makes high-fashion clothing needs a relatively high current ratio, since there is high risk involved in both this firm's accounts receivable and its inventory. On the other hand, a metals distributor may safely have a lower current ratio than the clothing manufacturer's, since the distributor's primary current asset would be inventories of steel, copper, and aluminum shapes, which do not become obsolete and whose prices may be increasing because of inflation.

ILLUSTRATION 5–5 Condensed Financial Statements

FRANKLIN COMPANY Balance Sheet As of December 31, 2010 (millions)	
Assets	
Current assets:	
Cash and temporary investments	$ 98.1
Accounts receivable (less allowances)	536.8
Inventories	403.1
Prepaid expenses	207.1
Total current assets	1,245.1
All other assets	2,992.0
Total assets	$4,237.1
Liabilities and Shareholders' Equity	
Current liabilities	$1,214.6
All other liabilities and stockholders' equity	3,022.5
Total liabilities and stockholders' equity	$4,237.1
Income Statement **For the Year Ended December 31, 2010** **(in millions)**	
Net sales and revenues	$6,293.9
Expenses*	5,613.2
Net income	$ 680.7

*Includes depreciation expense of $265.2 million.

Acid-Test Ratio

Some of the current assets are monetary assets. A ratio that focuses on the relationship of *monetary current assets* to current liabilities is called the **acid-test ratio,** or **quick ratio.** Quick current assets are those current assets that are also monetary assets; they therefore exclude inventories and prepaid items. The formula is

$$\text{Acid-test ratio} = \frac{\text{Monetary current assets}}{\text{Current liabilities}} = \frac{\$634.9}{\$1,214.6} = 0.52$$

Days' Cash

Although cash is a necessary asset, it earns little or no return. Thus, although too little cash is an obvious signal of difficulty, too much cash is a sign that management has not taken advantage of opportunities to put cash to work in, say, marketable securities.

One way to judge how well the company is managing its cash is to calculate roughly how many days' bills the cash on hand would pay. The first step is to use the income statement to estimate cash expenses: A rough approximation would be to take total expenses and subtract noncash expenses such as depreciation. This total is then divided by 365 days to arrive at daily cash needs:

$$\text{Cash costs per day} = \frac{\$5,348.0}{365 \text{ days}} = \$14.65$$

This amount can then be divided into the cash balance to determine approximately the "days' cash" on hand:

$$\frac{\text{Cash}}{\text{Cash costs per day}} = \frac{\$98.1}{\$14.65 \text{ per day}} = 7 \text{ days}^{24}$$

Combining these two steps, the formula for **days' cash** is

$$\text{Day's Cash} \frac{\text{Cash}}{\text{Cash expenses} \div 365}$$

It must be emphasized that this is a rough approximation. The calculation focuses on routine operating expenses; it does not take account of cash needed for major asset purchases or loan repayments. Thus, a firm might appear to have too much cash on hand because it has just received cash from bonds issued to finance construction of a new facility. On the other hand, firms with good cash management procedures would not let even that cash sit idle; they would invest it in short-term securities for as long as possible, even if that is only one or two days. In companies that manage their cash well, the days' cash will usually be only a few days. (Some analysts calculate this ratio using cash plus marketable securities in the numerator rather than just "pure" cash. The ratio then indicates short-term liquidity, rather than cash management.)

Days' Receivables

A calculation similar to that used in days' cash can be used to see how many days' worth of sales are represented in accounts receivable (days' sales outstanding, or DSOs). The formula is

$$\text{Day's receivables} = \frac{\text{Receivables}}{\text{Sales} \div 365} = \frac{\$536.8}{\$6,293.9 \div 365} = 31 \text{ days}$$

The result is also called the average **collection period** for the receivables. If available, the amount of sales in the denominator should be *credit* sales, which is more closely related to receivables than is total sales.

The collection period can be related roughly to the credit terms offered by the company. A rule of thumb is that the collection period should not exceed 11/3 times the regular payment period; that is, if the company's typical terms call for payment in 30 days, it is said that the average collection period should not exceed 40 days. Like all rules of thumb, this one has a great many exceptions. Changes in the ratio may indicate changes in the company's credit policy or changes in its ability to collect its receivables.

As with other ratios, comparisons should be made with the collection period of other firms in the same industry and also with a firm's own ratio for previous years. For example, in industries with excess capacity, looser credit policies are sometimes used as a competitive marketing tool, thus increasing the days' receivables. If a firm's collection period is significantly longer than its competitors', this may suggest inadequate collection procedures.

[24] This result needs to be interpreted in light of the fact that Franklin Company reports cash and highly liquid temporary investments as a single combined amount. For companies that separately report cash and marketable securities, basing the calculation on "pure" cash typically will give a result of only two or three days.

The aging schedule in Illustration 5–4 also provides useful information in analyzing the quality of the accounts receivable. An increase in the proportion of overdue amounts is a serious danger signal. Although aging schedules frequently are used within corporations, they are not disclosed in corporate annual reports to shareholders.

Indian Accounting Standard (Ind AS) on Revenue Recognition

Revenue is one of the most important financial statement measures for both makers and users of financial statements. The good news – finally revenue will be recognized in the same way across the globe as a substantially converged standard. The Ministry of Corporate Affairs (MCA) notified 39 Indian Accounting Standards (Ind AS) in 2015. These standards include Ind AS 115, which was converged with the International Financial Reporting Standards (IFRS). As explained by the Ministry of Corporate Affairs, Ind AS 115 lays down the principles to be applied by an entity in order to report useful information to users of financial statements. These principles include the nature, amount, timing, and uncertainty of revenue and cash flows arising from a contract with a customer.

Ind AS 115 offers clarity in areas involving multiple element contracts or bundled products, licensing, royalties for intellectual properties, financing components, and variable consideration. Experts believe that the new accounting standard will bring in much-needed transparency in the accounting and audit process by improving disclosures. This will impact a broad range of sectors in India, including technology, real estate, mining and metals, engineering-procurement-construction, and telecom as the standard incorporates new concepts of revenue recognition.

As discussed, the standard will impact all companies, with a varying degree depending on the industry sector, existing contracting practices and also their existing accounting policies. More importantly, the standard will require firms to apply judgment and use estimates in a number of areas. Depending on the nature of the industry and past practices, the new revenue standard may impact a range of issues including identification of performance obligations to be delivered, accounting for contract costs, accounting for the right of return, and evaluation of principal-agent relations. Moreover, the new standard may have an impact on a firm's budgeting and reporting process, IT systems, internal control systems, employee KPIs and bonuses, and tax liabilities.

India's real estate appears to be most affected by the transition in accounting standards. From this financial year on, listed real estate firms will need to switch to the Project Completion Method from the existing Percentage Completion Method (POC). This means that home buyer payments toward the purchase of under-construction projects will no longer be treated as turnover or profit from sales; rather they will be examined as advances or loans.

Conceptual Change – Transfer of Control vs Risks and Rewards

There is a fundamental and conceptual change in the standard for identifying the point of "revenue recognition." Under Ind AS 115, revenue is recognized when control over goods or services is transferred to a customer, which under current GAAP is based on the transfer of risks and rewards. A customer obtains control when it has the ability to direct the use of and obtain the benefits from the good or service; there is a transfer of title. The transfer of risk and rewards is now one of the many factors to be considered within the overall concept of control.

Ind AS 115 requires an entity to focus on the customer's point of view to decide revenue recognition. It details a five-stage process for revenue recognition.

The Five-Step Method

1. **Analyze closely the terms of the contract(s) with customer:** Contracts may be formally documented, verbal or implied by customary business practices, but revenue can be recognized only on those contracts that are enforceable and have commercial substance.

2. **Analyze the different performance obligations in the contract:** Performance obligations are explicitly or implicitly ensured goods or services to be delivered in a contract as well as those which are arising from customary business practices.

3. **Determine the transaction price:** The transaction price is the best estimate of consideration to which an entity expects to be benefited. It includes variable consideration, the impact of significant financing components, fair value of non-cash consideration and the impact of consideration payable to the customer.

4. **Apportion the transaction price to all the performance obligations separately:** The standard requires allocation of the total contract price to the various performance obligations based on their relative standalone selling prices.

5. **Revenue should be recognized when (or as) the entity fulfils a particular performance obligation:** Any recognition of revenue can occur either over time or at a point in time. Ind AS 115 moves away from "risk and rewards" model under Ind AS and focuses on the "control approach" to determine revenue recognition.

Another distinct feature of Ind AS 115 is that it prescribes detailed qualitative and quantitative disclosure templates for more transparency in the financial statements, e.g., disclosures for performance obligations still not complete and disaggregation of revenue.

Summary

Although a business earns income continuously, accounting recognizes revenue only in the period in which the entity has performed substantially what is required in order to earn income and in which the amount of income can be reliably measured. In the usual case of the sale of goods or services, this is the period in which goods are delivered or services performed. If income cannot be reliably measured at this time, as in certain types of installment sales, revenue recognition is postponed. If the earning process takes place over several accounting periods, the percentage-of-completion method recognizes revenue in each of these periods, provided that there is reasonable assurance of the profit margin and its ultimate realization.

The realization concept states that the amount of revenue recognized in a period is the amount that is reasonably certain to be collected from customers. Accordingly, the gross sales revenue is reduced by the estimated amount of bad debts that are hidden in credit sales. A corresponding reduction is made in the asset accounts receivable. Similar reductions may be made for warranty costs and for sales returns and allowances.

Monetary assets are money or claims to receive fixed sums of money. Cash, certificates of deposit, and accounts receivable are reported at realizable amounts (which, in the case of cash and certificates of deposit, are the same as the face amount). Marketable debt and equity securities are reported at either cost or current market value, depending on the company's intentions regarding holding the securities.

The current ratio, the acid-test ratio, days' cash, and days' receivables are useful tools in analyzing a company's monetary assets.

While the basic GAAP and IFRS revenue recognition standards differ, in most cases the revenue accounting outcome is the same.

Problems

Problem 5–1.

Below is a schedule of monthly credit sales and collections for Yzerman Company. Assuming Yzerman's cost of goods sold is always 65 percent of sales, calculate how much gross margin Yzerman will report each month (*a*) if revenues are recognized when the sale is made and (*b*) if the installment method is used.

	Jan.	Feb.	Mar.	Apr.	May	June
Sales	$12,000	$ 8,000	$13,000	$11,000	$ 9,000	$13,500
Collections	11,000	10,000	11,500	10,500	10,500	9,500

Problem 5–2.

The Giamatti Construction Company primarily builds houses, and rarely is a house only partially completed as of December 31. However, this year Giamatti is also building a motel, which it started in March and expects to complete next April. The motel calls for a fee of $5 million. Expected total costs are $4.25 million, and $2.55 million of these had been incurred as of December 31.

Required:

Assume that, *excluding* the motel project, Giamatti's income before taxes will be $1.25 million both this year and next. What will each year's income before taxes be, *including* the motel project, (*a*) if Giamatti uses the completed-contract method and (*b*) if it uses the percent-age-of-completion method? (Assume actual motel costs in fact turn out to be $4.25 million.) Which method *should* Giamatti use?

Problem 5–3.

Alcon Company decided to write off the $3,000 Wordel Corporation receivable as uncollectible. Subsequently, Wordel makes a $950 payment on the account. Prepare journal entries for these two transactions.

Problem 5–4.

Huron Corporation operates in an industry that has a high rate of bad debts. On December 31, before any year-end adjustments, the balance in Huron's Accounts Receivable account was $750,000 and the Allowance for Doubtful Accounts had a balance of $37,500. The year-end balance reported in the statement of financial position for the Allowance for Doubtful Accounts will be based on the aging schedule shown below.

Days Account Outstanding	Amount	Probability of Collection
Less than 16	$450,000	.99
16 to 30	150,000	.94
31 to 45	75,000	.80
46 to 60	45,000	.65
61 to 75	15,000	.50
Over 75	15,000	.00

Required:

a. What is the appropriate balance for the Allowance for Doubtful Accounts on December 31?

b. Show how accounts receivable would be presented on the balance sheet prepared on December 31.

c. What is the dollar effect of the year-end bad debt adjustment on the before-tax income for the year?

Problem 5–5.

Green Lawn Chemical Company sells lawn and garden chemicals through several hundred garden supply stores and department store garden shops. It was Green Lawn's policy to ship goods to these retailers in late winter on a consignment basis. Periodically, a Green Lawn field representative would count the Green Lawn products on hand at a retailer; based on this count, the previous count, and intervening shipments, it was determined how many items the retailer had sold since the previous count, and the retailer was billed for these goods by Green Lawn.

Required:

a. Assume Green Lawn shipped goods costing Green Lawn $8,400 and with a wholesale price (i.e., price to the retailer, not the end user) of $12,600 to Carson's Garden Shop. Prepare journal entries to record this entry (1) on Green Lawn's books and (2) on Carson's books.

b. Later, the field representative's count indicated that Carson's had sold some of these goods, totaling $6,720 at retail, $5,040 at wholesale, and $3,360 at Green Lawn's cost. Prepare journal entries to reflect these sales (1) on Green Lawn's books and (2) on Carson's books.

Problem 5–6.

Structco Construction Company entered into a long-term construction contract at a fixed contract price of $4,900,000 on September 1, 20x4. Work has proceeded since that time with the following results:

	20x4	20x5	20x6
Costs incurred (this year)	$ 721,000	$1,190,000	$1,715,000
Cost of work yet to be completed (at year-end)	3,430,000	2,240,000	525,000
Cash collections (this year)	560,000	1,120,000	1,540,000
Year-end percent complete	20%	50%	95%

Required:

Determine the amount of revenues, expenses, and income for 20x4, 20x5, and 20x6 by using the percentage-of-completion method.

Problem 5–7.

GRW Company has the following account balances at the end of the year, before adjusting and closing entries. (All numbers are in thousands of dollars.)

	Dr.	Cr.
Accounts receivable (gross; terms, net 30 days)	$ 34,650	
Accounts payable		$ 38,600
Allowance for doubtful accounts		1,850
Accumulated depreciation		61,600

Cash	23,100	
Common stock		231,000
Cost of goods sold	161,700	
Depreciation expense	15,400	
Goodwill	38,500	
Interest payable		25,000
Inventory, beginning	46,200	
Long-term debt (required to be repaid at a rate of $7,700 per year)		192,500
Other expenses	69,300	
Plant and equipment, at cost	346,500	
Purchases of inventory	184,800	
Retained earnings, beginning		46,200
Sales (23% were for cash)		323,400

Required:

Calculate and interpret the year-end
a. Quick and current ratios.
b. Number of days' cash on hand. (*Hint:* Total expenses minus noncash charges can be used as a proxy for operating cash needed for the year.)
c. Number of days' worth of sales represented by accounts receivable (i.e., collection period).

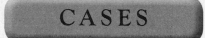

CASES

Case 5–1
Stern Corporation (A)*

On December 31, 2010, before the yearly financial statements were prepared, the controller of the Stern Corporation reviewed certain transactions that affected accounts receivable and the allowance for doubtful accounts. The controller first examined the December 31, 2009, balance sheet (Exhibit 1 on page 141). A subsequent review of the year's transactions applicable to accounts receivable revealed the items listed below:

1. Sales on account during 2010 amounted to $9,965,575.
2. Payment received on accounts receivable during 2010 totaled $9,685,420.

* Copyright © James S. Reece.

3. During the year, accounts receivable totaling $26,854 were deemed uncollectible and were written off.
4. Two accounts that had been written off as uncollectible in 2009 were collected in 2010. One account for $2,108 was paid in full. A partial payment of $1,566 was made by the Hollowell Company on another account that originally had amounted to $2,486. The controller was reasonably sure this account would be paid in full because reliable reports were circulating that the trustee in bankruptcy for the Hollowell Company would pay all obligations 100 cents on the dollar.

5. The Allowance for Bad Debts was adjusted to equal 3 percent of the balance in Accounts Receivable at the end of the year.

Questions

1. Analyze the effect of each of these transactions in terms of its effect on Accounts Receivable, Allowance for Doubtful Accounts, and any other account that may be involved, and prepare necessary journal entries.

2. Give the correct totals for Accounts Receivable and the Allowance for Doubtful Accounts as of December 31, 2010, after the transactions affecting them had been recorded.

3. Calculate the current ratio, acid-test ratio, and days' receivables figures as of December 31, 2010. Assume that amounts for items other than those described in the case are the same as on December 31, 2009.

Case 5–2
Grennell Farm*

Early in 2010, Denise Grey was notified by a lawyer that her recently deceased uncle had willed her the ownership of a 2,000-acre wheat farm in Iowa. The lawyer asked whether Grey wanted to keep the farm or sell it.

Grey was an assistant vice president in the consumer credit department of a large New York bank. Despite the distance between New York and Iowa, Grey was interested in retaining ownership of the farm if she could determine its profitability. During the last 10 years of his life, Jeremiah Grennell had hired professional managers to run his farm while he remained in semiretirement in Florida.

Keeping the farm as an investment was particularly interesting to Grey for the following reasons:

1. Recent grain deals with foreign countries had begun to increase present farm commodity prices, and many experts believed these prices would re-main high for the next several years.
2. Although the number of small farms had decreased markedly in the last 20 years, Grennell's use of mechanization and new hybrid seed varieties had proven to be profitable.
3. After some downward movement in the early 2000s, the value of good farmland in Iowa was beginning to appreciate at about 10 percent a year.

Included in the lawyer's letter were data on revenues and expenses for 2009 and certain information on balance sheet items, which are summarized below:

Beginning inventory	0	bushels
2009 wheat production	210,000	bushels
Shipped to grain elevator	180,000	bushels
Grain stored at farm at end of 2009	30,000	bushels

2009 Expenses for the Grennell Farm

A. Production costs per bushel:		
Seed	$	0.053
Fertilizer and chemicals		0.295
Machinery costs, fuel, and repairs		0.107
Part-time labor and other costs		0.058
Total production cost per bushel	$	0.513
B. Annual costs not related to the volume of production:		
Salaries and wages	$	72,500
Insurance		4,500
Taxes[a]		32,500
Depreciation		28,500
Other expenses		45,000
Total costs not related to production volume		$183,000

[a] This figure excludes income taxes since the corporation was taxed as a sole proprietorship.

Prices

The average price per bushel that the elevator operator had agreed to pay for wheat shipped to the grain elevator in 2009 was $2.90. The price per bushel at the time of the wheat harvest was $2.80. The closing price per bushel on December 31, 2009, was $3.07.

EXHIBIT 1

STERN CORPORATION
Balance Sheet
As of December 31, 2009

Assets

Current assets:

Cash		$ 671,344
Accounts receivable	$ 988,257	
Less: Allowance for doubtful accounts	29,648	958,609
U.S. Treasury securities at cost		274,060
Inventories		1,734,405
Total current assets		3,638,418

Other assets:

Investments		412,294
Land		186,563
Building	2,405,259	
Less: Accumulated depreciation	663,379	1,741,880
Factory machinery	3,425,585	
Less: Accumulated depreciation	1,642,358	1,783,227
Furniture and fixtures	56,484	
Less: Accumulated depreciation	40,400	16,084
Automotive equipment	58,298	
Less: Accumulated depreciation	37,156	21,142
Office machines	42,534	
Less: Accumulated depreciation	28,005	14,529
Tools		61,294
Patent		56,250
Prepaid expenses		100,190
Total assets		$ 8,031,871

Liabilities and Shareholders' Equity

Current liabilities:

Accounts payable	$ 510,000
Taxes payable	709,354
Accrued salaries, wages, and interest	141,478
Long-term debt, due within one year	69,300
Total current liabilities	1,430,132

Noncurrent liabilities:

Long-term debt	1,247,368

Shareholders' equity:

Common stock	2,503,275
Retained earnings	2,851,096
Total shareholders' equity	5,354,371
Total liabilities and shareholders' equity	$ 8,031,871

Accounts Receivable

At year-end, the proceeds from 20,000 bushels shipped to the grain elevator had not yet been received from the elevator operator. The average sales price of these 20,000 bushels of wheat had been $2.98 per bushel. There were no uncollected proceeds on December 31, 2009.

Cash

The farm had a checking account balance of $7,700 and a money market account balance of $23,200.

land

The original cost of the land was $375,000. It was appraised for estate tax purposes at $1,050 per acre.

Buildings and Machinery

Buildings and machinery with an original cost of $412,500 and accumulated depreciation of $300,000 are employed on the farm. The equipment was appraised at net book value.

Current Liabilities

The farm has notes payable and accounts payable totaling $33,000.

Owner's Equity

Common stock has a par value of $7,500 plus an additional paid-in capital of $450,000. There was no record of retained earnings. It was known that Jeremiah Grennell withdrew all of the farm's earnings in the last few years in order to continue the lifestyle to which he had become accustomed in Florida.

Looking over the data on revenues and expenses, Grey discovered that there were no monetary numbers for 2009's total revenues or ending inventory. The lawyer's letter explained that there was some doubt in his mind about when revenue for the farm should be recognized and about the appropriate way to value the grain inventory. The lawyer's understanding was that there are at least three alternative stages in the wheat growing cycle at which revenue could be counted in unaudited statements.

First, the *production method* could be used. Since wheat has a daily valuation on the Chicago Commodity Exchange, any unsold inventory as of December 31 could be valued at market price very objective-ly. In this way, revenue can be counted for all wheat produced in a given year, regardless of whether it is sold or not. A decision not to sell this wheat before December 31 is based on speculation about future wheat price increases.

Second, the *sales method* (also called the *delivery method*) could be used. This approach would recognize revenue when the grain is purchased and received from the farm by the grain elevator operator in the neighboring town. In this instance, the owner of the grain elevator had just sold control to a Kansas City company with limited experience in running such a facility. The manager of the Grennell Farm had expressed some concern about selling to an unknown operator.

Third, the *collection method* could be used. Under this approach, revenue is counted when the cash is actually received by the farm from the grain elevator operator. Full collection often took several months because a grain elevator operator might keep wheat for a considerable time in the hope that prices would rise so the elevator company could sell at a higher price than that paid the farmer.

Questions

1. Prepare the 2009 income statement and the related ending balance sheet for the Grennell Farm recognizing revenue by the
   a. Sales (delivery method).
   b. Collection method.
   c. Production method.
   (**Hint:** Under the collection method, accounts receivable are zero. Under the production method, ending inventory is zero. Under all three methods, assume beginning retained earnings are zero.)
2. Assume that the Grennell Farm had received a firm offer of $225,000 for 100 acres of the farm that would be used as the site of a new housing development. This development would have no effect on the use of the remaining acreage as a farm, and Ms. Grey planned to accept it. How would you account in the 2009 financial statements for the economic gain represented by this appreciation in land values?
3. Should Ms. Grey retain ownership of the farm?

Case 5–3
Joan Holtz (A)*

"Your course unfortunately doesn't give me the answer to a great many real-life problems," said Joan Holtz to an accounting professor. "I've read the text and listened to you attentively, but every once in a while I run across something that doesn't seem to fit the rules."

"Not all of life's complications can be covered in a first course," the professor replied. "As is the case with law, medicine, or indeed any of the professions, many matters are dealt with in advanced courses, and others are not settled in any classroom. Nevertheless, some problems that are not specifically discussed can be solved satisfactorily by relating them to principles that you already have learned. Let's take revenue recognition as a particularly difficult case in point. If you will write down some of the matters about which you are now uncomfortable, I'd be glad to discuss them with you—that is, after you have given some thought as to the most reasonable solution."

A week later, Holtz returned with the list given below.

1. **Electric utility bills.** When an electric utility customer uses electricity, the electric company has earned revenues. It is obviously impossible, however, for the company to read all of its customers' meters on the evening of December 31. How does the electric company know its revenue for a given year? Explain.

2. **Retainer fee.** A law firm received a "retainer" of $10,000 on July 1, 2010, from a client. In return, it agreed to furnish general legal advice upon request for one year. In addition, the client would be billed for regular legal services such as representation in litigation. There was no way of knowing how often, or when, the client would request advice, and it was quite possible that no such advice would be requested. How much of the $10,000 should be counted as revenue in 2010? Why?

3. **Cruise.** Raymond's, a travel agency, chartered a cruise ship for two weeks beginning January 23, 2011, for $200,000. In return, the ship's owner agreed to pay all costs of the cruise. In 2010, Raymond's sold all available space on the ship for $260,000. It incurred $40,000 in selling and other costs in doing so. All the $260,000 was received in cash from passengers in 2011. Raymond's paid $50,000 as an advance payment to the ship owner in 2011. How much, if any, of the $260,000 was revenue to Raymond's in 2010? Why? Does the question of whether passengers were entitled to a refund in 2011 if they canceled their reservations make any difference in the answer? Why?

4. **Accretion.** A nursery owner had one plot of land containing Christmas trees that were four years old on November 1, 2010. The owner had incurred costs of $3 per tree up to that time. A wholesaler offered to buy the trees for $4 each and to pay in addition all costs of cutting and bundling, and transporting them to market. The nursery owner declined this offer, deciding that it would be more profitable to let the trees grow for one more year. Only a trivial amount of additional cost would be involved. The price of Christmas trees varies with their height. Should the nursery owner recognize any revenue from these trees in 2010? Why?

5. **"Unbilled" receivables.** The balance sheet of an architectural firm shows a significant asset labeled Unbilled Receivables. The firm says this represents in-process projects, valued at the rates at which the customers will be charged for the architects' time. Why would a firm do this instead of valuing projects in process at their cost, the same as a manufacturing firm would value its in-process inventory? Does it make any difference in the reported owners' equity for the architectural firm to report such in-process work as receivables rather than as inventory? Why?

6. **Premium coupons.** A manufacturer of coffee enclosed a premium coupon with each $2.50 (at wholesale) jar of coffee that it sold to retailers. Customers could use this coupon to apply to $0.50 of the price of a new type of instant tea that the manufacturer was introducing and that sold for $2.00 wholesale. The manufacturer reimbursed retail stores $0.60 for each such coupon they submitted. (The extra $0.10 was to pay the grocer for coupon handling costs.) Past experience with similar premium offers indicated that approximately 20 percent of such coupons are eventually redeemed. At the end of 2010, however, only about 10 percent of the coupons issued in 2010 had been redeemed. In recording the revenues for the company for 2010, what allowance, if any, should be made for these coupons? Why?

* Copyright © Professor Robert N. Anthony.

If an allowance should be made, should it apply to the sales revenue of coffee or to the sales revenue of tea? Why?

7. **Traveler's checks.** A bank sells a customer $500 of American Express traveler's checks, for which the bank collects from the customer $505. (The bank charges a 1 percent fee for this service.) How does the bank record this transaction? How does the transaction affect American Express's balance sheet?

8. **Product repurchase agreement.** In December 2010, Manufacturer A sold merchandise to Wholesaler B. B used this inventory as collateral for a bank loan of $100,000 and sent the $100,000 to A. Manufacturer A agreed to repurchase the goods on or before July 1, 2010, for $112,000, the difference representing interest on the loan and compensation for B's services. Does Manufacturer A have revenue in 2010? Why?

9. **Franchises.** A national real estate brokerage firm has become highly successful by selling franchises to local real estate brokers. It charges $10,000 for the initial franchise fee and a service fee of 6 percent of the broker's revenue thereafter. For this it permits use of its well-known name and provides a one-week initial training course, a nationwide referral system, and various marketing and management aids. Currently, the franchise fee accounts for 25 percent of the national firm's receipts, but it expects that the United States market will be saturated within the next three years, and thereafter the firm will have to depend on the service fee and new sources of revenue that it may develop. Should it recognize the $10,000 as revenue in the year in which the franchise agreement is signed? Why? If it does, what will happen to its profits after the market has become saturated? Why?

10. **Computer systems.** In early 2010, the sales vice president of Tech-Logic reached agreement to deliver several computer systems with a total price of $570,000 to an organization in one of the newly independent countries established following the dissolution of the former Soviet Union. Tech-Logic management was very excited about this contract. The countries that were part of the former Soviet Union represented a major market that was just opening up for trade, and these countries especially needed the kinds of high-technology products that Tech-Logic sold. Tech-Logic manufactured and shipped the entire $570,000 order during 2010. Tech-Logic normally recognized revenue on the sale of its products when they were shipped. However, Tech-Logic's controller wondered whether the same revenue recognition policy should apply to this contract. First, contract law in these countries was evolving and it was hard to know if certain laws existed or what they were. In addition, the controller was uncertain when Tech-Logic would receive the $570,000 in cash. He had heard that in many of these countries it was difficult to obtain currencies needed for foreign exchange, although the customer kept assuring Tech-Logic that they would receive cash shortly. The controller pondered whether to recognize the entire $570,000 as revenue in 2010. If not, then when should this revenue be recognized? Why?

Question

Answer the questions raised by Holtz in each of the 10 issues on her list.

Case 5–4
Wareham SC Systems, Inc.*

Soma Desai, the chief financial officer of Wareham SC Systems, Inc., was reviewing the revenue recognition practices of the company's three divisions. Wareham SC Systems was a capital equipment and testing instrument manufacturer and supplier to a variety of highly cyclical electronics-based industries, includ-

* Copyright © 2003 President and Fellows of Harvard College. Harvard Business School case 110–015.

ing the semiconductor industry. Desai undertook the review in anticipation of disclosing in the company's third quarter 2000 Form 10-Q filing with the Securities and Exchange Commission (SEC) the possible impact on the company's financial statements of the revenue recognition and reporting guidelines set forth in the SEC's recently issued Staff Accounting Bulletin No 101, "Revenue Recognition in Financial Statements"

(SAB101). SAB 101 had to be adopted no later than the fourth quarter of 2000.

As a test of her own understanding of SAB 101, Desai selected from each of the company's three divisions a limited number of representative sale transactions to review.

Wareham SC Systems sales and net income for the last three year was (thousands).

	1999	1998	1997
Net Sales	$1,790,912	$1,489,151	$1,266,274
Net Income	$ 191,694	$ 102,117	$ 127,608

In addition to testing her understanding of SAB 101, Desai wondered what administrative actions she should take to prepare Wareham SC Systems for a successful adoption of SAB 101.

Revenue Recognition Policy

According to the company's 1999 annual report, its revenue recognition policy was as follows:

> Product revenue is recognized upon shipment. The Company's products are generally subject to warranty, and the Company provides for such estimated costs when product revenue is recognized. The Company recognizes service revenues as the services are provided or ratably over the period of the related contract, as applicable. The Company unbundles service revenue from product sales and installation services and maintenance services based upon amounts charged when such elements are separately sold. For certain contracts, revenue is recognized using the percentage-of-completion accounting method based upon an efforts-expended method.[1] In all cases, changes to total estimated costs and anticipated losses, if any, are recognized in the period in which determined.

SAB 101

Under US GAAP guidelines, the general rule governing revenue recognition is:

[1] The efforts-expended model recognizes revenue from long-term contracts as the work on the contract progresses. Typically, the revenue recognized to date is the percentage the costs to date bear to the contract's estimated total costs after giving effect to costs to complete based upon the most recent information.

- Revenue should be recognized when it is earned and realized or realizable.

Because the general rule had been abused by some companies, more specific criteria for revenue recognition were prescribed by the SEC in SAB 101. As a result, revenue was now considered to be earned and realized or realizablewhen the following conditionswere met:

- Persuasive evidence of an order arrangement exists;
- Delivery of the ordered goods has occurred or services have been rendered;
- The seller's price to the buyer is fixed or determinable; and,
- Collectibility of the sale proceeds is reasonably assured.

Glendale Division: Selected Transactions

Wareham SC System's Glendale Division was an equipment manufacturer whose main product was generally sold in a standard model. The contracts for sale of that model provided for customer acceptance to occur after the equipment was received and tested by the customer. The acceptance provisions stated that if the equipment did not perform to the division's published specifications, the customer could return the equipment for a full refund or a replacement unit, or could require the division to repair the equipment so that it performed by either a formal sign-off by the customer or by the passage of 90 days without a claim under the acceptance provisions. Title to the equipment passed upon delivery to the customer. The division did not perform any installation or other services on the equipment it sold. It tested each piece of equipment against the division's specifications before shipment. Payment was due under the division's normal payment terms, which was 30 days after customer acceptance.

In each of the following Glendale Division sales transactions reviewed by Desai, the above facts applied, in addition to those described in each of the Glendale Division sales transactions selected for review.

Onsetcom, Inc.

Onsetcom, Inc., a new Glendale Division customer, placed an order for a standard model of the division's main product. The sales contract included a customer-acceptance clause. It was based on the product meeting the division's published specifications for a standard model. Before shipping the equipment to Onsetcom, the division demonstrated that the equipment shipped met the required specifications. There was no reason to believe that the equipment would not operate in the same way in the customer's facility.

Cataumet Devices, Inc.

The Glendale Division entered into a sales arrangement with Cataumet Devices, Inc., a new customer, to deliver a version of its standard product modified as necessary to be integrated into the customer's new assembly line while still meeting all of the standard published vendor specifications with regard to performance. The customer could reject the equipment if it failed to meet the standard published performance specifications or could not be satisfactorily integrated into the new line. The division had never modified its equipment to work on an integrated basis in the type of assembly line the customer had proposed. In response to the request, the division designed a version of its standard equipment that was modified as believed necessary to operate in the new assembly line. The modified equipment still met all of the standard published performance specifications, and the division believed the equipment would meet the requested specifications when integrated into the new assembly line. However, the division was unable to replicate the new assembly line conditions in its testing.

Advanced Technology Division: Selected Transactions

Wareham SC System's Advanced Technology Division developed, manufactured, and sold complex manufacturing equipment. Desai selected two of the division's sales transactions involving a similar piece of equipment for review. (Although Advanced Technology sold its equipment separately to some customers without installation—meaning a general contractor would install the equipment—the sales transactions selected by Desai involved installation of the equipment by Advanced Technology employees.) The division sold its installation service on a time and materials basis. The uninstalled equipment sold for $19.5 million. In each of the installation contracts, the division's controller estimated that the fair value of the installation service approximated $500,000.

The division was experienced in the production and installation of the type of equipment involved in each of the two sales arrangements under review and had a history of successfully installing the type of equipment involved.

The division provided a warranty on all equipment sales that guaranteed that the delivered equipment would meet the division's published specifications and be free of defects in materials and workmanship. Title to the equipment passed to the customer upon delivery.

Sandham, Inc.

Sandham, Inc. ordered equipment that would be integrated into a larger production line that included other manufacturer's equipment. Advanced Technology had previously developed its own internal specifications for the model and demonstrated that the equipment met those specifications. At Sandham's request, the contract included a number of customer-specific technical and performance criteria regarding speed, quality, interaction with other equipment, and reliability. Because of the nature of the equipment, the division was unable to demonstrate that the equipment would meet the customer-specific specifications before installation. The contract included a customer-acceptance provision that obligated the division to demonstrate that the installed equipment met all specified criteria before customer acceptance. If customer acceptance was not achieved within 120 days of installation, Sandham could require the division to remove the equipment and refund all payments. Payment terms were 80% due 30 days after delivery, and 20% due 30 days after customer acceptance.

XL Semi, Inc.

The Advanced Technology Division also manufactured equipment to produce semiconductor wafers. The equipment was complex and sold for prices ranging from $500,000 to $10 million per unit. The equipment ordered by XL Semi sold for $9 million. The XL Semi order was typical. In the case of semiconductor equipment, the division published the performance specification (often stated in ranges) of its equipment based on results of prototype testing or, for established products, based on previously installed units. The equipment was extensively tested throughout the manufacturing process, which could range from 3 to 12 months, so the division was confident when the machine was shipped that it would ultimately perform in accordance with the customer's specifications.

Initial customer acceptance usually took place at the division's facility prior to shipment. Because of the size of the equipment, it was often partially disassem-bled for shipment and reassembled at the customer's site. The division, to minimize future warranty claims and due to the specialized nature of the equipment, used its own engineers to install and set up its products at the customer's facility; no other parties had installed the divisions equipment in the past. Frequently, although the divisions met its manufacturing and shipping deadlines, the customer would request that the division delay the final installation until a certain phase of the project was completed. The customer then tested and accepted the equipment. Payment of 90% of the total arrangement fee was due upon delivery and the remaining 10% was due upon final acceptance. The cost of the installation services was approximately 1% to 3% of the total arrangement fee.

Technical Devices Division:
Selected Transactions

Wareham SC System's Technical Devices Division developed, manufactured, and marketed a variety of electrical, electronic, and mechanical testing devices for use in production control, product testing, and research laboratory applications. The division used a combination of direct sales by its own sales force and independent distributors to market its products. Typically, the distributor network was used to sell products to low-volume customers, since most high-volume customers preferred to deal directly with the division.

Unlike Wareham SC System's other divisions, whose profitability rose and fell with changes in the business cycle, the Technical Devices Division under its current management had steadily increased its profits each quarter over a span of 37 consecutive quarters.

New Strategy

Only a few days before Desai was scheduled to begin her review of selected sales arrangements, the Technical Devices Division announced a change in its sales strategy. The direct marketing and shipment of the division's mechanical testing devices to high-volume customers would end.[2] In the future, all of this

business would be channeled through the division's independent distributors so that the division could free up resources to complete in the growing and increasingly more profitable and competitive electronic and electrical testing product markets. While it was not announced, Desai believed the change in sales strategy was motivated by a recognition by the division management that demand for mechanical testing devices was declining, uncertain, and increasingly less profitable.

She also suspected the division anticipated difficulties in reaching the quarter's profit goals.

As a result of the division's sales strategy shift, distributors were asked to increase their mechanical testing device inventory levels from their current several-weeks sales to as much as two-years sales. Moreover, these purchases had to be made, delivered, and have the title taken by September 30, the day the division closed its third quarter for financial reporting purposes. Distributors that did not comply were told they would lose their Technical Devices Division distributorships.

To help the dealers finance their larger inventories of mechanical testing devices, the division permitted distributors to make five small monthly payments following delivery with a final balloon payment of roughly 60% of the original amount owed six months after the initial deliveries. The monthly payment schedule was based on the distributor's expected sell-through of inventories. The normal payment terms extended to distributors was 1% upon delivery net 20 days.

While the division had not contractually agreed to take back any excess dealer inventories of mechanical testing devices, the division's past generous practices of allowing dealer returns of excess inventories led nearly all of the dealers to believe there was little risk to them in the new sales strategy. All but one of its company's distributors accepted the division's ultimation and payment schedule.

In 1998 the division had recorded a $23 million excess inventory charge, primarily for its excess mechanical testing instrument inventory.

Ashaban Industries, Ltd.

Just as the third quarter of 2000was to close, the Technical Devices Division delivered, and the Ashaban Industries, Ltd., the customer, accepted a $2million order for mechanical testing equipment. Ashaban Industries intended to use local contractors to install the equipment.

---

[2] High volume customers bought all of the division's products, including mechanical testing devices. Prior to the strategy change, distributor's were limited to selling to low-volume customers.

Ashaban Industries was a newly formed private company located in one of the former Soviet Republics established during the early 1990's as independent countries following the dissolution of the Soviet Union.

Ashaban Industries was a new customer. Is was also the division's first customer among the now independent former Soviet Union Republics, which was a market that some of the division's top management had long hoped to penetrate.

From the beginning of the negotiations preceding the signing of the Ashaban Industries firm purchase order, some of the division's top management had concerns about Ashaban Industries' ability to pay for the order and the division's ability to collect in the event of nonpayment. They noted that Ashaban and the division had been unable to secure bank, local government or international development agency payment guarantees. The concerned senior management also noted that contract law in Ashaban Industries' home country was evolving and it was hard to know what they were or how they might be interpreted. Later, just before the equipment was shipped, these same concerned managers noted that there was increasing unrest in the country and local importers seemed to be having difficulty obtaining foreign currency to pay for their foreign currency denominated imports. Despite these misgivings, based on Ashaban Industries assurances that Wareham SC Systems would be paid, the division accepted the purchase order and shipped the equipment.

Questions

1. What pre SAB 101 revenue recognition policies has Wareham SC Systems adopted? Which of these policies are most likely to be impacted by SAB 101?
2. Why might Soma Desai be concerned about the impact of SAB 101 on Wareham SC System's revenue recognition practice? Be as specific as possible.
3. What revenue recognition accounting is required by the facts of each of the sale transactions reviewed by Soma Desai? Justify your conclusions.
4. International Accounting Standards No. 18 states revenue from the sale of goods shall be recognized when all the following conditions have been satisfied:
   a. the entity has transferred to the buyer the significant risks and rewards of ownership of the goods;
   b. the entity retains neither continuing managerial involvement to the degree usually associated with ownership nor effective control over the goods sold;
   c. the amount of revenue can be measured reliably;
   d. it is probably that the economic benefits associated with the transaction will flow to the entity; and
   e. the costs incurred or to be incurred in respect of the transaction can be measured reliably.
   Would your answer to Question 3 change if you applied IAS No. 18 rather than SAB 101? Explain.
5. What administrative actions should Soma Desai take to prepare Wareham SC Systems for the adoption of SAB 101? Be specific.

Case 5–5
Cross-Selling: An Accounting Nightmare

Managers across functional areas have always appreciated the fact that the top line of any firm is driven by Revenue and therefore "marketing function" happens to be the key manifestation of any organizational growth strategy. Accounting has always acted as a "support function"; it never drives the strategy. All this while, accounting was silently recording the transactions and trying to make a sense of its impact on the bottom line. With growing competition and very demanding customers, companies are going all out to woo the customer. And the drive to "sell" at any cost is giving some sleepless nights to accountants when it comes to recording a transaction related to a

weird marketing offer. For example, a customer buys pizzas from Dominos using Paytm and gets an offer (redeemable voucher up to INR 100 or a discount of 10%) from both Dominos and Paytm which can be redeemed on a CCD Coffee or an Amazon purchase of minimum INR 500. On the face of it, looks like a perfect marketing offer with a very high chance of success and adoption rates. But, do have a heart for the poor accountant in either of the firms (Dominos and Paytm).

It is worth appreciating here that both the offers will definitely have a validity period and there is a very high probability that many original buyers from

Dominos will forget about the offer and may not actually use it but it is also true that before the expiry date, a customer may actually use it. All these possibilities throw an accounting challenge as the original firms can't record the revenue in full as they will have to adjust for the "possible redemption of vouchers or discounts."

Then there is this, almost ubiquitous, very attractive (from a marketing perspective) "free look period" or "no questions asked return policy" which gives the customers the option to have a close look at the product and can return, if not satisfied. How does an accountant treat this "free look period"? What if this offer is only on a selected product range or it is only in few limited geographies? All this makes the life of accountants a bit more challenging although, on the face of it, they look like a perfect "marketing recipe."

Questions

1. Do the "marketing" or "business development" team needs to take care of accounting challenges while proposing a "brilliant marketing offer."?
2. Suggest an accounting entry for Dominos example.
3. Suggest an accounting entry for the "Free Look" policy.

Cost of Sales and Inventories

CHAPTER
6

This chapter describes principles and procedures for measuring cost of sales as reported on the income statement and for the related measurement of inventory on the balance sheet.

We begin with a brief overview of accounting for inventory and cost of sales in three types of companies: merchandising, manufacturing, and service. Next, we describe in detail the procedures in merchandising companies. The procedures in manufacturing companies start with the same steps used in merchandising companies and incorporate additional aspects associated with the manufacturing process. We therefore limit the discussion of manufacturing companies to these additional matters. Service companies also are discussed.

Inventory costs may be accounted for by either the periodic inventory method or the perpetual inventory method; each method is described. The cost of individual units of inventory and of individual goods sold can be measured by any of several methods approved for use in the United States. These include specific identification; average cost; first-in, first-out (FIFO); and last-in, first-out (LIFO). All of these methods are described and compared in the chapter. With the exception of LIFO, all of these methods are also accepted by the International Accounting Standards Board. Inventory turnover, days' inventory, and gross margin percentage—three ratios used in inventory accounting—also are discussed.

Types of Companies

A single company may conduct merchandising, service, and/or manufacturing activities. For convenience, we shall assume that each company described here conducts only one type. If a company does conduct more than one type of activity, it will use the accounting method appropriate for each type.

Retail stores, wholesalers, distributors, and similar companies that sell tangible goods are merchandising companies.[1] A **merchandising company** sells goods in substantially

---

[1] The word *products* is often used when *goods* is intended. For clarity, throughout this book, we use *goods* for tangible items, *services* for intangibles, and *products* for the sum of goods and services. In other words, the outputs of an entity, whether tangible or intangible, are its products.

the same physical form as that in which it acquires them. Its cost of sales is therefore the acquisition cost of the goods that are sold.[2] On the balance sheet, a current asset, Merchandise Inventory, shows the cost of goods that have been acquired but not yet sold as of the balance sheet date.

A **manufacturing company** converts raw materials and purchased parts into finished goods. Its cost of sales includes the conversion costs as well as the raw material and parts costs of the goods that it sells. A manufacturing company has three types of inventory accounts: Materials, Work in Process, and Finished Goods.

Because both merchandising and manufacturing companies sell tangible goods, their income statements sometimes use the term **cost of goods sold** rather than *cost of sales*. We shall use the two terms interchangeably for merchandising and manufacturing companies, but use only *cost of sales* for service organizations.

Service organizations furnish intangible services rather than tangible goods. They include hotels, beauty parlors and other personal services organizations, hospitals and other health care organizations, educational organizations, banks and other financial institutions, and governmental units. Service organizations may have materials inventories—for example, the pipes and fittings of a plumbing company. Professional service firms, such as law, consulting, accounting, and architectural firms, may have intangible inventories consisting of costs that have been incurred on behalf of clients but that have not yet been billed to clients. These inventories, often called **jobs in progress** or **unbilled costs,** correspond to work in process inventories in a manufacturing company. Service organizations do not have finished goods inventories.

Supplies

In addition to inventory accounts for goods directly involved in the merchandising or manufacturing process, a company may have one or more inventory accounts for supplies. **Supplies** are tangible items that will be consumed in the course of normal operations. Examples include office and janitorial supplies, and lubricants and repair parts for equipment. Supplies are distinguished from merchandise in that they are not sold as such, and they are distinguished from materials in that supplies are not accounted for as an element of the cost of goods manufactured. Paper offered for sale is merchandise inventory in a stationery store; paper is materials inventory in a company that manufactures books; and paper intended for use in the office is supplies inventory in any organization. Supplies will not be discussed further in this chapter.

Merchandising Companies

We shall now describe in detail the principles and procedures related to accounting for inventories and cost of goods sold in merchandising companies.

Acquisition Cost

Merchandise is added to inventory at its cost, in accordance with the basic cost concept. Cost includes both the cost of acquiring the merchandise and also any expenditures made to make the goods ready for sale. Thus, merchandise cost includes not only the invoice cost of the goods purchased but also freight and other shipping costs of bringing the goods to the point of sale and the cost of unpacking the goods and marking prices on them. Since the recordkeeping task of attaching these latter elements of

---

[2] The U.S. tax code requires that the following costs also be included in the cost of inventory: (1) off-site storage and warehousing; (2) purchasing; (3) handling, processing, assembling, and repackaging; and (4) certain general and administrative expenses. Some companies add these costs to the inventory cost for financial reporting purposes. This practice is not a requirement of the tax code or generally accepted accounting principles.

ILLUSTRATION 6–1
Merchandise Inventory and Flows

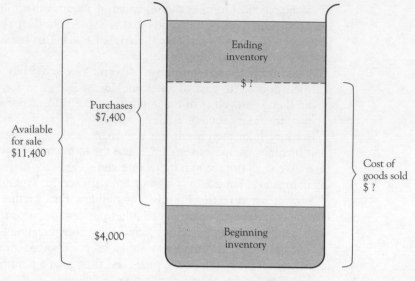

Inventory reservoir

cost to individual units of merchandise may be considerable, some or all of them may be excluded from merchandise product costs and reported as general operating expenses of the period in which they are incurred.

The purchase cost also is adjusted for returns and allowances and for cash discounts given by the suppliers of the merchandise. As was the case with sales discounts (see Chapter 5), purchase discounts can be accounted for either by recording the purchase amount as net of the discount or by recording the purchase amount at the invoice price and recording the discount when it is taken.

In accounting, the word *purchase* refers not to the placing of a purchase order but rather to the *receipt* of the merchandise that was ordered. No accounting entry is made when merchandise is ordered. The entry is made only when the merchandise becomes the property of the buyer.[3]

The Basic Measurement Problem

Think of merchandise inventory as a tank or a reservoir, as in Illustration 6–1. At the beginning of an accounting period there is a certain amount of goods in the reservoir; this is the beginning inventory. During the period, additional merchandise is purchased and added to the reservoir. Also during the period, merchandise sold is withdrawn from the reservoir. At the end of the accounting period, the amount of goods remaining in the reservoir is the ending inventory.

The amount of **goods available for sale** during the period is the sum of the beginning inventory plus the purchases during the period. This sum is $11,400 in Illustration 6–1. The problem to be discussed in this section, and indeed in most of the chapter, is how to divide the amount of goods available for sale between (1) the ending inventory and (2) cost of goods sold. How much of the $11,400 is still on hand at the end of the period, and how much was sold during the period? This is a significant problem because its resolution affects both the amount of inventory reported on the balance sheet and (perhaps more important) the amount of profit reported on the income statement for the period.

---

[3] Under commercial law, goods in transit usually belong to the buyer as soon as they are delivered to the transportation company if the terms are "FOB shipping point" (if the buyer pays the transportation costs). If the seller pays the transportation costs ("FOB destination"), title does not pass until the goods arrive at the buyer's warehouse.

There are two approaches to this problem:

1. We can determine the amount of ending inventory (i.e., the amount in the reservoir at the end of the period) and *deduce cost of goods sold* by subtracting the ending inventory from the goods available for sale. This is the periodic inventory method.
2. We can measure the amount actually delivered to customers and *deduce the ending inventory* by subtracting cost of goods sold from the goods available for sale. This is the perpetual inventory method.

Periodic Inventory Method

In the **periodic inventory method,** a physical count is made of merchandise in the ending inventory, and the cost of this inventory is determined. This process is called *taking a physical inventory.* Assume that the physical inventory shows the cost of the merchandise remaining at the end of the period to be $2,000. Cost of goods sold is deduced by subtracting the ending inventory from the amount of goods available for sale; thus:

Beginning inventory	$4,000
Plus: Purchases	7,400
Equals: Goods available for sale	11,400
Less: Ending inventory	2,000
Cost of goods sold	$ 9,400

The amount of beginning inventory in the above calculation is the amount found by the physical inventory taken at the end of the *preceding* period. (Recall that in accounting the end of one period and the beginning of the next period are the same instant in time, even though the dates say, June 30 and July 1 may make them appear to be different.)

Most companies do not show such a calculation in the cost of goods sold section of the published income statement itself. In contrast, in internal reports to management (as opposed to reports for shareholders), the calculation with additional detail is often presented. For example, if there are freight charges and the return of purchased merchandise, the internal income statement might show

Beginning inventory		$4,000
Plus: Purchases, gross	$7,000	
Freight-in	600	
	7,600	
Less: Purchase returns	200	
Net purchases		7,400
Goods available for sale		11,400
Less: Ending inventory		2,000
Cost of goods sold		$ 9,400

Accounts

When the cost of goods sold is deduced by the method described above, a separate account is established for each element in the calculation. Thus, a **Purchases** account is established and the invoice cost of merchandise received is debited to this account rather than directly to Merchandise Inventory. Accounts also are established for Freight-In, Purchase Returns, and any other items involved in the calculation.

Rules for debiting and crediting these accounts can be deduced from their relationship to other accounts. Since Purchases shows *additions* to the asset account Merchandise Inventory, it increases on the *debit* side. Purchase Returns is a *reduction* in Purchases and hence must have the opposite rule; return of goods to suppliers are thus recorded as *credits* to the Purchase Returns account. The Freight-In account *adds* to the cost of purchases and therefore increases on the *debit* side. The rules also can be deduced by thinking of the offsetting part of the transaction. Whenever possible, it is simplest to assume that the other account is Cash. Thus, a cash purchase involves a decrease in Cash, which is a credit; therefore, the entry to Purchases must be a debit.

As of the end of the period, these accounts are closed to Cost of Goods Sold. First, the balance in the Merchandise Inventory account is closed. (Recall that no entries were made to this account during the period, so the amount in the account is the *beginning* balance.) The entry is

Cost of Goods Sold	4,000	
Merchandise Inventory		4,000

Next, the temporary Purchases, Purchase Returns, and Freight-In accounts are closed to Cost of Goods Sold by entries that can be summarized as follows:

Cost of Goods Sold	7,400	
Purchase Returns	200	
Purchases		7,000
Freight-In		600

The new balance (from the physical inventory) is entered in Merchandise Inventory:

Merchandise Inventory	2,000	
Cost of Goods Sold		2,000

Finally, Cost of Goods Sold is closed:

Income Summary	9,400	
Cost of Goods Sold		9,400

Periodic Inventory Method

In the **perpetual inventory method,** a record is maintained of each item carried in the inventory. In a manual system, this record is a card similar to the sample shown in Illustration 6–2. In essence, this record is a subsidiary ledger account, and Merchandise Inventory is its control account. Purchases are entered directly on this record and also debited to Merchandise Inventory; the offsetting credit is to Accounts Payable or Cash. Deliveries of goods to customers are entered on this record and are credited to Merchandise

ILLUSTRATION 6–2
Perpetual Inventory Card

	Item: Cassette Deck, Model S150								
Date	Receipts			Shipments			Balance		
	Units	Unit Cost	Total	Units	Unit Cost	Total	Units	Unit Cost	Total
Jan. 2							40	100	4,000
12				32	100	3,200	8	100	800
14	70	100	7,000				78	100	7,800
25				56	100	5,600	22	100	2,200
27				2	100	200 *	20	100	2,000

*This entry is a purchase return to the manufacturer.

Inventory; the offsetting debit is to Cost of Goods Sold. The balance of the inventory record at the end of the period is the amount of that particular item in the ending inventory. The sum of the balances for all the items is the ending inventory for the entity.

Assuming for simplicity that a company had only the one item shown in Illustration 6–2, the journal entries for the transactions listed there would be
For purchases:

(1)

Merchandise Inventory	7,000	
Accounts Payable		7,000

For shipments to customers:

(2)

Cost of Goods Sold	8,800	
Merchandise Inventory		8,800

For purchase returns:

(3)

Accounts Payable	200	
Merchandise Inventory		200

In many perpetual inventory systems, freight-in is not entered on the perpetual inventory cards. Instead, it is accumulated in a separate account. Assuming the same $600 freight-in as in the previous example, the closing entry for this account would be

(4)

Cost of Goods Sold	600	
Freight-In		600

Cost of Goods Sold is closed to Income Summary, as in the periodic inventory method; that is:

(5)

Income Summary	9,400	
Cost of Goods Sold		9,400

These entries would be posted to ledger accounts as shown below:

Merchandise Inventory					Cost of Goods Sold			
Balance	4,000	(2) Shipments	8,800	→	8,800	(5) To Income Summary		9,400
(1) Purchases	7,000	(3) Returns	200	(4) Freight-In	600			
		To balance	2,000					
	11,000		11,000		9,400			9,400
Balance	2,000							

In the perpetual inventory method, no separate Purchases account is needed; purchases are debited directly to Merchandise Inventory.

Comparison of Periodic and Perpetual Methods

Both inventory methods match the cost of goods sold with the sales revenue for those same goods. Thus, either method is in accord with the matching concept. Without this matching, the gross margin amount for a period would not be meaningful.

The perpetual inventory method requires that a record be maintained for each item carried in inventory and therefore requires additional recordkeeping. This recordkeeping is not likely to be burdensome for a store offering at most a few hundred, relatively high-cost, items, such as a jewelry or an appliance store. Such recordkeeping may not be worthwhile in stores that stock many low-cost items, such as grocery stores and drugstores. (A large supermarket may stock 10,000 or more different items.) However, the development of electronic point-of-sale terminals, which have scanners that identify each item sold by reading a bar code on the item's package, has led many such stores to change to the perpetual inventory method.

The perpetual inventory method has three important advantages. First, the detailed record maintained for each item is useful in deciding when and how much to reorder and in analyzing customer demand for the item. In many stores using point-of-sale terminals with scanners, sales data are used as input to computer models that automatically prepare orders in a central warehouse to replenish the store's inventory and in some cases automatically to place orders with suppliers. This helps avoid both stock-outs and excess inventories of the various items carried by the store.

Second, the perpetual inventory record has a built-in check that is not possible with the periodic method. In the latter, the physical inventory at the end of the period is a necessary part of the calculation of cost of goods sold. The difference between the goods available for sale and the goods on hand is *assumed* to be the cost of goods sold. This assumption is not necessarily correct because some of the goods may have been pilfered, lost, thrown away, or overlooked when the physical inventory was taken. Goods that are not in inventory but were not sold make up the period's **inventory shrinkage.** In the perpetual inventory system, an actual count of the goods on hand can be used as a check on the accuracy of the inventory records. Shrinkage thus can be identified separately rather than buried in cost of goods sold.

Third, with a perpetual inventory system, an income statement can be prepared without taking a physical inventory. Thus, an income statement can be prepared every month, with the accuracy of the underlying perpetual inventory records being checked by an annual or semiannual physical inventory.

Retail Method

A store that does not maintain perpetual inventory records can nevertheless prepare reasonably accurate monthly income statements without taking a physical inventory by using the **retail method.** In this method, purchases are recorded at both their cost and their retail selling price. The gross margin percentage of the goods available for sale is calculated from these records. The *complement* of this percentage is applied to sales for the month (obtained from sales register records) to find the approximate cost of goods sold.

Example

Assume the following:

	At Cost	At Retail
Beginning inventory	$ 4,000	$ 6,000
Purchases	7,000	10,000
Goods available for sale	$11,000	$16,000

The gross margin percentage is ($16,000 − $11,000) ÷ $16,000 = 31 percent. The complement of this is 100 percent − 31 percent = 69 percent. If sales for the month were $13,000, it is assumed that cost of goods sold was 69 percent of this amount, or $8,970. In applying the retail method in practice, adjustments must be made for markdowns that are made from initial retail prices (e.g., in clearance sales).

A variation of this method, the **gross profit method,** simply applies a "normal" gross margin percentage to the amount of sales in order to arrive at an approximation of cost of goods sold. Records are not kept of the retail value of goods available for sale. With this method, a "normal" margin is determined for each department in the store, and the salesperson or checkout clerk records the department number of each item the customer purchases. A department's sales for the month are multiplied by the complement of the department's gross margin percentage to approximate the department's cost of goods sold. Some retailers that do not have a computer use these methods to approximate the cost of goods sold without taking a physical inventory.

The retail and gross profit methods are not methods in addition to the periodic and perpetual methods. Rather, they can be viewed as variations of the perpetual method in that cost of goods sold is determined without taking a physical inventory.

Manufacturing Companies

A manufacturing company has as a major function the conversion of raw materials and purchased parts into finished goods. In any company, cost of sales is the total of the acquisition cost plus conversion costs (if any) of the products that are sold.[4] The difference between accounting for the cost of sales in a merchandising company and in a manufacturing company arises because the merchandising company usually has no conversion costs.

The measurement of cost of goods sold is therefore more complicated in a manufacturing company than in a merchandising company. In a manufacturing company, this cost must be obtained by collecting and aggregating the several elements of manufacturing cost.

Inventory Accounts

A manufacturing company has three types of inventory accounts. Their names and the nature of their content are as follows:

1. **Materials Inventory:** Items of material that are to become a part of the ultimately salable goods that result from the manufacturing process. They are costed at acquisition cost, with the same types of adjustments for freight-in and returns as those made in calculating the net purchase cost of merchandise inventory, described above.
2. **Work in Process Inventory:** Goods that have started through the manufacturing process but have not yet been finished. They are costed as the sum of (1) the materials thus far issued for them plus (2) the conversion costs incurred on these items up to the end of the accounting period.
3. **Finished Goods Inventory:** Goods that have been manufactured but have not yet been shipped to customers. They are costed at the total cost incurred in manufacturing them. This account is essentially the same as Merchandise Inventory in a merchandising company, except that the items are recorded at the cost of manufacturing them rather than at their acquisition cost.

There are wide variations in the relative size of the three types of inventories among companies. Those companies with a short production cycle may have so little work in process at the end of the accounting period that they do not have a separate Work in

---

[4] Conversion costs include the cost of labor involved in the manufacture of the goods and other production costs. Other production costs might include depreciation of manufacturing plant and equipment, the cost of manufacturing-related utilities, factory supplies, indirect factory labor, and other production overhead costs, such as factory management and administration costs.

**ILLUSTRATION
6–3**
**Manufacturing
Inventories and
Flows**

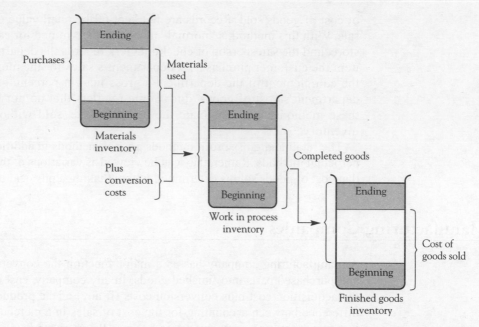

Process Inventory account. At the end of the period, they charge all manufacturing costs to Finished Goods Inventory (or to Cost of Goods Sold if there is no Finished Goods Inventory account). This process is called **back flushing.** Companies that produce items to customer order and ship to the customer as soon as the order is completed have little or no finished goods inventory.

A diagram of these accounts and the flow of costs from one to another is shown in Illustration 6–3. Using the periodic inventory method, we shall trace the flow of costs through these accounts. Each step is described by giving the relevant journal entries. The effect on ledger accounts is shown in Illustration 6–4.

In the merchandising company, we established a separate account to show the calculation of cost of goods sold. We could use similar accounts in a manufacturing company to show separately the calculation of materials used, cost of goods manufactured, and cost of goods sold. In the following description, however, we have not used these accounts. Instead, we arrive at the amounts by calculations made outside the accounts. There is no substantive difference between the two methods.

Materials Used

During an accounting period, various items of material are issued from a storage area to the production facilities for conversion into goods. The term **materials used** means the sum of all materials issued during the period. Such materials range in their degree of refinement from truly raw materials, such as crude oil or iron ore, to sophisticated components, such as motors or miniature circuit chips. Traditionally, all such purchased items were referred to as raw materials. However, there is nothing very "raw" about a motor or circuit chip. We shall use the term **materials inventory** to include the entire range of purchased items that are intended to become a part of salable goods during the production process.

In determining the cost of materials used, the periodic method may be used. That is, the assumption is made that the amount of materials used is the difference between the materials available for use during the period (which is the total of the beginning inventory and the period's net purchases) and the ending inventory. This assumption does not take into account anywaste or spoilage of materials that might have occurred. In practice, waste and

ILLUSTRATION 6–4
Flow of Costs through Inventories (000 omitted)

Materials Inventory			
Balance, Jan. 1	154	264	
① Purchases	273		Materials used: 154 + 273 − 163 = 264
Balance, Jan. 31	163	②	

Work in Process Inventory			
Balance, Jan. 1	19	570	
Materials used	264		Cost of goods manufactured: 19 + 264 + 330 − 43 = 570
③ Conversion costs	330		
Balance, Jan. 31	43	④	

Finished Goods Inventory			
Balance, Jan. 1	69	573	
Goods manufactured	570		Cost of goods sold: 69 + 570 − 66 = 573
Balance, Jan. 31	66	⑤	

Cost of Goods Sold		
573	573	⟶ Income Summary ⑥

Note: Circled numbers correspond to journal entries explained in the text.

spoilage are either disregarded or collected separately and removed from material costs by crediting Materials Inventory and debiting a separate manufacturing cost account.

We shall make this calculation in the Materials Inventory account. First, the amount of purchases made during the period, which includes $266,000 as the invoice cost of materials received plus $7,000 of freight charges on these materials, is added to Materials Inventory. These amounts would have first been debited to the temporary accounts, Purchases and Freight-In, and would have been credited to Accounts Payable. The $273,000 cost is then transferred to Materials Inventory by closing the two temporary accounts with this entry:

(1)

Materials Inventory	273,000	
Purchases		266,000
Freight-In		7,000

A physical inventory shows the amount of materials on hand as of the end of the period to be $163,000. Since $154,000 was on hand at the beginning of the period and $273,000 was added by the above entry, the total amount available was $427,000. By subtracting $163,000 from $427,000, we determine the amount of materials used: $264,000. It is subtracted from Materials Inventory and added to Work in Process Inventory by the following entry:

(2)

Work in Process Inventory	264,000	
Materials Inventory		264,000

Cost of Goods Manufactured

The sum of materials used and conversion costs is the total amount of cost added to Work in Process Inventory during the period. Given the amount in Work in Process Inventory at the beginning of the period and the amount remaining at the end of the period, the **cost of goods manufactured** (the goods completed and transferred to Finished Goods Inventory) can be deduced.

The cost of materials used was added by the preceding entry. Conversion costs incurred during the period are accumulated in various temporary accounts. For example, if employees directly involved in the conversion process earned $151,000 during the period, this amount would have been debited to a temporary Direct Labor account and credited to Wages Payable. The costs of direct labor and other resources used in the conversion process are added to Work in Process Inventory by closing the temporary accounts, as in the following entry:

(3)

Work in Process Inventory	330,000	
Direct Labor		151,000
Indirect Labor		24,000
Factory Heat, Light, and Power		90,000
Factory Supplies Used		22,000
Factory Insurance and Taxes		8,000
Depreciation, Plant and Equipment		35,000

A physical inventory shows the amount of work in process at the end of the period to be $43,000. Since $19,000 was on hand at the beginning of the period and $264,000 of materials and $330,000 of other manufacturing costs were added by entries 2 and 3, the total amount available was $613,000. By subtracting $43,000 from $613,000, we determine the cost of goods manufactured during the period to be $570,000. This figure is subtracted from Work in Process Inventory and added to Finished Goods Inventory by the following entry:

(4)

Finished Goods Inventory	570,000	
Work in Process Inventory		570,000

Cost of Goods Sold

Having determined the cost of goods manufactured, the cost of goods sold is found by (1) adding the cost of goods manufactured to the beginning finished goods inventory so as to find the total amount available for sale and then (2) subtracting the ending finished goods inventory. As with the periodic method in a merchandising company, the assumption is that if the merchandise is not in inventory, it has been sold.

A physical inventory shows the amount of finished goods at the end of the period to be $66,000. Since $69,000 was on hand at the beginning of the period and $570,000 of manufactured goods were completed during the period and added to finished goods inventory, the total amount available was $639,000. Subtracting $66,000 from $639,000 yields the cost of goods sold: $573,000. It is subtracted from Finished Goods Inventory and recorded as Cost of Goods Sold by the following entry:

(5)

Cost of Goods Sold	573,000	
Finished Goods Inventory		573,000

The balance in the Cost of Goods Sold account is then closed to Income Summary by the following entry:

(6)

Income Summary	573,000	
Cost of Goods Sold		573,000

Product Costing Systems

The foregoing entries assumed the use of the periodic inventory method. The same transactions could be accounted for using the perpetual inventory method. In a manufacturing company, the perpetual inventory method is called a **product costing system.** In such a system, the cost of each product is accumulated as it flows through the production process. The amounts involved in the journal entries are obtained directly from the cost records rather than deduced in the manner described above.

Product Costs and Period Costs

In the accounting process described above, items of cost included in the cost of producing goods are called **product costs.** Because these product costs "flow through" inventory accounts (see Illustration 6–3), they also are referred to as **inventory costs** or **inventoriable costs.** To arrive at gross margin, product costs are matched with, and subtracted from, the sales revenues in the period in which the goods are sold. Other items of cost that are matched with revenue in a given accounting period are called **period costs.** They are reported on the income statement of the period under a caption such as "selling, general, and administrative expense."

In accordance with generally accepted accounting principles, the cost of each product includes (1) materials cost; (2) costs incurred *directly* in bringing the product to its existing condition and location, such as direct labor costs; and (3) a fair share of the costs incurred *indirectly* in bringing the product to its existing condition and location, such as factory management costs.[5] These indirect costs are called **indirect production costs** or **production overhead.** Collectively, the materials, labor, and production overhead costs comprise the **full production cost** of a product.

Companies differ in their opinions on whether specific items should be treated as product costs or period costs. Some companies include the cost of such support functions as production administration, human resource management, industrial engineering, plant protection, and product cost accounting as production overhead and hence as product costs. Other companies include the cost of some or all of these functions as period costs.[6]

The way in which a manufacturing company classifies its costs into period costs and product costs can have an important effect on its reported net income. Period costs are expenses in the accounting period in which they are incurred, whereas product costs initially add to the total amount of the entity's assets. *Product costs do not have an impact on income until the product has been sold,* which may be in a later accounting period than the period in which the costs were incurred. The larger the inventory in relation to sales, the longer the time interval that elapses between the incurrence of a product cost and its impact on income.[7]

[5] *Accounting Research Bulletin No. 43,* Chapter 4, Statement 3.
[6] Some manufacturing companies follow the tax code rules for costing inventory; others do not. (See footnote 2.)
[7] *FASB Statement No. 34* requires that interest costs related to items produced as "discrete projects" (such as ships) be treated as product costs. (The accounting procedures for this are the same as for capitalized interest on assets produced for an enterprise's own use, described in Chapter 7.) "However, interest cost shall not be capitalized for inventories that are routinely manufactured or otherwise produced in large quantities on a repetitive basis" (*FASB Statement No. 34*).

Service Companies

In principle, product costing in service firms is the same as in manufacturing firms. Application of these principles is described below for three types of service organizations.

Personal services organizations such as barber shops, beauty parlors, and medical and dental practices have no inventories other than supplies inventory. Although these organizations may estimate the average cost of a haircut, a wash and set, or a routine office visit to aid them in pricing these services, these costs do not flow through inventory accounts as do product costs in a merchandising or manufacturing firm. A personal services organization may identify the labor costs of the people directly providing the service (e.g., a dental hygienist) and supplies costs (X-ray film) as elements of cost of sales, to distinguish them from "office overhead" costs (receptionist, rent, utilities, and so on).

Another category of service organization includes **building trade firms** (e.g., plumbing and electrical firms) and **repair businesses** that repair or maintain such items as appliances and automobiles. The inventories of repair parts and building materials carried by these firms are analogous to materials inventories in a manufacturing firm. Thus, the accounting for these inventories is conceptually the same as materials inventory accounting in a manufacturing firm. When materials are issued, they are recorded on some sort of cost sheet for the job. The labor costs of tradespersons or repair persons also are recorded on this sheet, which in effect is a subsidiary work in process inventory record for the job.

The third type of service company, **professional service firms** such as law and accounting firms, has labor product costs but no materials costs. The accounting procedures are similar to those for building trade and repair businesses. Each project that the firm works on is given a job number and a subsidiary account is set up for the job. Time spent by professionals on a job, and any related travel costs and long-distance telephone charges, are charged to that job's account. Collectively, these job costs constitute the firm's work in process inventory, which is the only inventory (other than supplies) that such firms have. When a point is reached in the project where the agreement with the client permits these job costs to be billed, a *markup* is added for office over-head and profit, and the client is billed. The related accounting entries record the revenues—usually called **billings**— and transfer the costs from the Jobs in Progress account to expense, as in this example:

Accounts Receivable	10,000	
Billings (or Revenues)		10,000
Project Expenses	4,000	
Jobs in Progress		4,000

Inventory Costing Methods

One important topic remains to be discussed: the measurement of inventory and cost of goods sold when the per-unit cost of one or more items in inventory changes during the accounting period. The basic problem is that shown in Illustration 6–1: How should the cost of goods available for sale be divided between (1) cost of goods sold and (2) ending inventory? Note that the goods available for sale are assumed to be either sold or still on hand in inventory. It follows that the higher the amount assigned to cost of goods sold, the lower the amount of ending inventory, and vice versa. Several acceptable methods of handling this problem exist and the choice of method can have a significant effect on reported income. We shall discuss four widely used methods:[8]

1. Specific identification.
2. Average cost.
3. First-in, first-out (FIFO).
4. Last-in, first-out (LIFO).

We shall illustrate these methods with an example from a merchandising company, but the same principles apply to a manufacturing company. In our illustration, we assume the following for a year:

	Units	Unit Cost	Total Cost
Inventory, January 1	100	$ 8	$ 800
Purchased June 1	60	9	540
Purchased October 1	80	10	800
Goods available for sale	240	$8.917	$2,140
Goods sold during the year	150	?	?
Ending inventory	90	?	?

Specific Identification Method

When there is a means of keeping track of the purchase cost of each item, such as with a code affixed to the item, it is possible to ascertain the actual cost of each item sold. This **specific identification method** is common practice with certain big-ticket items such as automobiles and with unique items such as paintings, expensive jewelry, and custom-made furniture; and bar codes and scanners are making it feasible with lower-cost items. In many cases, however, when a substantial number of physically similar items are sold, this method can be unsatisfactory because the cost of goods sold depends on what specific items happen to be sold. Indeed, a merchant can deliberately manipulate the cost of goods sold by selecting items that have a relatively high cost or a relatively low cost.

Example

In the illustration above, 150 units were sold. If the merchant selected the 100 units with a unit cost of $8 and 50 of the units having a unit cost of $9, the cost of goods sold would be (100 * $8) + (50 * $9) = $1,250. If the 150 units with the highest cost were selected, the cost of goods sold would be (80 * $10) + (60 * $9) + (10 * $8) = $1,420.

Average Cost Method

With the **average cost method,** the average cost of the goods available for sale is computed, and the units in both cost of goods sold and ending inventory are costed at this average cost. In the periodic inventory method, this average is computed for the whole period. It is a weighted average: Each unit cost is weighted by the number of units with that cost. In the perpetual inventory method, a new average unit cost is sometimes calculated after each purchase. In either case, the average cost is representative of the cost of all of the items that were available for sale during the period.

Example

Assuming the periodic inventory method, the 240 units available for sale have a total cost of $2,140; hence, the average cost is $2,140 ÷ 240 = $8.917. The calculations of cost of goods sold and ending inventory are as follows:

[8] As already noted, LIFO is not permitted under IFRS. Outside of the United States, LIFO is sometimes used where permitted by local accounting standards.

	Units	Unit	Cost Total*
Cost of goods sold	150	$8.917	$1,338
Ending inventory	90	8.917	802
Total	240		$2,140

* Rounded.

Some companies use a predetermined unit cost for all transactions during the period.

The average cost method gives results that are in between the next two methods to be described, FIFO and LIFO. It is therefore a compromise for those who do not find the arguments for one or the other of these methods to be compelling.

First-In, First-Out Method

The FIFO method assumes that the oldest goods are sold first and that the most recently purchased goods are in the ending inventory. In the illustration, for the 150 units sold, it is assumed that the 100 units in beginning inventory were sold first and that the other 50 units sold were from the purchase made on June 1.

	Units	Unit Cost	Total Cost
Cost of goods sold:			
From beginning inventory	100	$ 8	$ 800
From purchase of June 1	50	9	450
Cost of goods sold	150		$1,250
Ending inventory:			
From purchase of June 1	10	$ 9	$ 90
From purchase of October 1	80	10	800
Ending inventory	90		$ 890

We shall contrast the LIFO and FIFO methods below. For the moment, it is sufficient to note that with FIFO (1) cost of goods sold is likely to approximate the *physical* flow of the goods because most companies sell their oldest merchandise first and (2) the ending inventory approximates the *current cost* of the goods, since it is costed at the amounts of most recent purchases.

Last-In, First-Out Method

The LIFO method is the opposite of FIFO. Cost of goods sold is based on the cost of the most recent purchases, and ending inventory is costed at the cost of the oldest units available.

	Units	Unit Cost	Total Cost
Cost of goods sold:			
From purchase of October 1	80	$10	$ 800
From purchase of June 1	60	9	540
From beginning inventory	10	8	80
Cost of goods sold	150		$1,420
Ending inventory:			
From beginning inventory	90	$ 8	$ 720

Note that with LIFO (1) cost of goods sold does *not* reflect the usual physical flow of merchandise and (2) the ending inventory may be costed at amounts prevailing several years ago, which in an era of rapid inflation are *far below* current costs.

LIFO Dollar Value Method

Originally LIFO was used only by companies whose inventory consisted of fungible products, such as wheat, each unit of which is physically like every other unit. Other companies, however, successfully argued that this was unfair to them. Thus, LIFO may now be used for almost any kind of inventory. It is applied to an inventory of physically unlike items by the so-called **LIFO dollar value method.** In this method, items whose prices tend to move together are grouped into an *inventory pool.* For example, a pool may consist of all the items in the inventory of the housewares department in a store. The calculations required to determine cost of goods sold and inventory amounts with this method are beyond the scope of this book. Compared with the unit-by-unit LIFO method, dollar value LIFO saves a considerable amount of recordkeeping effort.

Changes in Inventory

In a year when the *physical size* of the inventory *increases* above the amount on hand at the beginning of the year, with LIFO the inventory account is increased by the additional quantity valued at the costs existing during that year. During a period of growth, the inventory account will therefore consist of a number of *layers,* a new layer being added each year. If subsequently the physical inventory should *decrease* in size, these layers are, in effect, stripped off, taking the most recently added layer first in accordance with the basic LIFO rule. This process can have a peculiar effect on the income statement. If inventory is decreased to the extent that several LIFO layers are stripped off, then inventory items will be moving into cost of goods sold at costs established several years previously. If there has been constant inflation during the interim, such a decrease in inventory can result in a significant increase in reported income. Some people assert that in a recession, some companies deliberately eat into their LIFO inventories in order to increase reported income in a lean year. Careful readers of financial statements are not fooled by this practice, since the profit effect of reducing LIFO inventories must be disclosed in the notes to the financial statements.

LIFO Reserve

Companies that use LIFO for determining their balance sheet valuation of inventory nevertheless keep their detailed inventory records on a FIFO or average cost basis. The inventory amounts on these other bases usually will be higher than the LIFO valuation shown on the balance sheet. At the end of each accounting period, the difference between the LIFO valuation and the FIFO or average cost valuation is determined. (This is a complex calculation that is covered in advanced accounting texts.) This difference is sometimes called the **LIFO reserve.** The terminology is unfortunate because "reserve" suggests something set aside or saved for some special future purpose. The LIFO reserve is nothing more than the mathematical difference between two inventory amounts, one based on LIFO and the other one based on a different method of valuing inventory. LIFO companies disclose their LIFO reserve in the notes for their financial statement.

Comparison of Methods

The following table summarizes the illustrative results of three of the four methods described above (the specific identification method depends on the specific items selected):

	Cost of Goods Sold	Ending Inventory	Total
FIFO	$ 1,250	$ 890	$ 2,140
Average cost	1,338	802	2,140
LIFO	1,420	720	2,140

All of the methods described are in accordance with generally accepted accounting principles (GAAP) and all are accepted by the Internal Revenue Service (IRS) for calculating taxable income.

Arguments for FIFO

A primary conceptual argument for using FIFO is that it matches the costs of the goods that are *physically* sold with the revenues generated by selling those goods. Also, many companies set selling prices by adding a gross margin to the cost of the actual goods to be sold. Conceptually, such a price results in the company's recovering the funds it had invested in the particular item to be sold, plus a margin to provide for recovery of selling and administrative costs and a reasonable profit. For example, this pricing philosophy is commonly applied in retailing companies such as grocery and department stores.

Example

This brief item from *The Wall Street Journal* reflects the idea of pricing based on the cost of the goods actually (physically) sold: "Retail coffee prices are being cut by supermarket chains around the nation. The reductions are selective because of lingering high-priced inventories; when these are gone, wholesale-price cuts can be passed on to the public."

Thus, it is argued, if a company's management thinks of gross margin as the difference between selling prices and the cost of the goods physically sold, then it should use FIFO, which will report this same margin in the company's income statement.

The other primary argument for FIFO reflects a balance sheet orientation. Many people feel that the amount shown for inventory on the balance sheet should be approximately equal to the current cost of that inventory. The mechanics of FIFO, which assume that the goods in inventory are those most recently acquired, result in an inventory valuation that is closer to current costs than would result if LIFO or average cost were used. (This is true irrespective of the rate of inflation.)

Arguments for LIFO

Proponents of LIFO also base their primary conceptual argument on the matching concept. They argue that gross margin should reflect the difference between sales revenues, which are necessarily current amounts, and the current cost of the goods sold. Although seldom made explicit, this LIFO matching argument assumes that a company's management sets selling prices by adding a margin to current costs rather than to historical costs. If this is indeed the case, then the gross margin reported using LIFO will reflect management's thinking with regard to the nature of gross margin.

It should be pointed out that although this conceptual argument for LIFO involves the notion of the current cost of goods sold, LIFO only approximates these current costs. Generally, **current cost of goods sold** means the cost of acquiring items identical in type and number to those sold to *replenish the inventory* immediately after a sale. This is also called **replacement cost inventory accounting,** or, more jocularly, *NIFO* (for next-in, first-out). True replacement cost accounting is not permitted by either GAAP or the income tax code.[9]

While focusing on income statement matching, LIFO proponents downplay the impact of LIFO on balance sheet inventory valuation. Because the base layer of inventory is valued forever in terms of price levels prevailing when LIFO was adopted, the LIFO inventory valuation departs further and further from reality as time goes on, thus reflecting neither actual purchase costs nor replacement costs. In periods of prolonged inflation, this LIFO valuation may be far below current costs, making the inventory figure of dubious usefulness. Thus, whereas FIFO leads to a cost of goods sold amount of questionable usefulness and thus casts doubt on the usefulness of the income statement, LIFO casts a similar doubt in the usefulness of the balance sheet amount for inventory and thus on the amounts for current assets, total assets, and owners' equity.

This problem with LIFO can be mitigated, however. Although the amount reported as inventory on the balance sheet may be unrealistically low, the company must provide the LIFO reserve date in the notes to the financial statements that permits the reader to convert the inventory to a FIFO basis by adding the LIFO reserve to the LIFO inventory amount.

Income Tax Considerations

FIFO, average cost, and LIFO are all permitted for U.S. income tax calculations—although once a method is chosen, a company cannot change it without seeking permission from the Internal Revenue Service (IRS). If a company chooses the LIFO method for tax purposes, it must also use LIFO in its published financial statements. This **LIFO conformity rule** is the only significant instance in which the IRS requires use of the same accounting method for income tax and "book" (financial reporting) purposes.

In periods of inflation, LIFO results in lower income than FIFO or average costs, and thus results in lower income taxes. If the physical size of inventory remains constant or grows, LIFO reduces taxable income indefinitely. Only if LIFO layers are stripped off in future years might taxable income under LIFO exceed taxable income under FIFO; and even in that case, LIFO will have postponed some income tax payments. These tax advantages of LIFO in periods of rising prices can improve a company's cash flow and therefore lead many companies to select the LIFO method regardless of the conceptual pros and cons of the various alternatives.

Why Not More LIFO?

Since LIFO can improve a company's after-tax cash flow, why don't *all* companies use it for *all* of their inventories? At least two reasons can be given.

First, although the economy as a whole may be experiencing inflation, the prices of the specific items in a company's inventory are not necessarily increasing. In some instances, particularly in the electronics industry, specific prices fall even while general inflation continues. For example, in 1970 the retail price of a four-function handheld calculator was $395; today, a similar item retails for under $10. Companies whose inventory replacement costs are trending downward will report lower taxable income and pay lower taxes by using FIFO rather than LIFO.

---

[9] Replacement cost inventory accounting is used outside the United States in countries with high inflation rates.

Second, in a company for which LIFO will reduce taxable income and thus lower income tax payments, the company also must report the lower LIFO income to its shareholders because of the LIFO conformity rule. This means that the cash flow improvement from LIFO will be accompanied by a decrease in reported earnings per share (relative to cash flows and earnings if FIFO were used). Although academic research studies suggest that the stock market does not penalize a company whose earnings drop because of a change to LIFO, many top managers of U.S. companies have long held the view that lower reported earnings per share are associated with lower stock prices, whatever the cause of the lower earnings. Thus, in considering LIFO, many managers see a dilemma: Increasing cash flow through lower tax payments is clearly good for the corporation, but they believe that the accompanying decrease in reported earnings is bad for the shareholders. Since top management serves at the pleasure of the board of directors and since the board is supposed to protect shareholders' interests, often the decision is to opt for FIFO and higher reported earnings rather than LIFO and improved cash flows.

Lower of Cost or Market

All the foregoing had to do with measuring the *cost* of inventory. The LIFO and FIFO methods are alternative ways of measuring cost. The general inventory valuation principle, deriving from the conservatism concept, is that inventory is reported on the balance sheet at the *lower of its cost or its market value.*

In the ordinary situation, inventory is reported at its cost. It is reduced below cost (i.e., written down) only when there is evidence that the value of the items, when eventually sold or otherwise disposed of, will be less than their cost. Such evidence may include physical deterioration, obsolescence, drops in price level, or other causes. When this evidence exists, inventory is stated at market.

Since the goods in inventory have not in fact been sold, their true market value is not ordinarily known and therefore must be estimated. *Accounting Research Bulletin (ARB) No. 43* states that this estimate should be the current *replacement* cost of the item; that is, what it would cost currently to purchase or manufacture the item.[10] The *ARB* further sets upper and lower boundaries on "market":

1. It should not be higher than the estimated selling price of the item less the costs associated with selling it. This amount is called the **net realizable value.**
2. It should not be lower than the net realizable value less a normal profit margin.

These principles can be compressed into the following rule: Use historical cost if that cost is lowest; otherwise, use the next-to-lowest of the other three possibilities.

Example

Assume four items with amounts as in the table shown below. The inventory amount to be used for each is starred.

	Item			
	1	2	3	4
a. Historical cost	$ 7*	$9	$9	$10
b. Current replacement cost	8	8*	7	9
c. Net realizable value (ceiling)	10	9	9	8*
d. Net realizable value less profit margin (floor)	9	7	8*	7

[10] *Accounting Research Bulletin No. 43*, Chapter 4.

As is true for the rules for marketable securities, which are applied to the individual securities in a portfolio, the rule for inventory is applied to each item in inventory (i.e., each unique part number or product number).

Analysis of Inventory

Inventory Turnover

The ratio most commonly used in analyzing the size of the inventory item is **inventory turnover:**

$$\text{Inventory turnover} = \frac{\text{Cost of goods sold}}{\text{Inventory}}$$

If the cost of goods sold for a year is $1 million and inventory is $250,000, then the inventory turnover is 4.0 times. This is equivalent to saying that the inventory turns over once every three months (quarter of a year).

Some companies calculate this ratio on the basis of the ending inventory, others on the basis of the average inventory. The average may be simply one-half the sum of beginning and ending inventories for the year, or it may be an average of monthly inventory levels. The end-of-period basis is more representative of the current state of the inventory if volume is expected to continue at previous levels. The average basis is a better reflection of events that occurred during the period because it measures the amount of inventory that supported the sales activity of that period.

Inventory turnover varies greatly with the nature of the business. It should be high for a store that sells fresh produce; otherwise spoilage is likely to be a problem. A supermarket may have an inventory turnover close to 50, a petroleum refinery 20. On the other hand, a jewelry store with a wide selection of expensive and unusual items may not turn its inventory as often as once a year, and most art galleries have a turnover much lower than 1.

One also must consider the seasonality of sales. For example, college bookstores have high inventories before the start of each new term, with lower inventories in between. In such entities, an annual calculation of inventory turnover has little meaning, and inventory measured at various seasonal high and low points is of more significance.

Inventory turnover indicates the velocity with which merchandise moves through a business. Turnover may fall either because of inventory buildup in anticipation of increased sales or because sales volume has declined, leaving excess merchandise on hand. The first is a favorable event; the second is unfavorable. The turnover number itself does not indicate which is the cause.

Days' Inventory

The same relationship can be expressed as the number of days' inventory on hand. If one has already calculated inventory turnover, then days' inventory is simply 365 ÷ inventory turnover. Days' inventory can be calculated directly as follows:

$$\text{Days' inventory} = \frac{\text{Inventory}}{\text{Cost of goods sold} \div 365} = \frac{\$250,000}{\$1,000,00 \div 365} = 91 \text{ days}$$

Of course, both the inventory turnover and days' inventory calculations are affected by the company's inventory costing method. Because, relative to FIFO, the LIFO method results in lower reported inventory value on the balance sheet and higher cost of goods sold, a company using LIFO will have a higher indicated inventory turnover ratio and a lower indicated number of days' inventory than if it were using FIFO. Such differences must be taken into account when comparing ratios for different entities.

One way this problem is resolved is to convert the LIFO data to their FIFO equivalent and use the adjusted data to compute the ratios.

Gross Margin Percentage

A ratio closely associated with inventory accounting is a company's gross margin (sales less cost of goods sold) expressed as a percentage of its net sales revenue. Since the gross margin figure is influenced by the cost of goods sold number, different inventory accounting methods can lead to different gross margins. The gross margin percentage is one of several different measures of a company's profitability. It measures the percentage of each sales dollar a company earns before considering period costs.

Example

Using the cost of goods sold figures from the FIFO and LIFO examples above and assuming $2,000 in sales, the FIFO-based gross margin is 37.5 percent ($750 ÷ $2,000); the LIFO-based gross margin is 29 percent ($580 ÷ $2,000).

To compute the gross margin of a LIFO accounting firm on a FIFO basis, the change in the company's LIFO reserve from the beginning of the accounting period to the end of the period is added to the LIFO-based cost of goods sold if the change is a positive amount. It is deducted if the change is negative. Similarly, to compute the FIFO inventory value of a LIFO firm, the LIFO reserve is added to the LIFO inventory value.

Cost of Goods Sold and Inventory (ND AS2)

Inventory in a firm has always been recorded as the main current asset (besides trade receivables and cash) which can take either of these three forms:

- Raw Material: the one in the form of materials and supplies to be consumed in the production process or in rendering the services
- Work in progress: the one which is in the process of production for sale
- Finished goods: the one which is held for sale in ordinary course of business

To ensure fair recognition of the inventory in books of accounts, the accountants draw upon from the accounting standards on Inventory to determine the cost of inventory and its subsequent recognition as an expense, including any writing down of value to its net realisable value. The standard applies to all inventories; except for special items like website cost, financial instruments and biological assets. Moreover, it also does not apply to measurement of inventories held by

(a) Producer of agricultural and forest products, agricultural produce after harvest and mineral products (measured at net realisable value)
(b) Commodity brokers and dealers (measure at fair value less cost to sell)

Inventory Valuation Inventories are valued at the lower of cost or net realisable value. Net Realisable Value is the estimated selling price in the normal course of business adjusted with estimated cost of completion and the estimated costs necessary to make the sale. The Cost here shall include:

1. Costs of purchase, (including import duties, non-refundable taxes, transportation and handling charges net of trade discount and rebates received)
2. Costs of conversion, (include all fixed and variable manufacturing overheads)
3. Other costs incurred in bringing the inventories to their present location and condition

However, the Cost shall not include any abnormal loss, Storage Cost (unless such cost are necessary), Administrative Overheads, Selling Costs, Interest cost in case the inventories are purchased with deferred settlement terms, Foreign exchange difference arising directly on the recent acquisition of inventories invoiced in a foreign currency etc.

Cost of Goods Sold (COGS/ Expense) Recognition

Inventories are probably one of those few items which appear in both Income statement as well as Balance Sheet although with different terminology, connotation and interpretation. When they appear in Balance Sheet, as described above, they are the closing stock of one of three categories of Inventory under Current Asset. While in Income statement, they are treated as an expense called Cost of Goods sold (COGS). Simply put it is the amount of material expensed or consumed in the relevant period.

- Inventories are recognised as an expense in the period in which the related revenue is recognised.
- Any write-down to Net Realizable Value or any inventory losses are also recognised as an expense when they occur.
- Also, reversal, if any of the "write down" should be recognised in the income statement in the period in which the reversal occurs.

Differences between Ind AS (IAS) and AS 2

1. While the older AS 2 did not deal with the inventory treatment related to Service Providers, the new IAS 2 details the treatment related to the cost of inventories of Service Providers too.
2. Ind AS 2 requires much larger disclosures in the financial statements when compared to AS 2. The additional disclosures in IND AS 2 as compared to existing AS 2 are:

    - The carrying amount of inventories carried at fair value less costs to sell.
    - The amount of inventories recognized as expense during the period.
    - The amount of any write-down of inventories recognized as an expense in the period.
    - The amount of any reversal of any write down that is recognized as a reduction in the amount of inventories recognized as an expense in the period.

3. In the earlier AS 2, Cost of Inventories did not include "selling and distribution costs" and it was expensed in the period in which they were incurred whereas IAS 2 specifically excludes only "Selling Costs" and not "Distribution Costs".
4. Whereas AS 2 required valuation of goods, which cannot be segregated for specific projects to be assigned using either First In First Out or Weighted Average Cost, the IndAS requires the same formula to be used for all the inventories with similar nature.

Example

Calculation of Net Realizable Value

If the Cost of inventory is 500 and its Net Realizable Value is 300 then Inventory value as per AS-2 is 300. However if Cost of Inventory is 500 and Net Realizable Value is 600 then Inventory value as per AS-2 is 600. If the Cost of inventory is 500, selling price is 700 and 30% is the commission, Net Realizable Value is 490 (700–30%*700) and Inventory value as per AS-2 is 490

Summary

The objectives of inventory accounting are (1) to match the cost of goods sold, an expense, with the revenue earned from the sale of those goods in an accounting period and (2) to measure the cost of inventory on hand at the end of the period, which is an asset.

A merchandising company has one inventory account. The separation of the cost of the goods available for sale into the amount determined to be cost of goods sold and the amount determined to be ending merchandise inventory can be accomplished by either the periodic inventory method or the perpetual inventory method. In the former, ending inventory is obtained by a physical count, and cost of goods sold is obtained by deduction. In the latter, both amounts are obtained directly from inventory records.

A manufacturing company has three inventory accounts: Materials, Work in Process, and Finished Goods. In the periodic inventory method, the amount in each account is determined by taking a physical inventory and then deducing the cost of materials used, the cost of goods manufactured, and the cost of goods sold. In a perpetual inventory system, also called a product costing system, these costs are obtained directly from the accounting records.

Inventory is ordinarily measured at its cost. In a merchandising company, cost is essentially the amount expended to acquire the goods. In a manufacturing company, product costs include, in addition to materials costs, the labor cost and other production costs incurred in converting the materials into finished goods. Other operating costs, in either type of company, are called period costs; they are expenses of the current period.

The flow of costs can be measured by any of several methods, including specific identification; average costs; first-in, first-out (FIFO); and last-in, first-out (LIFO). Although the LIFO method usually results in lower income taxes, some companies do not use it because the LIFO conformity rule would result in their reporting lower net income to their shareholders. IFRS does not permit the use of LIFO.

If the market value of an inventory item is below cost, the item is reported at its market value.

Two ratios helpful in analyzing inventories are inventory turnover and days' inventory.

The inventory accounting method adopted by management can influence a company's gross margin percentage.

Problems

Problem 6–1.

In the following table, there appear income statements for four hypothetical companies. Each income statement is missing three numbers; you are to determine these missing numbers. (Assume taxes are part of "period expenses.")

	Co. W	Co. X	Co. Y	Co. Z
Sales	$2,250	$ 1,800	$1,350	$ 2,100
Cost of goods sold:				
Beginning inventory	300	225	?	300
Plus: Purchases	975	?	850	1,200
Less: Ending inventory	225	300	300	?
Cost of goods sold	?	900	?	?
Gross margin	?	?	?	750
Period expenses	300	400	150	?
Net income (loss)	$?	$?	$ 150	$ (50)

Problem 6–2.

The Gardner Pharmacy uses the periodic inventory method. In its most recent fiscal year, 2010, Gardner had beginning inventory of $50,000; gross purchases of $167,000; freight-in of $4,000; purchases returned to suppliers totaling $8,000; and ending inventory of $77,500. Make the year-end adjusting and closing entries to reflect the above information in the inventory, cost of goods sold, and income summary accounts. Then, assuming sales of $325,000, other expenses (excluding taxes) of $95,000, and a tax rate of 30 percent, prepare an income statement for the year, including the derivation of the cost of goods sold amount.

Problem 6–3.

Gould's Company, which makes a single product, uses the perpetual inventory method. At the end of each accounting period, a physical inventory is taken to verify the perpetual inventory records. For its most recent accounting period, Gould's records showed beginning inventory of 673 units; goods added to finished goods inventory during the period, 5,700 units; and sales during the period of 5,800 units. Finally, during the period, 80 units in resalable condition were returned by Gould's customers. The unit cost was $15 throughout the period.

Required

a. Assuming Gould's sells this item for $23 per unit, prepare summary journal entries for the period's purchases, sales, and sales returns.

b. Prepare an income statement down to the gross margin line.

c. Assume that after the entries in part (*a*) were made, a physical count revealed that ending inventory was actually 610 units. What additional entry is required? How does this affect your income statement?

Problem 6–4.

On March 31, the Maple Shop had no alarm clocks on hand. During the next four months, it first purchased 50 clocks for $14 each, and then 75 more for $12 each. During these four months, 100 alarm clocks were sold.

Required

What will the July 31 alarm clock inventory amount and the four months' cost of goods be if the Maple Shop uses the periodic inventory method and (*a*) average cost; (*b*) FIFO; (*c*) LIFO?

Problem 6–5.

Electronic Heaven, Inc., sells electronic merchandise, including a personal computer offered for the first time in September, which retails for $695. Sales of this personal computer for the next six-month period (ending February 28) totaled $52,125. Purchase records indicate the following on the amounts purchased and prices paid by Electronic Heaven:

Purchase Date	Units	Cost per Unit
September 10	12	$370
October 15	20	375
November 2	32	360
December 10	11	350
February 3	10	335

Required

a. Prepare a statement for this personal computer showing its gross margin for the six-month period ending February 28 using the FIFO, average cost, and LIFO inventory methods.

b. What was the gross margin percentage earned on the $52,125 sales of this personal computer? (*Hint:* The answer depends on the inventory method used.)

c. If all of the purchases and sales of this personal computer were for cash, what was the net *pretax* cash flow resulting from the purchases and sales of this personal computer? Would the use of different inventory methods change the pre-tax cash flow figure you calculated?

d. Assume a tax rate of 30 percent. What would be the net *after-tax* cash flow using different inventory methods for tax purposes?

Problem 6–6.

Marks Manufacturing Company has the following beginning balances:

Materials inventory	$100,000
Work in process	370,000
Finished goods	60,000

During the period, the following occurred:

1. Purchased for cash $872,000 worth of raw materials. Delivery charges on these materials equaled $22,000.
2. Used $565,000 worth of direct labor in the production process.
3. Used $900,000 worth of materials in the production process.
4. The following costs were incurred:

Indirect labor	$27,000	Factory utilities	$147,000
Factory supplies used	46,000	Depreciation—manufacturing	46,000
Property taxes and insurance	14,000	Selling and administrative	28,000
Depreciation—factory	54,000		

5. Transferred $2,035,000 worth of work in process inventory to finished goods inventory.
6. Sales were $2,600,000.
7. The ending balance in Finished Goods Inventory was $93,000.

Required

a. Calculate the Ending Materials and Work in Process Inventory balances. (*Hint:* Refer to Illustration 6–4.)

b. What was Marks Manufacturing's gross margin during the period?

Problem 6–7.

You are given the following unit cost data for Sun-Power Company:

	A	B	C	D
Historical cost	$150	$183	$134	$113
Current replacement cost	145	177	126	116
Net realizable value	150	173	134	128
Net realizable value less profit margin	143	165	131	122
Number of units on hand	30	40	20	40

Required

Determine the carrying cost of each item, and record the adjusting entry to the inventory account.

CASES

Case 6–1

Browning Manufacturing Company*

The management of Browning Manufacturing Company annually prepared a budget of expected financial operations for the ensuing calendar year. The completed budget provided information on all aspects of the coming year's operations. It included a projected balance sheet as of the end of the year and a projected income statement.

The final preparation of statements was accomplished only after careful integration of detailed computations submitted by each department. This was done to ensure that the operations of all departments were in balance with one another. For example, the finance department needed to base its schedules of loan transactions and of collections and disbursements on numbers that were dependent on manufacturing, purchasing, and selling expectations. The level of production would be geared to the forecasts

of the sales department, and purchasing would be geared to the proposed manufacturing schedule.

In short, it was necessary to integrate the estimates of each department and to revise them in terms of the overall effect on operations to arrive at a coordinated and profitable plan of operations for the coming year. The budget statements ultimately derived from the adjusted estimated transactions would then serve the company as a reliable guide and measure of the coming year's operations.

At the time the 2010 budget was being prepared, in November of 2009, projected 2009 financial statements were compiled for use as a comparison with the budgeted figures. These 2009 statements were based on ten months' actual and two months' projected transactions. They appear as Exhibits 1, 2, and 3.

EXHIBIT 1 **Browning Manufacturing Company, Projected Balance Sheet, December 31, 2009**

Assets		
Current assets:		
Cash and marketable securities		$ 118,440
Accounts receivable (net of allowance for doubtful accounts)		311,760
Inventories:		
Materials	$ 110,520	
Work in process	172,200	
Finished goods	257,040	
Supplies	17,280	557,040
Prepaid taxes and insurance		66,720
Total current assets		1,053,960
Other assets:		
Manufacturing plant at cost	2,678,400	
Less: Accumulated depreciation	907,200	1,771,200
Total Assets		$ 2,825,160
Liabilities and Shareholders' Equity		
Current liabilities:		
Accounts payable	$ 185,760	
Notes payable	288,840	
Income taxes payable	9,000	
Total current liabilities		$ 483,600
Shareholders' equity:		
Capital stock	1,512,000	
Retained earnings	829,560	2,341,560
Total Liabilities and Shareholders' Equity		$ 2,825,160

*Copyright © by the President and Fellows of Harvard College. Harvard Business School case 198-047.

Below is the summary of expected operations for the budget year 2010 as finally accepted:

1. *Sales:* All on credit, $2,562,000; sales returns and allowances, $19,200; sales discounts taken by customers (for prompt payment), $49,200. (The sales figure is net of expected bad debts.)

2. *Purchases of goods and services:*
   a. New assets:
      i. Purchased for cash: manufacturing plant and equipment, $144,000; prepaid manufacturing taxes and insurance, $78,000.
      ii. Purchased on accounts payable: materials, $825,000; supplies, $66,000.

EXHIBIT 2 Browning Manufacturing Company, Projected 2009 Statement of Cost of Goods Sold

Finished goods inventory, 1/1/09			$ 218,820
Work in process inventory, 1/1/09		$ 137,760	
Materials used		663,120	
Plus: Factory expenses			
Direct manufacturing labor		419,040	
Factory overhead:			
Indirect manufacturing labor	$170,640		
Power, heat, and light	116,760		
Depreciation of plant	126,600		
Social Security taxes	42,120		
Taxes and insurance, factory	46,320		
Supplies	56,880	559,320	
		1,779,240	
Less: Work in process inventory, 12/31/09		172,200	
Cost of goods manufactured (i.e., completed)			1,607,040
			1,825,320
Less: Finished goods inventory, 12/31/09			257,040
Cost of goods sold			$1,568,280

EXHIBIT 3 Browning Manufacturing Company, Projected 2009 Income Statement

Sales		$2,295,600
Less: Sales returns and allowances	$17,640	
Sales discounts allowed	43,920	61,560
Net sales		2,234,040
Less: Cost of goods sold (per schedule)		1,568,280
Gross margin		665,760
Less: Selling and administrative expense		437,160
Operating income		228,600
Less: Interest expense		34,080
Income before federal and state income tax		194,520
Less: Estimated income tax expense		89,520
Net income		$ 105,000

b. Services used to convert materials into work in process, all purchased for cash: direct manufacturing labor, $492,000; indirect manufacturing labor, $198,000; social security taxes on labor, $49,200; power, heat, and light, $135,600.

c. Selling and administrative services, purchased for cash: $522,000.

3. *Conversion of assets into work in process:* This appears as an increase in the cost of work in process and a decrease in the appropriate asset accounts. Depreciation of manufacturing building and equipment, $140,400; expiration of prepaid taxes and insurance, $52,800; supplies used in manufacturing, $61,200; materials put into process, $811,000.

4. *Transfer of work in process to finished goods:* This appears as an increase in finished goods and a decrease in work in process. Total cost accumulated on goods that have been completed and transferred to finished goods, $1,901,952.

5. *Cost of finished goods sold to customers:* $1,806,624.

6. *Financial transactions:*
   a. $264,000 borrowed on notes payable to bank.
   b. Cash payment to bank of $38,400 for interest on loans.

7. *Cash receipts from customers on accounts receivable:* $2,604,000.

8. *Cash payments of liabilities:*
   a. Payment of accounts payable, $788,400.
   b. Payment of 2009 income tax, $9,000.

9. *Estimated federal income tax on 2010 income:* $58,000, of which $5,800 is estimated to be unpaid as of December 31, 2010.

10. *Dividends declared for year and paid in cash:* $36,000.

This summary presents the complete cycle of the Browning Manufacturing Company's budgeted yearly operations from the purchase of goods and services through their various stages of conversion to completion of the finished product to the sale of this product. All costs and cash receipts and disbursements involved in this cycle are presented, including the provision for federal income taxes and the payment of dividends.

The management was particularly interested in the budget's year-end cash position. The company's goal was to have a year-end cash balance of approximately $150,000 after paying off at least $350,000 and possibly as much as $400,000 of the note payable to the bank (not listed as a transaction in the budget). In addition, the company's budgeted year-end investment in inventory was of interest to management who had decided to work toward improving the company's inventory turnover ratio. Management was also aware of the need to maintain its satisfactory trade credit relationship with suppliers.

Questions

1. Prepare a projected statement of cost of goods sold for 2010, a projected income statement for 2010, and a projected balance sheet as of December 31, 2010. (*Hint:* Set up T accounts corresponding to the 2009 balance sheet accounts. Post the budgeted transactions to the accounts. Use the inventory T accounts to prepare the projected cost of goods sold statement and the retained earnings T account to prepare the income statement.)

2. Describe the principal differences between the 2010 estimates and the 2009 figures as shown in Exhibits 1, 2, and 3. In what respects is 2010 performance expected to be better than 2009 performance, and in what respects is it expected to be worse?

3. Does the budget indicate that management will achieve its note payable repayment goal? If not, what do you suggest they do to achieve their minimum objective?

4. Does the budget indicate management's inventory turnover goal will be achieved? If not, what do you suggest they do to improve the company's inventory turnover?

5. What does the budget indicate might happen to the company's trade credit standing?

Case 6–2
Lewis Corporation*

Lewis Corporation had traditionally used the FIFO method of inventory valuation. You are given the infor-mation shown in Exhibit 1 on transactions during the year affecting Lewis's inventory account. (The purchases are in sequence during the year. The company uses a periodic Inventory method.)

EXHIBIT 1 Inventory Transactions 2009–2011

2009				
Beginning balance	1,840	cartons	@	$20.00
Purchases	600	cartons	@	20.25
	800	cartons	@	21.00
	400	cartons	@	21.25
	200	cartons	@	21.50
Sales	2,820	cartons	@	34.00
2010				
Beginning balance	1,020	cartons		
Purchases	700	cartons	@	21.50
	700	cartons	@	21.50
	700	cartons	@	22.00
	1,000	cartons	@	22.25
Sales	3,080	cartons	@	35.75
2011				
Beginning balance	1,040	cartons		
Purchases	1,000	cartons	@	22.50
	700	cartons	@	22.75
	700	cartons	@	23.00
	700	cartons	@	23.50
Sales	2,950	cartons	@	35.75

Questions

1. Calculate the cost of goods sold and year-end inventory amounts for 2009, 2010, and 2011 using the (a) FIFO, (b) LIFO, and (c) average cost methods.
2. Lewis Corporation is considering switching from FIFO to LIFO to reduce its income tax expense. Assuming a corporate income tax rate of 40 percent, calculate the tax savings this would have made for 2009 to 2011. Would you recommend that Lewis make this change?
3. Dollar sales for 2012 are expected to drop by approximately 8 percent, as a recession in Lewis's market is forecasted to continue at least through the first three quarters of the year. Total sales are fore-casted to be 2,700 cartons. Lewis will be unable to raise its selling price from the 2011 level of $35.75. However, costs are expected to increase to

$24 per carton for the whole year. Due to these cost/price pressures, the corporation wishes to lower its investment in inventory by holding only the essential inventory of 400 cartons at any time during the year. What is the effect of remaining on FIFO, assuming Lewis had adopted FIFO in 2009? What is the effect of remaining on LIFO, assuming Lewis adopted LIFO in 2009? What method would you recommend now?
4. What is the LIFO reserve in 2009? What is the LIFO reserve in 2010? What is the significance of the LIFO reserve number? How much did the LIFO reserve increase in 2010? What is the significance of this increase?
5. Despite continuing inflation in the United States in the 1980s and the early 1990s, many companies continued to use FIFO for all or part of their domestic inventories. Why do you believe this was the case?

Case 6–3
Morgan Manufacturing*

Charles Crutchfield, manager of manufacturing operations at Morgan Manufacturing, was evaluating the performance of the company. Given his position, he was primarily interested in the health of the operating aspects of the business. At Morgan, the gross margin percentage was considered to be a key measure of operating performance; other measures considered to provide essential information on the health of business operations were pretax return on sales and pretax return on assets. Crutchfield considered the after-tax versions of these measures less relevant for his purposes because they combined information reflecting the health of operations with information reflecting the effectiveness of the tax accounting department, which was not under his control.

From Morgan Manufacturing's 2010 income statements and balance sheets, shown in Exhibit 1, Crutchfield computed Morgan Manufacturing's gross margin percentage (44.5%), pre-tax return on sales (14.5%), and pre-tax return on assets (13.4%). Crutchfield was especially interested in comparing his firm's perfor-

mance against that of its major competitor, Westwood, Inc. Crutchfield felt that Morgan had recently made significant productivity improvements over Westwood that would be reflected in the financial statements. When he looked at Westwood's 2010 financial statements (Exhibit 2), he was quite disappointed. Despite the similarities between the two companies based on the three key measures, he concluded that Westwood's financial performance was better.

Distraught, Crutchfield sought the advice of Edward Drewery, controller. "How can Westwood's results be better than ours, when I know that our operations are more efficient?" The controller responded, "I'm not sure about the relative efficiency of the two firms' operations, but I do know that we use a different method to account for inventory than Westwood uses. Have you taken that into account?" "Not really," replied Crutchfield. "Well, all you need to know," continued Drewery, "is that we use LIFO; Westwood uses FIFO; and our LIFO reserve was $10 million in 2009 and $70 million in 2010."

EXHIBIT 1 Morgan Manufacturing Financial Statements ($ millions)

Income Statement, for the year ended December 31	2009	2010
Sales	$1,500	$2,000
Cost of goods sold	810	1,110
Gross margin	690	890
Selling, general, and administrative expenses	450	600
Income before taxes	240	290
Income tax expense	96	116
Net Income	$ 144	$ 174

Balance Sheet, as of December 31	2009	2010
Cash	$ 100	$ 140
Accounts receivable	250	350
Inventory	120	100
Plant, property, and equipment (net)	1,385	1,580
Total assets	$ 1,855	$ 2,170
Current liabilities	$ 250	$ 325
Long-term liabilities	500	675
Common stock	400	400
Retained earnings	705	770
Total liabilities and owners' equity	$ 1,855	$ 2,170
LIFO reserve	$10	$70

*Copyright © Julie H. Hertenstein.

EXHIBIT 2 Westwood, Inc., Financial Statements ($ millions)

Income Statement, for the year ended December 31	2009	2010
Sales	$1,500	$2,000
Cost of goods sold	800	1,100
Gross margin	700	900
Selling, general, and administrative expenses	450	600
Income before taxes	250	300
Income tax expense	100	120
Net income	$150	$180

Balance Sheet, as of December 31	2009	2010
Cash	$ 100	$ 140
Accounts receivable	250	350
Inventory	140	170
Plant, property, and equipment (net)	1,385	1,580
Total assets	$1,875	$2,240
Current liabilities	$ 250	$ 330
Long-term liabilities	500	675
Common stock	400	400
Retained earnings	725	835
Total liabilities and owners' equity	$1,875	$2,240

Crutchfield wondered how the reported results could be adjusted so that the comparison could be done on a comparable basis.

Questions

1. What are Westwood's gross margin percentage, pre-tax return on sales (pre-tax income ÷ sales), and pre-tax return on assets (pre-tax income ÷ total assets)?

2. Which accounts that appear on the income statement or balance sheet and the various financial ratios and measurements incorporating these accounts are affected by the differing choices of inventory accounting method? Explain how the choice of different inventory accounting methods affects one's ability to directly compare the results of these two companies.

3. Using the information available in the exhibits, make the necessary adjustments to the 2010 results so that you can better compare the performance of the two companies on the three key measures.

4. Which of the two companies do you believe is performing better? Why?

Case 6–4
Joan Holtz (B)*

Because an earlier visit with the accounting instructor [see Case 5–3, Joan Holtz (A)] had cleared up some puzzling matters, Joan Holtz decided to prepare a new list of problems as a basis for a second discussion. As before, Holtz knew that the instructor expected that tentative answers to these questions be worked out prior to the meeting. The instructor also wanted Holtz

using numbers of her own choosing, to illustrate the issues she was raising and her tentative answers with simple numerical illustrations whenever possible. The list follows:

1. Evidently, there are three ways of handling purchase discounts: They can be deducted from the cost of the purchased goods, they can be reported as other income, or purchase discounts not taken can be reported as an expense of the period. But isn't the effect on

* Copyright © Professor Robert N. Anthony.

net income the same under all these methods? If so, why argue about which is preferable?

2. It is said that the perpetual inventory method identifies the amount of inventory shrinkage from pilferage, spoilage, and the like, an amount that is not revealed by the periodic inventory method. Having identified this shrinkage amount, however, how should it be recorded in the accounts?

3. People have said that the LIFO method assumes that the goods purchased last are sold first. If this is so, the assumption is clearly unrealistic because companies ordinarily sell their oldest merchandise first. Can a method based on such an unrealistic assumption be supported, other than as a tax gimmick?

4. A certain automobile dealer bases its selling prices on the actual invoice cost of each automobile. In a given model year, the invoice cost for similar automobiles may be increased once or twice to reflect increased manufacturing costs. Would this automobile dealer be wrong if it used the LIFO method? By contrast, a certain hardware dealer changes its selling prices whenever the wholesale price of its goods changes as reported in wholesalers' price lists. Would this hardware dealer be wrong if it used the FIFO method?

5. Are the following generalizations valid?
   a. The difference between LIFO and FIFO is relatively small if inventory turnover is relatively high.
   b. The average cost method will result in net income that is somewhere between that produced by the LIFO method and that produced by the FIFO method.
   c. If prices rise in one year and fall by an equal amount the next year, the total income for the two years is the same under the FIFO method as under the LIFO method.

6. If the LIFO method is used and prices are rising, ending inventory will normally be significantly

below prevailing market prices. Therefore, what justification is there for applying the lower-of-cost-or-market rule to LIFO inventories?

7. A certain distillery manufactured bourbon whiskey, which it aged in charred, white oak barrels for four years before bottling and selling it. Whiskey was carried in inventory at approximately $1 per gallon, which was the cost of ingredients, labor, and factory overhead of the manufacturing process. Barrels, which could not be reused, cost $0.70 per gallon. The distillery incurred $0.20 of warehousing costs per gallon per year, including costs involved in moving and testing the barrels. It also incurred $0.10 per gallon of interest costs per year. The costs of barrels, warehousing, and interest were charged directly to expense. If the distillery had consistently earned pretax profit of $600,000 per year on annual production and sale of 1 million gallons, what would happen to profits if it increased production to 1.2 million gallons per year? At what amounts should it carry its whiskey in inventory?

8. A company produced a "made for TV" movie at a total cost of $1 million. It sold the rights to the initial showing to a network for $1 million, and fully expected to sell the rights for a repeat showing the following year for $300,000. It thought that in future years, additional reruns would generate at least another $300,000 of revenue. Disregarding any GAAP dealing with this issue, how much should the company report as cost of sales for the first year? Would the answer be different if in the first year the producing company agreed to pay $100,000 for advertising and promoting the initial showing?

Question

Give your "tentative answers" to the above issues. Illustrate the issue and your answer whenever possible.

Case 6–5

Inventory at MMT, OYO etc

Traditionally, Inventory was always seen as a Current Asset item which was largely tangible and firms would pledge the inventory to raise short term loan from banks and financial institutions. Banks were also very comfortable in lending against inventory as they knew that eventually the final inventory will be sold to the

customers, money collected and passed on to the banks. If he firms were not able to pay back the loan because of any reason, the bank would sell their inventory (collateral) to recover their dues. It was a fairly simple understanding of the term "Inventory". With the new age firms coming in, this traditional way of understanding

Inventory appears to be a "historical" phenomenon. Today, we have firms whose relative size of the "Inventory" on the Balance Sheet is very large (sometimes as high as 75–80%) but actually they don't have any physical inventory as such. They have "virtual inventories" on their balance sheets and on top of it, "cost/price/net realizable value" of that "virtual inventory" is very volatile and can go up and down by more than 15–20% in a matter of few hours. Sounds weird, welcome to the world of aggregators, the likes of Makemytrip.com, Oyohotels.com, Uber.com, Ola.com, Swiggy.com who sell products and services by creating a virtual platform called "marketplace" without actually holding any of the product or providing services themselves. Take for example, makemytrip.com, an online firm which sells domestic and international airlines tickets, hotel rooms etc. Technically, the seats on the aircrafts of the various airlines whose tickets they sell are "inventory", the rooms of the hotels with whom they have a contract are their "inventory" but actually it is a virtual inventory (because they don't actually hold them) and the price of the same keeps on changing based on demand and supply. So, hypothetically their Balance sheet keeps changing every hour because of fluctuations in the value of their "inventory". Till the time, the "aircraft seats" and the "hotel rooms" are not sold, they contin-ue to be an unsold inventory and the firm may have to reduce the prices to actually sell them.

E-commerce companies in the retail space sell millions of products every day without actually holding any of those products as "inventory" on their own Balance Sheet. For a customer who is shopping at Amazon or Flipkart, the sections through which he or she navigates, items which he or she picks and put it in the " shopping cart" gives him/ her the feeling of actual shopping in a physical mall. At the end of the day, the "inventory" is delivered at his/ her place. What the customer doesn't realize that the "inventory" delivered was not actually owned by Amazon or Flipkart and therefore it doesn't reflect on its Balance Sheet.

Questions

1. With the change in the nature of "inventories" in new businesses, how will such an enterprise raise funds externally?
2. If "inventory" value keeps changing so frequently, suggest a robust method to carry on the valuation.
3. How are "Amazon" of the world helping the small traders etc by "virtually parking" their goods on their platforms?

Long-Lived Nonmonetary Assets and Their Amortization

Chapters 5 and 6 discussed monetary assets and inventories. Investments are discussed in Chapter 12. This chapter describes other categories of assets. The common characteristic of these assets is that they are nonmonetary and have long lives; they provide benefits to the entity for several future years. We describe the accounting principles involved in recording the acquisition of these long-lived assets, the conversion of their acquisition costs to expenses, and the disposition of such assets when they no longer provide service. Analytical techniques that give financial statement users a better understanding of a company's nonmonetary asset accounting decisions and transactions also are discussed.

Nature of Long-Lived Assets

When an entity makes an expenditure, the benefits from the goods or services acquired either are obtained in the current period or are expected to be obtained in future periods. If the benefits are obtained in the current period, the costs of the goods or services are *expenses*. If benefits are expected in future periods, the costs are *assets* in the current period and the expenditures are said to be **capitalized.** Although inventory and prepaid expenses also are assets because they benefit future periods, the term **capital assets** is usually taken to mean long-lived assets—assets that provide service for several future years.

A capital asset can usefully be thought of as a bundle of services. When a company buys a truck that is intended to last for 200,000 miles, it is in effect buying transportation services that will benefit the company over several future years. The cost of these services, that is, the cost of the truck, should be matched with the revenues that are obtained from its use in these future periods. The general name for this matching process is **amortization,** but other names are used for various types of capital assets, as will be described. The portion of the asset's cost that is charged to a given period is an expense of that period. A capital asset is therefore essentially similar to a prepaid insurance policy or other prepaid expense. It is initially recorded as an asset and is

ILLUSTRATION 7–1
Expenditures and Expenses

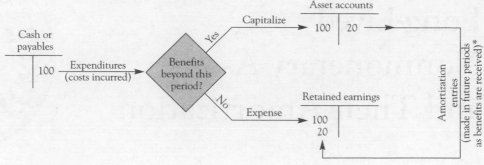

* Amortize over five years.

ILLUSTRATION 7–2
Types of Long-Lived Assets and Amortization Methods

Type of Asset	Method of Converting to Expense
Tangible Assets	
Land	Not amortized
Plant and equipment	Depreciation
Natural resources	Depletion
Intangible Assets	
Goodwill	Not amortized*
Intangible assets (other than goodwill)—limited life	Amortization
Intangible assets (other than goodwill)—indefinite life	Not amortized*
Leasehold improvements	Amortization
Deferred charges	Amortization
Research and development costs	Not capitalized

* Subject to periodic impairment test.

converted to an expense in one or more future periods. The difference is that the life of most capital assets is longer than that of most prepaid expenses.

Illustration 7–1 uses T accounts to depict how expenditures either are expensed in the current period (period costs) or are capitalized in an asset account and amortized (expensed) in later periods. Note that all costs *eventually* become expenses, but capital assets' costs do so over a period of several years, whereas period costs become expenses as they are incurred.

Types of Long-Lived Assets

Illustration 7–2 lists principal types of long-lived nonmonetary assets and the terminology used for the process of amortizing the cost of each type. The principal distinction is between tangible assets and intangible assets. A **tangible asset** is an asset that has physical substance, such as a building or a machine. An **intangible asset**, such as patent rights or copyrights, has no physical substance. Many such assets are referred to as **intellectual property.**

Long-lived tangible assets are usually listed on the balance sheet under the heading "property, plant, and equipment." The term **fixed assets** is often used in informal discussion and appears in several balance sheets in this book simply because it is shorter. Property includes *land,* which ordinarily is not amortized because its useful life is assumed to be indefinitely long. *Plant and equipment* includes buildings, machinery, office equipment, and other types of long-lived capital assets. The accounting process of converting the original cost of plant and equipment assets to expense is called

depreciation. Natural resources such as petroleum and natural gas in the ground are usually reported as a separate category (but *not* after they have been taken out of the ground and become inventory). The accounting process of converting the cost of these natural resource assets to expense is called **depletion.**

The several categories of intangible assets will be discussed separately in later sections of this chapter. When intangible assets are converted to expenses, the accounting process has no specific name (as in the case of fixed assets and natural resources); it is just called **amortization.**

Plant and Equipment: Acquisition

Distinction between Asset and Expense

The distinction between expenditures that are capitalized and expenditures that are expensed as period costs is not entirely clear-cut. Some borderline cases are described in the following paragraphs.

Low-Cost Items

In accordance with the materiality concept, items that have a low unit cost, such as calculators and hand tools, are charged immediately as expenses, even though they may have a long life. Each company sets its own criteria for items that are to be capitalized. Generally, the line is drawn in terms of the cost of an item, which may be anywhere from $25 to $1,000, or even more. Items costing less are expensed.

Nevertheless, the capitalized cost of a new facility may include the cost of the initial outfit of small items that do not individually meet the criteria for capitalization. Examples are the initial outfit of small tools in a factory, the books in a library, and the table-ware and kitchen utensils in a restaurant. When these items are replaced, the cost of the replacement items is charged as an expense, not capitalized.

Betterments

Repair and maintenance is work done to keep an asset in good operating condition or to bring it back to good operating condition if it has broken down. Repair and maintenance costs are ordinarily period costs; they are not added to the capitalized cost of the asset. A **betterment** is added to the cost of the asset. The distinction between maintenance expenses and betterments is this: Maintenance keeps the asset in good condition but in no better condition than when it was purchased; a betterment makes the asset better than it was when it was purchased or extends its useful life beyond the original estimate of useful life.

In practice, the line between the two is difficult to draw. A new accessory designed to make a machine operate more efficiently or perform new functions is a betterment; an overhaul during which worn-out parts are replaced with new ones is maintenance. In the interest of conservatism, some work that strictly speaking should be considered a betterment is often charged as an expense of the current period.

Replacements

Replacements may be either assets or expenses, depending on how the asset unit is defined. The replacement of an entire asset results in the writing off of the old asset and the recording of the new asset. The replacement of a component part of an asset is maintenance expense. For example, a few companies treat a building as a single asset unit, whereas most treat each major component (structure, plumbing, elevators, heating and air-conditioning system) as a separate asset. The replacement of an elevator would result in a maintenance charge in the former case and in a new asset in the latter. In general, the broader the definition of the asset unit, the greater will be the amount of costs charged as maintenance and, hence, expensed in the year the replacement parts are installed.

Items Included in Cost

The governing principle is that the cost of an item of property, plant, or equipment includes *all expenditures that are necessary to make the asset ready for its intended use.* In many cases the amount can be determined easily. For example, the cost of a truck purchased for cash is simply the amount of cash paid. In other cases, the problem is more complicated. The cost of a parcel of land includes the purchase price, broker's commission, legal fees, and the cost of grading or of tearing down existing structures so as to make the land ready for its intended use. The cost of machinery includes the purchase price, sales tax, transportation costs to where the machinery is to be used, and installation costs.

Despite the principle stated above, many organizations do not capitalize all the costs incurred to make the asset ready to provide service. Some capitalize only the purchase price. They do this both because it is simpler and it also minimizes property taxes, which may be calculated on the basis of the capitalized amount.

Self-Constructed Assets

When a company constructs a building or item of equipment for its own use, the amount of capitalized cost includes all the costs incurred in construction. As in the case of product costs, these costs include the materials and labor directly associated with the project, as well as a fair share of the company's indirect costs incurred during the construction period. The Financial Accounting Standards Board (FASB) requires that these capitalized costs also include interest.[1] The amount of interest capitalized is the amount related to borrowings made to finance the project (construction loans) if these are identifiable. If not, the company must estimate the interest cost that could have been avoided if the asset in question had not been constructed. The total amount of interest capitalized cannot exceed the company's total interest cost for the period. The interest capitalization period ends when the asset is substantially complete and ready for its intended use. If the company contracts with an outside party to build the asset and makes deposits or progress payments to the contractor, then interest costs associated with these funds are included in the capitalized cost.

As is the case with other items of cost, if interest cost is capitalized rather than expensed, this has the effect of increasing the income of the current period and decreasing income during the years of the asset's useful life. This decrease occurs because each year's depreciation expense for the asset is larger than it would have been had the interest cost not been capitalized.

Noncash Costs

In the great majority of cases, a capital asset is acquired for cash or for a note or other obligation whose cash equivalent is easily determined. When some other consideration, such as common stock, is given, there may be problems in determining the amount to be capitalized. The general principle is this: First, the fair market value of the consideration given for the asset should be determined; and, second, if it is not feasible to determine this value, then the fair market value of the new capital asset itself is used. (Special rules apply when one capital asset is traded in as part payment for a new asset, as described in a following section.)

---

[1] "Capitalization of Interest Cost," *FASB Statement No. 34.*

Acquisitions Recorded at Other Than Cost

There are a few exceptions to the basic rule that asset acquisitions are recorded in the accounts at cost. If the entity acquires an asset by donation or pays substantially less than the market value of the asset, the asset is recorded at its fair value.[2] This happens, for example, when a community donates land or a building in order to induce a company to locate there.

Such exceptions to the general rule are relatively rare, and their rarity emphasizes the importance of the general rule that *nonmonetary assets are recorded at cost.* Furthermore, as will be seen in the next section, increases in market value do not affect the accounting records for capital assets. Competent investors acquire or build apartment houses or shopping centers with the expectation that part of the profit from this investment will be derived from the appreciation of the property. This appreciation may in fact occur year after year, but it is not recorded in the accounts.[3]

The reason for the supremacy of the cost concept over a system geared to changes in current value is the importance of the basic criterion of objectivity. We may know in a general way that the value of an apartment house is increasing, but there is no objective way of measuring the amount of increase until a sale takes place. When this happens, a new cost is established, and the asset is recorded at this cost in the accounts of the new owner.

In contrast GAAP, IFRS allows property, plant, and equipment, after its initial recognition at cost, to be measured using the cost model (see above) or, if the assets fair value can be measured reliably, the revaluation model. Under the revaluation model, the asset is carried at its revalued amount (fair value) at its date of revaluation less any subsequent accumulated depreciation and subsequent impairment losses. If an asset's carrying amount is increased as a result of revaluation, the increase is treated as an increase in other comprehensive income (an owner's equity account). Revaluations resulting in a decrease in an asset's carrying amount are recorded as a reduction of other comprehensive income to the extent of previously recorded increases. Any excess loss of fair value is charged to income.[4]

Basket Purchases

Sometimes an entity acquires in one transaction several capital assets that are to appear in more than one balance sheet category. This is called a **basket purchase.** The company must divide the basket's cost between the categories on some reasonable basis. Usually this requires an appraisal of the relative value of each asset included in the basket purchase.

Such a separation is always required when land and a building are purchased in a single transaction; this is because the building will subsequently be depreciated, whereas the land will remain on the books at its cost. A separation also may be necessary if the capital assets in the basket have different useful lives, because they will then be depreciated at different rates.

Example

A parcel of land with a building thereon is purchased for $800,000. An appraiser states that the land is worth $90,000 and the building is worth $810,000, a total of $900,000, which is more than the $800,000 cost. Since the appraised value of the land is 10 percent of the total appraised value of the basket, the land is entered in the accounts at 10 percent of the total cost, or $80,000. The building is entered at 90 percent of the cost, or $720,000.

---

[2] "Accounting for Nonmonetary Transactions," *APB Opinion No. 29.*
[3] "Status of Accounting Research Bulletins," *APB Opinion No. 6,* "Property, plant and equipment should not be written up by an entity to reflect appraisal, market or current values which are above cost to the entity."
[4] "Property, Plant and Equipment", *IAS No. 16.*

Note that it would *not* be correct to use the appraised value of one asset as the amount to be capitalized and to capitalize the other asset at the remainder of the purchase price. Thus, it would not be correct to record the land at $90,000 and the building at $710,000.

Plant and Equipment: Depreciation

Unless otherwise indicated, the discussion of depreciation accounting in this section will relate to *financial reporting* (i.e., generally accepted accounting principles, or IFRS and GAAP), as distinguished from income tax reporting. Depreciation in financial reporting is based on the matching concept, whereas the tax code essentially eliminated the matching concept as the basis of income tax depreciation calculations. (Depreciation for income tax purposes is described in a later section.)

With the exception of land, most items of plant and equipment have a limited useful life; that is, they will provide service to the entity over a limited number of future accounting periods. A fraction of the cost of the asset is therefore properly chargeable as an expense in each of the accounting periods in which the asset provides service to the entity. The accounting process for this gradual conversion of plant and equipment capitalized cost into expense is called **depreciation.**[5]

Why is depreciation an expense? The answer is that the costs of *all* goods and services consumed by an entity during an accounting period are expenses. The cost of insurance protection provided in a year is an expense of that year even though the insurance premium was paid two or three years previously. Depreciation expense is conceptually just like insurance expense. The principal difference is that the fraction of total cost of an item of plant and equipment that is an expense in a given year is difficult to estimate, whereas the fraction of the total cost of an insurance policy that is an expense in a given year can be easily calculated. This difference does not change the fundamental fact that both insurance policies and plant and equipment provide benefits to the entity over a finite number of accounting periods, and a fraction of their original cost therefore must be charged as an expense of each of these periods.

The useful life of a tangible long-lived asset is limited by either deterioration or obsolescence. **Deterioration** is the physical process of wearing out. **Obsolescence** refers to loss of usefulness because of the development of improved equipment or processes, changes in style, or other causes not related to the physical condition of the asset. We will refer to the time until an asset wears out as its **physical life,** and the time until it becomes obsolete or is expected to be disposed of as its **service life.** Although the word *depreciation* is sometimes used as referring only to physical deterioration ("wear and tear"), this usage is incorrect. In many cases, a piece of equipment's service life is shorter than its physical life; computers are a good example.

Judgments Required

The depreciation expense for each accounting period is determined by one of several variations of this general formula:

$$\text{Depreciation expense} = \frac{\text{Original cost} - \text{Residual value}}{\text{Service life}}$$

---

[5] If the asset is used in the production process, its depreciation is properly chargeable as an item of product cost that is initially added to Work in Process Inventory, then flows through Finished Goods Inventory, and becomes an expense (cost of goods sold) in the period in which the product is sold, as described in Chapter 6. In the interests of simplicity, in this chapter we shall not distinguish between the depreciation that is a product cost and the depreciation that is a period expense.

In order to determine the depreciation expense for an accounting period, three judgments or estimates must be made for each depreciable asset:

1. The *service life* of the asset—the number of accounting periods over which the asset will be useful to the entity that owns it.
2. The asset's **residual value** at the end of its service life—any amount eventually recovered through sale, trade-in, or salvage. The **net cost** of the asset to the entity is its original cost less its residual value. It is this net cost that should be charged as an expense over the asset's life, not its original cost. In a great many situations, however, the estimated residual value is so small or uncertain that it is disregarded.
3. The *method of depreciation*— the method that will be used to allocate a fraction of the asset's net cost to each of the accounting periods in which it is expected to be used.

Managers, not being clairvoyant, cannot know in advance how long the asset will be used or what its residual value will be. Often they have no scientific or strictly logical way of deciding the best depreciation method. The amount of depreciation expense that results from these judgments is therefore an *estimate*. Because of the arithmetic precision of the calculations that take place *after* these judgments are made, the inexact nature of depreciation expense is sometimes overlooked.

Service Life

The service life of an asset is the period of time over which it is expected to provide service (i.e., benefits) to the entity that controls it. The service life may be shorter than the physical life because of obsolescence or because the entity may plan to dispose of an asset before its physical life ends. For example, although automobiles typically have a useful physical life of about 10 years, many companies trade in their automobiles every two years and buy new ones. In these companies, the service life is two years. If the asset's service life to a particular entity is clearly less than the asset's useful physical life, then the estimated residual value of the asset at the end of its service life should be greater than zero.

Estimating the service life of an asset is a difficult problem. Reference to the tax code is not helpful. The tax code uses "cost recovery periods" that generally are shorter than an asset's useful lives. (For example, a new apartment house has a cost recovery period of 271/2 years.) Since GAAP clearly indicates that depreciation is to be based on realistic service lives, companies should make their own estimates of the useful lives of their various categories of depreciable assets for financial reporting purposes rather than relying on income tax lives.

Depreciation Methods

Consider a piece of equipment purchased for $1,000 with an estimated service life of 10 years and estimated residual value of zero. The objective of depreciation accounting is to charge this net cost of $1,000 as an expense over the 10-year period. How much should be charged as an expense each year?

This question cannot be answered directly by observing the amount of asset value physically consumed in a given year. Physically the equipment continues to be equipment; usually, there is no observable indication of its decline in usefulness. Nor can the question be answered in terms of changes in the equipment's market value during the year, because equipment accounting is concerned with the amortization of cost, not with changes in market values. An indirect approach therefore must be used. Any method that is "systematic and rational" is permitted under GAAP.[6] IFRS is more explicit. It requires the depreciation method to reflect the pattern in which the asset's

---

[6] AICPA, *Accounting Research Bulletin No. 43*, Chap. 9, Sec. C.

future economic benefits are expected to be consumed.[7] Three conceptual ways of looking at the depreciation process are described below, together with the methods that follow from each.

Straight-Line Method

One concept views a fixed asset as providing its services in a level stream. That is, the service provided (benefit received) is equal in each year of the asset's life, just as a three-year insurance policy provides equal insurance protection in each of its three years. This concept leads to the **straight-line method,** which charges as an expense an equal fraction of the net cost of the asset each year. For a piece of equipment with a cost of $1,000, a zero residual value, and an estimated service life of 10 years, $\frac{1}{10}$ of $1,000 ($100) is the depreciation expense of the first year, another $\frac{1}{10}$ is the depreciation expense of the second year, and so on. Expressed another way, the equipment is said to have a **depreciation rate** of 10 percent per year, the rate being the reciprocal of the estimated service life.

Accelerated Methods

A second concept recognizes that the stream of benefits provided by a fixed asset may not be level. Rather, the benefits provided may be greatest in the first year of the asset's service life and least in the last year. This pattern may occur because the asset's mechanical efficiency tends to decline with age, because maintenance costs tend to increase with age, or because of the increasing likelihood that better equipment will become available and make it obsolete. Often, when a facility is not working at capacity, it is the older equipment that is not used. It is argued, therefore, that when an asset was purchased, the probability that the earlier periods would benefit more than the later periods was taken into account and that the depreciation method should reflect this. Such a line of reasoning leads to an **accelerated method** that charges a larger fraction of the cost as an expense of the early years than of the later years.[8]

Two accelerated depreciation methods, the double-declining-balance method and sum-of-the-years'-digits (or simply years'-digits) method, are described below. The effect of either of these methods is to write off approximately two-thirds of the asset's cost in the first half of its estimated life, as contrasted with the straight-line method, under which, of course, half the cost is written off in each half of the asset's estimated life. Thus, if an accelerated method is used, depreciation expense is greater in the early years and less in the later years as compared with the straight-line method.

In a **declining-balance method,** each year's depreciation is found by applying a rate to the net book value of the asset as of the beginning of that year. (In the straight-line method, the depreciation rate is applied to original cost net of residual value, not to each year's net book value.) The **net book value** of an asset at a point in time is the original acquisition cost less total depreciation accumulated up to that time. With a declining-balance method, the asset's estimated residual value, if any, has no effect on the annual depreciation charges because residual value is not included in the calculation of an asset's net book value.

The declining-balance rate is a stated percentage of the straight-line rate. Thus, for an asset with a useful life of 10 years (straight-line rate = 10 percent), 200 percent declining

---

[7] "Property, Plant and Equipment," *IAS No. 16.*
[8] An argument also can be made for an opposite approach: charging a smaller fraction of the cost in the early years and a larger fraction in the later years. This leads to an **annuity method.** It is rarely used in published financial statements.

balance would use a rate of 20 percent (200 percent ∗ 10 percent). Similarly, 150 percent declining balance would use a rate of 15 percent. The 200 percent declining-balance method is also called the **double-declining-balance method** because the depreciation rate is double the straight-line rate.

After several years, the annual depreciation charge with a declining-balance method will be lower than the annual charge with the straight-line method. The usual practice is to change at that time from declining-balance to straight-line depreciation for the remainder of the asset's life.

In the **years'-digits method**, also referred to as the sum-of-the-years' digits method (SYD), the numbers 1, 2, 3, . . ., *n* are added, where *n* is the estimated years of useful life. This sum (SYD) can be found by the equation (using 10 years for the example)

$$SYD = n\left(\frac{n+1}{2}\right) = 10\left(\frac{10+1}{2}\right) = 55$$

The depreciation rate each year is a fraction in which the denominator is the sum of these digits and the numerator is, for the first year, *n*; for the second year, *n* − 1; for the third year, *n* − 2; and so on. Thus, for a 10-year asset, the rate is $\frac{10}{55}$ the first year, $\frac{9}{55}$ the second year, $\frac{8}{55}$ the third year, and so on. As with the straight-line method, the rate is applied to the net cost—cost less residual value—of the asset.

Comparison of Methods

Illustration 7–3 shows graphically the way these three methods work out for a piece of equipment costing $1,000 with an estimated service life of 10 years and no residual value.

Units-of-Production Method

A third concept of depreciation also treats the asset as consisting of a bundle of service units; but it does not assume that these service units will be provided in a mathematical

ILLUSTRATION 7–3

Annual Depreciation Charges for Equipment with Net Cost of $1,000 and 10-Year Service Life

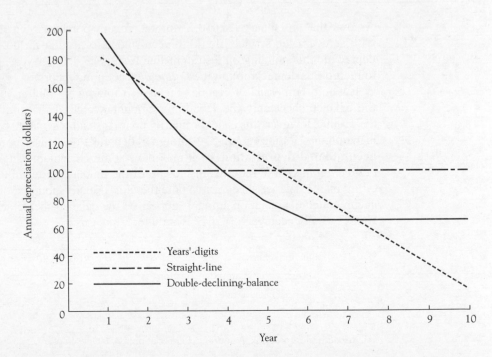

time-phased pattern, as is assumed by the straight-line and accelerated methods. Rather, with this concept, a period's depreciation is related to the *number of service units* provided by the asset during the period.

This view leads to the **units-of-production method,** in which the cost of each service unit is the net cost of the asset divided by the total number of such units. The depreciation charge for a period is then the number of units consumed in that period multiplied by the net cost of one unit. For example, if a truck has an estimated net cost of $60,000 and is expected to give service for 300,000 miles, depreciation would be charged at a rate of 20 cents per mile ($60,000 ÷ 300,000). The depreciation expense in a year in which the truck traveled 50,000 miles would be $10,000.

Choice of a Depreciation Method

Later in this chapter, depreciation methods allowed in computing taxable income for the IRS are described. In deciding on a depreciation method for *financial reporting* purposes, income tax considerations are kept entirely separate. For tax purposes, corporations in most instances use the tax code's accelerated depreciation rules, thereby receiving as quickly as possible the tax savings related to depreciation.

With respect to financial reporting, we have previously indicated that each type of method—straight-line, accelerated, and units-of-production—has its own conceptual basis as to the pattern in which an asset provides its bundle of services. In theory, GAAP allows a choice of methods so that a company can match the method to the pattern that an asset follows in that particular company. Strictly speaking, this means that different methods would apply to different types of assets in a given company. However, there is little evidence that companies think about service benefit patterns when selecting depreciation methods for their financial accounting. In most cases, a single method is applied to all of a company's depreciable assets. The method usually chosen is straight-line.

Accounting for Depreciation

Assume that on January 1, 2010, Trantor Company purchased for $1 million a building with an estimated service life of 40 years and zero residual value. Trantor decided to depreciate this building on a straight-line basis, $25,000 per year. Now consider how to record this depreciation in the *financial* accounting records.

It would be possible to reduce the asset value by $25,000 a year and to show on the balance sheet only the remaining amount, which at the end of 2010 would be $975,000. However, this is not ordinarily done. Instead, a separate contra-asset account is maintained for the cumulative amount of depreciation. This account is usually called **accumulated depreciation,** or it may have some other name such as *allowance for depreciation.* GAAP requires disclosure of the amount of accumulated depreciation, either on the balance sheet or in a note thereto.[9] Usually, both the original cost and the accumulated depreciation amounts appear on the balance sheet itself. For Trantor, the figures as of December 31, 2010, would look like this:

Building, at cost	$1,000,000	
Less: Accumulated depreciation	25,000	
Building, net		$975,000

---

[9] "Disclosure of Depreciable Assets and Depreciation," *APB Opinion No. 12.*

As of December 31, 2011, another year's depreciation would be added, and the balance sheet would then show

Building, at cost	$1,000,000	
Less: Accumulated depreciation	50,000	
Building, net		$950,000

The foregoing amounts can be interpreted as follows:

Original cost of the building	$1,000,000
That portion of the original cost charged as expense for all periods to date	50,000
That portion of original cost remaining to be charged as expense of future periods	$ 950,000

The $950,000 is the **book value** of the asset. This is often labeled **net book value** to distinguish it from original cost, which is called the **gross book value.** The term *book value* is intended to highlight the fact that the amount is not an appraisal or market value.

On the income statement, the expense item is usually labeled **depreciation expense.** In the income statement for 2010, this item for Trantor Company would be $25,000 (disregarding depreciation on assets other than this building); and $25,000 also would appear in the income statements for 2011, for 2012, and for following years until the building was either disposed of or fully depreciated.

The annual journal entry for depreciation on Trantor's building, which is one of the adjusting entries, would be as follows:

Depreciation Expense 25,000

Accumulated Depreciation 25,000

Change in Depreciation Rates

Suppose that in the year 2019 Trantor Company decides that the building is likely to last until 2054, which is longer than the 40 years originally estimated. In theory, Trantor should change the depreciation rate so that the book value remaining in 2019 would be charged off over the newly estimated *remaining* service life. Because of all the uncertainties and estimates inherent in the depreciation process, however, such changes in the depreciation rate are not always made in practice.

Fully Depreciated Assets

Even if Trantor Company should use its building for more than 40 years, depreciation would cease to be accumulated at the end of the 40th year, since by then the total original cost of the building would have been charged to expense. Until the asset is disposed of, it is customary to continue to show the asset on the balance sheet. Thus, as of December 31, 2050, and for as long thereafter as Trantor owned the building, the balance sheet would show the following:

Building, at cost	$1,000,000	
Less: Accumulated depreciation	1,000,000	
Building, net		$0

Partial-Year Depreciation

Often, half a year's depreciation is recorded in the year of acquisition and half a year's depreciation in the year of disposal, no matter what the actual date of acquisition or disposal is. This **half-year convention** is justified on the grounds that if the entity is acquiring and disposing of assets throughout the year, the inaccuracies in this procedure as regards specific assets will "wash out" over the course of the year. Other companies use an analogous half-quarter or half-month convention.

Disclosure

The amount of the depreciation charged off in the year must be disclosed in the financial statements. In a merchandising company, this can be done by reporting depreciation expense as a separate item on the income statement. In many manufacturing companies, a separate income statement item may not be feasible; this is because depreciation of production plant and equipment is part of cost of goods sold (product costs), whereas the depreciation of other assets is part of general and administrative expenses, which are period costs. In these circumstances, the total amount of depreciation expense is reported in a note accompanying the financial statements. The balance sheet, or a note thereto, must disclose the original cost of major classes of depreciable assets, the amount of accumulated depreciation, and the depreciation method or methods used.

Plant and Equipment: Disposal

Suppose that at the end of 10 years Trantor Company sells its building. At that time $^{10}/_{40}$ of the original cost, or $250,000, will have been built up in the Accumulated Depreciation account, and the net book value of the building will be $750,000. If the building is sold for $750,000 cash, the accounts are charged as follows:

```
Cash . . . . . . . . . . . . . . . . . . . . . . . . . . . . . . . 750,000
Accumulated Depreciation . . . . . . . . . . . . . . 250,000
     Building . . . . . . . . . . . . . . . . . . . . . . . . . . .         1,000,000
```

Since the building is no longer an asset of Trantor, both its original cost and its accumulated depreciation must be removed from the accounts. This is exactly what the preceding entry accomplishes.

If the building were sold for less than $750,000—for $650,000—the $100,000 difference is recorded as a loss, as in the following entry:

```
Cash . . . . . . . . . . . . . . . . . . . . . . . . . . . . . . . 650,000
Accumulated Depreciation . . . . . . . . . . . . . . 250,000
Loss on Sale of Building . . . . . . . . . . . . . . . . 100,000
     Building . . . . . . . . . . . . . . . . . . . . . . . . . . .         1,000,000
```

Note that the effect on the Building and the Accumulated Depreciation accounts is identical with that in the previous illustration: The amounts relating to this building disappear. The loss is a charge to earnings, reflecting the fact that the total depreciation expense recorded for the preceding 10 years was less than what Trantor now knows to have been the actual net cost of the building over that period of time. The actual net cost turns out to have been $350,000, whereas the total depreciation expense charged has amounted to only $250,000.

Since the depreciation expense as originally recorded turns out to have been incorrect, the Retained Earnings account, which reflects the net of all revenue and expenses to date, is also incorrect. There is therefore some logic in closing the Loss on Sale of

Building account directly to Retained Earnings, thus correcting the error contained therein. Nevertheless, the matching concept requires that this loss be shown as an expense on the income statement of the current period. An asset cost amount that no longer benefits future periods is an expense of the current period.

If an asset is sold for *more* than its book value, the entries are analogous to those described above. The account Gain on the Sale of Building (or other category of long-lived asset) is credited for the excess of the selling price over net book value. This account (as well as Loss on Sale of . . .) is usually included in "other income" on the income statement, rather than being shown as a separate line item.

Market Values

The net book value of an asset usually is not the same as its market value. However, if Trantor's building was sold at the end of 2015 for $650,000, this was by definition its market value at that time. Also, the $1 million original cost was presumably its market value on January 1, 2010, when it was acquired. Thus, the first and the last transactions for the building take account of market values. In the intervening periods under the cost model, changes in market values are disregarded in the financial statements and underlying accounting records.

Impaired Assets

An exception to this general rule is made in the case of an **impaired asset**— an asset for which its remaining benefits excluding the cost or benefits of financing activities and income taxes, as measured by the sum of the future cash flows the asset's use will generate, is less than its net book value. If the entity expects to hold such an impaired asset, it is written down to its fair value. If the entity plans to dispose of an impaired asset, it is valued at the lower of cost or fair value, less the cost of disposal. Any write-down is reported as an element of the period's income.[10] This is analogous to the lower-of-cost-or-market rule for inventories.

Example

On January 1, 20X1, a company paid $1 million for a specialized machine, expecting to use it to produce a specific item for six years. The equipment was depreciated using the straight-line method. By January 20X4 demand for the item had dropped so much that the company expected that the cash flows the item would generate over the remainder of its product life cycle would be less than the equipment's net book value ($500,000). The equipment was therefore written down to $300,000, its estimated fair value on January 1, 20X4. This write-down reduced 20X4 reported income.

The GAAP impairment test and subsequent measurement of any impairment loss described above is a two-step process. IFRS' recognition and measurement of any impairment loss is a one-step process. If, and only if, the recoverable amount of an asset accounted for using its cost model is less than its carrying amount, the carrying amount of the asset is reduced to its recoverable amount. Recoverable amount is higher of the assets' fair value less cost & sell and its value in use. Value in use is the present value of the future cash flows expected to be derived from an asset. Any reduction in the assets carrying amount is an impairment loss, which is a change to earnings.[11]

---

[10] "Accounting for the Impairment or disposal of Long-Lived Assets," *FASB Statement No. 144*.
[11] "Impairment of assets," *IAS No. 36*. If an asset is measured using the revaluation model, any impairment loss is treated as a revaluation decrease in accordance with "Property, Plant and Equipment," *IAS No. 16* (see page 187).

Exchanges and Trade-Ins

Some items of property and equipment are disposed of by trading them in or exchanging them for new assets. When this is done, the value of the old asset is used in calculating the acquisition cost of the new asset. The amount used in this calculation depends on whether or not the asset traded is similar to the new asset. If the trade-in is similar—of the same general type or performing the same function—its value is assumed to be its net book value. If the asset traded is dissimilar, its value is its estimated fair value.[12]

Example

Assume a company trades in two automobiles, each of which originally cost $20,000, of which $15,000 has been depreciated; thus, each has a net book value of $5,000. Each has a fair value of $7,000 as a used car.

The first automobile is traded for another automobile with a list price of $30,000, and $18,000 cash is given to the dealer in addition to the trade-in. In this case, the cost of the new automobile is recorded as $23,000, the sum of the $18,000 cash and the $5,000 *net book value* of the trade-in.

The second automobile is traded for a piece of equipment that also has a list price of $30,000, and $18,000 cash is given in addition to the trade-in. In this case, the cost of the new equipment is recorded as $25,000—the sum of the $18,000 cash and the $7,000 *fair value* of the trade-in.

Journal entries for these two transactions are as follows:

1. For an exchange of similar assets:

Automobile (New) 23,000		
Accumulated Depreciation (Automobile) 15,000		
Cash	18,000	
Automobile (Old)	20,000	

2. For other exchanges:

Equipment (New) 25,000		
Accumulated Depreciation (Automobile) 15,000		
Cash	18,000	
Automobile (Old)	20,000	
Gain on Disposal of Automobile	2,000	

In both cases, the cost and accumulated depreciation of the old asset are removed from the accounts. Also in both cases, the list price of the new asset is disregarded. In the case of an exchange of similar assets, no gain or loss is recognized; in other exchanges, the gain or loss is recognized. These rules are required for both financial reporting and income tax purposes. (For similar assets, tax regulations use the term *like-kind exchange.*)

The rationale behind these rules is that an exchange of similar assets does not result in the culmination of an earnings process, whereas an exchange of dissimilar assets does. For example, if a professional football team exchanges the contract of one of its players for cash and the contract of a player from another team, the team's process of generating earnings is not materially affected. On the other hand, if a farm owner exchanges a plot of tilled acreage for a new tractor, then the earnings process has ended on that portion of the farm that was exchanged.

Group Depreciation

The procedures described above related to a single fixed asset, such as one building or one automobile. To find the total depreciation expense for a whole category of assets, this procedure could be repeated for each single asset, and the total depreciation for

---

[12] "Accounting for Nonmonetary Transactions," *APB Opinion No. 29.*

all the assets in the category would then be recorded by one journal entry. This is **unit depreciation,** also called **item depreciation.**

An alternative procedure is to treat all similar assets (such as all automobiles or all office chairs) as a "pool," or group, rather than making the calculation for each one separately. The process is called **group depreciation.** Annual depreciation expense under group depreciation is computed in a manner similar to that described above for an individual asset. If the straight-line method is used, for example, the depreciation rate is applied to the total original cost of the entire group of assets.

If the group method is used, no gain or loss is recognized when an individual asset is sold or otherwise disposed of. Upon disposal, the asset account is credited for the asset's original cost, as in the entries given above. However, the difference between cost and the sales proceeds is debited or credited to Accumulated Depreciation rather than to a gain or loss account. This procedure assumes that gains on some sales in the group are offset by losses on others. This assumption is reasonable if the group contains a relatively large number of similar assets.

| **Example** | A used microcomputer with original cost of $3,000 is disposed of for $400 cash. Assuming group depreciation is used, the journal entry for this transaction is |

Cash 400	
Accumulated Depreciation, Microcomputers 2,600	
Microcomputers	3,000

Significance of Depreciation

The amount shown as accumulated depreciation on the balance sheet does *not* represent the "accumulation" of any tangible thing. It is merely that portion of the depreciable assets' original cost that already has been matched as expense against revenue.

Occasionally, an entity does set aside money for the specific purpose of purchasing new assets, a process sometimes called **funding depreciation.** This is a *financing* transaction, which is completely separate from the accounting process of *recording* depreciation—the operating expense associated with the use of fixed assets. If depreciation is funded, cash or securities are set aside in such a way that they cannot be used in the regular operation of the entity (e.g., a special bank account may be created). This practice is not common. It is mentioned here only to emphasize, by contrast, the point that the depreciation process itself is *not* a means of automatically creating a fund for the replacement of assets.

There is a widespread belief that in some mysterious way depreciation does represent money, specifically, money that can be used to purchase new assets. Sometimes this erroneous belief is reinforced by an entity's using the term *reserve for depreciation* to mean accumulated depreciation. Depreciation is *not* money; the money that the entity has is shown by the balance in its Cash account.

| **Example** | This quotation is from a well-known publication: "Most large companies draw much of the cash flow they employ for expanding and modernizing their operations from their depreciation reserves." This statement is not true in anything remotely approaching a literal sense. |

A widespread belief that the net book value of assets is related to their real value is equally erroneous.

Example

An auditor's report included the following statement: "Our inspection of insurance policies in force at the close of the year disclosed that the plant assets on the basis of book values were amply protected against fire." Such a statement has little if any significance. What investors want to know is whether the insurance protection equals the *replacement cost* of the assets, and this is unlikely to correspond to their book value.

The key to a practical understanding of depreciation is a sentence from *Accounting Research Bulletin No. 43:* "Depreciation is a process of allocation, not of valuation."[13] Depreciation expense does *not* represent the shrinkage in assets' market value during an accounting period. Particularly during periods of inflation, a depreciable asset's market value may be even higher at the end of the period than it was at the beginning. Neither does the net book value represent the market value of the depreciable assets. *Depreciation expense is the systematic allocation of the original cost of an asset to the periods in which the asset provides benefits to the entity.* It follows that the net book value of fixed assets reported on the balance sheet represents only that portion of the assets' original cost that has *not yet* been charged to expense through this systematic allocation process.

No one really knows how long an asset will last or what its residual value will be at the end of its life. Without this knowledge, each year's depreciation expense is necessarily an estimate, one of several estimates we have now discussed that affect the period's reported income.

Income Tax Considerations

Congress uses the income tax laws as a device to encourage corporations to invest in new productive assets. The key mechanism to encourage this capital formation has been depreciation allowances.[14]

Depreciation Allowances

Background

An incentive to invest in capital assets is provided in the tax code by allowing the use of accelerated depreciation in calculating taxable income for federal income tax purposes. This incentive is further increased by shortening asset lives for tax purposes to periods substantially shorter than the assets' actual service lives. The tax code calls this specified approach the **modified accelerated cost recovery system (MACRS).** MACRS provides for a series of asset classes, each class having its own depreciation life (called *recovery period* in the regulations) and method.[15] As with financial accounting declining-balance depreciation calculations, MACRS calculations ignore the estimated residual value of the asset.

Half-Year Convention

The tax rules also incorporate the **half-year convention.** Under this convention, most classes of property acquired or disposed of at any point during the year are assumed to have been acquired or disposed of at the *midpoint* of that year. Thus, an asset in, say,

---

[13] AICPA, *Accounting Research Bulletin No. 43,* Chap. 9, Sec. C.
[14] Our description of income tax matters throughout this text is intended to give general principles only. Details are spelled out in thousands of pages of Internal Revenue Service regulations.
[15] The tax laws also permit the use of straight-line depreciation over longer (realistic) asset lives. However, it is usually to a company's benefit to use the accelerated cost-recovery provisions.

the five-year class is actually depreciated over six years, with half a year's depreciation taken in both the first and sixth years and a full year's taken in each of the intervening four years.

| **Example** | Assume that a machine in the five-year class is acquired at some point in 20X1 for $100,000. This asset would have the following cost recovery schedule, based on the double-declining-balance method for this class and the half-year convention: |

Year	Cost Recovery Deduction	Computation
20X1	$ 20,000	½ * 40% * $100,000
20X2	32,000	40% * ($100,000 − $20,000)
20X3	19,200	40% * ($80,000 − $32,000)
20X4	11,520	40% * ($48,000 − $19,200)
20X5	11,520	Net book value at end of 20X4 is $17,280; this
20X6	5,760	is allocated to the remaining 1½ years, using the straight-line method.
Total	$100,000	

As a practical matter, MACRS is a complex combination of a declining-balance method, the half-year convention, and the change to straight-line depreciation for the latter portion of the recovery period that has made income tax depreciation calculations a "look-up" procedure. Instead of doing the calculations as illustrated above, the accountant uses an IRS table to look up the percentage of an asset's cost that can be depreciated in each year and applies this percentage to the asset's original cost. Thus, in the above example for the years 20X1–20X6, the accountant would find in a table the percentages 20.00, 32.00, 19.20, 11.52, 11.52, and 5.76, and would then multiply each year's percentage by the $100,000 original cost to arrive at that year's MACRS depreciation charge.

Investment Tax Credit

From time to time, the tax laws have permitted a reduction in the year's income taxes equal to a percentage—often 10 percent—of the cost of any business machinery and equipment (but not buildings) acquired by a company during the year. This is called the **investment tax credit (ITC).** The credit is a direct reduction in the company's income tax bill (as contrasted with an item deducted from revenues in arriving at the amount of taxable income). In effect, it is a *rebate* to the company acquiring a new fixed asset, except the rebate comes from the government rather than from the seller of the asset. For example, if a company acquired a $100,000 machine, it could deduct $10,000 from the federal income tax it would otherwise pay for that year.

Either one of two methods of accounting for the ITC is permitted for financial reporting purposes. The **flow-through method** reduces reported income tax expense by the amount of the ITC in the year in which the credit is taken. Conceptually, this method treats the ITC rebate as a tax reduction that is "earned" as a result of acquiring assets that qualify for the ITC.

The **deferral method** treats the ITC rebate as a reduction in the original cost of the asset (which, of course, is what a true rebate is). The deferral method spreads the tax credit over the years of the asset's useful life by reducing reported income tax expense in each of those years. Conceptually, the deferral method rejects the notion that the act of *acquiring* an asset should increase net income, which is the effect of the flow-through method. Rather, the credit is matched with the time periods in which the company is *using* the asset. Nevertheless, when the ITC was last in effect, almost all large companies used the flow-through method.

The income tax rules also permit special treatment of low-income housing, research expenditures, and restoration of historically important buildings, among other things. These provisions are beyond the scope of this introductory treatment.

A Caution

The tax code is subject to frequent change. The rules described above are those in effect as of 2010.[16]

Natural Resources

Natural resources (such as unextracted coal, oil, other minerals, and gas) are assets of the company that owns the right to extract them. The general principles for measuring the acquisition cost of these **wasting assets** are the same as those for other tangible assets. If purchased, the cost is the purchase price and related acquisition costs. Many companies acquire these assets as a consequence of exploring for them. There are two strongly held views on how these exploration costs should be accounted for, particularly for oil and gas companies.

A petroleum company, in a given year, may be exploring in many different locations; it probably will discover oil and gas reserves in only a few of them. Some people argue that *all* the exploration costs of a year should be capitalized as the asset value of the reserves that are discovered during the year; this is the **full cost method.** Others argue that only the costs incurred at locations in which reserves are discovered should be capitalized as the cost of these reserves and that the "dry-hole" costs should be immediately expensed; this is the **successful efforts method.** Both methods are used in practice, with larger companies typically using the successful efforts method.[17]

Example

A petroleum company explores 10 locations, incurring costs of $10 million at each. It discovers oil and gas reserves at three of these locations. If it uses the full cost method, the asset amount of the newly discovered reserves will be recorded as $100 million. If it uses the successful efforts method, the asset amount will be recorded as $30 million and the other $70 million will be charged to expense.

Depletion

The process of amortizing the cost of natural resources in the accounting periods benefited is called **depletion.** The objective is the same as that for depreciation: to allocate the cost in some systematic manner to the years of the asset's useful life. The units-of-production method is ordinarily used.

Example

If an oil property cost $250 million and is estimated to contain 50 million barrels of oil, the depletion rate is $5 per barrel. The total depletion for a year in which 8 million barrels of oil were produced would be $40 million.

---

[16] Remember that many states also levy corporate income taxes; as a result, this book uses a 40 percent rate in illustrations.

[17] In *Statement No. 19,* the FASB required the use of the successful efforts method. Subsequently, however, the SEC ruled that either method would continue to be acceptable for SEC filings. This SEC action led the FASB to issue *Statement No. 25,* which amended *Statement No. 19* to permit either method. This reversal by the FASB serves as a reminder that determining GAAP for public companies is formally the SEC's legislated responsibility, even though in most cases the SEC accepts the FASB's accounting standards.

For income tax purposes, however, the depletion allowance in certain cases may bear no relation to cost. Rather, in some situations, it is a percentage of revenue. The permitted percentage varies with the type of asset and, like other provisions of the tax law, is subject to change. Percentage depletion is an example of an income tax provision that is inconsistent with GAAP. Advocates of the tax law treatment of depletion claim that it stimulates exploration for and development of new supplies of natural resources and is therefore in the national interest.

Accretion and Appreciation

For timberland, cattle, tobacco, wine, and other agricultural products, the increase in value that arises through the natural process of growth or aging is called **accretion.** Since accretion does not represent realized revenue, it is ordinarily not recognized in the accounts. However, the costs incurred in the growing or aging process are added to the asset value, just as is done in the case of costs incurred in the manufacture of goods.

Appreciation is also an increase in the *value* of an asset. It is *not* the opposite of depreciation, which is a write-off of cost. Appreciation of assets is recognized in the accounts only under highly unusual circumstances. For example, if a business is purchased by a new owner and an appraisal discloses that the current fair value of certain assets is substantially above their book value, in some instances (described below) these assets' values are written up to their current value. Generally, however, increases in value are recognized in the accounts only when revenue is realized, whereas expiration of cost is recognized when it occurs.

Intangible Assets

A business can either acquire long-lived intangibles or develop them internally. The costs of internally developing, maintaining, or restoring intangibles that are not specifically identifiable, that have indeterminate lives, or that are inherent in a continuing business and related to the business as a whole, must be expensed as incurred.[18] Typically, acquired long-lived intangibles are capitalized.[19]

Intangibles recognized as long-lived assets fall into three categories: intangible assets with limited useful lives, intangible assets with indefinite useful lives, and goodwill.

Limited Useful Life

Intangible long-lived assets with limited useful lives—such as patents—are usually converted to expenses over a number of accounting periods. The systematic allocation of the costs of these assets to the periods in which they provide benefits is called **amortization.** (There is no specialized term for the process of amortizing these assets, as there is for fixed assets and natural resources.)

The amortization of limited-useful-life intangible assets is essentially the same process as the depreciation of tangible assets. The method of amortization should reflect the pattern in which the economic benefits of the intangible asset are consumed or otherwise used up. However, "if that pattern cannot be reliably determined, a straight-line amortization method shall be used."[20] Also, amortization of an intangible asset is usually credited directly to the asset account rather than being accumulated in a

[18] "Goodwill and Other Intangible Assets," *FASB Statement No. 142.*
[19] "Goodwill and Other Intangible Assets," *FASB Statement No. 142.*
[20] "Goodwill and Other Intangible Assets," *FASB Statement No. 142.*

separate contra asset account, as is the case with accumulated depreciation. Thus, the entry recording one year's amortization of a five-year nonrenewable license that originally cost $50,000 would be

Amortization Expense 10,000		
Licenses		10,000

Indefinite Useful Life

Intangibles recognized as long-lived assets with indefinite useful lives—such as a renewable broadcasting license—are not amortized. Rather they are subjected to periodic impairment tests. If it is determined that such an intangible asset is impaired, its carrying value is written down to its realizable value and a charge equal to the write-down is made to income. An intangible asset's useful life is considered to be indefinite if there are no legal, regulatory, contractual, competitive, economic, or other factors that limit its useful life.

Goodwill

When one company buys another company, the purchasing company may pay more for the acquired company than the fair value of its **net assets**—tangible assets plus recognized intangibles, net of any liabilities assumed by the purchaser. The amount by which the purchase price exceeds the fair value of the net assets is recorded as an asset of the acquiring company. Although sometimes reported on the balance sheet with a descriptive title such as "excess of acquisition cost over net assets acquired," the amount is customarily called **goodwill.**

It is important to note that goodwill arises only as part of a *purchase* transaction. (More details are given in Chapter 12.) The buying company may be willing to pay more than the fair value of the acquired net assets other than goodwill because the acquired company has a strong management team, a favorable reputation in the marketplace, superior production methods, or other unidentifiable intangibles.

The acquisition cost of the recognized assets other than goodwill is their fair value at the time of acquisition. Usually, these values are determined by appraisal, but in some cases the net book value of these assets is accepted as being their fair value. If there is evidence that the fair value differs from net book value, either higher or lower, the fair value governs.

Example

Company A acquires all the assets of Company B, giving Company B $1,500,000 cash. Company B has cash of $50,000, accounts receivable that are believed to have a realizable value of $60,000, and acquired assets other than goodwill that are estimated to have a fair value of $1,100,000. The amount of goodwill is calculated as follows:

Total purchase price		$1,500,000
Less		
Cash acquired	$ 50,000	
Accounts receivable	60,000	
Other acquired assets (estimated)	1,100,000	1,210,000
Goodwill		$ 290,000

Not Amortized

Goodwill cannot be amortized under any circumstances. It must be subjected to an annual impairment test. Any write-down due to impairment is charged to income.

Patents and Copyrights

Patents, copyrights, and similar intangible assets with limited useful lives are initially recorded at their cost. If they are purchased, the cost is the amount paid. If a patented invention is developed within the company, however, the costs involved ordinarily are not capitalized. These are considered to be research and development costs, which are discussed separately in a following section.

The cost of intangible assets with limited useful lives is amortized over the useful life of the asset. If the useful life is limited by agreement or by law (e.g., 17 years for a patent), the amortization period cannot be longer. It may be shorter if the company believes that, because of technological advances or other reasons, the practical life will be shorter than the legal life.

Leasehold Improvements

Leased property reverts to the owner at the end of the period of the lease. Any improvements made to the property belong to the owner; the lessee loses the use of them when the leased property is returned. Therefore, the useful life of such improvements corresponds to the period of the lease. The lease agreement may contain renewal options that effectively extend the life beyond the period of the original lease agreement. It follows that although improvements that otherwise meet the criteria for capitalization are capitalized, the useful life of these improvements is not determined by the physical characteristics of the improvements themselves but rather by the terms of the lease agreement.

Example

A company leases office space and spends $90,000 for remodeling to suit its needs. The lease is for an original period of three years with an option to renew for another three years. The physical life of the improvements is 10 years. The leasehold improvements are amortized over a period of six years, or $15,000 a year, if the lessee believes it likely that the lease will be renewed. Otherwise, they are amortized over three years, at $30,000 a year. In any event, they are not amortized over 10 years.

Deferred Charges

Deferred charges are conceptually the same as prepaid expenses, a current asset discussed in Chapter 2. They are included as long-lived assets only if they have a relatively long useful life—that is, if they benefit several future years. Patents, copyrights, and indeed all long-lived assets subject to amortization are deferred charges in the literal sense. However, the term is usually restricted to long-lived intangibles other than those listed in the preceding paragraphs.

Practice varies greatly with respect to these items. Some companies charge them off as expenses as the costs are incurred, even though there is no offsetting revenue. This reflects the conservatism concept. Other companies capitalize them. If capitalized, they are usually amortized over a relatively short period of time, often in the next year, but rarely more than five years.

Research and Development Costs

Research and development (R&D) costs are costs incurred for the purpose of developing new or improved goods, processes, or services. The fruits of R&D efforts can be increased revenues or lower costs. Since these fruits will not be picked until future periods, often five years or more after a research project is started, a good case can be made for capitalizing R&D costs and amortizing them over the periods benefitted. This practice was common at one time, but the FASB no longer permits it. Instead, it requires that R&D costs be treated as period costs—that is, charged off as an expense of the current period.

The reason given by the FASB for its requirement is that by their very nature, the future benefits to be derived from current R&D efforts are highly uncertain.

The efforts that are eventually unsuccessful cannot be identified in advance; otherwise, they would not have been undertaken. Although near the end of the development stage the success of certain projects seems reasonably assured, the FASB has concluded that there is no objective way of distinguishing between these projects and the unsuccessful ones.

The FASB decision is a particularly interesting example of the inherent conflict between certain concepts. Capitalizing R&D costs and then amortizing them over the future periods likely to benefit is consistent with the matching concept. However, it is inconsistent with the criterion that accounting should be reasonably objective, and it is not in accord with the conservatism concept. The FASB decided that the latter considerations were more important than the matching concept in this instance.

If a company does R&D work for a customer (i.e., another company or a government agency) and is paid for this work, these payments constitute revenue. The related costs are held as an asset in Work in Process Inventory. They are matched against revenue and therefore are charged as expenses in the period in which the revenue is earned.

IFRS requires expenditures for the research phase of R&D projects to be expensed as incurred. Generally IFRS requires expensing of development expenditures as incurred. However, IFRS requires development costs to be capitalized if they are expected to be recovered from future sales.[21]

Software Development

The costs of developing computer software to be sold, leased, or licensed are a type of R&D cost. These costs must be expensed as incurred up until the point that the technological feasibility of the software product has been established. Technological feasibility is established upon completion of a detailed program design or completion of a working model. Thereafter, the costs of bringing the software to market, such as producing product masters, can be capitalized. Capitalization of such costs ceases when the product is available for release to customers. Annual amortization of such costs is the greater of (1) the straight-line method amount or (2) the amount determined by the ratio of the year's revenues to the total anticipated revenues for the product. Thus, a product with an estimated market life of four years and with half of its estimated lifetime revenues coming in the first year would have half (not one-fourth) of its capitalized costs amortized in the first year.[22]

The costs of software developed for internal use are capitalized at the point where a commitment is made to its eventual development. The cost of internally developed software is amortized over its useful life.

Analysis of Nonmonetary Assets

Nonmonetary assets can be analyzed in a variety of ways to gain insights into the asset beyond the amount of the asset's book value reported on the balance sheet.

The average age of a company's depreciable assets can be estimated by dividing the asset's accumulated depreciation balance by the asset's annual depreciation expense.

A depreciable asset's depreciation period in years can be estimated by dividing the asset's gross cost by its related annual depreciation expense.

A company's annual expenditure for a particular intangible asset can be estimated by adding (an increase in the asset's balance) or deducting (a decrease in the asset's balance) to the asset's related annual amortization expense. The result is the estimated expenditure amount.

---

[21] "Intangible Assets," *IAS No. 38.*
[22] "Accounting for the Costs of Computer Software," *FASB Statement No. 86.*

Controversies Around Expense vs Capitalization in New Firms

(What's new in Ind-AS 16)

Ind AS 16, the accounting standard spells out the treatment for Property, Plant and Equipment (PPE). The standard includes the following issues related to PPE:

- Exact time when the asset is recognized
- Determining the carrying amounts of the asset
- Amount of depreciation to be recognized in the financial statement

Few of the changes in the new norms (Ind AS 16) from the existing ones (AS 10 and AS 6) and their treatment on PPE are:

1. **Change in the methods of depreciation**: Ind AS 16 considers such change as changes in the accounting estimate and is applied prospectively whereas AS10 necessitates retrospective recalculation of the depreciation and accounted for prospectively. This change is considered as the change in accounting policy.
2. **Reviewing residual value**: As per the new Ind AS 16, it is required that the firms carry out the review of the residual value at least once at the end of every financial year and change, if any, must be adjusted for as a change in the accounting estimate. The earlier AS 10 didn't require firms to re-estimate residual value so that they could be reviewed and updated.
3. **Reassessing the useful life**: Ind AS 16 requires reviewing at the end of every financial year and applied prospectively whereas AS 10 required periodical review and prospective application.
4. **Cost of major inspections**: As per AS 10, the cost of major inspections was usually expensed as and when they're incurred. In the new revised Ind AS 16, the cost of any major inspections needs to be capitalized and added to the existing amount of the PPE.
5. Furthermore, spare parts, servicing equipment and standby equipment which meet the definition criteria of PPE will be treated as PPE and will be accounted accordingly, and not as inventory.
6. Furthermore, the concept of component depreciation finds more weight in Ind-AS 16, though the erstwhile AS-10 (before revision) contained a short paragraph on component depreciation. The erstwhile AS-10 did not require the assets to be componentised and depreciated separately, although it stated that such an approach may improve the accounting for fixed assets. Component depreciation is likely to affect the quantum of depreciation and will require the corporates to be more particular with regards to record-keeping in relation to PPE.

Treatment in special situations as per the new standards

a. **Capitalization of the interest costs on the purchase of a machine on credit**: The cost of an item under PPE bought through a loan will be the cash price equivalent at the time of recognition. As per AS-16, the difference between the equivalent of the listed price and the actual payment made (if the payment is deferred beyond normal credit terms) will be recognized as an interest expense over credit period, unless it is a qualifying asset. For example, if a firm purchases machinery on a credit period of 5 years and paid Rs. 30 lakhs for the same. However, had the company gone for a "full down payment" and not opted for credit and, the machinery would have cost Rs. 25 lakhs. The additional payment of Rs.5 lakhs is attributable to the financing of the fixed asset rather than acquisition cost. In the previous accounting standard, the entire amount of Rs. 30 lakhs would have been capitalized. However, in the current

Ind-AS 16, only Rs. 25 lakhs would be capitalized and remaining Rs. 5 lakhs would be treated as interest cost which will be spread over a period of 5 years. This treatment is in line with the theme of substance prevailing over the form while recording transactions in accounting.

b. **Treatment of dismantling costs of certain assets**: There are certain assets which must comply with obligations related to decommissioning liabilities. In such kind of asset structure, Ind-AS 16 gives reference of Ind-AS 37 on Provisions, Contingent Assets, and Contingent Liabilities. All such liabilities are to be discounted and added to the cost of PPE. Subsequently, the unwinding of the discounted value will be recognized as an interest expense every year. In the IFRS terminology, decommissioning liabilities usually are referred as "Asset Retirement Obligations." Let us take an example, Milesh Telecom, a tower company got an order from a cellular operator to construct and lease 10 telecom towers in Mumbai. The land required for the construction of the towers was to be arranged by the operator. At the end of the 10-year period term, Milesh Telecom is required to dismantle the towers and restore the site/ land to its previous condition. The towers were constructed at a total cost of Rs. 100,00,000/-. The estimated cost of dismantling and restoration is Rs. 5,00,000/- and the yield on government bonds is 7% for a 10- year period. In this case, the present value of cost of dismantling (Rs. 500,000 discounted @7% for 10 years-) will be added to the cost of the telecom towers and will be correspondingly treated as a liability. The unwinding of the discounted value will be treated as an interest expense every year. The unwinding of the discounted value will finally increase the liability to increase to Rs. 5 lakhs at the end of year 10 and will be settled.

c. **Revaluation of assets**: Ind-AS 16 provides guidance on the revaluation model, and clarifies that if revaluation model is practiced, revaluation needs to be done with sufficient regularity to ensure that the book value does not differ significantly from the realizable value at the end of the reporting period. The earlier AS-10 (before revision) did not say anything about the frequency of revaluation. As per Ind-AS 16, the frequency of revaluation is dependent on the significance and volatility of changes in the realizable value of the asset.

Summary

Items of property, plant, and equipment are capitalized at their acquisition cost, which includes all elements of cost involved in making them ready to provide service. Except for land, a portion of this cost (less residual value, if any) is charged as depreciation expense to each of the accounting periods in which the asset provides service. A corresponding reduction is made each period in the net book value of the asset account. Any systematic method may be used for depreciation. The straight-line method is ordinarily used for financial accounting purposes, but declining-balance methods are the basis for the cost recovery deductions allowed for income tax purposes.

When an asset is disposed of, its cost and accumulated depreciation are removed from the accounts, and any gain or loss appears on the income statement (unless group depreciation is used).

Natural resources are accounted for in the same way as fixed assets, except that the expense item is called depletion rather than depreciation.

Intangible assets also are recorded at cost. In the case of goodwill, this cost is the difference between the price paid for a company and the fair value of the net assets acquired (acquired assets net of any liabilities assumed by the purchaser). If intangible assets have a limited useful life, their cost is amortized over that life. Intangible assets not subject to amortization are periodically tested for impairment. R&D costs are expensed as incurred;

exceptions are the costs of developing marketable computer software expected to be recovered from future sales, which are capitalized once the product's technical feasibility is established, and the costs of software developed for internal use, once the commitment is made to develop it.

Accounting for long-lived assets involves making estimates that result in each year's depreciation and amortization expense amounts being approximations. Since these amounts affect income in each year of an asset's life, reported income itself is an estimate. (Similar comments apply to the estimates described in earlier chapters for such assets as receivables and inventories and for the related expense amounts for bad debts and cost of sales.)

Problems

Problem 7–1.

Pemberton Corporation purchased a machine costing $300,000 that had an estimated useful life of six years and residual value of $18,000. The machine is expected to produce 3,525,000 units during its useful life, as follows:

Year	Units
1	930,000
2	800,000
3	580,000
4	500,000
5	415,000
6	300,000
	3,525,000

Required:

a. What will be each year's depreciation charge if Pemberton uses the units-of-production method?

b. Will this give significantly different depreciation charges in each year than the sum-of-the-years' digits method?

Problem 7–2.

Higher Company had the following disposals of production equipment during 2006:

Equipment ID Number	Purchase Date	Original Cost	Date of Disposal	Disposal Proceeds	Useful Life	Depreciation Method
301	2/28/98	$70,300	10/03/02	$14,300	10	Straight-line
415	7/03/05	96,000	7/19/02	63,000	5	150% declining-balance
573	6/15/04	94,500	3/21/02	38,000	6	Sum-of-the-years'-digits

Higher's policy is to charge a full year's depreciation in the year of purchase if an asset is purchased before July 1. For assets purchased after July 1, only one-half year's depreciation is charged. During the year of disposal, one-half year's depreciation is charged if the asset is sold after June 30. No depreciation is charged during the year of disposal if the asset is sold before July 1. In all three cases above, estimated residual value at the time of acquisition was zero.

Required:

Prepare journal entries to record the above disposals.

Problem 7–3.   During the year, Olsen Company traded an automobile plus $8,400 in cash to Barry Company for another automobile. The car Olsen used as a trade-in originally had cost $16,000, of which $14,500 has been depreciated.

Olsen also purchased new office furniture during the year. The list price of the furniture was $9,600. Olsen paid $3,350 cash plus gave the furniture company a used truck. This truck had a net book value of $6,250; it had originally cost $19,860, and had recently been appraised at $5,500.

Required:
Record the above transactions on Olsen Company's books.

Problem 7–4.   Chipper Company had the following transactions during the year:

1. Land was purchased for $75,000 cash. This land was to be used for a new office building. It was agreed that Chipper Company would pay for the razing of a building currently on the land; this would cost $5,600, to be paid in cash.
2. Chipper Company contracted with Cody Construction to build the new office building. It was agreed that Chipper would pay Cody with 3,000 shares of Chipper common stock, a $16,000 note, and $32,000 in cash. Chipper's common stock was currently selling for $30 a share.
3. Chipper purchased some office equipment from Northern Office Equipment for $9,600 cash. Mr. Chipper was a close personal friend of the owner of Northern Office Equipment, and accordingly was sold this equipment at a price lower than normally would be charged. The prices charged to "normal" customers were as follows:

Desks and chairs	$ 8,700
Bookcases	2,200
Filing cabinets	1,100
	$12,000

Required:
Prepare journal entries for the above transactions.

Problem 7–5.   Cleanburn Coal Company purchased coal-leasing land that contains 800,000 tons of coal for $21,700,000. Soil tests by geologists cost $35,250 for the purchased land, but tests at other sites that yielded negative results cost $116,250. Clearburn uses the full-cost method for exploration costs (i.e., the company's total exploration and testing costs are treated as one cost pool for the entire company rather than being associated with any one exploration project). Test permits were issued by the federal government at a cost of $41,000 to Cleanburn. The estimated salvage value of the purchased land will be $2,325,000 once the coal is removed. The coal is expected to be mined within 10 years.

Before mining could begin, the company had to remove trees and undergrowth at a cost of $387,500. In addition, storage facilities and a field office were constructed at a total cost of $271,250. These facilities will last an estimated 25 years but will serve no purpose once the coal is removed; hence, they have no residual value. Machinery that cost $1,162,500 was installed, but its service life is limited to the time required to remove the coal. The buildings will be depreciated on a straight-line basis, while the machinery will be depreciated by using the sum-of-the-years'-digits method.

In the first year of operation, Cleanburn mined 30,000 tons of coal; in the second year, 70,000 tons; and in the third year, 75,000 tons.

Required:

Prepare a schedule showing (*a*) unit and total depletion and (*b*) depreciation for the first three years of operation. Assume that the purchase occurred on January 1 and that Cleanburn uses a calendar fiscal year.

Case 7–1

Stern Corporation (B)*

After the controller of Stern Corporation had ascertained the changes in accounts receivable and the allowance for doubtful accounts in 2010, a similar analysis was made of property, plant, and equipment and accumulated depreciation accounts. Again the controller examined the December 31, 2009, balance sheet [see Exhibit 1 of Stern Corporation (A), Case 5–1]. Also reviewed were the following company transactions that were found to be applicable to these accounts:

1. On January 2, 2010, one of the factory machines was sold for its book value, $3,866. This machine was recorded on the books at $31,233 with accumulated depreciation of $27,367.
2. Tools were carried on the books at cost, and at the end of each year a physical inventory was taken to determine what tools still remained. The account was written down to the extent of the decrease in tools as ascertained by the year-end inventory. At the end of 2010, it was determined that there had been a decrease in the tool inventory amounting to $7,850.
3. On March 1, 2010, the company sold for $2,336 cash an automobile that was recorded on the books at a cost of $8,354 and had an accumulated depreciation of $5,180, giving a net book value of $3,174 as of January 1, 2010. In this and other cases of the sale of long-lived assets during the year, the accumulated depreciation and depreciation expense items were both increased by an amount that reflected the depreciation chargeable for the months in 2010 in which the asset was held prior to the sale, at rates listed in item 7 below.

4. The patent listed on the balance sheet had been purchased by the Stern Corporation. The cost of the patent was written off as an expense over the remainder of its legal life as of December 31, 2009, the patent's remaining legal life was five years.
5. On July 1, 2010, a typewriter that had cost $1,027 and had been fully depreciated on December 31, 2009, was sold for $75.
6. On October 1, 2010, the company sold a desk for $80. This piece of furniture was recorded on the books at a cost of $490 with an accumulated depreciation of $395 as of January 1, 2010.
7. Depreciation was calculated at the following rates:

Buildings	2%
Factory machinery	10*
Furniture and fixtures	10
Automotive equipment	20
Office machines	10

* Included in the factory machinery cost of $3,425,585 was a machine costing $85,000 that had been fully depreciated on December 31, 2009, and that was still in use.

Questions

1. In a manner similar to that used in Stern Corporation (A), analyze the effect of each of these transactions on the property, plant, and equipment accounts, accumulated depreciation, and any other accounts that may be involved. Prepare journal entries for these transactions.
2. Give the correct totals for property, plant, and equipment, and the amount of accumulated depreciation as of December 31, 2010, after the transactions affecting them had been recorded.

Case 7–2

Joan Holtz (C)*

Joan Holtz said to the accounting instructor, "The general principle for arriving at the amount of a fixed asset that is to be capitalized is reasonably clear, but there certainly are a great many problems in applying this principle to specific situations."

Following are some of the problems Joan Holtz presented:

1. Suppose that the Bruce Manufacturing Company used its own maintenance crew to build an additional wing on its existing factory building. What would be the proper accounting treatment of the following items?
   a. Architects' fees.
   b. The cost of snow removal during construction.
   c. Cash discounts earned for prompt payment on materials purchased for construction.
   d. The cost of building a combined construction office and toolshed that would be torn down once the factory wing had been completed.
   e. Interest on money borrowed to finance construction.
   f. Local real estate taxes for the period of construction on the portion of land to be occupied by the new wing.
   g. The cost of mistakes made during construction.
   h. The overhead costs of the maintenance department that include supervision; depreciation on buildings and equipment of maintenance department shops; heat, light, and power for these shops; and allocations of cost for such items as the cafeteria, medical office, and personnel department.
   i. The cost of insurance during construction and the cost of damages or losses on any injuries or losses not covered by insurance.

2. Assume that the Archer Company bought a large piece of land, including the buildings thereon, with the intent of razing the buildings and constructing a combined hotel and office building in their place. The existing buildings consisted of a theater and several stores and small apartment buildings, all in active use at the time of the purchase.

   a. What accounting treatment should be accorded that portion of the purchase price considered to be the amount paid for the buildings that are subsequently razed?
   b. How should the costs of demolishing the old buildings be treated?
   c. Suppose that a single company had owned this large piece of land, including the buildings thereon, and instead of selling to the Archer Company had decided to have the buildings razed and to have a combined hotel and office building constructed on the site for its own benefit. In what respect, if any, should the accounting treatment of the old buildings and the cost of demolishing them differ from your recommendations with respect to (*a*) and (*b*) above? Why?

3. Midland Manufacturing Company purchased a new machine. It is clear that the invoice price of the new machine should be capitalized, and it also seems reasonable to capitalize the transportation cost to bring the machine to the Midland plant. I'm not so clear, however, on the following items.

   a. The new machine is heavier than the old machine it replaced; consequently, the foundation under the machine has had to be strengthened by the installation of additional steel beams. Should this cost be charged to the building, added to the cost of the machine, or expensed? Why?
   b. The installation of the machine took longer and was more costly than anticipated. In addition to time spent by the regular maintenance crew on installation, it became necessary to hire an outside engineer to assist in the installation and in "working out the bugs" to get the machine running properly. His costs included not only his fee but also his transportation, hotel expense, and meals. Moreover, the foreman of the department and the plant superintendent both spent a considerable amount of time assisting in the installation work. Before the new machine was working properly, a large amount of material had been spoiled during trial runs. How should all of these costs be treated? Why?
   c. In addition to the invoice price and transportation, it was necessary to pay a state sales tax on purchasing the machine. Is this part of the machine's cost? Why?

d. In connection with payment for the new machine, the machine manufacturer was willing to accept the Midland Company's old machine as partial payment. The amount allowed as a trade-in was larger than the depreciated value at which the old machine was being carried in the books of the Midland Company. Should the difference have been treated as a reduction in the cost of the new machine or a gain on disposal of the old one? Why?

4. A computer manufacturing company sold outright about 25 percent of its products (in terms of dollar volume) and leased 75 percent. On average, a given computer was leased for four years. The cost of leased computers was initially recorded as an asset and was depreciated over four years. The company assisted new customers in installing the computer and in designing the related systems. These "applications engineering" services were furnished without charge, and the company's cost was reported as part of its marketing expense. Applications engineering costs averaged about 5 percent of the sales value of a computer, but about 20 percent of the first-year rental revenue of a leased computer. Recently, the company's installation of computers grew rapidly. Because the applications engineering cost was such a high percentage of lease revenue, reported income did not increase at all. Research and development costs must be expensed as incurred. Does the same principle apply to applications engineering costs, or could these costs be added to the asset value of leased computers and amortized over the lease period? If so, could other marketing costs related to leased computers be treated in the same way? Why?

5. An electronic component manufacturer announced a new product that would soon be available. This product, a new generation component, had features highly sought by customers for their next generation of electronics products. To meet the demands of its customers, many of whom had begun to impose quality standards on suppliers, the electronics component manufacturer would have to achieve a quality standard of 65 ppm, that is, 65 or fewer defective parts per million parts delivered to the customer.

The equipment intended to produce the new component at the 65 ppm quality standard was custom-built by the manufacturer. Once the equipment was physically installed in the plant, the company performed extensive testing and debugging efforts to ensure that the components met the required standard. A couple of months after installation, the new equipment was producing components that, while commercially viable, did not quite meet the quality standard. A key customer was eager to purchase the new component for use in its own new product, however. The customer agreed to purchase the component now if the electronics component manufacturer would continue to push to meet the quality standard.

Since the new manufacturing equipment was going to begin to generate revenue, the fixed asset accounting manager reviewed the costs capitalized as part of this asset. The costs of the material, labor, and overhead required to fabricate and install the equipment had been capitalized. In addition, the debugging and testing costs incurred to attempt to bring the new manufacturing equipment to the 65 ppm quality standard had also been capitalized, as these costs had been required to make the equipment ready for its intended use. The total costs were approximately one-half million dollars, and they would be amortized over the asset's productive life beginning with production for the eager first customer.

The engineers believed that at least $50,000 of additional debugging, fine-tuning, and testing would be required for the new equipment to reach the 65 ppm quality standard. Should those costs continue to be capitalized, despite the fact that the equipment was producing components that were sold commercially? Why? If so, once the quality standard was achieved and the full cost of the asset was known, should the amount of depreciation for the initial production periods be adjusted? Why? The 65 ppm standard was an extremely tough standard; the engineers who had designed the equipment were confident they could achieve it, although a few skeptics had expressed the concern that the standard might never be achieved. What implications, if any, might this have for capitalizing the cost of the asset? Explain.

Question

Answer the questions raised by Holtz in each of the five issues on her list.

Case 7–3

Stafford Press*

Stafford Press was founded in 2000 as a one-man job printing firm in a small southwestern town. Shortly after its founding, Lucas Stafford, the owner, decided to concentrate on one specialty line of printing. Because of a high degree of technical proficiency, the company experienced a rapid growth.

However, Stafford Press suffered from a competitive disadvantage in that the major market for its specialized output was in a metropolitan area over 300 miles away from the company's plant. For this reason, in 2010, having accumulated some extra cash to finance a move, the owner decided to move nearer his primary market. He also decided to expand and modernize his facilities at the time of the move. After some investigation, an attractive site was found in a suburb of his primary market, and the move was made.

A balance sheet prepared just prior to the move is shown in Exhibit 1. The transactions that arose from this move are described in the following paragraphs:

1. The land at the old site, together with the building thereon, was sold for $149,860 cash.

* © Professor Robert N. Anthony.

2. Certain equipment was sold for $35,200 cash. This equipment appeared on the books at a cost of $73,645 less accumulated depreciation of $40,890, for a net book value of $32,755.
3. A new printing press was purchased. The invoice cost of this equipment was $112,110. A 2 percent cash discount was taken by Stafford Press so that only $109,868 was actually paid to the seller. Stafford Press also paid $450 to a trucker to have this equipment delivered. Installation of this equipment was made by Stafford Press employees who worked a total of 60 hours. These workers received $15 per hour in wages, but their time was ordinarily charged to printing jobs at $30.50 per hour, the difference representing an allowance for overhead ($12.15) and profit ($3.35).
4. Stafford Press paid $140,000 to purchase land on which the new plant was to be built. A rundown building, which Stafford's appraiser said had no value, was standing on the plot of land. Stafford Press paid $21,235 to have the old building on the plot of land torn down. In addition, the company paid $13,950 to have permanent drainage facilities installed on the new land.

EXHIBIT 1

STAFFORD PRESS Condensed Balance Sheet (Prior to Move)					
Assets			**Liabilities and Owner's Equity**		
Current assets:					
Cash	$395,868		Current liabilities		$160,223
Other current assets	251,790		Common stock		400,000
Total current assets		$647,658	Retained earnings		358,648
Property and equipment:					
Land		34,034			
Buildings	$350,064				
Less: Accumulated depreciation	199,056	151,008			
Equipment	265,093				
Less: Accumulated depreciation	178,922	86,171			
Total assets		$918,871	Total liabilities and owner's equity		$918,871

5. A new composing machine with an invoice cost of $28,030 was purchased. The company paid $20,830 cash and received a trade-in allowance of $7,200 on a used piece of equipment. The used equipment could have been sold outright for not more than $6,050. It had cost $12,000 new, and accumulated depreciation on it was $5,200, making the net book value $6,800.

6. The company erected a building at the new site for $561,000. Of this amount, $136,000 was paid in cash and $425,000 was borrowed on a mortgage.

7. Trucking and other costs associated with moving equipment from the old location to the new location and installing it were $8,440. In addition, Stafford Press employees worked an estimated 125 hours on that part of the move that related to equipment.

8. During the moving operation, a piece of equipment costing $10,000 was dropped and damaged; $3,220 was spent to repair it. Management believed,

however, that the salvage value of this equipment had been reduced by $660 from the original estimate of $1,950 to $1,290. Up until that time, the equipment was being depreciated at $805 per year, representing a 10 percent rate after deduction of estimated salvage of $1,950. Accumulated depreciation was $3,220.

Questions

1. Analyze the effect of each of these transactions on the items in the balance sheet and income statement. For transactions that affect owner's equity, distinguish between those that affect the net income of the current year and those that do not. In most cases, the results of your analysis can be set forth most clearly in the form of journal entries.

2. Adjust the balance sheet in Exhibit 1 to show the effect of these transactions.

Case 7–4

Silic: Choosing Cost or Fair Value on Adoption of IFRS

In June 2002, the Council of Ministers of the European Union approved regulation requiring all companies quoted on European stock exchanges to use, with effect from January 1, 2005, International Financial Reporting Standards (IFRS) as the basis for their financial statements. Prior to this date, publicly listed companies in France used their domestic accounting standards for financial reporting purposes. Therefore, the transition to IFRS would have a substantial impact on their accounting practices. One company affected by the switch to the new accounting standards was Silic, a France-based investment property company. Before the implementation of IFRS, Silic was applying French accounting standards that required its investment properties to be reported using the historical-cost model. However, the introduction of International Accounting Standard 40 (IAS 40 Investment Properties) under IFRS would require the company to choose between historical-cost or fair-value accounting to report its investment properties.

Background

Silic (*Société Immobilière de Location pour l'Industrie et le Commerce*) was a major and historical player on the French commercial-property market. It was the first company in France to introduce the concept of business parks—areas of land, typically located close to major highways, railroads and airports, set aside for office space and light industry.

The company's strategy involved developing and operating business parks in the three largest business areas surrounding Paris. Specifically, the company built, refurbished and rented out office space in the La Défense business district to the west of the city and in the industrial poles located in close proximity to the Charles de Gaulle and Orly airports. Silic also owned and rented out multipurpose office and light industrial space in business parks located in the outer-lying Paris suburbs of Cergy, Courtaboeuf and Evry.

In the business parks that it managed, Silic also provided associated services and amenities, such as restaurants, convenience stores, fitness clubs and childcare facilities. In total, the company had over 700 individual tenants, ranging from small and medium-sized companies to

EXHIBIT 1 Silic's Shareholder Structure at December 31, 2004

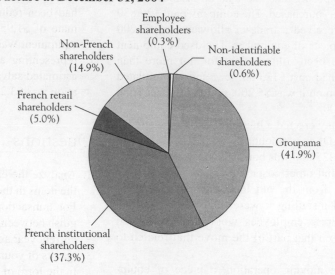

Source: Silic

major multinationals such as Air France, Alcatel Business Systems, Axa, France Telecom, Danone, LG, Microsoft, Nestle Waters, Peugeot and Xerox.

Silic had been listed on the Paris stock exchange in January 1973 and by 2004 had a largely institutional and relatively stable shareholder community. Groupama, a leading French insurance group, represented the company's reference shareholder (see Exhibit 1).[1]

At December 31, 2004, Silic had over €1.5 billion of investment properties valued on its balance sheet, including buildings recorded at over €1.1 billion and land reported at close to €449 million (see Exhibit 2),

[1] Groupama included Silic in its consolidated financial statements using the equity method. In Groupama's financial statements, land and buildings were reported at this historical cost.

and was profitable (see Exhibits 3, 4 and 5). The company's property portfolio consisted of 181 individual investment properties totaling almost 954,000 m^2 of office space (defined as premises where at least 70% of the floor area is occupied by offices) and multi-purpose business space (defined as premises providing a mix of both office and light-industrial space) (see Exhibit 6). In line with Silic's development strategy and its focus on both operating and developing business parks, the company was also constructing new office buildings that had been recorded at €62 million. Dominique Schlissinger, Silic's Chairman and Chief Executive Officer, explained that the company's Orly-Rungis site could be expanded by a further million square meters to further consolidate its position as Europe's largest business park.

EXHIBIT 2 Silic's 2003 and 2004 Balance Sheets (€ thousands)

ASSETS	2004	2003
Goodwill		
Other intangible assets	512	483
Less amortization and provisions	(483)	(444)
Net tangible assets	**29**	**39**
Tangible fixed assets		
Land	448,567	364,370
Fixed assets in course of construction	62,008	36,986
Buildings	1,139,063	1,096,824
Other tangible assets	2,181	14,475
	1,651,819	1,512,955
Less depreciation and provisions	(252,356)	(214,080)

(continued)

ASSETS	2004	2003
Net tangible fixed assets	**1,399,463**	**1,298,875**
Net long-term investments	**152**	**162**
Total fixed assets	**1,399,644**	**1,299,076**
Current assets		
Debtors	43,398	17,678
Marketable securities	1,524	–
Cash	7,009	4,753
Total current assets	**51,931**	**22,431**
Total assets	**1,451,575**	**1,321,507**
SHAREHOLDERS' EQUITY AND LIABILITIES		
Shareholders' equity		
Share capital	69,070	68,777
Share premiums	199,854	272,021
Revaluation surplus	430,967	448,456
Consolidated reserves	142,825	61,278
Other shareholders' equity	(7)	(42)
Net profit for the year	32,841	38,435
Total shareholders' equity	**875,550**	**888,925**
Provisions for liabilities and charges	1,280	2,154
Liabilities		
Bank loans	436,815	291,211
Security deposits	21,508	20,643
Other creditors	116,422	118,574
Total liabilities	**574,745**	**430,428**
Total shareholders' equity and liabilities	**1,451,575**	**1,321,507**

Source: Compiled by case writer from Silic annual reports

EXHIBIT 3 Silic's 2003 and 2004 Income Statements (€ thousands)

	2004	2003
Rental income	100,242	95,415
Fee income	5,898	4,914
Other services	32,447	31,288
Turnover	**138,587**	**131,617**
Fixed assets produced for own use	2,343	1,751
Purchases	(36,134)	(29,622)
Taxes, duties and similar	(14,918)	(14,592)
Staff costs	(8,224)	(7,704)
Other income and expense	10,101	7,387
EBITDA	**91,755**	**88,837**
Write-back of provisions and amortization	1,353	828
Charge to amortization, depreciation and provisions	(43,536)	(42,796)

(continued)

	2004	2003
Operating profit	**49,572**	**48,869**
Financial income and expenses	(10,995)	(11,025)
Consolidated profit on operating activities	**38,577**	**35,844**
Exceptional income and expenses	(5,274)	(2,355)
Corporation tax	(462)	4,946
Net profit	**32,841**	**38,435**

Source: Compiled by case writer from Silic annual reports

EXHIBIT 4 **Summary of Silic's 1999–2004 Financial Data (€ thousands)**

	1999	2000	2001	2002	2003[a]	2004
Balance sheet						
Total assets	546,863	577,353	711,915	742,577	1,321,507	1,451,575
Investment properties						
Buildings	542,132	565,167	689,007	771,467	1,096,824	1,139,063
Land	79,500	75,729	84,413	84,235	364,670	448,567
Replacement value[b]	975,715	1,092,538	1,319,272	1,352,300	1,419,719	1,681,493
Income statement						
Income	99,695	106,264	116,162	130,047	141,583	152,384
Expenses	59,954	62,467	62,204	79,168	94,714	102,812
Operating profit	43,797	39,741	49,958	50,879	46,869	49,572

(a) Following the adoption of SIIC status in 2003, Silic subjected its investment property portfolio to a one-off revaluation at the fair-value market by external appraisers.

(b) Open market value of investment properties, including any transfer taxes and acquisition-related expenses, as reported in the footnotes

Source: Compiled by case writer from Silic annual reports

EXHIBIT 5 **Silic's 2001–2004 Operating Profits (€ thousands)**

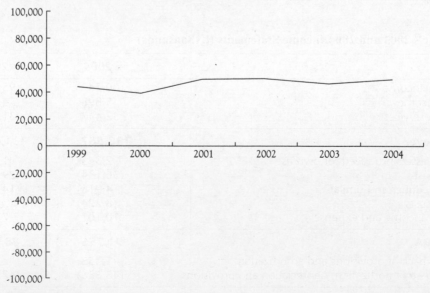

Source: Compiled by case writer from Silic annual reports

EXHIBIT 6 Silic's Investment Properties Portfolio at December 31, 2004

Investment Properties by Type

Type	Number
Office buildings[a]	96
Multi-purpose business space[b]	85
Total	**181**

(a) Premises where at least 70% of floor area is occupied by offices
(b) Premises providing both office and light-industrial space

Investment Properties by Location

Type	Orly-Rungis	La Défense	Roissy	Other[a]	Total
Buildings	85	30	23	43	181
Percentage	46%	17%	13%	24%	100%

(a) Multi-purpose office buildings in the Paris suburbs of Cergy, Courtaboeuf and Evry.

Floor Space by Location

Type	Multi-purpose[a]	Offices[b]	Other[c]	Total floor space
Orly-Rungis/Antony	173,889	197,377	68,548	439,814
La Défense	51,931	134,097	3,191	189,219
Roissy	22,263	107,286	1,868	131,417
Evry	30,081	25,909	974	56,964
Courtaboeuf	53,594	40,667	549	94,810
Cergy	40,201	0	0	40,201
Central Paris	0	1,452	0	1,452
Total portfolio	**371,959**	**506,788**	**75,130**	**953,877**

(a) Premises providing both office and light-industrial space
(b) Premises where at least 70% of floor area is occupied by offices
(c) Premises used for service or retail operations

Source: Compiled by case writer from Silic annual reports

French Investment Property Market and Property Values

Since 2001, the French real estate and property management industry had been growing steadily at an average rate of 2.8% per year, reaching a value of €23.8 billion in 2004. Revenues from non-residential properties, including offices and warehouses, accounted for over a fifth of the industry's value[i]. France represented Europe's third largest real estate management and development industry after the United Kingdom and Germany, generating 19.9% of the European industry's value. The industry was fore-cast to grow by a further 3.7% per year by 2010[ii]. Other major publicly listed companies in the French real estate management and development industry included Gecina, Icade, Klépierre, Société Foncière Lyonnaise and Unibail.

With 49 million m² of office space, the Paris region represented the largest commercial real estate market in Europe[iii]. Since the 1980s, the commercial property market of Paris and its surrounding region had experienced substantial upward and downward movements in the values of properties (see Exhibit 7). By the end of 2004, the commercial property market appeared to be on the cusp of an upswing, with sales prices rising on the year by 1.5%[iv].

Accounting for Investment Properties in France

Prior to the introduction of IFRS accounting standards in France, Silic reported its property assets in accordance with the French General Accounting Plan at historical cost, being either the purchase cost for the properties it had acquired or the cost price of its new

EXHIBIT 7 **Commercial Property Prices 1979–2003 in Paris and Surrounding Area (€/m²)**

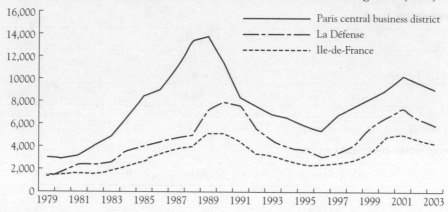

The graph represents the evolution of commercial property prices, measured in €/m², in central Paris, the La Défense business area to the west of the city centre and in the Ile-de-France region surrounding Paris

Source: Banque de France/CB Richard Ellis Bourdais[vi]

construction or redeveloped properties. The company depreciated its office and light industrial buildings on a straight-line basis over an average period of 40 years. Older buildings acquired were depreciated over a period taking into account their average age.

In 2003, Silic adopted SIIC status. Tile SIIC (*Sociétés d'Investissements Immobiliers Cotées)* tax regime was introduced by the French government in 2003 to create a strong and more efficient domestic real estate market. Inspired by the introduction of real estate investment trusts (REIT) in other countries, the SIIC legislation made real estate companies listed on the French stock exchange eligible for tax exemptions on their rental income and real estate capital gains, provided they distributed 85% of rental earning and 50% of capital gains to shareholders. Companies that elected the new regime had to pay a one-off 'exit tax' at a rate of 16.5% of latent capital gains on the buildings that they held.

Having chosen to adopt the new SIIC status, Silic followed the recommendations of the French accounting standards body (*Conseil National de la Comptabilité)* and financial market regulator (*Autorité des Marchés Financiers)* and had its buildings and land revalued by two independent external appraisers on an open-market and building-by-building basis. This one-off, fair-value revaluation had a significant impact on Silic's 2003 balance sheet. Indeed, the value of the company's investment properties and land increased from 2002 to 2003 by over €600 million or 70%.

Adoption of International Accounting Standards

The adoption of IFRS in January 2005 would have a number of effects on European property investment companies such as Silic. One major reporting issue related specifically to the International Accounting Standard 40 (IAS 40, Investment Properties). This standard allowed companies to report their investment properties using either a historical-cost model or a fair-value model.

Under the historical-cost model, investment property would be reported on the balance sheet at cost less accumulated depreciation and any impairment losses. Any changes in fair value would have to be evaluated by external appraisers and reported in the footnotes of annual reports. Companies that initially adopted the historical-cost model could switch to the fair-value model at a later date, if this would result in a more appropriate presentation of financial results.

Under the fair-value model, investment property (but not investment properties under construction or building land) would be revalued and reported on the balance sheet at its current market value, with all changes in value reported in the income statement. IAS 40 defined fair value as the amount for which an asset could be exchanged between knowledgeable, willing parties in an arm's-length transaction. Under the terms of IAS 40, companies adopting the fair-value method could not switch to the historical-cost method.

EXHIBIT 8 **Comments on Introduction of Fair-Value Accounting in France**

Investment Property Industry

Serge Grybowski (CEO, Gecina)

Fair value is more indicative of the development of the property .market than the operational

performance of a real estate company[vii]

Jean-Michel Gault (CFO, Klépierre)

Fair-value accounting complicates comparisons with historical accounting data[viii]

European Public Real Estate Association

Fair-value accounting will enhance uniformity, comparability and transparency of financial reporting by real estate companies. It allows performance benchmarking with direct property market indices.

Real estate companies should therefore account for their property investments based upon the fair-value model[ix].

International Accounting Firms and Associations

Rene Ricot (International Federation of Accountants)

Fair value is inevitable. Instability due to using market. values is a problem of the lack of education of market players and not that of accounting.

Françoise Bussac (Ernst & Young)

Fair value is the only single guideline to bring a real transparency in financial statements.

Financial Institution Investors

Federation of French Insurance Companies

Accounts reported at fair value can be deceptive and risk injecting a large dose of subjectivity into financial statements.

Sylvie Mathérat (General Secretary of the French Banking Commission)

The main problem of fair-value accounting is the volatility of earnings

Financial Analysts

Association of French Financial Analysts

The use of fair value can confuse interpretation of a company's operational results. Fair-value accounting is less reliable, allows greater manipulation of results and introduces volatility.

National Financial Authorities

French National Accounting Council (CNC)

The CNC endorsed neither historical-cost nor fair-value accounting since both methods were authorized under IAS 40.

French financial market regulator (AMF)

Fair-value accounting prevents the manipulation of results by managers by going in and out of the market to make the appearance of results at their will. However, it is better to avoid rushing through too audacious accounting reforms in a period of instability of markets.

Source: Compiled by case writer[x]

Although widely used outside of France, the concept of fair-value accounting was by and large unknown to the French. It called into question the country's long-established accounting traditions based on the principles of prudence and an avoidance of a valuation of assets which could lead to the disclosure of overvalued assets in financial statements[v]. The implementation of IFRS accounting standards triggered a lively public debate about the strengths and weaknesses of fair-value accounting versus historical-cost accounting (see Exhibit 8).

In the face of the implementation of IFRS, Dominique Schlissinger noted that Silic faced important cultural, sectoral and strategic dilemmas. It was against this background that the company's Board of Directors met on this issue on numerous occasions during 2003 and 2004 to better understand IAS 40. How would the two distinctive accounting models impact on Silic's financial statements? Which method would most transparently reflect Silic's real value? In short, which method should Silic ultimately adopt on January 1, 2005?

Endnotes

[i] Datamonitor (2006) *Real Estate Management & Development in France – Industry Profile* Data-monitor: London, available from Thomson Research, <http://research.thomsonib.com/> (accessed 24 September 2007)

[ii] Datamonitor (2006) *Real Estate Management & Development in France – Industry Profile* Data-monitor: London, available from Thomson Research, <http://research.thomsonib.com> (accessed 24 September 2007)

[iii] Paris Regional Economic Development Agency (2007) *Commercial Property in the Paris Region – 23 Strategic Business Sites* Paris Regional Economic Development Agency: Paris

[iv] Bank of International Settlements (2004) *Annual Report* Bank of International Settlements: Basel

[v] Bertoni, M, and Derosa, B. (2005) 'Comprehensive Income, Fair Value and Conservatism: A Conceptual Framework for Reporting Financial Performance', paper presented to the *5th International Conference on European Integration, Competition and Cooperation*, Lovran, April 22–23, 2005; Richard, J. (2004) 'The Secret Past of Fair Value: Lessons from History Applied to the French Case' in *Accounting in Europe*, Vol. 1, No.1, p95–107; Ricol, R. and Bonnet-Bernard, S. (2003) 'Fair Value Accounting: An Overworked Issue Over the Past Fifteen Years' in *Revue déconomie financière*, 71, p51–56

[vi] Banque de France (2004) *Is there a risk of a property bubble in France?* Banque de France: Paris

[vii] "Les foncières face à un enjeu de communication," *Les Echos,* May 13, 2004, available from Factiva, http://www.factiva.com (Accessed September 4, 2007)

[viii] "Les foncières face à un enjeu de communication," *Les Echos,* May 13, 2004, available from Factiva, http://www.factiva.com (Accessed September 4, 2007)

[ix] EPRA (2004) *Best Practices Policy Recommendations* European Public Real Estate Association: Amsterdam

[x] Richard, J. (2004) 'The Secret Past of Fair Value: Lessons from History Applied to the French Case' in *Accounting in Europe,* Vol. 1, No. 1, p95–107

Case 7–5

Accounting Fraud at WorldCom

WorldCom could not have failed as a result of the actions of a limited number of individuals. Rather, there was a broad breakdown of the system of internal controls, corporate governance and individual responsibility, all of which worked together to create a culture in which few persons took responsibility until it was too late.

—Richard Thornburgh, former U.S. attorney general[1]

[1] Matthew Bakarak, "Reports Detail WorldCom Execs' Domination," *AP Online,* June 9, 2003.

On July 21, 2002, WorldCom Group, a telecommunications company with more than $30 billion in revenues, $104 billion in assets, and 60,000 employees, filed for bankruptcy protection under Chapter 11 of the U.S. Bankruptcy Code. Between 1999 and 2002, WorldCom had overstated its pretax income by at least $7 billion, a deliberate miscalculation that was, at the time, the largest in history. The company subsequently wrote down about $82 billion (more than 75%) of its reported assets.[2] WorldCom's stock, once valued at $180 billion, became nearly worthless. Seventeen thousand employees lost their jobs; many left the company with worthless retirement accounts. The company's bankruptcy also jeopardized service to WorldCom's 20 million retail customers and on government contracts affecting 80 million Social Security beneficiaries, air traffic control for the Federal Aviation Association, network management for the Department of Defense, and long-distance services for both houses of Congress and the General Accounting Office.

Background

WorldCom's origins can be traced to the 1983 breakup of AT&T. Small, regional companies could now gain access to AT&T's long-distance phone lines at deeply discounted rates.[3] LDDS (an acronym for Long Distance Discount Services) began operations in 1984, offering services to local retail and commercial customers in southern states where well-established long-distance companies, such as MCI and Sprint, had little presence. LDDS, like other of these small regional companies, paid to use or lease facilities belonging to third parties. For example, a call from an LDDS customer in New Orleans to Dallas might initiate on a local phone company's line, flow to LDDS's leased network and then transfer to a Dallas local phone company to be completed. LDDS paid both the New Orleans and Dallas phone company providers for using their local networks, and the telecommunications company whose long-distance network it leased to connect New Orleans

to Dallas. These line-cost expenses were a significant cost for all long-distance carriers.

LDDS started with about $650,000 in capital but soon accumulated $1.5 million in debt since it lacked the technical expertise to handle the accounts of large companies that had complex switching systems. The company turned to Bernard J. (Bernie) Ebbers, one of its original nine investors, to run things. Ebbers had previously been employed as a milkman, bartender, bar bouncer, car salesman, truck driver, garment factory foreman, high school basketball coach, and hotelier. While he lacked technology experience, Ebbers later joked that his most useful qualification was being "the meanest SOB they could find."[4] Ebbers took less than a year to make the company profitable.

Ebbers focused the young firm on internal growth, acquiring small long-distance companies with limited geographic service areas and consolidating third-tier long-distance carriers with larger market shares. This strategy delivered economies of scale that were critical in the crowded long-distance reselling market. "Because the volume of bandwidth determined the costs, more money could be made by acquiring larger pipes, which lowered per unit costs," one observer remarked.[5] LDDS grew rapidly through acquisitions across the American South and West and expanded internationally through acquisitions in Europe and Latin America. In 1989, LDDS became a public company through a merger with Advantage Companies, a company that was already trading on Nasdaq. By the end of 1993, LDDS was the fourth-largest long-distance carrier in the United States. After a shareholder vote in May 1995, the company officially became known as WorldCom.

The telecommunications industry evolved rapidly in the 1990s. The industry's basic market expanded beyond fixed-line transmission of voice and data to include the transport of data packets over fiber-optic cables that could carry voice, data, and video. The Telecommunications Act of 1996 permitted long-distance carriers to compete for local service, transforming the industry's competitive landscape. Companies scrambled to obtain the capability to provide their customers a single source for all telecommunications services.

In 1996, WorldCom entered the local service market by purchasing MFS Communications Company, Inc., for $12.4 billion. MFS's subsidiary, UUNET, gave

---

[2] WorldCom's writedown was, at the time, the second largest in U.S. history, surpassed only by the $101 billion writedown taken by AOL Time Warner in 2002.

[3] Lynne W. Jeter, *Disconnected: deceit and betrayal at World-Com* (Hoboken, NJ: John Wiley & Sons, 2003), pp. 17–18.

[4] Jeter, p. 27.

[5] Jeter, p. 30.

WorldCom a substantial international presence and a large ownership stake in the world's Internet backbone. In 1997, WorldCom used its highly valued stock to outbid British Telephone and GTE (then the nation's second-largest local phone company) to acquire MCI, the nation's second-largest long-distance company. The $42 billion price represented, at the time, the largest takeover in U.S. history. By 1998, WorldCom had become a full-service telecommunications company, able to supply virtually any size business with a full complement of telecom services. WorldCom's integrated service packages and its Inter-net strengths gave it an advantage over its major competitors, AT&T and Sprint. Analysts hailed Ebbers and Scott Sullivan, the CFO who engineered the MCI merger, as industry leaders.[6]

In 1999, WorldCom attempted to acquire Sprint, but the U.S. Justice Department, in July 2000, refused to allow the merger on terms that were acceptable to the two companies. The termination of this merger was a significant event in WorldCom's history. World-Com executives realized that large-scale mergers were no longer a viable means of expanding the business.[a] WorldCom employees noted that after the turndown of the Sprint merger, "Ebbers appeared to lack a strategic sense of direction, and the Company began drifting."[b]

Corporate Culture

WorldCom's growth through acquisitions led to a hodgepodge of people and cultures. One accountant recalled, "We had offices in places we never knew about. We'd get calls from people we didn't even know existed." WorldCom's finance department at the Mississippi corporate headquarters maintained the corporate general ledger, which consolidated information from the incompatible legacy accounting systems of more than 60 acquired companies. WorldCom's headquarters for its network operations, which managed one of the largest Internet carrier businesses in the world, was based in Texas. The human resources department was in Florida, and the legal department in Washington, D.C.

None of the company's senior lawyers was located in Jackson. [Ebbers] did not include the Company's lawyers in his inner circle and appears to have dealt with them only when he felt it necessary. He let them know his displeasure with them personally when they gave advice—however Justified—that he did not like. In sum, Ebbers created a culture in which the legal function was less influential and less welcome than in a healthy corporate environment.[c]

A former manager added, "Each department had its own rules and management style. Nobody was on the same page. In fact, when I started in 1995, there were no written policies."[7] When Ebbers was told about an internal effort to create a corporate code of conduct, he called the project a "colossal waste of time."[d]

WorldCom encouraged "a systemic attitude conveyed from the top down that employees should not question their superiors, but simply do what they were told."[e] Challenges to more senior managers were often met with denigrating personal criticism or threats. In 1999, for example, Buddy Yates, director of World-Com General Accounting, warned Gene Morse, then a senior manager at WorldCom's Internet division, UUNET, "If you show those damn numbers to the f****ing auditors, I'll throw you out the window."[8]

Ebbers and Sullivan frequently granted compensation beyond the company's approved salary and bonus guidelines for an employee's position to reward selected, and presumably loyal, employees, especially those in the financial, accounting, and investor relations departments. The company's human resources department virtually never objected to such special awards.[9]

Employees felt that they did not have an independent outlet for expressing concerns about company policies or behavior. Several were unaware of the existence of an internal audit department, and others, knowing that Internal Audit reported directly to Sullivan, did not believe it was a productive outlet for questioning financial transactions.[f]

Expense-to-Revenue (E/R) Ratio

In the rapid expansion of the 1990s, WorldCom focused on building revenues and acquiring capacity sufficient to handle expected growth. According to Ebbers, in 1997, "Our goal is not to capture market

[6] *CFO Magazine* awarded. Sullivan its CFO Excellence award in 1998; *Fortune* listed Ebbers as one of its "People to Watch 2001."

[7] Jeter, p. 55.
[8] Personal correspondence, Gene Morse.
[9] Kay E. Zekany, Lucas W. Braun, and Zachary T. Warder, "Behind Closed Doors at WorldCom: 2001," *Issues in Accounting Education* (February 2004): 103.

share or be global. Our goal is to be the No.1 stock on Wall Street."[10] Revenue growth was a key to increasing the company's market value.[11] The demand for revenue growth was "in every brick in every building," said one manager.[g] "The push for revenue encouraged managers to spend whatever was necessary to bring revenue in the door, even if it meant that the long-term costs of a project outweighed short-term gains. . . . As a result, WorldCom entered into long-term fixed rate leases for network capacity in order to meet the anticipated increase in customer demand."[h]

The leases contained punitive termination provisions. Even if capacity were underutilized, WorldCom could avoid lease payments only by paying hefty termination fees. Thus, if customer traffic failed to meet expectations, WorldCom would pay for line capacity that it was not using.

Industry conditions began to deteriorate in 2000 due to heightened competition, overcapacity, and the reduced demand for telecommunications services at the onset of the economic recession and the aftermath of the dot-com bubble collapse. Failing telecommunications companies and new entrants were drastically reducing their prices, and WorldCom was forced to match. The competitive situation put severe pressure on WorldCom's most important performance indicator, the E/R ratio (line-cost expenditures to revenues), closely monitored by analysts and industry observers.

WorldCom's E/R ratio was about 42% in the first quarter of 2000, and the company struggled to maintain this percentage in subsequent quarters while facing revenue and pricing pressures and its high committed line costs. Ebbers made a personal, emotional speech to senior staff about how he and other directors would lose everything if the company did not improve its performance.[i]

As business operations continued to decline, however, CFO Sullivan decided to use accounting entries to achieve targeted performance. Sullivan and his staff used two main accounting tactics: accrual releases in 1999 and 2000, and capitalization of line costs in 2001 and 2002.[12]

[10] R. Charan, J. Useen, and A. Harrington, "Why Companies Fail," *Fortune* (Asia), May 27, 2002, pp. 36–45.
[11] Zekany et al., p. 103.
[12] The company also used aggressive revenue-recognition methods at the end of each reporting quarter to "close the gap" with Ebbers's aggressive revenue forecasts; see Zekany et al., pp. 112–114, and Beresford, Katzenbach, and Rogers, Jr., pp. 13–16.

Accrual Releases

WorldCom estimated its line costs monthly. Although bills for line costs were often not received or paid until several months after the costs were incurred, generally accepted accounting principles required the company to estimate these expected payments and match this expense with revenues in its income statement. Since the cash for this expense had not yet been paid, the offsetting entry was an accounting accrual to a liability account for the future payment owed to the line owner. When WorldCom paid the bills to the line owner, it reduced the liability accrual by the amount of the cash payment. If bills came in lower than estimated, the company could reverse (or release) some of the accruals, with the excess flowing into the income statement as a reduction in line expenses.

Throughout 1999 and 2000, Sullivan told staff to release accrual that he claimed were too high relative to future cash payments. Sullivan apparently told several business unit managers that the MCI merger had created a substantial amount of such overaccruals.

Sullivan directed David Myers (controller) to deal with any resistance from senior managers to the accrual releases.

In one instance, Myers asked David Schneeman, acting CFO of UUNET, to release line accruals for his business unit. When Schneeman asked' for an explanation, Myers responded: "No, you need to book the entry." When Schneeman refused, Myers told him in another e-mail, "I guess the only way I am 'going to get this booked is to fly to D.C. and book it myself. Book it right now, I can't wait another minute."[j] Schneeman still refused. Ultimately, staff in the general accounting department made Myers's desired changes to the general ledger. (See Exhibit 1 for a partial organizational chart.)

In another instance, Myers asked Timothy Schneberger, director of international fixed costs, to release $370 million in accruals. "Here's your number," Myers reportedly told Schneberger, asking him to book the $370 million adjustment. Yates, director of General Accounting, told Schneberger the request was from "the Lord Emperor, God himself, Scott [Sullivan]." When Schneberger refused to make the entry and also refused to provide the account number to enable Myers to make the entry, Betty Vinson, a senior manager in General Accounting, obtained the account number from a low-level analyst in

EXHIBIT 1 Partial WorldCom Organizational Chart, 2002

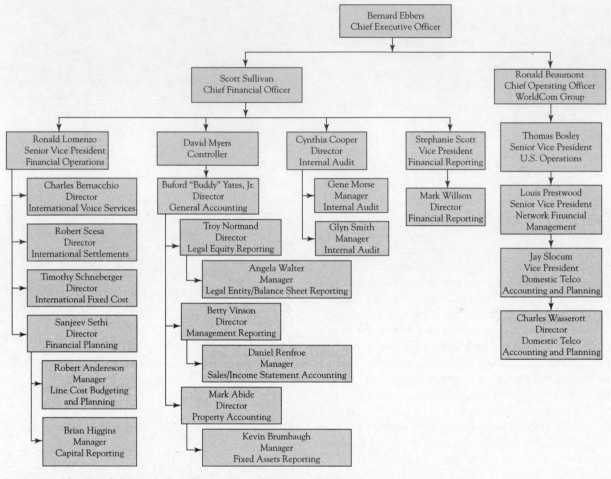

Source: Adapted from Beresford, Katzenbach, and Rogers, "Report of Investigation," 2003.

Schneberger's group and had one of her subordinates make the entry.[k] Employees in the general accounting department also made accrual releases from some departments without consulting the departments' senior management. In 2000, General Accounting released $281 million against line costs from accruals in the tax department's accounts, an entry that the tax group did not learn about until 2001.

Over a seven-quarter period between 1999 and 2000, WorldCom released $3.3 billion worth of accruals, most at the direct request of Sullivan or Myers. Several business units were left with accruals for future cash payments that were well below the actual amounts they would have to pay when bills arrived in the next period.

Expense Capitalization

By the first quarter of 2001, so few accruals were left to release that this tactic was no longer available to achieve the targeted E/R ratio.[l] Revenues, however, continued to decline, and Sullivan, through his lieutenants Myers and Yates, urged senior managers to maintain the 42% E/R ratio. Senior staff described this target as "wildly optimistic," "pure fantasy," and "impossible." One senior executive described the pressure as "unbearable—greater than he had ever' experienced in his fourteen years with the company."[m]

Sullivan devised a creative solution. He had his staff identify the costs of excess network capacity. He reasoned that these costs could be treated as a capital expenditure, rather than as an operating cost, since the contracted excess capacity gave the company an opportunity to enter the market quickly at some future time when demand was stronger than current levels. An accounting manager in 2000 had raised this possibility of treating periodic line costs as a capital expenditure but had been rebuffed by Yates: "David [Myers] and I have reviewed and discussed your logic of capitalizing excess capacity and can find no support within the current accounting guidelines that would allow for this accounting treatment."[n]

In April 2001, however, Sullivan decided to stop recognizing expenses for unused network capacity.[13] He directed Myers and Yates to order managers in the company's general accounting department to capitalize $771 million of non-revenue-generating line expenses into an asset account, "construction in progress." The accounting managers were subsequently told to reverse $227 million of the capitalized amount and to make a $227 million accrual release from ocean-cable liability.

WorldCom's April 26, 2001 press release and sub-sequent 10-Q quarterly report filed with the U.S. Securities and Exchange Commission (SEC) reported $4.1 billion of line costs and capital expenditures that included $544 million of capitalized line costs. With $9.8 billion in reported revenues, WorldCom's line-cost E/R ratio was announced at 42% rather than the 50% it would have been without the reclassification and accrual release.[o]

General Accounting Department

Betty Vinson, a native of Jackson, Mississippi, joined WorldCom in 1996, when she was 40 years old, as a manager in the international accounting division. She soon developed a reputation as a hardworking, loyal employee who would do "anything you told her" and often voluntarily worked extra hours at night, while at home, and on vacation.[14] Her good work soon led to a promotion to senior manager in General Accounting. In October 2000, Vinson and her colleague Troy Normand (another manager in General Accounting)

were called into their boss's office. Their boss, Yates, told them that Myers and Sullivan wanted them to release $828 million of line accruals into the income statement. Vinson and Normand were "shocked" by their bosses' proposal and told Yates that the proposal was "not good accounting."[15] Yates replied that he was not happy about the transfer either, but after Myers had assured him that it would not happen again, he had agreed to go along. After some debate, Vinson and Normand agreed to make the transfer. When the company publicly reported its third-quarter results, however, Vinson and Normand reconsidered their decision and told Yates that they were planning to resign.

Ebbers heard about the accountants' concerns and (according to another WorldCom employee) told Myers that the accountants would not be placed in such a difficult position again. A few days later, Sullivan talked to Vinson and Normand about their resignation plans: "Think of us as an aircraft carrier. We have planes in the air. Let's get the planes landed. Once they are landed, if you still want to leave, then leave. But not while the planes are in the air."[16]

Sullivan assured them that they were doing nothing illegal and that he would take full responsibility for their actions. Vinson decided against quitting. She earned more than her husband, and her WorldCom position paid for the family's insurance benefits. She knew that it would be difficult to find alternative work in the community with comparable compensation. Moreover, while she and Normand had doubts about the accounting transfers, they believed that Sullivan, with his "whiz kid" CFO reputation, probably knew what he was doing.

In April 2001, Vinson and Normand were again placed in a difficult position, except this time the position was, from Vinson's perspective, even less defensible. Revenues in the quarter were worse than expected, and Sullivan wanted them to transfer $771 million of line costs into capital expenditures.[17] Vinson was again shocked at the request but was reluctant to quit without another job. She knew Myers and Yates had already acquiesced to Sullivan's request. It was her job to distribute the amount across five capital accounts. She felt trapped but eventually made the entries and backdated them to February 2001.

---

[13] Sullivan's rationale, formally described in a two-page white paper, was rejected by the SEC, independent auditors, and WorldCom's own senior managers.

[14] Susan Pulliman, "WorldCom Whistleblowing," *The Wall Street Journal,* June 23, 2003.

[15] Ibid.

[16] Ibid., p. 1.

[17] This figure was subsequently reduced to $544 million when Sullivan and Myers found $227 million worth of accruals that could be released for the quarter.

Vinson continued to make similar entries throughout 2001 but began losing sleep, withdrawing from workers, and losing weight. Each time she hoped it would be the last, yet the pressure continued. In early 2002, she received a raise (to roughly $80,000) and a promotion to director. In April 2002, Yates, Normand, and Vinson reviewed the first-quarter report, which included $818 million in capitalized line costs. They also learned that achieving Ebbers's projections would require making similar entries for the remainder of the year. They made a pact to stop making such entries.

Internal Audit

Cynthia Cooper, a strong-willed, 38-year-old, nine-year WorldCom veteran, headed WorldCom's 24-member internal audit department. Cooper had grown up in Clinton, Mississippi, WorldCom's headquarters since 1998. Her high school teacher of accounting was the mother of one of her senior auditors. Gene Morse also was working in Internal Audit, as a senior manager; he had transferred after Yates threatened him, in October 1999, about speaking to external auditors. Internal Audit reported directly to CFO Sullivan for most purposes. It conducted primarily operational audits to measure business unit performance and enforce spending controls. Arthur Andersen, WorldCom's independent auditors, performed the financial audits to assess the reliability and integrity of the publicly reported financial information. Andersen reported to the audit committee of the company's board of directors.[18]

In August 2001, Cooper began a routine operational audit of WorldCom's capital expenditures. Sullivan instructed Myers to restrict the scope of Cooper's inquiry: "We are not looking for a comprehensive Capex audit but rather very in depth in certain areas and spending." Cooper's audit revealed that Corporate had capital expenditures of $2.3 billion. By way of comparison, WorldCom's operations and technology group, which ran the company's entire telecommunications network, had capital expenditures of $2.9 billion. Internal Audit requested an explanation of Corporate's $2.3 billion worth of projects. Cooper's team received a revised chart indicating that Corporate had only $174 million in expenditures. A footnote reference in this chart indicated that the remainder of the $2.3 billion included a metro lease buyout, line costs, and some corporate-level accruals.

In March 2002, the head of the wireless business unit complained to Cooper about a $400 million accrual in his business for expected future cash payments and bad-debt expenses that had been transferred away to pump up company earnings. Both Sullivan and the Arthur Andersen team had supported the transfer. Cooper asked one of the Andersen auditors to explain the transfer, but he refused, telling her that he took orders only from Sullivan. Morse recalled: "That was like putting a red flag in front of a bull. She came back to me and said, 'Go dig.'"[19]

Cooper brought the issue to WorldCom's audit committee but was told by Sullivan, after the audit committee meeting, to stay away from the wireless business unit. Cooper recalled Sullivan screaming at her in a way she had never been talked to before, by anyone.[p]

Also in March 2002, SEC investigators sent WorldCom a surprise "request for information." The SEC wanted to examine company data to learn how WorldCom could be profitable while other telecom companies were reporting large losses.

Cooper decided, unilaterally and without informing Sullivan, to expand Internal Audit's scope by conducting a financial audit. Cooper asked Morse, who had good computer expertise, to access the company's computerized journal entries. Such access was granted only with Sullivan's permission, which they definitely did not have. But Morse, anticipating a need for unlimited access to the company's financial systems, had previously persuaded a senior manager in WorldCom's IT department to allow him to use the systems to test new software programs.

The software enabled Morse to find the original journal entry for virtually any expense. Morse worked at night, when his activities were less likely to clog the network.[20] By day, Morse examined his downloaded materials in the audit library, a small windowless room.

---

[18] This audit was described as operational in nature, with an emphasis on actual spending in the field, capitalization of labor costs, and cash management. Internal Audit focused on operational and not financial statement audits at this time in order to avoid duplicating the work Andersen was doing; one employee told us that Internal Audit also wanted to avoid being seen as digging in Scott Sullivan's " backyard" when the group reported to him. (Beresford, Katzen-bach, and Rogers, Jr., p. 119.)

[19] Susan Pulliman and Deborah Solomon, "Uncooking the Books," *The Wall Street journal,* October 30, 2002.
[20] In an early effort, Morse attempted to download a large number of transactions from one account and crashed the system, which drew attention to his efforts.

He copied incriminating data onto a CD-ROM so that the company could not subsequently destroy the evidence. Morse, a gregarious father of three, was so concerned with secrecy that he did not tell his wife what he was doing and instructed her not to touch his briefcase.

The Outside Auditor: Arthur Andersen

WorldCom's independent external auditor from 1990 to 2002 was Arthur Andersen. Andersen considered WorldCom to be its "flagship" and most "highly coveted" client, the firm's "Crown Jewel."[q] Andersen viewed its relationship with WorldCom as long term and wanted to be considered as a committed member of WorldCom's team. One indicator of its commitment came after the company merged with MCI. Andersen, which had a Mississippi-based team of 10–12 people working full time on WorldCom's audits, underbilled the company and justified the lower charges as a continuing investment in its WorldCom relationship.

Originally, Andersen did its audit "the old-fashioned way," testing thousands of details of individual transactions and reviewing and confirming account balances in WorldCom's general ledger. As World-Com's operations expanded through mergers and increased scope of services, Andersen adopted more efficient and sophisticated audit procedures, based on analytic reviews and risk assessments. The auditors focused on identifying risks and assessing whether the client company had adequate controls in place to mitigate those risks, for example, for mistakenly or deliberately misrepresenting financial data. In practice, Andersen reviewed processes, tested systems, and assessed whether business unit groups received correct information from the field. Its auditors assumed that the information recorded by General Accounting was valid. It typically requested the same 20 to 30 schedules of high-level summaries to review each quarter, including a schedule of topside entries made by General Accounting directly to the corporate general ledger after the close of a quarter.[r]

Andersen also assessed the risk that expenditures for payroll, spare parts, movable parts, and capital projects were being properly recorded and classified as expenses or assets by reviewing the relevant approval process. For line costs, Andersen assessed the risk that line-cost liabilities might be understated or overstated by testing whether the domestic telco accounting group received accurate information from the field. It did not perform comparable tests for the international line-cost group even after WorldCom employees told Andersen's U.K. audit team about a corporate reversal of $34 million in line-cost accruals after the first quarter of 2000.[s] Andersen focused primarily on the risk that WorldCom revenues would be misstated because of errors or inaccurate records, not by deliberate misrepresentation.

Between 1999 and 2001, Andersen's risk management software program rated WorldCom as a "high-risk" client for committing fraud, a conclusion that its auditors upgraded to "maximum risk" because of volatility in the telecommunications industry, the company's active merger and acquisition plans, and its reliance on a high stock price for acquisitions. The Andersen concurring partner said at the time of the 1999 risk upgrade, "If this job is not maximum, none are."[t] The engagement manager stated that there were "probably few other engagements where [Andersen] ha[d] a higher risk."

But the Andersen audit team for WorldCom did not modify its analytic audit approach and continued to audit WorldCom as a "moderate-risk" client. Andersen could have identified the fraudulent topside entries (accrual reversals and capitalized line costs) from a review of the company's general ledger, its primary transactional accounting record.[u] WorldCom, however, repeatedly refused Andersen's request to access the computerized general ledger. Also, Andersen's analytic review procedures, properly performed, should have triggered a search for accounting irregularities when WorldCom's quarterly financial statements reported stable financial ratios during a period of severe decline in the telecommunications industry: "[M]anagement's ability to continue to meet aggressive revenue growth targets, and maintain a 42% line cost expense-to-revenue ratio, should have raised questions. Instead of wondering how this could be, Andersen appeared to have been comforted by the absence of variances. Indeed, this absence led Andersen to conclude that no follow-up work was required."[v]

Myers, Stephanie Scott, and Mark Willson instructed WorldCom staff about what information could and could not be shared with Andersen. When Andersen auditors asked to speak with Ronald Lomenzo, senior vice president of financial operations, who oversaw international line-cost accruals, the request was refused. One employee commented:

"Myers or Stephanie Scott would never permit it to happen."[w] In 1998, WorldCom's treasurer told the person in charge of security for WorldCom's computerized consolidation and financial reporting system never to give Andersen access. One employee said that she was specifically instructed not to tell Andersen that senior management orchestrated adjustments to domestic line-cost accruals. Myers told one employee who had continued to talk with Andersen's U.K. auditors, "Do not have any more meetings with Andersen for any reason. . . . Mark Willson has already told you this once. Don't make me ask you again."[x]

WorldCom also withheld information, altered documents, omitted information from requested materials, and transferred millions of dollars in account balances to mislead Andersen. In fact, special monthly revenue reports were prepared for Andersen:

> WorldCom provided Andersen with altered MonRevs [monthly revenue reports] that removed several of the more transparently problematic revenue items from the Corporate Unallocated schedule, and buried the revenue for these items elsewhere in the report . . . . After the third quarter of 2001, Stephanie Scott became concerned about how Andersen would react to the size of Corporate Unallocated revenue. . . .
> In the version prepared for Andersen, the Corporate Unallocated revenue items could no longer be identified by name and amount. . . . These items were removed from the Corporate Unallocated schedule and subsumed within a sales region's total/revenue number.[y]

Andersen rated WorldCom's compliance with requests for information as "fair," never informing the audit committee about any restrictions on its access to information or personnel.

The Board of Directors

Between 1999 and 2002, nonexecutive members made up more than 50% of WorldCom's Board of Directors. The board members, most of whom were former owners, officers, or directors of companies acquired by WorldCom, included experts in law, finance, and the telecommunications industry (see Exhibit 2). Bert Roberts, Jr., former CEO of MCI, was chairman from 1998 until 2002. His actual role, however, was hon-

orary. CEO Ebbers presided over board meetings and determined their agendas.

The board's primary interaction with WorldCom matters occurred at regularly scheduled meetings that took place about four to six times a year. With the occasional exception of Bobbitt (Audit) and Kellett (Compensation), none of the outside directors had regular communications with Ebbers, Sullivan, or any other WorldCom employee outside of board or committee meetings. Prior to April 2002, the outside directors never met by themselves.

A week prior to board meetings directors received a packet of information that contained an agenda, financial information from the previous quarter, draft minutes of the previous meeting, investor relations information such as analyst call summaries, and resolutions to consider at the upcoming meeting. The meetings consisted of a series of short presentations from the chairman of the compensation and stock option committee about officer loans and senior level compensation; the chairman of the audit committee;[21] the general counsel, who. discussed legal and regulatory issues; CFO Sullivan, who discussed financial issues at a high level of generality for 30 minutes to an hour; and, on occasion, COO Ron Beaumont. This format did not change, even when the board considered large multibillion-dollar deals.[22]

Sullivan manipulated the information related to capital expenditures and line costs presented to the board. His presentation of total capital spending for the quarter included a breakdown on spending for local, data/long haul, Internet, and international operations and major projects. The board, which was expecting cuts in capital expenditures, received information that reflected a steady decrease. However, the spending cuts were far greater than they were led to believe. The hundreds of millions of dollars of capitalized line costs inflated the capital expenditures reported to the board (see Table A).

Prior to the meetings, board members received line-cost information from a one-page statement of operations within a 15- to 35-page financial section. On this page, line costs were listed among roughly 10 other line items. In his hour-long PowerPoint presentations, Sullivan had a single slide that made quarterly comparisons of several budget items, including line costs. The investigative committee concluded:

---

[21] A nominating committee, responsible for filling vacancies on the board, met only when vacancies occurred.
[22] Committees met separately in hour-long sessions. Special executive sessions discussed mergers and acquisitions.

EXHIBIT 2 WorldCom Board of Directors, as of 2001

Clifford L. Alexander Jr., 67, joined the board after the merger with MCI in1998. He was previously a member of the MCI Board.

James C. Allen, 54, became a director in 1998 through the acquisition of Brooks Fiber Properties where he served as the vice chairman and CEO since 1983.

Judith Areen, 56, joined the board after the merger with MCI in 1998. She had previously been a member of the MCI Board. Areen was appointed executive vice president for Law Center Affairs and dean of the Law Center at Georgetown University in 1989.

Carl J. Aycock, 52, was an initial investor in LDDS and a director since 1983. He served as secretary of WorldCom from 1987 until 1995.

Ronald R. Beaumont, 52, was COO of WorldCom beginning in 2000 and had previously served both as the president and CEO of WorldCom's operations and technology unit and as the president of WorldCom Network Services, a subsidiary of WorldCom, Inc. Prior to 1996, Beaumont was president and CEO of a subsidiary of MFS Communications.

Max E. Bobbitt, 56, became a director in 1992 and served as chairman of the Audit Committee. He was president and CEO of Metromedia China Corporation from 1996 to 1997 and president and CEO of Asian American Telecommunications Corporation, which was acquired by Metromedia China Corporation in 1997.

Bernard J. Ebbers, 59, was the CEO of WorldCom since 1985 and a board member since 1983.

Francesco Galesi, 70, became a director in 1992. He was the chairman and CEO of the Galesi Group of companies, involved in telecommunications and oil and gas exploration and production.

Stiles A. Kellett Jr., 57, became a director in 1981 and served as chairman of the compensation and stock option committee.

Gordon S. Macklin, 72, became a director in 1998 after having served as chairman of White River Corporation, an information services company. He sat on several other boards and had formerly been chairman of Hambrecht and Quist Group and the president of the National Association of Securities Dealers, Inc.

Bert C. Roberts Jr., 58, was the CEO of MCI from 1991 to 1996 and served as chairman of the MCI Board beginning in 1992. He stayed on in this capacity after the WorldCom merger with MCI in1998.

John W. Sidgmore, 50, was the vice chairman of the board and a director at WorldCom beginning in 1996. From 1996 until the MCI merger, he served as COO of WorldCom. He had previously been president and COO of MFS Communications Company, Inc. and an officer of UUNET Technologies, Inc.

Scott D. Sullivan, 39, became a director in 1996 after he was named CFO, treasurer,. and secretary in 1994.

Source; "Annual Report for the Fiscal Year Ended December 31,2000, WorldCom, Inc., March 31, 2001.

TABLE A Report of Capital Expenditures to Board vs. Actual Capital Expenditures (in millions)

	3Q00	4Q00	IQ0I	2Q01	3Q01	4Q0I	1Q02
As reported to board	2,648	2,418	2,235	2,033	1,786	1,785	1,250
Actual spend, not shown to board			1,691	1,473	1,044	944	462

Source: Beresford, Katzenbach, and Rogers, Jr., p. 282.

The Board and the Audit Committee were given information that was both *false and plausible*[z] [emphasis added] . . . . [Audit Committee] members do not appear to have been sufficiently familiar and involved with the Company's internal financial workings, with weaknesses in the Company's internal control structure, or with its culture. . . . To gain the knowledge necessary to function effectively . . . would have required a very substantial amount of energy, expertise by at least some of its members, and time— certainly more than the three to five hours a year the Audit Committee met.[aa]

Ebbers, in addition to his full-time job as World-Com CEO, for which he was generously compensated,[23] had acquired and was managing several unrelated businesses, including hotels, real estate ventures, a Canadian cattle ranch, timberlands, a rice farm, a luxury-yacht-building company, an operating marina, a lumber mill, a country club, a trucking company, and a minor league hockey team.[bb] Ebbers financed the acquisitions of many of these businesses by commercial bank loans secured by his personal WorldCom stock. When WorldCom stock began to decline in 2000, Ebbers received margin calls from his bankers. In September 2000, the compensation committee began, at Ebbers's request, to approve loans and guarantees from WorldCom so that Ebbers would not have to sell his stock to meet the margin calls. The full board learned about the loans to Ebbers in November 2000, since the loans needed to be disclosed in the company's third-quarter l0-Q report. The board ratified and approved the compensation committee's actions. WorldCom did not receive any collateral from Ebbers or his business interests to secure these loans. Nor did the compensation committee oversee Ebbers's use of the funds, some of which were used to pay his companies' operating expenses. By April 29, 2002, the loans and guarantees to Ebbers exceeded $400 million.

According to the investigative committee, World-Com's board was "distant and detached from the workings of the Company."[cc] It did not establish processes to encourage employees to contact outside directors about any concerns they might have about accounting entries or operational matters.[dd]

The Board played far too small a role in the life, direction and culture of the company. The Audit Committee did not engage to the extent necessary to Understand and address the financial issues presented by this large and extremely complex business: its members were not in a position to exercise critical judgment on accounting and reporting issues, or on the nontraditional audit strategy of their outside auditor. The Compensation Committee dispensed extraordinarily generous rewards without adequate attention to the incentives they created, and presided over enormous loans to Ebbers that we believe were antithetical to shareholder interests and unjustifiable on any basis.[ee]

On April 26, 2002, the nonexecutive directors met by themselves, for the first time, to discuss Ebbers's delay in providing collateral for his loans from the company. The directors, dissatisfied with Ebbers's lack of strategic vision and his diminished reputation on Wall Street, voted unanimously to ask Ebbers for his resignation. Within three days, the board signed a separation agreement with Ebbers that included a restructuring of his loans into a five-year note and a promise of a $1.5 million annual payment for life.[ff],[24]

The Endgame

Cooper's internal audit team, by the beginning of June 2002, had discovered $3 billion in questionable expenses, including $500 million in undocumented computer expenses. On June 11, Cooper met with Sullivan, who asked her to delay the capital expenditure audit until after the third quarter. Cooper refused. On June 17, Cooper and Glyn Smith, a manager on her team, went to Vinson's office and asked her to explain several questionable capital expense accounting entries that Internal Audit had found. Vinson admitted that she had made many of the entries but did not have any support for them. Cooper immediately went to Yates's office, several feet away, and asked him for an explanation. Yates denied knowledge of the entries and referred Cooper to Myers, who acknowledged the entries and admitted that no accounting standards existed to support them. Myers allegedly said the entries should not have been made, but that once it had started, it was hard to stop.[25]

---

[23] Ebbers was ranked, for several years in a row, as among the highest paid CEOs in the United States.

[24] Subsequently, the corporate monitor and WorldCom's new management cancelled the $1.5 million annual payment and took control of some of Ebbers's personal business assets.

[25] Pulliman and Solomon.

On June 20, Cooper and her internal audit team met in Washington, D.C. with the audit committee and disclosed their findings of inappropriate capitalized expenses. When Sullivan could not provide an adequate explanation of these transactions, the board told Sullivan and Myers to resign immediately or they would be fired. Myers resigned. Sullivan did not and was promptly fired. On June 25, 2002, WorldCom announced that its profits had been inflated by $3.8 billion over the previous five quarters. Nasdaq immediately halted trading of WorldCom's stock. Standard & Poor's lowered its long-term corporate credit rating on WorldCom bonds from B+ to CCC-.

On June 26, the SEC initiated a civil suit of fraud against WorldCom. Attorneys in the U.S. Justice Department launched criminal investigations into the actions of Bernie Ebbers, Scott Sullivan, David Myers, Buford Yates, Betty Vinson, and Troy Normand.

Questions

1. Explain the nature of the accounting fraud.
2. What are the pressures that lead executives and managers to "cook the books?"
3. What is the boundary between earnings smoothing or earnings management and fraudulent reporting?
4. Why were the actions taken by WorldCom managers not detected earlier? What management control processes or systems should be in place to deter or detect quickly the types of actions that occurred in WorldCom?
5. Were the external auditors and board of directors blameworthy in this case? Why or why not?
6. Betty Vinson: victim or villain? Should criminal fraud charges have been brough against her? How should employees react when ordered by their employer to do something they do not believe in or feel uncomfortable doing?

Endnotes

[a] Dennis R. Beresford, Nicholas de B. Katzenbach, and C.B. Rogers,. Jr., "Report of Investigation," Special Investigative Committee of the Board of Directors of WorldCom, Inc., March 31, 2003, p. 49.

[b] Ibid.

[c] Ibid., p. 277.

[d] Ibid., p. 19.

[e] Ibid., p. 18.

[f] Ibid., p. 124.

[g] Ibid., p. 13.

[h] Ibid., p. 94.

[i] Ibid., pp. 94–95.

[j] Ibid., p. 83.

[k] Ibid., p. 71.

[l] Ibid., p. 16.

[m] Ibid., p. 94.

[n] Ibid., p. 99.

[o] Ibid., pp. 105–108.

[p] Ibid., p. 123.

[q] Ibid., p. 225.

[r] Ibid., p. 228.

[s] Ibid., p. 242.

[t] Ibid., p. 233.

[u] Ibid., p. 235.

[v] Ibid., p. 236.

[w] Ibid., p. 240.

[x] Ibid., p. 251.

[y] Ibid., p. 252.

[z] Ibid., p. 277.

[aa] Ibid., p. 286.

[bb] Ibid., pp. 294–295.

[cc] Ibid., p. 283.

[dd] Ibid., p. 290.

[ee] Ibid., p. 264.

[ff] Ibid., pp. 309–310.

Case 7–6

Valuation of Ecommerce Companies

Indian e-commerce companies have shown astonishing growth rates coupled with abnormal valuations but there are some very serious questions about some of their accounting practices and ownership patterns. The two questions are central to the operations of the poster boy of e-commerce in India: flipkart.com, the online retailer of books and electronics that was recently acquired by Walmart in a whopping deal of close to $16 billion. This deal also has a bearing on a clutch of other companies, including Byjus, Zomato, Myntra and Snapdeal.

Since then, there have been various theories going around on this abnormal valuation, as the company (Flipkart) has not made any profit until this date. There are people like K Vaitheeswaran, founder of Indiaplaza.com, who has lived through two crashes in his 12 years in this business who say "I think it (valuations in general) is a bubble, though I hope it is not." Mahesh Murthy, a venture capitalist, says "In these cases of high Indian valuation, the number seems to be driven by the 'find a greater fool theory' - where you believe it is okay to value someone at $1 billion because you think you can find a fool who will buy it from you at $3 billion in a few years."

Inflating Profits in Current Year

The key issue here is related to the credibility of the profit numbers that some e-commerce players are reporting. And to answer this, the key question arises over how they treat the discount expense (which is significant in many cases) in their books of accounts. Several companies are reportedly indulging in creative accounting of marketing expenses, including discounts. The net effect of this creative accounting is to postpone expenses to later years and inflate profits in the current one.

The math works like this. If the cost price of a book for an e-commerce firm is Rs.100 which it offers it for sale for Rs.120, but also offers a Rs.30 discount, be it in the form of cash or a gift certificate. A customer buys the book at an effective price of 90. But the firm doesn't record 90 as revenue and 10 as a loss. It breaks it down into two transactions. The first transaction records 120 as revenue and 20 (120–100) as profit. The second transaction records the 30 discount as an expense. But the same is not expensed the same year, rather it is capitalized and amortized over subsequent years, thus inflating profits in the current year.

When Sachin Bansal, co-founder of the company was asked about it, he conveyed ignorance. "I am not aware of such a practice in Flipkart." When asked specifically if any current expense was being capitalized, he replied: "I will not comment." It goes without saying that most e-commerce firms have done really well in the past 2-3 years, gaining huge popularity with the online consumer. Aided by cash from PE and VC firms, e-commerce companies have rolled out aggressive pricing and deals to drive revenues. Profits, though, are another matter and still remains elusive. Flipkart clocked revenues of Rs 30,164 crore in FY 2017-18, a 50% increase from its revenue in FY 2016-17. Losses increased to 46,000 crores, a jump of 5 times compared to previous year.

Questions

1. In what situations, an "expense" can be capitalized as "Assets".
2. Can you think of any other similar expense which has the discretion of "capitalization".
3. What could be the other triggers for firms to do (i) besides the accounting logic?
4. When there is a discretion available to managers between "expensing" and "capitalizing", which treatments are less likely to be objected by the auditors/markets and why?

Sources of Capital: Debt

Chapter 8 begins a more detailed description of the liabilities and owners' equity portion of the balance sheet. In this chapter we discuss liabilities and the related interest expense, while Chapter 9 discusses owners' equity. As mentioned in Chapter 2, liabilities and owners' equity represent the sources of the funds that have been used to finance the entity's investments in assets.

Identifying the needs for new funds and acquiring these funds are part of the function known as *financial management*. The financial executives in an organization need to have extensive knowledge about the various means of raising money and the legal and tax rules that relate to financing. Other members of management should have a general understanding of these matters even though they need not be familiar with all the details. This chapter discusses the accounting and financial analysis aspects of liabilities at a level that is intended to give the nonfinancial manager a general under-standing of the subject.

In the typical organization, arranging new sources of long-term liabilities is an event that occurs infrequently; but when it does occur, it is likely to have a major impact on the financial statements. The appendix to this chapter introduces the concept of present value, a fundamental concept in the balance sheet valuation of liabilities and the measurement of fair value.

Nature of Liabilities

In Chapter 2, *liability* was defined as an obligation to an outside party arising from a transaction or an event that has already happened. This definition is approximately correct. However, some accounting liabilities are not legally enforceable obligations, and some legal obligations are not liabilities in the accounting meaning of this word.

An estimated allowance for future costs under a warranty agreement is an example of a liability that is not a definite obligation at the time it is set up. When a warranty agreement applies, the liability account Allowances for Warranties is set up by a credit entry in the period in which the revenue is recognized, the offsetting debit being a charge to an expense account such as Estimated Warranty Expense. Later on, when repairs or replacements under warranty are made, the liability account will be debited and other balance sheet accounts such as Parts Inventory will be credited.

Executory Contracts

An example of a legal obligation that is not an accounting liability is an **executory contract**— a contract in which *neither* party has as yet performed. Understanding the nature of such agreements is important, not only in determining accounting liabilities but also in determining revenues and expenses. Five examples follow that illustrate the concept.

1. A sales order is placed for the future delivery of certain goods to the buyer. If the goods are not shipped in the current period, neither party has performed: The buyer has not paid anything and the seller has not shipped the goods. Thus, in accounting the sales order is not recognized—neither party has a liability and no revenue is recognized.

2. A baseball club signs a contract to pay a certain player $1 million per year for five years. The player works in the year in which the contract is signed; in this first year, the player has performed, so the contract is not an executory contract. If the baseball club has not paid all of the $1 million by the end of the first year, it has a liability for the unpaid amount. However, the agreement is currently an executory contract for the other four years; the remaining $4 million obligation is not recorded as a liability (or as anything) in the current year.

3. A law firm signs a contract in which it agrees to provide legal services next year. This is an executory contract in the current year; signing the contract does not constitute performance. This is conceptually the same as the sales order example, except that future provision of services is involved rather than future delivery of goods.

4. A law firm signs a contract in which it agrees to provide legal services next year on an as-needed basis; it receives a $50,000 retainer fee for so agreeing. This is not an executory contract because the client has performed by paying the $50,000. However, because the law firm has not yet performed, it records a liability of $50,000 in the current year; the $50,000 is not yet revenue. The law firm does earn $50,000 revenue in the following year, whether or not it is actually called upon by the client to perform any services.

5. The seller of a house receives $10,000 as a nonrefundable deposit from the buyer of the house; subsequently, the would-be buyer decides not to purchase the house after all. This is not an executory contract because the buyer has performed to the extent of $10,000. This $10,000 is a liability to the seller at the time the deposit is made; subsequently, when the buyer does not consummate the purchase, the $10,000 becomes revenue to the seller.

Important exceptions to the general rule that executory contracts do not create accounting liabilities are capital leases, discussed later in this chapter. Lease agreements are executory contracts. The lessor must provide the lessee with "quiet enjoyment" of the leased asset and the lessee must pay future lease payments. In the case of capital leases, the Financial Accounting Standards Board (FASB) decided the substance of the transaction rather than its legal form should dictate the accounting treatment.

Contingencies

A **contingency** is a set of circumstances involving uncertainty as to possible gain (a *gain contingency*) or loss (a *loss contingency*) that will ultimately be resolved when some future event occurs or fails to occur. Gain contingencies usually are not recorded because recording them would mean recognizing revenues before they are reasonably certain, which is not in accord with the conservatism concept. Accounting for loss contingencies is more judgmental. Examples of such contingencies include two items previously discussed—collectibility of receivables and future warranty costs—as well as threatened or pending litigation; guarantees of indebtedness to others; risk of damage or loss to property by fire, flood, earthquake, or other hazard; and actual or possible claims and assessments.

A loss contingency is recognized—recorded—as a liability (with an offsetting debit to an appropriate expense account to record the loss) only if *both* of the following conditions are met:

1. Information available prior to issuance of the financial statements indicates that it is probable that an asset had been impaired or a liability had been incurred.
2. The amount of loss can be reasonably estimated.

If one of the conditions is not met, the contingency must nevertheless be disclosed (but not recognized) if there is at least a reasonable possibility that a loss may have been incurred.[1]

For example, assume that during the period a lawsuit claiming damages has been filed against a company. If the company concludes that it is probable it will lose the lawsuit *and* if the amount can be reasonably estimated, a liability is recognized. If the amount of the probable loss can be estimated only within a range, the lower end of this range is the amount of the liability. The possible loss above this lower limit is disclosed in notes to the financial statements, but it is not recorded in the accounts.[2]

Example

A company's internal auditor discovered that an employee had made errors in calculating the amount of customs duties due on imported merchandise, resulting in underpayments totaling $100,000. The company immediately paid the $100,000 to the government. The penalty would be at the court's discretion, with a maximum of 10 times the value of the merchandise; in this instance, the maximum penalty could be $30 million. On the other hand, there would be no penalty if the court decided that the error was not willful. Based on the experience of other companies with similar violations, the company decided that the lower limit of the probable range of penalties was $300,000 and recorded this amount as a liability and an expense. It disclosed the possibility of paying up to $30 million in a note accompanying its balance sheet.

A company is said to be "contingently liable" if it has guaranteed payment of a loan made to a third party. But this is not a liability in the accounting sense unless available information indicates that the borrower has defaulted or will probably default.[3] The possibility of loss from future earthquakes or other natural catastrophes is not a liability because the events have not yet happened.

There are often practical difficulties in accounting for contingencies. *FASB Statement No. 5* distinguishes among three degrees of uncertainty— *probable* ("likely to occur"), *remote* ("slight" chance of occurring), and *reasonably possible* ("more than remote but less than likely"). In practice, judgment often must be exercised in deciding whether a contingency loss is probable, thus requiring its recognition, or only reasonably possible, thus requiring disclosure of the contingency but not its recognition. Losses that are remote need not be disclosed. The company's reported income for the period is affected by how this judgment is made, which raises the possibility that the judgment may be biased.

Liabilities as a Source of Funds

As described in Chapter 2, current liabilities are those that are to be satisfied in the near future. One noteworthy aspect of current liabilities is that they often provide funds (financial resources) to the company at no cost. For example, if suppliers

[1] "Accounting for Contingencies," *FASB Statement No. 5*; "Provisions, Contingent Liabilities and Contingent Assets," *IAS No. 37*.
[2] "Reasonable Estimation of the Amount of a Loss," *FASB Interpretation No. 14*.
[3] Even though such a guarantee may not create a liability, the nature and amount of the guarantee must be disclosed in a note to the balance sheet. See *FASB Statement No. 5* and "Disclosure of Indirect Guarantees of Indebtedness to Others," *FASB Interpretation No. 34*.

permit a company to pay for materials or supplies 30 days after delivery, this credit policy results in an interest-free, 30-day loan to the company. Similarly, unearned subscription revenue prepaid to a magazine publisher is, in effect, an interest-free loan from subscribers to the publisher.

With these exceptions, a company pays for the use of the capital that others furnish. Capital obtained from borrowing is called **debt capital.** Capital obtained from shareholders, either as a direct contribution (paid-in capital) or indirectly as retained earnings, is called **equity capital.** The rest of this chapter deals with debt capital. (Equity capital is dealt with in Chapter 9.)

Debt Capital

The debt instruments that a firm uses to obtain capital can be classified generally as either term loans or bonds. We will describe these instruments in general terms; additional details can be found in texts on financial management.

Term Loans

A business loan repayable according to a specified schedule is a **term loan.** The lender is usually a bank or an insurance company. Ordinarily a company's obligation to repay a term loan extends over a period of several years, making the loan a noncurrent liability. However, short-term loans also can be arranged, particularly for businesses with seasonal sales patterns that need cash to finance a buildup of inventories prior to the selling season (e.g., toy manufacturers). For major corporations, term loans are a less significant source of debt capital than bonds.

Bonds

A **bond** is a certificate promising to pay its holder (1) a specified sum of money at a stated date, called the **maturity date,** and (2) interest at a stated rate until the maturity date. Although bonds are usually issued in units of $1,000, the *price* of a bond is usually quoted as a percentage of this face value; thus, a price of 98 means $980. The stated interest rate is usually constant for the life of the bond. However, for some bonds, called **variable rate bonds,** the rate may be expressed in terms such as "the prime rate plus 2 percent"; the rate thus varies each interest period with that period's prime rate (the interest rate charged by banks on short-term loans to their best customers). Bonds may be issued to the general public through the intermediary of an investment banker, or they may be privately placed with an insurance company or other financial institution.

Long-term creditors usually require the borrowing entity to maintain certain minimum financial ratios (e.g., current ratio) and to refrain from taking actions that might endanger the safety of the money loaned. These requirements, called **covenants,** are spelled out in the loan or bond **indenture** (usually a lengthy document). If any of these covenants is not lived up to, the loan is technically in **default,** and the creditors can demand immediate repayment. In the event of default, however, creditors are more likely to require changes in the management or take other corrective action rather than demand immediate repayment.

A **mortgage bond** (or simply **mortgage**) is a bond secured by designated pledged assets of the borrower, usually land, buildings, and equipment. Should the firm default on the mortgage, the pledged assets may be sold to repay the mortgage. If the proceeds from the sale of the pledged assets are less than the amount of the mortgage, then the mortgage holder becomes a general creditor for the shortfall. If the bond is not secured by specific assets of the issuing entity, it is referred to as a **debenture.**

Bond Redemption

In an ordinary bond issue, the principal amount is paid in one lump sum at the maturity date. This payment is said to **redeem** the bond. In order to accumulate cash for redemption, the borrower (bond issuer) may be required to deposit money regularly in an account restricted for this purpose. Bonds that have such a requirement are **sinking fund bonds.** Sinking funds may be used to redeem bonds at maturity, or to redeem outstanding bonds at regular intervals by buying them in the open market or by redeeming certain bonds that are randomly selected. Bond sinking funds are usually controlled by a trustee, such as a bank; they appear in the "investments" or "other assets" section of the balance sheet.

Serial bonds also are redeemed in installments, the redemption date for each bond in the bond issue being specified on the bond itself. The primary difference between a sinking fund bond and a serial bond is that holders of serial bonds know the date when their bonds will be redeemed, whereas holders of sinking fund bonds do not. The latter may end up holding their bonds to maturity, or their bonds may be randomly selected for redemption by the sinking fund at some earlier time.

A bond also may be **callable**; the issuing entity may, at its option, call the bonds for redemption before the maturity date. If this is done, the corporation usually must pay a premium for the privilege.

Zero-coupon bonds do not make periodic interest payments. Rather, they are sold at a deep discount from their face value. Over the life of the bond, interest is accrued and added to the bond's carrying value. At maturity, the bond's carrying value is equal to its face value.

Other Features of Bonds

Some bonds are **convertible;** they may be exchanged for a specified number of shares of the issuing corporation's common stock if the bondholder elects to do so. Sinking fund bonds and serial bonds also may be callable, convertible, or both.

Finally, some bonds (and also some term loans) are **subordinated.** In the event a company goes bankrupt and is liquidated, the claims of the subordinated debtholders are subordinate (i.e., inferior) to the claims of any general or secured creditors. However, subordinated creditors' claims take precedence over those of the company's shareholders (equity investors).

Accounting for Bonds

We will now describe how a bond is recorded in the accounts when it is issued, how bond interest expense is recorded while the bond is outstanding, and how the bond's redemption is recorded.

Recording a Bond Issue

To illustrate the entries typically made to record the proceeds from an issue of bonds, assume Mason Corporation issues 100 bonds, each with a **par value** (also called **principal** or **face value)** of $1,000. The bonds have a stated interest rate, called the **coupon rate,**[4] of 10 percent. This means that the annual interest payment will be

---

[4] Before computers were widely used for keeping bondholder records, a bondholder requested each periodic interest payment by mailing in a coupon, printed on sheets attached to the bond certificate, to the bond issuer. That is the origin of the term *coupon rate* and also of the expression *coupon clipper* to describe someone with substantial financial investments.

10 percent of the par value—in this case, $100 per year.[5] The bonds will mature at the end of the 20th year after their issuance. They are not secured by any specific Mason Corporation assets. Such a bond would be called a "10 percent, 20-year debenture." If the corporation received $1,000 for each of these bonds, the following entry would be made:

Cash 100,000
    Bonds Payable   100,000

(In practice the liability account title describes the specific bond issue, with a separate account for each issue. The title is abbreviated here.)

Discount and Premium

A fundamental concept in finance is the relationship between risk and return: The higher the risk an investment represents, the higher the return the investor expects to receive from making the investment. For example, if an investor can earn 8 percent interest on a $1,000 investment in a federally insured certificate of deposit, the investor will expect a bond to provide more than an 8 percent return because there is some risk that either the bond's interest payments or its principal redemption will not be received in full by the bondholder. Similarly, if bonds of a given risk are currently providing a 12 percent return to their holders, investors will not be willing to pay $1,000 for a newly issued bond of comparable risk that has only a 10 percent coupon rate. By the same token, they would be willing to pay *more* than $1,000 for a bond having comparable risk and a 14 percent coupon rate.

There is always some delay between the time a bond's coupon rate is decided upon and when the bond is actually available to be issued to the public. During this delay the prevailing rate of return on bonds of comparable risk may have changed. For this reason, bonds often are issued for *less* than their par value—at a **discount.** This occurs when the prevailing market rate is *higher* than the bond's coupon rate. Recall that the bond's par value is fixed at $1,000, and the annual interest payment is fixed once the coupon rate is set (Interest payment = Par value * Coupon rate). Thus, in order to earn a return higher than the coupon rate, the bondholder must invest less than $1,000 in the bond. Similarly, if prevailing rates are *lower* than the bond's coupon rate, bondholders will be willing to invest *more* than the bond's par value, and the bond will be issued at a **premium.**[6]

Example

If the prevailing rate of interest in the bond market is more than 10 percent for bonds with a risk similar to those issued by Mason Corporation, potential investors will be unwilling to pay $1,000 for a Mason Corporation 10 percent bond. They would be willing to invest an amount such that the $100 annual interest payment on this bond would yield the market rate of interest. Assume that this market rate is 12 percent. The bond would therefore be sold at a price of $851, or at a discount of $149.[7]

---

[5] In practice, interest payments are usually made in semiannual installments, rather than annually—in this case, $50 every six months. For simplicity, we will usually assume annual payments.

[6] Although it is colloquially said that an investor "pays" for a newly issued bond and that corporations "sell" their bonds, a bond is *not* an asset of the corporation that is sold, as are goods. Rather, bonds are evidence of a contribution of funds—a long-term loan—to the firm by investors. To the investor, the bond *is* an asset, and it can be sold to another investor. Such an exchange between investors has no impact on the flow of cash into or out of the firm, however. (Similar comments apply to shares of a corporation's common stock.)

[7] The $851 is formally called the **present value** of the bond; the method of calculating it is described in the appendix to this chapter. The precise present value is $850.61. If the interest were received in $50 semiannual amounts, the present value would be $849.54.

The words *discount* and *premium* carry no connotation of bad or good. They reflect simply a difference between the coupon interest rate for the issue and the going market rate of interest at the time of issuance. The coupon rate is usually quite close to the market rate as of the date of issue.

From the standpoint of the bond issuer, the discount or premium on a bond is a function only of the interest rates prevailing at the time of issuance of the bonds. Subsequent changes in the level of interest rates (and hence in bond prices) do not affect the amount recorded in the accounts. To emphasize this fact, the discount or premium recorded by the bond issuer is often called **original issue discount** or **premium.**

Issuance Costs

The offering of a bond issue to the public is usually undertaken by an investment banking firm that charges the issuer a fee for this service. In addition to this fee, the issuer also incurs printing, legal, and accounting costs in connection with the bond issue. These **bond issuance costs** are recorded as a deferred charge, which is an asset analogous to prepaid expenses. The issuance costs are *not* subtracted from the bond liability on the balance sheet, nor are they combined with any bond discount or premium.[8]

Example

Mason Corporation's bonds, for which investors paid $851 each, also had issue costs to Mason averaging $21 per bond, resulting in a net cash inflow to Mason of $830 per bond. The discount is $149 per bond, not $170 ($149 + $21).

Accounting Entries

If the conditions of the preceding examples are assumed, and Mason Corporation received $83,000 net cash proceeds from the issuance of $100,000 face amount of bonds, the following entry would be made:

Cash	83,000	
Bond Discount	14,900	
Deferred Charges	2,100	
Bonds Payable		100,000

By contrast, if prevailing rates for similar bonds had been 9 percent, the bonds would have been issued at a premium of $91 per bond, and the entry would have been

Cash	107,000	
Deferred Charges	2,100	
Bond Premium		9,100
Bonds Payable		100,000

Balance Sheet Presentation

Bonds payable are shown in the long-term liabilities section of the balance sheet until one year before they mature, when ordinarily they become current liabilities. The description should give the principal facts about the issue—for example, "10 percent debentures due 2017." When a bond issue is to be *refunded* with a new long-term liability, however, it is not shown as a current liability in the year of maturity since it will not require the use of current assets. If the bonds are to be retired in installments (as with serial bonds), the portion to be retired within a year is shown in the current liabilities section.

---

[8] "Interest on Receivables and Payables," *APB Opinion No. 21.*

Bond discount or premium is shown on the balance sheet as a direct deduction from, or addition to, the face amount of the bond, as illustrated:

If a Discount:		*If a Premium:*	
Bonds payable:		Bonds payable:	
Face value	$100,000	Face value	$100,000
Less: Unamortized discount	14,900	Plus: Unamortized premium	9,100
	$ 85,100		$ 109,100

The principal amount less unamortized discount (or plus unamortized premium) is called the **book value** (or **net book value**) of the bond. It is the basis of calculating the bond's periodic interest expense, as described below. Note in the above two examples that the initial book value of a bond is equal to the proceeds from its issuance, ignoring any issuance costs. The book value less unamortized issuance costs (deferred charges) is called the **net carrying amount** of the bond.

Bond Interest Expense

To the *investor,* the return on a bond is made up of two components: (1) the periodic cash interest payments and (2) the difference between the bond's par value (received in cash at redemption) and the amount paid for the bond. The second component is a gain if the bond was purchased at a discount or a loss if purchased at a premium.

From the standpoint of the bond *issuer,* a bond's interest expense also has two components that are the mirror image of the investor's return components. **Bond interest expense** is made up of (1) the periodic cash interest payments to the bondholder and (2) amortization of original issue discount or premium. The amount of the issuer's interest expense when related to the initial proceeds from issuing the bond (ignoring issuance costs) determines the **effective rate of interest** on the bond. The effective rate is higher than the coupon rate for bonds issued at a discount; the effective rate is lower than the coupon rate for bonds issued at a premium.[9] (Calculation of the effective rate is described in the appendix to this chapter.)

Discount/Premium Amortization

Bond discount or premium is amortized using the **compound interest method,** also called the **effective interest method** or simply the **interest method.** (This method also is described in the appendix.) Straight-line amortization is not permitted unless the results would not differ materially from those obtained with the interest method.[10] With the interest method of amortization, the discount or premium is written off in such a way that each period's interest *expense* (as opposed to the cash interest payment) bears a constant ratio to the beginning-of-the-period book value of the bonds over the entire life of the issue. This ratio is the effective interest rate on the bonds. In the Mason example, if the bonds were issued for $851 each, this rate is 12 percent.[11]

Example

The first year's interest expense for the 10 percent Mason Corporation bonds that were assumed to have been issued for $851 each would be calculated as follows: *Interest expense is equal to the book value of the bonds at the start of the year* ($85,100) *times the effective*

---

[9] *APB Opinion No. 21* also requires disclosure of this effective rate of interest on the bond.
[10] *APB Opinion No. 21.*
[11] Readers checking our numbers with calculators may get slightly different results for our illustrative Mason bonds. Recall (from footnote 7) that the precise present value for a 12 percent return was $850.61 per bond, which we rounded to $851. This rounding changes the precise return to 11.994 percent, but we still use 12 percent.

interest rate (12 percent), which equals $10,212. Of this total interest expense for the year, $10,000 is the fixed cash interest payment (based on the bonds' par value and coupon rate) and the remaining $212 is the amortization of original issue discount. The entry is

Bond Interest Expense	10,212	
Bond Discount		212
Cash		10,000

This entry reduces the unamortized bond discount by $212 to a new balance of $14,688 ($14,900 – $212). Thus, at the beginning of the second year, the bond's book value will be $85,312 ($100,000 – $14,688). Next year's interest expense will be 12 percent of this book value, or $10,237; of this total, $237 is the second year's discount amortization and $10,000 is the fixed cash interest payment.

Continuing this process for the entire 20 years will completely amortize the original bond discount. Over the 20 years, the bonds' book value will gradually increase up to the $100,000 par value that must be paid to Mason's bondholders at maturity. Thus, the effect of bond discount/premium accounting procedures is that (1) when the bond is issued, its book value equals the cash proceeds received by the issuer (ignoring issuance costs) and (2) at maturity, the book value equals the amount of cash that must be paid out to fulfill the bond payable liability obligation. In other words, there is a matching of the cash flows and liability amounts at bond issuance and maturity, which would not be the case without the systematic amortization of discount or premium.

Adjusting Entries

If the interest payment date does not coincide with the closing of the company's books, an adjusting entry is made to record accrued interest expense and the amortization of discount or premium.

Example

Mason Corporation bonds are issued for $851 each on October 1. The first year interest date is September 30 of the following year, and the issue's fiscal year ends on December 31. The following entries would be made:

1. Adjustment on December 31 to record one-fourth year's interest accrued since October 1:

Bond Interest Expense	2,553	
Bond Discount		53
Accrued Interest Payable		2,500

2. Payment of annual interest on September 30; entry to record three-fourths of a year's interest expense and one year's payment:

Bond Interest Expense	7,659	
Accrued Interest Payable	2,500	
Bond Discount		159
Cash		10,000

Bond issuance costs, which are treated as a deferred charge, usually are amortized using the straight-line method. Thus, for Mason's bonds, the annual issuance cost amortization would be $105 ($2,100 ÷ 20 years).

Retirement of Bonds

Bonds may be retired in total, or they may be retired in installments over a period of years (i.e., as with sinking fund or serial bonds). In either case the retirement is recorded by a debit to Bonds Payable and a credit to Cash (or to a sinking fund that has been set up for this purpose). The bond discount or premium will have been completely amortized by the maturity date, so no additional entry is required for discount or premium at that time.

Refunding a Bond Issue

Callable bonds can be paid off before their maturity dates by paying investors more than the bonds' par value. In periods when interest rates have declined, a company may consider it advantageous to **refund** a bond issue, that is, to call the old issue and issue a new one with a lower rate of interest. At that point, the company must account for the **call premium** (the difference between the call price and par value), any other costs of the refunding, and any unamortized issue costs and discount (or premium) on the old bonds.

Recall that the bonds' face amount, adjusted for unamortized premium or discount and costs of issuance, is called the **net carrying amount** of the debt to be refunded. The amount paid on refunding, including the call premium and miscellaneous costs of refunding, is called the **reacquisition price.** The difference between these two amounts must be reported as a separate loss or gain on the income statement for the period in which the refunding takes place.

Example

Suppose that the 100 Mason Corporation bonds are called at the end of five years by paying the call price of the bonds at that time, $1,050 per bond, to each bondholder. Assume that miscellaneous refunding costs are $1,000 in total. Also, much of the bond discount and issuance costs will not have been amortized. The $13,553 of unamortized discount is determined using the compound interest method. Unamortized bond issuance costs after five years (one-quarter of the bonds' scheduled life) would be ¾ * $2,100 = $1,575. The loss is determined as follows:

Reacquisition price ($105,000 + $1,000)		$106,000
Net carrying amount:		
Face value	$100,000	
Less: Unamortized discount	(13,553)	
Less: Unamortized issuance costs	(1,575)	84,872
Loss on retirement of bonds		$ 21,128

The accounting entry is

Bonds Payable	100,000	
Loss on Retirement of Bonds	21,128	
Cash		106,000
Bond Discount		13,553
Deferred Charges (Issuance Costs)		1,575

Leased Assets

In a **lease** agreement, the owner of property, the **lessor**, conveys to another party, the **lessee**, the right to use property, plant, or equipment for a stated period of time. Leases are a form of lessee financing. For many leases, this period of time is short relative to the total life of the asset. Agencies lease—or **rent**, which is another term for lease—automobiles for a few hours or days, and space in an office building may be leased on an annual basis. These leases are called **operating leases**. The lease payments are expenses of the accounting period to which they apply. The entry to record a period's operating lease payments of, say, $10,000 is thus

Rental Expense	10,000	
Cash		10,000

Capital Leases

Other leases cover a period of time that is substantially equal to the estimated life of the asset, or they contain other provisions that give the lessee almost as many rights to the use of the asset as if the lessee owned it. Such leases are called **capital leases** or **financial leases.** Assets acquired under a capital lease are treated as *if they had been purchased.* The lease obligation is a liability, which is treated in the same manner as long-term debt.

The Financial Accounting Standards Board (FASB) has ruled that a lease is a capital lease if one of the following criteria are met: (1) Ownership is transferred to the lessee at the end of the term of the lease, (2) the lessee has an option to purchase the asset at a "bargain" price, (3) the term of the lease is 75 percent or more of the economic life of the asset, or (4) the present value of the lease payments is 90 percent or more of the fair value of the property (subject to certain detailed adjustments).[12] The idea of these criteria is to establish the substance (as opposed to the form) of the lease transaction. Even if only one of the four criteria is met, the transaction is viewed in substance as a sale of the asset to the lessee, with the lessor acting both as a seller of assets and as a finance company. In sum, a capital lease is, in effect, just another name for an asset purchase financial an installment loan.

The lease payments in a capital lease are usually set so that over the life of the lease the lessor will recover (1) the cost of the asset and (2) interest and a profit on the lessor's capital that is tied up in the asset. The amount debited as the cost of the asset acquired with a capital lease, and the offsetting liability for lease payments, is the *smaller* of (1) the fair value of the asset or (2) the present value of the stream of minimum lease payments required by the lease agreement. *Fair value* means the cash price that the acquirer of the leased item would have to pay for it if the seller were not providing financing to the acquirer in the form of a lease. The method of calculating the present value of the lease payments is described in the appendix to the chapter. These two amounts are approximately the same in most lease transactions.

The asset amount is depreciated just as would be any item of plant or equipment owned by the organization.[13] When lease payments are made to the lessor, part of the payment reduces the liability, and the remainder is interest expense of the period.

Example

A company leases an item of equipment whose useful life is 10 years. Lease payments are $1,558 per year payable at the end of each of the next 10 years. This is a capital lease because the lease term exceeds 75 percent of the asset's life. The fair value of the equipment is $10,000 (as is the present value of the lease payments). When the equipment is acquired, the entry is

Equipment 10,000		
Capital Lease Obligations	10,000	

Assume that the first annual lease payment consists of $900 of interest expense and $658 to reduce the liability. The entry for this payment is as follows:

Interest Expense 900	
Capital Lease Obligations 658	
Cash	1,558

Also, depreciation on the asset would be charged as an expense each year, just as if the entity had bought the asset for cash. Assuming the straight-line method is used, the entry is

Depreciation Expense 1,000	
Accumulated Depreciation	1,000

---

[12] "Accounting for Leases," *FASB Statement No. 13.*

[13] If the lease agreement includes an automatic ownership transfer of the leased property to the lesee at the end of the lease or a bargain purchase provision, the lesee depreciates the leased asset over its useful life, otherwise the leased asset is depreciated over the leased term.

At the end of the 10 years, all of the $10,000 asset cost will have been charged to expense via the depreciation mechanism. Also, the capital lease obligation will have been reduced to zero, and the annual interest expense will have been recognized in each of the 10 years via entries such as the one shown above. Note that once the leased item is acquired and the initial equipment asset and lease obligation liability entry is made, accounting for the leased asset and for the lease obligation are separate, unrelated processes.

Most assets of an entity are legally owned by that entity. Assets acquired by a capital lease are an exception to this general rule. They are legally owned by the lessor, but they are accounted for as if they were owned by the lessee. In this way, the lease obligation, which is in substance a long-term loan, is disclosed as a liability.

IFRS refers to "finance leases" and "operating leases," finance leases are similar what the FASB refers to as "capital leases." Under IFRS, a lease agreement that transfers substantially all the risks and rewards incidental to ownership of an asset to the lessee is classified as a "finance lease." The above lease accounting entry discussion applies equally to finance and operating leases.[14]

Sale and Leaseback

A sale and leaseback is a financing transaction whereby the owner of the property sells it and simultaneously leases it back from the buyer. Any losses on the sale are recognized in income immediately. Gains on the sale are deferred and in most cases are recognized over the life of the lease.

Other Liabilities

This chapter thus far has focused on debt capital—long-term loans, bonds, and leases. For completeness, two other liabilities will be discussed briefly.

Current Liabilities

As explained in Chapter 2, current liabilities are obligations that are expected to be satisfied either by the use of current assets (usually by cash) or by the creation of other current liabilities within one year or less. The largest current liability for most entities is accounts payable (i.e., amounts owed to suppliers of goods and services). These amounts are recorded based on an invoice (i.e., a bill) from the supplier of the goods or services. Entries to other current liability accounts usually arise from adjusting entries; accrued wages payable, accrued interest payable, and estimated taxes payable are examples that have previously been described.

Deferred Taxes

Another liability section item of significant size for many corporations is *deferred income taxes*. This is a complicated topic and its mechanics are described in Chapter 10. Suffice it to say here that deferred taxes arise when a company uses different accounting methods in preparing its corporate income tax return than is used in preparing its financial statements for shareholder reporting purposes. For example, most corporations use straight-line depreciation over an asset's useful life for shareholder reporting but use the tax law's accelerated cost recovery provisions for income tax reporting.

Analysis of Capital Structure

Debt Ratios

The relative amount of a company's capital that was obtained from various sources is a matter of great importance in analyzing the soundness of the company's financial position.

---

[14] "Leases," *IAS No. 17.*

In illustrating the ratios intended for this purpose, the following summary of the liabilities and owners' equity side of a company's balance sheet will be used:

	$ Millions	Percent
Current liabilities	$1,600	23%
Long-term liabilities	1,800	26
Shareholders' equity	3,600	51
Total liabilities and owners' equity	$ 7,000	100%

Attention is often focused on the sources of **invested capital** (also called **permanent capital**): **debt capital** (long-term liabilities) and **equity capital** (owners' equity). From the point of view of the company, debt capital is risky because if bondholders and other creditors are not paid promptly, they can take legal action to obtain payment. Such action can, in extreme cases, force the company into bankruptcy. Equity capital is much less risky to the company because shareholders receive dividends only at the discretion of the directors and the shareholders cannot force bankruptcy.[15] Because the shareholders have less certainty of receiving dividends than the bondholders have of receiving interest, investors usually are unwilling to invest in a company's stock unless they see a reasonable expectation of making a higher return (dividends plus stock price appreciation) than they could obtain as bondholders. Investors would be unwilling to give up the relatively certain prospect of receiving 8 percent or 9 percent interest on bonds, unless the probable, but less certain, return on an equity investment were considerably higher, say, 12 percent or more.

Leverage

From the company's standpoint, the greater the proportion of its invested capital that is obtained from shareholders, the less worry the company has in meeting its fixed obligations. But in return for this lessened worry, the company must expect to pay a higher overall cost of obtaining its capital. Conversely, the more funds that are obtained from bonds, the more the company can use debt funds obtained at relatively low cost in the hopes of earning more on these funds for the shareholders.

The relatively low cost of debt capital arises not only from the fact that investors typically are willing to accept a lower return on bonds than on stocks but also because debt interest (including bond interest payments) is tax deductible to the corporation, whereas dividends are not. Assuming a 40 percent tax rate, for every $1 that a company pays out in interest, it receives a tax saving of $0.40. Thus, its net cost is only 60 percent of the stated interest rate. For example, debt capital obtained from a bond issue with a yield of 10 percent costs the company only about 6 percent. By contrast, if equity investors require a return of 12 percent, the cost of obtaining equity capital is the full 12 percent.

Debt/Equity Ratio

A company with a high proportion of long-term debt is said to be highly **leveraged.** The **debt/equity ratio** shows the balance that the management of a particular company has struck between these forces of risk versus cost. This is often called simply the **debt ratio.** It may be calculated in several ways. Debt may be defined as total liabilities, as interest-bearing current liabilities plus noncurrent liabilities, or as only

[15] Note that risk is here viewed from the standpoint of the company. From the viewpoint of *investors,* the opposite situation prevails. Thus, bondholders have a relatively low risk of not receiving their payments, whereas stockholders have a relatively high risk. Based on this latter perspective, equity capital is called **risk capital.**

noncurrent liabilities. The user must always be careful to ascertain which method is used in a given situation. Including current liabilities, the debt/equity ratio for the illustrative company is

$$\frac{\text{Total liabilities}}{\text{Shareholders' equity}} = \frac{\$3,400}{\$3,600} = 94 \text{ percent}$$

Excluding current liabilities, the ratio is

$$\frac{\text{Long-term liabilities}}{\text{Shareholders' equity}} = \frac{\$1,800}{\$3,600} = 50 \text{ percent}$$

Debt/Capitalization Ratio

The mix of debt and equity in the capital structure also may be expressed as the ratio of long-term debt to total invested capital (debt plus equity). This ratio is called the **debt/capitalization ratio.** For our illustrative company, it is the ratio of $1,800 to $5,400, or 33 percent. Note that this ratio is based on the same data as is the debt/equity ratio; it is just another way of expressing the relationship. (As an analogy, one can say that the female/male ratio in a class is 100 percent, or that females make up 50 percent of the total enrollment in the class.) The debt/capitalization ratio varies widely among industries but is less than 50 percent in the majority of industrial companies.

Times Interest Earned

Another measure of a company's financial soundness is the **times interest earned**, or **interest coverage ratio**. This is the relationship of a company's income to its interest requirements. The numerator of this ratio is the company's *pretax* income *before* subtraction of interest expense. Assuming that for our illustrative company this amount was $1,000, and that interest expense was $200, the calculation is

$$\text{Times interest earned} = \frac{\text{Pretax income before interest}}{\text{Interest expense}} = \frac{\$1,000}{\$200} = 5.0 \text{ times}$$

Bond Ratings

Organizations such as Standard & Poor's and Moody's provide ratings on bonds to indicate their probability of going into default. A number of factors are considered in rating a corporation's bonds, including various financial ratios and evaluation of the prospects of the company's industry and the company's market position in that industry. The debt/capitalization ratio and interest coverage ratio are especially important. For example, the typical industrial company meriting Standard & Poor's top "AAA" rating might have a debt/capitalization ratio in the preceding three years of about 22 percent and interest coverage of about 17 times. (Standard & Poor's debt/capitalization ratio definition includes interest-bearing current liabilities, as well as long-term debt.) An AAA rating indicates a company's capacity to pay interest and repay principal on time is extremely strong.

Indian Debt Markets

The accounting standard IND AS 109 deals with all the issues related to Financial Instruments (both Assets and Liabilities). It covers all the aspects related to the instruments starting from recognition and measurement to classification and to de-recognition.

FVTPL vs FVTOCI: Accounting of Financial Assets and Liabilities

When it comes to recognizing financial assets and liabilities to a firm they are always valued at fair value except where the original transaction price is not indicative of fair value of a financial instrument evidenced by either a quoted price of a similar asset or liability or is based on a valuation tool which takes input data from public markets. The difference (which could be either a gain or loss) is recognized in Profit and Loss statement.

The two choices available under IND AS 109 are:

Fair value through the OCI route (other comprehensive income) (FVOCI): the financial assets are classified and measured at **fair value via the OCI route** if they are held in a business model where the objective is largely achieved by both collecting contractual cash flows and selling financial assets.

Fair value through profit or loss (FVTPL): it means that on each balance sheet date, the asset or liability is marked to **fair value** and any movement in that **fair value** is taken directly to the **income** statement

Financial assets are classified by one of these methods depending on the category of financial assets they were classified at the time of first recognition. Depending on whether they were classified as "Held for trade" or not, FVTPL or FVOCI is used. Debt assets usually follow FVTPKL and Equity follows FVOCI.

Financial Liabilities are classified as FVTPL when:

- they meet the definition for Held for Trade
- They are designated so at the time of recognition
- It eliminates or reduces significantly measurement or a recognition inconsistency
- The financial liability has embedded derivative features.

Derecognition of financial liabilities

An entity shall remove a part or full financial liability from its Balance Sheet when it is extinguished. In other words, all contract obligation is discharged or canceled or is legally transferred to another party. Moreover, any existing liability is also considered derecognized if there is a significant alteration in the terms of the instrument, for example where the discounted present value of net cash flows is different from the previous cash flow by at least 10%.

Some of the special situations that can emerge as part of derecognition of financial liabilities are as follows:

- **Exchange between existing borrower and lender with substantial modification**: The accounting treatment in such a situation would be quite straight forward; Removal of the original financial liability and the recognition of a new financial liability.
- **Transferred to another party (entirely or part):** the accounting treatment is totally different this time; the difference between the carrying amount and the consideration paid (including any non-cash assets) to be recognized as a gain/loss in the P&L Account.
- **Repurchase of a part of a financial liability:** again here, the previous carrying amount is split between the part that continues to be recognized and the part that is de-recognized depending on the fair values as on the date of the repurchase.

India's Corporate Debt Markets

An active and broad corporate bond market is essential for the efficiency and stability of any country's financial system and the overall growth of its economy. It takes away a lot of burden from the traditional main suppliers of "debt capital" in an economy, i.e., the banks. Firms who wish to raise debts and debt investors see the debt markets as a medium that provides opportunities for financial diversification and facilitates necessary financing, which benefits not only good rated corporations but also less known, average grade corporations and infrastructure developers.

ILLUSTRATION 8–1

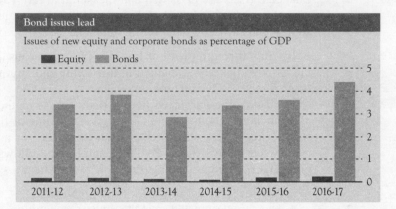

The Indian corporate bond market is quite small as compared to other emerging markets that have similar depth in their financial sectors. Its volume of outstanding debt amounting is not even 5 percent of gross domestic product. Mobilisation of capital through the issue of corporate bonds has just about crept up to 4.4 percent of the GDP (Illustration 8–1). Though that is substantially higher than the 0.2 percent of GDP for mobilisation through new equity issues, it is way short of the figure (varying from 15 to 50 percent) for most similarly placed emerging markets. Compared to the size of its economy, India's corporate bond market is undoubtedly too small (Illustration 8–2).

ILLUSTRATION 8–2

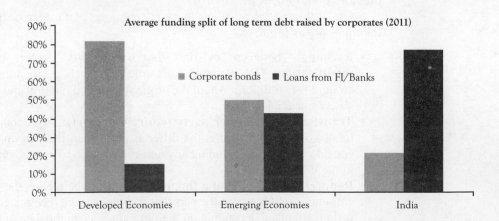

Why do we even need a Corporate Debt market?

In any economy, Debt markets along with the equity markets play a very crucial role for firms in accessing the long-term financing needed for growth. The development of a corporate bond market is particularly important, given that Indian corporations today have limited access to long-term funding from financial institutions, and banks are more inclined toward retail lending, where the risks are comparatively lower. The corporate bond market provides that window of alternative funding source for corporations, which could act as a buffer in the face of sudden interruptions in bank credit or international capital flows. Moreover, the banks' willingness to make long-term loans is also limited by the asset-liability mismatch on their balance sheets as the majority of their deposits are short-term and most of the loans made for large infrastructure projects (a common feature in a developing economy) are usually long-term. This essentially means that any financial system which is dominated by bank is supported with relatively short-term deposits as capital. Using short-term deposits to finance capital-intensive investments or long gestation projects would involve serious liquidity and maturity mismatches that can lead to huge systemic risk to the economy.

What plagues Indian corporate debt markets?

Some of the constraints facing the Indian corporate debt market are structural while some emanate from a too regressive and archaic regulatory framework. The prominent factors behind such small size of the market are basically very low amount of primary issuance of corporate bonds leading to very poor liquidity in the secondary market, narrow investor base, comparatively high costs of issuance, almost no debt market accessibility to small and medium enterprises, almost non-existence of a well-functioning derivatives market that could have partially absorbed risks emanating from interest rate fluctuations and default possibilities. Excessive regulatory restrictions on the investment mandate of financial institutions, large fiscal deficit, high interest rates and the dominance of issuances through private placements which in turn also prevent retail participation and further aggravate the dependence on bank financing.

Summary

Liabilities and owners' equity represents the sources of the funds that are invested in the firm's assets. Liabilities and owners' equity consists of current liabilities, other liabilities (primarily long-term debt), and owners' equity. Current liabilities are distinguished from other liabilities by their payment time horizon (one year or less). Liabilities are distinguished from owners' equity by their nature as obligations to outside parties. Executory contracts are not liabilities (except for capital leases) because neither party has performed. Loss contingencies create liabilities only if it is probable that a liability has been incurred and the amount of loss can be reasonably estimated.

The liability arising from the issuance of bonds is shown at its face amount (par value), adjusted for any difference between this face amount and the amount of cash actually paid by investors for the bonds; this difference is recorded as bond premium or discount. Premium or discount is amortized over the life of the issue using the interest method. This amortization plus the periodic cash interest payments equal the bonds' interest expense of each period. No gain or loss results when a bond is redeemed at maturity, but early retirement will lead to such a gain or loss.

If a company has leased equipment but the lease is, in effect, a vehicle to finance the purchase of the equipment, then under GAAP this capital lease obligation is reported as a liability. Similarly under IFRS, if the lease agreement transfers substantially all the risks and rewards incidental to ownership to the lease, the lease is classified as a finance lease and reported as a liability. In both cases an offsetting asset is recorded. Other liabilities include current liabilities and deferred income taxes.

Debt/equity ratios and interest coverage indicate the level of risk associated with the amount of a company's debt capital.

Appendix

Present Value

The concept of present value underlies the valuation of many liabilities. The concept is also applied in valuing many monetary assets (which is the nature of most of a bank's assets). Related to these liability and asset valuations is the interest method, which is used to amortize discount, premium, and the principal amount of all long-term debt, including capital leases. Finally, the present value concept is used in analyzing proposals to acquire new long-lived assets and to measure the fair value of impaired long-lived assets. These asset acquisition proposals are called *capital investment decisions.*

Concept of Present Value

Many people have difficulty understanding the present value concept because it differs from what we were taught as children—that it is a good thing to put money into a piggy bank. We are congratulated when the bank is finally opened and the accumulated coins are counted. Children are taught that it is better to have a given amount of money in the future than to use that money today. More formally, children are taught that a dollar received at some future time is more valuable than a dollar received today.

Business managers think differently, however. They expect a dollar invested today to *increase* in amount as time passes, because they expect to earn a profit on that investment. It follows that an amount of money available for investment today is *more* valuable to the manager than an equal amount that will not be available until some future time. Money available today can be invested to earn still more money, whereas money not yet received obviously cannot be invested today. To the manager, therefore, the value of a given amount of money today—its *present value*— is more than the value of the same amount received at some future time.

Compound Interest

To make the idea of present value more concrete, consider first the idea of **compound interest.** Suppose we invest $1,000 in a savings account that pays interest of 5 percent compounded annually. (Interest is invariably stated at an annual rate; thus, "5 percent" means 5 percent per year.) *Compounded annually* means that the interest earned the first year is retained in the account and, along with the initial $1,000, earns interest in the second year, and so on for future years. If we make no withdrawals from this account, over time the account balance will grow as shown below:

Based on this table, one can make the following statement: "$1,000 invested today at 5 percent interest, compounded annually, will accumulate to $1,628.89 after 10 years."

Year	Beginning-of-Year Balance	Interest Earned*	End-of-Year Balance
1	$1,000.00	$50.00	$1,050.00
2	1,050.00	52.50	1,102.50
3	1,102.50	55.13	1,157.63
4	1,157.63	57.88	1,215.51
5	1,215.51	60.78	1,276.29
.	.	.	.
.	.	.	.
10	1,551.32	77.57	1,628.89

* Some amounts may appear to be off by 0.01, because the actual calculations were carried to four decimal places and then rounded.

An equivalent statement is that the *future value* of $1,000 invested for 10 years at 5 percent interest is $1,628.89.[1]

Rather than obtaining a future value (*FV*) from a table, it can be calculated using the compound interest formula:

$$FV = p(1+i)^n$$

where
   p = Principal (initial investment)
   i = Interest rate
   n = Number of periods
Thus, the future value of $1,000 invested at 5 percent for 10 years is given by

$$FV = \$1,000(1+0.05)^{10} = \$1,628.89$$

Discounting

To arrive at *present* values, we reverse the future value concept. The reverse of interest compounding is called **discounting.** For example, if the future value of $1,000 at 5 percent interest for 10 years is $1,628.89, then we can also say that the *present value* of $1,628.89 *discounted* at 5 percent for 10 years is $1,000. The interest rate (5 percent in the example) in present value problems is commonly referred to as the **discount rate.** This illustration leads to a more formal definition of **present value:**

The present value of an amount that is expected to be received at a specified time in the future is the amount that, if invested today at a designated rate of return, would cumulate to the specified amount.

Thus, assuming a 5 percent rate of return, the present value of $1,628.89 to be received 10 years hence is $1,000, because (as we have illustrated) if $1,000 were invested today at 5 percent, it would cumulate to $1,628.89 after 10 years.

[1] Interest may be compounded more frequently than once a year. Interest on savings accounts, for example, may be compounded quarterly, monthly, or even daily. In such a case, both the number of periods and the rate per period must be converted to the period used in compounding. For example, with quarterly compounding, the number of periods is 40 (i.e., 40 quarters in 10 years), and the interest rate *per quarter* would be 1.25 percent (5 percent ÷ 4). Thus, the future value of $1,000 invested for 10 years at 5 percent compounded quarterly is $1,000(1.0125)^{40} = $1,643.62. The results of the formulas given in this chapter are available in published tables and are programmed into many handheld calculators and personal computers.

Finding Present Values

The present value (PV) of an amount p to be received n years hence, discounted at a rate of i, is given by the formula

$$PV = \frac{p}{(1+i)n}$$

Appendix Table A (at the back of the book) is a table of present values that were derived from this formula. The amounts in such a table are expressed as the present value of $1 to be received some number of years hence, discounted at some rate. To find the present value of an amount other than $1, we multiply the amount by the appropriate present value factor from Table A.

Example

To find the PV of $400 to be received 10 years hence, discounted at a rate of 8 percent, we first find the 10 year/8 percent factor from Table A, which is 0.463. Hence, the PV of $400 is $400 * 0.463 = $185.20. This means that $185.20 invested today at a return of 8 percent will accumulate to $400 by the end of 10 years.

Inspection of Table A reveals two basic points about present value:

1. Present value decreases as the number of years in the future in which the payment is to be received increases.
2. Present value decreases as the discount rate increases.

Present Value of a Series of Payments

In many business situations, the entity expects to receive a series of annual payments over a period of several years, rather than simply receiving a single amount at some future point. The present value of a series of payments is found by summing the present values of the individual payments. Computational procedures generally assume that each payment in the series is to be received at the *end* of its respective period rather than in a continuous flow during the period.

Example

Using a 10 percent discount rate, what is the present value of the following series of payments: year 1, $1,000; year 2, $1,500; year 3, $2,000; and year 4, $2,500?

Solution:

Present Year	Payment	Discount Factor (Table A)	Value
1	$1,000	0.909	$ 909
2	1,500	0.826	1,239
3	2,000	0.751	1,502
4	2,500	0.683	1,708
Present value of the series			$ 5,358

Equal Payments

In many situations, such as the repayment of loans, the series of payments is comprised of equal amounts each period. (Technically, such a series of equal payments is called an **annuity**.) If the payments are $1,750 per year for four years, then the present value of the series discounted at 10 percent would be

Year	Payment	Discount Factor	Present Value
1	$1,750	0.909	$ 1,591
2	1,750	0.826	1,446
3	1,750	0.751	1,314
4	1,750	0.683	1,195
Present value of the series			$5,546

Rather than look up discount factors for each year in such a problem, one can use a table such as Appendix Table B (at the back of the book). In that table, the factor shown for four years at 10 percent is 3.170. This number is the same (except for rounding error) as the sum of the individual years' factors in the previous example: 0.909, 0.826, 0.751, and 0.683; and 3.170 * $1,750 = $5,548. This example illustrates that each factor in Table B was obtained by cumulating the factors for the corresponding year and all preceding years in the same interest rate column of Table A. Thus, the present value of a level series can be found in one step using Table B.

The values in Table B also can be used to find the present value of a series of equal payments between any two points in time. The procedure is to subtract the Table B factor for the year *preceding* the year of the first payment from the factor for the last year of payment.

Example

What is the present value of $1,000 a year to be received in years 6 through 10, assuming a 12 percent discount rate?

Solution:

Time Period	*PV* Factor (Table B)
Years 1–10	5.650
Years 1–5	3.605
Difference (years 6–10)	2.045
PV = $1,000 * 2.045 =	$2,045

Present Values and Liabilities

The amount shown on the balance sheet for a liability such as a loan is often thought of as being the amount the borrower must repay to satisfy the obligation. This is only partly true. Certainly, the borrowing entity must repay the amount borrowed, called the *principal* in the case of a term loan or bond; and the amount shown on the balance sheet of the borrower *is* the amount of unpaid principal. However, the borrower's future payments to satisfy the obligation far exceed the amount of unpaid principal because interest must be paid on the amount of outstanding principal over the life of the loan.

In many cases, the balance sheet liability is properly interpreted as meaning not the dollar amount of the principal but rather the *present value* of the series of future interest payments plus the *present value* of the future principal payments.

Example

Kinnear Company borrowed $25,000, with interest at 10 percent (i.e., $2,500) to be paid annually and the principal to be repaid in one lump sum at the end of five years. The balance sheet liability would be reported as $25,000. This can be interpreted as the sum of the present values, as follows:

	Present Value
Interest, $2,500 * 3.791 (Table B)	$ 9,478
Principal, $25,000 * 0.621 (Table A)	15,525
Total present value	$ 25,003*

* Does not add exactly to $25,000 because of rounding.

If the annual repayments are of a constant amount, with each payment including both interest and a reduction of principal, Table B can be used to find the amount of these payments.

Example

Kinnear Company borrowed $25,000 with interest at 10 percent to be repaid in equal annual amounts at the end of each of the next five years. The present value of this obligation is $25,000. The amount of the annual installments is $6,595. It is found by dividing $25,000 by the 5 year/10 percent factor in Table B, which is 3.791.

Each payment of $6,595 in the above example consists of two components: (1) interest on the amount of principal outstanding during the year and (2) reduction of that principal. These two components of each payment can be calculated as shown in Illustration A8–1, which is called a **loan amortization schedule.**

ILLUSTRATION A8–1   **Loan Amortization Schedule***

Year	(a) Principal Owed at Beginning of Year	(b) Annual Payment	(c) Interest Portion of Payment (a) * 10%	(d) Reduction of Principal Principal (b) – (c)	(e) Ending Year (a) – (d)
1	$25,000	$ 6,595	$2,500	$ 4,095	$20,905
2	20,905	6,595	2,090	4,505	16,400
3	16,400	6,595	1,640	4,955	11,445
4	11,445	6,595	1,145	5,450	5,995
5	5,995	6,595	600	5,995	0
Totals		$32,975	$7,975	$25,000	

* Some numbers may appear to be off by 1 owing to rounding.

Column *c* of the schedule shows how much interest expense on this loan Kinnear Company should recognize each year. Column *e* shows the proper balance sheet valuation of the loan liability as of the end of each year (or, equivalently, as of the beginning of the next year, as shown in column *a*). The amounts in columns *c* and *d* represent the only conceptually correct way to divide each year's payment between interest expense and principal reduction (amortization). This approach is called the **compound interest method** (or **effective interest method** or simply **interest method)** of debt amortization.

Note how the amounts in column *c* decrease over time, whereas the amounts in column *d* increase. Someone not familiar with the compound interest method might assume that each year's $6,595 payment reflects a principal reduction of $5,000 ($25,000 ÷ 5 years) and interest expense of $1,595 ($6,595 − $5,000). Such an assumption is incorrect.

Note also that the compound interest method amounts are calculated such that the interest expense is always a constant *percentage* of the principal outstanding during the year (10 percent in the illustration). This means that Kinnear Company's interest expense on this loan is a true 10 percent in *every* year the loan is outstanding and that the true interest rate on the loan over its entire life is 10 percent. This is the same principle mentioned in the chapter text in the illustration of bond discount amortization. The interest expense, the sum of the cash interest costs and the discount amortization on Mason Corporation's 10 percent bonds issued for $851, will be a constant rate (12 percent) of the book value of the bonds for each of the 20 years they are outstanding, provided that the initial discount is amortized using the compound interest method.

Present Values and Assets

Accounting for interest-bearing receivables and similar monetary assets is the mirror image of accounting for monetary liabilities. For example, in the Kinnear Company loan illustration above, column *c* in Illustration A8–1 shows how much interest *revenue* Kinnear's lender should report each year on this loan. Similarly, column *e* shows the proper year-end valuation of the loan *receivable* asset on the lender's balance sheet. We can therefore conclude that the amount shown for a loan receivable or similar monetary asset is the present value of the future payments the asset holder will receive in satisfaction of the credit the asset holder has extended to the borrower (Kinnear Company in the illustration).

Calculating Bond Yields

The **yield** on a bond is the rate of return that the bondholder earns as a result of investing in the bond. The investor's return is made up of two parts: (1) the bond's interest payments and (2) any difference between what the investor paid for the bond and the proceeds she or he receives upon selling the bond. This difference is referred to as the investor's **capital gain** or **loss** on the bond. Both the interest stream and future proceeds must be adjusted to present values to be comparable with the current market price.

Current Yield

The yield to maturity on a bond (described below) should not be confused with the **current yield,** which is the annual interest payment divided by the current price.

Example

If at a given point in time Mason Corporation's 10 percent bonds were selling on a bond market at a price of 94 (i.e., $940), then the current yield at that time would be $100 ÷ $940 = 10.6 percent.

Yield to Maturity

The yield on a bond actually is investor-specific because the capital gain (or loss) portion of the yield depends on what a specific investor paid for the bond and how much he or she sells it for. Thus, in calculating a bond's yield to maturity, it is assumed that (1) the bond will be purchased at the current market price and (2) the bond will then be held until maturity. Also, income tax effects are ignored in calculating bond yields. The **yield to maturity** of a bond is the discount rate that will make the sum of (1) the present value of the series of future interest payments plus (2) the present value of the bond redemption proceeds equal to the current *market price* of the bond.

Example

Exactly 10 years before their maturity, Mason Corporation 10 percent bonds have a market price of $887. Mason makes the $100 per year interest payments in a lump sum at year-end. The yield to maturity is the discount rate that will make the present value of the 10-year series of future $100 annual interest payments plus the present value of the $1,000 bond redemption proceeds 10 years hence equal to the bond's current market price of $887. This rate is 12 percent, which can be demonstrated as follows:

PV of interest stream ($100 * 5.650*)	$ 565
PV of redemption proceeds ($1,000 * 0.322*)	322
Sum of *PVs* (market price)	$ 887

* Ten-year/12 percent factors from Tables B and A, respectively.

This 12 percent yield to maturity is also called the **effective rate of interest** on the bond.

The calculation of yield to maturity can be a fairly cumbersome trial-and-error procedure if present value tables are used. This procedure is programmed into personal computers and relatively inexpensive business calculators, which can find the yield in a few seconds.

Bond Prices

A similar calculation can be used to determine the "rational" market price of a bond, given current yields on bonds of similar quality (or risk).

Example

When Mason's 20-year, 10 percent bonds were *issued* the prevailing market interest rate (yield) of similar bonds was 12 percent. The market price of Mason's bonds should be the price that would result in a yield of 12 percent to a Mason bondholder. This price will be the present value of the 20-year interest stream and the proceeds at maturity (20 years hence):

PV of interest stream ($100 * 7.469*)	$ 747
PV of redemption proceeds ($1,000 * 0.104*)	104
Market price for 12% yield	$ 851

* Twenty-year/12 percent factors from Tables B and A, respectively.

This $851 is the amount that was given in the text in the Mason Corporation example of 10 percent bonds that were issued at a discount because the prevailing market rate for comparable bonds was 12 percent.

| Problem | *Note*: The problems may require the use of the present value tables found in the textbook appendix. Handheld calculators may yield slightly different results due to the rounding of factors used in the tables. |

Problem 8-1.

As a manager in charge of information processing for a fast-growing company, you realize that your current computer will only serve your needs for the next six years. At that time, you will replace it with a more efficient model, which at that time will cost an estimated $750,000. If the anticipated rate of interest is 8 percent for the next six years, how much money should you place in a special investment fund today so that you will have a balance of $750,000 six years from now? (Assume annual compounding and ignore taxes.)

Problem 8-2.

In 2010, a compact disc costs $14. If the price of CDs continues to increase at an annual compound rate of 4 percent, how much will a disc cost in 10 years? 25 years? 50 years?

Problem 8-3.

For each of the following situations, the present value concept should be applied:

1. Your wealthy aunt has just established a trust fund for you that will accumulate to a total of $100,000 in 12 years. Interest on the trust fund is compounded annually at an 8 percent interest rate. How much is in your trust fund today?
2. On January 1, you will purchase a new car. The automobile dealer will allow you to make increasing annual December 31 payments over the following four years. The amounts of these payments are $4,000; $4,500; $5,000; $6,000. On this same January 1, your mother will lend you just enough money to enable you to meet these payments. Interest rates are expected to be 8 percent for the next five years. Assuming that you can earn annual compounding interest by depositing the loan from your mother in a bank, what is the minimum amount your mother must loan you to enable you to meet the car payments?
3. In settlement of a claim for your recently wrecked car, your insurance company will pay you either a lump sum today *or* three annual payments of $3,100 starting one year from now. Interest rates are expected to be 6 percent for the next five years. What is the least amount of money that you should be willing to accept today?
4. What is the present value of $3,000 a year to be received in years 3 through 11, assuming a 12 percent discount rate?

Problem 8-4.

Clearwater Company borrowed $164,440 with interest at 12 percent to be repaid in equal annual amounts at the end of each of the next six years. Prepare a loan amortization schedule (i.e., schedule showing principal outstanding after each annual payment) for the repayment of this obligation. Round to the nearest whole dollar.

Problem 8-5.

How would the following be disclosed on W&H Company's financial statements? The balance sheet was dated December 31, 2010, and the financial statements were issued February 14, 2011.

1. The Internal Revenue Service has claimed that W&H Company owes $450,000 of additional taxes for the first quarter of 2010; the claim was made in a suit filed on January 25, 2011. W&H Company's tax adviser estimates that the actual amount that will be paid is between $270,000 and $318,000.
2. On January 15, 2011, a fire destroyed one of W&H Company's warehouses. The warehouse had a net book value of $2,735,000 on the year-end balance sheet.
3. During 2010, a lawsuit was filed against W&H Company that claimed $750,000 in punitive damages and $400,000 for personal injury, which the plaintiff alleges occurred when using one of W&H Company's products. The suit was not settled as

of December 31, 2011, but the company's attorney is convinced insurance would pay 75 percent of any award.

4. In late December, 2010 several dissident shareholders had informed the company that they intended to sue the W&H board of directors for $5,000,000 because the board had rejected a merger offer proposed by a major supplier. The company has indemnified the directors; thus, any judgment against the directors would be paid by the company. W&H Company's attorney felt any such suit would be without merit.

Problem 8–6.

On April 1, 2008, the Texidor Company issued bonds with a face value of $250,000 for $260,000 cash. These bonds paid an annual interest of 8 percent. The interest was paid semi-annually on April 1 and October 1. The bonds were to be repaid on April 1, 2018. Record the entries that should be made on the following dates: April 1, 2008; October 1, 2008; December 31, 2008; and April 1, 2009. (Assume for simplicity that the bond premium is to be amortized on a straight-line basis.)

Problem 8–7.

During the year, Shor Company issued several series of bonds. For each bond, record the journal entry that must be made upon the issuance date. (Round to the nearest dollar; a calculator is needed for 2 and 3.)

1. On March 15, a 20-year, $5,000 par value bond series with annual interest of 9 percent was issued. Three thousand of these bonds were issued at a price of 98. Interest is paid semiannually.
2. On January 20, a series of 15-year, $1,000 par value bonds with annual interest of 8 percent was issued at a price giving a current yield to maturity of 6.5 percent. Issuance costs for the 7,000 bonds issued were $250,000. Interest is paid annually.
3. On October 31, a 10-year, $1,000 par value bond series with annual interest of 7 percent was issued at a price to give a current yield to maturity of 8 percent. Interest on the 5,000 bonds issued is paid semiannually.

Problem 8–8.

On January 1, 2008, the Evans Company issued callable bonds with a face value of $5,000,000 for $4,750,000 cash. These bonds paid an annual interest of 10 percent payable semiannually on January 2 and July 1. The bonds were to be repaid on January 1, 2018. On January 1, 2013, the bonds were called and redeemed for $5,250,000. Make the journal entries for January 1, 2008, and January 1, 2013. (Assume that the bond discount was being written off on a straight-line basis. Ignore bond issuance and reacquisition costs.)

Problem 8–9.

On January 1, 1982, Jackson Corporation issued 4,000 bonds with face value of $1,000 each and a coupon rate of 5 percent. The bonds were purchased by investors at a price of $1,030. Jackson incurred costs of $80,000 in issuing the bonds. On January 1, 2002, which was five years prior to the bond's maturity date, Jackson redeemed the bonds at a call price of $1,080. Jackson also spent $75,000 in calling the bonds. What accounting entries should Jackson make to reflect this early redemption? (Assume that the bond premium was being written off on a straight-line basis.)

CASES

Case 8–1

Norman Corporation (A)*

Until 2010, Norman Corporation, a young manufacturer of specialty consumer products, had not had its financial statements audited. It had, however, relied on the auditing firm of Kline & Burrows to prepare its income tax returns. Because it was considering borrowing on a long-term note and the lender surely would require audited statements, Norman decided to have its 2010 financial statements attested by Kline & Burrows.

Kline & Burrows assigned Jennifer Warshaw to do preliminary work on the engagement, under the direction of Allen Burrows. Norman's financial vice president had prepared the preliminary financial statements shown in Exhibit 1. In examining the information on which these financial statements were based, Ms. Warshaw discovered the facts listed below. She referred these to Mr. Burrows.

1. In 2010 a group of female employees sued the company, asserting that their salaries were unjustifiably lower than salaries of men doing comparable work. They asked for back pay of $250,000. A large number of similar suits had been filed in other companies, but results were extremely varied. Norman's outside counsel thought that the company probably would win the suit but pointed out that the decisions thus far were divided, and it was difficult to forecast the outcome. In any event, it was unlikely that the suit would come to trial in 2011. No provision for this loss had been made in the financial statements.

2. The company had a second lawsuit outstanding. It involved a customer who was injured by one of the company's products. The customer asked for $500,000 damages. Based on discussions with the customer's attorney, Norman's attorney believed that the suit probably could be settled for $50,000. There was no guarantee of this, of course. On the other hand, if the suit went to trial, Norman might win it. Norman did not carry product liability insurance. Norman reported $50,000 as a Reserve for Contingencies, with a corresponding debit to Retained Earnings.

3. In 2010 plant maintenance expenditures were $44,000. Normally, plant maintenance expense was about $60,000 a year, and $60,000 had indeed been budgeted for 2010. Management decided, however, to economize in 2010, even though it was recognized that the amount would probably have to be made up in future years. In view of this, the estimated income statement included an item of $60,000 for plant maintenance expense, with an offsetting credit of $16,000 to a reserve account included as a noncurrent liability.

4. In early January 2010 the company issued a 5 percent $100,000 bond to one of its stockholders in return for $80,000 cash. The discount of $20,000 arose because the 5 percent interest rate was below the going interest rate at the time; the stockholder thought that this arrangement provided a personal income tax advantage as compared with an $80,000 bond at the market rate of interest. The company included the $20,000 discount as one of the components of the asset "other deferred charges" on the balance sheet and included the $100,000 as a noncurrent liability. When questioned about this treatment, the financial vice president said, "I know that other companies may record such a transaction differently, but after all we do owe $100,000. And anyway, what does it matter where the discount appears?"

5. The $20,000 bond discount was reduced by $784 in 2010, and Ms. Warshaw calculated that this was the correct amount of amortization. However, the $784 was included as an item of nonoperating expense on the income statement, rather than being charged directly to Retained Earnings.

6. In connection with the issuance of the $100,000 bond, the company had incurred legal fees amounting to $500. These costs were included in nonoperating expenses in the income statement because, according to the financial vice president, "issuing bonds is an unusual financial transaction for us, not a routine operating transaction."

7. On January 2, 2010, the company had leased a new Lincoln Town Car, valued at $35,000, to be used for various official company purposes. After three years

* Copyright © Professor Robert N. Anthony.

EXHIBIT 1

NORMAN CORPORATION Proposed Income Statement (condensed) For the Year 2010		
Net sales		$1,658,130
Cost of sales		1,071,690
Gross margin		586,440
Operating expenses		329,100
Operating income		257,340
Nonoperating income and expense (net)		9,360
Pretax income		247,980
Provision for income taxes		99,300
Net income		$ 148,680

Proposed Balance Sheet (condensed)
As of December 31, 2010
Assets

Current assets:		
Cash and short-term investments		$ 107,026
Accounts receivable, gross	$262,904	
Less: Allowance for doubtful accounts	5,250	257,654
Inventories		376,006
Prepaid expenses		10,814
Total current assets		751,500
Plant and equipment, at cost	310,996	
Less: Accumulated depreciation	139,830	171,166
Goodwill		101,084
Development costs		124,648
Other deferred charges		166,878
Total assets		$ 1,315,276

Liabilities and Shareholders' Equity

Current liabilities	$ 421,770
Noncurrent liabilities	228,704
Total liabilities	650,474
Common stock (100,000 shares)	100,000
Capital surplus	82,500
Retained earnings	432,302
Reserve for contingencies	50,000
Total liabilities and shareholders' equity	$ 1,315,276

of $13,581 annual year-end lease payments, title to the car would pass to Norman, which expected to use the car through at least year-end 2014. The $13,581 lease payment for 2010 was included in operating expenses in the income statement.

Although Mr. Burrows recognized that some of these transactions might affect the provision for income taxes, he decided not to consider the possible tax implications until after he had thought through the appropriate financial accounting treatment.

Questions

1. How should each of the above seven items be reported in the 2010 income statement and balance sheet?
2. (Optional—requires knowledge of appendix material.) The bond described in item 4 above has a 15-year maturity date. What is the yield rate to the investor who paid $80,000 for this bond? Is the $784 discount amortization cited in item 5 indeed the correct first-year amount? (Assume that the $5,000 annual interest payment is made in a lump sum at year-end.)
3. (Optional) If the lease in item 7 is determined to be a capital lease, what is its effective interest rate?

Case 8–2
Paul Murray*

Paul Murray would soon graduate from business school with his MBA. He had accepted a fine job offer. Paul's wife, Nancy, was an attorney with a local firm specializing in corporate law. Paul and Nancy were expecting their first child a few months after Paul's graduation. With the experience of paying for their own graduate educations fresh in their minds, Paul and Nancy recognized that they would have to plan early to accumulate enough money to send their child through four years of college.

Paul wanted to accumulate a fund equal to four times the first year's tuition, room, and board by the time his child entered college. Paul and Nancy assumed that these fees might increase, perhaps annually, through the four years of college. However, if they invested the funds appropriately, the investments would yield enough to cover the increase in fees through the four years of college.

Ideally, Paul and Nancy wanted their child to be able to choose among an array of public or private colleges with good academic reputations. A recent newspaper article had indicated that the average tuition, room, and board at private four-year institutions

was about $15,000. They felt that if their child were entering college this coming fall, $18,000 per year for tuition, room, and board would provide the range of choice they sought.

Questions

1. In the recent past, college fees had been increasing at about 8 percent per year. Because this rate of increase exceeded the general inflation rate, Paul and Nancy felt it would decline to a level closer to measures of general inflation, such as the Consumer Price Index. Thus, they decided to assume that college fees would increase 6 percent per year. At this rate, how much will one year of college cost 18 years from this fall?
2. Assume the Murrays want to accumulate a fund equal to four times the first year's tuition by the end of year 18. Assume further that they make a single payment into this fund at the end of each year, including the 18th year. How much would they have to contribute to this fund each year, assuming that their investments earn 6 percent per year?
3. How would their annual contributions differ if their investments earned 8 percent? 10 percent? 4 percent?

* © Professor Robert N. Anthony.

Case 8–3
Joan Holtz (D)*

Having recently studied liabilities and the concept of present value, Joan Holtz was interested in discussing with the accounting professor several matters that had recently come to Joan's attention in the newspaper

and on television. Each of these matters is described below.

1. On a 2010 late-night talk show, a guest described having found a bond in the attic of his home in a small Missouri town. The bond had been issued in 1883 by the town, apparently to finance a municipal water

* © Professor Robert N. Anthony.

system. The bond was payable to the bearer (who-ever happened to have the bond in his or her posses-sion), rather than to a specifically named individual. The face amount of the bond was $100, and the stated interest rate was 10 percent. According to the terms of the bond, it could be redeemed at any future time of the bearer's choosing for its face value plus accumulated *compound* interest. Joan was anxious to discuss the terms of the bond with has professor and to use her calculator to determine what this bond was worth because only the amount "several million dollars" was mentioned during the show.

2. Joan also had read about "zero-coupon" bonds, which are bonds that pay no interest. Therefore, they are offered at a substantial discount from par value, since the investor's entire return is the differ-ence between the discounted offering price and the par value. In particular, Joan had read that one com-pany had issued eight-year, zero-coupon bonds at a price of $327 per $1,000 par value. Joan wanted to discuss the following with the accounting professor: (*a*) Was the yield on these bonds 15 percent, as Joan had calculated? (*b*) Assuming that bond dis-count amortization is tax deductible by the issuing corpo-ration, that the issuer has a 40 percent income tax rate, and that for tax purposes a straight-line amor-tization of original discount is permissible, what is the effective or "true" after-tax interest rate to the issuer of this bond? And (*c*) if, instead of issuing these zero-coupon bonds, the company had issued 15 percent coupon bonds with issue proceeds of $1,000 per bond (i.e., par value), what would the issuer's effective after-tax interest rate have been on these alternative bonds?

3. Joan also had read about a new financing gimmick called a "debt-for-equity swap." The technique works as follows: A company's bonds are currently trading on the New York Bond Exchange at a sizable discount because their coupon rate is well below current market interest rates. The company arranges with an investment banking firm to buy up these bonds on the open market. The company then issues new shares of common stock to the investment banker in exchange for the bonds (which are then retired). The shares issued have a value about 4 percent higher than the amount the investment banker has spent acquiring the bonds. Finally, the investment banker sells these shares on the open market, real-izing the 4 percent profit. According to the article

Joan had read, Exxon Corporation had swapped 1.4 million common shares valued at $43 million for bonds with a face value of $72 million, thereby real-izing a tax-free gain of $29 million. Joan wondered two things about such a transaction: (*a*) Why doesn't the company issue the shares directly and use the proceeds to buy back the bonds on the open market, instead of using an investment banker as an inter-mediary? And (*b*) should the gain on such a swap be treated as income for financial reporting purposes since, in a sense, the company has done nothing of substance to earn it?

4. Joan was aware that major airlines had "frequent flyer" plans, through which a traveler could earn upgrades from coach to first class, or tickets for free travel. Joan wondered how the airlines should account for upgrade and free travel coupons that had been issued to travelers but had not as yet been redeemed. Were they a liability? If so, how would the amount be determined, and what would be the offsetting debit?

5. Joan had noticed that many retailers, especially those dealing in high-ticket consumer goods like stereos, computers, and VCRs, offered to sell cus-tomers extended warranty contracts when they pur-chased the product. Joan had heard that retailers earned a much higher margin on an extended war-ranty contract than on the product it covered. For example, for a projection TV that cost $2,000, the customer might be offered the option to purchase a three-year warranty contract for $180. The margin on the projection TV might be 8 percent, or $160; the margin on the extended warranty contract might be 75 percent, or $135. Hence, when a customer purchased both the projection TV and the warran-ty, the margin on the total purchase was $295 or 13.5 percent. The proportion of customers purchas-ing extended warranty contracts depended on the product but, because consumers wanted to protect their investment in high-ticket items, the vast major-ity purchased extended warranty contracts, and the proportion was very predictable.

Joan wondered how to account for this combined purchase. One alternative, which she called Alterna-tive A, was to treat the purchase of the projection TV and the purchase of the warranty contract completely separately. For the projection TV, revenue of $2,000 and cost of goods sold of $1,840 would be recognized immediately. For the three-year warranty, the payment received would be treated as deferred revenue, and one-third of the revenue ($60) and one-third of the cost of the service ($15) would be recognized each year for three years. Under this alternative, the accounting would reflect the immediate sale of a low-margin product followed by three years' sale of a high-margin service.

Joan was not satisfied with this alternative. She figured that the purchase of the projection TV and the service contract was really a single purchase, not two separate purchases, and thus the margin earned on the sale was really the 13.5 percent combined margin. Using this reasoning, Joan saw two alternative ways to treat the sale. First, all of the revenue from the sale of the projection TV and the three-year warranty ($2,180) as well as all of the cost associated with both ($1,885 = $1,840 + $45) could be recognized immediately (Alternative B). Retailers had reasonably accurate information regarding historical service costs to predict the $45 future service cost. However, if actual service costs differed from those estimated, a subsequent adjustment could be made.

Another approach (Alternative C) was to defer recognition of some proportion of the revenue until the warranty period expired. The proportion of the revenue to be recognized immediately would depend on the proportion of the costs associated with the product versus the proportion associated with the service contract. In this example, $1,840 ÷ $1,885 = 97.6 percent of the revenue (or $2,128) would be recognized immediately, with a cost of goods sold of $1,840, and a margin of 13.5 percent; similarly, $45 ÷ $1,885 = 2.4 percent of the revenue (or $52) would be deferred and recognized over the three-year life of the service contract, with an associated cost of $15 per year and a margin of 13.5 percent.

Joan wondered from the point of view of management which alternative provided the most appropriate representation of the profitability of extended warranties. She also wondered how the different choices would affect both the balance sheet and the income statement.

Question

Answer the questions raised by Joan Holtz on each of the five issues on her list.

Case 8–4
Leasing Computers at Persistent Learning*

Persistent Learning, an early-stage educational software company, was in the midst of making the largest equipment investment decision in its history. Persistent Learning was finally starting to see significant orders for its newly expanded product line, but it was clear that the company's aging computer systems would not be able to support the increased demand. The entire management team agreed that new systems and more machines were needed. The big decision now was whether to do a "one-dollar-purchase" lease, essentially providing financing for a purchase, or a "fair-market-value" lease, which would be more like a rental agreement. Persistent Learning was under the watchful eye of analysts and customers concerned over its profitability and staying power. The perceptions of its financial performance had suddenly become extremely important to the company. As a newly public company, Persistent Learning was faced with not only its biggest single investment decision but also its first major financial reporting and investor relations decision.

Priya Gupta was convinced the financial reporting consequences of Persistent Learning Corporation's new-computer lease decision would be significant. If she was going to convince the management team, however, she needed to prepare a complete analysis of the effects for their next meeting.

Industry

According to the National Center for Education Statistics, there were 123,385 public and private elementary and secondary schools in the U.S. for the 2001–2002 academic year, with the number of schools slowly climbing. Roughly 25% of those schools, enrolling roughly 10% of K-12 students, were private, meaning that they were funded and run independently of the government. The remaining 75% of the schools were public schools run by government education agencies and publicly elected or appointed boards and funded by federal, state, and local governments.[1] School enrollment was expected to set new records every year from 2006 until 2014, the last year for which the National Center for Education Statistics had projected enrollment, with almost 55 million students enrolled in 2003 and a projected 56.7 million students for 2014.[2] For the 2001–2002 school year, spending by public schools on instructional supplies topped $11 billion, and spending on purchased services was nearly $7 billion, with total per student spending expected to increase in coming years.[3] In addition, schools spent heavily on computers, and by the fall of 2002, 99% of public schools had Internet access. Nationwide, there was a computer with Internet access for every 4.8 students, and schools were increasingly incorporating computer-based learning. Persistent Learning's competitors estimated the U.S. public school market for educational software at roughly $600 million–$800 million per year, with continued growth expected for the future.[4]

Due to the academic year and budgeting cycle, most software purchase decisions were made near the beginning and end of the academic year. This resulted in a high level of cyclicity for order placement and cash collections, with few sales made in December, January, and February. Both the cyclicity and the approval process for large purchases also created extremely long and unpredictable sales cycles for the industry, with companies having to pursue a sale for several months, and sometimes over a year, before any orders were placed.

[1] Martha Naomi Alt and Katharin Peter, *Private Schools: A Brief Portrait,* NCES 2002 1/N 2013, U.S. Department of Education, National Center for Education Statistics, Washington, DC, 2002.
[2] The National Center for Education Statistics, a part of the U.S. Department of Education and the Institute of Education Sciences, provides summary statistics and detailed reports on its website, at http://nces.ed.gov.
[3] Crecilla Cohen and Frank Johnson, *Revenues and Expenditures for Public Elementary and Secondary Education: School Year 2001–02* (Washington, DC: U.S. Department of Education, National Center for Education Statistics, June 2004).
[4] Plato Learning 2005 10-K, The American Education Corporation 2005 10-K, Scientific Learning Corporation 2005 10-K.

The industry was marked by diverse competition. Pearson Digital Learning was one example of an educational software division within a larger educational-service and-product company. Pearson's parent company had over $7 billion in sales and over 30,000 employees. There were also several smaller private companies in the industry. The most comparable companies to Persistent Learning, being small and publicly traded, were Plato Learning, Scientific Learning Corporation, The American Education Corporation and Renaissance Learning, with sales ranging from less than $10 million to roughly $120 million and with employee counts ranging from round 60 to nearly 1,000.

Persistent Learning's History

Persistent Learning designed, marketed, and sold educational software and online tools for school students, focusing on computer-related topics such as typing and computer use for younger students and computer programming and Web-page design for more advanced students. Persistent Learning had started in 1998 when the founder, James Bogle, a computer programmer, became frustrated that his children were spending hours at home playing video games on the computer but no time learning computer science topics. The company started with a simple program with interactive elements, extensive graphics use, and audio explanations to teach Web design. The first program was marketed to the founder's local school district. While several companies had entered the educational software market for math, reading, and other core subjects, there was almost no competition for computer topics. Within this area the company was able to grow quickly, hiring additional programmers and educational professionals for content development and quickly expanding the product line.

Persistent Learning soon developed a large set of proprietary knowledge for creating and running inter-active tools, lessons with game-like components, and cross-school project competitions. Its systems included tools to help parents and teachers track student progress. Preliminary data from these tracking tools and some additional research data suggested that Persistent Learning's programs significantly increased student learning, primarily through increasing student involvement, motivation, and particularly the time students spent on the lessons outside of the classroom.

Knowing that the core subjects of math, reading, and writing were tied to much larger markets than computer topics, Persistent Learning began to slowly expand into those core subject areas, using its unique platform and teaching methods.

During the initial growth period, Persistent Learning financed its growth through venture capital (VC) funding. With the success of its early math and reading/writing attempts, the company decided to launch a large-scale product-line expansion into these areas. To finance this new project, the company went to public equity markets, completing its initial public offering and listing on NASDAQ in 2004. With both the product-line expansion and its first large-scale nation-wide marketing push under way, the company expected dramatic growth in the following few years. The company expected to maintain gross margin percentages at roughly the same levels, but with much higher volumes. In the short term, research and development as well as sales and marketing expenditures would increase disproportionately, but long term the company expected the rates as a percentage of sales to go down. The product-line expansion was expected to improve profit levels within a couple of years.

The Meeting

Both product development and sales and marketing were under high pressure to perform with the planned nation-wide launch. Both groups were starting to experience problems with their computer systems that were damaging productivity. The programmers and content developers relied on high-end desktops and test servers for their work, and sales staff needed high-end laptops for demonstrations. Finally, cross-country networking and increased video content were both key selling points of the new edition, but both of these required newer and faster servers and expanded storage space.

The management team met to discuss all three options for the new computer acquisition: a cash purchase, a "fair-market-value" lease, or a "one-dollar-purchase" lease. They concluded the following:

- In order to maintain enough cash for operations, particularly given the new initiatives, the company would have to borrow the full $6.3 million for the computers, at an interest rate of 12%, if it chose to purchase them. While lease rates varied greatly, the

leases Persistent Learning were considering were a slightly cheaper form of financing than other forms of debt. This allowed management to rule out the cash-purchase option. (See **Exhibit 1** for Persistent Learning's 2006 financial statements and its most recent projections for 2007, assuming the company made a cash purchase for the new computers.)

- The cash outlay for the one-dollar-purchase lease was slightly higher than for the fair-market-value lease. The one-dollar-purchase lease gave the lessee (Persistent Learning) the option to purchase the computers at the end of the three-year lease term for one dollar each, far below the expected fair market value at the time. The fair-market-value lease, on the other hand, only allowed the lessee to purchase at the fair market value. Because the one-dollar-purchase lease contained this valuable option, the monthly payments were higher. (See Exhibit 1 for the payment schedule for each option.)

- The company intended to use the computers for three years, however if they owned the computers at the end of three years they could sell them or decide to use them for a longer period, depending on conditions at that time.

- Both leases gave the lessee the option to upgrade computers at any time during the lease term, renewing the original three-year lease term from that point in time. The leases also made it easier to acquire additional machines. This flexibility would be valuable if Persistent Learning's technology needs grew faster than predicted.

- With either lease, the lessor would take responsibility for the machines at the end of the lease term if the lessee (Persistent Learning) chose not to purchase. This could save Persistent Learning from having to sell or dispose of the computers itself, a potentially costly and time-consuming process.

Based upon this discussion, the management team was able to rule out the cash purchase but was unable to decide between the fair-market-value and one-dollar-purchase-option leases. Gupta suggested another dimension they should consider:

> We met today to discuss the economics of the two options. Since there's no clear winner from that discussion, I believe we should also consider our financial reporting environment. We are a newly public firm, and the market is just getting to know us.

EXHIBIT 1 **Persistent Learning Financial Statements and Projections**

Balance Sheet as of December 31, 2006, and Projection for 2007 (in $ thousands)

	2004	2005	2006	2007 Projected
ASSETS				
Current Assets:				
Cash and Cash Equivalents	$ 23,319	$ 11,029	$ 2,616	$ 2,725
Accounts Receivable (net)	10,844	10,678	14,995	20,999
Inventories	1,445	1,362	1,786	2,500
Deferred Tax Asset	0	0	120	700
Prepaid Expenses and Other Current Assets	1,451	1,602	1,908	2,331
Total Current Assets	$ 37,059	$ 24,670	$ 21,425	$ 29,255
Property and Equipment (net)	2,370	1,720	1,470	5,945
Deferred Tax Asset	$ 6,351	$ 11,380	$ 13,193	$ 12,439
Total Assets	$ 45,780	$ 37,770	$ 36,088	$ 47,638
LIABILITIES AND STOCKHOLDERS' EQUITY				
Accounts Payable	$ 1,219	$ 1,082	$ 1,080	$ 1,302
Accrued Liabilities	3,227	5,487	5,021	6,133
Deferred Revenue	6,888	6,400	8,661	12,125
Total Current Liabilities	$ 11,335	$ 12,970	$ 14,762	$ 19,560
Long-term deferred revenue	223	189	268	375
Long-term debt	0	0	0	6,300
Total Liabilities	$ 11,558	$ 13,158	$ 15,030	$ 26,235
Common Stock	2,100	2,100	2,100	2,100
Additional Paid-In Capital	44,100	44,100	44,100	44,100
Accumulated Deficit	(11,978)	(21,588)	(25,141)	(24,797)
Total Stockholders' Equity	$ 34,222	$ 24,612	$ 21,059	$ 21,403
Total Liabilities and Stockholders' Equity	$ 45,780	$ 37,770	$ 36,088	$ 47,638

This year is supposed to be our first positive earnings year and our first year with positive cash from operations. Those are both pretty significant milestones. Plus, even though we've forecasted taking on debt again this year, I imagine the market would be pretty happy if we could put that off by one year. All of this is particularly important considering that the VCs and some of out other early invertors are selling off their shares fairly aggressively, so the market is going to be particularly sensitive about our financials.

We made our forecasts assuming we would purchase the machines. And we used the depreciation method that seems most appropriate given our experience with computer assets: straight-line deprecation over three years and a residual value of $1.575 million. We gave earnings guidance based on these assumptions, and when we gave our earnings guidance, we told the market to expect $0.06 per share. But now with the leases, I don't know what the numbers will look like.

Finally, I checked their financial statement footnotes, and Scientific Learning, Plato Learning, and

EXHIBIT 1 Computer Lease or Purchase Pricing

Computers to be leased: a combination of high-end laptops, desktops, servers, and storage machines, all with the appropriate peripherals.

These computers are expected to have an economic life of five years. Useful life to the company of purchased computers is currently expected to be three years, but may be extended depending on future conditions. The computers are expected to have a resale value at the end of three years of roughly $1.575 million, with the resale value declining as the computers age.

Effective Interest Rate: 12%

Payment Schedules ($ thousands)

	At Signing/Purchase	Annually for Three Years (end-of-year)
Fair-value lease		$2,197.04
One-dollar-purchase lease		2,497.43
Purchase	$6,300	

Source: Casewriter.

Renaissance Learning all own their machines[5], so the industry analysts and the investors aren't used to seeing leases in the financials. I'm not sure investors will understand the effect of the leases on our numbers. Basically, I'm concerned about investors *thinking* that we've missed our numbers when it's just an accounting issue.

Ultimately the group agreed that they needed to figure out *exactly* what these alternatives would do to their financial statements and how hard it would be for investors to understand. They would meet again the next day to discuss the ultimate decision. Gupta was put in charge of presenting what the financial statements would look like under the different options and reporting back to the rest of the management team.

3. How would the company account for the "fair market value" lease and the "one-dollar purchase" lease for the computers in each of the three years? Please calculate the dollar amount of each of the journal entries (debits/credits). Assume that the leases are signed on January 1, 2007.

4. The Financial Accounting Standards Board (FASB) is currently reevaluating *FASB Statement No. 13*, "Accounting for Leases." They have proposed eliminating the distinction between capital and operating leases and requiring all leases to be recorded as capital leases. What are the principal arguments for and against the current treatment?

Questions

1. Why has Persistent Learning's management abandoned the outright purchase of the equipment and is focusing on leasing the equipment?
2. Which leasing alternative would you choose? Why? (The earnings per share in 2007 will be 5¢ under the "fair market value" lease and under the "one-dollar purchase" lease.)

[5] Scientific Learning Corporation 2005 10-K, Plato Learning 2005 10-L, and Renaissance Learning 2005 10-K, all available from the SEC Edgar database at http://www.sec.gov.

Case 8–5

Kim Park*

Following her plan to explore interesting accounting questions with her study group, Kim Park prepared a set of short case studies dealing with the recognition and measurement of liabilities. Kim knew from her earlier study group discussions that her fellow students expected prior to the meeting she would prepare tentative answers to the questions she raised. In addition, the study group had encouraged her to illustrate her tentative answers with numerical illustration using case data.

Prior Knowledge

Kim understood from the background readings assigned for her accounting course that Generally Accepted Accounting Principles (GAAP) defined liabilities as:

> "[P]robable future sacrifices of economic benefits arising from present obligations of a particular entity to transfer assets or provide services to other entities in the future as a result of past transactions or events."[1]

Kim also knew under International Financial Reporting Standards liabilities were recognized in the balance sheet when

> "[I]t is probable that an outflow of resources embodying economic benefits will result from the settlement of a present obligation and the amount at which the settlement will take place can be measured reliably."[2]

Austral Electronics Company

Before Kim went to business school, she had a friend who worked for Austral Electronics Company ("Austral"). As Kim recalled, during her friend's time with the company, it had issued a US $1Million equivalent local currency eight-year zero-coupon bond priced to yield 10 percent at maturity.[3]

Kim had three questions for her study group: How should Austral have accounted for its zero-coupon bond at the issue date? How should the company have accounted for the zero-coupon bond at the end of the first year following its issuance? At the end of the third year?

United Airlines, Inc.

Prompted by her observation that different airlines appear to account for their unredeemed frequent flier mileage obligations differently, Kim decided to ask her study group the question—how ought an airline account for its unredeemed frequent flier mile obligations.

To focus the study group discussion, Kim prepared a short description of United Airlines Inc.'s Mileage Plus program. United Airlines ("United") through its frequent flier rewards program, Mileage Plus, rewarded frequent fliers with mileage credits that could be redeemed for free, discounted or upgraded travel, and non-travel awards. More than 54 million members were enrolled in the program.

United had considerable leeway in changing the Mileage Plus program's expiration policy, program rules, and program redemption opportunities. For example, effective December 31, 2007, United announced it was reducing the expiration period for inactive accounts from 36 months to 18 months.

A United subsidiary, UAL Loyalty Services administered much of the Mileage Plus program along with a number of United's non-core marketing businesses, such as United's e-commerce activities.

---

[1] Financial Accounting Standards Board, *Statements of Financial Accounting Concepts No. 6*, "Elements of Financial Statements."

[2] International Accounting Standards Board, "Framework for the Preparation and Presentation of Financial Statements."

* Copyright © 2009 President and Fellows of Harvard College. Harvard Business School case 110-018.

[3] A zero-coupon security makes no periodic interest payments but instead is sold at a deep discount from its face value (US$1 million in the case of the Austral Electronics zero-coupon bond). The buyer of such a bond received the specified rate of return by gradual appreciation of the security, which is redeemed at face value on a specified maturity date. (John Downes and John Elliot Goodman. Dictionary of Financial and Investment Terms. Barron's Financial Guides).

At December 31, 2008, the outstanding Mileage Plus frequent flier miles was approximately 478.2 billion miles of which management estimated 362 billion miles would ultimately be redeemed based on certain mileage redemption and expiration pattern assumptions.

Exhibit 1 presents selected 2008 United operating statistics.

Exhibit 2 shows United's 2008 mainline operating expenses.

Intel Corporation[4]

While preparing a term paper on the development of Intel Corporation's (Intel's) Pentium chip for her technology innovations course, Kim came across a major accounting issues Intel faced in 1994 when a flaw was

EXHIBIT 1 United Airlines, Inc.

Selected 2008 Mainline Operating Statistics

Revenue passengers (millions)	63
Revenue passenger miles ("RPMs")[a]	110,061
Available seat miles ("ASMs")[b]	135,861
Passenger lead factors[c]	81.0%
Yield[d]	$13.89
Passenger revenue per ASM[e]	$11.29
Operating revenue per ASM[f]	$12.58
Operating expense per ASM[g]	$15.74
Fuel gallons consumed	2,182
Average price per gallon of jet Fuel, including tax and hedge impact	353.90¢

Source: United Airlines, Inc. 2008 From 10-K

[a] RPMs are the number of miles flown by revenue passengers. (millions)

[b] ASMs are the number of seats available for passengers multiplied by the number of miles those seats are flown. (millions)

[c] Passenger load factor is derived by dividing RPMs by ASMs.

[d] Yield is passenger revenue excluding industry and employee discounted fare per RPM.

[e] PRASM is mainline passenger revenue per ASM.

[f] RASM is operating revenues per ASM.

[g] CASM is operating expenses per ASM.

[4] This case consists of selected excerpts from "Accounting for the Intel Pentium Chip Flaw" prepared by Professors Gregory S. Miller and V.G. Narayanan. Harvard Business School case 9-101-072.

EXHIBIT 2 United Airlines, Inc.

2008 Operating Expenses (millions)

Aircraft fuel	$7,722
Salaries and related costs	4,311
Regional affiliates	3,248
Purchased services	1,375
Aircraft maintenance materials and outside repairs	1,096
Depreciation and amortization	932
Landing fees and other rent	862
Aircraft rent	409
Cost of third party sales	272
Goodwill impairment	2,277
Other impairments and special items	339
Other operating expenses	1,079
Total operating expenses	$ 24,632

Source: United Airlines, Inc. 2008 From 10-K

discovered in the company's 500 Pentium-based PC's microprocessor chip.[5] Microprocessors are the "brains" of computers for both home and business use.

Kim had three questions for her study group: Should Intel have recorded a liability for the potential future costs associated with the chip's flaw? If so, when should it have recorded the liability? What would be a reasonable estimate of the liability?

Flaw Discovered

Early in the summer of 1994 mathematics professor Dr. Thomas Nicely of Lynchburg College in Virginia discovered inconsistencies in his calculations performed on his Pentium-driven PC. Nicely was trying to prove that PCs could do mathematical work heretofore only performed on larger systems and thus was involved in intense and continuous number crunching far beyond that of a typical user. Nicely discovered the division flaw occurred only with rare

[5] As one example of the flaw, the solution to the following calculation, $4,195,835 - ((4,195,835 / 3,145,727)) \times 3,145,727$, should be zero, but a computer with a flawed Pentium chip provides an answer of 256. Walter A. Mossberg, "Intel Isn't Serving Millions Who Bought Its Pentium Campaign," The *Wall Street Journal*, December 15, 1994, p. 81.

combinations of numbers, and was not in his software, but in the processor of his Pentium.

The problem arose in the floating-point processing unit of the chip, which handled numbers expressed in scientific notation. At the end of October, Nicely published a note on the Internet querying other users about the Pentium flaw. A discussion soon emerged at the Internet news group "comp.sys.intel." The tone quickly changed from a calm discussion of arcane technical tests to flaming accusations and threats aimed at Intel.

On November 7, 1994, an Electrical Engineering Times article by Alexander Wolfe, based on the Inter-net discussions, prompted Intel's response that it had uncovered the flaw during tests the previous June. However, Intel had run a series of tests and concluded that an error would occur only once every nine billion random calculations, or every 27,000 years for most users. Further, Intel had remedied the problem for the next planned version of the Pentium, but had not informed customers who had purchased a flawed processor. Following the article, Intel offered to replace the flawed chips, but only on a limited basis: users first had to demonstrate that the flaw was likely to occur in the work they performed on their computer. The Internet discussion group continued to "flame" the company on-line and eventually attracted the attention of reporters. On November 22, 1994, CNN broadcasted a story that revealed the chip flaw for the first time to the general public, Intel's own computer-making customers, and the rest of the media.

On November 24, the beginning of the Thanksgiving holiday weekend, the front-page of the *New York Times* Business Section headlined "Flaw undermines the accuracy of Intel's Pentium." The *Boston Globe* carried the same story on its front page, and the news continued to unfold over the next month. By November 25 Intel's stock had dropped two percentage points from its high in late September.

The mounting consumer pressure to fix the Pentium flaw was hitting PC manufacturers as well as Intel. But who would take responsibility for fixing the flaw? Dell, a computer manufacturer, began advertising its Pentium with a built-in computer fix to remedy the latent flaw. On November 28, Sequent, a mainframe manufacturer, stopped shipping Pentium machines until a software solution could be installed. On November 30, IBM—a major Intel customer— announced that it would replace the Pentium processor in any of its machines at the customer's request. IBM, however, did not have Intel's support to fulfill such a promise and ran the risk of having to purchase replacements on its own account.

As the second week of December passed, the media coverage began to abate and Pentium flaw stores lost their front-page status. December Pentium sales continued to increase as planned, but several thousand Pentium owners were calling Intel daily. Intel rallied over a thousand of its employees to respond to these calls and carefully assess whether the users were performing functions that would be at risk of engaging the flaw in the floating point unit.

On December 12, 1994, IBM, without prior notice to Intel, dropped a bomb by halting shipments of their Pentium PCs. News coverage and consumer fears re-ignited. IBM claimed that further testing had revealed the bug to be more common that Intel had reported. On certain spreadsheet programs, IBM researchers claimed the problematic number combinations were not random and occurred much more frequently. Calculations for a continuous 15 minutes per day could produce an error once every 24 days. Intel's stock plummeted $2.50 within an hour of IBM's announcement.

Cost of Replacement

Clearly, Intel was faced with the prospect of replacing some of the defective chips.

The actual cost of producing the replacement chip and the accompanying heat sinks (the devices that release heat from operating chips) was estimated to be between $50 and $100 per chip. Other replacement costs, which included the actual labor and incidental costs, were estimated to range from $31 to $750 and average over $400 per chip replaced. The amount paid out by Intel depended on what method it used to implement the repair. Intel could pay for the entire cost of accessing the unit, the direct labor to replace the flawed chip, and any shipping or transportation costs incurred by customers. Alternatively, Intel could send the replacement chip to the customers, leaving them to decide how to replace the chip. Another possibility was to negotiate with computer manufacturers and sellers to offer discounted or free replacement service to end-user customers. In any case, the end user seeking replacement would have to bear some costs. One information technology consultancy estimated that "[t]he amount borne by companies in a typical scenario will be $289 per system, including administrative, labor, and downtime costs.

Other Potential Costs

Intel had other costs to account for as well. It had produced almost eight million flawed chips, so in addition to the six million chips currently in computers it would need to account for the two million chips in inventory.

The potential of lawsuits from consumers, computer manufacturers, and shareholders loomed as an imminent threat. *The Wall Street Journal* reported that "at least 10 suits in three states" accusing Intel of securities fraud, false advertising, and violation of consumer protection laws, had been filed seeking "hundreds of millions of dollars in damages." Some suits also looked to force Intel to replace the flawed chips. In addition, attorneys general of four states were in the process of filing suits against Intel on the grounds that the company violated unfair-trade-practices laws.

Case 8–6
Who will Rate the "Rating Agencies"

Normally, when a company tries to raise funds through the Debt route (either through public at large or from a bank or a financial institution), the issuing company seeks a Credit Rating for itself. There are third party agencies who specialise in such activities and are called Credit Rating Agencies. Credit rating is predominantly an analysis of the credit risks (default risk; inability to pay back) associated with a debt instrument issued by a firm that is trying to raise funds via the debt route. It is a rating given to a particular company based on their past credentials and the extent to which the financial statements of the entity are sound, in terms of their capability to repay the borrowings that have been done in the past. It may also include the "repayment capability position" after the current round of issuance too. It is basically a representation of the creditworthiness of an individual, entity or commercial instrument, considering various factors, representing the capability and willingness, to pay various financial commitments on time.

Generally, it is in the form of a detailed report based on the past records of borrowing or lending and creditworthiness of the company obtained from largely the statements of its assets and liabilities with an aim to determine their ability to meet the debt obligations. Some of the better known global Credit Rating agencies are Standard & Poor's, Moody's Investors Service, Fitch and ICRA, to name a few. Their ratings and guidance were hugely respected and they were always seen as organizations with very high integrity and impeccable record.

Come 2006, all this changed with serious questions being raised about the kind of ratings given by these credit rating agencies in "The Subprime Crisis" in the United States to the mortgage lenders. It is quite evident now that these big Credit rating agencies were involved as a key player in the "fraudulent conveyance" of the quality of mortgage backed securities to the investors. The agencies have been blamed for exaggerated ratings of risky mortgage-backed securities, giving investors false confidence that they were safe for investing. To the extent that just six days before Lehman Brothers collapsed five years ago, the premier rating agency Standard & Poor's maintained the firm's investment-grade rating of "A". Moody's, another globally respected agency waited even longer, downgrading Lehman one business day before it collapsed. All this has led to a serious question mark on the "credibility" of these rating agencies and it will take a while before that confidence and trust are brought back.

The same phenomenon repeated recently in India where large organizations like ILFS almost "bought" good ratings from these agencies to fool the investors. The credit rating agencies have been charged with neglecting all code of conduct and ethics in the business. It has been revealed by investigating agencies that numerous cases of favours and gifts extended by the erstwhile top management to senior officials of rating agencies and their family members were given in exchange for a good rating. The so-called "gifts" included tickets for a Real Madrid football match, steep discounts on a luxurious villa, Fitbit watch, etc. The investors anger is at all time high.

Questions

1. Why aren't equity instruments rated just like debt instruments?
2. What are the differences in the role of "credit rating agencies" and "auditors"?
3. Suggest some regulatory structures that can be brought to prevent rating agencies from committing similar mistakes again.

Sources of Capital: Owners' Equity

This chapter continues our more detailed description of the liabilities and owners' equity portion of the balance sheet. A company obtains its permanent capital (also called *invested capital*) from two sources: debt and equity. Debt capital consists principally of bonds and long-term loans, as discussed in Chapter 8. This chapter discusses equity capital, the capital supplied by the entity's owners.

The chapter begins with a discussion of the characteristics of the several legal forms of business organizations—proprietorships, partnerships, and corporations. This is followed by a description of the accounting for owners' equity in each form. The primary emphasis is on the ownership interests of a corporation as evidenced by its common and preferred stock. The next section deals with some financial instruments that blur the line between debt and equity. Equity in nonprofit organizations is discussed in the final section.

Forms of Business Organization

The three principal legal forms of business ownership are the sole proprietorship, the partnership, and the corporation.

Sole Proprietorship

A business entity owned by an individual is a **sole proprietorship**. This is a simple form for a business organization. Essentially all that one does to form a proprietorship is to begin selling goods or one's services. There are no incorporation fees to pay, no special reports to file (except an additional schedule on the proprietor's personal income tax return), and no co-owners with whom to disagree, to share liability for their actions, or to share the profits of the business. The profits of a proprietorship, whether withdrawn by the proprietor or retained in the firm, are taxed at the proprietor's personal income tax rate, which may be lower than the corporate tax rate.

On the other hand, sole proprietorships cannot issue stock or bonds, so it is difficult for them to raise large amounts of capital. They can borrow money from banks or individuals, but they cannot obtain outside equity capital because, by definition, investors who provide equity capital have an ownership interest. Moreover, the proprietor is personally responsible for the entity's debts. In the event of the firm's failure, creditors have claims not only against the assets of the proprietorship but also against the *personal* assets of the proprietor.

Partnership

A **partnership** is a business with the same features as a proprietorship, except that it is owned jointly by two or more persons, called the **partners.** A partnership also is a relatively simple and inexpensive kind of organization to form. In a partnership, each partner is personally liable for all debts incurred by the business; in the event of the firm's failure, each partner's personal assets are jeopardized. Also, each partner is responsible for the business actions of the other partners. For example, if one partner in an architectural firm makes a mistake in designing a building that ultimately results in a lawsuit, the potential liability extends to *all* the partners. Each partner pays a personal income tax on his or her share of the partnership's taxable income whether or not the profits are actually distributed to the partners in cash.

Some partnerships are **limited partnerships.** They are managed by a general partner, who receives a larger share of the income in exchange for shouldering all potential liability of the partnership. The limited partners provide capital but have little say about operations. Such partnerships are common in oil exploration and real estate investment ventures.

A common variation of the partnership structure is the limited liability company. It may be taxed as a partnership while providing limited liability to its members.

Corporation

A **corporation** is a legal entity with essentially perpetual existence. It comes into being under the auspices of a state, which grants it a *charter* to operate. The corporation is an artificial person in the sense that it is taxed on its net income as an *entity,* and legal liability accrues to the corporation itself rather than to its owners.

Compared with a proprietorship or a partnership, the corporate form of organization has several disadvantages:

1. There may be significant legal and other fees involved in its formation.
2. The corporation's activities are limited to those specifically granted in its charter.
3. It is subject to numerous regulations and requirements.
4. It must secure permission from each state in which it wishes to operate.
5. Its income is subject to *double taxation.* The corporation's income is taxed, and distributions of any net income to shareholders in the form of dividends are taxed again.[1]

On the other hand, in addition to its limited liability and indefinite existence, a corporation has the advantage of being able to raise capital from a large number of investors through issuing bonds and stock. Moreover, corporate shareholders can usually liquidate their ownership by selling their shares to others, and organized securities exchanges exist to facilitate such sales. A corporation whose shares are traded on a securities exchange is called a **public corporation,** in contrast with a private or "tightly held" corporation, whose shares are owned by an individual or by a relatively few individuals and their families. The financial reports and certain other activities of larger public corporations are regulated by the Securities and Exchange Commission (SEC).

While about 80 percent of U.S. business firms are partnerships or proprietorships, they account for only about 10 percent of total business measured in sales. Corporations account for the other 90 percent of total business activity.

[1] An exception is an **S corporation** (formerly a *Subchapter S* corporation). If certain conditions are met, including having no more than 75 shareholders, these firms pay no corporate income tax. Instead, as in a partnership, the owners are taxed on their respective shares of the entity's taxable income at their personal tax rates.

Accounting for Proprietor's and Partners' Equity

Proprietorship Equity

Not much more need be said about the owner's equity accounts in a sole proprietorship than the comments made in Chapter 2. There may be one capital account in which all entries affecting the owner's equity are recorded. A separate **drawing account** may be set up for recording periodic withdrawals made by the owner. The drawing account may be closed into the capital account at the end of the accounting period, or it may be kept separate so as to show the owner's original contribution of capital separate from the effect on owner's equity of operating transactions.

As far as the ultimate effect is concerned, it is immaterial whether the owner regards withdrawals as salary or as a return of profit. However, if a proprietor wishes to compare the proprietorship's income statement with that of a corporation, a certain part of the owner's drawings must be viewed as being salary expense and only the remainder as equivalent to corporate dividends. Consistent with this quasi-corporate approach to proprietorship accounting, some proprietorships maintain a separate owner's equity account that is analogous to Retained Earnings in a corporation. Whatever the *format* chosen for reporting proprietorship equity, in *substance* it is the same as owners' equity in a corporation.

Partnership Equity

A partnership has an owner's equity account for each partner. The amounts credited to each account depend on the terms of the partnership agreement. In the absence of a specific agreement, the law assumes that net income is to be divided equally among the partners. This is also common in written partnership agreements. If such is the case, in a three-person partnership the capital account, or the drawing account, of each partner is credited with one-third of net income. It is debited with the actual amount of the partner's withdrawals.

Partnership agreements also may provide that the partners receive stated salaries and a stated share of residual profits after salaries, or a stated percentage of interest on the capital they have invested and a stated share of residual profits, or a combination of salary and interest. The accounting required in connection with such arrangements depends on the specific terms of the agreement.

Example

The partnership agreement of Jackson and Curtin provided that Jackson (who worked half-time) would receive a salary of $20,000 and Curtin a salary of $40,000; that each would receive 8 percent interest on their invested capital; and that they would share equally in the remainder of net income. In the current year, the average balance in Jackson's capital account was $30,000 and in Curtin's was $70,000. The partnership net income (before partners' salaries) was $80,000.

The amount to be credited to each partner's equity account would be computed as follows:

	Total	Jackson	Curtin
Salary	$60,000	$20,000	$40,000
Interest on capital	8,000	2,400	5,600
Remainder	12,000	6,000	6,000
Total	$80,000	$28,400	$51,600

Whatever the partnership arrangement, the law does not regard salaries or interest payments to the partners as being different from any other type of withdrawal, since the partnership is not an entity legally separate from the individual partners. Nevertheless, some partnerships prepare income statements that include partners' salaries as an expense, and balance sheets with equity accounts analogous to Paid-In Capital and Retained Earnings. This enables the partners to compare their statements with those of similar businesses that are incorporated.

Ownership in a Corporation

Preferred Stock

Ownership in a corporation is evidenced by a **stock certificate.** This capital stock may be either *common* or *preferred.* Each corporation is authorized in its charter to issue a maximum number of **shares** of each class of stock. Each stock certificate shows how many shares of ownership it represents. Because a corporation's owners hold stock certificates that indicate their shares of ownership, owners' equity in a corporation is called **shareholders' equity** or **stockholders' equity.**

Preferred stock pays a stated dividend, much like the interest payment on bonds. However, the dividend is not a legal liability until it has been declared by the directors, nor is it a tax-deductible expense to the corporation. Preferred stock has preference, or priority, over common as to the receipt of dividends, distribution of assets in the event of liquidation, and other specified matters. Preferred stock may be cumulative or noncumulative. With **cumulative preferred stock,** if the corporation is unable to pay the dividend, the unpaid dividends accumulate and must be paid before the firm can resume payment of common stock dividends. The undeclared dividends are not, however, recorded as a liability.

Example

In 2010 Cotting Corporation did not pay the $9 dividend on each share of its $9 cumulative preferred stock. Hence, no dividend could be paid on the common stock In 2010. In 2011 holders of Cotting's common stock cannot be paid any dividend unless $18 is paid on the $9 cumulative preferred (2011's $9 dividend plus the $9 from 2010).

Preferred stock is usually issued with a face, or par, value of $100 per share. The dividend rate (9 percent in the above example) is analogous to the coupon rate on a bond, although in practice the dividend is usually stated at its dollar amount rather than as a percentage of par value. Also, like bonds, a preferred stock may be convertible into a specified number of shares of common stock; this is called a **convertible preferred.** Although preferred stock is usually outstanding indefinitely, some issues of preferred stock are redeemable on a specified date or at the holder's option. These **redeemable preferreds** are discussed later in this chapter.

If a corporation is liquidated, preferred stockholders are entitled to receive par value for their shares, provided that enough assets exist after all liabilities have been settled. Also, whereas bondholders can force the firm into bankruptcy if an interest payment on the bonds is missed, preferred stockholders have no such re-course if their dividend is not paid. Interest on bonds is an expense, both for financial accounting purposes and for income tax purposes, whereas a dividend on stock, including preferred stock, is not an expense. It is a distribution of owners' equity. Accounting treatment of preferred stock is substantially the same as for common stock, described below.

Contrary to a common misconception, issuance of bonds is a much larger source of funds for corporations than is issuance of either common or preferred stock. A principal reason for the unpopularity of preferred and common stock is that their dividends are not a deductible expense for income tax purposes, whereas interest on bonds is.

Common Stock

Every corporation has **common stock.** Common shareholders have a residual interest in profits and assets, below that of all other creditors and preferred stockholders. Common stock may have a par value, or it may be no-par stock. No-par stock usually has a stated value analogous to par value. In the following description, statements about par value apply also to stated value.

The **par value** of a share of stock[2] is usually a nominal amount, such as $1. Whereas par value on a bond or on preferred stock has meaning, par value on a common stock amount is an essentially meaningless amount. Many years ago, shareholders had an obligation to a corporation's creditors for the difference between the amount paid for the stock and its par value if the shareholders had purchased their shares (when issued by the corporation) at an amount less than par. This is not the case today because most states' corporation laws forbid issuing stock at a price below its par value. The important thing to remember about par value is that in isolation it is meaningless and tells us *nothing* about the proceeds received by the corporation upon issuance of the stock.

The **book value** of common stock is the total common shareholders' equity as reported on the balance sheet.[3] This section of the balance sheet consists of two parts: (1) the amount invested in the firm by its shareholders, called **paid-in capital,** and (2) retained earnings. The amount of paid-in capital can be reported as a single amount. Nevertheless, many corporations report this amount in two pieces: (1) the par or stated value of the outstanding shares of capital stock, usually called **common stock at par,** and (2) the amount by which the proceeds from issuing common stock have exceeded the par value of the shares issued, usually called **additional paid-in capital** or **other paid-in capital.** (The Financial Accounting Standards Board suggests the more descriptive but cumbersome title "capital contributed in excess of the par or stated value of shares.") Generally accepted accounting principles (GAAP) do not require that the two components be separately reported. The practice started decades ago when par value *did* mean something, and certain old accounting habits die hard.

Recording a Common Stock Issue

To illustrate the issuance of stock, let us consider Kuick Corporation, which received a charter from the state authorizing the issuance of 200,000 shares of $1 par value common stock. If 100,000 shares of this stock were issued at a price of $7 per share and the proceeds were received by Kuick immediately, this financing transaction could be recorded in either of two ways. The most useful way from the standpoint of statement users would be

Cash	700,000	
Common Stock.		700,000

However, in practice, many corporations may record the transaction this way:

Cash	700,000	
Common Stock at Par.		100,000
Additional Paid-In Capital		600,000

Issuance Costs

The offering of an issue of stock is often handled by an investment banking firm that receives a fee, or "spread," for this service. Usually the corporation records only the net

---

[2] Henceforth, the word *stock* unmodified by *common* or *preferred* will mean common stock.

[3] The book value of a *corporation* is a term sometimes used to mean the amount of owners' equity. If a corporation has no preferred stock, then the book value of the corporation equals the book value of its owners' equity. The book value of a corporation is also called its *net assets* because book value equals owners' equity (i.e., owners' equity equals assets minus liabilities).

amount received from the investment banker (the amount remitted by shareholders less the banker's spread).

In addition to this spread, the corporation incurs legal, auditing, and printing costs. These issuance costs are usually also deducted from the amount received from the issue. (The entry would debit Additional Paid-In Capital and credit Cash or Accounts Payable.) Note that because of the spread and other issuance costs, the amount actually remitted by the shareholders is greater than the amount by which paid-in capital (i.e., par value plus additional paid-in capital) increases on the balance sheet. Note also that there is a paid-in capital transaction between the company and its shareholders only when the shares are issued. When a shareholder sells stock to another party, the amounts in the company's accounts are not affected in any way; the only change is in the company's detailed record of the identity of its shareholders.

Treasury Stock

Treasury stock is a corporation's own stock that has been issued and subsequently reacquired by purchase. The firm may reacquire its shares for a number of reasons: to obtain shares that can be used in the future for acquisitions, bonus plans, exercise of warrants, and conversion of convertible bonds or preferred stocks; to increase the earnings per share and therefore the market price of each share; to thwart an attempt by an outsider to accumulate shares in anticipation of a takeover attempt; or to increase the market price of each share of the stock.

Treasury stock is clearly not an "economic resource" of an entity. A corporation cannot own part of itself. Therefore, treasury stock is not an asset, and it has no voting, dividend, or other shareholder rights. Rather, it is reported on the balance sheet as a reduction in shareholders' equity—as a reduction in the number and book value of the shares outstanding.

Two methods of accounting for treasury stock are permitted. For a given situation, either method has the same effect on total owners' equity. With the simpler method, called the **cost method,** when treasury stock is purchased, the amount debited to Treasury Stock (contra equity account) is its reacquisition cost, regardless of its par value. It continues to be shown at this reacquisition cost until it is canceled or reissued, at which time adjustments are made in shareholders' equity to dispose of any differences between this cost, the paid-in value (i.e., the net proceeds at the time the stock was originally issued), and, in the event of reissuance, the amount then received.[4]

If treasury shares are reissued, any excess of selling price above cost is credited to a paid-in capital account (such as Paid-In Capital from Treasury Stock Transactions). If treasury stock is sold at a price below its reacquisition cost, the loss may be deducted from the related paid-in capital account if such an account already exists from prior transactions; otherwise the loss is debited to Retained Earnings. Any gain or loss on the resale of treasury stock is *not* shown on the income statement, nor is it recognized for income tax purposes.[5]

Retained Earnings

The remaining owners' equity account is Retained Earnings. As pointed out in previous chapters, the amount of **retained earnings** represents the *cumulative* net income

---

[4] An exception occurs if stock is reacquired at an amount significantly in excess of its fair value. This may occur when the company wants to buy out a stockholder who is contemplating an "unfriendly" takeover attempt or who is otherwise viewed by the corporation's board of directors as being problematical. When such a so-called greenmail transaction takes place, only the fair value of the treasury stock is recorded as the cost of the treasury shares, and the excess of the price paid over the fair value is recorded as an expense. *FASB Technical Bulletin No. 85-6.*

[5] The other permissible method is the *par value method.* It is more complicated and is described in advanced texts.

of the firm since its beginning, less the total dividends (or drawings, in the case of unincorporated businesses) that have been paid to owners over the entire life of the entity. Stated from more of a financial management point of view, retained earnings shows the amount of assets that have been financed by "plowing profits back into the business," rather than paying all of the company's net income out as dividends.

Reserves

Some shareholders do not understand that there is no connection between the amount shown as retained earnings and the corporation's ability to pay cash dividends to the shareholders. In an attempt to lower these shareholders' dividend aspiration levels, a corporation may show on its balance sheet an appropriation, or **reserve,** as a separate item that is subtracted from Retained Earnings. For example, a *reserve for future expansion* signals to shareholders the corporation's intention to use internally generated funds (rather than a new bond or stock issue) to finance the acquisition of new assets. Also, if some contingency does not meet the criteria (described in Chapter 8) for recording it as a liability, then a *reserve for contingencies* may be shown.

None of these reserves represents money, or anything tangible; the assets of a business are reported on the assets side of the balance sheet, not in the shareholders' equity section. The accounting entry creating the reserve involves a debit to Retained Earnings and a credit to the reserve account. This entry simply moves an amount from one owners' equity account to another. It does not affect any asset account, nor does the reserve represent anything more than a segregated portion of Retained Earnings. Because the use of the word *reserve* tends to be misleading to unsophisticated readers of financial statements (it connotes something stashed away), such usage fortunately is on the decline.

Dividends

Dividends are ordinarily paid to shareholders in cash, but they occasionally are paid in other assets. Dividends are debited to Retained Earnings on the date they are declared (i.e., voted) by the board of directors, even though payment is made at a later date. On the date of declaration, the dividends become a legal liability.

Example

If Kuick Corporation declared a $6,000 dividend on December 15 to be paid on January 15 to holders of record as of January 1, the entries would be as follows:

1. Declaration of dividend on December 15:
   Retained Earnings 6,000
      Dividends Payable (a liability account)   6,000

2. Payment of dividend on January 15:
   Dividends Payable 6,000
      Cash   6,000

Stock Splits

In a **stock split,** each shareholder receives a multiple of the number of shares previously held. For example, in a two-for-one split, the holder of 100 shares would receive 100 additional shares at no cost, doubling the total held before the split. A stock split merely increases the number of shares of stock outstanding with no change in each shareholder's proportional interest in the company. Such a split has no effect on the amount of shareholders' equity; its effect is solely to repackage the evidence of owner-ship in smaller units.

No transfer is made from Retained Earnings to Paid-In Capital when a stock split is effected. However, the par value *per share* is reduced proportionately; if the stock was

$1 par prior to a two-for-one split, it would automatically become $0.50 par after the split. Since the number of outstanding shares doubled and the par value per share halved, the total of Common Stock at Par remains unchanged, as does the amount in Additional Paid-In Capital.

Stock splits are usually effected to reduce the price of a share of stock, thus allegedly making the stock appealing to a wider range of investors (including those who prefer to trade only in round lots of 100 shares). Theoretically, a stock split should automatically reduce the market price of a share of stock in inverse proportion to the split: A two-for-one split should exactly halve the market price. In practice, however, the price reduction sometimes is less than proportional to the split, indicating that the split may add value in the eyes of shareholders.

Stock Dividends

Sometimes a company wants to retain funds in the business to finance expansion, and this precludes paying a cash dividend; yet the company still wants its shareholders to receive a dividend of some kind. Such a company may declare a **stock dividend,** which increases every shareholder's number of shares by the same percentage. For example, if a 5 percent stock dividend were declared, the holder of 100 shares would receive 5 more shares at no cost from the corporation (either newly issued or from treasury stock). Since each shareholder's holdings are increased by the same proportion, every shareholder's equity in the corporation remains unchanged.

Like a stock split, a stock dividend does increase the number of shares outstanding without changing the corporation's earnings, its assets, or each shareholder's proportionate equity interest in the company. In theory, therefore, such a dividend should reduce the market price per share of the stock. For the 5 percent stock dividend example, if the price before the dividend was $10.50 per share, theoretically it should drop to $10 ($10.50 ÷ 105%) after the stock dividend. However, studies indicate that shareholders do perceive a stock dividend as having some value because, in some cases, the price per share does not drop as much as theory would predict.[6]

To record a stock dividend, Retained Earnings is debited with the *fair* value of the additional shares issued, with the credit being to the paid-in capital accounts.

Example

If Kuick Corporation declared a 5 percent stock dividend to the holders of its 100,000 outstanding shares (par value of $1) when the market price of a share was $10.50, the entry would be

Retained Earnings 52,500		
Common Stock at Par	5,000	
Additional Paid-In Capital.	47,500	

The $52,500 is the fair value, at $10.50 per share, of the 5,000 additional shares issued as a dividend. The $47,500 is the difference between the $52,500 fair value and the par value of the newly issued shares. Note that the total amount of owners' equity is *not* changed by this transaction; there is just a shift of $52,500 out of Retained Earnings and into the paid-in capital accounts.

Stock dividends and splits are similar. They increase the number of shares outstanding without changing the stockholders' current proportional interests in the company. As can be seen from the above example, accounting treats stock dividends and stock splits differently. The Accounting Principles Board (APB) believed the difference

---

[6] These cases are usually situations where the stock dividend is accompanied by an increase in dividends.

between a stock dividend and a stock split was a matter of intent. The intent of a stock dividend is to give shareholders "ostensibly separate evidence" of their interests in the firm without having to distribute cash. The intent of a stock split is to reduce the market price of the shares to improve their marketability. The presumption is that any increase in shares smaller than 20 to 25 percent is a stock dividend, *not* a stock split.[7,8]

Spin-Offs

The stock referred to in the preceding paragraphs is the company's own stock. If the company owns shares of some *other* corporation's stock that it distributes to its shareholders, this distribution is called a **spin-off.** It is essentially similar to a cash dividend, and it is recorded in the same manner except that the credit is to the Investments asset account rather than to Cash. Most spin-offs are of the stock of a company's wholly owned subsidiary, as opposed to stock that was being held as an investment.

Warrants and Stock Options

Warrants

The right to purchase shares of common stock at a stated price within a given time period is called a **warrant.** For example, a warrant could give its holder the right to buy 100 shares of Sterling Company common stock for $25 per share anytime between January 1, 2010, and December 31, 2014. If during this period the market price of Sterling's common stock rises to $31, the holder of the option can *exercise* it by paying Sterling $25. The share of stock received can then be sold for $31, so the warrant holder gains $6. Warrants are negotiable; they can be bought and sold. Some companies have warrants that are traded on stock exchanges, just like other corporate securities. In this case the warrant holder can sell the warrant and realize its value without actually exercising it.

Stock Options

A **stock option** is essentially the same as a warrant except that it is not negotiable. Many corporations grant options to certain officers and employees, either to obtain widespread ownership among employees or as a form of compensation.

The *fair value–based* method is used to account for stock options.[9] The fair value–based method requires the issuing corporation to estimate the fair value of the options granted using an option pricing model (described in advanced finance courses). This value is then charged ratably to Salaries Expense over the vesting period of the option. (*Vesting* means that the option can be exercised even if the employee leaves the company.)

Example

An employee is granted an option to buy 5,000 shares of her company's common stock at a stated price, and the estimated fair value of this option is $150,000. The option's vesting period is five years. The company will charge $30,000 per year to Salaries Expense (the offsetting credit is to Paid-In Capital) over each of the next five years to account for this option.

Employee Stock Ownership Plans

Some corporations have a program of setting aside stock for the benefit of employees as a group (as distinguished from options, which are granted to certain employees as individuals). This is called an **employee stock ownership plan (ESOP).** Such a plan

---

[7] *Accounting Research Bulletin No. 43,* Chapter 7B.
[8] As a general rule, stock dividends and splits are not taxable to the recipient.
[9] "Accounting for Stock-Based Compensation," *FASB Statement No. 123* (revised 2004). "Share-based Payments," *IFRS No. 2.*

ILLUSTRATION 9–1
Presentation of Owners' Equity

PRESTON COMPANY AND SUBSIDIARIES Consolidated Balance Sheet At December 31 (millions)		
	2009	**2010**
Shareholders' Equity		
Common stock, $.25 par value	$ 77.6	$ 77.5
Capital in excess of par value	72.0	69.2
Retained earnings	3,409.4	3,033.9
Treasury stock, at cost	(1,653.1)	(1,105.0)
Total shareholders' equity	$1,905.9	$2,075.6

can have important income tax benefits to the corporation. (Contributions to the plan are tax-deductible employee compensation.) The plan's manager can vote the ESOP's shares, and the plan receives dividends. The plan is a separate entity whose assets (i.e., the stock that it holds and reinvested dividends) do not appear on the balance sheet of the corporation (just as the accounting records of other shareholders do not appear). However, the ESOP amounts are disclosed in notes to the financial statements.

Balance Sheet Presentation

In sum, the shareholders' equity section of the balance sheet maintains a distinct separation between capital invested by the shareholders and equity resulting from the retention of earnings in the business. There is a separation between paid-in capital—which in turn is usually subdivided into par value and additional paid in capital   and retained earnings. If a company has more than one class of stock, a note to the balance sheet provides details on each class. As an example, Illustration 9–1 shows the owners' equity section of a corporation's balance sheet.

Earnings per Share

In analyzing the financial statements of a corporation, investors pay particular attention to the amounts called *basic* and *diluted* **earnings per share.** The FASB and IASB require these figures be reported on the income statement and have provided detailed guidelines for making the calculations.[10]

Basic earnings per share is a measurement of the corporation's per share performance over a period of time. It is computed by dividing net income **applicable to the common stock** (explained below) by the number of shares of common stock outstanding. (Recall that treasury stock is not considered to be stock outstanding.)

Example

The 2010 income statement of McLean Corporation showed net income of $7 million. The corporation had 1 million shares of common stock outstanding during 2010. McLean's basic earnings per share was $7 ($7,000,000 ÷ 1,000,000 shares).

---

[10] "Earnings per Share," *FASB Statement No. 128.* "Earnings per Share," *IAS No. 33.*

The various classes of equity stock that a corporation might issue can be divided into one of two categories: (1) senior securities and (2) common stock. **Senior securities,** usually preferred stock, are those that have a claim on net income ahead of the claim of the common shareholders. The income figure used in the calculation of basic earnings per share is the amount that remains *after* the claims of the senior securities have been deducted from net income.

Example

Nugent Corporation in 2010 had net income of $7 million. It had outstanding 100,000 shares of $8 preferred stock (i.e., preferred stock whose annual dividend is $8 per share) convertible into 200,000 shares of common stock and 1 million shares of common stock. The preferred stock dividend of $800,000 must be subtracted from net income to arrive at net income applicable to common stock. Nugent's basic earnings per share was therefore ($7,000,000 − $800,000) ÷ 1,000,000 shares = $6.20 per share.

If the number of shares of common stock outstanding fluctuates within a year, then the *weighted-average* number of shares outstanding is computed and used to determine basic earnings per share.

Example

Optel Corporation in 2006 had net income of $7 million. On January 1 it had outstanding 1 million shares of common stock. On July 1 it issued an additional 500,000 shares, which were therefore outstanding for half of the year. Its weighted-average number of common shares outstanding was 1,000,000 + (500,000 * ½) = 1,250,000. Its basic earnings per share was $7,000,000 ÷ 1,250,000 = $5.60.

Diluted earnings per share is another measurement of a corporation's per share performance. It is the amount of earnings for the period applicable to each share of common stock outstanding (basic earnings per share) adjusted to reflect dilution (lower earnings per share) assuming all potentially dilutive common shares were outstanding during the period. Potentially dilutive common stock shares include stock options, warrants, and convertible securities (such as convertible preferred stock and convertible debt). Diluted earnings per share reflects the potential dilution of earnings per share that could occur if these contracts and securities were exercised or converted into common stock. The FASB's objective in requiring disclosure of diluted earnings per share is to alert financial statement users to this potential dilution. Typically, investors use diluted earnings per share to judge a corporation's per share performance and to value its common stock.

The diluted earnings per share calculation can be complex. Only two of its commonly used requirements—the if-converted and treasury stock methods—will be covered.

The *if-converted* method, as its name implies, is used to measure the potential dilutive effect on basic earnings per share from convertible securities. It assumes the convertible security has been converted. (It is important to remember the securities have not been converted. They are only *assumed* to be converted for this calculation.)

Example

Nugent Corporation in 2010 had net income of $7 million (see above example). It had outstanding 100,000 shares of $8 preferred stock (i.e., preferred stock whose annual dividend is $8 per share) convertible into 200,000 shares of common stock and 1 million shares of common stock. The preferred stock dividend of $800,000 must be subtracted from net income in the calculation of basic earnings per share to arrive at net income applicable to common stock. Nugent's basic earnings per share was therefore $6.20 per share [($7,000,000 − $800,000) ÷ 1,000,000 shares].

Since the preferred stock is convertible into common stock, two adjustments must be made to the basic earnings per share calculation to determine Nugent's diluted earnings per share. First, assuming conversion of the preferred stock, the $800,000 preferred stock dividends that would not have to be paid are added back to the $6,200,000 income applicable to common stock used in the basic earnings per share calculation. Second, again assuming conversion of the preferred stock, the 200,000 shares that would be issued upon conversion of the preferred stock are added to the actual 1 million common shares outstanding. Reflecting these two adjustments, Nugent's diluted earnings per share was $5.83 ($7,000,000 ÷ 1,200,000 shares).

The *treasury stock* method is used to calculate the potential dilutive effect on basic earnings per share from options and warrants. This method assumes the options or warrants are exercised and the cash received by the corporation is used to purchase its own stock at the average price of the stock during the period. The net of the number of common shares issued when the options or warrants are assumed to be exercised and the assumed number of common shares purchased is added to the denominator of the basic earnings per share calculation to calculate diluted earnings per share.

Example

The average price of the Veba Corporation's common stock during 2010 was $20 per share. The company had net income of $7 million for 2010. It had stock options for 100,000 common shares issued in 2009 at an exercise price of $10 per share and 1 million shares of common stock outstanding during 2010. Since the stock options are for common stock, their potential dilutive effect on basic earnings per share must be incorporated in the diluted earnings per share figure. First, it is assumed the options are exercised and the corporation issued 100,000 common shares and received $1 million. Next, it is assumed the corporation used the $1 million to buy 50,000 ($1 million ÷ $20 per share) of its own common stock. The net effect of these two assumed transactions is a 50,000-share (100,000 shares − 50,000 shares) increase in the outstanding common stock. Veba's diluted earnings per share was $6.67 ($7 million ÷ 1,050,000 shares).

If-converted and treasury stock–method adjustments enter into the calculation of diluted earnings per share only if the effect on diluted earnings per share is dilutive. That is, the adjustment reduces diluted earnings per share.

Example

During the third quarter of 2010 the average price of the Veba common stock was $5 per share. The company had stock options for 100,000 common shares issued at an exercise price of $10 per share in 2009 and 1 million common shares outstanding during the quarter. For the purpose of calculating dilutive earnings per share, the corporation used the treasury stock method to determine the dilutive effect of the stock options. (The treasury stock and if-converted calculations are made quarterly.) The corporation assumed the stock options were converted at the beginning of the quarter and 100,000 common shares were issued in return for $1 million (100,000 shares * $10 per share). Next, the corporation assumed the $1 million was used to buy 200,000 common shares of the corporation ($1 million ÷ $5 per share). The net result of these two assumed transactions is a reduction of 100,000 common shares in the denominator of the diluted earnings per share calculation (1 million shares − 100,000 shares). This reduction would be antidilutive (i.e., it would increase diluted earnings per share). Therefore, the stock options would not enter into the diluted earnings per share calculation for the third quarter. (They also would not be treated as outstanding during this quarter for the purpose of determining the weighted-average number of dilutive shares outstanding for the year.)

The control number for determining if a potentially dilutive security is dilutive or antidilutive is earnings before discontinued operations, extraordinary items, and the cumulative effect of accounting principle changes.

The Line between Debt and Equity

Chapter 8 described the trade-off between the lower after-tax cost of debt capital (relative to equity capital) and the risk that financial leverage adds to the shareholders' investment. In general, corporate financial managers favor leverage and the tax-deductible interest associated with debt capital *up to a point,* but they are concerned about the exposure to risk beyond that point. Although they like the lower risk of equity capital, they also realize that equity capital is inherently more expensive than debt capital. Thus, they want as much debt in the capital structure as is practicable without alarming investors by having an excessively high debt/equity (or equivalently, debt/capitalization) ratio.

In recent years, investment banking firms have developed a variety of financial instruments that are intended both to suit the needs of various types of investors and also to provide the corporation with securities of different risk characteristics. Some of these instruments tend to blur the line between debt and equity, and their existence requires that caution be exercised in using the debt/equity or debt/capitalization ratio to analyze capital structure. Two examples, each previously mentioned in passing, will be described.

Zero-Coupon Bonds

A company may issue bonds that pay no interest but whose face value is payable in, say, five years. These are called **zero-coupon bonds.** They may be issued by a start-up corporation that anticipates having little cash flow in the near future with which to make interest payments. Because there are no interest payments, zero-coupon bonds are sold at a deep discount from their par value. As described in the preceding chapter, this discount is determined by finding the present value of the bonds' future principal redemption payment at maturity. If investors view the issuing corporation's prospects as somewhat shaky, they will use a high discount rate in arriving at this present value.

Example

If investors discount a five-year, zero-coupon bond at 14 percent, at the date of issuance they will pay only $519 for each $1,000 par value bond (using Table A, as explained in the appendix to Chapter 8).

Although no cash interest is paid, the annual amortization of the $481 discount is reported as interest expense by the corporation. This noncash interest expense resulting from the discount amortization is tax deductible to the corporation (and, usually, is taxable interest revenue to the investor). However, the corporation has no cash interest payments to worry about for the five-year period. Thus, a zero-coupon bond meets the traditional definition of a debt security, but its burden may be less onerous to the corporation than that of cumulative preferred stock, which is not debt but whose dividends are expected to be declared and paid annually.

Debt with Warrants

Some corporations issue warrants in conjunction with the issuance of bonds, putting an exercise price on the warrants of about 15 to 20 percent above the current market price of the common stock. If the investor expects the firm to prosper and expects this prosperity to be reflected in the market price of the common stock, then the warrant has value. The investor will then accept a correspondingly lower interest rate on the bond, thus reducing the interest cost of the bond to the issuer. Also, some small firms that investors regard as being very risky would not be able to attract investors to their bonds without using warrants as a "sweetener."

The accounting for debt issued with warrants depends on whether the warrants are detachable (i.e., the warrants can be removed from the debt and used to purchase

Chapter 9 *Sources of Capital: Owners' Equity* **285**

the issuer's stock or sold to a third party) or nondetachable (i.e., the debt must be surrendered to get the issuer's stock).[11] If the warrants are *nondetachable,* the debt is accounted for as if it were a convertible debt security. That is, no recognition is given to the equity character of the debt. It is accounted for as regular debt. The Accounting Principles Board adopted this approach in the belief that the debt and equity features could not be separated.

If the warranties are detachable, the proceeds of the offering must be allocated between the debt and warrant based on their relative fair values. The value of a warrant at the time it is issued can be a matter of opinion. If a market for the warrant does not exist, this value sometimes can be approximated by estimating the higher interest rate that would have been required for the bonds if there were no warrants; the warrant's value is then assumed to be the difference between the present value of the bonds using this higher rate and the actual bond proceeds. Whatever the value is judged to be, the warrants are recorded separately from the bond liability by an entry such as

```
Cash . . . . . . . . . . . . . . . . . . . . . . . . . . . . . . . . . . . 210,000
     Bonds Payable . . . . . . . . . . . . . . . . . . . . .          200,000
     Bond Premium. . . . . . . . . . . . . . . . . . . . .             6,000
     Warrants Outstanding . . . . . . . . . . . . . . .                4,000
```

Warrants Outstanding is a shareholders' equity account.

Redeemable Preferred Stock

A corporation may issue preferred stock that not only pays annual dividends but also may be redeemed by the investor on or after a certain date, say five years hence. This **redeemable preferred stock** may be issued, for example, as part of the payment made to the owner of a small company when it is acquired by a larger one. The redemption price may be considerably higher than its par value. Redeemable preferred stock is evidence of ownership in the company and is therefore an equity security; yet the company's obligation to pay the redemption price may be fully as certain as that for the redemption of bonds when they mature, which is a liability. The FASB requires the issuer to classify this security as a liability.[12]

Equity in Nonprofit Organizations

Nonprofit organizations do not receive equity capital from shareholders; however, they do receive equity capital from contributions. These capital contributions are usually in the form of endowment or contributed "plant." **Endowment** consists of contributions whose principal is to be kept intact indefinitely, with the earnings on that principal being available to finance current operations. **Contributed plant** consists of contributed buildings, works of art and other museum objects, or the funds to acquire these or similar assets. Endowment and plant contributions are distinguished from contributions intended for operating purposes, such as contributions to an annual alumni/alumnae fund; operating contributions are revenues, not contributed capital.

In both for-profit and nonprofit organizations, equity is increased by earning net income. In a nonprofit organization, the cumulative net income amount is usually labeled "operating equity" rather than "retained earnings." Since nonprofit organizations do

---

[11] "Accounting for Convertible Debt and Debt Issued with Stock Purchase Warranties," *APB Opinion No. 14.* The FASB is reconsidering the accounting for hybrid securities that have both debt and equity components.
[12] "Accounting for Certain Financial Instruments with Characteristics of both Liabilities and Equity," *FASB Statement No. 150.*

not pay dividends, their equity does not decrease as does a dividend-paying entity's equity when it declares a dividend. However, a nonprofit organization's equity does decrease in any year in which its operations were unprofitable.

This difference in the source of equity funds is the only substantive difference in accounting for the two types of organizations. Many other differences are found in practice, but these result from nonprofit accounting traditions and terminology differences rather than from actual differences in substance.

Multiple Share Classes: Voting Rights and Control

Facebook's CEO and founder Mark Zuckerberg has close to 54% voting rights in the company although he doesn't hold as many shares in the firm. He actually holds roughly 28% of a special class of shares, called Class B shares. Why are his voting rights then so much higher? What are class B shares? Some companies, especially start-ups in the technology space have two types of share classes, one with enhanced voting rights and the other with limited voting rights; which are known as dual class shares. For example, in Facebook, the class B shares have 10 votes per share. Dual class shares serve dual purpose; it helps the promoter retain management control and also gives limited voice to other shareholders.

Recently many companies, specifically in the IT industry, find this a useful way to grow. Start-ups, especially those who are exploring new technology often don't have a proven market, typically called POC (proof of concept). Moreover, the inherent dynamic nature of such businesses always keeps seeking additional capital to fund growth as they "burn" a lot of cash in this phase. At the same time, the expertise required is specialised and, in many cases, restricted to founders. This combination results in the idea of raising equity funds without diluting control and, hence, the need for dual class shares.

Firms (like Facebook, etc,) that have decided to have multiple classes of common shares issue two categories of shares usually denoted as Class A and Class B shares. The primary objective is to assign more voting rights to one class of stock than the other. Generally, when a private firm decides to go public; it will usually issue a large number of common shares, but some specific firms, mostly start-ups will also provide its founders, executives, or other investors like private equity firms or venture capitalists with a slightly different category of equity shares that carries multiple votes for every single share. Generally, the "super-voting" multiple is about 10 votes per higher class share, although occasionally companies might choose to make them even higher. Usually, Class A shares are superior to Class B shares, but there is no standard nomenclature for multiple share classes. Sometimes Class B shares have more votes than their Class A counterparts. Because of this difference in categories of shares being issued, it becomes imperative for investors to do some research related to the details of a company's share classes if they are considering investing in a firm with more than one class.

Classic Example of Dual Class Shares

One classic example of multiple class shares is Google and its parent firm, Alphabet, Inc. The firm has all the three class of shares namely Class A, Class B and Class C. All the three shares have different ticker symbols on the stock exchange. While GOOG stock represents Class C shares, GOOGL stock represents Class A shares. The Class C shares (GOOG) have no voting rights, the Class A shares (GOOGL) have one vote each. These classes were issued subsequent to the stock split during the restructuring which resulted in the formation of Alphabet as the parent company. Any investor who owned Google stock before the split got one share of the voting GOOGL stock and one share of the non-voting GOOG stock. Moreover, there are Class B shares of Google stock too which actually do not trade on the stock market The Class B shares are owned by Google insiders and early investors and each share gets 10 votes, making them super-voting shares.

Objective of Dual Class Shares

Pros and cons

What are the pluses and minuses of issuing such dual class shares? On one hand, it works well for the founders as the company grows in size and public shareholding expands, the skewness in control of the firm via voting rights appears a little unfair. Also, there is no assurance that the stupendous performance of the company will continue indefinitely. If things go wrong, public shareholders have little influence or control over future courses of action as without a vote they cannot provide oversight to boards and management. It can also compromise issues of governance as there is possible scope for misuse of majority control. With such clear limitations, it is not seen as a very popular way of managing control in companies. However, some experts argue that to expand business growth in new-age sectors, this route of raising funds can work more effectively.

There is another side to it though. Many investors, particularly venture capitalists want to be perceived as "founder friendly," and therefore generally will not like to take a stand where the founders' long-term control" over the company is seen as a bad thing. In the worst case, they may make an observation by pointing out that their interests are being compromised by having low vote shares while the founders have high vote shares. But this is generally not the case, because VCs will require that a startup company agree to certain "protective provisions" in a term sheet as a pre-condition to their investment. It is therefore recommended that in financial markets where retail participation is large and significant, but legal recourse against rogue companies (read shady promoters) is weak and not viable, exchanges and regulators need to create awareness for outcomes of dual class shares to the common investors. Also, regulators must intervene quickly and on time, whenever they see a possibility of general investors interests being compromised.

The Indian Context: DVR

Back home, Indian companies, can create differential shares called differential voting right shares or DVRs; for diluting stake. These are exactly same as dual class shares, and voting rights on DVRs are different from those of the regular shares issued by the company. However, only a very small number of listed companies in India have so far gone this way. Another reason why DVRs are not very popular as that because they normally trade at a relative discount to the full voting right share class. It's not a very attractive option for India as most companies are closely held by promoters and public shareholding is very low (often a minority) to begin with.

How Dual-Stock Structure can Work for a Startup Firm

It is commonly suggested for startup founders to at least consider the most basic dual-class of Common Stock structure, where the one class has 10 voting rights and the other class has one voting right, but otherwise the classes are largely identical.

The high voting power shares could have some other features too:

- Automatic conversion to low vote normal share class on a transfer or sale to a third party
- Protective provisions like necessary approval of the holders of high vote shares for certain corporate actions, like M&A.

Summary

Although the legal forms of organization—proprietorship, partnership, and corporation—differ, all three conceptually have paid-in capital and retained earnings as components of owners' equity. Most corporations report two separate components of paid-in capital: par value and additional paid-in capital. Neither number is meaningful in isolation; their sum shows the proceeds the corporation received when the stock was issued.

Preferred stock pays a stated dividend, which may be cumulative. Although this dividend is analogous to bond interest, it is not a liability. Preferred shareholders have precedence over common shareholders in matters of dividend payments and distribution of proceeds of a corporate liquidation.

Treasury stock is stock that a corporation has reacquired by purchase. It is not an asset and is not counted as either paid-in capital or outstanding shares. Ordinarily, it is recorded at its reacquisition cost. Subsequent reissuance of the stock may lead to a reported loss or gain, which is not included in income.

Retained earnings is the cumulative amount of net income an entity has earned since its inception, less the cumulative amount of dividends it has paid to its owners. Stock dividends and stock splits do not affect the relative holdings of shareholders nor the total amount of owners' equity. Creation of a reserve account also does not affect the total of owners' equity; a reserve is simply a reclassification of a portion of retained earnings. The calculation of basic earnings per share is based on the amount of net income applicable to common stock (net income less preferred stock dividends) and the number of outstanding shares. The diluted earnings per share calculation reflects the potential dilution of basic earnings per share from contracts and securities that may require the issuance of common stock at some time in the future.

Securities such as zero-coupon bonds and redeemable preferreds have blurred the distinction between debt capital and equity capital, and thus complicate the ratio analysis of capital structures.

The nature of nonprofit organizations' equity capital differs from that of for-profit organizations, but otherwise accounting for the two types of entities is substantively similar.

Problems

Problem 9–1.

The following information was taken from the balance sheet of Laribee Company (amounts are in thousands of dollars):

Current liabilities*	$ 24,480
Long-term debt	73,440
Common stock, par value	61,200
Paid-in capital	15,300
Retained earnings	70,380
	$244,800

*Includes $6,120 current portion of long-term debt.

Required:

    a. Calculate the debt/equity and debt/capitalization ratios.

    b. What do these ratios measure?

Problem 9–2. During its fiscal year, Morey Corporation had outstanding 600,000 shares of $6.50 preferred stock and 2,000,000 shares of common stock. Morey's net income for the year was $19,550,000. The company also had granted stock options to employees for 2,00,000 shares of common stock at $10 per share (exercise price). The average price of the company's common stock during the fiscal year was $20 per share.

Required:

    a. Calculate the company's basic earnings per share.

    b. Calculate the company's diluted earnings per share.

Problem 9–3. The Power Corporation had the following common shares outstanding during the fiscal year: 1,00,000 during the first quarter of the fiscal year and 3,00,000 during the balance of the fiscal year. What was the weighted-average number of common shares outstanding during the fiscal year?

Problem 9–4. Two recent business school graduates, Jane Johns and Lou Schwartz, started a shop called Exports Unlimited on January 1. Their partnership agreement stipulated that each would receive 10 percent on capital contributed and that they would share equally any net income in excess of this 10 percent payment. Jane had contributed $50,000 and Lou, $70,000. They also agreed that Jane, who could devote only part time to the venture, would receive a salary of $15,000, while Lou would receive $40,000. Net income for the first year (after deducting both partners' salaries) was $66,000. What was each partner's total income (including salaries) from the business?

Problem 9–5. The Owner's Equity section of the balance sheet of Ovlov Corporation on December 31, 2009, was as follows:

$8.00 preferred stock (40,000 shares, par value $100)	$ 4,000,000
Common stock (no par value, 5,000,000 shares issued and outstanding)	21,000,000
Retained earnings	7,000,000
Total owner's equity	$32,000,000

The board of directors took the following actions:

December 31, 2010:

1. A 2-for-1 stock split of common stock was declared.
2. 12,000 shares of its outstanding preferred stock were purchased by Ovlov at $114 per share.

January 1, 2011:

1. The preferred dividend of $8.00 was declared.
2. A cash dividend of $.15 a share on common stock outstanding on January 1 was declared.
3. A stock dividend of $\frac{1}{10}$ of a share was declared on common stock, effective February 1.

February 1, 2011: The dividends declared in January were paid.

Required:
Prepare journal entries to record the transactions.

Problem 9–6.

The shareholders' equity section of Valade Corp.'s balance sheet is:

	2010	2009
Preferred stock (8%, $50 par value)	$ 300,000	$ 150,000
Common stock ($10 par value, 80,000 shares authorized, 80,000 shares issued, 10,000 shares in treasury)	800,000	650,000
Additional paid-in capital:		
Preferred stock	200,000	175,000
Common stock	525,000	300,000
Retained earnings	679,000	505,000
Less: treasury stock	150,000	—
Total shareholders' equity	$2,654,000	$1,780,000

Required:
a. How many shares of common stock were issued during 2010? What was their average issue price?
b. How many shares of preferred stock were issued during 2010? What was their average issue price?
c. Give the entry for the company's purchase of treasury stock. What was the average repurchase price?
d. What was the company's book value at the end of 2009? 2010?

Problem 9–7.

Eastman, Inc., incorporated in New Hampshire on April 15, 2007. Since the date of its inception, the following transactions occurred:
a. On April 15, 2007, Eastman was authorized to issue 2,000,000 shares of $6 per value common stock.
b. On April 15, 2007, the company issued 100,000 shares of common stock for $15 per share.
c. The company issued and paid a 25 percent stock dividend on December 21, 2007. The market value on that date was $16 per share.
d. On July 1, 2008, Eastman sold 30,000 shares of common for $30.
e. On November 15, 2008, the company repurchased 10,000 shares of stock for $42 per share.
f. On December 15, 2008, Eastman issued 5,000 shares of treasury stock at $46 per share.
g. On February 1, 2009, the stock split 2 for 1.
h. On September 15, 2009, the remaining treasury stock was sold for $35 per share.
i. On December 24, 2009, Eastman declared a cash dividend of $150,000.
j. On January 24, 2010, the cash dividend was paid.

Required:
Prepare the necessary journal entries.

CASES

Case 9–1

Xytech, Inc.*

Xytech was a high-tech company that had been started by three partners in early 20X0. Their successful product designs led to rapid growth of the company, with resulting needs for additional capital to support the growth. This case describes the major financing transactions entered into by Xytech in its first 10 years of existence. The firm's earnings history also is given.

You are to write a journal entry for each transaction as it is described. You should be explicit about what noncurrent liability and owners' equity—that is, invested capital—accounts are affected by the transactions, but effects on assets (including cash) and current liabilities can be recorded in a single account, "A&CL."

20X0: The firm began as a partnership on January 10, with the three equal partners, Able, Baker, and Cabot, each contributing $100,000 capital. The accountant set up a capital account for each of the three partners. On April 1 the partners arranged with a bank a $100,000, 8 percent, five-year "balloon" note, which meant that only quarterly interest was payable for five years, with the principal due in full as a lump sum at the end of the fifth year. The firm's net loss for 20X0 was $54,000. A salary for each partner was included in the calculation of net loss; no other payments were made to the partners.

20X1: To help the firm deal with a short-term liquidity problem, on April 26, Cabot liquidated some personal securities and loaned the firm the $50,000 proceeds. Cabot expected to be repaid these funds in no more than one year. In October Baker's ownership interest in the firm was sold out equally to Able and Cabot, with Baker receiving a total of $110,000 in notes and cash from Able and Cabot. The firm had $12,000 net income for the year. Able and Cabot planned to incorporate the firm as of January 1, 20X2. Prepare a statement of invested capital for the partner-ship as of December 31, 20X1.

20X2: The firm was incorporated on January 1, as planned. The articles of incorporation authorized 500 shares of $100 par value common stock, but only 100 shares were issued, 50 each to Able and Cabot.

On March 21 the bank agreed to increase the $100,000 balloon note to $150,000; the $50,000 proceeds were used to repay Cabot's $50,000 loan. The net income for the year was $26,000.

20X3: In anticipation of a public woffering of Xytech, Inc., stock, the firm effected a 1,000-for-1 stock split in November. The year's net income was $43,000. Calculate the 20X3 basic earnings per share amount.

20X4: In January the firm went public. An investment banker sold 100,000 newly issued shares at $7.75 per share. The banker's fee and other issuance costs amounted to $55,000. The year's net income (after stock issuance costs) was $68,000. Prepare a statement of invested capital as of December 31, 20X4.

20X5: In January the company issued 500 20-year bonds with a face value of $1,000 each and a coupon rate of 6 percent. Although the bonds were issued at par, because of issuance costs the proceeds were only $950 per bond. Part of the proceeds was used to repay the firm's prior long-term debt. The year's net income was $85,000.

20X6: In April Able and Cabot each sold 25,000 of their common shares, receiving proceeds of $11 per share. The company earned net income of $111,000. On December 31, the firm declared a dividend of $0.15 per share, payable January 31, 20X7, to holders of record as of January 15. Prepare a statement of invested capital as of December 31, 19X6.

20X7: Feeling that the market was undervaluing the company's stock, in June the management decided to purchase 20,000 shares on the open market. The purchase was effected July 1 at a price of $10 per share. The shares were held as treasury stock, available for possible reissuance. The year's net income was $152,000. In December, a $0.20 per share dividend was declared, payable the following month. Calculate the year's earnings per share.

20X8: In January the company issued 4,000 shares of convertible cumulative preferred stock with an annual dividend rate of $5 per share. Proceeds of the issuance were $200,000. Each share was convertible upon the holder's demand into two shares of Xytech common stock. Net income before preferred dividends was $186,000. In December, a dividend of $0.25 per common share was declared, payable the following month. Calculate the basic and diluted earnings per share of common stock in 20X8.

20X9: Net income before preferred stock dividends was $252,000. Instead of paying a cash dividend to common stock shareholders, on December 31, the firm declared a 5 percent stock dividend. The market price of the common stock on December 31 was $17 per share. No shares of preferred stock were converted during the year. Calculate the basic and diluted earnings per share for 20X9 and prepare a statement of invested capital as of December 31. What is the company's debt/capitalization ratio at year-end?

Case 9–2
Innovative Engineering Company*

Innovative Engineering Company was founded by two partners, Meredith Gale and Shelley Yeaton, shortly after they had graduated from engineering school. Within five years, the partners had built a thriving business, primarily through the development of a product line of measuring instruments based on the laser principle. Success brought with it the need for new permanent capital. After careful calculation, the partners placed the amount of this need at $1.2 million. This would replace a term loan that was about to mature and provide for plant expansion and related working capital.

At first, they sought a wealthy investor, or group of investors, who would provide the $1.2 million in return for an interest in the partnership. They soon discovered, however, that although some investors were interested in participating in new ventures, none of them was willing to participate as partner in an industrial company because of the risks to their personal fortunes that were inherent in such an arrangement. Gale and Yeaton therefore planned to incorporate the Innovative Engineering Company, in which they would own all the stock.

After further investigation, they learned that Arbor Capital Corporation, a venture capital firm, might be interested in providing permanent financing. In thinking about what they should propose to Arbor, their first idea was that Arbor would be asked to provide $1.2 million, of which $1.1 million would be a long-term loan. For the other $100,000, Arbor would receive 10 percent of the Innovative common stock as a "sweetener." If Arbor would pay $100,000 for 10 percent of the stock,

this would mean that the 90 percent that would be owned by Gale and Yeaton would have a value of $900,000. Although this was considerably higher than Innovative's net assets, they thought that this amount was appropriate in view of the profitability of the product line that they had successfully developed.

A little calculation convinced them, however, that this idea (hereafter, proposal A) was too risky. The resulting ratio of debt to equity would be greater than 100 percent, which was considered unsound for an industrial company.

Their next idea was to change the debt/equity ratio by using preferred stock in lieu of most of the debt. Specifically, they thought of a package consisting of $200,000 debt, $900,000 preferred stock, and $100,000 common stock (proposal B). They learned, however, that Arbor Capital Corporation was not interested in accepting preferred stock, even at a dividend that exceeded the interest rate on debt. Thereupon, they approached Arbor with a proposal of $600,000 debt and $600,000 equity (proposal C). For the $600,000 equity, Arbor would receive $\frac{6}{15}$ (i.e., 40 percent) of the common stock.

The Arbor representative was considerably interested in the company and its prospects but explained that Arbor ordinarily did not participate in a major financing of a relatively new company unless it obtained at least 50 percent equity as part of the deal. They were interested only in a proposal for $300,000 debt and $900,000 for half of the equity (proposal D). The debt/equity ratio in this proposal was attractive, but Gale and Yeaton were not happy about sharing control of the company equally with an outside party.

Before proceeding further, they decided to see if they could locate another venture capital investor who might be interested in one of the other proposals. In calculating the implications of these proposals, Gale and Yeaton assumed an interest cost of debt of 8 percent, which seemed to be the rate for companies similar to Innovative, and a dividend rate for preferred stock of 10 percent. They assumed, as a best guess, that Innovative would earn $300,000 a year after income taxes on operating income but before interest costs and the tax savings thereon. They included their own common stock equity at $900,000.

They also made pessimistic calculations based on income of $100,000 (instead of $300,000) per year and optimistic calculations based on income of $500,000 a year. They realized, of course, that the $100,000 pessimistic calculations were not necessarily the minimum amount of income; it was possible that the company would lose money. On the other hand, $500,000 was about the maximum amount of income that could be expected with the plant that could be financed with the $1.2 million. The applicable income tax rate was 34 percent.

Questions

1. For each of the four proposals, calculate the return on common shareholders' equity (net income after preferred dividends − common shareholders' equity) that would be earned under each of the three income assumptions. Round calculations to the nearest $1,000 and $\frac{1}{10}$ percent.
2. Calculate the pretax earnings and return on its $1.2 million investment to Arbor Capital Corporation under each of the four proposals. Assume that Arbor receives a dividend equal to its portion of common stock ownership times Innovative's net income after preferred dividends (if any); assume a "negative dividend" if Innovative has a net loss.
3. Were the partners correct in rejecting proposals A and B?
4. Comment on the likelihood that Innovative Engineering Company could find a more attractive financing proposal than proposal D.

Case 9–3
UPC Inc.*

Beginning in late 1997 and continuing into 1998, UPC Inc., a manufacturer of complex circuit boards, raised new debt and equity capital to finance its rapidly growing business. In addition, as part of its management incentive program, the company granted a number of stock options to key employees. All of the previously issued stock options have been exercised.

Statement 128

The *Financial Accounting Standards Board's Statement 128,* "Earnings per Share," became effective for fiscal years beginning after December 15, 1997. As a result, UPC's 1998 earnings per share disclosures were the company's first earnings per share figures to be calculated using this new standard. This case describes the effect of the 1997–98 capital and financial incentive transactions on the company's 1998 annual basic and diluted earnings per share figures.

Capital- and Incentive-Related Transactions

UPC's 1997–98 capital- and incentive-related transactions were

(a) In the second quarter of 1997, 600,000 shares of *convertible preferred stock* were issued for assets in a purchase transaction. The quarterly dividend on each share of the convertible preferred stock was $0.05, payable at the end of the quarter. Each share was convertible into one share of common stock. Holders of 500,000 shares of the convertible preferred stock converted their preferred stock into common stock on June 1, 1998.

(b) In the last quarter of 1997, 4 percent *convertible debentures* with a principal amount of $10,000,000 due in 20 years were sold for cash at $1,000 (par). Interest was payable semiannually on May 1 and November 1. Each $1,000 debenture was convertible into 20 shares of common stock. No debentures were converted in 1997. The entire issue was converted on April 1, 1998, because the issue was called by the company.

* This case is based on an illustrative example included in *Statement of Financial Accounting Standards No. 128.*

(c) *Warrants* to buy 500,000 shares of common stock at $60 per share for a period of five years were issued on January 1, 1998. All outstanding warrants were exercised on September 1, 1998.

(d) *Options* to buy 1,000,000 shares of common stock at $85 per share for a period of 10 years were granted to employees on January 1, 1998. No options were exercised during 1998 because the exercise price of the options exceeded the market price of the common stock.

(e) On March 1, 1998, 100,000 shares of *common stock* were issued for cash.

Selected Financial Data

UPC's 1998 quarterly and annual operating results were

1998	Income (Loss) Before Extraordinary Item and Accounting Change	Extraordinary Loss[a]	Cumulative Effect of an Accounting Change[a]	Net Income (Loss)
First quarter	$3,000,000			$3,000,000
Second quarter	4,500,000			4,500,000
Third quarter	(500,000)	$(2,000,000)		(1,500,000)
Fourth quarter	(500,000)		$ 4,250,000	3,750,000
Full year	$7,500,000	$(2,000,000)	$ 4,250,000	$9,750,000

[a] Net of tax.

The number of shares of UPC's common stock outstanding at the beginning of 1998 was 3,300,000.

The company's 1998 tax rate was 40 percent. UPC's average market prices of common stock for the calendar-year 1998 were as follows:

First quarter	$59
Second quarter	$70
Third quarter	$72
Fourth quarter	$72

Full-Year

UPC's 1998 full-year earnings per share computation was

Income before extraordinary item and accounting change	$7,500,000
Less: Preferred stock dividends	(45,000)
Income available to common stockholders	7,455,000
Extraordinary item	(2,000,000)
Accounting change	4,250,000
Net income available to common stockholders	$9,750,000

Dates Outstanding	Shares Outstanding	Fraction of Period	Weighted Average Shares
January 1–February 28	3,300,000	2/12	550,000
Issuance of common stock on March 1	100,000		
March 1–March 31	3,400,000	1/12	283,333
Conversion of 4% debenture on April 1	200,000		
April 1–May 31	3,600,000	2/12	600,000
Conversion of preferred stock on June 1	500,000		
June 1–August 31	4,100,000	3/12	1,025,000
Exercise of warrants on September 1	500,000		
September 1–December 31	4,600,000	4/12	1,533,333
Weighted average shares			3,991,666

$$\text{Income before extraordinary item and accounting change} = \frac{\$7,455,000}{3,991,666} = \underline{\$1.87}$$

$$\text{Extra oridinary item} = \frac{\$(2,000,000)}{3,991,666} = \underline{\$(0.50)}$$

$$\text{Accounting change} = \frac{\$4,250,000}{3,991,666} = \underline{\$1.06}$$

$$\text{Net income} = \frac{\$9,705,000}{3,991,666} = \underline{\$2.43}$$

Diluted Earnings per Share

The equation used by UPC to compute diluted earnings per share was

$$\text{Diluted earnings per share} = \frac{\text{Income available to common stockholders} + \text{Effect of assumed conversions}}{\text{Weighted average shares} + \text{Dilutive potential commonshares}}$$

Full Year

UPC's 1998 full-year diluted earnings per share disclosure was

Income before extraordinary item and accounting change	$ 1.73
Extraordinary item	(0.46)
Accounting change	0.97
Net income	$2.24

These amounts were based on these figures:

Income available to common shareholders		$7,455,000[a]
Plus: Income impact of assumed conversions		
Preferred stock dividends	$45,000	
Interest on 4% convertible debentures	60,000	
Effect of assumed conversions		105,000
Income available to common stockholders + assumed conversions		7,560,000
Extraordinary item		(2,000,000)
Accounting change		4,250,000
Net income available to common stockholders + assumed conversions		$9,810,000

[a] See annual basic earnings per share calculations.

Weighted average shares		3,991,666[a]
Plus: Incremental shares from assumed conversions		
Warrants	30,768[b]	
Convertible preferred stock	308,333[c]	
4% convertible debentures	50,000[d]	
Dilutive potential common shares		389,101
Adjusted weighted average shares		4,380,767

[a] See annual basic earnings per share calculations.   [b] $\left(71,429 \text{ shares} \times \frac{3}{12}\right) + \left(51,643 \text{ shares} \times \frac{3}{12}\right)$.
[c] $\left(60,000 \text{ shares} \times \frac{5}{12}\right) + \left(10,000 \text{ shares} \times \frac{7}{12}\right)$.   [d] $200,000 \text{ shares} \times \frac{3}{12}$.

Question

Be prepared to explain the calculations shown above for arriving at the annual income available to common stockholders, weighted average shares, and the basic and diluted earnings per share amounts disclosed by UPC.

Case 9–4

Maxim Integrated Products, Inc.

Expensing stock options for financial reporting purposes became mandatory for most firms in mid 2005.[1] Under the heading "Two Sets of Books," *Investor's Business Daily* reported:

> Take Maxim Integrated Products. The chipmaker told analysts August 1 that expensing employee stock options would reduce its earnings per share by about 20% this quarter.
>
> Maxim said expensing options would cut its first-quarter earnings by 7 or 8 cents a share, resulting in GAAP EPS of 30 to 31 cents.
>
> Maxim Chief Executive John Gifford said he believes free cash flow and pro forma EPS "will be a truer indication of our performance."
>
> When pushed by analysts for details on the impact of expensing stock options, Gifford said, "I don't even care . . . I will do whatever they require us to do for GAAP. But I don't pay any attention to it . . ."
>
> Will Wall Street ignore options?[2]

The Company

Maxim Integrated Products, Inc. (Maxim), incorporated in 1983, is headquartered in Sunnyvale, California. Maxim designs, develops, manufactures, and markets a broad range of linear and mixed-signal integrated circuits, commonly referred to as analog circuits. Maxim also provides a range of high-frequency design processes and capabilities that can be used in custom designs. Maxim is a global company with manufacturing facilities in the United States, testing facilities in the Philippines and Thailand, and sales offices throughout the world. Its products are sold to customers in numerous markets, including automotive, communications, consumer, data processing, industrial control, instrumentation, and medical industries.[3]

The company's stock is traded on the NASDAQ national market under the symbol MXIM. During fiscal year 2005, the high and low closing prices by quarter for fiscal year 2005 were

	Quarter Ended			
	June 25, 2005	March 26, 2005	December 25, 2004	September 25, 2004
Fiscal year 2005				
High	$41.86	$44.40	$44.70	$52.42
Low	$36.60	$38.17	$40.87	$39.27

Source: Maxim Integrated Products, Inc., 2005 Form 10-K.

Exhibits 1–4 present selected Maxim financial statement data. These data are from periods when expensing stock options was not mandatory. Like most companies, Maxim used the intrinsic value method to account for stock options.[4] The effect on earnings of expensing stock options was a required disclosure.

---

[1] *FASB Statement 123(R)* (*FAS 123R*) required companies to expense the cost of stock options. Management had considerable latitude in selecting the method to value stock option grants. Prior to the issuance of *FAS 123R,* most companies simply disclosed the effect on income of stock option expensing in the financial statement notes.

[2] *Investor's Business Daily,* September 7, 2005.

[3] Maxim Integrated Products, Inc., 2005 Form 10-K.

[4] Under the intrinsic value method, no expense was ever recognized for stock options issued with an exercise price equal to the stock's price at the grant date.

EXHIBIT 1

MAXIM INTEGRATED PRODUCTS, INC. Consolidated Statements of Income for the Years Ended June 28, 2003; June 26, 2004; and June 25, 2005 (amounts in thousands, except per share data)			
	June 25, 2005	June 26, 2004	June 28, 2003
Net revenues	$1,671,713	$1,439,263	$1,153,219
Cost of goods sold	463,664	433,358	348,264
Gross margin	$1,208,049	$1,005,905	$ 804,955
Operating expenses:			
Research and development	$ 328,164	$ 306,320	$ 272,322
Selling, general, and administrative	98,513	93,550	85,597
Total operating expenses	$ 426,677	$ 399,870	$ 357,919
Operating income	$ 781,372	$ 606,035	$ 447,036
Interest income and other, net	28,265	20,461	15,055
Income before provision for income taxes	$ 809,637	$ 626,496	$ 462,091
Provision for income taxes	268,800	206,744	152,490
Net income	$ 540,837	$ 419,752	$ 309,601
Earnings per share:			
Basic	$ 1.66	$ 1.28	$ 0.96
Diluted	$ 1.58	$ 1.20	$ 0.91

Source: Maxim Integrated Products, Inc., 2005 Form 10-K.

EXHIBIT 2

MAXIM INTEGRATED PRODUCTS, INC. 2005 Consolidated Statement of Stockholders' Equity (amounts in thousands)					
	Common Stock		Additional Paid-in Capital	Retained Earnings	Other Accumulated Comprehensive (Loss) Income	Total Stockholders' Equity
	Shares	Par Value				
Balance, June 26, 2004	324,444	$325	$ 80,137	$2,038,820	(6,964)	$2,112,318
Components of comprehensive income:						
Net income	—	—	—	540,837	—	540,837
Unrealized gain on forward-exchange contracts, net of tax	—	—	—	—	795	795
Unrealized loss on available-for-sale investments, net of tax	—	—	—	—	(361)	(361)
Total comprehensive income						$ 541,271
Exercises under the Stock Option and Purchase Plans	7,112	7	105,986	—	—	105,993
Repurchase of common stock	(4,062)	(5)	(168,452)	—	—	(168,457)
Tax benefit on exercise of nonqualified stock options and disqualifying dispositions under stock plans	—	—	117,000	—	—	117,000
Dividends declared and paid	—	—	—	(123,943)	—	(123,943)
Balance, June 25, 2005	327,494	$327	$134,671	$ 2,455,714	$(6,530)	$2,584,182

Source: Maxim Integrated Products, Inc., 2005 Form 10-K.

EXHIBIT 3

MAXIM INTEGRATED PRODUCTS, INC. Consolidated Statements of Cash Flows for the Years Ended June 28, 2003, June 26, 2004, and June 25, 2005 (amounts in thousands)			
	June 25, 2005	June 26, 2004	June 28, 2003
Cash flows from operating activities:			
Net income	$540,837	$419,752	$309,601
Adjustments to reconcile net income to net cash provided by operating activities:			
Depreciation, amortization, and other	76,849	61,860	61,036
Tax benefit related to stock-based compensation plans	117,000	152,500	113,473
Changes in assets and liabilities:			
Accounts receivable	4,813	(70,398)	3,052
Inventories	(49,994)	3,407	18,014
Deferred taxes	45,483	23,500	48,404
Income tax refund receivable	668	9,034	41,918
Current assets	946	(7,029)	106
Accounts payable	(37,590)	51,815	(3,243)
Income tax payable	13,834	8,439	267
Deferred income on shipments to distributors	(2,633)	1,276	(5,601)
All other accrued liabilities	(11,153)	41,298	(4,533)
Net cash provided by operating activities	699,060	695,454	582,494
Cash flows from investing activities:			
Additions to property, plant, and equipment	(132,445)	(231,618)	(84,060)
Other noncurrent assets	(308)	2,873	(5,148)
Purchases of available-for-sale securities	(1,150,968)	(1,002,154)	(1,620,085)
Proceeds from sales/maturities of available for-sale securities	808,885	994,296	1,259,990
Net cash used in investing activities	(474,836)	(236,603)	(449,303)
Cash flows from financing activities:			
Issuance of common stock	105,993	183,856	83,671
Repurchase of common stock	(168,457)	(601,244)	(153,949)
Dividends paid	(123,943)	(104,570)	(25,879)
Net cash used in financing activities	(186,407)	(521,958)	(96,157)
Net increase (decrease) in cash and cash equivalents	37,817	(63,107)	37,034
Cash and cash equivalents:			
Beginning of year	147,734	210,841	173,807
End of year	$185,551	$147,734	$210,841
Supplemental disclosures of cash flow information:			
Cash paid (refunds received), net during the year for:			
Income taxes	$93,622	$13,275	$(51,562)

Source: Maxim Integrated Products, Inc., 2005 Form 10-K.

EXHIBIT 4 2005 Stock-Based Compensation Note

The company accounts for its stock option and employee stock purchase plans using the intrinsic value method prescribed in Accounting Principles Board's Opinion No. 25 (APB 25), "Accounting for Stock Issued to Employees." Accordingly, employee and director compensation expense is recognized only for those options whose price is less than fair market value at the measurement date. In addition, the company discloses pro forma information related to its stock plans according to SFAS No. 123, "Accounting for Stock-Based Compensation," as amended by, SFAS No. 148, "Accounting for Stock-Based Compensation—Transition and Disclosure . . ."

The valuation of options granted in fiscal years 2005, 2004, and 2003 reported below has been estimated at the date of grant using the Black-Scholes option pricing model with the following weighted average assumptions:

	Stock Option Plans			Employee Stock Participation Plan		
	2005	2004	2003	2005	2004	2003
Expected option holding period (in years)	4.5	4.8	4.5	1.1	0.5	0.5
Risk-free interest rate	3.3%	2.9%	2.7%	2.5%	1.2%	1.3%
Stock price volatility	0.33	0.42	0.43	0.33	0.42	0.43
Dividend yield	1.0%	.63%	.46%	1.0%	.63%	.46%

Source: Maxim Integrated Products, Inc., 2005 Form 10-K.

The Black-Scholes option pricing model was developed for use in estimating the value of traded options that have no vesting restrictions and are fully transferable. In addition, option valuation models require the input of highly subjective assumptions, including the expected stock price volatility. Because the company's options have characteristics significantly different from those of traded options, and because changes in the subjective input assumptions can materially affect the estimate of value, in the opinion of management, the existing models do not provide a reliable single measure of the value of the options. The following is a summary of weighted average grant values generated by application of the Black-Scholes model:

	Weighted Average Grant Date for the Years Ended		
	June 25, 2005	June 26, 2004	June 28, 2003
Stock Option Plans	$12.08	$15.63	$10.25
Employee Stock Participation Plans	$11.99	$11.63	$ 6.23

Source: Maxim Integrated Products, Inc., 2005 Form 10-K.

As required under *SFAS 148,* the reported net income and earnings per share have been presented to reflect the impact had the company been required to include the amortization of the Black-Scholes option value as an expense. The adjusted amounts are as follows:

	For the Years Ended		
	June 25, 2005	June 26, 2004	June 28, 2003
Net income—as reported	$540,837	$419,752	$309,601
Deduct: Total stock-based employee			
compensation expense			
determined under the fair value			
method, net of tax	155,904	134,734	139,684

(continued)

	For the Years Ended		
	June 25, 2005	June 26, 2004	June 28, 2003
Net income—pro forma	$384,933	$285,018	$169,917
Basic earnings per share—pro forma	$ 1.18	$ 0.87	$ 0.53
Diluted earnings per share—pro forma	$ 1.13	$ 0.82	$ 0.50

Source: Maxim Integrated Products, Inc., 2005 Form 10-K.

Role of Stock Options

At JP Morgan's Annual Technology Conference, John Gifford stated:

We are the innovative leader in mixed-signal analog in the world. We intend to continue to be. We got here and we will go forward because we have been able to collect and will continue to collect the best engineers in the world. They are world class. If you're not world class, you cannot do these things I have been talking about.

We cannot hire them out of college. The ones we do hire, it takes five years to train, and there is a huge dropout rate. We need to recruit and continue to recruit and also retain and collect engineers.

Stock options are important to do that. The cost of options to our shareholders is approximately, without taking into account the repurchasing of options by the company, about 4% a year. That is equivalent to—that is paid for if we grow at 25.8% instead of 25%. We do repurchase shares in the past. That has reduced the dilutive effect to less than 2%.

As always, we are completely committed to increasing your equity. It is a religion with us because that increases our value and our employees' value, and we cannot do that without taking care of our customers. And we know that if we provide security for our people, both of the two things at the top will happen. We are a very competitive group of people, and we intend to be even more important going forward.[5]

Questions

1. Why are stock options important to the operating effectiveness of companies like Maxim? Are their stock option grants a form of compensation?
2. How might changes in the assumptions Maxim uses in its option pricing model influence the grant date valuations?
3. How would you handle stock option grants in (a) measuring Maxim's performance and (b) valuing its equity? Do you think Wall Street should ignore options?
4. Gifford suggests free cash flow (cash flow from operations less capital investments) as a better indicator of Maxim's performance than net income. Do you agree?
5. Do you believe the tone and substance of Gifford's statements communicating his view of net income (after expensing stock options) is appropriate for a CEO?
6. Do you believe the requirement to expense stock options will change the way employees are compensated? For example, will restricted stock grants and cash bonuses become more popular? How should you account for these alternative forms of compensation?
7. Do you believe the Financial Accounting Standards Board has adopted the best measure of stock option expense?

[5] JP Morgan 33rd Annual Technology Conference.

Case 9–5

New Private Banks in India

Size of Promoters' Equity:

Generally, when a firm is incorporated, it kick-starts its operations with something called Issued Capital, also called promoter's contribution, which is nothing but the amount of money the founders bring in at the time of start of business. Subsequent to bringing this equity capital, a firm can raise money through debt or other routes. This issued equity capital goes up naturally every year by the amount of undistributed business profits that are ploughed back in the business after distributing dividends. This can also go up by issuing shares to the public at large either by diluting the stake of promoters or by issuing fresh shares to the new set of investors. In either case, the promoter's stake will go down after every round of raising equity capital.

In Indian banking space, recently during the tenure of Dr. Raghuram Rajan, the ex-central banker, many entities were given a banking license after a fairly long due diligence process. Since these entities had the largest shares held by the promoter's or their group companies, it was recommended that they should bring down their equity stake in the banks below 20% in a phased manner in a predefined timeline, a fixed time (5 years) from the date of allotment of a banking license. Whereas, the existing large private banks are majorly foreign owned, the new ones are finding it difficult to meet this requirement of diluting their stakes to 20% or less. The objective of such kind of rules is that diverse ownership would prevent concentration of power and that would lead to better governance but what is being observed is that such shareholding dilution primarily ends up with foreign investors. India's four of the top five *banks* are majorly foreign owned. The foreign ownership in HDFC *Bank* is around 72 percent, ICICI *Bank* (60 percent), Axis *Bank* (52 percent), IndusInd *Bank* (73 percent) and Kotak Mahindra *Bank* (47 percent).

The reason why the Central Bank is insisting on reduction in promoter's equity stake is not very difficult to understand. The Central bankers are not worried without a reason. There have been cases in the past where banks have loaned to their own promoter's group companies violating Central Bank norms and putting at huge risk the depositor's money. The erstwhile Bank of Rajasthan, owned by the Tayal Group had an exposure of more than 40% to its own group companies. When such gross violations were noticed, the bank almost went down and was merged with a much strong and large bank, ICICI Bank. There are many such instances across the world where such conflict of interest has created serious problems for the depositors and the state had to intervene pushing tax payer's money to save these banks. Right now, both Kotak Bank and Bandhan Bank are facing significant challenges to meet this equity dilution norm of the Central Bank, but performance-wise they are excellent banks with healthy returns and fundamentally much cleaner balance sheets than their counterparts.

On the whole, it is a very interesting phenomenon because generally, we would like promoter involvement to be there in the company once it starts growing big and therefore their stakes should be high so that they take an active interest in taking forward the company. But in the case of banks, we want it the other way round. Therefore, estimating the optimal amount of promoter's equity in a firm is not a very simple task and will depend on multiple factors.

Questions

1. Why is promoter's stake such a significant variable in valuation, image and overall market sentiments of a firm?
2. Why would the requirement be slightly different in the case of a bank or a financial institution?
3. Bring out the merits and demerits of a large promoter holding (more than 60%) in some firm vis-a-vis a smaller holding (say less than 20%).

Other Items That Affect Net Income and Owners' Equity

Owners' equity consists of four components: common stock, preferred stock, retained earnings, and accumulated items that are direct debits or credits to owners' equity rather than to net income. The preceding chapters discussed the accounting treatment of many transactions that affect owners' equity either directly or by the process of closing the Net Income account to Retained Earnings. This chapter completes the more detailed discussion of income statement and balance sheet items that began in Chapter 5. It discusses the treatment of nonowner transactions that directly change owners' equity and its disclosure requirements. Also discussed is the accounting for extraordinary items, discontinued operations, accounting changes, accounting errors, foreign currency translation adjustments, and derivatives. How each of these items affects net income and ultimately owners' equity and its components is covered also.

Total and Other Nonowner Changes in Owners' Equity

The FASB and IASB require companies to report each accounting period's **total nonowner changes in owners' equity** and to disclose the details of its measurement.[1] This figure is the sum of the period's net income and the changes in the balances of those items that affect owners' equity directly that do not involve transactions with owners (collectively referred to as **other nonowner changes in owners' equity**).[2]

---

[1] "Reporting Comprehensive Income," *FASB Statement No. 130.* "Presentation of Financial Statements," *IAS No. 1.*

[2] *FASB Statement No. 130* and *IAS No. 1* refer to the total of this sum as *comprehensive income*. This caption is misleading. It implies by its name and its elements (net income plus other nonowner changes in owners' equity) that it is a superior number to net income. This is not the case. Many commentators on the *Statement's* exposure draft expressed this view to the FASB, which responded by retaining the term *comprehensive income* in the final *Statement* while giving corporations the right to select their own descriptive caption. The caption adopted for this book is one suggested by the FASB as a possible alternative to comprehensive income.

ILLUSTRATION 10–1 Total and Other Nonowner Changes in Owners' Equity

	Total	Total Nonowner Changes in Owners' Equity	Retained Earnings	Accumulated Other Nonowner Changes in Owners' Equity	Common Stock	Paid-In Total Capital
BASEL CORPORATION Statement of Changes in Owners' Equity Year Ended December 31, 2010 (in thousands)						
Beginning balance	$132,457		$ 99,111	$2,502	$10,000	$20,844
Total nonowner changes in owners' equity						
Net income	6,034	$6,034	6,034			
Other nonowner changes in owners' equity, net of tax:						
Unrealized gains on securities, net of reclassification adjustment (see disclosure below)	702	702				
Other nonowner changes in owners' equity	702	702				
Total nonowner changes in owners' equity		$6,736				
Dividends declared on common stock	(3,000)		(3,000)			
Ending balance	$136,193		$102,145	$3,204	$10,000	$20,844
Disclosure of reclassification amount:						
Unrealized holding gains arising during period		$ 802				
Less: Reclassification adjustment for gains included in net income		(100)				
Net unrealized gains on securities		$702				

These items include the accumulated balances of unrealized gains and losses on available-for-sale securities (discussed in Chapter 5), foreign currency–denominated net investment translation adjustments, gains and losses on certain derivatives (these latter two topics are discussed in this chapter), and several other items not discussed in this book.[3]

Companies have considerable leeway in how they present and label their nonowner changes in owners' equity disclosures. Illustration 10–1 employs a statement of changes in owners' equity display to satisfy the FASB's requirement. As shown in the illustration, the Basel Corporation's total nonowner changes in owners' equity is $6,736,000. This figure is the sum of net income ($6,034,000) and unrealized gain on securities, net of reclassification adjustments ($702,000). The reclassification adjustment shown at the bottom of the illustration indicates that the Basel Corporation had unrealized gains on its available-for-sale securities during the period ($802,000). These unrealized gains are directly credited to owners' equity.

[3] For a list of these highly technical additional items, see *FASB Statement No. 130.*

In addition, the corporation sold some of its securities and realized a gain, some part of which had previously been included as unrealized gains in the beginning accumulated other nonowner changes in equity balance ($2,502,000). To avoid double accounting, the previously recorded unrealized gain related to the sold securities ($100,000) must be deducted (a debit entry) from owners' equity and included as part of the total realized gain recognized in net income (a credit entry). The owners' equity section of the Basel Corporation's balance sheet would report only the ending balances of the last four columns of Illustration 10–1.

FASB Statement No. 130 and *IAS No. 1* were issued in response to what was perceived to be the concerns of some financial statement users about the increasing number of items being taken directly to equity and the effort required to analyze these items. It is difficult to see how *FASB Statement No. 130* solves this problem by requiring disclosure of items that were already disclosed and a sum of net income and the changes in the accumulated balances of these items, which has little, if any, analytical or economic significance. It is anticipated that net income, rather than total nonowner changes in owners' equity, will be used in most situations requiring a bottom-line earnings figure.

Discussed next are four display requirements of the FASB and IASB that do have considerable information value to financial statement users.

Nonoperating Items

To the extent feasible, the income statement should show the results of the year's normal results from continuing operations separately from those parts of the business that are to be discontinued and special and presumably nonrecurring events that affected net income and retained earnings. This permits the reader to see more clearly the profitability of normal ongoing activities. This section describes four types of transactions that are reported separately from the revenues and expenses of recurring operations: extraordinary items, discontinued operations, changes in accounting principles, and adjustments to retained earnings. The first three of these affect net income for the period, whereas the fourth does not. The method of reporting these four types of transactions on a statement of income and retained earnings is shown in Illustration 10–2. (Notes A and B are not given here. They would explain the two items in some detail.)

Extraordinary Items

At one time, companies had considerable latitude in deciding on the types of transactions that should be classified as extraordinary. Companies reported a variety of losses as "extraordinary" in the hope that readers would regard them as abnormal and not likely to recur. The publication of *APB Opinion No. 30* greatly reduced this discretion.[4] Today extraordinary items are rare.

APB Opinion No. 30 requires that in order to qualify as an extraordinary item, an event must satisfy two criteria:

1. The event must be *unusual;* it should be highly abnormal and unrelated to, or only incidentally related to, the ordinary activities of the entity.
2. The event must occur *infrequently;* it should be of a type that would not reasonably be expected to recur in the foreseeable future.

---

[4] "Reporting the Results of Operations," *APB Opinion No. 30.* See also "Reporting the Results of Operations," *APB Opinion No. 9.*

ILLUSTRATION 10–2 Separation of Continuing Operations Income from Other Items

BASEL CORPORATION Condensed Statement of Income and Retained Earnings Year Ended December 31, 2010 (in thousands)		
Net sales and other revenue		$60,281
Expenses		46,157
Income from continuing operations before income taxes		14,124
Provision for income taxes		5,650
Income from continuing operations		8,474
Discontinued operations (Note A):		
Loss from operations of Division X (less applicable income taxes of $320)	$480	
Loss on disposal of Division X (less applicable income taxes of $640)	960	(1,440)
Extraordinary loss (less applicable income taxes of $525) (Note B)		(1,000)
Net income		$6,034

The words of these criteria do not convey their narrowness as clearly as do the illustrations that are used to explain them. The following gains and losses are specifically *not* extraordinary:

1. Write-down or write-off of accounts receivable, inventory, or intangible assets.
2. Gains or losses from changes in the value of foreign currency.
3. Gains or losses on disposal of a segment of a business (discussed in the next section).
4. Gains or losses from the disposal of fixed assets.
5. Effects of a strike.

Accounting Treatment

In those rare cases in which extraordinary gains or losses can be identified, they are reported separately on the income statement below "income from continuing operations," as shown in Illustration 10–2. The amount reported is the net amount after the income tax effect of the item has been taken into account.

Example

If a company had an extraordinary loss of $1 million, its taxable income presumably would be reduced by $1 million. At an income tax rate of 40 percent, its income tax would be reduced by $400,000, and the ultimate effect on net income would therefore be only $600,000.

The IASB took a different approach than that adopted by the IASB to resolve the extraordinary items controversy. The IASB eliminated the concept of extraordinary items and prohibited their presentation in the income statement.[5]

Pro Forma Earnings

In recent years, many companies have highlighted in supplemental disclosures what they call pro forma earnings (in contrast to the reported net income figure). Pro forma earnings exclude certain items included in the measurement of net income, such as

[5] "Presentation of Financial Statements," *IAS No. 1.*

restructuring charges and impairment of goodwill. Sometimes other names are used to describe pro forma earnings. These include "operating earnings" and "recurring earnings." The Securities and Exchange Commission requires that pro forma earnings not be misleading and not exclude recurring items in their calculation. Managements publish pro forma earnings in the belief they are better indicators of their performance and are more useful to investors than their company's reported net income.

Discontinued Operations

Another type of transaction that, if material, is reported separately on the income statement is the gain or loss from the discontinuance of a division or other identifiable segment of the company.[6] The transaction must involve a whole business unit, as contrasted with the disposition of an individual asset or discontinuance of one product in a product line. Discontinuance may occur by abandoning the segment and selling off the remaining assets or by selling the whole segment as a unit to some other company. In the former case, a loss is likely; in the latter case, there may be either a gain or a loss, depending on how attractive the segment is to the other company.

If a loss is expected from discontinuing a segment, the loss is recorded in the period in which the *decision* to discontinue is made, which may be earlier than the period in which the actual transaction is consummated. Usually, the amount of this loss is an estimate. This estimate may be quite complicated, for it must take into account (1) the estimated revenues and expenses of the discontinued segment during the period in which it continues to be operated by the company; (2) the estimated proceeds of the sale; and (3) the book value of the assets that will be written off when the segment is disposed of. If a gain is expected, it is not recognized until it is realized, which ordinarily is the disposal date.

Accounting Treatment

The amounts related to discontinued operations are reported after their income tax effect has been taken into account. As shown in Illustration 10–2, two amounts are reported:

1. The net income or loss attributable to the operations of the segment until it is sold.
2. The estimated net gain or loss on disposal after taking account of all aspects of the sale, including the amount received and the write-off of assets that are not sold.

Change in Accounting Principles

The third type of nonrecurring item reported on the income statement is the effect of a change in accounting principles. Sometimes a change is required by a new FASB or IASB *Statement*. In most other circumstances, the consistency concept requires that a company use the same accounting principles from one year to the next. But if a company has a sound reason for doing so, it may occasionally shift from one generally accepted principle to another one. For example, several methods of depreciation are acceptable; if a company has a sound reason for doing so, it may shift from one method to another.

Voluntary change in an accounting principle should be accounted for retrospectively and all prior periods should be restated as if the newly adopted accounting policy had always been used, except when retroactive application is impracticable. When the effects of retroactive application of an accounting change for particular prior years are not determinable, the cumulative effect on prior years of retroactive application should be recorded directly in opening retained earnings (or other balance sheet caption as appropriate) of the first year presented on the new basis. When an accounting change is made

---

[6] *APB Opinion No. 30.* "Non-Current Assets Hold for Sale and Discontinued Operations," *IFRS No. 5.*

in other than the first interim period, the change should be reported as if it were adopted at the beginning of the fiscal year.[7]

Errors

Errors are mathematical mistakes, mistakes in the application of accounting principles, or oversight or misuse of facts that existed at the time the financial statements were prepared. Corrections of errors must be made retrospectively.[8]

The remainder of this chapter discusses the accounting for personnel costs (which affects net income and ultimately retained earnings), income taxes (which affects both net income and ultimately retained earnings, and the other nonowner changes in owners' equity component of owners' equity), and foreign currency translation adjustments (which affects the other nonowner changes in owners' equity component of owners' equity).

Personnel Costs

Personnel costs include wages and salaries earned by employees and other costs related to their services. (Customarily, the word *wages* refers to the compensation of employees who are paid on a piece-rate, hourly, daily, or weekly basis, whereas the word *salaries* refers to compensation expressed in longer terms; we use *wages* to denote either category.) The effect on the accounting records of earning and paying wages is more complicated than merely debiting Wages Expense and crediting Cash. This is because when wages are earned or paid, certain other transactions occur almost automatically.

Employees are rarely paid the gross amount of wages they earn, since from their gross earnings the following must be deducted:

1. An amount representing the employee's FICA (Federal Insurance Contribution Act) contributions for Social Security and Medicare coverage.
2. An amount withheld from gross earnings to apply toward the employee's personal state and federal income taxes.
3. Deductions for charitable contributions, savings plans, union dues, and a variety of other items.

None of these deductions represents a cost *to the employer*. In the case of the tax deductions, the employer is acting as a collection agent for the state and federal governments. The withholding of the tax amounts and their subsequent transfer to the government does not affect net income or owners' equity. Rather, the withholding creates a liability, and the subsequent transfer of the taxes to the government pays off this liability. Similarly, the employer is acting as a collection agent in the case of the other deductions. The employee is paid the net amount after these deductions have been taken.

When wages are earned, certain other costs are automatically created. The employer must pay a tax equal in amount to the employee's FICA tax, and the employer also must pay an additional percentage of the employee's pay for the *unemployment insurance tax*. The *employer's* share of these taxes *is* an element of cost.

---

[7] "Accounting Changes and Error Corrections," *FASB Statement No. 154*. "Accounting Policies, Changes in Accounting Estimates and Errors," *IAS No. 8*. Most accounting estimate changes are applied prospectively.
[8] "Accounting Changes and Error Corrections," *FASB Statement No. 154*. " Accounting Policies, Changes in Accounting Estimates and Errors," *IAS No. 8*.

Example

If an employee with three dependents earned $600 for work in a certain week, and $45.90 for FICA tax contribution and $63.00 for withholding tax was deducted from this $600, the employee's take-home pay would be $491.10. (Other possible deductions are omitted.) The *employer* also would incur an expense of $45.90 for FICA and an additional expense of, say, $54 for federal and state unemployment insurance taxes, or a total of $99.90 for employment taxes.

The journal entries for these transactions are as follows:

1. When wages are earned:

Wages Cost[9]	600.00	
Wages Payable		600.00
Employment Tax Cost	99.90	
FICA Taxes Payable		45.90
Unemployment Taxes Payable		54.00

2. When the employee is paid:

Wages Payable.	600.00	
Cash.		491.10
FICA Taxes Payable		45.90
Withholding Taxes Payable		63.00

3. When the government is paid:

FICA Taxes Payable (45.90 _ 45.90)	91.80	
Unemployment Taxes Payable	54.00	
Withholding Taxes Payable	63.00	
Cash.		208.80

In practice, the above entries would be made for all employees as a group. The government does require, however, that a record be kept of the amount of FICA tax and withholding tax accumulated for each employee.

In addition to cash wages or salaries, most organizations provide **fringe benefits** to their employees. Among these are pensions, life insurance, health care, and vacations. Such fringe benefits may amount to as much as 40 percent of payroll. These amounts are costs of the period in which the employee worked, just as are the cash earnings. Accounting for many of these fringe benefits is relatively straightforward. However, that is not the case with pensions.

Pensions

Payments that employees will receive after they retire are called **pensions.** Pension costs are typically in the range of 5 to 10 percent of payroll. In some organizations, employees contribute part of their pension cost, and this cost is a payroll deduction that is treated just like the other deductions mentioned above. It does not involve a cost to the organization. The employer's promise to pay pension benefits *is* a cost to the employer, just as are other fringe benefits.

In the United States, pension plans are regulated under the Employee Retirement Income Security Act (ERISA). The provisions of this act are such that, in most cases, pension plans must be **funded.** This means that the company must make pension plan contributions in cash, stock, or other assets to a bank, insurance company, or other trustee for the pension fund. However, the law does not require that a plan be *fully* funded.

---

[9] As pointed out previously, manufacturing labor costs are a product cost debited to Work in Process Inventory. Other labor costs are period costs debited to Wage and Salary Expense. We use the account Wages Cost here to include either of these.

That is, at a given point in time, the plan assets do not have to be sufficient to provide all future plan benefits that have already been earned by employees if no further contributions were made to the plan.

The trustee invests the contributions and pays pension benefits directly to employees after they retire. The pension fund is therefore a separate entity, with its own set of accounts.

Types of Pension Plans

There are two general types of pension plans: (1) defined contribution plans and (2) defined benefit plans.

In a **defined contribution plan,** the employer contributes to the pension fund an agreed amount each year for each employee, often determined as a percentage of the employee's salary. The employee's pension benefits thus depend on how much has been accumulated (contributions plus gains on the investments of those contributions) for her or him as of the date of retirement. There is no promise about how much those benefits (*outputs* of the plan) will be; the agreement relates only to plan contributions (*inputs)*. Thus, by definition, a defined contribution plan is never underfunded or over-funded. In such plans, the organization's pension cost for a year is simply the agreed-on contribution. The entry recording this cost is

```
Pension Cost . . . . . . . . . . . . . . . . . . . . . . . . 100,000
    Cash . . . . . . . . . . . . . . . . . . . . . . . . . .          100,000
```

In a **defined benefit plan** the employer agrees to contribute to the pension fund an amount large enough so that employees will receive a specified amount of monthly benefits after retirement. This amount depends on the employee's years of service before retirement, the employee's average earnings during some period immediately preceding retirement, and possibly other factors. Thus, this plan's benefits (outputs) are agreed on and the company must determine the amount of contributions (inputs) necessary to provide these benefits.

Pension Cost

The determination of the amount of annual pension cost for a defined benefit plan is extremely complicated. *FASB Statement No. 87*[10] is 132 pages long, including 11 pages of definitions. While *IAS No. 19* is not as long, it is just as complicated.[11] We will provide only a conceptual overview of these matters.

To calculate its pension contribution in a given year, the company must first make a number of estimates: how many years employees will work until they retire; employee turnover; average earnings on which the pension benefits will be calculated; how many years the employee will live after retirement; probable increases in benefit payments due to inflation, new union contracts, or other factors; and the amount that the pension fund will earn on funds invested in it. The pension calculations incorporating these estimates are based on the present value concept.

A company's pension cost is the sum of a number of elements. The year's **service cost** element is the present value of the future benefits employees have earned during the year. The year's **interest cost** element is the amount by which the present value of the plan's beginning-of-the-year obligations are projected to increase during the year.

---

[10] "Employers' Accounting for Pensions," *FASB Statement No. 87. FASB Statement No. 87* has been amended by a series of subsequent FASB pronouncements including "Employers' Accounting for Defined Pension Benefit and Other Postretirement Plans," *FASB Statement No. 158.*
[11] "Employee Benefits," *IAS No. 19.*

Offsetting these two cost elements is the **assumed return on plan assets element**, which is the gain assumed by management based on the pension asset's expected return over the long run (assumed return percentage times plan assets).

The fourth element of pension cost relates to the amortization of several other pension-related items. One of these is the **prior service cost element**. This cost arises if a new pension plan is instituted and it takes into account employees' service prior to the initiation of the new plan. Prior service cost also can arise if a plan is amended or "sweetened"—the terms are made more generous with the result that the contributions to date are inadequate to meet the amended obligations. Rather than having the cost of such a "sweetening" impact only the year in which the plan is amended, the present value of the added benefits is amortized over the expected service life of the employees affected by the amendment.

The year's **net pension cost** is the algebraic sum of the four elements just described: service cost plus interest cost minus assumed return plus amortization. (In some situations, additional elements may be included in the pension cost, but they are not discussed in this book.) Not surprisingly, most companies engage an **actuary,** a professional who specializes in such matters, to make all of the estimates and calculations that eventually boil down to this one amount for net pension cost.[12]

Accounting Entries

The year's pension cost for a defined benefit plan is an adjusting entry, analogous to the entry for accrued interest expense payable. If the net pension cost for the year were $500,000, the entry would be

Net Pension Cost	500,000	
Accrued Pension Cost (a liability)		500,000

If a subsequent contribution of $450,000 were made to the plan by the employer, the entry would be

Accrued Pension Cost	450,000	
Cash		450,000

Note that the remaining $50,000 accrued pension cost liability is related to how much of the employer's accrued pension cost has not as yet been contributed to the separate pension plan entity. If the employer has contributed *more* than the amount of its accrued pension cost, then the excess is recorded as Prepaid Pension Cost, an asset.

Employers must recognize the funded status of their employee defined benefit plans and other postretirement plans (see below)—measured as the difference between the fair value of plan assets and the benefit obligation—in their balance sheets.

Disclosure

In addition to reporting the period's net pension cost and unfunded plan position, for each of its defined benefit plans, a company must disclose a number of detailed items, such as each of the four components of net pension cost and the elements of the calculation of a plan's funding position. These details are reported in a note to the financial statements. Also, the plan itself must make certain disclosures as an entity.[13]

---

[12] The FASB uses the term *net pension cost* rather than *net pension expense* for the same reason we used Wages Cost rather than Wages Expense in the previous section: Pension costs for manufacturing employees may be capitalized as part of the cost of inventory rather than treated as a period expense.
[13] "Accounting and Reporting by Defined Benefit Pension Plans," *FASB Statement No. 35.* "Accounting and Reporting by Retirement Benefit Plans," *IAS No. 26.*

Other Postretirement Benefits

Employees often receive other retirement benefits (**other postretirement benefits**), such as health care and life insurance benefits. The substance of the accounting for these benefits is similar to that for pensions: The total costs that will be incurred by retirees is estimated and a portion of the present value of these costs is charged as an expense in each year that an employee works.[14] For health care costs, this requires estimating employees' needs for postretirement health care services as well as the future cost of such services. These are even more difficult and uncertain estimates than those required for pensions.

For many companies, the requirement to accrue other retirement costs has resulted in a huge obligation for unfunded and unrecognized future nonpension postretirement benefits that employees already had earned.

Compensated Absences

In some organizations, any vacation and sick leave days that were *earned* this year but *not used* this year can be carried forward and used at some future time. If the amount can be reasonably estimated, the cost of these **future compensated absences** is treated as an expense of the period in which the future absence time is *earned.* The offsetting credit is to an accrued liability account. When the employee is later compensated, the liability account is debited and Cash is credited.[15]

Income Taxes

To the beginning accounting student, accounting for income taxes might seem to be straightforward. One might think that all that is involved is calculating the year's income tax liability—the year's tax bill—and then debiting this amount to Income Tax Expense and crediting it to Income Taxes Liability. (Some companies call the tax expense account **Provision for Income Taxes.** Also, the liability account may be called **Taxes Payable.**) Unfortunately, income tax accounting is not so simple. As a result, the tax expense of most corporations is the sum of two components: **current income tax expense** (this year's tax bill) and **deferred income tax expense** (see below).

Book-to-Tax Differences

For most revenue and expense transactions, the amount used in calculating taxable income for income tax purposes is the same as the amount used in calculating pre-tax income in the income statement as prepared for shareholders. (The term **taxable income** always means income as reported to the taxing authorities; **pretax accounting income,** or **pretax book income,** refers to the amount reported in the income statement that is prepared in accordance with GAAP.) Taxable income and pretax book income are affected in the same way by most revenue and expense transactions. However, *most* is not the same as *all* transactions. Those transactions that are *not* reported in the same way for book and tax purposes cause a difference between pretax book income and taxable income and the carrying amounts of assets and liabilities for book and tax purposes.

Example

A company buys personal computers costing over $15,000 for each for its managers. For tax purposes, it elects to use an accelerated depreciation method to depreciate the computers. For financial reporting purposes, it decides to use the straight-line method. As a result, in the first year, the depreciation charge for tax purposes will be higher than the depreciation

---

[14] "Employers' Accounting for Postretirement Benefits Other Than Pensions," *FASB Statement No. 106* and *FASB Statement No. 158.*
[15] "Accounting for Compensated Absences," *FASB Statement No. 43.*

charge for financial reporting purposes. If all other items are accounted for in the same way for tax and financial reporting purposes, the company's taxable income for this year will be lower than its book pretax income. In addition, at the end of the year, the net carrying amount of the computers (cost less accelerated depreciation charge) on the company's tax books will be lower than their net carrying amount (cost less straight-line depreciation charge) on the company's financial reporting books. (The difference between these two carrying amounts is the cumulative difference between the book and tax depreciation charges.)

It is these **book-to-tax balance sheet differences** that create the complications in accounting for income taxes.

Why the Difference?

Before further explaining these complications, we should consider why the difference between taxable income and book income and the tax basis and book value of balance sheet items arises. The answer essentially is that the process of income taxation has little to do with the reporting of financial information to shareholders and other interested outside parties. Income tax laws are formulated, in part, to encourage certain kinds of behavior by taxpayers on the premise that such behavior is good for the economy as a whole. For example, the accelerated depreciation provisions of corporate tax law are intended to encourage investment in fixed assets. By contrast, GAAP is formulated to accomplish the objectives of financial reporting (described in Chapter 1), including providing information that is useful to investors and creditors in making rational investment and credit decisions.

As a specific example of the different perspectives of taxation and financial reporting, consider depreciation. If a corporation acquires an asset that qualifies for accelerated depreciation over six years for tax purposes, the corporation should take advantage of that provision of the law; it should depreciate the asset as rapidly as the law permits. Assuming nonincreasing tax rates over time, the present value of the tax savings associated with reporting a dollar of depreciation expense now is greater than the present value of the savings if the expense is reported in the future. On the other hand, if the corporation believes that the asset will give up its benefits in a *level stream* over an *eight-year* period, the depreciation method customarily used in financial reporting is the straight-line method, which, for an eight-year life, would have an annual rate of 12.5 percent. Over the useful life of the asset, this method will provide the appropriate *matching* of the asset's original cost with the benefits received from using the asset. Thus, the company would be completely justified in using straight-line depreciation for book purposes while at the same time using accelerated depreciation for tax purposes.

Some critics of business like to suggest that there is something cynical or evil about these book versus tax differences. But there is nothing wrong with a corporation's (or an individual's) doing everything legally permitted to reduce income taxes. As Supreme Court Justice Learned Hand wrote:[16]

> Over and over again courts have said there is nothing sinister in so arranging one's affairs as to keep taxes as low as possible. Everybody does so, rich or poor, and all do right, for nobody owes any public duty to pay more than the law demands; taxes are enforced exactions, not voluntary contributions. To demand more in the name of morals is mere cant.

Permanent and Temporary Differences

There are two important classes of book-to-tax differences. First, the income tax regulations prohibit certain deductions from taxable income that are expenses under GAAP, and they permit certain revenue items to be excluded from taxable income.

[16] *Commissioner v. Newman.*

For example, fines are an expense for book purposes but are not tax deductible, and interest revenue on municipal bonds is income for book purposes but it is not taxable. These exceptions create **permanent differences** between pretax book income and tax income. The differences are permanent in the sense that they will not reverse or "turn around" in some subsequent year.

In other situations, the income tax regulations permit or require revenues or expenses to be recognized in a *different period* than the recognition method used in financial reporting. For example, the tax law permits certain types of business to use a form of the installment method for recognizing revenues, even though the company may use the sales method for financial reporting. Another example is estimated warranty expense; GAAP requires that this be accrued in the period in which the warranted items are sold, whereas the tax law does not permit a deduction until the period in which warranty costs are actually incurred. These book-to-tax accounting recognition differences lead to **temporary differences.** These differences *do* reverse or "turn around" in later periods. For example, for a given installment sale contract, the total amount of revenue recognized for book (delivery method) and tax (installment method) purposes is the same over the *entire life* of the contract, but the amount recognized in *any one year* for book and tax purposes will differ if the installment contract collections span more than one year.

No special accounting problem arises in the case of permanent differences. For a "tax preference," such as the municipal bond interest exclusion, the amount reported to shareholders as income tax expense of the current period is simply lower than it would be if the preferential treatment did not exist. Permanent differences lower the effective tax rate that is applied to pretax book income. For an unallowable deduction, such as a fine, the reported income tax expense will be higher than if the expense could also be deducted for tax purposes.

By contrast, temporary differences do create complications in accounting for income tax expense. The reason has to do with the matching concept and not misleading statement users. The FASB and IASB feel that in each period a company's financial statements should reflect the tax consequences of *all* of the events recognized in the financial statements that have current tax or taxable temporary difference consequences.[17] This means that, ignoring permanent differences and for the purposes of illustrating the FASB and IASB point of view, the amount of reported income tax expense is the amount of tax that would be due *if* the amount of pretax book income had also been reported to the government as taxable income. (As discussed later, this is not the way deferred taxes are actually measured under GAAP and IFRS.) For example, assuming a 40 percent tax rate, if in some year a corporation reports $1 million pretax income, then it also should report $400,000 income tax expense, *irrespective of the amount of the company's actual tax obligation for that year.* The FASB and IASB believe that it would be misleading or confusing to users of the income statement if an amount of income tax expense other than $400,000 were reported when $1 million pretax income is reported and the tax rate is 40 percent.

Deferred Income Taxes

It might occur to the reader that if Income Tax Expense is debited without regard to the company's *actual* tax bill but Cash must be credited based on the payment of that actual bill, then the dual aspect principle of accounting will be violated—less formally, "the books won't balance."

---

[17] "Accounting for Income Taxes," *FASB Statement No. 109.* "Income Taxes," *IAS No. 12.*

Example

Because of temporary differences, in 2010 a corporation reported $1 million pretax income to its shareholders and an income tax expense of $400,000 but only $800,000 taxable income to the taxing authorities. Thus, its income tax expense was $400,000, but its actual income taxes were only $320,000 ($800,0000 * .40). Assume that these taxes have been paid (i.e., the taxes have all been credited to Cash; none is still a credit in Taxes Payable). Since an expense reduces Retained Earnings, we can think of these transactions solely in terms of their impact on the balance sheet:

Assets	=	Liabilities	+	Owners' equity
Cash – 320,000 (reflecting actual tax bill payments)				Retained Earnings – 400,000 (reflecting tax expense used to measure book income)

Question: Is the missing $80,000 ($400,000 _ $320,000) credit entry a further reduction in assets, or is it an increase in a liability account or an owners' equity account?

The answer is that the credit entry is an increase in a liability account. In journal entry form, the combined income tax expense and income tax payment transaction is

Income Tax Expense—Current 320,000		
Income Tax Expense—Deferred 80,000		
Cash	320,000	
Deferred Income Taxes Liability	80,000	

Deferred Tax Measurement

FASB Statement No. 109 and *IAS No. 12* require that the *asset and liability method* (also called *balance sheet liability method)* be used to measure deferred income taxes.

The balance liability sheet method measures deferred income tax expense in two steps. First, the deferred income taxes liability or asset (discussed below) is calculated using the differences between the tax basis (remaining balance for income tax purposes) and book values of the individual taxable items on the corporate reporting balance sheet. (Remember the example given at the beginning of the income tax discussion.) Next, the deferred income tax expense is calculated. It is the change in the Deferred Income Taxes Liability account for the period. This procedure is demonstrated in Illustrations 10–4, 10–5, and 10–6 using the following $1 million asset example.

The example illustrates temporary differences created by the use of different depreciation methods for book and tax purposes, which is the most common source of timing differences in practice. Assume that a company purchased for $1 million a single depreciable asset. For tax purposes, it is depreciated over a five-year period using the years'-digits method (discussed in Chapter 7). For financial reporting purposes, the company depreciates the asset over a five-year period using a straight-line method with zero residual value. There are no other differences between the company's book and tax accounting. The company's income for tax and book purposes is $1 million each year, *before* subtracting depreciation and tax expense. Finally, assume that the applicable tax rate is 40 percent (this includes both federal and state taxes).[18]

Illustration 10–3 shows how the company would calculate its income taxes due to the government in each of the five years. Note how the company's tax depreciation charge falls each year, leading to higher taxable income and taxes due. If the company reported its taxes due to the government as its tax expense for financial reporting purposes, its profit after taxes (net income) would decline each year from $733,300 in 2010

---

[18] For the purpose of this illustration, we will ignore the income tax depreciation rules and methods discussed in Chapter 7.

ILLUSTRATION 10–3 Calculation of Taxes Due (thousands of dollars)

Year	Income before Depreciation and Taxes (1)	Depreciation Charge (2)*	Taxable Income (3)†	Taxes Due (at 40 percent rate) (4)‡
2010	$1,000.0	$ 333.3	$ 666.7	$ 266.7
2011	1,000.0	266.7	733.3	293.3
2012	1,000.0	200.0	800.0	320.0
2013	1,000.0	133.3	866.7	346.7
2014	1,000.0	66.7	933.3	373.3
	$5,000.0	$1,000.0	$4,000.0	$1,600.0

*Assets' original depreciable cost times years'-digits rate (⁵⁄₁₅ in 2010, ⁴⁄₁₅ in 2011, ³⁄₁₅ in 2012, ²⁄₁₅ in 2013, and ¹⁄₁₅ in 2014).
†Column (1) less column (2).
‡Column (3) times .4.

ILLUSTRATION 10–4 Tax Basis Calculation (thousands of dollars)

Year	Original Depreciable Cost (1)	Annual Tax Depreciation (2)*	Cumulative Tax Depreciation (3)†	Tax Basis (4)‡
2010	$1,000	$333.3	$ 333.3	$666.7
2011	1,000	266.7	600.0	400.0
2012	1,000	200.0	800.0	200.0
2013	1,000	133.3	933.3	66.7
2014	1,000	66.7	1,000.0	–0–

* Column (1) times years'-digits rate (⁵⁄₁₅ in 2010, ⁴⁄₁₅ in 2011, ³⁄₁₅ in 2012, ²⁄₁₅ in 2013, and ¹⁄₁₅ in 2014).
† Cumulative sum of column (2).
‡ Column (1) less column (3) (year-end balance).

($1 million – $266,700) to $626,700 in 2014 ($1 million – $373,300) as a consequence of its tax depreciation schedule. Thus, inherent in each year's net income is a future tax consequence that reduces future net income below the previous year's figure, making the current net income a misleading indication of future net income. Accounting for deferred taxes overcomes this problem by properly matching costs and revenues.

Illustration 10–4 shows the annual calculation of the $1 million asset's tax basis. The values in the last column are the asset's tax basis (undepreciated balance for tax purposes).

Illustration 10–5 presents the annual calculation of the $1 million asset's book value (undepreciated balance for financial reporting purposes).

Illustration 10–6 shows the calculation of the company's deferred income taxes liability (step number one) and deferred income tax expense (step number two). Column (3) in Illustration 10–6 is the key column. It shows the temporary differences between the $1 million asset's book value and tax basis. Using the balance sheet liability method, the deferred income taxes liability is 40 percent (the tax rate) of the values in this column [see column (4)]. The last column in Illustration 10–6, column (5), shows the annual change in the deferred income taxes liability balance. This change is the deferred income tax expense (credit) for the year.

ILLUSTRATION 10–5 Net Book Value Calculation (thousands of dollars)

Year	Original Book Cost (1)	Annual Tax Depreciation (2)*	Cumulative Book Depreciation (3)†	Net Book Value (4)‡
2010	$1,000.0	$200.0	$ 200.0	$800.0
2011	1,000.0	200.0	400.0	600.0
2012	1,000.0	200.0	600.0	400.0
2013	1,000.0	200.0	800.0	200.0
2014	1,000.0	200.0	1,000.0	–0–

* Column (1) times .2.
† Cumulative sum of column (2).
‡ Column (1) less column (3) (year-end balance).

ILLUSTRATION 10–6 Deferred Income Tax Liability and Deferred Income Tax Expense (credit) Calculation: Balance Sheet Method (thousands of dollars)

Year	Net Book Value (1)*	Tax Basis (2)†	Net Book Value Less Tax Basis (3)‡	Deferred Income Taxes Liability (4)§	Deferred Income Tax Expense (Credit) (5)ı
2010	$800.0	$666.7	$133.3	$53.3	$53.3
2011	600.0	400.0	200.0	80.0	26.7
2012	400.0	200.0	200.0	80.0	0.0
2013	200.0	66.7	133.3	53.3	(26.7)
2014	–0–	–0–	–0–	–0–	(53.3)

* See Illustration 10–5 Column (4) (year-end balance).
† See Illustration 10–4 Column (4) (year-end balance).
‡ Column (1) less column (2).
§ Column (3) times .4. (Beginning balance assumed to be zero.) Tax rate is 40 percent.
ı Change in column (4).

Accounting Entries

The actual income tax due for 2010 is calculated as in Illustration 10–3 and is recorded in the following journal entry (for 2010):

    Income Tax Expense—Current 266,700
        Income Taxes Payable   266,700

The 2010 income tax expense amount is then adjusted to reflect the income tax that should be matched with pretax accounting income. For 2010, this requires an addition of $53,300 to Income Tax Expense (Illustration 10–6), so the entry is

    Income Tax Expense—Deferred 53,300
        Deferred Income Taxes Liability   53,300

After this entry, Income Tax Expense totals $320,000, which is the amount reported on the income statement for 2010.

When the taxes are paid, the entry is[19]

    Income Taxes Payable 266,700
        Cash   266,700

---

[19] In practice, corporations must make estimated payments throughout the year, just as individuals do.

Combining all three 2010 entries, the *net* effect is as shown in this single entry:

Income Tax Expense 320,000		
Cash	266,700	
Deferred Income Taxes Liability	53,300	

Nature of Deferred Income Taxes Liability

Deferred Income Taxes is a liability account. It is shown separately from Income Tax Liability (or Taxes Payable), which is the amount actually owed the government at the time. Deferred Income Taxes is not a liability in the sense that the amount is an obligation owed to the government as of the date of the balance sheet. It is a liability only in the sense of a deferred credit to income. It is an amount that will reduce income tax expense in the years in which the temporary differences between book and tax accounting reverse (the years 2010–14 in Illustration 10–6).

For any year during the five-year period in the above $1 million asset example, the balance in Deferred Income Taxes Liability account can be thought of as an interest-free loan from the government that has resulted from Congress passing a tax law that allows accelerated depreciation for calculating taxable income rather than allowing only straight-line depreciation. For example, the deferred tax liability balance at the end of 2012 means that the company has been able to *postpone* (or defer) paying income taxes of $80,000 ($200,000 * .4) by taking advantage of the tax law's accelerated depreciation provision. This is like having an interest-free $80,000 loan, compared with what would be the case if straight-line depreciation had to be used for tax purposes.

Permanent Deferrals

As shown in Illustration 10–6, column (*4*), at the end of the life of the asset, the balance in the Deferred Income Taxes Liability account is zero. This is always the case with respect to a single asset. If, however, we drop the assumption that the company operates with only a single asset and make instead the more realistic assumption that a company acquires additional assets each year, a strange situation develops in the Deferred Income Taxes Liability account.

As long as the company grows in size, the credit balance in Deferred Income Taxes Liability continues to increase. Even if the company stops growing in size, a sizable credit balance remains in the account. This balance remains permanently; there will always be a credit balance in the Deferred Income Taxes Liability account unless the company stops acquiring assets (i.e., it begins to shrink).

Furthermore, since replacement costs of assets increase in periods of inflation, the credit balance will continue to grow even if the physical size of the company remains constant. For these reasons, many companies report a large deferred income taxes liability on their balance sheet. This is not an obligation owed to some outside party, and it is unlikely that the balance in the account ever will be eliminated, or even that it will decrease. The effective permanency of this increasing credit balance has led many companies to argue against deferred tax accounting.

Deferrals are not necessarily permanent, however. For example, for professional service firms such as architectural and consulting firms, the IRS has generally permitted recognizing revenues when clients pay their bills (the collection method), as opposed to when the firm has performed the services for the client. If a firm's revenues are growing, this results in an increasing balance of deferred taxes, because collections always lag behind the performance of work. However, if a firm were to cease operations, the full amount of the deferred taxes would come due as the clients for whom work had already been performed sent in their cash payments.

(A similar but less extreme effect occurs if the firm's revenues decrease, rather than the firm completely ceasing operations.) This phenomenon causes the FASB to believe that deferred taxes are indeed a liability. The FASB draws an analogy with an item that is clearly a liability—accounts payable. Even though the balance in Accounts Payable increases as a firm grows, there is turnover within the account—that is, old payables are paid (debits) as new ones are recorded (credits). Similarly, the fact that the balance in Deferred Income Taxes Liability is growing (or constant) does not mean that reversals of old deferrals are not taking place.

Deferred Tax Assets

In some circumstances, book-to-tax differences result in a deferred tax asset. For example, GAAP requires a company to charge estimated future warranty costs as an expense of the period in which the warranted goods are sold, but U.S. tax law does not permit deducting such costs until they actually are incurred. This means that an appliance manufacturer with increasing sales (assuming corresponding increasing warranty costs) will show an increasing balance in a deferred income taxes asset account; this happens because (other things being equal) each period's lower warranty costs on its tax return will result in higher taxable income than its pretax book income. Similarly, a magazine publisher is required for income tax purposes to recognize subscription payments when they are received, whereas GAAP requires that these prepayments be treated as a liability (Deferred Subscription Revenues). With a growing subscription base (or a constant base but increasing subscription prices), the publisher also will experience an increasing balance in a deferred income tax asset account, because each year's taxable income will be greater than its pretax book income.

Also giving rise to a deferred tax asset are **tax-loss carryforwards.** These are deductions or credits that a company cannot make use of on its current tax return that may be carried forward to reduce taxable income in a future year.

The amount of the deferred tax asset cannot exceed the amount of future tax benefits that the company actually expects to receive. If the company believes that "it is more likely than not (a likelihood of more than 50 percent) that some portion or all of the deferred tax assets will not be realized," a *valuation allowance* must be established to reduce the nominal amount of the deferred tax asset to its estimated realizable amount.

Recognition of a deferred tax asset (a debit entry) gives rise to a deferred tax credit. The deferred tax credit reduces the income tax expense. For any accounting period, the total deferred tax credit is equal to the change in the recognized deferred tax asset during the period.

Tax Rate Changes

The discussion of deferred taxes thus far has assumed that the tax rate would indefinitely remain constant. This assumption masked an issue in deferred tax accounting. We will state the issue in the form of two questions: (1) Should the amount of tax deferral caused by a temporary difference be based on the tax rate in effect when the difference arose or on the rate expected to be in effect when the difference reverses? (2) If corporate tax rates change, should deferred income taxes assets and liabilities be restated, based on the new rates?

The FASB's answer to these questions is that new deferrals are entered in the accounts based on the tax rates that currently enacted tax laws state will be in effect when the temporary differences will reverse. The balance in a deferred income taxes account is adjusted if a later change in the tax law changes the rates from those that were expected to apply. This adjustment affects reported (book) net income in the year in which the tax rate change is enacted; the adjustment is a component of income tax expense.

Example

A new tax law is passed that reduces the corporate income tax rate from 40 percent to 35 percent. This change requires that the balance in Deferred Income Taxes Liability be reduced from $680,700, which was calculated based on a 40 percent rate, to $595,613, a reduction of $85,087. The journal entry is

Deferred Income Taxes Liability 85,087

    Income Tax Expense—Deferred   85,087

Financial Statement Disclosure

The FASB requires that deferred tax asset and liability amounts be reported separately; they cannot be combined into a single net asset or net liability amount. Also, deferred tax assets and liabilities must be classified as current or noncurrent based on the classification of the related asset or liability for financial reporting. Thus, for example, a deferred tax liability related to fixed asset depreciation timing differences would be classified as noncurrent because the depreciable asset is noncurrent. On the other hand, a deferred tax liability relating to using the installment method for tax purposes would be classified as current (assuming the related installment receivables were classified as current).

In contrast to GAAP, IFRS does not permit the classification of deferred tax assets and liabilities as current assets and liabilities.[20]

Foreign Currency Accounting

Changes in the price of a foreign currency vis-à-vis the dollar—that is, fluctuating **exchange rates**— cause problems in preparing financial statements involving a foreign subsidiary.[21] These problems are foreign currency *translation* accounting problems. Also, whether or not a company has a foreign subsidiary, the company may engage in transactions with foreign entities; these transactions lead to foreign currency *transaction* accounting problems. Both types of problems are discussed below.

Foreign Currency Transactions

If an American firm buys or sells goods abroad or borrows from, or grants credit to, a foreign entity, the firm may experience a **foreign currency transaction** gain or loss as a result of exchange rate fluctuations between the date the transaction was entered into and the date cash is transmitted.

Example

Shipley Shoe Store received from an Italian manufacturer a shipment of shoes with an invoice for 50,000 euro (€). On the date the invoice was received and the transaction journalized, the U.S. dollar–euro exchange rate was $1.10 per euro, giving a $55,000 account payable for the shoes received. Thirty days later, when Shipley paid its bill in euro, the exchange rate had increased to $1.30 per euro. Thus, Shipley had to pay $65,000 to buy the required euro, and a currency exchange loss of $10,000 was realized. This would be accounted for as follows:

Accounts Payable 55,000

Loss on Foreign Exchange 10,000

    Cash.   65,000

---

[20] "Income Taxes," *IAS No. 12.*

[21] As will be explained in Chapter 12, a *subsidiary* is an entity controlled by another entity, called its *parent.* Consolidated financial statements report on the parent and all of its subsidiaries as if they were a single economic entity.

Note that this transaction loss occurred because the transaction was denominated in a currency other than the dollar. If Shipley had originally agreed to pay $55,000 rather than €50,000 for the shipment, no transaction loss would have occurred.

Transaction gains and losses are included in the calculation of net income for the period in which the exchange rate changes. This is true whether or not the gain or loss has been realized. For example, if Shipley had still owed the €50,000 as of December 31, 2010, and if at that time the exchange rate was anything other than $1.10 per euro, then Shipley would have recognized a transaction gain or loss in its 2010 income statement. If the payment were then made on January 12, 2011, another gain or loss would have been recognized if the exchange rate were different on January 12, 2011, than it was on December 31, 2010.[22] The sum of these two *recognized* transaction gains or losses would equal whatever gain or loss was ultimately *realized*.

Foreign Currency Translation Adjustments

Usually the accounts of a foreign subsidiary are kept in the currency of the country in which the subsidiary operates. In preparing consolidated statements, the American parent must translate these foreign currency amounts into dollars (called more generally the **reporting currency**). Because exchange rates fluctuate, the question arises as to the date or dates that should be used to determine the exchange rates used in this **foreign currency translation** process.

FASB Statement No. 52

There are various possible answers to this question, but *FASB Statement No. 52* limited the possibilities to two.[23] The nature of the subsidiary's **functional currency** determines which translation method is used. A company's functional currency is the currency of the primary economic environment in which the company operates.[24] If that currency is other than the dollar, the subsidiary's financial statements are translated into dollars using the **net investment,** or **current rate, method.** With this method, the parent's investment in a foreign subsidiary is considered to be an investment in the subsidiary's net assets (i.e., assets minus liabilities). Accordingly, *all* of the foreign entity's assets and liabilities are translated at the *current* exchange rate as of the balance sheet date. All revenue and expense items are translated at the *average* rate for the period.

Example

The Franco Company, a French subsidiary of its U.S. parent, Americo, Inc., was formed on January 1, 2010. Americo's initial investment in Franco was $6.5 million, which at the time was equivalent to € 5 million because the January 1, 2010, exchange rate was $1.30 per euro. Franco's 2006 financial statements are shown in Illustration 10–7. All year-end assets and liabilities are translated at the $1.20 per euro exchange rate as of December 31, 2010. All income statement items are translated at the average 2010 exchange rate, which was $1.25 per euro. Franco's capital stock is translated at the rate in effect when it was contributed by Americo, $1.30 per euro. The dollar amount for retained earnings is simply the beginning balance (zero) plus net income ($1.25 million) less dividends (zero).

---

[22] "Foreign Currency Translation," *FASB Statement No. 52.* "The Effects of Changes in Foreign Currency Exchange Rates," *IAS No. 21.*

[23] IFRS foreign currency translation standards are similar to *FASB Statement No. 52.*

[24] The salient economic factors management should consider when determining a foreign subsidiary's functional currency are (1) the currency denomination of its cash flows, sale prices, expenses and financings and (2) the degree to which the foreign subsidiary's activities are integrated with its parent company. For example, if the foreign subsidiary operates primarily in dollars and as an integrated extension of its parent, the dollar is its functional currency. *IAS No. 21* places emphasis in the functional currency decision on the currency of the economy that determine the pricing of transactions, as opposed to the currency in which transactions are denominated.

**ILLUSTRATION
10–7**
Foreign Statement
Translations

FRANCO COMPANY Balance Sheet As of December 31, 2010 (in thousands except exchange rates)			
	Euro	**Exchange Rate**	**Dollars**
Assets			
Cash	€1,000	$1.20	$ 1,200
Receivables	5,000	1.20	6,000
Inventories	3,000	1.20	3,600
Equipment (net)	4,000	1.20	4,800
	€13,000		$15,600
Liabilities and Owners' Equity			
Liabilities	€7,000	1.20	$ 8,400
Capital stock	5,000	1.30*	6,500
Retained earnings[†]	1,000		1,250
Accumulated translation adjustment[‡]	—		(550)
	€13,000		$15,600

**Income Statement
For the Year Ended December 21,2010
(in thousands except exchange rate)**

	Euro	**Exchange Rate**	**Dollars**
Revenues	€20,000	$1.25	$25,000
Cost of Sales	12,000	1.25	15,000
Other Expenses	7,000	1.25	8,750
Net Income	€1,000		$1,250

* Exchange rate as of the date capital stock issued (€ = $1.3).
[†] €1,000 net income added to retained earnings.
[‡] Calculation of translation loss:

Jan. 1, 2010, net assets = €5,000 (Capital stock):			
Translated at December 31, 2010, rate = 5,000 * $1.20	=	$6,000	
Translated at January 1, 2010, rate = 5,000 * $1.30	=	$6,500	
Loss on beginning-of-year net assets		($500)	
Increment in net assets during 2010 = €1,000:			
Translated at December 31, 2010, rate = €1,000 * $1.20	=	$1,200	
Translated at average 2010 rate = €1,000 * $1.25	=	1,250	
Loss on incremental net assets		($50)	
Total loss in dollar value of net assets		$(550)	

Collectively, these translation calculations leave the dollar balance sheet's sum of liabilities and owners' equity $550,000 greater than the total assets. The negative $550,000 translation adjustment restores the dollar balance sheet's equality. But this $550,000 downward adjustment can be viewed as more than just a "plug" figure. Since Americo held euro net assets while the value of the euro fell relative to the dollar, Americo sustained a holding loss in the dollar value of this net assets investment. The calculation of this loss is shown at the bottom of Illustration 10–7. The translation loss (or gain) does *not* appear on the translated income statement. Rather, this amount will be disclosed and accumulated in a separate account in the owners' equity portion of the translated balance sheet. This account appears as a component of other non-owner changes in owners' equity, with a name such as "Cumulative foreign currency translation adjustments." The translated foreign subsidiary's statements are then consolidated with the parent's statements, as described in Chapter 12.

If a foreign subsidiary's functional currency is the dollar, its financial statements are translated into dollars using the **remeasurement method (temporal method)**.[25] The objective of the remeasurement method is to report the foreign subsidiary's financial statement amounts as if its activities were carried out as an integral part of its parent's operations rather than as a separate entity. This approach is consistent with the characteristics of the foreign subsidiary's operations and financing that determined the dollar is its functional currency. The remeasurement method translates most financial statement items using the same exchange rates as the current rate method. There are several exceptions. Long-lived assets and inventories are translated using the exchange rate as of the date the asset was acquired (**historical rate**). For example, if the € 4,000 Equipment (net) balance shown in Illustration 10–7's December 31, 2010, balance sheet had been acquired on January 1, 2010, and the dollar was the functional currency, it would be translated into dollars using the $1.30 exchange rate (the January 1, 2010, rate). Similarly, the December 31, 2010, €3000 Inventories balance would be translated into dollars using the average exchange rate for its holding period. The expenses related to assets translated at their historical rate are also translated at the same historical rate. For example, the 2010 euro-denominated depreciation expense for the equipment acquired on January 1, 2010, would be translated at the same $1.30 exchange rate used to translate the related equipment's euro balance (not shown on financial statement). The use of historical rates results in the foreign subsidiary's assets and their related expenses being recorded in dollars at the same dollar cost as if they had been originally acquired by the parent. Unlike the current rate method's treatment of translation gains and losses, the temporal method requires translation gains or losses (also referred to as remeasurement gains or losses) to be included in the measurement of net income.

Derivatives

A derivative instrument is a financial instrument or other contract that derives its value by direct references to the changes in the values of one or more **underlyings.** Under
-lyings can be the return or yield on another security or contract, a per share price, an interest rate, an index of prices, or some other variable. An underlying is not transferred from one party to another at the inception of the contract and may or may not be transferred on maturity of the contract.

Example

You own 100 shares of Example Corporation, which on September 12, 2010, traded for $135 per share. You sell to someone the right to buy your 100 shares at any time during the next six months at a price of $145 per share. The right you sold is a *derivative*— over the next six months, its value will change by direct reference to the per share price of Example's stock.[26] If the price of an Example share does not go over $145 during the next six months, the buyer of your contract will not exercise the right to obtain your shares. Alternatively, if the price goes over $145, the holder of the right may ask you to deliver the 100 shares or you may keep your shares and pay over to the holder the difference between the current price of the shares and $145.

[25] Under GAAP and IFRS, this method also must be used when the three-year cumulative inflation rate in the foreign subsidiary's domicile country is approximately 100 percent. See "Financial Reporting in Hyperinflationary Economics," *IAS No. 29*.

[26] Such contracts as the one described in the example are traded on many of the major exchanges. The $145 is known as the *strike* or *exercise price*. This type of contract is called a *call* option (the buyer has the option to "call" for your 100 shares). The seller of the option is referred to as the *writer*. You could have bought an option to sell your stock at a specified price within some future period. This is a *put* option.

Derivatives are used by companies both for investment purposes and for hedging their risks from swings in security prices or fluctuations in interest rates, currency rates, or the prices of commodities.

The FASB and IASB require all derivatives held or written by a company to be recognized as assets or liabilities on the company's balance sheet and to be measured at their fair value. Any unrealized gains or losses on derivatives enter directly into the measurement of current income or owners' equity, depending on the reason for entering into the derivative contract.[27]

Pro Forma Earnings

Companies sometimes supplement their GAAP net income announcements with an additional earnings number labeled **pro forma earnings**.[28] The principal characteristic of these supplemental numbers is that they exclude certain items included in the measurement of GAAP earnings, such as merger-related charges, nonrecurring items, and goodwill impairment write-offs. These pro forma earnings announcements are not covered by GAAP, but the Securities and Exchange Commission insisted that they not be misleading.

Net Income

The bottom line on the income statement is labeled **net income** or **net earnings** (or **loss**), without any qualifying phrase. The term *net income* never appears as a label for any other item on the income statement. Note that in Illustration 10–2 the label is "In-come from continuing operations," not "Net income from continuing operations."

Net income therefore means the net addition from the income statement to Retained Earnings during the accounting period, regardless of whether it arises from ordinary operations or from other events and regardless of whether the transactions entering into its determination are recurring or are highly unusual.

Other Comprehensive Income

Firms could be generating revenue which is still not realized but notional, for example gains on investments in financial assets that have appreciated in price but firm has not sold the concerned asset and realized that gain. Such kind of "notional gains" could easily pass through the Income statement and affect the Equity. But if we see it from market participants' point of view, this increase in equity is not realizable. This issue gave birth to the concept of Other Comprehensive Income (OCI). Therefore, apart from Balance Sheet, Income Statement and Cash Flow statement, reporting of OCI is now part of IFRS compliance and more recently

---

[27] "Accounting for Derivative Instruments and Hedging Activities," *FASB Statement No. 133.* "Financial Instruments: Recognition and Measurement," *IAS No. 39.*

[28] Other terms used to describe this type of earnings number include *core, adjusted, cash,* and *recurring earnings.*

GAAP requirements. Other comprehensive income, or OCI, consists of those revenue, expenses, gains or losses that are *not* reported on the company›s standard income statement but have an effect on the balance sheet amounts. These changes are reported on the statement of comprehensive income along with the amount of net income from the income statement. Also, these items don't have any impact on corporation's retained earnings since the OCI items do not affect the net income. Instead, the current period's OCI items will affect the accumulated other comprehensive income, which is altogether a different component of stockholders' equity. Although a company's performance on current operations can be very well understood by looking at its Profit and Loss statement, it will be always useful to look at the unrealized profit or loss as it can provide a useful guide to investors for the future and also help them to take decisions accordingly.

Sections of Other Comprehensive Income

Some items, which are classified as other comprehensive income include:

- Unrealized gains or losses on investments that are classified as available for sale
- Unrealized gains/losses on hedge/derivative financial instruments bought or sold to hedge risk to the firm
- Foreign currency translation adjustments
- Unrealized gains/losses on postretirement benefit plans
- Gains on Revaluation of Assets

How to distinguish OCI from Profit and Loss or Change in Equity: Net Assets

A common area of confusion among the market participants is what is the exact difference between other comprehensive income and profit or loss? What is the difference between other comprehensive income and changes in equity? The easiest way to handle this confusion is to simply understand what is net assets. Net assets are simply total assets less total liabilities of a company which is similar to equity or the residual interest in the assets of an entity after deducting all of its liabilities. Positive equity (or net assets) happens for a firm when total assets are greater than total liabilities. Conversely, there is negative equity (or net assets) when total assets are lower than total liabilities. Therefore net assets are nothing but share capital, share premium, reserves, retained earnings or losses and some other items, too.

Any change (increase or decrease) in Net assets or equity could be because of one or more such events like:

- Existing shareholders bring fresh capital to the firm
- A firm makes a profit or loss
- A firm gets into a buyback of its own shares from the market
- A firm pays dividends to shareholders
- A firm carries out a revaluation of certain assets.

To easily identify the difference between a regular profit or loss, other comprehensive income and changes in equity, it is advisable to track where are these changes coming from. For better comprehension, it is recommended to group factors causing changes in net assets or equity into two broad heads:

1. **Capital changes** – changes that happen because of fresh induction or return of capital to shareholders. Most common such corporate events are:

   o IPO/FPO or Issuance of new shares
   o Distributing dividends to shareholders
   o Buy-back of own shares from the market

Such changes are reported **in the standard SCE (statement of changes in equity)**.

2. **Performance changes** – changes on account of the natural business of the company and not because of the shareholders.

Performance changes can be divided into two subcategories:

i. The main revenue-producing and expense incurring activities of the company that are reported in Income Expense Statement. Some of them are:

- Revenue generated from sales of goods or services
- Expenses incurred directly towards the sales of goods or services
- All other indirect, non-operating income and expenses, such as finance, administrative, marketing, personnel, etc.
- Gains on sale of property, plant and equipment, etc

ii. Other non-primary or non-revenue producing activities of the company that are not captured in the Income Expense Statement. Some of them are:

- Increase/Decrease in revaluation reserves related to property, plant and equipment
- Gains and losses related to actual vs expected pension payments
- Gains and losses because of translating the financial statements of a foreign operation
- The effective portion of gains and losses on hedging instruments in a cash flow hedge
- Gains and losses on the revaluation of financial assets
- Changes in the fair value of financial liabilities because of changes in the liability's issuers credit risk or ratings.

All the above items are reported in other comprehensive income (OCI) of the firm.

Treatment of OCI in case of Revaluation of Assets

IND AS 16 is the accounting standard for treatment for Property, Plant and Equipment. When the cost incurred for acquiring a property, plant or equipment is determined as an asset cost then the company must determine the carrying amount. Carrying amount is the amount at which the asset is recognized after deducting the accumulated depreciation and accumulated impairment loss. But subsequently, if revaluation of assets is chosen, the assets must be revalued on a particular date. The revalued amount is the realizable fair value as on revaluation date adjusted with subsequent accumulated depreciation and impairment loss. When the asset is revalued, the amount can be more or less than the carrying amount. Hence, this gain or loss on revaluation will be part of Other Comprehensive Income.

The treatment of revaluation gains or loss as per Ind AS 16 is as follows:

- If the carrying amount of the asset increases on account of a revaluation, the increase shall be recognised as Other comprehensive income and is recorded on the liabilities side in Equity under Revaluation reserves. However, in certain cases, the increase can be recognised in the Income Statement to the extent that it reverses a revaluation decrease of the same asset previously recognised in the Income Statement.
- However, if the carrying amount of the asset decreases on account of a revaluation, the decrease shall be recognised in the Income Statement. However, the decrease shall be recognised in Other comprehensive income to the extent of credit balance existing in the revaluation reserves in respect of that asset. The decrease recognised in Other comprehensive income reduces the Equity by reducing the revaluation reserve on the liabilities side.

For example, Trident Ltd purchases a machinery for Rs. 25,00,000 on 25th January 2019 and opts for the revaluation method. On 30th June 2019, it goes for revaluation and the asset is now valued at Rs. 30,00,000. The difference of Rs. 5,00,000 will be shown under Other Comprehensive income and on the liabilities side under Equity as Revaluation reserves. If on 30th September 2019, the company again does a revaluation of the asset and the revalued amount is Rs. 24,00,000. Now the decrease of Rs. 6,00,000 will be treated as follows:

- Rs. 5,00,000 will be reduced from revaluation surplus
- Rs. 1,00,000 will be shown in the profit and loss account.

Summary

The FASB and IASB require disclosure of a company's total nonowner changes in owners' equity (comprehensive income). This is not a particularly helpful disclosure and may be subject to misinterpretation if not correctly described.

A few unusual items are reported on the income statement separately from revenues and expenses of recurring operations. These include extraordinary losses or gains (GAAP only), gain or loss from discontinued operations, and the adjustment that results from changing accounting principles.

In analyzing transactions regarding wages costs, a careful distinction must be made between the amount earned by the employee, the additional cost that the employer incurs for payroll taxes, and the amount collected from employees that is to be transmitted to the government. Employee pension and other postretirement benefit costs are costs associated with work done in the current period, although the actual pension payments and provision of other benefits may not begin until many years later. Accounting for defined contribution plans is straightforward, but accounting for defined benefit plans and other postretirement benefits requires complicated estimates and computations.

A period's income tax expense is the sum of the two tax items: current income taxes and deferred income taxes. The resulting difference between reported income tax expense and the income tax actually payable is recorded in the Deferred Income Taxes Liability or Asset account. This account does not represent an amount due the government; Taxes Payable shows the amount that is currently due.

Foreign currency *transaction* gains or losses arise from transactions between a domestic company and a foreign entity, where the transaction is denominated in the foreign entity's currency; they are included in net income. Foreign currency *translation* gains or losses arise from a domestic parent holding an investment in the net assets of a foreign subsidiary; depending on the functional currency designation they are included in income or directly accumulated in the other nonowner changes in owners' equity component of the owners' equity section of the parent's consolidated balance sheet.

The FASB and IASB require that all derivatives of a company be recognized as assets or liabilities on the company's balance sheet and be measured at their fair value.

Sometimes companies include in their earnings announcements an amount referred to as "pro forma" earnings. It must not be misleading.

Problems

Problem 10–1.

Robin Bradley received a paycheck from her employer in the amount of $776.35. The paycheck stub indicated that in calculating her $776.35 net pay, $139.75 had been withheld for federal income tax, $34.25 for state income tax, and $74.65 for FICA. Assuming that Robin's employer had to match her share of FICA tax, and in addition had to pay unemployment insurance tax of $40.05, prepare journal entries that record these transactions in Robin's employer's accounts.

Problem 10–2.   Ryan's Snack Shacks, Inc., had a 2010 pension cost of $85,000. The company's 2010 cash contribution to the defined pension plan trust was $40,100. Prepare journal entries to record these pension cost and funding transactions.

Problem 10–3.   Acton Design Group is an incorporated architectural firm that began operations on January 1, 2007. It reports to its shareholders on the accrual basis, but to the Internal Revenue Service on the cash basis. Following is a schedule of its 2007–2010 revenues, expenses, receipts, and disbursements. For each year shown, calculate the company's income tax payment and income tax expense (provision for income taxes). Assume that in all four years the effective tax rate was 30 percent.

	2007	2008	2009	2010
Revenues	$456,000	$696,000	$840,000	$780,000
Expenses	270,000	672,000	798,000	618,000
Receipts	336,000	636,000	894,000	690,000
Disbursements	288,000	528,000	750,000	606,000

Based on your calculations, do you feel the company was wise in using the cash basis for its tax returns? Explain.

Problem 10–4.   During 2010, Kirkpatrick Corporation purchased a new electric generator for $2,750,000. The generator is expected to have a five-year useful life and will be disposed of in 2015 without any anticipated residual value. The company uses straight-line depreciation on its income statement. The company will charge $275,000 depreciation in 2010 and 2015 and $550,000 per year in 2011–2014, inclusive. For tax purposes, the generator falls into a special five-year cost recovery class. The cost recovery percentage rates applicable to the generator are as follows (i.e., 20 percent of the cost is deducted for tax purposes in 2010):

Year	Cost Recovery Class Rate
2010	20.0%
2011	32.0
2012	19.2
2013	11.5
2014	11.5
2015	5.8

Kirkpatrick expects its income before depreciation and income taxes to be $1,500,000 per year for years 2010–2015. The combined federal and state income tax rate is 40 percent.

Required:
Prepare a schedule showing
   a. Each of the six years' income tax payments, starting in 2010.
   b. Each year's provision for income taxes.
   c. The balance in the deferred tax account at the end of each year. (Assume a zero beginning balance.)

As you develop your schedule, for each year make a posting to the following T accounts: Cash (for payments), Income Tax Expense, and Deferred Taxes. In what year does the temporary difference reverse?

Problem 10–5. The Smith Corporation disclosed $1.2 million as an unusual loss on its internal income statement this year. The footnotes to the financial statements disclose the following occurrences this year:
1. Accounts receivable of $85,000 were written off.
2. A loss of $125,000 was incurred when a storage facility in Louisiana was damaged in a hurricane.
3. A loss of $325,000 was incurred when a warehouse in northern New Mexico was damaged by a flood.
4. The company lost $365,000 when Smith sold one of its operating divisions.
5. A loss of $300,000 was incurred when a manufacturing facility in Washington state was damaged by an explosive device placed by a disgruntled ex-husband of an employee.

Required:
a. Are the items above extraordinary items for external reporting purposes? Discuss.
b. Show how the extraordinary items section of the income statement should have been reported (the tax rate is 30 percent).

Problem 10–6. Heritage, Ltd., is a U.S. company doing business in 20 countries. Local exchange rates for U.S. $1 at year-end before the introduction of the Euro were

British pound (£)	.52
Spanish peseta (PTA)	90.00
Italian lira (£)	1200.00
Australian dollar ($A)	1.25

The company's records indicate the following transactions for the year:

1. Purchased inventory from Roma Fine Skins in exchange for a note payable of £72,000,000. The exchange rate at that time was £1,250 to $1.
2. While the exchange rate was peseta 100 to $1, sold raw materials to Lopez Trading Company in exchange for a PTA 270,000 note receivable.
3. While the exchange rate was £.5 to $1, sold equipment to U.K. Copies, Ltd., in exchange for an account receivable of £360,000.
4. Purchased from Containers Ltd. (Australia) spare bottles for $A149,500 (Australian). The exchange rate, when the accounts payable was incurred, was $A1.25 (Australian) to $1.

Required:
a. What is the U.S. dollar equivalent for the above transactions?
b. Record the transactions in journal entries.
c. If these payables and receivables are outstanding at year-end, would there be an exchange gain or loss for each of the above transactions?

Case 10–1

Norman Corporation (B)*

In addition to the transactions listed in Norman Corporation (A) [Case 8–1], several other matters were referred to Allen Burrows for his opinion as to how they should be reported on the audited 2010 income statement and balance sheet.

1. Norman had purchased advertising brochures costing $125,000 in 2010. At the end of 2010, one-fifth of these brochures were on hand; they would be mailed in 2011 to prospective customers who sent in a coupon request for them. As of March 1, 2011, almost all the brochures had been mailed. Norman had charged $100,000 of the cost of these brochures as an expense in 2010, and showed $25,000 as a deferred charge as of December 31, 2010.
2. In 2010 the company had placed magazine advertisements, costing $75,000, offering these brochures. The advertisements had appeared in 2010. Because the sales generated by the brochures would not occur until after prospective customers had received the brochures and placed orders, which would primarily be in 2011, Norman had recorded the full $75,000 as a deferred charge on its December 31, 2010, balance sheet.
3. Norman's long-standing practice was to capitalize the costs of development projects if they were likely to result in successful new products. Upon introduction of the product, these amounts were written off to cost of sales over a five-year period. During 2010, $55,000 had been added to the asset account and $36,000 had been charged off as an expense. Preliminary research efforts were charged to expense, so the amount capitalized was an amount that related to products added to Norman's line. In the majority of instances, these products at least produced some gross profit, and some of them were highly successful.
4. In 2010, the financial vice president decided to capitalize, as a deferred charge, the costs of the

company's employee training program, which amounted to $35,000. He had read several books and articles on "human resource accounting" that advocated such treatment because the value of these training programs would certainly benefit operations in future years.

5. For many years, Norman's practice had been to set its allowance for doubtful accounts at 2 percent of accounts receivable. This amount had been satisfactory. In 2010, however, a customer who owed $19,040 went bankrupt. From inquiries made at local banks, Norman Corporation could obtain no reliable estimate of the amount that eventually could be recovered. The loss might be negligible, and it might be the entire $19,040. The $19,040 was included as an account receivable on the proposed balance sheet.
6. Norman did not carry fire or theft insurance on its automobiles and trucks. Instead, it followed the practice of self-insurance. It charged $5,000 as an expense in 2010, which was the approximate cost of fire and theft insurance policies, and credited this amount to an insurance reserve, a noncurrent liability. During 2010, only one charge, for $3,750, was made to this reserve account, representing the cost of repairing a truck that had been stolen and later recovered. The balance in the reserve account as of January 1, 2010, was $20,900.
7. In 2010, the board of directors voted to sell a parking lot that the company had operated for several years. Another company had expressed an interest in buying the lot for approximately $125,000. In 2010, the pretax income generated by this lot was $19,000. The book value of the assets that would be sold was $50,000 as of the end of 2010. Norman did not reflect this transaction in its financial statements because no final agreement had been reached with the proposed buyer and because the sale would not take place until well into 2011, even if a final agreement were reached in the near future.
8. During 2010, the president of Norman exercised a stock option and the corporation used treasury stock

* Copyright © Professor Robert N. Anthony, Harvard Business School.

for this purpose. The treasury stock had been acquired several years earlier at a cost of $10,000 and was carried in the shareholders' equity section of the balance sheet at this amount. In accordance with the terms of the option agreement, the president paid $13,000 for it. He immediately sold this stock, however, for $25,000. Norman disregarded the fact that the stock was clearly worth $25,000 and recorded the transaction as

```
Cash . . . . . . . . . . . . . . . . . . 13,000
    Gain on Treasury Stock . . . . . . . . . .    3,000
    Treasury Stock . . . . . . . . .               10,000
```

The $3,000 gain was included as a nonoperating income item on the income statement.

9. Norman's long-standing practice was to declare an annual cash dividend of $50,000 in December and to pay it in January. When the dividend was paid, the following entry was made:

```
Retained Earnings . . . . . . . . . 50,000
    Cash . . . . . . . . . . . . . . . .         50,000
```

Questions

1. What changes in the financial statements [see Norman Corporation (A)] is Norman required to make in accordance with generally accepted accounting principles? Ignore income taxes and assume that all the transactions are material.
2. As Mr. Burrows, what additional changes, if any, would you recommend be made in the proposed income statement in order to present the results more fairly?

Case 10–2

Silver Appliance Company*

Silver Appliance Company operated a large retail appliance store in San Diego. The store sold all sorts of household appliances, plus auto and home sound equipment. The company's owner, Brian Silver (known by his customers as "Big Brian" because of his rather ample proportions), had for many years been an extremely productive salesman in a San Diego store of the Highland Appliance chain. Having built up a large personal clientele during those years, Mr. Silver felt he could easily shift customers to a new store, were he to open one. In 2003, he did just that, and the store had rapidly achieved an annual sales volume of over $5 million.

In 2006 Mr. Silver decided he could increase the store's volume, plus earn interest revenue, if he established an installment credit program to assist customers in financing their major purchases. The program was a success, with the amount of installment receivables growing in each successive year (except for 2010).

In early 2011 Mr. Silver decided the firm had outgrown its sole-practitioner accounting firm. He therefore retained a national public accounting firm to provide Silver Appliance with various auditing, tax, and consulting services. The accounting firm's partner assigned to the Silver account was Suzi Chung. After reviewing Silver's accounting practices, Ms. Chung met with Mr. Silver to review these practices. Of particular interest to Ms. Chung was the fact that Silver used the typical sale method (formally, the "delivery method") to recognize sales—and hence cost of sales and gross margin—on all sales, irrespective of whether the sales were for cash, were charged to a Visa or Master Card account, or were financed on Silver's installment credit plan. Although she felt this made good sense and was in accord with GAAP for preparing income statements for Mr. Silver's use, Ms. Chung pointed out that the federal income tax laws permit the use of the installment method of revenue and gross margin recognition on installment plan sales.

With the installment method, the retailer recognizes revenues as installment payments are made and then applies the store's normal gross margin percentage to these payments to determine the gross margin for tax purposes. For example, suppose a customer bought a $700 refrigerator having a cost of $490; then the gross margin percentage is 30 percent ($210 ÷ $700). If the customer's first installment payment were $50

* Copyright © James S. Reece.

EXHIBIT 1 Installment Sales Data (thousands of dollars)

	2006	2007	2008	2009	2010
Installment receivables as of December 31	$190.1	$351.9	$526.2	$559.4	$489.1
Pretax profit as reported	332.6	415.3	478.2	492.5	461.3
Gross margin percentage	34.6%	35.1%	34.2%	33.4%	32.2%

Notes:
1. All installment sales contracts were for periods of one year or less.
2. The company's effective federal income tax rate in each year was approximately 34 percent.

(ignoring interest), the store would at that time recognize $15 (30% ∗ $50) gross margin for tax purposes.[1] The effect of using this method for calculating taxable income is that it delays, relative to the delivery basis, the reporting of gross margin, and hence defers the taxes on that margin until the margin is realized through the customer's cash installment payments.

After Ms. Chung's explanation of the installment method, Mr. Silver expressed a definite interest in changing to this method for tax purposes. "However," he said, "I want to keep using the regular basis for our monthly and annual income statements because I really feel we earn the margin when the customer signs the installment agreement and we deliver the appliances. But before we change, I'd like to see how much we've been overpaying in taxes the past few years by not using the installment method." To address this question, Ms. Chung gathered the data shown in Exhibit 1.

Mr. Silver raised several other questions with Ms. Chung. "I understand in general the impact that this method would have on our tax payments; but it's not clear to me what the impact would be on our balance sheet, given that I don't want to change methods on our income statement. I've seen an item called 'deferred taxes' on balance sheets in the annual reports of some companies that I own stock in. I know this is somehow related to using different accounting for shareholder and income tax reporting. Would we have such an account if we make this change? If so,

[1] The formal accounting treatment is to recognize $50 of revenues, match with that $35 cost of goods sold, and thus recognize $15 gross margin, as explained in Chapter 5.

you will have to explain to me how I should interpret the balance in that account.

"Also, I have a friend who owns an architectural firm that reports on the cash basis for tax purposes. She was telling me the other day that her billings have really dropped this year because of the downturn of local construction activity, and yet she is still having to make tax payments as big as last year's. Could this happen to us if we change our method for reporting installment sales for tax purposes?

"Finally, it occurs to me that we have already paid taxes on the installment sales profits we recognized in 2010, even though many of those sales have not yet been collected. If we change methods for 2011, are we going to end up paying taxes twice on those uncollected 2010 installment sales—once in 2010 and again in 2011?"

Questions

1. If Silver Appliance Company had used the installment method for tax purposes in the years 2006–2010, how different would its tax payments have been in each of those years? What would the year-end balance in deferred taxes have been in each of those years? (Round calculations to the nearest $10.)

2. How would you respond to Mr. Silver's questions concerning (*a*) interpretation of the amount of deferred taxes, (*b*) tax payments in a period of declining sales, and (*c*) double taxation of installment sales made in 2010?

Case 10–3

Freedom Technology Company*

Freedom Technology Company produced various types of household electronic equipment, which it sold primarily through two large retail store chains in the United States. On October 1, 20x1, Freedom established a wholly owned subsidiary in South Korea, called Freedom-Korea, for the purpose of assembling a small home version of a video arcade game that Freedom had been licensed to produce. The Korean subsidiary sold its output directly to the U.S. retailers that carried the game (as opposed to selling its output to its U.S. parent for resale to U.S. retailers).

Exhibit 1 shows the subsidiary's condensed balance sheet as of September 30, 20x2 (fiscal year-end) and an income statement for its first year of operations. Freedom's controller, Marion Rosenblum, asked a member of the accounting staff to translate these statements into dollars, following the standards of *FASB Statement No. 52*.

* Copyright © Professor Robert N. Anthony, Harvard Business School.

The accounting staff person assembled the following information to assist in preparing the two sets of translated statements:

1. The South Korean unit of currency is the won (abbreviated W). As of October 1, 20x1, the exchange rate was one won = $0.00140; as of September 30, 20x2, the rate was one won = $0.00124.
2. As of October 1, 20x1, Freedom-Korea's assets were W400 million cash and W600 million fixed assets. No additional fixed assets were acquired during the first year of operations. On average, the year-end inventories had been on hand 11/2 months; the exchange rate on August 15, 20x2, was one won = $0.00126.
3. The capital stock of Freedom-Korea had been issued to Freedom-Technology on October 1, 20x1; no additional capital stock transactions had taken place during the fiscal year.

EXHIBIT 1

FREEDOM-KOREA
Balance Sheet
As of September 30, 20x2
(millions of won)

Assets		Liabilities and Owners' Equity	
Cash	W 591	Current liabilities	W 624
Receivables	1,182		
Inventories	552	Capital stock	1,000
Fixed assets	575	Retained earnings	1,276
	W2,900		W2,900

Income Statement
For the Year Ended September 30, 19x2
(millions of won)

Revenues	W7,090
Cost of sales	4,415
Other expenses	1,399
Net income	W1,276

Questions

1. Prepare translated year-end statements for Free-dom-Korea using the current rate method.
2. Prepare a translated (i.e., measured) year-end statement for Freedom-Korea using its temporal method. This method requires any translation gain or loss to be included as an item in the translated income statement. You may treat any such gain or loss as a "plug" figure; that is, you are not expected to calculate it in detail.
3. Compare your two sets of translated statements and comment on any differences between them. If the company were permitted a choice as to which method to use, which method do you think they would prefer?

Case 10–4

Proxim, Inc.*

Julie Cassidy, a financial analyst with a major institutional investor, was puzzled by the large number of what appeared to be "nonrecurring" items in Proxim, Inc.'s 2001 income statement (Exhibit 1). In particular,

*Based on case research previously conducted by Professor Mark Bradshaw, Harvard Business School.

she was confused as to what income figure or figures she should use to judge the performance of management and value of the company's common stock.

Earlier, in mid-January, Proxim had issued a press release announcing its fourth quarter and year-end

EXHIBIT 1

PROXIM, INC. Statement of Operations for the Year Ended December 31, 2001 (in thousands, except per share data)		
	GAAP	**Pro Forma**
Revenue	$85,536	$85,536
Cost of revenue excluding amortization and provision	49,367	49,367
Amortization of intangible assets	2,832	—
Provision for excess and obsolete inventory	50,000	—
Gross profit (loss)	(16,663)	36,169
Research and development 13,235 13,235 Purchased in-process research and development 1,373 — Selling, general, and administrative	22,057	22,057
Provision for doubtful accounts	4,500	—
Restructuring charges 13,585 — Impairment of goodwill and intangible assets 10,372 — Terminated merger costs	2,950	—
Patent litigation costs	2,600	—
Amortization of goodwill	5,252	—
Income (loss) from operations	(92,587)	877
Interest income, net	1,905	1,905
Impairment gain (losses) on investments	(12,074)	—
Income (loss) before taxes	(102,756)	2,782
Provision for income taxes	5,043	974
Net income (loss)	($107,799)	$1,808
Basic net income (loss) per share	($3.87)	$0.06
Diluted net income (loss) per share	($3.87)	$0.06

Source: Proxim Inc., 2001 form 10-K.

EXHIBIT 2 **Selected Excerpts from Proxim Inc., Q4 and Year-End 2001 Earnings Announcement**

Excluding the provisions and charges discussed below, and the amortization of intangible assets and goodwill in the respective periods, the pro forma loss for the fourth quarter of 2001 was $(1,093,000), or $(0.04) per share, compared to pro forma net income of $4,943,000, or $0.17 per share (diluted) for the fourth quarter of 2000, and pro forma net income for the year ended December 31, 2001, was $1,808,000, or $0.06 per share (diluted), compared to pro forma net income of $14,631,000, or $0.51 per share (diluted) for the year ended December 31, 2000.

Including the provisions and charges discussed below, and the amortization of intangible assets and goodwill in the respective periods, the loss for the fourth quarter of 2001 was $(16,002,000), or $(0.53) per share, compared to net income of $1,970,000, or $0.07 per share (diluted) for the fourth quarter of 2000, and the loss for the year ended December 31, 2001, was $(107,799,000), or $(3.87) per share, compared to net income of $2,149,000, or $0.07 per share (diluted) for the year ended December 31, 2000.

During the fourth quarter of 2001, the Company recorded a restructuring charge of $12,635,000 related to a reduction in workforce and closing certain facilities. The fourth quarter 2001 restructuring charge includes $1,400,000 related to severance payments and closed facilities lease costs during the quarter, and $11,235,000 related to closed facilities lease commitments, net of estimated future sublease receipts for the closed facilities.

During the fiscal year ended December 31, 2001, the Company recorded the following charges and provisions: restructuring charges of $550,000 in the second quarter, $400,000 in the third quarter, and $12,635,000 in the fourth quarter; provisions for excess and obsolete inventory and purchase commitments totaling $44,000,000 in the second quarter and $6,000,000 in the third quarter; increases in the allowance for doubtful accounts of $2,000,000 in the second quarter and $2,500,000 in the third quarter; a charge for purchased in-process research and development related to the acquisition of Card Access, Inc., of $1,373,000 in the third quarter; a charge for the impairment of goodwill and purchased intangible assets of $10,372,000 in the second quarter; a charge for expenses related to a terminated merger of $2,950,000 in the first quarter; a charge for expenses related to patent litigation of $2,600,000 in the first quarter; charges for the impairment of equity investments in five companies of $5,694,000 in the first quarter, $1,000,000 in the second quarter, and $5,380,000 in the third quarter; and a provision for deferred tax assets net of deferred tax liabilities of $5,043,000 in the second quarter.

Source: Business Wire, January 22, 2002.

2001 financial results. This release indicated fourth quarter revenues were $16.7 million (compared to $33.6 million in the prior year's fourth quarter) and $85.5 million for the year (compared to $107.5 million for the prior year). Excerpts from the release are included in Exhibit 2.

Questions

1. Why do you think Proxim has so many "nonrecurring"-type charges during 2001?
2. As the management of Proxim, what income figure do you believe best reflects your 2001 performance?

3. What 2001 income figure would you use to calculate Proxim's 2001 trailing year price-earnings ratio?
4. Should the Securities and Exchange Commission be concerned with any proliferation of pro forma earnings announcements? If you had to write a new Securities and Exchange regulation covering pro forma earnings announcements, what might your regulation require?
5. Should the Financial Accounting Standards Board issue guidance on reporting earnings information. For example, should it define what constitutes acceptable measurements of pro forma earnings? What guidance, if any, do you recommend the Financial Accounting Standards Board issue?

The Statement of Cash Flows

Our attention thus far has been focused on the analysis of transactions in terms of their effect on the balance sheet and the income statement. In this chapter, we describe the third accounting report that a company must prepare, the **statement of cash flows** (or **cash flow statement**).

The discussion of the cash flow statement was deferred to this point because this statement does not affect the way in which transactions are recorded in the accounts. The accounts provide information that is summarized in the balance sheet and the income statement. Information used in preparing the cash flow statement is derived from data reported in the other financial statements and therefore does not require any new accounts to be added to the recordkeeping system.

Purpose of the Cash Flow Statement

The income statement focuses on the economic results of the entity's *operating* activities during a period. Key concepts in the measurement of the period's income are revenue recognition and the matching of expenses. Revenue is recognized in the period in which the entity performs its revenue-generating tasks (e.g., delivering goods or providing services), irrespective of whether the customer pays cash at that time or agrees to pay later. Expenses measure the resources consumed in generating the period's revenue and in administering the entity during the period, irrespective of when cash was used to pay for those resources. Thus, the period's income bears no direct relationship to the cash flows associated with the period's operations. Also, because of its focus on the results of operations, the income statement does not provide information about the entity's investing or financing activities during the period.

The purpose of the cash flow statement is to provide information about the *cash flows associated with the period's operations* and also about the entity's *investing and financing activities* during the period. This information is important both to shareholders, part of whose investment return (dividends) is dependent on cash flows, and also to lenders, whose interest payments and principal repayment require the use of cash. The welfare of other constituencies of a company—including its employees, its suppliers, and the local communities that may levy taxes on it—depends to varying degrees on the company's ability to generate adequate cash flows to fulfill its financial obligations.

The numbers on the cash flow statement are objective: *Cash is cash,* and the amounts of cash flows are not influenced by the judgments and estimates that are made in arriving at revenues, expenses, and other accruals.[1] Because of this objectivity, many analysts pay considerable attention to the cash flow statement. It must be remembered that despite the judgments and estimates that influence balance sheet and income statement amounts, the numbers in those statements provide better information about an entity's financial status and operating performance than do cash flow statement numbers.

Sources and Uses of Cash

The activities that the cash flow statement describes can be classified in two categories: (1) activities that generate cash, called *sources* of cash, and (2) activities that involve spending cash, called *uses* of cash. Of course, an entity's operations routinely generate cash (especially from cash sales to customers and collection of customer accounts receivable) and use cash (for most operating expenses, especially the payment of wages and accounts payable). The user of a cash flow statement is interested primarily in the *net* amount of cash generated by operations rather than in the detailed operating cash inflows and outflows. Thus, rather than separately showing operating cash inflows as sources and outflows as uses, this net amount is shown. Operations ordinarily are a net source of cash; however, operations are a net use of cash if they use more cash than they generate. A net use of cash is common in start-up companies and in companies that are expanding rapidly.

Treating this net of operating inflows and outflows as a single number, here are the following major types of cash sources and uses:

Sources	Uses
1. Operations	1. Cash dividends
2. New borrowings	2. Repayment of borrowings
3. New stock issues	3. Repurchase of stock
4. Sale of property, plant, and equipment	4. Purchase of property, plant, and equipment
5. Sale of other noncurrent assets	5. Purchase of other noncurrent assets

Inspection of the above lists suggests why cash flow statements are felt to be useful. They help the user answer questions such as the following:

- How much cash was provided by the normal, ongoing operations of the company?
- In what other ways were significant amounts of cash raised?
- Is the company investing enough in new plant and equipment to maintain or increase capacity and to replace old facilities with more efficient ones?
- Is the company reinvesting excess cash in productive assets, or is it using the cash to retire stock?
- To what extent are the company's investments being financed by internally generated cash and to what extent by borrowing or other external sources?
- For the cash obtained externally, what proportion was from debt and what from equity?
- Is the company having to borrow cash in order to maintain its cash dividend payments?

[1] Despite the objectivity of cash flows, their classification between operating, investing, and financing cash flows can be manipulated by accounting decisions by management. For example, classifying a cost as a noncurrent asset rather than an expense changes the related cash flow to an investing cash flow rather than an operating cash flow.

Although the cash flow statement cannot provide complete answers to all of these questions, it can at least suggest answers and highlight areas where it would be desirable to gather more information before deciding, for example, whether to buy, sell, or hold one's investment in the company's common stock.

Meaning of Cash

Companies using modern cash management techniques invest any temporary excess amounts of cash in highly liquid (i.e., can be readily sold at current market prices), short-term investments (e.g., money market funds and Treasury bills) for periods as short as one or two days. As a result, for purposes of the cash flow statement, *cash* means the sum of actual cash and these short-term investments; the sum is formally called **cash and cash equivalents.** The FASB defines *cash equivalents* as highly liquid investments that are readily convertible to known amounts of cash and that mature in no more than 90 days from the date of the financial statement.[2] The IASB has a slightly different definition. It defines cash equivalents as short-term, highly liquid investments that are readily convertible to known amounts of cash that are subject to an insignificant risk of changes in value.[3]

The Cash Flow Statement

Imagine that you have a checking account in which amounts over some minimum balance, say $1,000, are automatically invested in highly liquid interest-bearing securities. Instead of your account representing just cash, it constitutes the sum of cash and cash equivalents. In your checkbook register, you record all deposits and other increases in the account (debit entries), and you also record all checks written and other withdrawals from the account (credit entries). Now assume that at the end of each year, you wish to prepare a summary of the sources of the items that you deposited in your account and a summary of the various uses you made of the cash in the account. For example, the sources categories might be wages, investment earnings, and gifts, and the uses categories might be housing costs, other living expenses, recreation/entertainment, health care, taxes, and major purchases (such as a new television set or a car). You could first classify each entry in your checkbook register according to one of these categories, and then add the amounts of all of the items in each category and report the totals of the various categories. The end result could reasonably be called a *personal cash flow statement.*

In substance, the cash flow statement for a business entity is analogous in that it summarizes a myriad of specific cash transactions into a few categories. However, in practice, the information for the statement of cash flows is not taken directly from the Cash and Cash Equivalents accounts but rather is derived from income statement and balance sheet data. This section describes these derivation techniques.

---

[2] "Statement of Cash Flows," *FASB Statement No. 95,* as amended by "Statement of Cash Flows—Exemption of Certain Enterprises and Classification of Cash Flows from Certain Securities Acquired for Resale," *FASB Statement No. 102,* and "Statement of Cash Flows—Net Reporting of Certain Cash Receipts and Cash Payments and Classification of Cash Flows from Hedging Transactions," *FASB Statement No. 104.*

[3] "Statement of Cash Flows," *IAS No. 7.* Outside the United States, the definition of *cash* may be different. Users of non-U.S.GAAP cash flow statements should always determine the definition of *cash* adopted before using the cash flow statement data.

Statement Categories

FASB 95 and IAS No. 7 do not use as many major categories for sources and uses as we listed above. Instead, those 10 types of sources and uses are combined into three major categories: operating activities, investing activities, and financing activities.

Operating activities are defined to be all transactions that are *not* investing or financing activities. These transactions include the cash inflows associated with sales revenues and the cash outflows associated with operating expenses, including payments to suppliers of goods or services and payments for wages, interest, and taxes.

Investing activities include acquiring long-lived assets such as property, plant, equipment, and investments in securities that are not cash equivalents; and lending money (i.e., loans receivable). Investing activities also include the opposites of these transactions: disinvesting activities such as disposing of long-lived assets, and collecting loans. Note that increases or decreases in accounts receivable and inventory are not treated as investment activities; the changes in these current assets are included in operating activities.

Financing activities include the borrowing of cash (notes payable, mortgages, bonds, and other noncurrent borrowings) and the issuance of equity securities (common or preferred stock). Repayments of borrowings are also financing activities, as are dividend payments to shareholders and the use of cash to repurchase and retire issued stock. Changes in accounts payable, wages payable, interest payable, and taxes payable are not treated as financing activities; they are operating activities.

IAS No. 7 gives managers more flexibility than *FASB 95* when it comes to classify interest and dividend cash flows. *IAS No. 7* permits, as long as it is done in a consistent manner, interest and dividend cash flows to be classified as either operating, investing, or financing activities depending on the nature of the transaction.

Because the procedures for developing the net cash flow from operations are more complex than those for developing cash flows related to investing and financing activities, we will describe the latter two cash flow statement categories first. The descriptions for all three categories are based on the financial statements shown in Illustrations 11–1 and 11–2 and the resulting statement cash flows shown in Illustration 11–3.

Investing Activities

Illustration 11–1 shows that during 2010 investment in plant and equipment (at cost) *increased* by $350,000 (from $2,000,000 to $2,350,000). This is the *net* increase in investment during the year: Additional plant and equipment investments minus disposals amounted to a net increase (at cost) of $350,000. From the balance sheet alone one cannot determine whether there was $350,000 of new fixed assets acquired and no disposals or some combination of acquisitions and disposals that amounted to a net increase of $350,000. Thus, the preparer of the cash flow statement would need to examine the Plant and Equipment account to make this determination. In this instance it happens that the investment in new equipment was $500,000 and the original cost of equipment disposed of was $150,000, resulting in the $350,000 net increase.

Conceptually, this net amount should be broken down into the portion that represents a cash outflow and the portion that represents a cash inflow, and we do this in the description that follows. However, as a practical matter, flows that are not material in amount are often netted.

If $500,000 cash was paid for the new assets and $20,000 cash received for the old assets, then the cash flow statement would report each of these investing transactions as follows:

Acquisition of plant and equipment	$(500,000)
Proceeds from disposals of plant and equipment	20,000

ILLUSTRATION 11–1

FAIRWAY CORPORATION Balance Sheets As of December 31, 2009, and 2010 (in thousands)	2009	2010	Change
Assets			
Current assets:			
Cash and cash equivalents	$ 230	$ 326	$ 96
Accounts receivable	586	673	87
Inventories	610	657	47
Total current assets	1,426	1,656	230
Noncurrent assets:			
Plant and equipment, at cost	2,000	2,350	350
Accumulated depreciation	(1,000)	(970)	30
Plant and equipment, net	1,000	1,380	380
Investment securities	450	400	(50)
Total noncurrent assets	1,450	1,780	330
Total assets	$2,876	$3,436	$560
Liabilities and Shareholders' Equity			
Current liabilities:			
Accounts payable	$ 332	$ 388	$ 56
Income taxes payable	9	10	1
Short-term borrowings	147	126	(21)
Total current liabilities	488	524	36
Long-term debt	500	835	335
Deferred taxes	65	70	5
Total liabilities	1,053	1,429	376
Shareholders' equity:			
Common stock ($1 par)	50	60	10
Additional paid-in capital	133	167	34
Retained earnings	1,640	1,780	140
Total shareholders' equity	1,823	2,007	184
Total liabilities and shareholders' equity	$2,876	$3,436	$560

Thus, inflows and outflows related to a specific type of asset are shown as separate gross amounts rather than as a single net amount (i.e., a $480,000 net outflow in the example just given).

A similar approach is applied to the 2010 *decrease* of $50,000 in investment securities (from $450,000 to $400,000). If that decrease were the result of selling $50,000 of securities (at cost) during the year and receiving $50,000 cash, then one line on the cash flow statement would describe the transactions:

Proceeds from sales of investment securities	$50,000

**ILLUSTRATION
11–2**

FAIRWAY CORPORATION Income Statement and Statement of Retained Earnings For the Year Ended December 31, 2010 (in thousands)		
Sales revenues		$3,190
Cost of sales		2,290
Gross margin		900
Expenses:		
Depreciation	$120	
Other expenses	477*	
Income taxes	103	700
Net income		$ 200
Retained earnings, December 31, 2009		$1,640
Add: 2010 net income		200
Less: Cash dividends		(60)
Retained earnings, December 31, 2010		$1,780

* Net of $20,000 gain on disposal of equipment.

On the other hand, if the $50,000 were the net of $75,000 cash inflows from securities sales and $25,000 outflows for purchases, then the cash flow statement would show

Purchases of investment securities	$(25,000)
Proceeds from sales of investment securities	75,000

Finally, if the $50,000 net change in investment securities on the balance sheet were different from the associated net *cash flow,* then the cash flow would be reported. For example, if securities with a balance sheet carrying amount of $50,000 were sold for $53,000, the cash inflow reported would be $53,000, even though the balance sheet Investment Securities account decreased by $50,000.

The company's investing activities are summarized in the middle section of the cash flow statement shown in Illustration 11–3. Note that all of the individual items are summarized to arrive at a single net amount of cash flow associated with investing activities, in this case an outflow (use) of $430,000.

**Financing
Activities**

During 2010 Fairway Corporation's short-term borrowings decreased by $21,000 (from $147,000 to $126,000). The underlying records reveal that this was the net effect of $15,000 of new borrowings and $36,000 repayments of old borrowings. Rather than reporting the net amount, the cash flow statement would show

Proceeds of short-term debt	$15,000
Payments to settle short-term debt	(36,000)

Similarly, analysis of the underlying transactions reveals that the $335,000 increase in long-term debt was the net of $375,000 new borrowings and $40,000 repayments of previous long-term debt. This would be reported as follows:

Proceeds of long-term debt	$375,000
Payments on long-term debt	(40,000)

**ILLUSTRATION
11–3**

FAIRWAY CORPORATION Statement of Cash Flows For the Year Ending December 31, 2010 (in thousands)	
Net cash flow from operating activities:	
Net income	$200
Noncash expenses, revenues, gains, and losses included in income:	
Depreciation	120
Deferred taxes	5
Increase in accounts receivable	(87)
Increase in inventories	(47)
Increase in accounts payable	56
Increase in taxes payable	1
Gain on sale of equipment	(20)
Cash flow from operating activities	228
Cash flows from investing activities:	
Acquisition of plant and equipment	(500)
Proceeds from disposals of plant and equipment	20
Purchase of investment securities	(25)
Proceeds from sales of investment securities	75
Net cash used by investing activities	(430)
Cash flows from financing activities:	
Proceeds of short-term debt	15
Payments to settle short-term debt	(36)
Proceeds of long-term debt	375
Payments on long-term debt	(40)
Proceeds from issuing common stock	44
Dividends paid	(60)
Net cash provided by financing activities	298
Net increase (decrease) in cash and cash equivalents	96
Cash and cash equivalents at beginning of year	230
Cash and cash equivalents at end of year	$326

The $40,000 cash payments are a reduction in the *principal* of the long-term debt; interest payments are treated as an operating transaction rather than as an investing or financing activity.

Also during 2010, Fairway issued 10,000 additional shares of $1 par value common stock resulting in cash proceeds to the corporation of $44,000. On the balance sheet, this appears as a $10,000 increase in common stock at par and a $34,000 increase in additional paid-in capital. On the cash flow statement, the following line would appear:

Proceeds from issuing common stock	$44,000

Finally, *FASB 95* treats dividend payments to shareholders as a financing activity. As shown at the bottom of Illustration 11–2, cash dividends amounted to $60,000. This would appear on the cash flow statement thus:

Dividends paid	$(60,000)

Note that it is the amount of cash dividends *paid* during the year, as opposed to the amount of dividends *declared* for the year, that appears on the cash flow statement. In this instance, the amount paid was the same as the amount declared: $60,000. However, because the dividend declared for the last quarter of the year ordinarily is not paid until early in the following year, it is not unusual for the amount of dividends declared for the year to be different from the amount paid *during* that year.

The bottom section of the cash flow statement in Illustration 11–3 reports and summarizes all of the company's 2010 financing activities. The net cash flow from these activities was a $298,000 inflow (source). We emphasize that although the level of detail we have shown is conceptually correct, certain immaterial flows would be netted in practice.

Noncash Transactions

Some significant investing and financing activities do not involve cash flows at all, such as the conversion of a convertible bond into common stock. Certain other investing and financing activities, although affecting cash, do not affect it in the full amount of the investment or financing transaction. For example, if an entity acquires a fixed asset costing $500,000 by making a $200,000 cash payment and giving the seller an equipment note payable for the other $300,000. The cash flow statement report only the $200,000 cash outflow associated with the fixed asset investment transaction.[4] However, both the FASB and IASB require disclosure of the $300,000 noncash portion of the transaction in a narrative statement or supplemental schedule.

A transaction involving the conversion of $400,000 face value of bonds into common stock results in no cash inflows or outflows. Thus, it is not reported in the statement of cash flows. However, the substance of such a conversion is that stock is issued, resulting in a cash inflow, and then the proceeds of the issuance are used to retire the bonds, an equal and offsetting outflow. *FASB 95* and *IAS No. 7* require that the conversion be reported in a supplemental disclosure, thus: "Additional stock was issued upon conversion of $400,000 of bonds payable."

Cash Flow from Operating Activities

As mentioned above, the cash flow statement reports the net cash flow generated by the period's operations. This net amount can be presented in two ways: the direct method and the indirect, or reconciliation, method.

Direct Method

With the **direct method** of reporting cash flows from operating activities, summaries of operating inflows and outflows are shown and then combined to arrive at the net

---

[4] In our view, the FASB's way of recording this transaction does not adequately capture its substance. In effect, there was a $300,000 *financing* transaction that momentarily increased cash, representing the note payable proceeds. Then this $300,000 plus another $200,000 cash was used to make the $500,000 investment in the fixed asset. Thus, in substance, there was a $300,000 financing activity inflow and a $500,000 investing activity outflow rather than a $200,000 investing activity outflow.

cash flow from operations. For Fairway Corporation in 2010, the presentation would appear as follows:

Cash flows from operating activities:	
Cash received from customers	$3,103,000
Dividends and interest received	19,000
Cash provided by operating activities	3,122,000
Cash paid to suppliers and employees	2,729,000
Interest paid	67,000
Income taxes paid	98,000
Cash disbursed for operating activities	2,894,000
Net cash flow from operating activities	$ 228,000

FASB 95 "encourages" companies to use the direct method. It results in a straightforward presentation that is intuitively understandable by users with little or no accounting training. However, it does not suggest why the year's net operating cash flow ($228,000) differed from the year's net income ($200,000). However, because one of the FASB's stated purposes of a statement of cash flows is to help users understand the differences between net income and the associated cash receipts and payments, if the direct method is used, then a reconciliation of net income and net cash flow from operating activities must be provided in a separate schedule.

Indirect Method

Because it does not clearly show why the year's net income differs from the year's net operating cash flow, the direct method is not the preferred one in practice. Most companies prefer a presentation that helps the user understand the reasons for the difference between the period's net income and the period's net cash flow from operations—the **reconciliation,** or **indirect, method**.

The indirect method is much harder to understand than the direct method. We will first illustrate the presentation and then explain the calculations on which the indirect method is based. The presentation is as shown in the top portion of Illustration 11–3, labeled "Net cash flow from operating activities."

Indirect Method Calculations

The approach of the indirect method is to start with the net income amount and adjust it for differences between revenues (or gains) and operating cash inflows, and for differences between expenses (or losses) and operating cash outflows. For many companies, the largest adjustment relates to depreciation.

Depreciation

To understand the depreciation adjustment, consider the adjusting entry made to record depreciation expense:

Depreciation Expense 120,000	
Accumulated Depreciation	120,000

Note that this entry reduces income by $120,000 but has *no effect* on Cash. (To affect Cash, the credit would have to be to Cash rather than to Accumulated Depreciation.) Now assume for the moment (contrary to fact) that (1) revenues were equal to operating cash inflows (Cash was debited whenever Sales Revenues was credited) and (2) total expenses *excluding* depreciation expense were equal to operating cash outflows (except for depreciation, Cash was credited whenever an expense account was debited). Then net income would be $120,000 lower than net operating cash flow because $120,000 depreciation expense was subtracted in the calculation of net income, but this $120,000 expense did not reduce Cash. Thus, if we add $120,000 back to the amount of net income, then the resulting amount is the net cash flow from operations. Because of our assumptions, this is the only adjustment needed to take account of revenues that were not also cash inflows and expenses that were not also cash outflows. Note in the Illustration 11–3 reconciliation presentation that $120,000 is added to the net income of $200,000 as one of the adjustments.

Deferred Taxes

To understand the adjustment labeled "Deferred taxes," we must review the nature of the Deferred Income Taxes account. This account will increase (be credited) if the period's income tax *expense* is larger than the period's income tax *payments*. Note in Illustration 11–1 that the balance in Deferred Taxes increased by $5,000 (from $65,000 to $70,000) during the year. Fairway's 2010 tax expense was $5,000 larger than its 2010 tax payments. Thus, the amount subtracted for income taxes in preparing Fair-way's income statement overstated the *cash outflows* for taxes by $5,000. To adjust the income statement to a cash basis, therefore, requires that this $5,000 overstatement of cash outflows be added back to the net income figure. Note that in the indirect method presentation, $5,000 is added to net income for this adjustment.

Analogously, if the balance in Deferred Income Taxes decreases during the year, then the amount of the decrease must be subtracted from net income. This is because the year's tax payments were greater than the amount of reported tax expense, and the income statement thus overstates operating cash flows. (An understatement of an out-flow is equivalent to the overstatement of an inflow.)

Accounts Receivable

To understand this adjustment, assume all sales are credit sales and recall that the nature of the period's entries to Accounts Receivable is as follows:

Accounts Receivable

Beginning balance	Collections (debit to Cash)
Sales revenue	Ending balance
Beginning balance of next period	

The following equation describes these relationships:

$$\text{Beginning balance} + \text{Sales revenues} = \text{Collections} + \text{Ending balance}$$

For purposes of developing the operating cash flow amount, the amount of *collections* is of interest, because this is the amount of cash inflows that resulted from sales. Yet the period's net income is calculated based on the amount of revenues, not collections. The necessary adjustment can be calculated by a simple rearrangement of the above equation:

$$\text{Collections} = \text{Sales revenues} - (\text{Ending balance} - \text{Beginning balance})$$

Thus, if the balance in Accounts Receivable *increased* during the year, collections can be deduced by *subtracting* the increase in receivables from sales revenues.

This was the case with Fairway Corporation in 2010: Collections = $3,190,000 − $87,000 = $3,103,000. (The $87,000 increase in receivables is the difference between the ending balance of $673,000 and the beginning balance of $586,000, as shown in Illustration 11–1.) Note that this result, $3,103,000, is the amount that was reported in the direct method as "Cash received from customers."[5]

In a similar manner, it can be demonstrated that a *decrease* in the amount of accounts receivable during the period should be *added* to net income because such a decrease means that the period's cash inflows from customers (i.e., collections) exceeded the amount of sales revenue reported on the income statement.

Inventories

The adjustment related to inventories can also be developed by focusing on the T account:

Inventories

Beginning balance	Cost of sales
Purchases (credit Cash)	Ending balance
Beginning balance of next period	

In this case, the equation that is the basis of the adjustment is

$$\text{Purchases} = \text{Cost of sales} + (\text{Ending balance} - \text{Beginning balance})$$

If inventories increased during the period, cost of sales understates the cash outflows for purchases, and the inventory increase must therefore be added to cost of sales to deduce the cash outflows. But adding to cost of sales, an expense amount, is equivalent to subtracting from net income. Thus, if inventories *increased,* the amount of the increase is *subtracted* from net income to adjust income to a cash flow basis. For Fairway Corporation, the inventories' increase during 2010 was $47,000 ($657,000 − $610,000). Thus, $47,000 must be subtracted from 2010 net income to adjust cost of sales from an expense amount to a cash outflow amount.

Similarly, a *decrease* in inventory would be *added* to net income, which is equivalent to subtracting the amount of the decrease from cost of sales. If inventory decreases during the period, then the cost of sales amount overstates the cash outflows for the period's inventory purchases, and this overstatement of outflows must be added back to net income to convert it to an operating cash flow amount.

Accounts Payable

The adjustment related to changes in inventory converted the cost of sales expense item to a cash basis on the implicit assumption that all purchases for inventory were made for cash. The adjustment related to Accounts Payable relaxes this assumption and deals at the same time with purchases of resources that are expenses of the period, such as selling expenses, rather than assets. Since, in a sense, Accounts Payable is a mirror image of Accounts Receivable, the payables adjustment is algebraically the opposite of the receivables adjustment. Thus, if the balance in Accounts Payable *increases* during the period, the amount of the increase is *added* to net income to reflect the fact that the

---

[5] We have assumed that all sales are made on credit, which is the case with many nonretailing companies. The adjustment procedure is the same if some sales are made for cash. The reader can simply imagine that, for a cash sale, Accounts Receivable is simultaneously debited for the sales revenue and credited for the collection of this revenue.

period's expenses overstate the cash outflows for payments to suppliers. If the balance in Accounts Payable declines during the period, then suppliers have been paid more than is reflected in expenses; thus, a *decrease* in Accounts Payable is *subtracted* from net income to adjust it to operating cash flows. For Fairway Corporation in 2010, the $56,000 increase in Accounts Payable must be added to net income to adjust it to a cash flow amount.

Similar comments and the same rules apply to other payables related to operations—Interest Payable, Wages Payable, and Taxes Payable. However, there is no adjustment made for Notes Payable because that account relates to financing activities, not operating activities.

Prepaid Expenses

Fairway Corporation had no prepaid expenses. If there are prepaid expenses, the adjustments related to them are the same as for inventories. An increase in the balance in Prepaid Expenses during the period is subtracted from the period's net income. A decrease in the balance of Prepaid Expenses is added to net income.

Gains and Losses

The final type of adjustment made to net income to convert it to cash flow from operations relates to gains or losses reported on the accrual-basis income statement. Such gains or losses ordinarily are related to the sale or disposal of property, plant, and equipment or of marketable securities. The income statement will report the difference between the proceeds (if any) from the asset's sale or disposal and the asset's carrying amount at the time of sale (net book value in the case of fixed assets). If the proceeds exceed the carrying amount, a gain will be reported; if the proceeds are less than the carrying amount, a loss will be reported.

However, from the standpoint of the cash flow statement, the write-off of the asset's carrying amount is not relevant; the cash outflow associated with that amount occurred in some earlier period when the asset was acquired. Only the cash proceeds from the sale are of concern. Thus, the carrying amount of the asset must be added back to net income, since it was a write-off of a capitalized cost, not a cash outflow. Moreover, any cash proceeds from the asset's disposal are treated as an investing activity inflow in that section of the cash flow statement. Therefore, if no adjustment was made, the disposal proceeds would get double-counted—once in the operating activities section and again in the investing section. Hence, the cash proceeds must be subtracted from net income to avoid this double-counting. When both adjustments are taken into account—adding back the asset's carrying amount and subtracting the proceeds—the net effect simply reverses the reported gain or loss.

To illustrate such an adjustment, recall that Fairway Corporation sold a fixed asset in 2010 for $20,000 cash. The original cost of the asset was $150,000, but it was fully depreciated, so its net book value was zero.[6] Thus, the sale resulted in a $20,000 gain that would have been recorded by this entry:

Cash	20,000	
Accumulated Depreciation	150,000	
Equipment, at Cost		150,000
Gain on Disposal of Equipment		20,000

[6] Note in Illustrations 11–1 and 11–2 that Fairway's accumulated depreciation as of year-end 2009 was $1,000,000 and 2010 depreciation expense was $120,000, a sum of $1,120,000. Yet 2010 year-end accumulated depreciation was $970,000, or $150,000 less than $1,120,000. Thus, the amount of accumulated depreciation associated with the asset disposed of during 2010 was $150,000.

In this case, because the carrying amount of the asset was zero, the gain and the cash proceeds are the same, $20,000. But recall that the $20,000 proceeds were treated as an inflow in the investing activities section of the cash flow statement. To report this $20,000 also as an inflow from operations would double-count it. Thus, the $20,000 gain must be subtracted in the cash flow from operating activities section to avoid this double-counting.

Book Value

Suppose instead that equipment with a net book value of $10,000 had been disposed of with no resultant cash proceeds. In this case, the income statement would have reported a $10,000 loss; yet this would not have been associated with a $10,000 cash out-flow. Thus, the adjustment to net income to convert it to net operating cash flow would be to add back the $10,000 loss; otherwise, net income would understate cash outflows and thus understate net cash flow from operating activities.

As a final example, assume that property with a net book value of $10,000 was disposed of with cash proceeds of $15,000. The income statement would report a $5,000 gain. Since the sale of long-lived productive assets is treated as an investing activity, the $15,000 cash inflow from the disposal would be reported in that section of the cash flow statement. Thus, this $5,000 gain that is part of net income must be subtracted in the cash flow from operating activities section to preclude (1) double-counting the $15,000 proceeds and (2) counting the write-off of the $10,000 net book value as though it were a cash outflow when it is not.

In sum, the cash flow statement must accurately report the cash inflow (if any) associated with the sale or disposal of long-lived assets, not the difference between cash proceeds and net book value, which is reported in the income statement. Because the cash inflow proceeds are reported in the investing activities section of the statement and the write-off of the carrying amount of the asset does not involve a simultaneous cash outflow, any gain or loss reported in the income statement must be reversed in developing the amount for cash flow from operating activities.

Operating Activities: Summary

With the adjustment for gains or losses, the indirect method format for the operating activities section of the cash flow statement is complete. Collectively, the adjustments constitute a reconciliation of net income and net cash generated by operating activities. As seen in Illustration 11–3, the $228,000 net inflow is the same as would have been reported had the direct method been used. (Indeed, some of the adjustment techniques described for the indirect method can be used to obtain the numbers reported by the direct method; the direct method simply reports the results of the adjustments rather than showing the adjustments themselves.) Illustration 11–4 is presented as a summary of the adjustments we have described under the indirect method.

Summary of the Cash Flow Statement

The cash flow statement is divided into three major sections: operating, investing, and financing activities. Cash flow from operating activities can be prepared using the direct method or the indirect (reconciliation) method. Assuming use of the indirect method, the steps in preparing the statement of cash flows are as follows:

1. Find cash generated by operations by adjusting the net income as reported on the income statement using the procedures summarized in Illustration 11–4.
2. Identify any investing activities—for example, acquisition or sale of property, plant, and equipment or marketable securities. Report only the cash outflows associated with acquisitions; any portion of the cost of an acquisition that was financed by a

ILLUSTRATION 11–4 Calculating Operating Cash Flow from Net Income

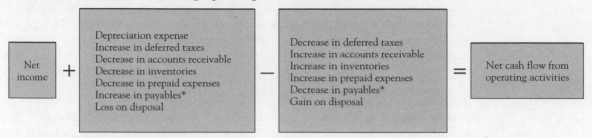

* Includes accounts payable, wages payable (accrued wages), interest payable (accrued interest expense), and taxes payable; does not include notes payable, short-term borrowings, or current portion of long-term debt.

directly related liability (e.g., a mortgage) must be subtracted in arriving at the cash outflow associated with the acquisition. Report only the cash proceeds from the sale of an asset.

3. Identify any financing activities, such as new borrowings or repayments on existing borrowings, issuance or retirement of stock, and cash dividend payments. If a convertible security was converted, do not report it in the cash flow statement, but dis-close it in a supplementary narrative.

4. Sum the subtotals for the three sections of the statement to determine the increase or decrease in cash (and equivalents). This amount is then added to the beginning cash balance to arrive at the ending cash balance, as shown in the bottom portion of Illustration 11–3.

Misconceptions about Depreciation

The way in which cash generated by operations is determined in the indirect method can lead to confusion about the nature of depreciation. Hence, this calculation warrants further discussion. Instead of calculating net cash flow from operations by showing cash inflows from customers and other revenue sources and then subtracting cash outflows for operating costs (the direct method), the starting point in the indirect method (as shown in Illustration 11–3) was the net income figure, to which depreciation was added. This add-back of depreciation was done because depreciation was an expense in Fairway's accrual-basis income statement that did not represent an outflow of cash during the period. (As was shown by the journal entry to record depreciation expense, depreciation was neither a source nor a use of cash.)

Unfortunately, many people misunderstand the nature of the calculation deriving operating cash flow from net income. They have the misconception that depreciation is a source of cash. Their misunderstanding is compounded by the failure of some companies to label the add-back of depreciation as an adjustment needed to convert net income to cash generated by operations. Instead, these companies simply list both net income and depreciation under the heading, "cash flow from operations." This confusion is exemplified by statements in the business press such as the following:

Depreciation should not be considered as a part of cash flow that can be used to pay dividends; rather, it should be considered as a source of funds to replace plant.

This kind of capital expenditure we write off fairly quickly . . . so that it becomes part of the financing. It's the cash flow.

The weaker airlines generally leased rather than bought their planes, thus forfeiting the chance to boost cash flow from depreciation. When ticket sales are an airline's only source of cash, a plunge in bookings can quickly put a carrier out of business.

The loan may be repaid . . . through cash generated from the gradual liquidation of a fixed asset (represented by depreciation) or the earnings of the borrower . . . These two items—depreciation and earnings—constitute cash flow.

These statements are fallacious. *Depreciation is not a source of cash.*

Some people argue that depreciation is a source of cash because depreciation expense reduces taxable income and hence reduces the cash outflow in payment of taxes. For example, if Fairway Corporation acquires more equipment in 2011, the additional depreciation expense will reduce its 2011 taxable income from what it would be if the equipment were not acquired, and hence will reduce the cash outflow for tax payments. This does not mean, however, that depreciation is a source of cash. The cash transaction is the income tax payment, and depreciation merely enters into the calculation of taxable income and hence reduces the tax payment. By the same token, Fairway could reduce its taxes in 2011 by increasing *any* expense, such as by giving every employee a 25 percent wage increase. Would one then say that increased wages expense is a source of cash?

Cash Flow Earnings

Since in most companies depreciation is the principal expense item that does not involve the use of cash, the sum of net income plus depreciation is often a good *approximation* of the cash generated by operations. (This is presumably what the author of the final quotation had in mind.) This total is often called **cash flow earnings.** Although depreciation enters into the calculation of this amount, depreciation is not itself a source of cash. The cash is generated by earnings activities, not by an adjusting entry for depreciation. The FASB specifically prohibits reporting an item labeled *cash flow income* or *cash earnings per share*.

Preparation of the Cash Flow Statement

Unlike the balance sheet and income statement, which are prepared directly from the firm's accounts, the cash flow statement is derived *analytically* from those accounts. This statement explains the changes in the cash and cash equivalents accounts between the beginning and ending balance sheets of the period. Since it is impractical to analyze every transaction recorded in those accounts, we analyze the changes in all other asset accounts, as well as liabilities and owners' equity, to determine their effect on cash during the period. Therefore, a logical way to prepare a cash flow statement is to identify and analyze the causes of differences between account amounts in the beginning and ending balance sheets. This analysis can be done in one of three ways: (1) by directly analyzing differences calculated from the comparative balance sheets, (2) by using a worksheet, or (3) by using T accounts.

The first approach is essentially the same as we have already used in explaining the derivation of amounts shown in Illustration 11–3, based on amounts in Illustration 11–1. The worksheet and T account approaches are not conceptually different but are more methodical and hence reduce the chance of errors. We will demonstrate the worksheet method below.

We emphasize that these descriptions contain no new concepts. The two alternative approaches are merely mechanical devices for arriving at the amounts to be reported on the statement of cash flows.

ILLUSTRATION 11–5

FAIRWAY CORPORATION Worksheet to Develop the Cash Flow Statement For the Year Ended December 31, 2010					
	Beginning Balances	Analytical Entries		Ending Balances	Net Change
		Debit	Credit		
Debit-balance accounts:					
Cash	230,000			326,000	96,000 dr.
Accounts receivable	586,000			673,000	87,000 dr.
Inventories	610,000			657,000	47,000 dr.
Plant and equipment, at cost	2,000,000			2,350,000	350,000 dr.
Accumulated depreciation	(1,000,000)			(970,000)	30,000 dr.
Investment securities	450,000			400,000	50,000 cr.
	2,876,000			3,436,000	560,000 dr.
Credit-balance accounts:					
Accounts payable	332,000			388,000	56,000 cr.
Income taxes payable	9,000			10,000	1,000 cr.
Short-term borrowings	147,000			126,000	21,000 dr.
Long-term debt	500,000			835,000	335,000 cr.
Deferred taxes	65,000			70,000	5,000 cr.
Common stock ($1 par)	50,000			60,000	10,000 cr.
Additional paid-in capital	133,000			167,000	34,000 cr.
Retained earnings	1,640,000			1,780,000	140,000 cr.
	2,876,000			3,436,000	560,000 cr.
Cash from operations:		Sources	Uses		
Cash from investing activities:					
Cash from financing activities:					

Cash Flow Worksheet

Illustration 11–5 is the worksheet for preparation of Fairway Corporation's 2010 cash flow statement. On it have been entered the beginning and ending account balances from Illustration 11–1, and changes in these account balances have been calculated in the final column. We must explain the $96,000 increase in Cash. For each of the other accounts, we will reconstruct the journal entries that caused the changes. Entries that affect the amount of cash will be classified as one of three types: cash from operations, cash from investing activities, and cash from financing activities. Because these classifications correspond to the format of the cash flow statement, using them will facilitate its final preparation. The numbers in the entries that follow correspond to those on the completed worksheet in Illustration 11–6.[7]

[7] Asset balances on Illustration 11–6 are shown as being debit-balance accounts, which is how they are recorded in the company's general ledger. Similarly, liability and owners' equity accounts are credit balances. Accumulated depreciation is a credit balance account included among the asset balances as a negative amount.

ILLUSTRATION 11–6

FAIRWAY CORPORATION					
Completed Cash Flow Statement Worksheet					
For the Year Ended December 31, 2010					

	Beginning Balances	Analytical Entries*		Ending Balances	Net Change
		Debit	Credit		
Debit-balance accounts:					
Cash	230,000	96,000	326,000		96,000 dr.
Accounts receivable	586,000	(7a) 87,000	673,000		87,000 dr.
Inventories	610,000	(7b) 47,000	657,000		47,000 dr.
Plant and equipment, at cost	2,000,000	(4) 500,000	(5) 150,000	2,350,000	350,000 dr.
Accumulated depreciation	(1,000,000)	(5) 150,000	(3) 120,000	(970,000)	30,000 dr.
Investment securities	450,000	(9a) 25,000	(9b) 75,000	400,000	50,000 cr.
	2,876,000			3,436,000	560,000 dr.
Credit-balance accounts:					
Accounts payable	332,000		(7c) 56,000	388,000	56,000 cr.
Income taxes payable	9,000		(7d) 1,000	10,000	1,000 cr.
Short-term borrowings	147,000	(10b) 36,000	(10a) 15,000	126,000	21,000 dr.
Long-term debt	500,000	(11b) 40,000	(11a) 375,000	835,000	335,000 cr.
Deferred taxes	65,000		(8) 5,000	70,000	5,000 cr.
Common stock ($1 par)	50,000		(12) 10,000	60,000	10,000 cr.
Additional paid-in capital	133,000		(12) 34,000	167,000	34,000 cr.
Retained earnings	1,640,000	(2) 60,000	(1) 200,000	1,780,000	140,000 cr.
	2,876,000	1,041,000	1,041,000	3,436,000	560,000 cr.

		Sources	Uses		
Cash from operations:					
Net income		(1) 200,000			
Depreciation expense		(3) 120,000			
Gain on disposal			(6) 20,000		
Increase in accounts receivable			(7a) 87,000		
Increase in inventories			(7b) 47,000		
Increase in accounts payable		(7c) 56,000			
Increase in taxes payable		(7d) 1,000			
Increase in deferred taxes		(8) 5,000			
Cash from investing activities:					
Equipment acquisition			(4) 500,000		
Proceeds from disposal		(6) 20,000			
Purchase of securities			(9a) 25,000		
Sale of securities		(9b) 75,000			
Cash from financing activities:					
Dividends paid			(2) 60,000		
Short-term debt proceeds		(10a) 15,000			
Short-term debt payments			(10b) 36,000		
Long-term debt proceeds		(11a) 375,000			
Long-term debt payments			(11b) 40,000		
Proceeds from stock issuance		(12) 44,000			
		911,000	815,000		96,000 dr.

* Numbers in parentheses correspond to entries described in the text.

Worksheet Entries

Retained Earnings A good starting point for the analysis is the $140,000 change in Retained Earnings. Illustration 11–2 showed a condensed version of Fairway's income statement and a reconciliation of the beginning and ending balances of Retained Earnings. From these statements we can see that two things affected the level of retained earnings: net income ($200,000), a "source" of cash; and payment of cash dividends ($60,000), a "use" of cash. We thus can record these two entries on the worksheet:

(1)

Cash from Operations 200,000

    Retained Earnings   200,000

(2)

Retained Earnings 60,000

    Cash from Financing Activities[8]   60,000

At this point, note that these two entries result in a net credit to Retained Earnings of $140,000. The last column of the worksheet shows that a change of $140,000 cr. was the amount we needed to explain. Thus, the analysis of the change in Retained Earnings is complete.

Plant and Equipment

The changes in the plant and equipment balance sheet accounts can be caused by acquisition or disposal of fixed assets and by changes in accumulated depreciation. As explained above, depreciation is an expense that is quite properly subtracted in arriving at net income but that, unlike most expenses, does not affect cash. Hence, we must add back the depreciation expense to net income; otherwise, Cash from Operations would be understated. The $120,000 depreciation expense for the period is shown in the income statement in Illustration 11–2. The entry for the worksheet is

(3)

Cash from Operations. 120,000

    Accumulated Depreciation   120,000

Other company records indicate that $500,000 of new equipment was purchased during the year. Thus, as another entry we have

(4)

Plant and Equipment, at Cost 500,000

    Cash from Investing Activities   500,000

Entries 3 and 4 do not completely explain the net increase of $350,000 in Plant and Equipment, at Cost, or the net increase of $30,000 in Accumulated Depreciation. (Since Accumulated Depreciation is a contra asset, its changing from $1,000,000 to $970,000 constitutes an increase in assets.) The disposal of a fully depreciated asset, having original cost of $150,000, needs to be included in the analysis:

(5)

Accumulated Depreciation 150,000

    Plant and Equipment, at Cost   150,000

[8] In the case of the statement of cash flows shown at the bottom of Illustration 11–6, since all three of the major category (operating, investing, and financing) captions are stated in terms of "cash *from*" (a "source" of cash), a debit cash entry is a "source" of cash and a credit cash entry is a "use" of cash. For example, a credit entry to cash *from* financing activities is a "use" of cash, which, in this case, is a payment of dividends. *Source* and *use* are shown in quotation marks since some of the adjustments do not necessarily represent a movement in the cash account, such as the net income adjustment.

Entries 3, 4, and 5 now collectively explain the $350,000 increase in Plant and Equipment, at Cost, and the $30,000 increase in Accumulated Depreciation.

Note that the write-off transaction in entry 5 does not affect cash flow. However, we also know that there were $20,000 cash proceeds from the disposal, which must be shown as a source in the investing activities section of the cash flow statement. This $20,000 was treated as a gain on the income statement since the net book value of the equipment disposed of was zero. But net income, including this $20,000, has already been reflected as a source of cash from operations in entry 1. Thus, we need to reclassify this $20,000 from an operating activity source to an investing activity source, as with this entry:

(6)

Cash from Investing Activities 20,000	
Cash from Operations	20,000

Other Adjustments to Net Income

Entries 3 and 6 constitute two of several adjustments that must be made to convert the net income amount, $200,000 in entry 1, to the net cash flow from operations. Illustration 11–4 reminds us of the other adjustments, which are related to changes in receivables, inventories, and payables. These adjustments are made with the following entries:

(7a)

Accounts Receivable 87,000	
Cash from Operations	87,000

(7b)

Inventories 47,000	
Cash from Operations	47,000

(7c)

Cash from Operations 56,000	
Accounts Payable	56,000

(7d)

Cash from Operations 1,000	
Income Taxes Payable	1,000

Also, the $5,000 increase in deferred taxes, representing income tax expense that did not require a current outflow of cash, leads to this adjustment:

(8)

Cash from Operations 5,000	
Deferred Taxes	5,000

The analysis has now taken care of all items affecting cash from operations but is incomplete with regard to investing and financing activities.

Investment Securities

The one remaining unexplained asset change (other than Cash, which is what we are explaining overall) is the $50,000 decrease in Investment Securities. Underlying records show that this was the net effect of both new investments ($25,000) and securities sales ($75,000). The FASB wants each component reflected separately in the cash flow statement, which will require these entries:

(9a)

Investment Securities 25,000	
Cash from Investing Activities	25,000

(9b)

Cash from Investing Activities 75,000

    Investment Securities   75,000

Debt Transactions

Short-Term Borrowings and Long-Term Debt both changed during 2010. As with other balance sheet changes, the net amount of a change in debt is explained by reporting both the inflows and outflows contributing to the net change. For Short-Term Borrowings, underlying records reveal that the net decrease of $21,000 is explained by new short-term debt of $15,000 and repayments on earlier short-term debt of $36,000. This leads to the following entries:

(10a)

Cash from Financing Activities 15,000

    Short-Term Borrowings   15,000

(10b)

Short-Term Borrowings. 36,000

    Cash from Financing Activities   36,000

Similarly, the net increase in Long-Term Debt of $335,000 is explained thus:

(11a)

Cash from Financing Activities 375,000

    Long-Term Debt   375,000

(11b)

Long-Term Debt 40,000

    Cash from Financing Activities   40,000

Paid-In Capital

The remaining two account changes to be analyzed are those in Common Stock ($1 par) and Additional Paid-In Capital: that is, total paid-in capital. During the year, 10,000 shares of Fairway Corporation $1 par common stock were issued, for which the firm received $44,000. This financing activity leads to this worksheet entry:

(12)

Cash from Financing Activities 44,000

    Common Stock ($1 par)   10,000

    Additional Paid-In Capital   34,000

This entry completes the analysis of changes on the worksheet (Illustration 11–6). The change of every noncash account has been explained, and the offsetting entries have been classified as sources of cash (debits in the lower portion of the worksheet) or as uses of cash (credits); and these sources and uses have been further classified as arising from operations, investing activities, or financing activities. As a check, the debits (sources) and credits (uses) below the double line are added and the net change compared with the top line of the worksheet. Both changes are $96,000 dr., showing the accuracy of the amounts of the analytical entries.

Statement Preparation

The actual preparation of the cash flow statement is now straightforward. All of the amounts needed for the statement of cash flows appear on the worksheet in Illustration 11–6. All that is necessary is to put these amounts in the proper format, as shown in Illustration 11–3. We have used the indirect method to develop the amount for cash from operating activities because it is illustrative of usual practice. The direct method is also permitted; but if it is used, a reconciliation of net income with net cash flow from operations must be presented in a separate schedule.

Summary of Preparation Procedures

To prepare a cash flow statement, the following steps are taken:

1. From the company's balance sheets, enter the beginning and ending balances of each account and the change in each account's balance on a worksheet (such as in Illustration 11–6).
2. For each account (other than Cash), analyze the nature of the transactions causing the amount of net change and classify the change from each such transaction as either cash from operations, cash from investing activities, or cash from financing activities. This analysis will require reference to the income statement (e.g., to explain the change in Retained Earnings) and, in some cases, to other financial records of the company. Illustration 11–7 summarizes the nature of such transactions and the place where information about them is likely to be found.
3. After the account changes have been analyzed and classified, the debits and credits are totaled and then combined as a check to see that their net amount is equal to the amount of change in Cash.
4. The cash flow statement is prepared directly from the worksheet, using the format shown in Illustration 11–3.

ILLUSTRATION 11–7 Locating Amounts for a Cash Flow Statement

Item	Location on Financial Statements
1. *Cash from operations:*	
a. Net income	Income statement
b. Plus: Depreciation expense	Income statement (or note thereto)
c. Plus: Amortization of prepaid expense, goodwill, and other intangibles	Income statement (or note thereto) or change in balance sheet item
d. Plus: Increase (or Minus: Decrease) in deferred income taxes	Change in deferred tax liability
e. Minus: Increase in accounts receivable, inventories; Plus: Increase in payables	Changes in balance sheet items
f. Plus: Decrease in accounts receivable, inventories; Less: Decrease in payables	Changes in balance sheet items
g. Plus: Loss (or Minus: Gain) on disposal of assets (Note 1)	Income statement
2. *Cash from investing activities:*	
a. Purchase of noncurrent assets	Increase in asset account (Note 1), net of related financing
b. Proceeds from asset disposals	Decrease in net book value less loss (or plus gain) from income statement (Note 1)
c. Loans made to (or collected from) another entity	Change in loans receivable account (Note 2)
3. *Cash from financing activities:*	
a. Borrowings or debt repayments	Changes in liability accounts (Note 2)
b. Issuance or retirement of stock	Changes in paid-in capital accounts (Note 2)
c. Cash dividends	Retained earnings statement

Notes:
1. The change in the asset account is affected by depreciation, sale of assets, and purchase of assets. The amount of each is reported in a note accompanying the balance sheet and in detailed accounting records within the organization.
2. Only the net change can be determined from the balance sheet, whereas the FASB requires that any increases and decreases be reported separately.
3. Conversion of bonds and stock (Balance sheet changes). The conversion of bonds or preferred stock to common stock does not affect the total amount of cash flow. Such transactions are not reported in the statement itself, but are disclosed supplementally.

Analysis of the Cash Flow Statement

At the outset of this chapter, several questions were mentioned that analysis of the cash flow statement can help answer. In specifying the operating, investing, and financing activities classifications as the basic format for this statement, the FASB and IASB intended to aid in the analysis of the statement's contents.

For example, for Fairway Corporation, the statement in Illustration 11–3 indicates that operations did not generate enough cash ($228,000) to fund the company's 2010 investing activities ($430,000). The $202,000 difference was financed through borrowings and a common stock issue, which also provided funds for dividend payments and a $96,000 buildup in cash and cash equivalents. Given this relatively large increase in cash (42 percent higher than at the start of the year), the question is raised about why Fairway borrowed the additional $375,000 in long-term debt rather than a lesser amount, or why the $44,000 stock issuance was undertaken. Perhaps the company plans to make some significant investments early in 2011. (Statement analysis often raises as many questions as it answers.)

Ratios

In addition to the classification of the information into three categories, three specific analytic techniques will now be suggested.

Cash Realization Ratio

The cash realization ratio is defined as

$$\frac{\text{Cash generated by operations}}{\text{Net income}}$$

This ratio indicates how close net income is to being realized in cash. A ratio higher than one is considered to signal high-quality earnings. The ratio is sometimes called the quality of earnings ratio. It should be used with caution since cash management tactics, such as a slowdown in paying accounts payable, can increase the numerator and the ratio.

Coverage Ratios

Two "coverage" ratios, *times interest earned* and *fixed charges coverage,* were described in Chapter 8. Both of these ratios would be conceptually sounder if the numerator were based on cash generated by operations rather than on income, because interest, lease payments, and similar fixed charges must be paid by using cash. The amount for cash generated by operations should be adjusted to a pretax, prefixed-charges basis (as was the case when these ratios were based on income in Chapter 8). These coverage ratios will ordinarily be higher when based on operating cash rather than on income because cash generated by operations is usually a larger amount than net income.

Source and Use Percentages

Despite the FASB's prescribed cash flow statement format, some analysts find it useful to reorganize the data into the previously popular sources and uses format, as is done in Illustration 11–8. As shown in that illustration, the amount of total sources of cash can be treated as 100 percent; then each cash flow statement item can be expressed as a percentage of total sources. For example, internally generated cash provided 30 percent ($228,000 ÷ $757,000) of the total sources; equipment purchases used 66 percent ($500,000 ÷ $757,000) of the total sources; and dividends used another 8 percent.

A ratio used by credit officers in evaluating corporations' creditworthiness for long-term debt is the **ratio of cash generated by operations to total debt** (both short- and

ILLUSTRATION 11–8
Cash Flows
Presented in
Sources and Uses
Format

FAIRWAY CORPORATION Sources and Uses of Cash For the Year Ended December 31, 2010 (dollars in thousands)		
	Amount	**Percent**
Sources of Cash		
Cash generated by operations	$228	30.1%
Short-term borrowings	15	2.0
Long-term debt	375	49.5
Issuance of common stock	44	5.8
Proceeds from disposal of equipment	20	2.6
Sale of investment securities	75	9.9
Total sources of cash	757	100.0%
Uses of Cash		
Acquisition of plant and equipment	$500	66.1%
Purchase of investment securities	25	3.3
Dividends paid	60	7.9
Repayment of short-term debt	36	4.8
Repayment of long-term debt	40	5.3
Total uses of cash	661	87.4%
Net increase in cash	$ 96	12.6%

long-term debt). For a corporate bond to qualify for the highest credit rating issued by the rating agencies, this ratio must be at least 100 percent (that is, 1 to 1).

"Free" Cash Flow

Cash Flow Projections

Some analysts calculate the amount of **"free" cash flow,** which is cash from operations minus three items: (1) cash used by essential investing activities (e.g., fixed asset replacements necessary to maintain existing capacity); (2) scheduled debt repayments; and (3) normal dividend payments. If positive, the amount indicates cash available to retire additional debt, increase dividends, or invest in new lines of business. If negative, it indicates the amount of financing needed just to support current operations and programs.

The purpose of analyzing cash flow statements is not solely to understand what has happened in the past. In addition, this analysis serves as a means of projecting what cash flows may look like in the future.

A projected cash flow statement is an essential device for planning the amount, timing, and character of new financing. These projections are important both to management in anticipating future cash needs and to prospective lenders for appraising a company's ability to repay debt on the proposed terms. Estimated uses of cash for new plant and equipment, for increased receivables and inventories, for dividends, and for the repayment of debt are made for each of the next several years. Estimates also are made of the cash to be provided by operations. If cash uses exceed cash sources, cash that must be obtained by borrowing or the issuance of new equity securities. If the indicated amount of new cash required is greater than management thinks it is feasible to raise, then the plans for new plant and equipment acquisitions and dividend policies are reexamined so that the uses of cash can be brought into balance with anticipated sources of financing them.

For shorter-term financial planning, cash flow projections are made for each of the next several months or several quarters. This **cash budget** is useful in anticipating seasonal financing needs; for example, toy manufacturers need short-term financing for inventories prior to the major holiday sales season. Similarly, the cash budget will indicate when excess cash will be available to invest in short-term marketable securities.

How does it looks for a Start up

Cash as an Asset

Cash or Cash Equivalents, as part of current asset, sits on the Balance Sheet and is normally ignored by value searching investment bankers who usually dismiss it as an unproductive asset. The generic interpretation is that when a firm doesn't know what to do with the surplus created out of business operations, the undistributed profits lie in form of Cash. Also, as per the general understanding of the business, firms should invest surplus into productive assets like PPE, Inventory to expand operations or sometimes, reward the shareholders by paying dividends. Although, there is some exception to this interpretation but it is largely true. Moreover, at times, the reason why the firm is not able to use the cash to expand its operations could be because of the state restrictions on expansion.

What kind of firms keep lot of Cash and why?

One of the categories of industries who would normally have very high proportion of "Cash and Cash equivalents" on their Balance Sheet would be IT companies or companies which are more into technology innovation. These companies usually have "asset light" balance sheet as they don't require a lot of "tangible assets." They develop and sell unique products and therefore have huge margins and then since they don't need a lot of PPE, the surplus money normally is shown as "Cash Equivalents." Typical examples would be firms like Apple, Facebook, Microsoft, TCS, etc. Other reasons for holding large volume of cash range from "technology firms need to have enough money to pay salaries to the employees who are the main asset of such firms (intellectual capital driven firms will normally have to pay very attractive salaries to retain top talent and there could be long periods of cash flowing out without any new innovation; therefore they hold sufficient cash to keep paying salaries to their best executives)" to "keep making all cash acquisitions every now and then (in technology space, there are a lot of small firms who keep developing new technologies but are primarily waiting to be bought over by the big technology giants." Sometimes, such companies use the surplus Cash to buy back their own shares from the markets basically to send a signal that markets are not pricing their shares appropriately, which also results in increase of promoters shares in the firm. This could also be an exercise to thwart any attempt of a possible takeover by a competitor.

Cash and Profits

Can there be a firm which have never made any profit since its birth and continues to make perennial losses but still be flushed with Cash? Looks like a very unlikely scenario but the fact of the matter is that many of the Unicorns (one who has a value of more than $10 billion) fall into this category. They have to still make any profit out of their operations but attract very high valuations which translates into a lot of Cash on their Balance Sheet. Actually some of these startups are also referred as "Cash burning" firms because they keep on incurring losses by making huge expenses including hiring very costly talent but still attract abnormal valuations from the markets. Till the time, the firm can attract investors who believe that the firm can become profitable in future, it can have positive cash balances despite negative margins. Therefore, there can be firms with losses in PL but Cash positive in Balance Sheet because that "Cash" is not coming from Operations but is actually coming from outside investors.

The next obvious question would be why and how are investors putting so much money on such loss making firms. One of the main reasons is that these investors believe that the current stress resulting in loss is temporary and once the business scales up and gathers more acceptability in the market, the current trend will reverse because volumes will increase pushing the revenue and therefore the margins from red to profits. Who will drive these businesses still remains a challenge as such companies continue to hire very costly talent, spend huge money on Research and Development and also on Branding and Publicity. The investors (normally Private Equity firms like Sequoia Capital, etc.) normally sit on the Boards of such companies and observe very closely the direction in which the firm is heading. Although when the company will generate profits still remains an elusive question.

Summary

A statement of cash flows provides information about an entity's investing and financing activities during the accounting period, as well as showing how much cash was generated by the period's operations.

The net amount of cash generated by operations is not the same as net income. Some expenses (notably depreciation) subtracted in arriving at net income for the period do not use cash. The net amount of cash generated by operations can be derived indirectly from the net income figure by making adjustments for those income statement amounts that were not accompanied by an equal amount of cash flow. These adjustments take account of changes in accounts receivable, inventories, payables, and deferred taxes. Also, depreciation is added back to net income because it is an expense that does not involve a corresponding use of cash. However, one must not infer from this calculation that depreciation is itself a source of cash, for it definitely is not. The net cash flow from operating activities also can be developed directly from cash receipts and payments related to operations.

The cash flow statement does not include certain financing and investing activities that do not cause a change in cash, such as the purchase of fixed assets with a long-term mortgage note or the conversion of a bond into common stock. However, these noncash transactions are supplementally disclosed in order to give a full picture of investing and financing activities.

Cash flow statements are also prepared prospectively so that an organization can anticipate both short-term and longer-term needs to raise additional cash through sale of assets, borrowing, or issuing additional shares of stock.

Problems

Problem 11–1.

The Bee Company shows the following account amounts:

	2009	2010
Sales	$8,743,000	$8,337,000
Accounts receivable 12/31	511,000	641,000

Required:
Determine how much cash was generated from sales during 2010.

Problem 11–2.   Explain what effect the following transactions would have on cash and how they would be shown in a cash flow statement.

1. A $2,000,000 piece of equipment is purchased with the proceeds of a new 12-month note.
2. Mortgage bonds are retired with $790,000 cash and the proceeds of an issue of 150,000 shares of common stock.
3. $2,000,000 of inventory is purchased on account.
4. A dividend of $0.25 per share is declared on the 750,000 outstanding shares.
5. A piece of machinery is sold for $1,500,000 cash. When originally purchased, it cost Anwat $5,000,000, and currently has $2,500,000 of accumulated depreciation.

Problem 11–3.   Kids 'n Caboodle, a children's clothing store, had the following cash receipts and disbursements for its first year of operations:

Receipts:	
Cash sales	$155,000
Loan proceeds	21,000
Total receipts	176,000
Disbursements	
Merchandise purchases (all sold this year)	84,000
Wages	33,000
Rent and lease payments	22,000
Other operating outlays	7,900
Purchase equipment	10,500
Total disbursements	157,400
Increase in Cash Balance	$18,600

The store has no accounts receivable (it accepts only cash or bank cards for payment). At year-end, an employee had earned $200, which the store had not yet paid. Also, at year-end, the store had not paid its most recent utilities bills, which totaled $150.

Required:
Prepare a cash flow statement for the year.

Problem 11–4.   Lori Crump owns a small trucking operation. The bookkeeper presented Crump with the following income statements and balance sheets for 2010 and 2009.

INCOME STATEMENTS				
	2010		**2009**	
Revenues		$191,400		$182,600
Operating expenses:				
Depreciation	$26,400		$ 26,400	
Fuel	77,000		46,200	
Drivers' salaries	44,000		35,200	
Tax and licenses	22,000		17,600	
Repairs	30,800		19,800	
Miscellaneous	2,200	202,400	1,100	146,300
Income (Loss)		$(11,000)		$36,300

(continued)

Balance Sheets		
	12/31/10	12/31/09
Cash	$ 22,000	$ 4,400
Accounts receivable	8,800	26,400
Net fixed assets	198,000	224,400
Total Assets	$228,800	$255,200
Accounts payable	$ 30,800	$ 22,000
Accrued salaries	8,800	5,500
Other accruals	3,300	1,100
Long-term debt	100,100	129,800
Crump, capital	85,800	96,800
Total Liabilities and Capital	$228,800	$255,200

Crump does not understand how the company can be $17,600 ahead of last year in terms of cash on hand and yet show an $11,000 loss for the year.

Required:
Prepare a cash flow statement (indirect method) to use in explaining this to Lori Crump.

Problem 11–5.   The owner of a small business has asked you to prepare a statement that will show him where his firm's cash came from and how it was used this year. He gives you the following information based on the Cash account in his general ledger:

Balance at beginning of year		$ 3,450
Collection of accounts receivable		34,500
Interest on savings account		345
Sale of old machine		3,105
Cash sales		27,600
Total		69,000
Payment on vendor accounts	$17,250	
Cash purchase of supplies	345	
Cash purchase of inventory	17,250	
Down payment on new truck	3,450	
Rent payments	8,625	
Utilities	2,070	
Interest payment	1,035	
Other miscellaneous expenses	1,725	
Payment on debt	3,450	
Part-time help	6,900	62,100
Balance at end of year		$ 6,900

In addition, the following is available from company records:

1. Sales were $61,410 for the year.
2. The Accounts Receivable balance decreased by $690.
3. Cash operating expenses totaled $54,165 (including cost of sales, supplies, rent, utilities, part-time help, and other miscellaneous expenses).
4. Accounts Payable decreased by a net of $2,760 during the year.
5. The Inventory balance remained constant throughout the year.
6. Depreciation of $1,725 was taken this year.

Required:
Prepare a cash flow statement using the direct method.

CASES

Case 11–1

Medieval Adventures Company*

Medieval Adventures Company was founded by Aaron Reinholz to produce a game marketed under the name "Castles and Unicorns." Each "Castles and Unicorns" cost the company $35 to produce. In addition to these production costs that varied in direct proportion to volume (so-called variable costs), the company also incurred $10,000 monthly "being in business" costs (so-called fixed costs) irrespective of the month's volume. The company sold its product for $55 each.

As of December 31, Reinholz had been producing "Castles and Unicorns" for three months using rented facilities. The balance sheet on that date was as follows:

MEDIEVAL ADVENTURES COMPANY Balance Sheet As of December 31	
Assets	
Cash	$146,250
Accounts receivable	68,750
Inventory	35,000
	$250,000
Equities	
Common stock	$250,000
Retained earnings	0
	$250,000

Reinholz was very pleased to be operating at a profit in such a short time. December sales had been 750 units, up from 500 in November, enough to report a profit for the month and to eliminate the deficit accumulated in October and November. Sales were expected to be 1,000 units in January, and Reinholz's projections showed sales increases of 500 units per month after that. Thus, by May monthly sales were expected to be 3,000 units. By September that figure would be 5,000 units.

Reinholz was very conscious of developing good sales channel relationships in order to increase sales, so "Castles and Unicorns" deliveries were always prompt. This required production schedules 30 days in advance of predicted sales. For example, Medieval Adventures had produced 1,000 "Castles and Unicorns" in December for January sales, and would produce 1,500 in January for February's demand. The company billed its customers with stated terms of 30 days net, but did not strictly enforce these credit terms with the result that customers seemed to be taking an additional month to pay. All of the company's costs were paid in cash in the month in which they were incurred.

Reinholz's predictions came true. By March, sales had reached 2,000 "Castles and Unicorns," and 2,500 units were produced in March for April sale. Total profit for the year by March 31 had reached $60,000. In order to get a respite from the increasingly hectic activities of running the business, in mid-April Reinholz went on a family vacation.

Within the week, the company's bookkeeper called. Medieval Adventures' bank balance was almost zero, so necessary materials could not be purchased. Unless Reinholz returned immediately to raise more cash, the entire operation would have to shut down within a few days.

Questions

1. Prepare monthly income statements, balance sheets, and cash budgets based on sales increases of 500 units per month and 30-day advance production for January through September. When will the company need extra funds? How much will be needed? When can a short-term loan to cover the need be repaid?

2. How is it possible that a company starts with $250,000 in capital and has profitable sales for a period of six months and still ends up with a zero bank balance? Why did Medieval Adventures need money in April? How could this need have been avoided?

3. From your calculations and financial statements for Question 1, *derive* cash flow statements for the months of March, May, and July from each month's beginning and ending balance sheets and income statement. Compare these derived cash flow statements with the cash budgets prepared directly in Question 1.

Case 11–2

Amerbran Company (A)*

Amerbran Company was a diversified company that sold various consumer products, including food, to

* Copyright © James S. Reece.

bacco, distilled products, and personal care products and financial services. Financial statements for the company are shown in Exhibit 1.

EXHIBIT 1

AMERBRAN COMPANY Balance Sheets As of December 31, 20x1 and 20x0 (in thousands)		
	20x1	20x0
Assets		
Cash	$ 28,912	$ 23,952
Accounts receivable	756,152	687,325
Inventories	1,244,912	1,225,402
Prepaid expenses	76,140	77,167
Total current assets	2,106,116	2,013,846
Investments	1,116,534	1,058,637
Property, plant, and equipment, at cost	1,566,268	1,366,719
Less accumulated depreciation	723,442	645,734
Net property, plant, and equipment	842,826	720,985
Goodwill	645,210	577,606
Other assets	115,826	62,374
Total assets	$4,826,512	$4,433,448
Liabilities and Shareholders' Equity		
Accounts payable	$ 271,452	$ 238,377
Short-term debt	430,776	351,112
Accrued expenses payable	922,990	728,262
Total current liabilities	1,625,218	1,317,751
Long-term liabilities	880,674	932,828
Total liabilities	2,505,892	2,250,579

(continued)

Convertible preferred stock	33,828	42,611
Common stock, at par	322,834	161,417
Additional paid-in capital	53,641	57,072
Treasury stock, at cost	(110,948)	(102,705)
Retained earnings	2,021,265	2,024,474
Total shareholders' equity	2,320,620	2,182,869
Total liabilities and shareholders' equity	$4,826,512	$4,433,448

Income Statement
For the year ended December 31, 20x1
(in thousands)

Sales revenues, net	$7,622,677
Cost of sales	2,803,623
Excise taxes on goods sold	2,887,616
Gross margin	1,931,438
Selling, general, and administrative expenses	1,328,107
Income before income taxes	603,331
Provision for income taxes	274,558
Net income	$328,773

The 20x1 financial statements reflect the following transactions (dollar amounts are in thousands):

1. Depreciation and amortization expense was $115,974.
2. Net income included a loss of $66,046 resulting from the write-off of some obsolete equipment. The equipment had not yet been disposed of.
3. Net income included $59,610 from Amerbran's investment in a subsidiary; none of this income had been received in cash.
4. The year-end balance in Deferred Income Taxes was $17,548 lower than it was at the start of the year.
5. New property, plant, and equipment purchases totaled $260,075, all paid for with cash. Disposals of fixed assets generated $33,162 cash proceeds.
6. Acquisition of another company that was made for cash resulted in additional depreciable assets of $31,691 and goodwill of $102,030.
7. Cash dividends were paid in the amount of $216,158.
8. The firm declared and issued a 100 percent common stock dividend effective September 10, 20x1; that is, each shareholder received as a dividend a number of shares equal to his or her holdings prior to the dividend. The newly issued shares were valued at par in recording this transaction.
9. The firm spent $30,609 to purchase treasury stock on the open market. Some of the shares so acquired were reissued to certain employees as a bonus.
10. The firm increased its short-term debt as indicated on the balance sheet in Exhibit 1. Long-term borrowings decreased by $34,606.

Question

Prepare a statement of cash flows for the year 20x1. In order for your statement to show the correct increase in cash ($4,960), you will need to add a "miscellaneous activities" category; this will capture several transactions that were not described because they are more complicated than those covered in the text.

Case 11–3

Tesla Ltd

Read the following Financial Statements and answer the questions:

TESLA LTD Income Statement (values in 000's)				
Period Ending:	**12/31/2017**	**12/31/2016**	**12/31/2015**	**12/31/2014**
Cash and Cash Equivalents	$3,523,237	$3,498,735	$1,219,536	$1,923,660
Net Receivables	$515,381	$499,142	$168,965	$226,604
Inventory	$2,263,537	$2,067,454	$1,277,838	$953,675
Other Current Assets	$268,365	$194,465	$115,667	$76,134
Total Current Assets	$6,570,520	$6,259,796	$2,782,006	$3,180,073
Long-Term Investments	$456,652	$506,302	$0	$0
Fixed Assets	$14,144,126	$9,117,037	$5,194,737	$2,596,011
Goodwill	$60,237	$0	$0	$0
Intangible Assets	$361,502	$376,145	$12,816	$0
Other Assets	$7,062,335	$6,404,796	$78,380	$54,583
Total Assets	$28,655,372	$22,664,076	$8,067,939	$5,830,667
Accounts Payable	$4,121,616	$3,070,369	$1,338,946	$1,046,829
Short-Term Debt/Current Portion of Long-Term Debt	$896,549	$1,150,147	$627,927	$611,099
Other Current Liabilities	$2,656,505	$1,606,489	$844,162	$449,238
Total Current Liabilities	$7,674,670	$5,827,005	$2,811,035	$2,107,166
Long-Term Debt	$9,418,319	$5,969,500	$2,021,093	$1,818,785
Other Liabilities	$4,752,192	$4,101,872	$1,658,717	$642,539
Deferred Liability Charges	$1,177,799	$851,790	$446,105	$292,271
Misc. Stocks	$397,804	$375,823	$47,285	$58,196
Minority Interest	$997,346	$785,175	$0	$0
Total Liabilities	$24,418,130	$17,911,165	$6,984,235	$4,918,957
Common Stocks	$169	$161	$131	$126
Capital Surplus	$9,178,024	$7,773,727	$3,409,452	$2,345,266
Retained Earnings	($4,974,299)	($2,997,237)	($2,322,323)	($1,433,660)
Other Equity	$33,348	($23,740)	($3,556)	($22)
Total Equity	$4,237,242	$4,752,911	$1,083,704	$911,710
Total Liabilities & Equity	$28,655,372	$22,664,076	$8,067,939	$5,830,667

(continued)

TESLA LTD Income Statement (values in 000's)				
Period Ending:	**12/31/2017**	**12/31/2016**	**12/31/2015**	**12/31/2014**
Annual Income Statement (values in 000's)				
Total Revenue	$11,758,751	$7,000,132	$4,046,025	$3,198,356
Cost of Revenue	$9,536,264	$5,400,875	$3,122,522	$2,316,685
Gross Profit	$2,222,487	$1,599,257	$923,503	$881,671
Research and Development	$1,378,073	$834,408	$717,900	$464,700
Sales, General and Admin.	$2,476,500	$1,432,189	$922,232	$603,660
Operating Income	($1,632,086)	($667,340)	($716,629)	($186,689)
Add'l income/expense items	($105,687)	$119,802	($40,144)	$2,939
Earnings Before Interest and Tax	($1,737,773)	($547,538)	($756,773)	($183,750)
Interest Expense	$471,259	$198,810	$118,851	$100,886
Earnings Before Tax	($2,209,032)	($746,348)	($875,624)	($284,636)
Income Tax	$31,546	$26,698	$13,039	$9,404
Minority Interest	$279,178	$98,132	$0	$0
Net Income-Cont. Operations	($1,961,400)	($674,914)	($888,663)	($294,040)
Net Income	($1,961,400)	($674,914)	($888,663)	($294,040)
Net Income Applicable to Common Shareholders	($1,961,400)	($674,914)	($888,663)	($294,040)

Question

1. Can a company which is running into losses repeatedly have huge positive cash balances? Give argument citing the information in Case?
2. Looking at the Income Statement and Balance Sheet, comment on the nature/ specific characteristics of the industry? (Use factors like Fixed assets, Inventory, R&D expenses, SGA Expenses to comment)
3. Comment on the overall trend (increasing or decreasing) revenue, profit and other major expenses.
4. Would you suggest to buy the shares of this company or not?

Acquisitions and Consolidated Statements

Many corporations acquire an ownership interest in other corporations. Depending primarily on the percentage of ownership acquired, these investments in other corporations can be accounted for (1) at their fair value, (2) at cost, (3) on an equity basis, or (4) on a consolidated basis. This chapter describes these four methods of accounting. Because the most difficult problems arise in accounting for consolidated entities, most of the chapter deals with such entities. The chapter also describes the recording of an acquisition of another company—the acquisition method—and the preparation of consolidated financial statements.

Accounting for Investments

If Company A owns securities of Company B, then A is the *investor* company and B is the *investee* company. A's holdings of B's securities are reported on A's balance sheet as an asset, Investments.

Fair-Value Method

If the investor company's holdings constitute less than 20 percent of the common stock of the investee company, and if the stock's fair value is readily determinable, then *FASB 115* (described in Chapter 5) applies. Such stock is treated as an "available-for-sale" equity security and the **fair-value method** is used: The stock is reported on the balance sheet at fair value with unrealized gains or losses excluded from earnings and entered directly in the owners' equity account Other Comprehensive Income.[1] Dividends received do not affect the carrying amount of the investment. Rather, they are treated as revenues:

Cash	50,000	
Dividend Revenues		50,000

These revenues are usually included on the income statement under the caption "other income."

---

[1] "Accounting for Certain Investments in Debt and Equity Securities," *FASB Statement No. 115. FASB 115* does not apply if the equity method (described later) is used.

Cost Method

If an investor company owns less than 20 percent of an investee company's common stock, *and* the stock's fair value is not readily determinable, the investment is reported at its cost. Under the cost method, dividends are treated as revenues (a credit entry). The debit entry is to Cash.

Equity Method

If the investing company's holdings constitute a large enough fraction of the ownership interest in the investee company so that the investing company can significantly influence the actions of the investee, the investment is accounted for by the **equity method.** Unless the investing company can demonstrate that it does *not* "exercise significant influence" on the investee company, ownership of 20 percent or more of the investee company's common stock requires the use of the equity method.[2] If the investor company can demonstrate it does not exercise significant influence on the investee company, the investment is accounted for at fair value if the value of the investment is readily determinable. If this value is not readily- determinable, the investment is accounted for at cost.

The IASB's equity method standard does not incorporate the FASB's 20 percent test. Rather it requires that the equity method be used to account for investments in "associates." An associate is an entity over which the investor has significant influence and is neither a subsidiary nor an interest in a joint venture.[3]

In the equity method, the investment is initially recorded at its cost. Thereafter, the balance sheet investment amount is increased (debited) to reflect the investing company's share in the investee's net income; the offsetting credit is to a revenue account. If a dividend is received from the investee, the balance sheet investment amount is decreased (credited) and the offsetting debit is to Cash. Thus, in the fair-value and cost methods (described above), the income statement reports dividends; in the equity method, the income statement reports the investing company's share of the investee's net income, irrespective of how much of that income is distributed in the form of dividends.

Recording the Acquisition

To illustrate the entries made in the equity method, assume that Merkle Company acquired 25 percent of the common stock of Pentel Company on January 2, 2010, for $250,000 cash. Merkle Company's entry for this transaction would be

Investments.	250,000	
Cash.		250,000

Recording Earnings

If Pentel Company's net income for 2010 was $100,000, Merkle Company would increase the amount of its investment by its share (25 percent) of this amount, or $25,000. The following entry would be made on December 31, 2010:

Investments.	25,000	
Investment Revenue		25,000

[2] "Equity Method for Investments in Common Stock," *APB Opinion No. 18;* and "Criteria for Applying the Equity Method of Accounting for Investments in Common Stock," *FASB Interpretation No. 35.*
[3] "Investments in Associates," *IAS No. 28.* A subsidiary is an entity that is controlled by another entity (known as the parent). A joint venture is contractually agreed sharing of control over an economic activity.

Dividends

If Merkle Company received $10,000 in dividends from Pentel Company during 2010, Merkle would make the following entry:

Cash	10,000	
Investments		10,000

Note that this dividend entry reduces the amount of investments on the balance sheet but does not affect the income statement. (Equity method income is usually reported as a separate line item on the income statement.)

Consolidated Basis

If an investing company owns more than 50 percent of the stock of another company, it reports on a **consolidated basis.**[4] Such an acquisition is carried on the accounts of the investing company in accordance with the equity method. Consolidated financial statements are prepared by adjusting this account, as will be described in detail later in the chapter.

In summary, the most common methods of reporting an investment encountered in practice are as follows:

Amount of Ownership	Method of Reporting
Over 50%	Consolidated statements
20–50%	Equity method
Less than 20%	Fair-value or cost method

The IASB's consolidation standard has a 50 percent plus ownership consolidation test that is similar to the FASB's quantitative test for consolidation.[5] It is anticipated that the IASB will replace its 50 percent plus consolidation test with a requirement that requires consolidation of an entity by a parent when the parent "controls" the entity. The proposed definition of control of an entity is "the power to direct the activities of another entity to generate return for the reporting entity."[6] An investor company under the IASB proposal that has the power to control could consolidate an entity in which it holds a less than 50 percent ownership interest.

Business Combinations

A business combination occurs when two companies are brought together in a single accounting entity. In some cases, an acquiring company dissolves the acquired corporation and incorporates the latter's assets and liabilities with its own assets and liabilities. In other cases, the acquired company continues to exist as a separate corporation. It then becomes a **subsidiary** of the acquiring company. The acquiring company is its **parent.**

---

[4] "Consolidation of All Majority-Owned Subsidiaries," *FASB Statement No. 94. FASB 94* is an amendment to the basic consolidation standard " *Consolidated Financial Statements,*" *Accounting Research Bulletin No. 51.*

[5] "Consolidated and Separate Financial Statements," *IAS No. 27.*

[6] "IASB Exposure Draft," "Consolidated Financial Statements."

ILLUSTRATION 12–1

Preacquisition Balance Sheets As of Proposed Date of Acquisition (in thousands)	Corporation A	Corporation B
Assets		
Cash and marketable securities	$ 6,000	$1,000
Accounts receivable	5,000	1,400
Inventories	6,400	1,800
Total current assets	17,400	4,200
Plant and equipment (net of accumulated depreciation)	10,600	2,800
Total assets	$28,000	$7,000
Liabilities and Shareholders' Equity		
Accounts payable	$ 6,000	$1,700
Other current liabilities	1,500	300
Total current liabilities	7,500	2,000
Long-term debt	8,200	1,600
Total liabilities	15,700	3,600
Common stock (par plus paid-in capital)*	2,500	700
Retained earnings	9,800	2,700
Total shareholders' equity	12,300	3,400
Total liabilities and shareholders' equity	$28,000	$7,000
*Number of shares outstanding	1,000,000	100,000

Purchase versus Pooling

Under GAAP and IFRS, the acquisition method must be used to account for the acquisition of another company.[7] Prior to the issuance of *FASB Statement 141* (2002) and *IFRS No. 3* (2004), another accounting method, referred to as the pooling of interests, also was required if the acquisition transaction met certain conditions.[8]

To illustrate accounting for the pooling and purchase methods, we will use the balance sheets for two hypothetical corporations, shown in Illustration 12–1. We assume that Corporation A plans to acquire on January 1 all 100,000 shares of Corporation B stock and that it will pay for this stock with 200,000 shares of its own stock, which has a market value of $30 per share, a total of $6 million.

Accounting as a Pooling

The underlying premise of pooling accounting is that there is a "marriage" of the two entities, with the two shareholder groups agreeing to a simple merging of the two firms' resources, talents, risks, and earnings streams. Accordingly, under pooling treatment, the balance sheets of A and B would simply be added together to arrive at the new consolidated balance sheet for A, which is the surviving entity. Any intercorporate obligations involved (for example, a receivable on A's balance sheet that was due from B) would be eliminated. With this exception, the new enterprise (the A–B combination) is accounted for as the sum of its parts, as shown in the first column of Illustration 12–2.

---

[7] "Business Combinations," *FASB Statement No.141* (revised 2007). "Business Combinations," *IFRS No. 3*.

[8] The pooling of interests method is discussed since those using pre-July 2002 financial statements of U.S. corporations will encounter this method of accounting for business combinations.

**ILLUSTRATION
12–2**

CORPORATION A Pro Forma Consolidated Balance Sheets As of Proposed Date of Acquisition (in thousands)		
	Pooling Accounting	Purchase Accounting
Assets		
Cash and marketable securities	$ 7,000	$ 7,000
Accounts receivable	6,400	6,400
Inventories	8,200	8,200
Total current assets	21,600	21,600
Goodwill	—	1,500
Plant and equipment (net of accumulated depreciation)	13,400	14,500
Total assets	$35,000	$37,600
Liabilities and Shareholders' Equity		
Accounts payable	$ 7,700	$ 7,700
Other current liabilities	1,800	1,800
Total current liabilities	9,500	9,500
Long-term debt	9,800	9,800
Total liabilities	19,300	19,300
Common stock (par plus paid-in capital)*	3,200	8,500
Retained earnings	12,500	9,800
Total shareholders' equity	15,700	18,300
Total liabilities and shareholders' equity	$35,000	$37,600
*Number of shares outstanding	1,200,000	1,200,000

The assets and liabilities of the combined firm are carried at the sum of their previous *book* values. Similarly, the Common Stock and Retained Earnings accounts of the combining firms are simply added to determine the combined firm's shareholders' equity. Note that when one compares A's preacquisition balance sheet in Illustration 12–1 with the *pro forma* (projected) pooling balance sheet in Illustration 12–2, there is no evidence of the fact that A paid stock worth $6 million for B's net assets, which had a book value of only $3.4 million (as indicated by its shareholders' equity). This $2.6 million difference appears nowhere on the balance sheet.

**Accounting as
a Acquisition**

The underlying premise of acquisition accounting is that instead of a marriage of A and B, A is buying the *net* assets of B.[9] A is buying B's assets and assuming B's liabilities, the equivalent to buying B's shareholders' equity. In accordance with the cost concept, the net assets of B go onto A's balance sheet at the amount that Corporation A paid for them: $6 million. This treatment involves three steps.

First, B's tangible assets and those intangible assets that A will have a legal or contractual right to and those that are separable and salable (such as patents and licenses) are revalued to their *fair* value.[10] In Illustration 12–2, it is assumed that all of the assets

[9] The acquisition method (GAAP terminology) and the acquisition method (IFRS terminology) are similiar in nearly all respects

[10] Fair value is the amount at which an asset (or liability) could be bought (or incurred) or sold (or settled) in a current transaction between willing parties.

on B's preacquisition balance sheet were reported at amounts approximately equal to their fair values, except for plant and equipment. Plant and equipment had a book value of $2.8 million but a fair value of $3.9 million, an increase of $1.1 million. Hence, with acquisition accounting, the consolidated plant and equipment account shows $14.5 million ($10.6 million for A's preacquisition plant and equipment plus the acquired fixed assets of B, newly valued at $3.9 million).

Second, the assumed liabilities must be revalued to their fair value. The illustration assumes the fair value of B's liabilities assumed by A is equal to their value as reported on B's balance sheet.

Third, after the revaluation of B's assets and liabilities, any excess of the purchase price over the net amount of B's revalued assets and liabilities is shown on the consolidated balance sheet as an asset called **goodwill** (also referred to as *positive goodwill*).[11] This amount is $1.5 million, as shown in the second column of Illustration 12–2. It is calculated as follows:

Purchase price	$6,000,000
Less: Book value of net assets acquired	3,400,000
	2,600,000
Less: Write-up of acquired assets other than goodwill to fair value	1,100,000
Goodwill	$1,500,000

Hence, of the $2.6 million excess of the purchase price over the book value of Corporation B (which did not appear under pooling accounting), $1.1 million has been assigned to plant and equipment, and the remaining $1.5 million is shown on the balance sheet as goodwill. Goodwill must not be amortized under any circumstances; rather, it is subject to an annual impairment test.[12] (For income tax purposes, so-called Section 197 Intangibles, which include goodwill acquired after August 10, 1993, are amortized on a straight-line basis over 15 years; goodwill acquired prior to that date is not tax deductible.)

Intangible assets other than goodwill acquired in a business combination transaction fall into two categories. They have either limited useful lives or indefinite lives. Limited-life intangible assets are amortized over their useful life. Indefinite-life intangible assets are not amortized; rather, they are subjected periodically to an impairment test.

If the purchase price is less than the fair value of the net assets acquired, the cost concept requires that the acquired tangible asset be written down on a pro rata basis by the excess of the fair value over the purchase price. If any excess remains, it is recognized as extraordinary gain.

Consolidated Statements

A "company," as it is thought of by its management, its employees, its competitors, and the general public, may actually consist of a number of different corporations created for various legal, tax, and financial reasons. The existence of a family of corporations is by no means peculiar to big business. A fairly small enterprise may consist of one

[11] The preferred caption for this account is "Excess of cost over net assets of acquired companies."
[12] "Goodwill and Other Intangible Assets," *FASB Statement No. 142.* "Impairment of Assets," *IAS No. 36.* Generally, IFRS allows reversal of previously taken impairment losses when justified by changing circumstances. Goodwill is an exception. A goodwill impairment loss cannot be reversed in a subsequent period. The IASB believed the reversal is most probably the result of internally generated goodwill, which cannot be recognized.

corporation that owns its real estate and buildings, another that primarily handles production, another for marketing activities, and over them all a *parent corporation* as the locus of management and control. Each of these corporations is a legal entity, and each therefore has its own financial statements. Although the company itself may not be a separate legal entity, it is an important *economic* entity, and a set of financial statements for the whole business enterprise may be more useful than the statements of the separate corporations of which it consists.

Such statements are called **consolidated financial statements.** They are prepared by first adjusting and then combining the financial statements of the separate corporations. No separate journals or ledgers are kept for the consolidated entity. The adjustments are made on worksheets using data from the accounts of the separate corporations. Also, only legal entities are involved in the consolidation process. If an acquired corporation has been dissolved and as a result its assets have come under the legal ownership of the acquiring company, its assets and liabilities are already reflected in the acquiring company's accounts.

Basis for Consolidation

The legal tie that binds the other corporations, or *subsidiaries,* to the parent is the ownership of their stock. A subsidiary is not consolidated unless more than 50 percent of its voting common stock is owned by the parent. The FASB and IASB require a majority-owned subsidiary be consolidated, irrespective of whether or not its activities are homogeneous with those of its parent. This requirement can lead to confusing consolidated financial statements when unlike entities are consolidated, such as when a finance subsidiary and a manufacturing subsidiary are reported as one consolidated entity.

Consolidation Procedure

Illustration 12–3 shows the consolidation process in the simplest possible situation, consisting of the parent company and one subsidiary company, named Parent and Subsidiary, respectively. Parent owns 100 percent of Subsidiary's stock, this stock is an

ILLUSTRATION 12–3 Consolidation Worksheet

	Separate Statements		Intercompany Eliminations*		Consolidated Balance Sheet
	Parent	Subsidiary	Dr.	Cr.	
Assets					
Cash	45,000	12,000			57,000
Accounts receivable	40,000	11,000		(1) 5,000	46,000
Inventory	30,000	15,000		(4) 2,000	43,000
Fixed assets, net	245,000	45,000			290,000
Investment in subsidiary	55,000	—		(2) 55,000	—
	415,000	83,000			436,000
Liabilities and Shareholders' Equity					
Accounts payable	20,000	13,000	(1) 5,000		28,000
Other current liabilities	25,000	9,000			34,000
Long-term liabilities	100,000	—			100,000
Capital stock	100,000	40,000	(2) 40,000		100,000
Retained earnings	170,000	21,000	(2) 15,000		
			(4) 2,000		174,000
	415,000	83,000			436,000

* Parenthetical numbers correspond with text description.

asset shown on Parent's balance sheet as Investment in Subsidiary. The investment is recorded at cost. It is assumed here that Parent purchased Subsidiary for $55,000, and this purchase price was equal to Subsidiary's book value (capital stock plus retained earnings) as of the time of acquisition.

The two companies have been operating for a year. At the end of that year, their separate balance sheets are as summarized in the first two columns of Illustration 12–3. If the two columns were simply added together, the sum of the balance sheet amounts would contain some items that, so far as the consolidated entity is concerned, would be counted twice. To preclude this double counting, adjustments are made in the next two columns; these are explained below. Essentially, these adjustments eliminate the effect of transactions that have occurred between the two corporations as separate legal entities. Since the consolidated financial statements should report only assets owned by the consolidated entity and the liabilities and owners' equity of parties *outside* the consolidated entity, these internal transactions must be eliminated. The consolidated balance sheet that results from these adjustments appears in the last column. The adjustments are as follows:

1. **Intercompany Financial Transactions.** The consolidated balance sheet must show as accounts receivable and accounts payable only amounts owed by and to parties outside the consolidated business. Therefore, amounts that the companies owe *to one another* must be eliminated. Assuming that Parent owes Subsidiary $5,000, this amount is eliminated from their respective Accounts Payable and Accounts Receivable accounts. The effect is shown in the following hypothetical journal entry (remember that no journal entries actually are made in the books of either corporation):

   Accounts Payable (Parent) 5,000
      Accounts Receivable (Subsidiary)   5,000

   The payment of dividends by the subsidiary to the parent is a financial transaction that has no effect on the consolidated entity. In the separate statements, this was recorded on Parent's books as a credit to Investment Revenue (which was closed to Parent's Retained Earnings) and on Subsidiary's books as a debit to Dividends (which was closed to Subsidiary's Retained Earnings). Since this transaction ultimately affected only the two retained earnings accounts, adding to one account the same amount that was subtracted from the other, the act of combining the two of them automatically eliminates its effect. Therefore, no further adjustment is necessary.

2. **Elimination of the Investment.** Parent company's investment in Subsidiary's stock is strictly an intrafamily matter and must therefore be eliminated from the consolidated balance sheet. Because it is assumed that the stock was purchased at book value, the $55,000 cost shown on Parent's books must have equaled Subsidiary's capital stock plus retained earnings at the time of purchase. We know that capital stock is $40,000; the difference, $15,000, must therefore be the amount of retained earnings at that time. To eliminate the investment, therefore, the entry is as follows:

   Capital Stock (Subsidiary) 40,000
   Retained Earnings (Subsidiary). 15,000
      Investment in Subsidiary (Parent)   55,000

The additional $6,000 of retained earnings ($21,000 – $15,000) now shown on Subsidiary's books has been earned by Subsidiary subsequent to its acquisition by Parent.

3. Intercompany Sales. In accordance with the realization concept, the consolidated company does not earn revenue until sales are made to the outside world. The revenue, the related costs, and the resulting profit for sales made between companies in the consolidated entity must therefore be eliminated from the consolidated accounts.

The sales and cost of sales on intercompany transactions are subtracted from the total sales and cost of sales amounts on the consolidated income statement. If this were not done, the amounts would overstate the volume of business done by the consolidated entity with the outside world. To do this, records must be kept that show the sales revenue and the cost of sales of any sales made within the family.

Example

Subsidiary sold goods costing it $52,000 to Parent for $60,000. Parent then sold these goods to outside customers for $75,000. The consolidated entity's gross margin on these sales was $23,000 ($75,000 – $52,000). Of this amount, $8,000 ($60,000 – $52,000) appeared on Subsidiary's income statement and $15,000 ($75,000 – $60,000) appeared on Parent's income statement. Hence, the consolidated *income* amount would not be overstated. However, the correct consolidated sales revenue amount is $75,000, not $135,000 ($60,000 + $75,000). Similarly, the correct consolidated cost of sales amount is $52,000, not $112,000. Thus, Subsidiary's sales and Parent's cost of sales must be reduced by the $60,000 intercompany transfer to avoid double counting:

Sales (Subsidiary)	60,000	
Cost of Sales (Parent)		60,000

These adjustments would be made on the worksheet for the consolidated income statement. (This worksheet is not illustrated here, but it is similar to the worksheet for the consolidated balance sheet.) Also, as mentioned above, any accounts receivable and payable amounts arising from Subsidiary's sales to Parent would be eliminated.

4. Intercompany Profit. If goods sold by Subsidiary to Parent have not been sold by Parent to the outside world, these intercompany sales transactions will affect the Inventory account of the buyer (Parent) and the Retained Earnings account of the seller (Subsidiary). Adjustments to these accounts are required. Assume that, in the preceding example, Parent sold to outside customers only three-fourths of the products it acquired from Subsidiary and the other one-fourth remain in Parent's inventory at the end of the year at its cost to Parent of $15,000. The products sold to the outside world present no problem because they have disappeared from inventory and the revenue has been realized. The $15,000 remaining in Parent's inventory, however, is regarded by Subsidiary as a sale, and the $2,000 gross margin on that amount (one-fourth of Subsidiary gross margin of $8,000) appears in Subsidiary's Retained Earnings. This portion of the profit must be eliminated from the consolidated balance sheet. This is done by reducing Subsidiary's Retained Earnings and Parent's Inventory by the amount of the gross margin, as in the following entry:

Retained Earnings (Subsidiary)	2,000	
Inventory (Parent)		2,000

(To avoid double-counting, the entry shown in the example—eliminating Subsidiary's $60,000 sales to Parent and Parent's $60,000 cost of sales—must still be made, even though some of these goods remain in Parent's inventory.)

The necessary eliminations having been recorded, the amounts for the consolidated balance sheet can now be obtained by carrying each line across the worksheet, as shown in Illustration 12–3.

In the preceding example, two of the most difficult problems in preparing consolidated statements did not arise because of simplifying assumptions that were made. These problems are described below.

Asset Valuation

In the example it was assumed that Parent purchased Subsidiary's stock at its *book* value. But a subsidiary's stock is often purchased at an amount higher than its book value. As explained earlier, purchase accounting for an acquisition requires that the book value of the acquired identifiable assets be adjusted to show their fair value and that any remaining excess of purchase price over the revalued net assets be shown as an asset called *goodwill*. In the above illustration, if Parent had paid $70,000 rather than $55,000 for Subsidiary's stock and if Subsidiary's assets were found to be recorded at their fair value, there would be goodwill of $15,000, and adjustment 2 (elimination of the investment) would have been

Goodwill	.15,000	
Capital Stock (Subsidiary)	40,000	
Retained Earnings (Subsidiary)	15,000	
Investment in Subsidiary (Parent).		70,000

Minority Interest

If Parent had purchased less than 100 percent of Subsidiary's stock, then there would exist a **minority interest**— the equity of Subsidiary's other owners in the acquired entity. On the consolidated balance sheet, this minority interest appears as a separate equity item, in shareholders' equity.[13] For example, if Parent owned 80 percent of Subsidiary's stock, for which it had paid 80 percent of Subsidiary's book value, or $44,000, adjustment 2 would have been as follows:

Capital Stock (Subsidiary)	.32,000	
Retained Earnings (Subsidiary)	.12,000	
Investment in Subsidiary (Parent).		44,000

As this elimination suggests, at the time Parent acquired 80 percent of Subsidiary's stock, the minority interest amount was $11,000, the sum of the remaining 20 percent of Subsidiary's capital stock and retained earnings.

After the acquisition, this minority interest would increase by 20 percent of the increase in Subsidiary's retained earnings, *after* elimination of Subsidiary's $2,000 profit on sales to Parent. This intercompany profit adjustment is prorated between Parent and the minority shareholders in proportion to their respective ownership. Hence, if Parent owned 80 percent of Subsidiary, on the consolidated balance sheet, the following amounts would appear:

Minority interest	$ 11,800
Shareholders' equity:	
Capital stock	100,000
Retained earnings	173,200

[13] "Consolidated and Separate Financial Statements," *IAS No. 27.* "Noncontrolling Interests in Consolidated Financial Statements," *FASB Statement 160.* Under the purchase method, *FASB Statement 141R* ("Business Combinations") requires any minority interest remaining in the acquired entity to be valued at its fair value at the acquisition date.

The amount for minority interest is the net of four items:

20% of Subsidiary capital stock	$ 8,000
20% of Subsidiary retained earnings at time of acquisition	3,000
20% of the $6,000 increase in Subsidiary retained earnings since acquisition	1,200
Less 20% of the $2,000 intercompany profit	(400)
Total minority interest	$11,800

Similarly, the consolidated retained earnings amount, which was $174,000 when we assumed Parent owned 100 percent of Subsidiary, is now $800 less ($173,200), reflecting the $1,200 minority interest in the $6,000 post acquisition increase in Subsidiary's retained earnings, adjusted downward for the $400 minority interest share of the $2,000 intercompany profit elimination.

Related Party Transactions and Arm's Length Transaction

The objective of any commercial business is to maximize shareholder's wealth keeping in mind the larger good of the society in which the business operates. To try and optimally re-distribute the wealth for the overall betterment of those working for the business is a very important mission of firms now. The larger an organization becomes, the more it is expected to spread its benefits into the society by reaching into more people's pockets. The overall impact of a business is directly proportional to the impact it creates on all its major stakeholders' interests. In such circumstances, even the slightest skewness towards a particular interest group can lead to adverse repercussions upon the other stakeholders. Although such balancing is largely self-regulated, many times, regulatory supervision is needed to ensure fair representation of all the stakeholders. One of such regulatory measures is to ensure proper regulation of "related party transactions," which managers might use for private benefits and can indirectly promote fraudulent activities in the firm.

What is a related party transaction (RPT)?

A related party is a firm or a business related to a company in any other way other than by pure business transactions. It means that there is a special relationship that pre-exists between the parties even before the transaction takes place. Section 2(76) of the Companies Act, 2013 defines a related party with reference to a company, as:

a. a firm, private company in which the partner, director manager or his relative is a partner or

b. a private company or a public company in which a director or manager is a director and holds along with his relatives, more than 2% of its paid-up share capital.

The provisions of related party transactions are applicable to both private and public companies.

For instance, if Company A rents office premises from Y, a relative of its director X, and pays higher than market rent in a sweetheart deal, it helps Y and indirectly X, but harms shareholders of Company A. That said, RPTs need not always be bad for a company's shareholders. In many cases, RPTs make commercial and operational sense for the company. So, the Companies Act has not banned RPTs but instead laid down safeguards to be followed.

Arm's Length Transactions

Contrary to a related party, if the business transactions are conducted and carried out in a fair, transparent manner without any signs of influence of the parties' relation upon itself, it qualifies as a transaction at arm's length. It basically means any business transactions which are not influenced by the relationship between the parties and are conducted as if it is being done with an unrelated party.

Related Party Transactions: Are They Allowed or Banned?

As such, Related Party Transactions are not really banned in businesses but they are regulated by certain conditions as provided in Section 188 of the Act. The basic premise is that if there are any such transactions, they need to be disclosed to the Board and shareholders for ratification. Moreover, prior approval from the Audit Committee is to be obtained if the transactions fall within the meaning of RPT as defined in Section 188. Justification is also required to be given in support of the transactions. However, if the transactions are big and beyond a pre-decided threshold limits, they need to be disclosed in the Annual General Meeting for approval by a special resolution.

Related Party Transactions Which Require Special Resolution in AGM

a. In case of a sale, purchase or supply of any goods or materials where the transaction size exceeds 10% of the turnover of the firm or Rs.100 crore, whichever is lower;

b. In case of selling or otherwise disposing of, or buying, property of any kind; where the transaction amount is more than 10% of the net worth of the company or Rs.100 crore, whichever is lower

c. In case of leasing of property of any kind where the amount involved exceeds ten percent of net worth of the company or ten per cent of turnover of the company or 100 crore.

d. In case the firm is availing any services from another firm where the transaction amount is exceeding 10% of the turnover of the company or INR 50 crore, whichever is lower

If these conditions are satisfied, then the transactions qualify for Arm's Length Transaction and can be proceeded with. Companies are expected to adopt policies whereby they have a SOP (standard operating procedures) to deal with related parties to be in compliance with the regulations. However, there is a rider clause too; no member of the related party is allowed to vote in a special resolution to approve any contract or arrangement which the company is proposing to enter into.

What are the costs of Non-Compliance?

Whenever any contract is signed by a director or any other employee of a firm, to a third party without the ratification of the Board or it is done without the approval by a special resolution in the general meeting or if it is not approved by the Board or by the shareholders within three months from the date on which such contract is made, then the Board can cancel such contract or arrangement and declare it null and void.

What is there for common shareholders to worry about?

Simply because a shareholder's money is at stake and if a company in which he has invested is fooling him through unfavorable RPTs, he will be better off heading for the exit door. Such practices tantamount to misrepresentation and bad corporate governance eventually come to bite shareholders even if they're not the villains.

Summary

Depending primarily on the fraction of stock owned, a corporation reports an investment in other companies (1) at fair value, (2) at cost, (3) on the equity basis, or (4) by the preparation of consolidated financial statements.

Acquisitions of other companies are reported on the basis of their purchase cost. If treated as a purchase, acquisitions often give rise to an asset called *goodwill,* which is the excess of the acquisition cost over the fair value of the net identifiable assets acquired. Goodwill must not be amortized. It is subjected to an annual impairment test.

Consolidated balance sheets and income statements are prepared by combining the accounts of the separate corporations in a corporate family. In combining these accounts, the effects of transactions occurring within the family are eliminated so that the consolidated statements reflect only transactions between members of the family and the outside world.

Problems

Problem 12–1.

On January 1, Company P purchased 40 percent of the voting stock of Company S for $600,000 cash. Company P exercises significant influence over Company S. During the year, Company S had net income of $300,000 and declared and paid dividends of $100,000. What accounting method should Company P use to record this investment? Why? Show how Company P would account for this investment on January 1, and for the subsequent income and dividends of Company S, using journal entries. Show the explanations of the journal entries and your calculations. How would the investment appear on Company P's books as of December 31?

Problem 12–2.

During its fiscal year, Company P purchased 50,000 shares of voting stock of Company S for $1,000,000. Company S has 312,500 shares of voting stock outstanding. Company S had a profit of $156,250 for the current year. Both companies have the same fiscal year. Company S paid dividends of $0.50 per share during the year. What accounting method should be used by Company P to account for this investment and why? Show the journal entries with explanations to record the original investment and make any adjustments necessary for Company S's profits and dividends.

Problem 12–3.

XYZ Company had the following transactions related to ABC Company over a two-year period:

Year 1

1. On January 1, XYZ purchased 35 percent ownership of ABC Company for $700,000 cash.
2. ABC Company had net income of $70,000 for the year.
3. At year-end, ABC Company paid its shareholders dividends of $60,000.

Year 2

1. XYZ Company purchased on January 1 an additional 5 percent of ABC Company's stock for $75,000 cash.
2. ABC Company declared a 10 percent stock dividend.
3. ABC Company had net income of $150,000 for the year.
4. At year-end, ABC Company paid its shareholders dividends of $100,000.

Required:

Prepare the journal entries for XYZ Company's books for the above transactions.

Problem 12–4. Elder Co. acquired for cash all of the outstanding stock of BaBe Co. on December 31 for $870,000. The balance sheets of the two companies just prior to the acquisition were as follows:

	Elder	BaBe
Current assets	$ 1,974,000	$138,000
Net fixed assets	32,814,000	537,600
Other assets	14,412,000	134,400
Total assets	$49,200,000	$810,000
Current liabilities	$ 3,600,000	$ 42,000
Long-term debt	15,582,000	150,000
Common stock	24,000,000	462,000
Paid-in capital	5,418,000	120,000
Retained earnings	600,000	36,000
Total equities	$49,200,000	$810,000

An independent appraiser valued the assets of BaBe Co. as follows:

	Market Value
Current assets	$150,000
Net fixed assets	555,600
Other assets	134,400

Required:

Prepare a consolidated balance sheet as of the acquisition date. Assume that no intercompany transactions have occurred in the past and that Elder will assume BaBe's liabilities.

Problem 12–5. Sandvel Company is a wholly owned subsidiary of Pebble, Inc. Each company maintains its own financial statements, but consolidated statements are prepared at the end of each fiscal year. At the end of the present fiscal year, the following items will affect the consolidated statements:

1. During the year, Sandvel sold chemicals to Pebble at a total price of $337,000; Sandvel's cost of these chemicals was $285,000. Pebble has sold all of these goods to outside customers.
2. Pebble owes Sandvel $73,000 of accounts payable.
3. Sandvel is indebted to Pebble on a long-term loan for $396,000. Pebble realized $32,000 of interest revenue from this long-term loan during the year.
4. As of the beginning of the year, Sandvel was carried at an equity amount of $3.1 million on Pebble's balance sheet.

Required:

Describe the elimination journal entries that would be needed in preparing consolidated statements.

Problem 12–6.   After much analysis, Company A, a non-U.S. company, is considering the acquisition of Company B. Under A's local GAAP, two alternative methods of acquisition accounting are available to the company. It can either buy all of Company B's stock on the market for a cash outlay of $650,000, or Company A can exchange authorized but un issued Company A shares with a value of $650,000 (currently selling for $50 per share) for all of the outstanding shares of Company B. In either case, Company A will assume Company B's liabilities, and Company B will be preserved as a wholly owned subsidiary. The following data were collected immediately before the acquisition:

	Company A		Company B	
	Book Value	Market Value	Book Value	Market Value
Current assets	$ 500,000	$ 635,000	$150,000	$175,000
Fixed assets	700,000	840,000	250,000	325,000
Totals	$1,200,000	$1,475,000	$400,000	$500,000
Current liabilities	$ 250,000		$ 75,000	
Long-term liabilities	175,000		50,000	
Capital stock, $20 par	400,000		—	
Capital stock, $10 par	—		170,000	
Additional paid-in capital	175,000		60,000	
Retained earnings	200,000		45,000	
Totals	$1,200,000		$400,000	

Required:

a. Present the balance sheet that would result immediately after the acquisition assuming a stock exchange is consummated and pooling accounting is to be followed. Use only the facts given and assume no others.

b. Present the balance sheet that would result immediately after the acquisition is consummated assuming that the Company B stock is purchased for cash rather than exchanged. Assume that of the $650,000 purchase price, Company A took out a term loan for $550,000 of the total and used $100,000 cash on hand for the remainder.

CASES

Case 12–1

Hardin Tool Company*

The management of Pratt Engineering Company had agreed in principle to a proposal from Hardin Tool Company to acquire all its stock in exchange for Hardin securities. The two managements were in general agreement that Hardin would issue 100,000 shares of its authorized but unissued stock in exchange for the 40,000 shares of Pratt common stock. Hardin's investment banking firm had given an opinion that a new

public offering of 100,000 shares of Hardin common stock could be made successfully at $8 per share.

Condensed balance sheets for the two companies, projected to the date of the proposed acquisition, and condensed income statements estimated for the separate organizations are given in Exhibit 1. The income statements reflect the best estimate of results of operations if the two firms were not to merge but were to continue to operate as separate companies. There were no intercompany receivables or payables, and no intercompany sales or other transactions were contemplated.

EXHIBIT 1

Condensed Balance Sheets As of the Proposed Acquisition Date (thousands of dollars)		
	Hardin	**Pratt**
Assets		
Current assets	$ 432	$246
Plant and equipment	690	312
Total assets	$1,122	$558
Liabilities and Equity		
Current liabilities	$ 263	$107
Long-term debt	195	10
Common stock ($1 par)	100	40
Additional paid-in capital	218	94
Retained earnings	346	307
Total liabilities and equity	$1,122	$558
Condensed Income Statements For the First Year after Combination (thousands of dollars)		
Sales	$2,100	$1,500
Expenses	1,620	1,120
Income	480	380
Income tax expense	168	133
Net income	$312	$247

An appraiser had been retained by the two firms and had appraised Pratt's net assets (assets less liabilities) at $600,000. The difference between this amount and Pratt's $441,000 book value was wholly attributable to the appraiser's valuation of Pratt's plant and equipment.

Although an exchange of common stock was the most frequently talked about way of consummating the merger, one Pratt shareholder inquired about the possibility of a package consisting of 50,000 shares of Hardin common stock and $400,000 of either cumulative preferred stock with a 10 percent dividend or debentures with a 10 percent interest rate.

Questions

1. Prepare consolidated balance sheets as of the proposed acquisition date, assuming the exchange of 100,000 shares of Hardin common stock on a purchase basis.

2. Assuming that in its first year of operations the combined company would achieve the same results of operations as the sum of the two firms' independent operations, what would be the combined company's net income and earnings per share on a pooling basis? (Assume plant and equipment life of 10 years, straight-line depreciation, and an income tax rate of 35 percent. Round results—except earnings per share—to the nearest thousand dollars.)

3. What would be the combined net income and earnings per share under (*a*) the preferred stock package and (*b*) the debenture package? Is either of these proposals preferable to the all-common-stock proposal?

Case 12–2

Carter Corporation*

Early in 20x1, Carter Corporation acquired Diroff Corporation. Diroff continued to operate as a Carter subsidiary. At the end of 20x1, the president of Carter asked the company's public accounting firm to prepare consolidated financial statements. Data from the separate financial statements of the two corporations are given in Exhibit 1. (For the purpose of this case, these data have been condensed and rounded.)

The following additional information was provided:

1. During 20x1 Diroff delivered and billed to Carter goods amounting to $34,000. Diroff's cost for these goods was $25,500. Carter had paid Diroff invoices billed through November 30 that totaled $28,900. All of the Diroff goods were sold to outside customers in 20x1.

2. Late in December 20x1, Carter took a loan from Diroff for $32,300 cash. The loan was evidently a five-year note. (No interest on this loan was recorded in the accounts of either company because the transaction occurred so near the end of the year.)

The accountant proceeded to prepare consolidated financial statements. In discussing them with the president, however, the accountant discovered that he had made two assumptions:

1. He had assumed that Carter had acquired 100 percent of Diroff's stock, whereas, in fact, Carter had acquired only 75 percent.

2. He had assumed that Diroff's dividend was included in Carter's $37,400 of other income, whereas, in fact, Carter had not received the dividend in 20x1 and had made no entry to record the fact that the dividend had been declared and was owed to Carter as of December 31, 20x1.

The accountant thereupon prepared revised consolidated statements.

After these revised statements had been mailed, the accountant received a telephone call from Carter's president: "Sorry, but I was wrong about our sales of Diroff merchandise," he said. "Carter's sales were indeed $1,040,400 but only $20,400 was from sales of Diroff products. We discovered that $13,600 of Diroff products were in Carter's inventory as of December 31, 20x1. Don't bother to prepare new statements, however. Tell me the changes, and I'll make them on the statements you sent me."

EXHIBIT 1 Financial Statement Information

Balance Sheet Data As of December 31, 20x1	Carter	Diroff
Assets		
Cash	$ 57,800	$ 20,400
Accounts receivable	110,500	35,700
Inventory	120,700	54,400
Investment in subsidiary	142,800	—
Plant (net)	477,700	134,300
Loans receivable	—	32,300
Total assets	$909,500	$277,100
Liabilities and Equity		
Current liabilities	$ 88,400	$ 62,900
Noncurrent liabilities	170,000	54,400
Capital stock	255,000	102,000
Retained earnings	396,100	57,800
Total liabilities and equity	$909,500	$277,100
Income Statement Data, 20x1		
Sales	$1,040,400	$408,000
Cost of sales	816,000	299,200
Gross margin	224,400	108,800
Expenses (including income taxes)	234,600	61,200
Operating income (loss)	(10,200)	47,600
Other income	37,400	—
Net income	27,200	47,600
Dividends	—	30,600
Added to retained earnings	$27,200	$17,000

Questions

1. Reconstruct the consolidated financial statements that the accountant originally prepared.

2. Prepare revised consolidated financial statements based on the information that the accountant learned in his first conversation with the president.

Case 12–3

The Politics and Economics of Accounting for Goodwill at Cisco Systems

On March 2, 2000, Dennis Powell, vice president and corporate controller for Cisco Systems, appeared before the Senate Committee on Banking, Housing, and

Urban Affairs. Powell was testifying on a recent proposal by the Financial Accounting Standards Board (FASB) to abolish the **pooling-of-interests method** of accounting for mergers. Powell expressed his opposition to the FASB proposal, arguing that the accounting method firms would be required to use in lieu of pooling (i.e., the **purchase method)** would "stifle technology development, impede capital formation and slow job creation . . . ."[1] The Senate heard from eight other expert witnesses that day; all but one—Ed Jenkins, chairman of the FASB—argued against the proposal to abolish pooling.[2]

Six months later, by September 2000, Powell had abandoned his support for the pooling method. In leading a group of industry representatives at a meeting with members of the FASB, Powell argued for a regime that permitted only the purchase method, provided **goodwill** recognized under that method be solely subject to **impairment testing** (rather than **amortization** as the FASB had proposed).[3]

Accounting for Mergers: Purchase and Pooling Methods

Until 2001, U.S. generally accepted accounting principles (GAAP) had two methods to account for mergers: the purchase method and the pooling-of-interests method. Under the purchase method, acquired tangible assets, certain acquired intangible assets (e.g., contracts, patents, franchises, customer and supplier lists, and favorable leases), and all acquired liabilities were revalued to their current **fair values** before being added to the acquiring firm's books. Any excess of the total price paid for the acquisition over the sum of the revalued net assets was added to acquirer's books as goodwill. In the years following the acquisition, goodwill was amortized in the acquirer's income statement. Further, under the purchase method, the acquiring firm only recognized the acquired firm's income from the date of the acquisition.

Under the pooling method, the surviving firm in an acquisition simply added the book value of all acquired assets and liabilities to its own assets and liabilities. There were no asset and liability revaluations and no goodwill was recorded. Accordingly, there was no

goodwill expense associated with pooling transactions. Further, under the pooling method, the acquiring firm recognized the acquired firm's income for the entire fiscal year in which the acquisition occurred. Thus, the balance sheets and income statements of firms doing pooling method acquisitions looked very different from those of firms doing purchase method acquisitions.

Firms were required to use the purchase method unless they met certain criteria to qualify for pooling accounting. The most important of these criteria were (1) that each of the companies in an acquisition was independent of the other and (2) that the acquiring firm issued only common stock (with rights identical to its own outstanding common stock) in consideration for the acquired firm.[4]

Cisco and the Making of Mergers Accounting

In September 1999, the FASB proposed abolishing the pooling method of accounting for mergers; all firms were asked to use purchase method accounting with amortization required for any, goodwill.[5] The vast difference between pooling and purchase method accounting, the FASB argued, had led to situations whereby "two transactions that [were] not significantly different [could] be accounted for by methods that produce[d] dramatically different financial statement results."[6] The FASB solicited public comments on its proposal; about 60% of corporate respondents opposed the idea.[7] Ciscowas among these opponents, and Powell took a lead role in expressing Cisco's concerns.

At Cisco, Powell oversaw global financial reporting international tax strategies and implementation, corporate procurement, and internal auditing.[8] In a December 1999 letter to the FASB, Powell wrote expressing "serious concerns" with the proposed elimination of pooling accounting in favor of the purchase method with goodwill amortization. "While we understand that pooling accounting has its critics," he wrote,

---

[1] Prepared statement of Dennis Powell before the Senate Committee on Banking, Housing, and Urban Affairs (Washington: U.S. Government Printing Office, 2000).

[2] Karthik Ramanna, The implications of unverifiable fair-value accounting: Evidence from the political economy of goodwill accounting, *Journal of Accounting and Economics* (forthcoming).

[3] Dennis Powell, Business Combination Purchase Accounting: Goodwill Impairment Test, appendix to the minutes of the September 29, 2000 FASB Board meeting (Norwalk, CT: FASB, 2000).

[4] Accounting Principles Board Opinion No. 16: *Business Combinations,* (New York: AICPA, 1970).

[5] Exposure Draft 201-A: *Business Combinations and Intangible Assets,* (Norwalk, CT: FASB, 1999).

[6] Ibid., p. 34.

[7] See footnote 2.

[8] Dennis Powell's biography, www.cisco.com, accessed July 19, 2997.

"we believe on balance, for equity funded transactions, it is less problematic that the purchase accounting model in representation the economic reality of operating results of the combined entity."[9]

Powell's opposition to the purchase method was based on the idea that goodwill was not an asset.[10] "[G]oodwill is simply the amount of purchase price that is left over after allocating value to identifiable assets . . .," he noted. "It has no value on its own; it can't be borrowed against, sold separately or generate any cash flow."[11]

Powell also expressed doubts about the purchase method in general and about goodwill amortization in particular:

> The purchase method of accounting was designed for accounting for tangible assets that have reliable measurable fair values. However, in the acquisitions of New Economy technology companies, an overwhelming portion of the purchase price is attributable to intangibles. It is this situation that makes the purchase method inadequate. Identifying intangibles is difficult, but determining the fair value of identified intangible assets with some level of consistency or reliability is impossible. . . .[12]
>
> While Cisco continues to grow our business by combining with similar companies with the same long term strategic goals, our operating results would decrease because of the amortization of goodwill. This decrease in operating results would continue even if the acquisitions we complete were successful resulting in an increase to our market capitalization . . . . Our operating results would not be comparable to companies who develop technology internally. [13]

Powell concluded his letter to the FASB with a passionate defense of pooling accounting: "We believe the retention of pooling of interests accounting is particularly critical considering the adverse impact its elimination will have on the merger activity in the United States, which in turn will negatively impact the ecosystem that is driving technology development in this country today.[14]

Concerns from corporations like Cisco over the FASB proposal to abolish pooling quickly reached Congress. In March and May of 2000, the Senate Banking Committee and the House Finance Subcommittee, respectively, held hearings on the issue. Several of the corporate respondents who had already expressed their opposition to the FASB testified at these hearings.[15] Cisco was among them: Powell appeared before both the Senate and House on Cisco's behalf, reiterating his arguments above. In comments to the House, he added that extant accounting rules for mergers accounting had "for the past 50 years, generated and supported the strongest capital markets in the world.[16]

Sometime after the hearings in Congress, two separate groups of opponents to the FASB proposal met with members of the FASB Board.[17] Powell led the second group. This meeting, held in September of 2000, included experts from the American Business Conference, Merrill Lynch, the Technology Network, and United Parcel Service, besides Powell on Cisco's behalf. Both Powell's group and the group before it did not discuss retaining pooling accounting at their respective meetings. Instead, they proposed an alternative to goodwill amortization under a regime that permitted only the purchase method. In the years after an acquisition, they argued for goodwill to be periodically tested for impairment. The impairment test, they proposed, would be based on a comparison of good-will's recorded book value and an estimate of the current fair value of goodwill.[18]

The FASB, after some field testing and an additional round of comment solicitation, accepted the

---

[9] Dennis Powell, Letter of Comment No.: 25A, FASB file reference: 1033–201 (Norwalk, CT: FASB, 1999), p. 2.

[10] *FASB Concept Statement No. 6* defines "assets" as "probable future economic benefits obtained or controlled by a particular entity as a result of past transactions or events."

[11] See footnote 9, p. 2.

[12] Ibid., p. 3. Note that when Powell was speaking of "identified intangibles," he was referring to their definition at the time, that is, "intangible assets that can be identified and named." *APB Opinion 16, paragraph 88e, p. 319*. The current definition of "identified intangibles" includes any asset that arises from legal rights (regardless of whether those rights are transferable or separable) or any asset that is capable of being separated or divided for sale, rent, and so on (regardless of whether there is intent to do so). *SFAS141, paragraph 39, p. 17*.

[13] Ibid., pp. 4–5.

[14] Ibid., p. 5.

[15] See footnote 2.

[16] Prepared statement of Dennis Powell before the House Subcommittee on Finance and Hazardous Materials (Washington: U.S. Government Printing Office, 2000).

[17] See footnote 2.

[18] Trevor Harris, Accounting for Business Combination: A Workable Solution, appendix to the minutes of the May 31, 2000 FASB Board meeting (Norwalk, CT: FASB, 2000); see also footnote 3.

goodwill impairment alternative. In June 2001, the FASB formally promulgated new accounting standards that abolished pooling accounting, requiring all firms to use the purchase method, with impairment testing for any acquired goodwill.[19]

According to the 2001 standards, an acquiring firm must—upon completing the acquisition—allocate any acquired goodwill among its **reporting units** (a reporting unit is a segment within the acquiring firm with discrete financial information that is regularly reviewed by management). If the acquired goodwill represents synergies from a merger, managers are required to disaggregate and allocate those synergies to reporting units based on estimates of how they are expected to be realized. In the years after an acquisition, goodwill must be tested for impairment within the reporting unit to which it was allocated. The goodwill impairment test in a reporting unit is a two-step procedure. In the first step, managers must estimate the current fair value of the reporting unit (as a whole) and compare it to the unit's total book value. If the unit's fair value is greater than the unit's book value, step two is ignored and no goodwill impairment is recognized. If the unit's fair value is less than its book value, step two is conducted as follows. Managers calculate the current fair value of the unit's goodwill as the difference between the estimate of the unit's total fair value (as calculated in step one) and an estimate of the current fair value of the unit's net assets (excluding goodwill). The current fair value of goodwill is then compared to the goodwill's book value. The excess (if any) of the goodwill's book value over its current fair value is the unit's goodwill impairment.

Managers are not required to disclose the assumptions that underlie their estimates of goodwill's fair value (both at the initial stage of allocating goodwill to reporting units and at the subsequent stage of testing for goodwill impairment within units). The goodwill impairment of reporting units (if any) are aggregated and reported at the firm level.

Cisco Systems in the 1990s

Cisco Systems was founded in 1984 by two computer scientists from Stanford University. The company developed technologies that enabled computer networks to communicate with one another. Cisco went public in February 1990 with a market capitalization of about $224 million. By the close of the 1990 fiscal year, Cisco had 251 employees and $69 million in revenues. The 1990s were a period of extraordinary growth for Cisco. As it was a key supplier of computer networking technologies, the company's fortunes grew with the rise of the Internet. By 1999, Cisco employed nearly 21,000 people, had sales of about $12.2 billion, and had a market capitalization of over $235 billion. On March 27, 2000, Cisco briefly became the world's most valuable company, with a market capitalization of $569 billion.[20]

Cisco's growth was fueled in large part by an acquisitions strategy. This strategy was laid out in a 1993 plan put forth by then Chief Technology Officer John Chambers (Chambers became CEO in 1995).[21] Cisco made its first acquisition in September 1993. From then through the end of 2000, Cisco acquired 75 other companies at a combined price of over $36 billion. Most of these deals were to acquire key intangibles. As Chambers noted, "Most people forget that in a high-tech acquisition, you really are acquiring only people. . . . At what we pay, $500,000 to $2 million an employee, we are not acquiring current market share. We are acquiring futures."[22] Of the combined purchase price of Cisco's acquisitions through February 2000, Powell attributed 95% to goodwill and other intangible assets.[23]

Cisco operations for the quarter ending April 29, 2000, were classified into four broad areas: routers, switches, access, and "other." Routers and switches each accounted for about $2 billion of the quarter-ending sales, while access and "other" accounted for about $0.6 billion and $0.8 billion, respectively. Unallocated negative sales adjustments were about $0.5 billion.[24]

[19] See *Statement of Financial Accounting Standards No. 141*, "Business Combinations" (Norwalk, CT: FASB, 2001) and *Statement of Financial Accounting Standards No. 142*, "Goodwill and Other Intangible Assets" (Norwalk, CT: FASB, 2001). The FASB, in collaboration with the International Accounting Standards Board, is in the process of revising the current rules of purchase method accounting in order to harmonize them with international accounting practices. Under the new rules, expected to be released in the third quarter of 2007, the purchase method will be known as the "acquisition method." See FASB Project Updates: Business Combinations, www.fasb.org, accessed August 20,2007.

[20] Cisco Systems Corporate Timeline, www.cisco.com, accessed July 19, 2007.
[21] "Cisco Systems, Inc.: Acquisition Integration for Manufacturing (A)," HBS Case No. 600–015 (Boston: Harvard Business School Publishing, 2000).
[22] John Byrne, "The Corporation of the Future," *BusinessWeek*, August 31,1998, quoted from HBS Case No. 600–015.
[23] See footnote 1.
[24] Cisco Systems Form 10-Q, filed June 13,2000.

EXHIBIT 1 **Accounting Standard-Setting in the United States**

Accounting standards for public companies in the United States were unregulated until the early 1930s. The Securities Acts of 1933 and 1934, promulgated in the wake of the stock market crash of 1929, created the Securities and Exchange Commission (SEC) and charged it with the responsibility to set accounting standards. Since the late 1930s, the SEC has relied on private standard-setting bodies to establish accounting rules, reserving for itself the right to veto, amend, and enforce those rules. The first such standard-setting body was the Committee on Accounting Procedure (CAP), in existence from 1938 to 1959. The second was the Accounting Principles Board (APB), in existence from 1959 to 1973. The members of both the CAP and the APB served on a part-time basis. Most members were either public accountants affiliated with audit firms and listed public companies or accounting academics.

In 1973, the FASB replaced the APB as the SEC-designated accounting standard setter for public company financial reports. FASB members serve full time. They are appointed by the FASB's governing board, the Financial Accounting Foundation (FAF). The FAF was initially charged with both raising (from the private sector) and administering funds for the FASB. Since the Sarbanes-Oxley Act of 2002, voluntary private-sector funds no longer support FASB activities. Instead, all listed companies are assessed a mandatory tax to pay for the administration of the FASB.

The FASB encourages a collaborative decision-making process on standard-setting. When board members propose a change to accounting standards, they solicit feedback from users and preparers of financial statements. This feedback, in the form of letters, testimonials, or presentations, is often incorporated by the FASB in determining the nature of the final standard. The U.S. Congress rarely involves itself directly in the accounting standard-setting process. However, as former FASB chair Dennis Beresford points out, when congressional hearings do take place, they are taken "very seriously" by the FASB. Rice University accounting historian Professor Stephen Zeff notes how persistent industry criticisms of the CAP and the APB may have led to their respective demises, suggesting that there is precedent for the dissolution of accounting standard-setting bodies in the face of strong opposition.

Sources:

1. Dennis Beresford, "Congress Looks at Accounting for Business Combinations," *Accounting Horizons* (March 2001): 73–86.
2. Facts about FASB, www.fasb.org, accessed August 8, 2007.
3. Financial Accounting Foundation 2006 Annual Report (Norwalk, CT: FAF, 2007).
4. Stephen Zeff, "The Evolution of US GAAP: The Political Forces Behind Professional Standards Part 1," *CPA Journal* (January 2005): 18–27.

Cisco Systems' Acquisition of ArrowPoint Communications

On May 5, 2000, one day after Powell testified before the U.S. House, Cisco Systems announced its acquisition of ArrowPoint Communications. ArrowPoint was a Boston-based provider of Internet content switches that help Web hosts optimize and track their website performance.[25] The switches allow Web hosts to direct their preferred customers through priority routes and to limit access to their websites based on security or privacy concerns.[26]

ArrowPoint had only just completed its IPO (April 5, 2000) when the Cisco deal was announced.[27] On May 3, 2000, ArrowPoint's stock opened at $102, giving it a market capitalization of over $3.6 billion; by May 5, ArrowPoint stock closed at $140. In a press release dated May 5, Cisco announced that it would exchange for every outstanding share and option in ArrowPoint 2.1218 shares in Cisco. Based on Cisco's closing price of $63.625 on May 4, the deal was worth over $5.7 billion (including nearly $1 billion for converted Arrow-Point options).

Cisco announced that it was acquiring ArrowPoint "to provide its customers with a feature-rich, flexible content switching platform."[28] A press release announcing the merger added:

> Coupled with Cisco's Internet infrastructure, ArrowPoint's products will provide a new level of intelligence that will enable ISPs, Web hosting companies and other customers to create a faster, more reliable Web experience. In addition, ArrowPoint's solutions strengthen Cisco's presence

[25] "Cisco Systems to Acquire ArrowPoint Communications," press release, www.cisco.com, accessed July 19, 2007.
[26] ArrowPoint Corporate Profile, www.hoovers.com, accessed July 19, 2007.
[27] ArrowPoint Communications Form 10-Q, filed May 2, 2000.

[28] See footnote 25.

EXHIBIT 2 Cisco and ArrowPoint Balance Sheets prior to the Merger Announcement

	Cisco Systems as of April 29, 2000	ArrowPoint Communications[a] as of April 30, 2000
Cash and Equivalents	4,653	187
Accounts Receivable, net	1,922	8
Inventory	878	4
Other Current Assets	1,627	–
Total Current Assets	9,080	199
Investments, net	11,589	–
Property, plant, and equipment, net	1,153	6
Goodwill and Other Intangibles, net	3,214	–
Other Assets	1,049	1
Total Assets	26,085	206
Accounts Payable, net	596	4
Other Current Liabilities	4,503	5
Total Current Liabilities	5,099	9
Other Liabilities	960	35
Preferred Stock[b, c]	–	–
Common Stock[d, e]	10,701	222
Retained Earnings	7,624	(60)
Other Comprehensive Income[f]	1,701	–
Total Stockholders' Equity	20,026	162
Total Liabilities and Stockholders' Equity	26,085	206

Source: Cisco Systems and ArrowPoint Communications financial statements and case writer.
Note: All figures in millions of U.S. dollars, except as indicated.

[a] The ArrowPoint balance sheet in this exhibit is an *estimate* of the company's financial position post-IPQ (ArrowPoint's only publicly available balance sheet is dated prior to its IPO, completed April 5, 2000). At the IPO, ArrowPoint converted all of its "Preferred Stock" into "Common Stock" and raised $172 million in cash.

[b] For Cisco: no par value; 5 million shares authorized; none issued or outstanding.

[c] For ArrowPoint: $0.01 par value; 699,837 shares authorized; none issued or outstanding.

[d] For Cisco: $0.001 par value; 20 billion shares authorized; 7 billion shares issued and outstanding.

[e] For ArrowPoint: $0.001 par value; 200 million shares authorized; 35 million shares issued and outstanding.

[f] Other comprehensive income is an account accumulating changes in equity from sources other than transactions with owners that do not pass through the income statement.

in emerging markets that include ASPs (Application Service Provider), AIPs (Application Infrastructure Provider) and "dot com" companies. [29]

Cisco stated that after the acquisition the 337-person ArrowPoint group would continue to be led by its CEO, Cheng Wu. ArrowPoint employees would join Cisco's Public Carrier IP Group, and Wu would report to a senior vice president at Cisco. Exhibits 2 and 3 detail Cisco's and ArrowPoint's most recent balance sheets and income statements before the acquisition announcement.[30]

[29] Ibid.

[30] Note: Quarterly income statements are presented because ArrowPoint never released an annual report.

EXHIBIT 3 Cisco and ArrowPoint Income Statements prior to the Merger Announcement

	Cisco Systems Quarter ending April 29, 2000	ArrowPoint Communications Quarter ending March 31, 2000
Net Sales	4,919	10
Cost of Sales	1,748	4
Selling, General, and Administrative	1,169	9
Research and Development	719	2
Amortization of Intangible Assets	51	–
In-process Research and Development[a]	488	–
One-time Expenses	–	–
Interest Expenses, net	(313)	–
Other Expenses, net	–	3
Provision for Income Taxes	395	–
Total Expenses	4,257	18
Net Income	662	(8)

Source: Cisco Systems and ArrowPoint Communications financial statements. Note: All figures in millions of U.S. dollars, except as indicated.

[a] In consolidating financials after an acquisition, the in-process research and development of the acquired firm that is considered not to have any alternate use to the acquirer is expensed in the acquirer's income statement.

Questions

1. What is Cisco getting from its acquisition of Arrow-Point? Why does Cisco's offer price differ from both the book value and the market value of ArrowPoint?
2. (a) Assume Cisco used the purchase method to account for the acquisition of ArrowPoint. Estimate what Cisco's balance sheet would look like after the acquisition (you will need to allocate the purchase price among acquired net assets; be ready to defend any assumptions you make). What are the acquisition's income-statement effects on Cisco?

(b) Now assume Cisco used the pooling-of-interest method to account for the acquisition of Arrow-Point. Estimate the acquisition's balance-sheet and income-statement effects on Cisco?
3. Given your answers above, what is your assessment of the effectiveness of the pooling and purchase methods in reflecting the economics of the acquisition? Do you agree with Dennis Powell that the "purchase method of accounting was designed for accounting for tangible assets?"
4. Why do you think Dennis Powell switched from supporting the pooling method to proposing the purchase method with goodwill impairment testing?

Case 12–4

Productos Finas*

Recent adoption of International Financial Reporting Standards (IFRS) required "full consolidation" for financial reporting by Spanish companies. David Ortiz,

*Copyright © President and Fellows of Harvard College. Harvard Business School case 106-037.

president and principal stockholder of Productos Finas, a Spanish operating and holding corporation, was concerned about this new law's impact on his plans for a small public issue of his company's common stock. Currently, Productos Finas only prepared parent company statements. The cost method was used to account

EXHIBIT 1 Company P and Subsidiary Company S Working Papers for Consolidated Statements for the Year Ended December 31, 2006 (millions of euros; parentheses indicate deductions)

	Company P	Company S	Adjustment and Eliminations Dr.	Cr.	Consolidated Statements
Income Statement					
Sales	1,500	1,800			
Cost of sales	(900)	(1,400)			
	600	400			
Depreciation	(40)	(20)			
Operating expenses	(440)	(290)			
Net income from operations	120	90			
Dividend income	24				
Minority net income					
Goodwill					
Net income	144	90			
Retained Earnings Statement					
Retained earnings, January 1, 2006					
Company P	248				
Company S		70			
Net income (as above)	144	90			
Dividends:					
Company P	(72)				
Company S		(30)			
Retained earnings December 31, 2006	320	130			
Balance Sheet					
Cash	110	150			
Accounts receivable (net)	375	410			
Inventories	310	75			
Plant and equipment	885	200			
Less: accumulated depreciation	(265)	(60)			
Investment in Company S (at cost)	290				
Goodwill					
Total	1,705	775			
Accounts payable	385	345			
Minority interest					
Capital stock:					
Company P	1,000				
Company S		300			
Retained earnings (as above)	320	130			
Total	1,705	775			

for the parent company's various subsidiaries in these statements.

David Ortiz was unfamiliar with consolidation accounting. In order to understand the accounting mechanics and financial ratio implications of consolidated statements, David Ortiz asked his chief accountant to prepare a short presentation illustrating the preparation of consolidated statements.

ILLUSTRATIVE CASE

The chief accountant intended to use the following case example to illustrate consolidation accounting.

Company P purchased 80% of the outstanding capital stock of Company S from individual stockholders for €290 million cash, on January 1, 2002. On this date, the retained earnings of Company S were €30 million.

Company S was primarily, but not exclusively, engaged in marketing goods purchased from Company P. Company S's purchases from Company P during the year 2006 were €1,200 million. The inventory held by Company S at the beginning or the close of the year did not include any merchandise acquired from Company P. On December 31, 2006, the balance due to Company P for intercom-pany purchases was €280 million.

All plant and equipment owned by Company S was acquired for cash from Company P on January 1, 2004, and has been depreciated on the basis of its estimated life of 10 years, using the straight-line method without salvage value. In 2004, Company P had recorded a €50 million profit on the sale of these fixed assets to its subsidiary.

A 10% cash dividend was declared and paid by Company S on its outstanding capital stock on July 1, 2006.

Financial statements of Company P and of Company S are presented in vertical form on the accompanying worksheet (Exhibit 1) to facilitate assembly of information for consolidation statements.

Using this illustrative case and ignoring taxes, the chief accountant intended in his presentation to David Ortiz to:

1. Complete the worksheet and prepare
   a. A consolidated income statement.
   b. A consolidated retained earnings statement.
   c. A consolidated balance sheet.
2. Compare the financial condition of Company P on an unconsolidated basis with that presented by the consolidated statements. His planned comparison included computation of
   a. Working capital (current assets – current liabilities).
   b. Total assets.
   c. Long-term capital.
   d. Any other ratios he thought significant.
3. Compare the profitability of Company P on an unconsolidated basis with that shown by the consolidated statements.
4. Discuss with David Ortiz the significance of consolidated statements to
   a. A stockholder of Company P.
   b. A minority stockholder of Company S.

To simplify the presentation the chief accountant decided to assume that Company P used the cost method to account on its books for Company S. This was consistent with Productos Finas' present accounting policy. Under IFRS goodwill was not amortized.

Case 12–5

Indigo Airlines and Related Party Transactions

There is a Mahabharata-like war that has erupted at India's top airlines, IndiGo Airlines, where one of the promoters, Rakesh Gangwal has accused another promoter, Rahul Bhatia of irregular related party transactions (RPTs) among other misdoings. Although Bhatia has refuted and denied these charges strongly, citing that the concerned transactions are a regular and proper arm's length transaction, the controversy refuses to die and the shareholders of this airline are now sounding a bit concerned. However, such disputes over RPTs have been a recurring theme in India Inc. from time to time and it is not an absolutely new thing to happen.

Related party transactions are transactions that a company does with parties related to it. So, if Company A buys goods or services from its director X, it counts as an RPT. Similarly, if Company A takes some buildings on rent and the concerned premises are actually owned by Y, a relative of director X, it is also an RPT.

The list of persons and entities that are considered related parties by the law include the company's directors, key managerial persons, and their relatives. Moreover, firms or private companies in which such directors, managers, or even their relatives are partners or directors are also covered under the definition. Also holding companies, subsidiaries and associate companies fall under related party definition. Simply put, any person or entity that can give rise to the risk of vested interest for the company is considered a related party. Conceptually, there is a risk that the related party may be favored with terms that could harm the interests of the company's shareholders and therefore there could be a bias in awarding the contract.

As a result, RPTs, in general, need the stamp of the company's Board of Directors and clearance from the Audit Committee in general. In some cases, they may have to get approval from the majority of the shareholders (excluding interested parties) through special resolutions. Such approvals are not required if the RPT is done on arm's length basis which basically means that the transaction is done on purely commercial terms as it would be done with any other unrelated parties.

In case of Indigo Airlines, one of the promoters, Gangwal, an ex-United Airlines, and US Airways veteran, who has been aggressively leading IndiGo's emergence as one of the fastest-growing carriers in the world has charged that the co-promoter Rahul Bhatia has not followed due diligence in many related party transactions. Gangwal, who is a US citizen, almost single-handedly strategized IndiGo's record-breaking plane orders, its aggressive expansion in India and the ambition to make it a global carrier, which resulted in major changes to the senior management. Bhatia ran the show in India, ably supporting the airline's growth and getting regulatory clearances. The specific issues here are related party transactions, which are deals or arrangements between two parties who are joined by a pre-existing business relationship or common interest. In IndiGo's case, Gangwal is charging Bhatia of undue favor to Novotel for the award of accommodation contract of Indigo's crew. The airline's contract with Novotel, locally owned in part by Bhatia's Interglobe Enterprises who has the contract for crew accommodation is not really an arm's length transaction. However, top executives at Indigo reject the charges and claim that the transactions are done at "arm's length" and through a tendering process and Interglobe owned companies don't always win the contracts.

Earlier, Rakesh Gangwal has raised serious objections over slack corporate governance in the company, by claiming that there are clear related party transactions in at least four different areas: real estate leased to IGAL, simulator training facilities, General Sales Agreements (GSAs) for limited foreign markets, and crew accommodation at Accor Hotels. The Bhatia group has come out even more strongly refuting those charges and further claims that the related party transactions in the four areas accounted for only 0.53% of IGAL's consolidated turnover of 2018-19. The Bhatia group maintains that all related party transactions have been executed on an arm's length basis and in the ordinary course of business.

So, what appears to be a simple business contract whereby employees of one airline company are traveling and staying in a hotel for a day or so, turns out to be a possible related party transaction because one of the owners of the airline also holds share in the hotel company too. Organizations all over the world are becoming increasingly complex and so is the ownership structure. What appears to be a straight forward business deal could be actually done for a personal benefit at the cost of the poor and unaware shareholders. Many times, the internal employees of the firm may not be even aware of related party transaction and they may see it as a fair deal. This issue is more related to corporate governance where the Board (especially the independent directors) and the Audit Committee needs to play a very proactive role by timely red-flagging such contracts if there is even an iota of suspicion that it could be a related party transaction. They have to ensure that the due process is followed while awarding the contracts through a comprehensive tender process and that no bidder is granted any special favor so that the transaction remains an arm's length transaction.

Financial Statement Analysis

CHAPTER
13

In previous chapters, the principal focus has been on conveying an understanding of the information contained in the three basic financial statements: the balance sheet, the income statement, and the cash flow statement. This chapter describes how this information is analyzed, both by parties outside the firm and by the company's own management.

All analyses of accounting data involve comparisons. An absolute statement, such as "Company X earned $1 million profit," is by itself not useful. It becomes useful only when the $1 million is compared with something else. The comparison may be quite imprecise and intuitive. For example, if we know that Company X is an industrial giant with tens of thousands of employees, we know intuitively that $1 million profit is a poor showing because we have built up in our minds the impression that such companies should earn much more than that. Or the comparison may be much more formal, explicit, and precise, as is the case when the $1 million profit this year is compared with last year's profit. In either case, the process of comparison makes the number meaningful.

Business Objectives

Comparisons are essentially intended to shed light on how well a company is achieving its objectives. In order to decide the types of comparisons that are useful, we need first to consider what a business is all about—what its objectives are. Let us say as a generalization that *the overall objective of a business is to create value for its shareholders while maintaining a sound financial position.*[1] Implicit in this statement is the assumption that value creation can be measured. But if a company's equity securities are not publicly traded and hence the total market valuation of its equity securities cannot be calculated, then shareholder value creation cannot be directly measured. Nevertheless, profit and return on investment, which are indicators of value creation, can be measured in all cases. Of course, employee satisfaction, social responsibility, ethical

[1] This statement is not necessarily consistent with the *profit maximization* assumption often made in economics. The techniques in this chapter are equally applicable under a profit maximization assumption, however, so there is no point in arguing here whether the profit maximization assumption is valid and useful.

considerations, and other nonmeasurable objectives are also important and must be taken into account whenever possible in appraising the overall success of an enterprise. The measurement of profit has already been discussed; below we briefly discuss return on investment and maintaining a sound financial position.

Return on Investment

Return on investment (ROI) is broadly defined as net income divided by investment.[2] The term **investment** is used in three different senses in financial analysis, thus giving three different ROI ratios: return on assets, return on owners' equity, and return on invested capital.

Return on assets (ROA) reflects how much the firm has earned on the investment of *all* the financial resources committed to the firm. Thus, the ROA measure is appropriate if one considers the investment in the firm to include current liabilities, long-term liabilities, and owners' equity, which are the total sources of funds invested in the assets. It is a useful measure if one wants to evaluate how well an enterprise has used its funds, without regard to the relative magnitudes of the sources of those funds (short-term creditors, long-term creditors, bondholders, and shareholders). The ROA ratio often is used by top management to evaluate individual business units within a multi-divisional firm (e.g., the laundry equipment division of a household appliance firm). The division manager has significant influence over the assets used in the division but has little control over how those assets are financed because the division does not arrange its own loans, issue its own bonds or capital stock, or in many cases pay its own bills (current liabilities).

Return on owners' equity (ROE) reflects how much the firm has earned on the funds invested by the shareholders (either directly or through retained earnings). This ROE ratio is obviously of interest to present or prospective shareholders, and is also of concern to management because this measure is viewed as an important indicator of shareholder value creation. The ratio is not generally of interest to division managers, however, because they are primarily concerned with the efficient use of assets rather than with the relative roles of creditors and shareholders in financing those assets.

The third ROI ratio is **return on invested capital (ROIC).** Invested capital (also called **permanent capital)** is equal to noncurrent liabilities plus shareholders' equity and hence represents the funds entrusted to the firm for relatively long periods of time. ROIC focuses on the use of this permanent capital. It is presumed that the current liabilities will fluctuate more or less automatically with changes in current assets and that both will vary with the level of current operations.

Invested capital is also equal to working capital plus noncurrent assets. This equivalency points out that the owners and long-term creditors of the firm must in effect finance the plant and equipment, other long-term assets of the firm, and the portion of current assets not financed by current liabilities.

Some firms use ROIC to measure divisional performance, often labeling the ratio **return on capital employed (ROCE)** or **return on net assets (RONA).**[3] This measure is appropriate for those divisions whose managers have a significant influence on decisions regarding asset acquisitions, purchasing and production schedules (which determine inventory levels), credit policy (accounts receivable), and cash management and also on the level of their divisions' current liabilities.

---

[2] As described later, net income may be subject to an adjustment for interest expense when calculating ROI.

[3] In this context, the companies are using *net assets* to mean assets less *current* liabilities, whereas the formal accounting meaning is assets minus *all* liabilities.

Sound Financial Position

In addition to desiring a satisfactory return, investors expect their capital to be protected from more than a normal amount of business risk of capital loss. The return on the shareholders' investment could be increased if incremental investments in the assets for new projects were financed solely by liabilities, provided the return on these incremental investments exceeds the interest cost of the added debt. This "financial leverage" policy, however, would increase the shareholders' risk of losing their investment, because interest charges and principal repayments on the liabilities are fixed obligations and failure to make these payments could throw the company into bankruptcy. The degree of risk in a situation can be measured in part by the relative amounts of liabilities and owners' equity and by the funds available to discharge the liabilities. This analysis also involves the use of ratios.

Structure of the Analysis

Many ratios have been described in previous chapters. In this section, these ratios and others are discussed in a sequence intended to facilitate an understanding of the total business. Thus, we shall assume here that one first looks at the firm's performance in the broadest terms and then works down through various levels of detail in order to identify the significant factors that accounted for the overall results. If the values of the ratios used in this analysis are compared with their values for other time periods, this comparison is called a **longitudinal,** or **trend, analysis.**

Dozens of ratios can be computed from a single set of financial statements. Each analyst tends to have a set of favorite ratios, selected from those described below and probably from some we do not describe. (Certain ratios that are useful only in a specific industry, such as banking, are not described here.) Although we describe many frequently used ratios, the best analytical procedure is not to compute all of them mechanically but rather to decide first which ratios might be relevant in the particular type of investigation being made.

Illustration 13–1 shows some of the important ratios and other relationships that aid in the analysis of how satisfactory a company's performance was.[4] These ratios can be grouped into four categories: overall measures, profitability measures, tests of investment utilization, and tests of financial condition. The ratios calculated below are based on the Franklin Company's financial statements shown in Illustration 13–2. The Franklin Company's financial statements are typical of these companies with major market shares that produce and sell breakfast cereals and similar products.

Overall Measures

Return on Investment

As explained above, return on investment can be calculated in three different ways, depending on whether one views investment as being total assets, invested capital, or shareholders' equity. These ratios are calculated as follows:

$$\text{Return on assets} = \frac{\text{Net income} + \text{Interest}(1 - \text{Tax rate})}{\text{Total assets}}$$

$$= \frac{\$680.7 + \$33.3(.66)}{\$4,237.1} = 16.6 \text{ percent}$$

[4] Diagrams analogous to Illustration 13–1 can be drawn to show return on invested capital or return on assets, as alternative ROI measures.

ILLUSTRATION 13–1   Factors Affecting Return on Investment*

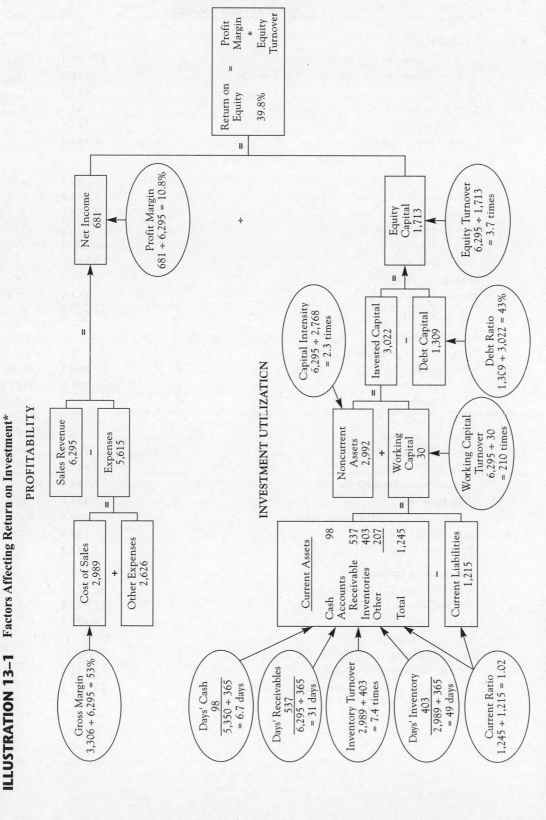

* Numbers based on 2010 data in Illustration 13–2, rounded.

ILLUSTRATION 13–2

FRANKLIN COMPANY AND SUBSIDIARIES Consolidated Balance Sheet At December 31 (dollars in millions)	2010	2009
Current Assets		
Cash and temporary investments	$ 98.1	$ 126.3
Accounts receivable, less allowances of $6.0 and $6.2	536.8	519.1
Inventories	403.1	416.4
Deferred income taxes	85.5	66.2
Prepaid expenses	121.6	108.6
Total current assets	1,245.1	1,236.6
Property		
Land	40.6	40.5
Buildings	1,065.7	1,021.2
Machinery and equipment	2,857.6	2,629.4
Construction in progress	308.6	302.6
Accumulated depreciation	(1,504.1)	(1,331.0)
Property, net	2,768.4	2,662.7
Intangible assets	59.1	53.3
Other assets	164.5	62.4
Total assets	$4,237.1	$4,015.0
Current Liabilities		
Current maturities of long-term debt	$ 1.5	$ 1.9
Notes payable	386.7	210.0
Accounts payable	308.8	313.8
Accrued liabilities:		
Income taxes	65.9	104.1
Salaries and wages	76.5	78.0
Advertising and promotion	233.8	228.0
Other	141.4	135.2
Total current liabilities	1,214.6	1,071.0
Long-term debt	521.6	314.9
Nonpension postretirement benefits	450.9	407.6
Deferred income taxes	188.9	184.6
Other liabilities	147.7	91.7
Shareholders' Equity		
Common stock, $.25 par value	77.6	77.5
Capital in excess of par value	72.0	69.2
Retained earnings	3,409.4	3,033.9
Treasury stock, at cost	(1,653.1)	(1,105.0)
Currency translation and pension adjustments	(192.5)	(130.4)
Total shareholders' equity	1,713.4	1,945.2
Total liabilities and shareholders' equity	$4,237.1	$4,015.0

(continued)

ILLUSTRATION 13–2
(continued)

FRANKLIN COMPANY AND SUBSIDIARIES
Consolidated Earnings and Retained Earnings
Year Ended December 31
(dollars in millions, except per share amounts)

	2010	2009	2008
Net sales	**$6,295.4**	$6,190.6	$5,786.6
Cost of goods sold	**2,989.0**	2,987.7	2,828.7
Gross margin	**3,306.4**	3,202.9	2,957.9
Selling and administrative expense	**2,237.5**	2,140.1	1,930.0
Other expenses (revenue)	**1.5**	(36.8)	(14.6)
Interest expense	**33.3**	29.2	58.3
Earnings before income taxes and extraordinary item	**1,034.1**	1,070.4	984.2
Income taxes	**353.4**	387.6	378.2
Earnings before extraordinary item	**680.7**	682.8	606.0
Extraordinary item (net of income tax benefit of $144.6)		(251.6)	
Net income—$2.94, $1.81, $2.51 a share	**680.7**	431.2	606.0
Retained earnings, beginning of year	**3,033.9**	2,889.1	2,542.4
Dividends paid—$1.32, $1.20, $1.075 a share	**(305.2)**	(286.4)	(259.3)
Retained earnings, end of year	**$3,409.4**	$3,033.9	$2,889.1

Consolidated Statement of Cash Flows [Condensed]
Year Ended December 31
(dollars in millions)

	2010	2009	2008
Operating Activities			
Net income	**$680.7**	$ 431.2	$ 606.0
Depreciation	**265.2**	231.5	222.8
Net amount of other adjustments for noncash items included in calculation of net earnings	**(145.7)**	79.2	105.6
Cash provided by operating activities	**800.2**	741.9	934.4
Investing Activities			
Additions to properties	**(449.7)**	(473.6)	(333.5)
Property disposals	**114.6**	133.8	25.2
Other	**(25.1)**	(10.6)	(11.6)
Cash used by investing activities	**(360.2)**	(350.4)	(319.9)
Financing Activities			
New borrowings	**676.5**	504.0	186.4
Reduction of borrowings	**(293.2)**	(440.9)	(400.0)
Issuance of common stock	**2.9**	13.4	17.7
Purchase of treasury stock	**(548.1)**	(224.1)	(83.6)
Cash dividends	**(305.2)**	(286.4)	(259.3)
Other	**2.9**	11.4	1.1

**ILLUSTRATION
13–2**
(concluded)

Cash used by financing activities	(464.2)	(422.6)	(537.7)
Effect of exchange rate changes on cash	(4.0)	(20.6)	0.7
Increase (decrease) in cash and temporary investments	(28.2)	(51.7)	77.5
Cash and temporary investments at beginning of year	126.3	178.0	100.5
Cash and temporary investments at end of year	**$98.1**	$126.3	$178.0

Notes:
1. Earnings per share amounts are based on the weighted-average number of shares outstanding—231.5, 238.9, and 241.2 million shares respectively for 2010, 2009, and 2008.
2. The market price of Franklin Company stock on December 31, 2010, 2009, and 2008 was, respectively, $65 3/8, $67, and $56 3/4.

$$\text{Return on invested capital} = \frac{\text{Net income} + \text{Interest}\ (1 - \text{Tax rate})}{\text{Long-term liabilities} + \text{Shareholders' equity}}$$

$$= \frac{\$680.7 + \$33.3(.66)}{\$1,309.1 + \$1,713.4} = 23.2 \text{ percent}$$

$$\text{Return on shareholders' equity} = \frac{\text{Net income}}{\text{Shareholders' equity}} = \frac{\$680.7}{\$1,713.4} = 39.7 \text{ percent}$$

Treatment of Interest

These formulas immediately raise a question: Why is after-tax interest expense added back to net income when figuring ROA or ROIC but not when calculating ROE? The answer is that, in calculating these returns, the analyst is attempting to determine how well management has used a pool of capital, whether that pool includes all liabilities plus shareholders' equity (which equal total assets), invested capital, or just shareholders' equity. The analyst can then compare these returns with the cost of using the pools of funds. However, in arriving at the net income amount, *part* of the cost of capital— the interest on the debt portion—was subtracted as an expense. The resulting net income therefore understates the earnings generated by using either the total equities pool or the invested capital pool.

Note that the amount of the adjustment is the *after-tax* interest cost of the firm. Because interest expense is tax deductible, the after-tax interest cost is the interest expense multiplied by the complement of the tax rate. Franklin's tax rate in 2010 was 34 percent ($353.4 ÷ $1,034.1).

On the other hand, in determining the return on the shareholders' investment, interest expense *should* be included in the earnings calculation, since the earnings accruing to the shareholders (i.e., net income) must reflect the fact that payments (in the form of interest) have been made to the creditors for the use of their funds.

Thus, the returns calculated using the above equations reflect the earnings generated by using a pool of funds, *excluding* the cost of the funds in the pool. This is the conceptually correct way to calculate the ratios. However, because making the interest adjustments adds complexity, some analysts ignore them in practice and simply use net income as the numerator in all three of the ROI ratios.

Average Investment

In many situations, a more representative return percentage is arrived at by using the *average* investment during the period rather than the year-end investment. Ordinarily, the average investment is found by taking one-half the sum of the beginning and ending investment. If, however, a significant amount of new debt or equity funds was obtained near the end of the year, using the beginning-of-year amounts rather than the simple average would be more meaningful. Ending balance sheet amounts have been used in the examples so that they can be easily traced back to Illustration 13–2.

Tangible Assets

ROA is sometimes calculated on the basis of tangible assets rather than total assets—goodwill and other intangible assets are excluded. When so calculated, the return is clearly labeled **return on tangible assets.** A similar approach can be used for calculating ROIC or ROE.

Liabilities

The calculations above treated deferred income taxes as a liability. A few analysts include deferred taxes as well as minority interest as a component of owners' equity. (Franklin has no minority interest.) Some analysts include as a part of invested capital any short-term notes and long-term debt maturing in one year, even though these are classified as current liabilities. These analysts maintain that debt capital includes all funds supplied by investors who expect a return in the form of interest. In any event, the description of the ratio should make clear which approach is used.

Investment Turnover and Profit Margin

Return on investment is equal to net income divided by investment. As Illustration 13–1 suggests, ROI also can be looked at as the combined effect of two factors: profitability and investment utilization. A ratio can be associated with each of these factors. Algebraically, it is clear that the following is in fact an equality:

$$\frac{\text{Net income}}{\text{Investment}} = \frac{\text{Net income}}{\text{Sales}} * \frac{\text{Sales}}{\text{Investment}}$$

Each of the two terms on the right-hand side of the equation has investment meaning of its own. Net income divided by sales is called **profit margin** or **return on sales (ROS);** it is an overall ratio for profitability. Sales divided by investment is called **investment turnover;** it is an overall ratio for investment utilization. Investment turnover is called, more specifically, **asset turnover, invested capital turnover,** or **equity turnover,** depending on which definition of investment is being used.

These relationships suggest the two fundamental ways that the ROI can be improved. First, it can be improved by increasing the profit margin—by earning more profit per dollar of sales. Second, it can be improved by increasing the investment turnover. In turn, the investment turnover can be increased in either of two ways: (1) by generating more sales volume with the same amount of investment or (2) by reducing the amount of investment required for a given level of sales volume.

As shown in Illustration 13–1, these two factors can be further decomposed into elements that can be looked at individually. The point of this decomposition is that no one manager can significantly influence the overall ROI measure, simply because an overall measure reflects the combined effects of a number of factors. However, the items on the left side of Illustration 13–1 do correspond with the responsibilities of individual managers. For example, the manager who is responsible for the firm's credit policies and procedures influences the level of accounts receivable. Thus, the outside analyst, as well as the firm's management, can use the ROI chart to identify potential problem areas in the business, as described in the separate sections on profitability ratios and investment utilization ratios.

The following equation is also often used by outside analysts and management to understand how a company achieved its ROI. Franklin's 2010 financial statement data is used to illustrate the equation's application.

$$
\begin{array}{c}
\text{Return on} \\
\text{shareholders' equity}
\end{array}
=
\begin{array}{c}
\text{Pretax margin} \\
\text{percentage}
\end{array}
*
\begin{array}{c}
\text{Asset turnover} \\
\text{ratio}
\end{array}
*
\begin{array}{c}
\text{Financial} \\
\text{leverage ratio}
\end{array}
*
\begin{array}{c}
\text{Tax retention} \\
\text{rate}
\end{array}
$$

$$
\frac{\text{Net income}}{\text{Shareholders' equity}} = \frac{\text{Pretax profit}}{\text{Sales revenues}} * \frac{\text{Sales revenues}}{\text{Total assets}} * \frac{\text{Total assets}}{\text{Shareholders' equity}} * (1 \text{ Tax rate})
$$

$$
\frac{\$680.7}{\$1,713.4} = \frac{\$1,034.1}{\$6,295.4} * \frac{\$6,295.4}{\$4,237.1} * \frac{\$4,237.1}{\$1,713.4} * (1-.34)
$$

$$
.397 = .164 * 1.49 * 2.47 * *.66
$$

The above analysis shows that Franklin's 2010 39.7 percent return on shareholders' equity was achieved by a combination of operating results (pretax margin and asset turnover) and financial policies (financial leverage and tax retention rate). The tax retention rate is the percentage of pretax income that flows down to net income.

Price/Earnings Ratio

The broadest and most widely used overall measure of performance is the **price/earnings,** or **P/E, ratio:**

$$
\frac{\text{Market price per share}}{\text{Net income per share}} = \frac{\$65.375}{\$2.94} = 22 \text{ times}
$$

This measure involves an amount not directly controlled by the company: the market price of its common stock. Thus, the P/E ratio is the best indicator of how *investors* judge the firm's future performance.[5] (We say *future* performance because, conceptually, the market price indicates shareholders' expectations about future returns—dividends and share price increases—discounted to a present value at a rate reflecting the riskiness of these returns.) Management, of course, is interested in this market appraisal, and a decline in the company's P/E ratio not explainable by a general decline in stock market prices is cause for concern. Also, management compares its P/E ratio with those of similar companies to determine the marketplace's relative rankings of the firms.

P/E ratios for industries vary, reflecting differing expectations about the relative rate of *growth in earnings* in those industries. At times, the P/E ratios for virtually all companies decline because predictions of general economic conditions suggest that corporate profits will decrease and/or interest rates will rise.

Franklin does not have a complex capital structure (i.e., it does not have potentially dilutive securities). Therefore, the net income per share figure used to compute its P/E ratio is its basic earnings per share. If Franklin's capital structure included potentially dilutive securities, its diluted earnings per share would typically be used to compute its P/E ratio. Often one-time charges and credits to income are excluded from the earnings per share figure used to compute P/E ratios on the grounds that the market price of a stock reflects investors' expectations about the company's future earnings power. (Franklin's 2010 extraordinary item charge is an example of a one-time item.) Since

---

[5] Major newspapers such as *The Wall Street Journal* print firms' P/E ratios along with the firm's daily stock quotations. These data are also available in many sites on the Internet.

different earnings per share figures for the same company can be used to compute a company's P/E ratio, users of P/E ratios should always check to see which earnings per share figure is being used.[6]

Profitability Ratios

Each of the items on the income statement in Illustration 13–2 can be expressed as a percentage of sales. Examining relationships within a statement in this way is called a **vertical analysis.** As noted in Chapter 3, net sales is usually taken as 100 percent. Of the percentages that can be calculated, gross margin ($3,306.4 ÷ $6,295.4 ÷ 52.5 percent), income before taxes ($1,034.1 ÷ $6,295.4 = 16.4 percent), and net income ($680.7 ÷ $6,295.4 = 10.8 percent) are all important. Retailing firms tend to pay particular attention to their gross margin percentage. A discount retailing strategy, for example, is based (in part) on the premise that selling goods at a lower gross margin percentage will generate more volume so that *total* dollar gross margin will compare favorably with that of firms having a larger gross margin percentage but lower sales volume and lower asset turnover.

Profit Margin

As mentioned previously, the profit margin is a measure of overall profitability. Some people treat this measure as if it were the most important single measure of performance. Critics of the social performance of a company or an industry, for example, may base their criticism on its relatively high profit margin. This is erroneous. Net income, considered either by itself or as a percentage of sales, does not take into account the investment employed to produce that income. For example, utilities have a relatively high ROS, but their ROE is below average, reflecting the very large fixed asset base that a utility must finance. On the other hand, supermarkets have a low ROS, but their ROE is above average. This reflects the facts that (1) supermarkets do not have any accounts receivable to finance, (2) their inventory turnover is very rapid, and (3) many rent their premises, which, if they are operating leases, therefore do not appear as balance sheet assets; that is, their investment turnover is high.

Illustration 13–1 suggests the things top management needs to examine if the profit margin is unsatisfactory. Perhaps dollar sales volume has declined, either because fewer items are being sold or because they are being sold at lower prices, or both. Perhaps the gross margin is being squeezed because cost of sales increases cannot be passed along to customers in the form of higher prices. Cost of sales may be up because of production inefficiencies. Perhaps other expenses have gotten out of control: Maybe management has gotten lax about administrative expenses or is spending more for marketing costs than the sales results would seem to justify.

Common-Size Financial Statements

Common-size financial statements are often used to obtain answers to the question raised in the above paragraph. A common-size income statement expresses each item on the income statement as a percentage of net sales. A common-size balance sheet uses total assets as the base. To identify changes in a company's operating results, investment mix and sources of capital, common-size financial statements for two or more periods are prepared and the percentage figures for each line item are compared. For example, a comparison of Franklin's 2008–2010 common-size income statements

[6] Financial analysts often exclude one-time items from income when calculating profitability ratios. In addition to extraordinary items, one-time items often include restructuring changes, inventory write-downs, asset impairments, contingency losses and gains, and gains and losses on asset dispositions.

would show the company's selling and administrative expense as a percentage of net sales has risen from 33.3 percent in 2008 to 35.5 percent in 2009. The reason for this 2.2-percentage-point increase should be examined.

Investment Utilization Ratios

Ratios that deal with the lower branch of Illustration 13–1 represent tests of *investment utilization.* Whereas profitability measures focus on income statement figures, utilization tests involve both balance sheet and income statement amounts. We have already looked at the all-encompassing utilization ratio, return on investment (ROI). In this section, narrower measures will be examined.

Investment Turnover

As with other ratios involving investment, three turnover ratios can be calculated:

$$\text{Asset turnover} = \frac{\text{Sales revenue}}{\text{Total assets}} = \frac{\$6,295.4}{\$4,237.1} = 1.5 \text{ times}$$

$$\text{Invested capital turnover} = \frac{\text{Sales revenue}}{\text{Invested capital}} = \frac{\$6,295.4}{\$3,022.5} = 2.1 \text{ times}$$

$$\text{Equity turnover} = \frac{\text{Sales revenue}}{\text{Shareholders' equity}} = \frac{\$6,295.4}{\$1,713.4} = 3.7 \text{ times}$$

Because of industry disparities in investment turnover, judgments about the adequacy of a firm's turnover must be made carefully. ROI is profit margin multiplied by investment turnover. Thus, if two firms have different turnover ratios, the firm with the lower turnover will need to earn a higher profit margin to achieve a given level of ROI, as is the case with utilities. Comparing the turnover ratios of two similar companies in the same industry is valid, of course, and may help explain why one achieves a higher ROI than the other. Similarly, comparing profit margins of companies in the same industry is valid, provided the companies are similar enough that the implicit assumption of their having equal investment turnover is valid. (Gap and Nordstrom are in the same industry—nonfood retailing—but it is not valid to compare them solely on the basis of either profit margin or investment turnover, because their different marketing strategies should cause these ratios to differ.)

Capital Asset Intensity

Several investment utilization ratios that are less encompassing than investment turnover can be calculated. One of these is the **capital asset intensity ratio:**

$$\text{Capital asset intensity} = \frac{\text{Sales revenue}}{\text{Property, plant, and equipment}} = \frac{\$6,295.4}{\$2,768.4} = 2.3 \text{ times}$$

The capital asset intensity ratio (sometimes called **fixed asset turnover**) focuses only on the property, plant, and equipment item. Companies that have a high ratio of plant to sales revenue, such as steel companies, are particularly vulnerable to cyclical fluctuations in business activity. Because the costs associated with this plant are relatively fixed, when these companies' sales revenue drops in a recession, they are unable to cover these costs. Conversely, a company that is not capital intensive, as is the case with many service businesses, can reduce its costs as its revenues decline and therefore has less difficulty in a recession.

Working Capital Measures

Management is interested in the velocity with which funds move through the various current accounts. Ratios for days' cash, days' receivables, days' inventory, and inventory turnover (described near the ends of Chapters 5 and 6) provide the information on these flows. The reader can review the calculations of these ratios by referring to Illustration 13–1.

Working Capital Turnover

In addition to the ratios that focus on specific working capital items (see below), it is often useful to look at the turnover of working capital (Current assets − Current liabilities) as a whole:

$$\text{Working capital turnover} = \frac{\text{Sales revenue}}{\text{Working capital}} = \frac{\$6,295.4}{\$30.5} = 206 \text{ times}$$

Some analysts prefer to look at working capital as a percentage of sales. For Franklin, this is 0.5 percent. Since this is simply the inverse of the working capital turnover ratio, it conveys the same information but in a slightly different way.

Days' Payables

An analogous ratio can be calculated for days' payables:

$$\text{Days' payables} = \frac{\text{Operating payables}}{\text{Pretax cash expenses} \div 365}$$

Pretax cash expenses can be approximated by adding all expenses except taxes and then subtracting noncash expenses such as depreciation. (This is the same procedure as for the days' cash ratio, except that taxes usually are included there.) Operating payables include accounts payable, accrued salaries and wages, and other items that represent deferred payments for operating expenses. A note payable would be included if its proceeds financed accounts receivable or inventories; otherwise, short-term debt is excluded. For Franklin, the ratio is

$$\text{Days' payables} = \frac{\$308.8 + \$76.5 + \$233.8 + \$141.4}{\$4,996.1 \div 365} = 56 \text{ days}$$

Cash Conversion Cycle

Days' receivables, days' inventory, and days' payables can be combined to determine the **cash conversion cycle.** This is the length of time for cash to complete the operating cycle shown in Illustration 5–1, after incorporating payment deferrals. It is calculated as follows (using numbers for Franklin):

	Days
Receivables conversion period (days' receivables)	31
Plus: Inventory conversion period (days' inventory)	49
Operating cycle	80
Less: Payment deferral period (days' payables)	56
Cash conversion cycle	24

The result of this calculation is a measure of liquidity (discussed in the next section); it also indicates the time interval for which additional short-term financing might be needed to support a spurt in sales.

Each of these measures of turnover gives an indication of how well the firm is managing some particular subset of its assets. The investment turnover figures permit a comparison of similar firms' investment bases vis-à-vis the sales generated by those firms. The days' cash, receivables, and inventory ratios help identify whether a firm is tying up excessive amounts of funds in current assets. Excess levels of assets hurt performance because they require additional capital, and there is a cost associated with this capital. To the extent that debt could be reduced by cutting the level of assets, interest costs would fall, increasing net income, and the investment base would decrease, thus having a doubly favorable impact on ROI.

Financial Condition Ratios

Liquidity and Solvency

Whereas the ratios previously discussed are indicators of the firm's success in marketing management and operations management, financial condition ratios are related to the firm's financial management. Financial condition ratios look at the company's liquidity and solvency. **Liquidity** refers to the company's ability to meet its current obligations. Thus, liquidity tests focus on the size of, and relationships between, current liabilities and current assets. (Current assets presumably will be converted into cash in order to pay the current liabilities.) **Solvency,** on the other hand, pertains to the company's ability to meet the interest costs and repayment schedules associated with its long-term obligations.

Most of the ratios used for this purpose have been discussed in previous chapters: current ratio, acid-test (or quick) ratio, debt/equity ratio, debt/capitalization ratio, times interest earned, and cash generated by operations/total debt. Also, the cash conversion cycle, described previously, is related to liquidity.

Dividend Policy

Two other ratios are related to another aspect of financial management: dividend policy. These ratios are the **dividend yield** and **dividend payout:**

$$\text{Dividend yield} = \frac{\text{Dividends per share}}{\text{Market price per share}} = \frac{\$1.32}{\$65.375} = 2.0 \text{ percent}$$

$$\text{Dividend payout} = \frac{\text{Dividends}}{\text{Net income}} = \frac{\$305.2}{\$680.7} = 45 \text{ percent}$$

A company must reach decisions on how its growth should be financed. Each company has a target debt/equity ratio it attempts to maintain. To do so, it must raise a certain fraction of additional capital from debt sources and the remainder from equity sources. Equity capital can be raised either by issuing new stock or by retaining earnings. If a company finds it expensive to raise new equity capital directly from investors, it can obtain its additional equity capital by retaining earnings. The more of the net income it retains in this fashion, the less it can pay out to shareholders as dividends. Of course, this applies only to a profitable company. If a company is in financial difficulty, it simply may not be able to afford to pay dividends.

The dividend yield on stocks is often compared with the yield (interest) on bonds, but such a comparison is not valid. The earnings of bondholders consist entirely of their interest (adjusted for amortization of discount or premium), whereas the earnings of shareholders consist not only of their dividends but also of retained earnings. Although shareholders do not receive retained earnings, the fact that part of the net income has been retained in the business (and presumably invested in income-producing assets) should enhance future earnings per share and dividends. This, in turn, should increase the market value of the shareholders' investment.

The ratios described in this book are summarized in Illustration 13–3.

ILLUSTRATION 13–3 Summary of Ratios

Name of Ratio	Formula	State Results as	Discussed in Chapter
Overall Performance Measures			
1. Price/earnings ratio	$\dfrac{\text{Market price per share}}{\text{Net income per share}}$	Times	13
2. Return on assets	$\dfrac{\text{Net income + interest (1 – Tax rate)}}{\text{Total assets}}$	Percent	13
3. Return on invested capital	$\dfrac{\text{Net income + interest (1 – Tax rate)}}{\text{Long-term liabilities + Shareholders' equity}}$	Percent	13
4. Return on shareholders' equity	$\dfrac{\text{Net income}}{\text{Shareholders' equity}}$	Percent	13
Profitability Measures			
5. Gross margin percentage	$\dfrac{\text{Gross margin}}{\text{Net sales revenues}}$	Percent	6, 13
6. Profit margin	$\dfrac{\text{Net income}}{\text{Net sales revenues}}$	Percent	13
7. Earnings per share	$\dfrac{\text{Net income}}{\text{No. shares outstanding}}$	Dollars	9
8. Cash Realization	$\dfrac{\text{Cash generated by operations}}{\text{Net income}}$	Times	11
Tests of Investment Utilization			
9. Asset turnover	$\dfrac{\text{Sales revenues}}{\text{Total assets}}$	Times	13
10. Invested capital turnover	$\dfrac{\text{Sales revenues}}{\text{Long-term liabilities + Shareholders' equity}}$	Times	13
11. Equity turnover	$\dfrac{\text{Sales revenues}}{\text{Shareholders' equity}}$	Times	13
12. Capital intensity	$\dfrac{\text{Sales revenues}}{\text{Property, plant, and equipment}}$	Times	13
13. Days' cash	$\dfrac{\text{Cash}}{\text{Cash expenses} \div 365}$	Days	5
14. Days' receivables (or collection period)	$\dfrac{\text{Accounts receivable}}{\text{Sales} \div 365}$	Days	5
15. Days' inventory	$\dfrac{\text{Inventory}}{\text{Cost of sales} \div 365}$	Days	6
16. Inventory turnover	$\dfrac{\text{Cost of sales}}{\text{Inventory}}$	Times	6
17. Working capital turnover	$\dfrac{\text{Sales revenues}}{\text{Working capital}}$	Times	13
18. Current ratio	$\dfrac{\text{Current assets}}{\text{Current liabilities}}$	Ratio	5
19. Acid-test (quick) ratio	$\dfrac{\text{Monetary current assets}}{\text{Current liabilities}}$	Ratio	5

(continued)

ILLUSTRATION 13–3 *(continued)*

Name of Ratio	Formula	State Results as	Discussed in Chapter
Tests of Financial Condition			
20. Financial leverage ratio	$\dfrac{\text{Assets}}{\text{Shareholders' equity}}$	Times	13
21. Debt/equity ratio	$\dfrac{\text{Long-term liabilities}}{\text{Shareholders' equity}}$ or	Percent	8
	$\dfrac{\text{Total liabilities}}{\text{Shareholders' equity}}$	Percent	8
22. Debt/capitalization	$\dfrac{\text{Long-term liabilities}}{\text{Long-term liabilities + Shareholders' equity}}$	Percent	8
23. Times interest earned	$\dfrac{\text{Pretax operating profit + Interest}}{\text{Interest}}$	Times	9
24. Cash flow/debt	$\dfrac{\text{Cash generated operations}}{\text{Total debt}}$	Percent	11
Tests of Dividend Policy			
25. Dividend yield	$\dfrac{\text{Dividends per share}}{\text{Market price per share}}$	Percent	13
26. Dividend payout	$\dfrac{\text{Dividends}}{\text{Net income}}$	Percent	13

Notes:

1. *Averaging.* When one term of a formula is an income statement item and the other term is a balance sheet item, it is often preferable to use the average of the beginning and ending balance sheet amounts rather than the ending balance sheet amounts.

2. *Tangible assets.* Ratios involving noncurrent assets or total assets often exclude intangible assets such as goodwill and trademarks. When this is done, the word *tangible* is usually used in identifying the ratio.

3. *Debt.* Debt ratios may exclude accounts payable, accrued liabilities, deferred income taxes, and other noninterest-bearing liabilities. The reader often has no way of knowing whether this has been done, however. Conceptually, *debt* means interest-bearing liabilities.

4. *Coverage ratios.* Times interest earned and other coverage ratios can be calculated using pretax cash generated by operations instead of pretax operating profit.

Growth Measures

Analysts are also interested in the growth rate of certain key items such as sales, net income, and earnings per share. These rates are often compared with the rate of inflation to see if the company is keeping pace with inflation or experiencing real growth. Common growth rate calculations include average growth rate and compound growth rate. Both involve looking at information over a period of years, typically 5 or 10. The calculations will be illustrated using Franklin's 2005–2010 sales data (expressed in millions):

	2010	2009	2008	2007	2006	2005
Net sales	$6,295	$6,191	$5,787	$5,181	$4,652	$4,349

To calculate **average growth rate,** growth is first calculated on a year-to-year basis. From 2005 to 2006, this was 6.97 percent ($4,652 ÷ $4,349 − 100 percent); from 2006 to 2007, 11.37 percent; and so on. These five year-to-year rates are then averaged; the result is an average growth rate in sales of 7.74 percent.

The **compound growth rate** calculation uses the compound interest/present value concepts described in the appendix to Chapter 8. In this instance, the question is: At what rate would $4,349 have to grow to reach the amount of $6,295 after five years? (More formally: What rate of return gives a present value of $4,349 to a future value of $6,295 in five years?) Using Table A at the end of this book, this rate can be approximated as almost 8 percent (since $4,349 ÷ $6,295 = 0.691, which falls near the 0.681 factor for 8 percent on the five-year line); using a preprogrammed calculator, the rate can be calculated as 7.68 percent.

In some cases, the compound growth rate method can give misleading results because either the base year number (here, for 2005) or the final year number (for 2010) is abnormally high or low. In such a case, the average growth rate method is preferable.

The **implied growth rate equation** is used to project a company's *potential* to grow its sales and profits. The implied growth rate equation is

$$\text{Implied growth rate} = \text{Return on shareholders' equity} * \text{Profit retention rate}$$

$$\text{Implied growth rate} = \frac{\text{Assets}}{\text{Shareholders' equity}} * (1 - \text{Dividend payout})$$

$$21.8 \text{ percent} = .397 * (1 - .45)$$

The implied growth rate equation indicates that Franklin has the potential to grow its sales profits 21.8 percent per year without an injection of new equity capital if it achieves a 39.7 percent return on equity and maintains a dividend payout of 45 percent. It is important to note that the implied growth rate equation does not predict that Franklin will grow at a 21.8 percent rate. The company's actual growth rate will depend on many factors, such as product market conditions.[7]

Making Comparisons

Difficulties

An approximately accurate report of actual performance can be obtained from a company's financial statements. Finding an adequate standard with which these actual amounts can be compared, however, is often difficult. Some of the problems are described below. Financial statement analysis is used as an example, but the same problems arise in analyzing other types of quantitative data.

Deciding on the Proper Basis for Comparison

In general, a youth who can high jump six feet is a better high jumper than a youth who can only jump five feet. In business, however, there are situations in which one cannot tell whether a higher number represents better performance than a lower number.

A high current ratio is not necessarily better than a low current ratio. For example, the current ratio for Franklin on December 31, 2010, was 1.03 to 1. Suppose that on January 2, 2011, Franklin borrowed $300 million of long-term debt and used these funds to pay down accounts payable. A balance sheet prepared subsequent to this transaction would show $1,245 million of current assets and $915 million of current liabilities, and the current ratio would accordingly be 1.36 to 1, 11/3 times the ratio two days earlier. Yet one could scarcely say that a company that had increased its long-term debt in order to pay current liabilities was in an improved financial condition.

---

[7] A company's implied growth rate is often used in dividend and net income–based equity valuation models to normalize dividend and net income growth for future periods beyond five years.

In some comparisons the direction of change that represents "better" is reasonably apparent. Generally, a high profit margin is better than a low one, and a high ROI is better than a low one. Even these statements have qualifications, however. A high return may indicate that the company is only skimming the cream off the market; a more intensive marketing effort now could lead to a more sustained growth in the future.

Many standards can usefully be thought of as a *quality range* rather than as a single number. Actual performance that goes outside the range in *either* direction is an indication of an unsatisfactory situation. For a certain company, the current ratio may be considered satisfactory if it is within the range 1.5:1 to 2.5:1. Below 1.5:1 there is the danger of being unable to meet maturing obligations. Above 2.5:1 there is an indication that funds are being left idle rather than being efficiently employed.

Differences in the Situations

No reasonable person would expect a 12-year-old youth to run as fast as a 19-year-old athlete; the youth's performance should be compared to others of the same age, sex, and training. Differences in the factors that affect a company's performance this year as compared with last year are complex. Nevertheless, some attempt must be made to allow for these differences. The task is more difficult when we attempt to compare one company with another, even if both are of the same size and in the same industry. It becomes exceedingly difficult if the two companies are in different industries or if they are of substantially different size.

Changes in the Dollar Measuring Stick

Accounting amounts are expressed in historical dollars. A change in price levels may therefore seriously lessen the validity of comparisons of ratios computed for different time periods. Also, a ratio whose numerator and denominator are expressed in dollars of significantly different purchasing power (e.g., the capital asset intensity ratio when the fixed assets were acquired many years ago) may have no useful meaning. The fact that plant and equipment amounts are stated as unexpired historical dollar costs causes particular difficulty in making comparisons of ratios. Two companies, for example, might have physically identical facilities in all respects except age, and they might operate exactly the same way and earn exactly the same net income. If, however, the facilities of one company were purchased at a time when prices were low and the facilities are almost fully depreciated, and if the facilities of the other company were purchased at a time of higher prices and those facilities are relatively new, then the ROI of the company that carried its assets at a low book value would be much higher than the ROI of the other company.

Differences in Definition

The term *six feet* used to measure the high jumper's leap is precisely defined and easily measured. But the individual elements making up such terms as *current assets* and *current liabilities* are by no means precisely defined, and there is considerable diversity in practice as to how they should be measured. Similarly, profit may mean (1) net income as determined by using generally accepted accounting principles (which in turn can be a range of values, depending on the particular methods used for depreciation, inventory valuation, and so forth); (2) income after taxes, based on the firm's income tax return; (3) profit as determined by procedures required by a regulatory agency; or (4) profit as shown on a report intended for the use of management only.

Hidden Short-Run Changes

A balance sheet may not reflect the typical situation. It reports as of one moment in time and tells nothing about short-term fluctuations in assets and equities that have occurred within the period between two balance sheet dates. Many department stores, for example, publish annual balance sheets as of January 31. By that date, the December holiday season inventories have been sold out, and payments of many of the holiday season receivables have been received; but Easter merchandise has not started to arrive, and payables for this merchandise have not yet been generated. Current assets (other than cash) and current liabilities as reported on the January 31 balance sheet are therefore likely to be lower than at other times of the year. As a result, ratios such as inventory turnover and the average collection period may not be representative of the situation in other seasons.

Moreover, companies have been known to deliberately clean up their balance sheets just before the end of the year. They may reduce inventories, which increases the inventory turnover ratio, and then build up inventories again early in the next year. Such "window dressing" of the balance sheet is difficult for an outside analyst to discern.

The Past as an Indication of the Future

Financial statements are historical documents, and financial ratios show relationships that have existed in the past. Managers and analysts alike are primarily interested in what is happening now and what is likely to happen rather than what did happen. Often, outside analysts must rely on past data as an indication of the current situation. But they should not be misled into believing that the historical ratios necessarily reflect current conditions—much less that they reflect future conditions. With this caveat in mind, past financial ratios can be a useful tool to construct future pro forma, financial statements that the outside analyst can use as a basis for making operating and financial condition predictions.

Possible Bases for Comparison

An actual financial statement amount or ratio can be compared against four types of standards: (1) experience, (2) a budget, (3) a historical amount, and (4) an external benchmark.

Experience

Managers and analysts gradually build up their own ideas about what constitutes good or poor performance. One important advantage that experienced people have is that they possess a feeling for what the "right" relationships are in a given situation. These subjective standards of a competent analyst or manager are more important than standards based on mechanical comparisons.

Budgets

Almost all companies prepare budgets that show what performance is expected to be under the circumstances prevailing. If actual performance corresponds with budgeted performance, there is a reasonable inference that performance was good.

Two important qualifications affect this inference, however. First, the budgeted amounts may not have been developed very carefully. The comparison can, of course, be no more valid than the validity of the standards. Second, the budgeted amounts were necessarily arrived at on the basis of various assumptions about the conditions that would be prevailing during the period. If these assumptions turn out to be incorrect, the amounts are also incorrect as a measure of results "under the circumstances prevailing." If, because of a recession or other economic phenomenon outside the control of management, net income is lower than the amount budgeted, it cannot fairly be said that the difference indicates poor management performance. Nevertheless, the budget is a type of standard that has fewer inherent difficulties than either historical or external standards. Of course, outside analysts frequently do not have access to a company's budget; but some overall budget parameters (such as earnings per share and return on investment) are publicly stated by top management as corporate financial goals.

Historical Standards

A comparison of a company's current performance with its past performance raises relatively few comparison problems and is consistent with a management philosophy of continuous improvement. Such a comparison does not run into the problem of differences in accounting methods. If a method has changed, the change must be reported in the financial statements. Moreover, the analyst also can recollect or find out from supplementary data some of the circumstances that have changed between the two periods and thus allow for these changes in making the comparison. At best, however, a comparison between a current amount and a historical amount in the same company can show only that the current period is better or worse than the past. This may not provide a sound basis for judgment because the historical amount may not have represented an acceptable standard. A company that increases its ROE from 1 percent to 2 percent has doubled its ROE, but it nevertheless is not doing very well.

External Benchmarks

When one company is compared with another, environmental and accounting differences may raise serious problems of comparability. If, however, the analyst is able to allow for these differences, then the outside data provide a performance check that has the advantage of being arrived at independently. Moreover, the two companies may have been affected by the same set of economic conditions, so this important cause of noncomparability may be neutralized.

Some companies use the results of a highly regarded competitor as a benchmark. Others identify the best performer among their various quasi-independent business units and use this unit's results as a benchmark against which to compare the other units' performance. Such comparisons may involve overall results or specific parameters such as inventory turnover or production efficiency.

Several organizations, including Dun & Bradstreet, various industry associations, and the Department of Commerce, publish average ratios for groups of companies in the same industry. Several online database services provide access to financial and statistical information for several thousand industrial companies and utilities in the United States and Canada; ratios can be calculated from these data. A reference librarian can assist in locating these various sources.

Use of industrywide ratios involves all the difficulties of using ratios derived from one other company plus the special problems that arise when the data for several companies are thrown together into a single average. Nevertheless, they may give some useful impressions about the average situation in an industry.

Use of Comparisons

The principal value of analyzing financial statement information is that it *suggests questions* that need to be answered. Such an analysis rarely provides the answers. A large unfavorable difference between actual performance and whatever standard is used indicates that something may be wrong, and this leads to an investigation. Even when the analysis indicates strongly that something *is* wrong (as when one company's income has declined while incomes of comparable companies have increased), the analysis rarely shows the underlying causes of the difficulty. Nevertheless, the ability to pick from thousands of potential questions those few that are really worth asking is an important one.

Keep in mind the basic relationships shown in Illustration 13–2, or some variation applicable to the situation being analyzed. The only number that encompasses all these relationships is an ROI ratio. A change in any less inclusive ratio may be misleading as an indication of better or worse performance, because it may have been offset by compensating changes in other ratios. An increase in dollars of net income indicates improved performance only if there was no offsetting increase in the investment required. An increase in the net profit margin indicates improved performance only if there was no offsetting decrease in sales volume or increase in investment. An increase in the gross margin percentage indicates improved performance only if there was no offsetting decrease in sales volume, increase in investment, or increase in selling and administrative expenses.

In short, the use of any ratio other than ROI, taken by itself, implies that all other things are equal. This *ceteris paribus* condition ordinarily does not prevail, and the validity of comparisons is lessened to the extent that it does not. Yet the ROI ratio is so broad that it does not give a clue about which of the underlying factors may be responsible for changes in it. It is to find these factors, which if unfavorable indicate possible trouble areas, that the subsidiary ratios of profitability are used. Furthermore, an ROI ratio tells nothing about the financial condition of the company; liquidity and solvency ratios are necessary for this purpose.

Accounting Performance versus Market Performance

Performance of a firm can always be viewed from two perspectives; how is the firm doing in the markets, i.e., its valuation in the stock markets (captured through ratios like Price/Earnings, Price/Book Value, etc.) or how is the firm doing basically on Balance sheet and Income Statement (captured in terms of liquidity, solvency, turnover, margins, etc.). Ideally, both these measures of performance should merge and move together but there could be a time lag between them because of information asymmetry. Markets may react early or late to a financial information about the firm. They may even over-react or under react to a piece of information coming from the firm. Therefore, in many situations, the two measures of performance may contradict each other. The firm might continue to get strong valuations in the markets even though its fundamentals may be weakening up or the firm may attract poor valuations in the markets although its numbers on Balance Sheet and Income Statement might have improved. In such situations, the central question is which performance is more objective and which one matters more.

Most observers and researchers will argue that in such situation where the Accounting and Market performance are not synchronized and that either of them is indicating something fundamentally flawed, market performance will be seen as more true indication of the firm's actual performance. The reason is two-fold; one that accounting performance gets affected by managerial discretion on treatment of some items (thanks to the subjective language of the accounting standards) and two because of the fact that markets consist of collective wisdom of millions of people and the chances of all of them estimating the valuations wrong is very small. There will be someone in the markets definitely who will catch hold of the information, analyse it and accordingly the markets will start reflecting that information in the price. Accounting performance can have undesirable effects of individual biases related to the treatment of items like depreciation and provisioning which continue to be at the end of the day, an estimate only.

Let us take an example. A firm which is showing fundamental weakness in their Revenue numbers can decide to reduce the provisioning for bad debts by claiming that they have started doing stricter background check of the customer as compared to the previous year and therefore lesser provisioning requirements. The real objective of the firm could be to report better profit numbers but that is happening not because of any fundamental change on the ground in the business but just because of a change in accounting policy. This change will send a message to the markets that although the firm is showing slower growth in Sales volumes, their profits are still increasing. This tantamount to a phenomenon called "fraudulent conveyance" where the firm is masking its poor performance by tinkering with accounting policy. In doing so they are window dressing the performance. Now, fundamentally, we believe that there would be some "smart people" in the market who will observe this "revision in accounting estimates" and reveal it to the markets that the numbers which are looking "little better" is not because of any genuine change in performance and therefore will educate the entire market about it. So, in real sense the efforts of the firm to hide its poor performance will get exposed and such firms will lose credibility and may be seen as companies with less integrity, and it may affect their long-term valuations in the markets too.

However, events in the recent past, both in developed and developing markets point towards a situation where markets have got it wrong completely. Be it the infamous Lehman collapse or the most recent ILFS (Infrastructure Leasing and Financial Services Ltd) collapse, both these companies were getting good valuations even just before the collapse. Thus, pointing out a very basic argument that markets can get it wrong or in the short run get carried away. Although, there were huge weaknesses in the Balance sheet of the firm; specifically, in terms of huge asset-liability mismatch but markets failed to read it and it was only when the company announced its inability to meet the obligations related to a bond repayment, the markets erupted. Later on, it was discovered that the role of auditors and the Board committees including the Risk Management and Audit Committee was nothing short of highly unprofessional working with a mala fide intent. Therefore, blindly saying that market-based matrices are always superior and the markets will identify a "crack in the wall" may not be always true.

EBITDA versus PAT

Continuing with the argument in the previous section about the superiority of Market performance over Accounting performance, we try and find a mid-way between the two approaches. We understand and acknowledge that some items in the financial statements are subject to managerial discretion (primarily because of the subjective language of the accounting standards) and therefore the treatment of such items may significantly impact the reported profits for a firm but if somehow we can neutralize the influence of such discretionary items, we may have a purer variable which better captures the underlying performance of the firm. One of such variables commonly used is EBITDA (Earnings before interest, tax, depreciation and amortization) which is commonly referred to as Operating Cash flows. This variable adds back the discretionary items (which were earlier included in estimating PAT) like Depreciation and Amortization. There is a discretion available to managers when it comes to estimating the depreciation or amortization expenses of a firm as it is based on estimated useful life whose estimate could have a personal bias and can change subsequently on account of usage, maintenance, etc. Similarly interest expense is a non-operating expense as it is on borrowed money and has nothing to do with the direct operations of the firm. Just because a firm has borrowed money for its operations rather than sourcing it from internal sources must not give the firm any advantage or disadvantage as such in its overall valuation. The same logic can be extended to the tax paid to the state. That is the reason why interest and tax are added back.

Therefore, in a way, EBITDA removes all the "noise" in the reported Accounting Profit by making PAT look purer as it captures only the revenue and expenses directly related to the main operations of the business. Such is the popularity of the variable EBITDA that most internal management decision in firms are getting benchmarked on EBITDA margins rather than PAT margins. Firms are getting increasingly valued on the basis of the Enterprise Value divided by EBITDA as EV/EBITDA is seen as the best indicator of valuation matrix. As discussed earlier, the interest expense and tax expense shouldn't have a major impact on valuation as they are not part of Operating expenses.

Summary

The numbers on financial statements are usually most useful for analytical purposes when they are expressed in relative terms in the form of ratios. ROI measures overall performance, but other ratios help the analyst find more specific areas affecting ROI where investigation may be fruitful. Categories of ratios include those related to profitability, investment utilization, and financial condition. Although a great many ratios can be calculated, only a few are ordinarily necessary in connection with a given problem.

The essential task is to find a standard or norm with which actual performance can be compared. In general, there are four types of standards: (1) subjective standards, derived from the analyst's experience; (2) budgets, set in advance of the period under review; (3) historical data, showing performance of the same company in the past; and (4) the performance of other companies, as shown by their financial statements or by industry averages. None of these is perfect, but a rough allowance for the factors that cause noncomparability often can be made. The comparison may then suggest important questions that need to be investigated; it rarely indicates answers to the questions.

Problems

Problem 13–1.

You are given the following data on two companies, M and N (figures are millions):

	M	N
Sales	$1,080	$1,215
Net income	54	122
Investment	180	105

Required:

a. Which company has the higher profit margin?

b. Which company has the higher investment turnover?

c. Based solely on the data given, in which firm would you prefer to invest?

Problem 13–2.

As the manager of Losen division of McCarthy Corporation, you are interested in determining the division's return on investment. As division manager, you have no control over financing assets, but you control acquisition and disposition of assets. The division controller has given you the following data to aid you in calculating return on investment:

Fiscal Year, January 1 to December 31 (000 omitted):	
Total assets, January 1	$400,000
Total assets, December 31	525,000
Long-term debt, January 1	75,000
Long-term debt, December 31	96,000
Owners' equity, January 1	278,000
Owners' equity, December 31	303,000
Net income for the year	54,000
Interest expense on long-term debt	4,200

Tax rate = 30%.

Required:

What method would be most appropriate for calculating the division's return on investment (ROI)? Why? Using this method, what is ROI for the current year?

Problem 13–3.   The president of Kelly Company is interested in determining how effective the company's newcontroller has been in controlling cash on hand. You have the following information available from the fiscal year preceding the new controller's arrival, and the current year:

	Current Year	Preceding Year
Cash on hand	$ 5,479,296	$ 6,123,704
Cash expenses	83,138,408	99,748,943

Required:

Does it appear that the new controller has been effective in managing cash?

Problem 13–4.   The treasurer of Gould's Stores, Inc., was interested in what effect, if any, new credit terms have had on collections of customer accounts. The usual 30-day payment period was shortened to 20 days in an attempt to reduce the investment in accounts receivable. The following information for the current year and the preceding year (prior to the payment period change) is available:

	Current Year	Preceding Year
Accounts receivable (net of bad debt allowance)	$ 1,392,790	$ 1,207,393
Credit sales	13,035,085	11,597,327

Required:

What effect has the new credit policy apparently had?

Problem 13–5.   Tara Whitney was interested in controlling her company's inventory because she knew that excess inventories were expensive in that they tied up funds. On the other hand, insufficient inventory levels could result in lost sales. Whitney obtained the following inventory information from her trade association, which reported average figures for companies similar to hers:

Days' inventory	38 days
Inventory turnover	11 times

Whitney had the following information from last year, which she considered to be a typical year for her company:

Cost of sales	$300,000
Beginning inventory	58,160
Ending inventory	62,880

Required:

How does Tara Whitney's company's inventory compare with that of other similar companies?

Problem 13–6. Ralite Company had net income for the year of $20 million. It had 2 million shares of common stock outstanding, with a year-end market price of $82 a share. Dividends during the year were $5.74 a share.

Required:

Calculate the following ratios: (*a*) price/earnings ratio, (*b*) dividend yield, and (*c*) dividend payout.

Problem 13–7. Unisonic Company had sales revenues for the year of $1,750. Average working capital; property, plant, and equipment; and shareholders' equity were $250, $525, and $1,500, respectively. (All figures are millions.)

Required:

Calculate (*a*) working capital turnover, (*b*) capital asset intensity, and (*c*) equity turnover.

Case 13–1

Genmo Corporation*

On the night of February 27, 2012, certain records of the Genmo Corporation were accidentally destroyed by fire. Two days after that, the principal owner had an appointment with an investor to discuss the possible sale of the company. The owner needed as much information as could be gathered for this purpose, recognizing that over a longer period of time a more complete reconstruction would be possible.

On the morning of February 28, the following were available: (1) a balance sheet as of December 31, 2010, and an income statement for 2010 (Exhibit 1) and (2) certain fragmentary data and ratios that had been calculated from the current financial statements

*Copyright © Professor Robert N. Anthony. 2011?

(Exhibit 2). The statements themselves had been destroyed in the fire. (In ratios involving balance sheet amounts, Genmo used year-end amounts rather than an average.) And (3) the following data (in thousands):

2011 revenues	$10,281
Current liabilities, December 31, 2011	2,285

Questions

1. Prepare a balance sheet as of December 31, 2011, and the 2011 income statement.
2. What was the return on shareholders' equity for

EXHIBIT 1

Genmo
Corporation
Financial
Statements
(thousands of
dollars)

Balance Sheet As of December 31, 2010		
Assets		
Current assets:		
Cash		$ 18
Marketable securities		494
Accounts receivable		728
Inventories		972
Prepaid expenses		214
Total current assets		2,426
Investments		898
Real estate, plant, and equipment	$4,727	
Less: Accumulated depreciation	2,433	2,294
Special tools		171
Goodwill		594
Total assets		$6,383
Liabilities and Shareholders' Equity		
Current liabilities:		
Accounts payable		$ 732
Loans payable		266
Accrued liabilities		1,232
Total current liabilities		2,230
Long-term debt		250
Other noncurrent liabilities		951
Total liabilities		3,431
Shareholders' equity:		
Preferred stock		25
Common stock		54
Additional paid-in capital		667
Retained earnings		2,206
Total shareholders' equity		2,952
Total liabilities and shareholders' equity		$6,383
Income Statement, 2010		
Total revenues		$9,779
Cost of sales (excluding depreciation and amortization)	$8,165	
Gross margin	1,614	
Other expenses		
Depreciation	278	
Amortization of goodwill and special tools	343	
Selling, general, and administrative expenses	430	
Provision for income taxes	163	
Total costs and expenses		9,379
Net income		$ 400

EXHIBIT 2

Selected Ratios

	2011	2010
Acid-test ratio	0.671	0.556
Current ratio	1.172	1.088
Inventory turnover (times)	10.005	8.400
Days' receivables	39.66	27.17
Gross margin percentage	15.12	16.50
Profit margin percentage	2.831	4.090
Invested capital turnover (times)	2.091	2.355
Debt/equity ratio (percentage)	62.15	40.68
Return on shareholders' equity	?	13.55

Case 13–2

Amerbran Company (B)*

Using the 20x1 financial statements in Amerbran Company (A), Case 11–2, together with the 20x0 income statement shown in Exhibit 1 below, calculate the ratios listed below for 20x0 and 20x1. Use year-end amounts for ratios that involve balance sheet data. The company's

EXHIBIT 1

AMERBRAN COMPANY Income Statement For the Year Ended December 31, 20x0 (in thousands)	
Sales revenue, net	$6,577,480
Cost of sales	2,573,350
Excise taxes on goods sold	2,354,350
Gross margin	1,649,780
Selling, general, and administrative expenses	974,121
Income before income taxes	675,659
Provision for income taxes	296,877
Net income	$378,782

* Copyright © James S. Reece.

interest expense in 20x0 and 20x1 was (in thousands) $105,165 and $102,791, respectively.

1. Return on assets.
2. Return on equity.
3. Gross margin percentage.
4. Return on sales.
5. Asset turnover.
6. Days' cash (20x1 only).
7. Days' receivables.
8. Days' inventories.
9. Inventory turnover.
10. Current ratio.
11. Acid-test ratio.
12. Debt/capitalization ratio.
13. Times interest earned.

Questions

1. Comment on Amerbran's treatment of excise taxes as part of the calculation of gross margin.
2. As an outside analyst, what questions would you want to ask Amerbran's management based on the ratios you have calculated?

Case 13–3

Identify the Industries*

Common-sized balance sheets of 12 firms are presented in the following pages, along with some useful ratios (see Exhibit 1, page 421). These companies were chosen because they consist of primarily one major business segment and the relationships between balance sheet items, profit, and operations are fairly typical of these industries. The companies involved are

- Regional bank
- Temporary office personnel agency
- For-profit hospital chain
- Warehouse club

- Major passenger airline
- Major regional utility company
- Manufacturer of oral, personal, and household care products
- Hotel chain
- Upscale department store chain
- Discount department store chain
- International oil company
- Defense contractor

The financial statement dates are noted at the top of each column. Use the ratios, common-sized statements, and your knowledge of business operations and conditions at the time these data were generated to identify the companies.

Case 13–4

Supplement to Identify the Industries*

Presented in Exhibit 1 (see page 422) are balance sheets, in percentage form, and selected ratios drawn from the balance sheets and operating statements of seven different firms in seven different industries. Recognizing the fact of certain differences between firms in the same industry, each firm whose figures are summarized is broadly typical of those in its industry.

See if you can identify the industry represented. Then, be prepared as best you can to explain the distinctive asset structures and ratios of each industry.

- Basic chemical company
- Maker of name-brand, quality men's apparel
- Meat packer
- Retail jewelry chain (which leased its store properties)
- Coal-carrying railroad
- Automobile manufacturer
- Advertising agency

Case 13–5

Springfield National Bank*

John Dawson Jr., president of Dawson Stores, Inc., had a discussion with Stefanie Anderson, a loan officer at Springfield National Bank. Both Mr. Dawson and

Dawson Stores, Inc., were deposit customers of the bank and had been for several years. Dawson's comments were directly to the point:

It appears that we are going to have some working capital needs during the next year at Dawson

EXHIBIT 1 For Case 13–3

Fiscal Year End	Jun A	Dec B	Dec C	Jan D	Dec E	Jan F	Dec G	Dec H	Dec I	Dec J	Dec K	Sep L
Cash and marketable securities	13.5	2.1	2.1	0.9	32.7	0.2	13.4	3.4	0.2	1.2	17.7	2.1
Receivables	7.9	9.4	7.6	32.7	63.1	2.3	7.2	14.6	6.0	13.4	55.4	2.8
Inventories	—	37.8	6.2	22.9	—	42.6	0.5	10.1	1.6	2.0	—	30.6
Other current assets	5.4	4.3	3.1	2.5	—	1.1	2.4	2.8	1.6	4.5	4.6	1.8
Total current assets	26.8	53.6	19.0	59.0	95.8	46.2	23.5	30.9	9.4	21.1	77.7	37.3
Plant and equipment	55.6	16.1	71.7	40.4	1.8	50.3	55.4	28.2	81.1	49.0	11.7	58.8
Investments	6.0	1.9	6.2	—	—	—	19.4	—	0.7	10.5	—	—
Goodwill	2.2	25.7	—	—	0.3	—	—	35.9	—	17.6	7.7	1.0
Other noncurrent assets	9.4	2.7	3.1	0.6	2.1	3.5	1.7	5.0	8.8	1.8	2.9	2.9
Total noncurrent assets	73.2	46.4	81.0	41.0	4.2	53.8	76.5	69.1	90.6	78.9	22.3	62.7
Total Assets	100.0	100.0	100.0	100.0	100.0	100.0	100.0	100.0	100.0	100.0	100.0	100.0
Accounts payable	12.6	10.6	9.3	10.1	84.7	17.2	10.0	9.7	3.7	4.2	7.4	25.3
Notes payable	—	12.2	1.9	8.5	6.0	6.5	—	2.7	3.5	—	—	1.2
Current portion of L/T debt	0.8	0.1	0.5	2.7	—	0.9	7.1	0.5	2.8	1.2	—	0.2
Unearned revenues	11.6	3.5	—	—	—	—	—	—	—	—	—	—
Other current liabilities	4.8	11.1	8.8	9.1	0.9	5.9	0.4	10.1	5.2	8.4	26.3	9.4
Total current liabilities	29.8	37.5	20.5	30.4	91.6	30.5	17.5	23.0	15.2	13.8	33.7	36.1
L/T debt	17.8	15.1	8.5	13.4	0.5	28.3	35.0	39.2	31.8	35.9	—	25.0
Other noncurrent liabilities	30.5	3.8	26.7	4.1	—	1.9	6.5	15.9	20.0	14.5	—	2.7
Total liabilities	78.1	56.4	55.7	47.9	92.1	60.7	59.0	78.1	67.0	64.2	33.7	63.8
Preferred stock	1.1	—	—	—	—	—	—	5.3	5.9	—	—	—
Common stock	1.8	2.4	3.2	6.2	0.3	0.6	4.2	2.4	1.2	0.0	5.5	0.0
Additional paid-in capital	21.5	2.6	—	—	3.0	1.5	—	13.5	18.8	22.6	1.0	6.6
Retained earnings	(1.0)	38.5	58.6	47.7	4.5	38.3	41.7	31.3	7.1	12.9	60.6	31.1
Adjustments to retained earnings	1.0	0.1	1.5	—	0.1	(1.1)	(0.2)	(11.7)	—	0.3	—	(1.5)
Treasury stock	(2.5)	—	(18.9)	(1.8)	—	—	(4.7)	(18.9)	—	—	(0.8)	—
Total stockholders' equity	21.9	43.6	44.3	52.1	7.9	39.3	41.0	21.9	33.0	35.8	66.3	36.2
Total Liabilities & Stockholders' Equity	100.0	100.0	100.0	100.0	100.0	100.0	100.0	100.0	100.0	100.0	100.0	100.0
Selected Ratios												
Current ratio	0.90	1.43	0.92	1.94	1.05	1.51	1.34	1.34	0.62	1.53	2.31	1.03
Inventory turns (X)	N.M.	2.5	8.9	4.5	N.M.	5.0	N.M.	5.8	2.6	N.M.	N.M.	11.9
Receivables collection period	28	29	27	79	N.M.	3	51	49	49	55	54	3
Net sales/Total assets	1.019	1.191	1.357	1.505	0.066	2.524	0.539	1.094	0.447	0.890	3.741	3.983
Net profits/Net sales	0.053	0.068	0.052	0.040	0.71	0.029	0.105	0.021	0.069	0.060	0.026	0.013
Net profits/Total assets	0.054	0.080	0.071	0.060	0.011	0.073	0.057	0.023	0.031	0.053	0.096	0.051
Net profits/Net worth	0.217	0.185	0.160	0.116	0.144	0.186	0.138	0.102	0.113	0.147	0.145	0.140

Notes: * "Adjustments to retained earnings" consists primarily of foreign translation adjustments. *"N.M." means that the ratio is not meaningful, even if calculable, for this company.

EXHIBIT 1 For Case 13–4

	A	B	C	D	E	F	G
Cash and marketable securities	4.0	7.6	5.1	14.7	4.1	3.2	17.0
Receivables	3.9	8.6	16.4	26.8	21.5	27.6	72.1
Inventories	—	24.9	11.0	23.2	61.0	49.2	—
Other current assets	0.9	3.5	—	1.2	0.2	1.6	0.8
Plant and equipment (net)	78.7	44.6	49.5	33.4	10.9	17.1	7.4
Other assets	12.5ᵃ	10.8ᵇ	18.0ᶜ	0.7	2.3	1.3	2.7
Total assets	100.0	100.0	100.0	100.0	100.0	100.0	100.0
Notes payable	—	—	12.8	—	5.1	2.0	—
Accounts payable	2.9	23.9	5.3	29.3	12.6	10.5	50.3
Accrued taxes	2.6	3.7	1.9	1.4	6.6	3.1	—
Other current liabilities	0.6	4.9	5.7	—	1.2	5.8	2.6
Long-term debt	35.2	3.4	30.4	1.7	5.8	20.6	3.3
Other liabilities	3.8	6.4	—	1.6	1.0	—	1.0
Preferred stock	—	—	—	—	2.2	0.1	—
Capital stock	16.7	6.8	27.8	9.4	31.0	17.4	6.8
Retained earnings	38.2	50.0	16.1	56.6	34.5	40.5	36.0
Total liabilities & stockholders' equity	100.0	100.0	100.0	100.0	100.0	100.0	100.0
Selected Ratios							
Current assets/Current liabilities	1.45	1.38	1.25	2.15	3.41	3.81	1.44
Cash, marketable securities, and receivables current liabilities	0.96	0.50	1.20	1.35	1.62	1.44	1.24
Inventory turnover (X)	—	6.4X	6X	23X	2.1X	3.1X	—
Receivables collection period (days)	20	19	64	18	64	66	42
Total debt/Total assets	0.412	0.356	0.565	0.339	0.313	0.420	0.663
Long-term debt/Capitalization	0.403	0.055	0.425	0.025	0.078	0.262	0.090
Net sales/Total assets	0.32	1.61	0.69	5.40	1.30	1.51	5.33
Net profits/Total assets	0.052	0.059	0.057	0.080	0.085	0.065	0.081
Net profits/Total net worth	0.102	0.105	0.137	0.121	0.124	0.112	0.240
Net profits/Net sales	0.167	0.037	0.083	0.015	0.065	0.043	0.015

Note: Investments in affiliated companies accounted for using the equity method including some nonhomogeneous subsidiaries that under U.S. GAAP should be accounted for on a full consolidation basis.

ᵃ Includes 10.1% of investments in affiliated companies.

ᵇ Includes 9.2% of investments in affiliated companies.

ᶜ Includes 14.4% of investments in affiliated companies.

Stores, Inc. I would like to obtain a $1,000,000 line of credit, on an unsecured basis, to cover these short-term needs. Could you set up the line of credit for a year to be reviewed when next year's statements are available?

I know from my friends that you need information about the company in order to grant this request, so I have brought a copy of the company's statements for the last four years for you. Could you let me know about the line of credit in a few days? We are having a board meeting in two weeks, and I would like to get the appropriate paperwork for you at that time.

In reviewing the reports of previous contacts by bank personnel with Dawson Stores, Inc., Ms. Anderson found the information summarized below:

Dawson Stores, Inc., had been incorporated in 1881. The stock had been widely dispersed upon the death of John Dawson Sr., who had divided his share among his 5 children and 14 grandchildren.

Dawson Stores, Inc., had maintained its deposit accounts with Springfield for many years, even during the years John Dawson Sr. had managed the company. The accounts had varied over the past few years. Average balances of the accounts were $350,000 for the past year. The company had occasionally purchased certificates of deposits for short periods.

Dawson Stores, Inc., had not used bank credit in the last 10 years. A recent Dun& Bradstreet (D&B) report requested by a business development officer reported all trade accounts satisfactory and contained only satisfactory information. The D&B report showed the officers were John as president and his brother Bill as vice president and treasurer. The directors were the officers, their two sisters, and two cousins, the latter four residing in other states. Credit terms included both revolving (30-day) accounts and installment sales.

Dawson Stores, Inc., has operated seven stores for the past six years. All store locations have been modernized frequently. One store location was moved during the past year to a new location two blocks from the previous location.

The call report from the business development officer reported the premises orderly and well located for this chain of small retail soft-goods and hard-goods stores (based upon visits to three of seven locations), all located in the Springfield trade area. The president was happy with his present bank services, but in the opinion of the business development officer there was little possibility for further business.

The audited financial statements left with Ms. Anderson by John Dawson are summarized in Exhibits 1, 2, and 3. Notes accompanying these financial statements gave the following additional information.

ACCOUNTS RECEIVABLE

Retail customer accounts receivable are written off in full when any portion of the unpaid balance is past due 12 months. The allowance for losses arising from un-collectible customer accounts receivable is based on historical bad debt experience and current aging of the accounts.

	2007	2008	2009	2010
Accounts receivable (in thousands):				
Thirty-day accounts	$ 68	$ 75	$ 40	$ 32
Deferred payment accounts	2,606	2,709	3,102	3,595
Other accounts	245	310	348	251
Less: Allowance for losses	(57)	(87)	(112)	(111)
	$2,862	$3,007	$3,378	$3,767

Thirty-day accounts are revolving charge accounts that are billed every 30 days. Deferred payment accounts are accounts requiring monthly principal payments of at least 10 percent of the outstanding balance plus interest at 15 percent. Other accounts are for sales contracts from three to five years from the sales of office properties. The above is an aging schedule of accounts receivable as of January 31, 2010:

EXHIBIT 1

DAWSON STORES, INC. Comparative Balance Sheets As of January 31 (amounts in thousands)				
	2007	**2008**	**2009**	**2010**
Assets				
Current assets:				
Cash	$ 107	$ 141	$ 709	$ 916
Accounts receivable (net)	2,862	3,007	3,378	3,767
Inventories	2,600	2,383	2,821	3,090
Supplies and prepaid expenses	70	100	91	75
Total current assets	5,639	5,631	6,999	7,848
Investments and other assets	287	318	162	201
Property, plant, and equipment (net)	4,917	5,186	5,385	5,707
Total assets	$10,843	$11,135	$12,546	$13,756
Liabilities and Shareholders' Equity				
Current liabilities:				
Accounts payable	$ 1,153	$ 1,166	$ 1,767	$ 2,272
Taxes other than income taxes	379	389	414	418
Accrued liabilities	410	454	676	792
Income taxes, currently payable	221	229	491	480
Deferred income taxes, installment sales	374	401	484	589
Current portion of long-term debt	119	143	181	141
Total current liabilities	2,656	2,782	4,013	4,692
Long-term debt	3,494	3,430	3,136	2,942
Deferred credits	266	292	244	302
Shareholders' equity:				
Capital stock	130	130	130	130
Retained earnings	4,297	4,501	5,023	5,690
Total liabilities and shareholders' equity	$10,843	$11,135	$12,546	$13,756

(in thousands)	30 Days or Less	30 to 60 Days	Over 60 Days
Thirty-day	$28	$3	$1
Deferred payment	3,201	288	106
Other	228	23	–0–

without regard to last-in, first-out principles (amounts in thousands):

2007	2008	2009	2010
$283	$519	$560	$660

INVENTORIES

Substantially all inventories are recorded at cost on the last-in, first-out (LIFO) method. Inventories on January 31 are stated less the following amounts that would have been determined under the retail method

PLANT

Property, plant, and equipment is carried at cost less accumulated depreciation. Depreciation is computed using the straight-line method for financial reporting purposes and accelerated methods for tax purposes.

EXHIBIT 2

DAWSON STORES, INC. Comparative Statements of Income and Retained Earnings For the Years Ending January 31 (amounts in thousands)				
	2007	**2008**	**2009**	**2010**
Revenues	$18,297	$19,558	$21,976	$24,128
Cost of sales	12,816	13,884	15,163	16,527
	5,481	5,674	6,813	7,601
Operating expenses	4,789	5,023	5,422	5,830
Earnings before income taxes	692	651	1,391	1,771
Income taxes:				
Current	246	275	690	813
Deferred	91	48	34	104
	337	323	724	917
Net income	355	328	667	854
Retained earnings, beginning of the year	4,058	4,297	4,501	5,023
Less: Dividends	116	124	145	187
Retained earnings, end of year	$ 4,297	4,501	5,023	$ 5,690
Earnings per share (100,000 shares issued and outstanding)	$ 3.55	$ 3.28	$ 6.67	$ 8.54

	2007	2008	2009	2010
Land	$1,128	$1,285	$ 948	$1,023
Building and improvements	4,643	5,050	5,760	5,969
Fixtures and equipment	1,311	1,426	1,427	1,602
Construction in progress	329	304	266	351
Accumulated depreciation	(2,494)	(2,879)	(3,016)	(3,238)
	$ 4,917	$5,186	$5,385	$5,707

Annual minimum rentals on long-term noncancellable leases are as follows:

2010	$ 245
2011	238
2012	226
2013	222
2014	219
Beyond 2014	1,848

Contingent rentals are based upon a percentage of sales. Most leases require additional payments for real estate taxes, insurance, and other expenses that are included in operating costs in the accompanying statement of income and retained earnings.

INCOME TAXES

Deferred income taxes are provided for income and expenses that are recognized in different accounting periods for financial reporting than for income tax purposes. The temporary differences and the related deferred taxes are as follows:

EXHIBIT 3

DAWSON STORES, INC. Statements of Cash Flows For the Years Ending January 31 (amounts in thousands)				
	2007	2008	2009	2010
Cash flows from operating activities:				
Net income	$355	$328	$ 667	$ 854
Adjustments for differences between net income and cash flows from operating activities:				
Depreciation and amortization expense	329	358	388	424
Equity in loss of joint venture	—	—	37	38
(Increases) Decreases in current assets: Accounts receivable (net)	(379)	(145)	(371)	(389)
Inventories	(28)	217	(438)	(269)
Supplies and prepaid expenses	(7)	(30)	9	16
Increases (decreases) in current liabilities: Accounts payable	89	13	601	505
Accrued liabilities and others	157	54	247	120
Income taxes currently payable	(10)	8	262	(11)
Deferred income taxes	30	27	83	105
Cash provided by operations	536	830	1,485	1,393
Cash flow for investing activities:				
Additions to property, plant, and equipment	(725)	(656)	(416)	(933)
Receipts from disposals of property and equipment	126	138	29	287
Mortgages assumed by purchasers of office properties and prepayment on long-term debt	(103)	(168)	(209)	(102)
Investments	(17)	(27)	—	(46)
Other (net)	64	81	80	29
Cash used for investing activities	(655)	(632)	(516)	(765)
Cash flow for financing activities:				
Proceeds from long-term debt	229	104	97	218
Reductions of long-term debt	(119)	(144)	(353)	(452)
Cash dividends	(116)	(124)	(145)	(187)
Cash used for financing activities	(6)	(164)	(401)	(421)
Increase (decrease) in cash	(125)	34	568	207
Cash at beginning of the year	232	107	141	709
Cash at end of the year	$107	$141	$709	$916

	2007	2008	2009	2010
Excess of tax over book depreciation	$28	$22	$25	$ 5
Deferred income on installment sales	66	23	77	104
Other	(3)	3	(68)	(5)
Total	$91	$48	$34	$104

LONG-TERM DEBT

The long-term debt of Dawson Stores, Inc., is composed of mortgage loans from three savings institutions on the store properties that the company occupies. There is no debt agreement that places restrictions on the company's operations or financing.

Questions

1. Appraise the recent performance and financial position of Dawson Stores, Inc., using selected financial ratios as appropriate.

2. As Stefanie Anderson, would you conclude that the company is a good credit risk?

Case 13–6

Butler Lumber Company*

After a rapid growth in its business during recent years, the Butler Lumber Company in the spring of 2011 anticipated a further substantial increase in sales. Despite good profits, the company had experienced a shortage of cash and had found it necessary to increase its borrowing from the Suburban National Bank to $247,000 in the spring of 2011. The maximum loan that Suburban National would make to any one borrower was $250,000, and Butler had been able to stay within this limit only by relying very heavily on trade credit. In addition, Suburban was now asking that Butler secure the loan with its real property. Mark Butler, sole owner and president of the Butler Lumber Company, was therefore looking elsewhere for a new banking relationship where he would be able to negotiate a larger and unsecured loan.

Butler had recently been introduced by a friend to George Dodge, an officer of a much larger bank, the Northrop National Bank. The two men had tentatively discussed the possibility that the Northrop Bank might extend a line of credit to Butler Lumber up to a maximum amount of $465,000. Butler thought that a loan of this size would more than meet his foreseeable needs, but he was eager for the flexibility that a line of credit of this size would provide. After this discussion, Dodge had arranged for the credit department of the Northrop National Bank to investigate Mark Butler and his company.

The Butler Lumber Company had been founded in 2001 as a partnership by Mark Butler and his brother-in-law, Henry Stark. In 2008 Butler bought out Stark's interest for $105,000 and incorporated the business. Stark had taken a note for $105,000, to be paid off in 2009; to give Butler time to arrange for the financing necessary to make the payment of $105,000 to him.

The major portion of the funds needed for this payment was raised by a loan of $70,000, negotiated in late 2008. This loan was secured by land and buildings, carried an interest rate of 11%, and was repayable in quarterly installments at the rate of $7,000 a year over the next 10 years.

The business was located in a growing suburb of a large city in the Pacific Northwest. The company owned land with access to a railroad siding, and two large storage buildings had been erected on this land. The company's operations were limited to the retail distribution of lumber products in the local area. Typical products included plywood, moldings, and sash and door products. Quantity discounts and credit terms of net 30 days on open account were usually offered to customers.

Sales volume had been built up largely on the basis of successful price competition, made possible by careful control of operating expenses and by quantity purchases of materials at substantial discounts. Much of the moldings and sash and door products, which constituted significant items of sales, were used for re-pair work. About 55% of total sales were made in the six months from April through September. No sales representatives were employed, orders being taken exclusively over the telephone. Annual sales of $1,697,000 in 2008, $2,013,000 in 2009, and $2,694,000 in 2010 yielded after-tax profits of $31,000 in 2008, $34,000 in 2009, and $44,000 in 2010.[1] Operating statements for the years 2008–2010 and for the three months ending March 31, 2011, are given in Exhibit 1.

*Copyright © 1991 President and Fellows of Harvard College. Harvard Business School case 292–013.

[1] Sales in 2006 and 2007 amounted to $728,000 and $1,103,000, respectively; profit data for these years are not comparable with those of 2008 and later years because of the shift from a partnership to a corporate form of organization. As a corporation, Butler was taxed at the rate of 15% on its first $50,000 of income, 25% on the next $25,000 of income, and 34% on all additional income above $75,000.

EXHIBIT 1 **Operating Statements for Years Ending December 31, 2008–2010, and for First Quarter 2011 (thousands of dollars)**

	2008	2009	2010	First Quarter 2011
Net sales	$1,697	$2,013	$2,694	$ 718[a]
Cost of goods sold Beginning inventory	183	239	326	418
Purchases	1,278	1,524	2,042	660
	$1,461	$1,763	$2,368	$1,078
Ending inventory	239	326	418	556
Total cost of goods sold	$1,222	$1,437	$1,950	$ 522
Gross profit	475	576	744	196
Operating expense[b]	425	515	658	175
Interest expense	13	20	33	10
Net income before taxes	$ 37	$ 41	$ 53	$ 11
Provision for income taxes	6	7	9	2
Net income	$ 31	$ 34	$ 44	$ 9

[a] In the first quarter of 2010 sales were $698,000 and net income was $7,000.

[b] Operating expenses include a cash salary for Mr. Butler of $75,000 in 2008, $85,000 in 2009, $95,000 in 2010, and $22,000 in the first quarter of 2011. Mr. Butler also received some of the perquisites commonly taken by owners of privately held businesses.

Mark Butler was an energetic man, 39 years of age, who worked long hours on the job. He was helped by an assistant who, in the words of the investigator of the Northrop National Bank, "has been doing and can do about everything that Butler does in the organization." Other employees numbered 10 in early 2011, 5 of whom worked in the yard and drove trucks and 5 of whom assisted in the office and in sales.

As part of its customary investigation of prospective borrowers, the Northrop National Bank sent inquiries concerning Mark Butler to a number of firms that had business dealings with him. The manager of one of his large suppliers, the Barker Company, wrote in answer:

The conservative operation of his business
appeals to us. He has not wasted his money in
disproportionate plant investment. His operating
expenses are as low as they could possibly be.
He has personal control over every feature of his
business, and he possesses sound judgment and a
willingness to work harder than anyone I have ever
known. This, with a good personality, gives him a
good turnover; and from my personal experience
in watching him work, I know that he keeps close
check on his own credits.

All the other trade letters received by the bank bore out this opinion.

In addition to owning the lumber business, which was his major source of income, Butler held jointly with his wife an equity in their home. The house had cost $72,000 to build in 1989 and was mortgaged for $38,000. He also held a $70,000 life insurance policy, payable to his wife. She owned independently a half interest in a house worth about $55,000. Otherwise, they had no sizeable personal investments.

The bank gave particular attention to the debt position and current ratio of the business. It noted the ready market for the company's products at all times and the fact that sales prospects were favorable. The bank's investigator reported: "Sales are expected to reach $3.6 million in 2011 and may exceed this level if prices of lumber should rise substantially in the near future." On the other hand, it was recognized that continuation of the current general economic downturn might slow down the rate of increase in sales. Butler Lumber's sales, however, were protected to a considerable degree from fluctuations in newhousing construction because of the relatively high proportion of its repair business. Projections beyond 2011 were difficult to make, but the prospects appeared good for a continued growth in the volume of Butler Lumber's business over the foreseeable future.

The bank also noted the rapid increase in Butler Lumber's accounts and notes payable in the recent past, especially in the spring of 2011. The usual terms of purchase in the trade provided for a discount of 2% for payments made within 10 days of the invoice date. Accounts were due in 30 days at the invoice price, but suppliers ordinarily did not object if payments lagged somewhat behind the due date. During the last two years, Butler had taken very few purchase discounts because of the shortage of funds arising from his purchase of Stark's interest in the business and the additional investments in working capital associated with the company's increasing sales volume. Trade credit was seriously extended in the spring of 2011 as Butler strove to hold his bank borrowing within the $250,000 ceiling imposed by the Suburban National Bank. Balance sheets at December 31, 2008–2010 and March 31, 2011, are presented in Exhibit 2.

The tentative discussions between George Dodge and Mark Butler had been about a revolving, secured 90-day note not to exceed $465,000. The specific details of the loan had not been worked out, but Dodge had explained that the agreement would involve the standard covenants applying to such a loan. He cited as illustrative provisions the requirement that restrictions on additional borrowing would be imposed, that net working capital would have to be maintained at an agreed level, that additional investments in fixed assets could be made only with prior approval of the bank, and that limitations would be placed on withdrawals of funds from the business by Butler. Interest would be set on a floating-rate basis at 2 percentage points above the prime rate (the rate paid by the bank's most credit-worthy customers). Dodge indicated that the initial rate to be paid would be about 10.5% under conditions in effect in early 2011. Both men also understood that Butler would sever his relationship with the Suburban National Bank if he entered into a loan agreement with the Northrop National Bank.

EXHIBIT 2 **Balance Sheets at December 31, 2008–2010, and March 31, 2011 (thousands of dollars)**

	2008	2009	2010	First Quarter 2011
Cash	$ 58	$ 48	$ 41	$ 31
Accounts receivable, net	171	222	317	345
Inventory	239	326	418	556
Current assets	$468	$596	$776	$ 932
Property, net	126	140	157	162
Total assets	$594	$736	$933	$1,094
Notes payable, bank	$ —	$146	$233	$ 247
Notes payable, Mr. Stark	105	—	—	—
Notes payable, trade	—	—	—	157
Accounts payable	124	192	256	243
Accrued expenses	24	30	39	36
Long-term debt, current portion	7	7	7	7
Current liabilities	$260	$375	$535	$ 690
Long-term debt	64	57	50	47
Total liabilities	$324	$432	$585	$ 737
Net worth	270	304	348	357
Total liabilities and net worth	$594	$736	$933	$1,094

Questions

1. How well is Butler Lumber doing?
2. What has been the company's financial strategy? Why does Mr. Butler have to borrow so much money to support this seemingly profitable business? Has he been managing his company's cash flow wisely?
3. Do you agree with Mr. Butler's estimate that he will need up to $465,000 in 2011. How much will he need to borrow to finance his expected expansion in sales in 2011 (assume sales volume hits $3.6 million)? To answer these questions, construct pro forma income statements and balance sheets for 2011 and make the following assumptions:
   - Mr. Butler reduces the payables period to 10 days
   - Discounts are recorded as a separate line item on income statements
   - The tax rate is a flat 34%
   - Interest expense in 2011 is based on bank debt of $465,000
   - Bank debt is also used to repay any trade notes payable
4. How much will Mr. Butler need over the next few years if sales grow at 25% per year?
5. Would you recommend that Mr. Butler proceeds with his expansion plans?

Understanding Financial Statements

The first section of this chapter describes certain information contained in corporate annual reports that has not yet been discussed. The next section reviews the criteria and concepts introduced in Chapters 1, 2, and 3, bringing together amplifications and qualifications to the concepts that have been developed in later chapters. Alternative treatments of accounting transactions that are possible within the framework of these concepts are described. Finally, this chapter discusses the meaning of information contained in financial reports, in view of all the above.

Additional Information in Annual Reports

The annual report that a company prepares for the use of shareholders, financial analysts, and other outside parties contains important information in addition to the three primary financial statements. At its option, a company may include information about products, personnel, facilities, environmental protection practices, or any other topic. Often, this information is accompanied with color photographs and diagrams of various kinds.[1] A listed company is *required* to provide certain other types of information, including the auditors' opinion, notes to the financial statements, management's discussion and analysis (a narrative identification and explanation of operating and financial highlights), operating segment information, and certain comparative data for previous years.

Auditors' Opinion

All companies whose securities are listed on an organized stock exchange, most other corporations, and a great many unincorporated businesses have their financial statements and the underlying accounting records examined by independent, outside public accountants called **auditors.** Usually, these are certified public accountants (CPAs) who meet prescribed professional standards and are licensed to practice by the state in which they do business. The auditors' examination relates only to the financial statements, including notes, not to nonfinancial material that may appear in a company's annual report.

---

[1] Increasingly it has become its practice of corporations registered with the SEC to dispense with the traditional annual report and simply send sections of their Form 10-K SEC annual filing to stockholders.

**ILLUSTRATION
14–1**
Auditors' Report

Standard Report

We have audited the accompanying balance sheets of X Company as of December 31, 2010 and 2011, and the related statements of income, retained earnings, and cash flows for each of the three years in the period ended December 31, 2011. These financial statements are the responsibility of the Company's management. Our responsibility is to express an opinion on these financial statements based on our audits.

We conducted our audits in accordance with generally accepting auditing standards. Those standards require that we plan and perform the audit to obtain reasonable assurance about whether the financial statements are free of material misstatement. An audit includes examining, on a test basis, evidence supporting the amounts and disclosures in the financial statements. An audit also includes assessing the accounting principles used and significant estimates made by management, as well as evaluating the overall financial statement presentation. We believe that our audits provide a reasonable basis for our opinion.

In our opinion, such financial statements present fairly, in all material respects, the financial position of X Company as of December 31, 2011, and 2010, and the results of its operations and its cash flows for each of the three years in the period ended December 31, 2011, in conformity with generally accepted accounting principles.

Illustrative Required Paragraph to Report an Inconsistency

As discussed in Note X to the financial statements, the Company changed its method of computing depreciation in 2011.

Illustrative Required Paragraph to Report an Uncertainty

As discussed in Note Y to the financial statements, the Company is a defendant in a lawsuit alleging infringement of certain patent rights and claiming royalties and punitive damages. The ultimate outcome of the litigation cannot presently be determined. Accordingly, no provision for any liability that may result upon adjudication has been made in the accompanying financial statements.

Illustrative Required Paragraph to Report Going-Concern Doubt

The accompanying financial statements have been prepared assuming that the Company will continue as a going concern. As discussed in Note Z to the financial statements, the Company has suffered recurring losses from operations and has a net capital deficiency that raises substantial doubt about the entity's ability to continue as a going concern. Management's plans in regard to these matters are also described in Note Z. The financial statements do not include any adjustments that might result from the outcome of this uncertainty.

The results of the auditors' examination are presented in a report commonly called the **auditors' opinion.** The paragraphs required by the American Institute of Certified Public Accountants (AICPA) for a standard report, and additional paragraphs required under certain circumstances, are shown in Illustration 14–1.[2]

Scope

The first and second paragraphs of the opinion discuss the scope of the auditors' work. Specifically noted is that it is management's responsibility, not the auditors', to prepare the financial statements. The scope section also stresses that the auditors are responsible for deciding what audit procedures are necessary to provide *reasonable assurance* that the financial statements do not include *material misstatements*. Management cannot ask the auditors, for example, to "perform as much of an audit as you can for $100,000."

[2] AICPA, "Reports on Audited Financial Statements," *Statement on Auditing Standards No. 58.*

In making their examination, auditors do not rely primarily on a detailed rechecking of the analysis, journalizing, and posting of each transaction. Rather, they satisfy themselves that the accounting *system* is designed to ensure that the data are processed properly. The auditors (1) make test checks of how well the system is working; (2) verify the existence of assets (for example, they must observe the taking of physical inventory); (3) ask a sample of customers to confirm, or verify, the accuracy of the accounts receivable; (4) check bank balances and investment securities; and (5) make sure that especially important or nonroutine transactions are recorded in conformity with generally accepted accounting principles.

These checks provide reasonable assurance that material errors have not been committed through oversight or carelessness and that there has been no misstatement of financial statements due to fraudulent activity.[3] They do not provide absolute assurance, however; almost any system can be beaten by someone intent on doing so. Although spectacular frauds receive much publicity, they are infrequent relative to the number of companies audited every year.

Opinion

The third paragraph is known as the **opinion paragraph.** The key phrases in this paragraph are *present fairly* and *in conformity with generally accepted accounting principles.*

Fairness   The word *fairly* should be contrasted with the word *accurately.* The auditors do not say that the reported net income is the only, or even the most accurate, number that could have been reported. Rather, they say that of the many alternative accounting principles that could have been used, those actually selected by management do give a fair picture in the circumstances relevant to the particular company. This contrast between fairness and accuracy is further emphasized by the fact that the auditors' report is called an *opinion.* Auditors do not certify the accuracy of the statements; instead, they give their professional opinion that the presentation is fair.

When two or more alternative practices are permitted by GAAP to account for the same transaction, management, not the auditors, decides which one to use. In the opinion letter, the auditors do not state that management has necessarily made the *best* choice among alternative principles but only that the choice made by management was an acceptable one.

Principles   The second phrase means that each of the accounting principles used in preparing the statements is "generally accepted." For many transactions there are several generally accepted alternative treatments, and the auditors' opinion merely states that management has selected one of these. If the Financial Accounting Standards Board (FASB), or one of its predecessor bodies, has issued a pronouncement on a certain point, this constitutes a generally accepted accounting principle. Rule 203 of the AICPA Code of Professional Ethics states that no departures from such pronouncements can be regarded as a generally accepted accounting principle "unless the member can demonstrate that due to unusual circumstances the financial statements would otherwise have been misleading." Such circumstances are exceedingly rare. If they do exist, the report must describe the departure, give the reasons for making it, and show its approximate effect on the reported results. For all practical purposes, generally accepted accounting principles are what the FASB and the Securities and Exchange Commission (SEC) say they are.

[3] AICPA, "Consideration of Fraud in a Financial Statement Audit," *Statement on Auditing Standards No. 99.*

Qualified Opinions

An auditors' report containing only the three paragraphs described above is informally called a **clean opinion.** Other reports are said to be **qualified opinions.** Qualification may occur for any of three reasons: (1) a lack of consistency, (2) existence of a major uncertainty, or (3) doubt as to the entity's ability to continue as a going concern.

Consistency If a company has changed an accounting method from the method used in the preceding year, the auditors' report must point this out in a paragraph following the opinion paragraph. Consistency here does not mean, for example, that the method used to measure plant and equipment is consistent with that used to measure inventory; nor does it mean that the company's practices are consistent with industry practices, or even that the several corporations within a consolidated enterprise have used the same methods. Rather, consistency refers solely to use of the same methods in successive years' financial statements. The details of any inconsistency are spelled out in a note to the financial statements cited in this additional report paragraph. (See Illustration 14–1 for an example.)

Uncertainty Sometimes a major uncertainty (such as a pending lawsuit) may ultimately have a material effect on the company's financial position. Auditors are required to call attention to such uncertainties in an additional report paragraph following the opinion paragraph, without making a prediction of the eventual outcome. The nature of the uncertainty is described in a statement note cited in this extra report paragraph. (An example is given in Illustration 14–1.)

Going-Concern Doubt Auditors *in every audit* evaluate whether there is a substantial doubt about the company's ability to continue as a going concern over the next year. If the auditors conclude that there is substantial doubt, then this must be disclosed in a report paragraph following the opinion paragraph.[4] Again, a statement note cited in this additional report paragraph explains in some detail why the going-concern doubt exists. (See Illustration 14–1 for an example.)

In rare cases, the auditors' opinion may be a **disclaimer;** they report that they are unable to express an opinion. This may happen because limitations were placed on the scope of the audit by management. If the auditors conclude that the financial statements do *not* "present fairly" the situation, they write an **adverse opinion.** This may occur if the company has departed from GAAP or clearly is no longer a going concern. Adverse opinions and disclaimers are extremely serious matters. They usually result in a suspension of trading in a public company's securities.

Notes to Financial Statements

We have discussed three required financial statements: the balance sheet, the income statement, and the statement of cash flows. A fourth type of required information is also important—the notes that accompany and are deemed to be an integral part of the financial statements themselves. The requirements for these **notes to financial statements** are becoming increasingly elaborate and detailed.

One of these notes, usually the first, summarizes the accounting policies the company has followed in preparing the statements. Among other topics, this note usually describes the basis of consolidation (if the statements are consolidated statements),

---

[4] AICPA, "The Auditor's Consideration of an Entity's Ability to Continue as a Going Concern," *Statement on Auditing Standards No. 59.* Formerly, major uncertainties, including doubt as to ability to continue as a going concern, were reported by inserting a phrase beginning "subject to [ultimate resolution of the uncertainty]" in the opinion paragraph, and such opinions were hence called **subject-to opinions.**

depreciation methods, policies with respect to the amortization of intangible assets, inventory methods, and policies regarding the recognition of revenues.

Other notes give details on long-term debt (including the maturity date and interest rate of each bond issue), a description of stock option plans and other management incentive plans, a description of postretirement benefits, and the total rental expense and the minimum amount of rent that must be paid in the future under current lease commitments. Additional detail on the composition of inventories and of depreciable assets is given. A note on income taxes reconciles the company's book tax rate with the federal income tax rate as well as the details of the company's deferred tax asset and liability balances. (Temporary differences in reporting depreciation expense for book and tax purposes are often the major cause of this difference.) Major contingencies must be discussed.

In addition to these notes, the Securities and Exchange Commission requires that the annual report of a public company include a discussion of the company's financial condition and results of operations written by senior management (usually the chief executive officer). Also required is a statement from management accepting responsibility for the financial statements (to counter the incorrect impression that the outside auditors have this responsibility)[5] and for the system of internal controls that is intended to ensure that the numbers are reliable. The chief executive officer and the chief financial officer of a public company also must certify that the company has adequate internal controls and the financial statements are not misleading.

Segment Reporting

Current economic and political forces affect different business activities and countries in different ways. Moreover, typical margins, return on assets, and other financial ratios vary widely among industries. Analysts therefore find it difficult to estimate the effect of these forces and to use typical financial ratios if the financial statements of a multiple-industry company operating in many countries report only the aggregate results.

For this reason, corporations are required to supplement the overall financial statements with additional information about the principal operating segments through which they operate. Operating segments are components of a corporation about which separate financial information is available that is evaluated regularly by the chief operating decision maker in deciding how to allocate resources and in assessing performance. As a result, operating segment disclosures reflect the way a corporation is organized and the data used internally by management. No company is required to report on more than 10 operating segments.

For each operating segment, the company reports (1) revenues from external and intercompany customers; (2) operating profit or loss; (3) interest expense; and (4) identifiable assets, including depreciation expense on these assets. In addition to this report on operating segments, corporations also are required to provide other information, including amounts of sales and long-lived assets in each country where the company has material operations and sales to single customers if these sales constitute a significant fraction of the total.[6]

Full Disclosure

A fundamental accounting principle is that the financial statements and the accompanying notes must contain a **full disclosure** of *material* financial information.

[5] Note that the first paragraph of the auditors' standard report also stresses that the statements are management's responsibility.
[6] "Disclosures about Segments of an Enterprise and Related Information," *FASB Statement No. 131*. "Operating Segments", *IFRS No. 8*.

This includes not only information known as of the balance sheet date but also information that comes to light after the end of the accounting period that may affect the information contained in the financial statements. For example, if in January 2011 one of the company's plants was destroyed by fire, this fact should be disclosed in the company's 2010 annual report, even though the amount of plant on the December 31, 2010, balance sheet was properly reported as of that time.

Disagreement arises as to what constitutes full disclosure. In general, if an item of economic information would cause informed investors to appraise the company differently than would be the case without that item of information, it should be disclosed. Clearly, there is room for differences of opinion as to what such items are, but recent court decisions have taken an increasingly broad view of disclosure requirements.

Comparative Statements

In addition to the financial statements for the current year, the annual report also must contain the previous year's balance sheet and the preceding two years' income and cash flow statements. Many companies also include summaries of important past financial statement items for a period of 5 or 10 years.

The information from prior years that is published in the current annual report is usually the same information as that originally published. The financial statements for prior years must be restated to reflect voluntary changes in accounting principles.[7] Prior to 2006, with a few exceptions, however, prior-year statements were not restated. Instead, when a company made a change in its accounting practices that affected the net income reported in prior periods, the *cumulative* effect of this change on the net income of all prior periods was calculated, and this amount was reported on the *current* year's income statement as a cumulative accounting principle change item.

The accounting for a change in depreciation, amortization or depletion method for long-lived nonmonetary assets is accounted for in a manner similar to a change in estimate: that is, propectively. This treatment is a major exception to the requirement that changes in accounting principles be accounted for retroactively.

If a company believes that estimates that affected the reported net income in prior years were incorrect (such as when subsequent events show that the estimated service life of depreciable assets was too long or too short), it does not go back and correct the financial statements for the prior years. The new estimate is only applied prospectively.

Management's Discussion and Analysis

Annual reports of companies regulated by its Securities and Exchange Commission (SEC) include a section referred to as Management's Discussion and Analysis, which is a discussion by management of their company's operating results, liquidity, solvency, important developments during the periods covered by the primary financial statements, and the possible impact on future financial statements of known trends and events. Also covered is the potential impact of new accounting standards on the company's financial statements.

Securities and Exchange Commission (SEC) Reports

In addition to the annual report to its shareholders, companies under the jurisdiction of the SEC must file an annual report with the SEC. This report is filed on SEC Form 10–K and is therefore known as the **10–K report.** In general, the financial data in this report are consistent with, but in somewhat more detail than, the data in the annual report. Rules governing the preparation of Form 10–K are contained

---

[7] "Accounting Changes and Error Corrections," *FASB Statement No. 154.* "Accounting, Policies, Changes in Accounting Estimates and Errors," *IAS No. 8.*

in various SEC publications. With few exceptions, they are consistent with the standards of the FASB.[8]

The SEC also requires that certain financial data be included in the notice of annual meeting sent to all shareholders. These include the compensation of each top executive; the compensation, stock options, and common stock holdings in the company of officers and directors as a group; a description of proposed changes in incentive compensation plans; and a description of any of the company's financial transactions that involved officers and directors as individuals (such as loans made by a bank whose president was a director of the company).

Interim Statements

Companies under the jurisdiction of the SEC also file quarterly reports on **Form 10–Q.** These interim statements contain a summary of financial statements for the current quarter and for the year to date. Although they are not audited in the strict sense, the auditors go over them to ensure that they appear to be reasonable. If significant events occur at any time, such as a major investment by one company in the stock of another or a decision to dispose of a division, the company must report these events promptly to the SEC on **Form 8–K.** Earnings announcements also must be filed on Form 8–K.

All SEC reports are available electronically and upon request are provided by most companies.[9] Because they often contain more detailed information than the company's annual report and because the data are set forth in a standard format, financial analysts use these reports more than reports published by the company.

Review of Criteria and Concepts

In Chapter 1, we listed three criteria that governed financial accounting concepts and principles; in Chapters 2 and 3, we described 11 basic concepts. It is appropriate here that we reconsider these criteria and concepts with the benefit of the additional material that has been discussed in the intervening chapters.

Criteria

There are three basic accounting criteria:

1. Accounting information should be **relevant.** Accounting reports should provide information that describes as accurately and completely as possible the status of assets, liabilities, and owners' equity, the results of operations, and cash flows.
2. Accounting information should be **objective.** The amounts reported should not be biased, particularly by the subjective judgments of management. (The FASB uses the term *reliable* in the same way we use *objective.*)
3. The reporting of accounting information should be **feasible.** Its value should exceed the cost of collecting and reporting it.

There is an inevitable conflict between the criterion of *relevance* on the one hand and the criteria of *objectivity* and *feasibility* on the other. Accounting concepts and principles reflect a workable compromise between these opposing forces. Failure to appreciate this fact is behind the feeling of many of the uninitiated that "accounting doesn't make sense."

[8] Non-U.S. companies registered with the SEC must file Form 20–F showing a reconciliation between the accounting practices employed by the company and U.S. GAAP.
[9] Instructions on how to obtain these reports from the company's investor relations department are provided in most annual reports as well as on the company's Web site. SEC filings can be obtained by accessing the SEC's Web site (http://www.sec.gov).

Of the many examples of this conflict, perhaps the most clear-cut is that relating to the measurement of property, plant, and equipment. In general, the most relevant rule for stating the amounts of these items—the rule that would provide readers of financial statements with what they really want to know—would be to state these assets at their current fair value, what they are really worth. But such a rule would be neither objective nor feasible in most situations.

Conceptually, the worth of property, plant, and equipment is measured by the present value of the future cash flows they will generate. However, there is no feasible way of making this calculation. In the first place, the subjective opinions of management as to future cash flows and the appropriate discount rate would have to be used. Second, for many assets, such as administrative offices, it is not really meaningful to think of the asset as generating cash flows (at least not *positive* cash flows). Although more feasible, even replacement cost numbers can have a high degree of subjectivity, especially if the asset is a specialized piece of equipment and is not, in fact, likely to be replaced at the end of its service life. Furthermore, an entity is more than the sum of its individual assets, and the financial statements cannot possibly report what the *total* resources, both physical and human, are actually worth.

At the other extreme, the most objective and feasible rules for measuring property, plant, and equipment would be either (1) to state these assets at acquisition cost and report them as an asset at cost until they are disposed of or (2) to write them off the books immediately. In most cases, either rule would be perfectly simple to apply and would involve little, if any, subjective judgment. But with either rule, accounting could not report the depreciation expense that is properly charged to the operations of each accounting period. A net income figure that includes such an estimate of asset cost expiration is much more relevant for most purposes than one that omits depreciation altogether.

Accounting takes a middle ground. Assets are originally booked at cost, which is an objectively determined amount in most cases, and, in the case of nonmonetary assets (with the exception of land), this cost then is systematically charged as an expense in the accounting periods over the useful life of the asset. The annual depreciation charge is an estimate, and several ways of making this estimate are permitted; but the number of accepted alternatives is small, and freedom to tamper with the estimates is further restricted by the concept of consistency.

Concepts

Eleven basic financial accounting concepts were stated in Chapters 2 and 3. Other persons might classify and describe basic concepts somewhat differently than we have.[10] The 11 concepts are repeated below, with amplifications and qualifications given for some of them.

1. Money Measurement

Accounting records only those facts that can be expressed in monetary terms. In the accounts, there are no exceptions to this concept, although nonmonetary information is often provided as supplementary data. Assets are recorded at the number of dollars (or dollar equivalents) paid to acquire them. Although the purchasing power of the monetary unit changes because of inflation, accounting does not reflect these changes in purchasing power. Thus, the monetary unit used in accounting is *not* a unit of constant purchasing power.

---

[10] The FASB has published seven Concepts Statements that together set out the "concepts" that underlie the GAAP governing the preparation and presentation of financial statements for external uses. The IASB has published a "framework" that serves the same purpose.

2. Entity

Accounts are kept for entities, as distinguished from the persons who are associated with those entities. In small businesses, particularly unincorporated ones, some problems arise in distinguishing between transactions affecting the entity and transactions affecting the owners. In parent companies that have subsidiaries, a subsidiary is considered to be part of the consolidated entity if the parent owns more than 50 percent of its common stock. Because governments and other nonprofit organizations may not control subunits by stock ownership, there may be difficulties in defining the entity in many such organizations.

3. Going Concern

Accounting assumes that an entity will continue to operate indefinitely and that it is not about to be liquidated. The going-concern concept does not assume that the entity will exist forever. Rather, it assumes that the entity will continue to operate long enough to use up its long-lived assets and to pay off its long-term liabilities as they mature—that is, for the foreseeable future. This concept explains why accounting ordinarily does not attempt to keep track of the liquidation value or current market value of individual long-lived assets.

There is one important qualification to this statement. If there is strong evidence that the entity will *not* continue in existence, asset amounts are recorded at their estimated liquidation value.

4. Cost

An asset is ordinarily entered in the accounts at the amount paid to acquire it, and this cost rather than current market value is the basis for subsequent accounting for the asset. There are important qualifications to this concept. If the amount paid is obviously less than the fair value of the asset (as in the case of donated assets), the asset is recorded at fair value. There are differences of opinion as to how the cost of products manufactured by a company should be measured, as noted in Chapter 6.

Also, market value does affect the subsequent accounting for certain types of assets. Inventory is reported at the lower of its cost or market value. Nearly all monetary assets are reported at fair value. Certain investments are reported at the book value of the equity of the company whose stock is owned (i.e., the equity method), rather than at cost.

Depreciation, depletion, and amortization are write-offs of an asset's cost as the asset's benefits are consumed by the entity; these write-offs are not intended to reflect changes in market value.

5. Dual Aspect

The total amount of assets equals the total amount of liabilities and owners' equity. There are absolutely no exceptions to this concept. It is important not only because mechanically it lessens the possibility of making errors in recording transactions but also because conceptually it aids in understanding the effect of transactions on an accounting entity. The fact that "for every debit there must be a credit" helps one to remember to take account of both aspects of a transaction.

6. Accounting Period

Accounting measures activities for a specified interval of time, usually one year. Reporting on results at frequent intervals, both to management and to outside parties, is obviously necessary. The need for doing this, however, causes most of the difficult problems in accounting: the problems associated with accrual accounting.

In measuring the net income of an accounting period, the revenues and expenses that properly belong to that period must be measured. These measurements depend in part on estimates of what is going to happen in future periods, which is unknown.

7. Conservatism

Revenues are recognized only when they are reasonably certain, whereas expenses are recognized as soon as they are reasonably possible. The conservatism concept explains why certain assets are recorded at the lower of cost or market value. It is also a reason behind certain FASB decisions, such as the one that most research and development (R&D) costs should be expensed as incurred rather than be capitalized. Although these R&D costs may benefit future periods, it is possible they will not. Also, the conservatism concept suggests that revenues should usually be recognized in the period in which goods were delivered to customers or services were rendered, since at that point it is reasonably certain that the revenues have been earned.

8. Realization

The amount recognized as revenue is the amount that is reasonably certain to be realized, that is, paid by customers. Many problems arise in deciding on both the period in which the revenue for a given transaction should be recognized and the amount of such revenue. The conservatism concept suggests *when* to recognize revenue; the realization concept suggests *how much* to recognize. In unusual circumstances, the amount of revenue recognized may reflect a considerable amount of optimism about future earnings, but the auditors will ordinarily detect and call attention to revenues whose realization is not reasonably certain. Chapter 5 is suggested as a refresher for exceptions and clarifications of this concept.

9. Matching

When a given event affects both revenues and expenses, the effect on each should be recognized in the same accounting period. Costs are reported as expenses in the period when (1) there is a direct association between costs and revenues of the period, (2) costs are associated with activities of the period itself, or (3) costs cannot be associated with revenues of any future period.

This concept explains why bad debt expense is recognized in the period in which the related sales revenues are recorded, rather than later when some customers actually default on their payments. Similarly, the concept is the basis for recognizing future warranty costs as an expense in the period in which the warranted goods are sold, rather than later when the warranty costs are paid.

Differences of opinion about the application of this concept and the realization concept are at the heart of most accounting controversies. We shall elaborate on these in connection with our discussion of the income statement.

10. Consistency

Once an entity has decided on a certain accounting method, it should use the same method for all subsequent events of the same character unless it has a sound reason to change methods. This concept is always adhered to in theory, but the practical problem is to decide when a "sound reason" for a change exists. At the root of some changes in method is the desire to increase the amount of net income reported in the current period. This is definitely not an acceptable reason for making a change. Nevertheless, some companies make a change for this purpose and devise other reasons to justify it.

11. Materiality

Insignificant events may be disregarded, but there must be full disclosure of all import-ant information. This concept is probably the least precise of any. The SEC's definition of materiality is often referred to as the guiding concept. It states that "[t]he omission or misstatement of an item in a financial report is material if, in the light of surrounding circumstances, the magnitude of the item is such that it is probable that the judgment of a reasonable person relying upon the report would have been changed or influenced by the inclusion or correction of the item."[11]

The materiality concept also can be invoked as a reason to depart from the other concepts in the interest of simplicity, when the effect of such a departure is not mate-rial. For example, FASB *Statements* include as the last sentence of every standard: "The provisions of this Statement need not be applied to immaterial items."

Importance of the Concepts

These 11 concepts govern the accounting in all business organizations. Governments and certain nonprofit organizations follow somewhat different accounting practices, which are not consistent with the conservatism, realization, and matching concepts. A discussion of these differences is outside the scope of this book.[12]

The many practices and procedures described in earlier chapters were amplifications and applications of these basic concepts rather than additions to them. As a matter of practice, for example, accumulated depreciation is shown in a separate account rather than being credited directly to the asset account. But the basic idea of depreciation accounting is nevertheless in accordance with the concepts that assets are recorded at cost and costs are matched with revenues.

Any conceivable transaction, provided it is clearly described, can be analyzed in terms of its effect on the assets, liabilities, and owners' equity of the entity in accordance with the basic accounting concepts. For an extremely large fraction of the transactions in a typical business, the analysis is simple: For a cash sale, debit Cash and credit Sales Revenue; for receipts from a credit customer, credit Accounts Receivable and debit Cash.

In a relatively small number of transactions, the analysis is difficult. For example, a number of transactions involve a credit to Cash or Accounts Payable for the purchase of goods or services. The question is whether the offsetting debit is to an asset account or to an expense account. The answer to this question depends on whether the entity has or has not acquired something that has beneficial value beyond the end of the accounting period, which is sometimes a matter of judgment.

Many of these difficult situations require judgment because of inevitable uncer-tainties about the future. How long will the building really be of value to the busi-ness? Is a decline in the market value of inventory only temporary, or should the inventory be written down? There are no unequivocal answers to such questions and hence no way of arriving at a result with which everyone would agree.

Misconceptions about Concepts

Some of the basic concepts are intuitively sensible—for example, the idea that account-ing data are expressed in monetary terms. Certain concepts, however, are rather dif-ferent from the impression that typical laypersons have about accounting information.

---

[11] "Materiality," *SEC Staff Accounting Bulletin No. 99.*
[12] For such a discussion, see "Objectives of Financial Reporting by Nonbusiness Organizations," *FASB Concepts Statement No. 4;* and "Elements of Financial Statements," *FASB Concepts Statement No. 6.*

Undoubtedly, the greatest misconception relates to the cost concept. To those who do not understand accounting, it seems only reasonable that the accountant should report the *value* of all assets—what they are really worth—rather than in the case of nonmonetary assets merely the flow of costs. They find it difficult to believe that the balance sheet is not, even approximately, a statement showing what the entity is worth, especially when they see or hear the owners' equity of an entity referred to as its *net worth.* Even if they eventually recognize that the balance sheet does not report current values for all items, they criticize accounting and accountants for not doing this.

A related misconception results from a failure to appreciate the significance of the going-concern concept. Only after accepting the idea that productive assets are held not for sale but for their future usefulness can there be an appreciation that the fair value of these assets does not have enough significance to warrant using fair value rather than the more objective historical cost data.

The matching concept is also a difficult one to comprehend. When people make a personal expenditure to the grocer, to the service station, and so on, they know that they are that much "out of pocket." They have difficulty understanding the fact that many business expenditures are merely the exchange of one asset for another, with the business getting as much as it gives up. Expenses occur in the time period when costs expire—when they are used up—and this time period is not necessarily the same as the time period in which the expenditure is made.

Those who do understand the basic concepts do not necessarily agree with all of them. The accounting profession is constantly involved in debates over one or another of the currently accepted accounting principles. Since these principles are not laws of nature, they are subject to change and in recent years have been changing with increasing frequency. At the same time, although financial statement *users* may wish that certain principles were different, these users need to know how the statements *were* prepared, not how they *might have been* prepared.

Accounting Alternatives

Notwithstanding the basic concepts and generally accepted accounting principles, there are considerable differences in the way certain transactions may be recorded. These differences result from (1) requirements imposed by regulatory agencies in certain industries, (2) the latitude that exists within GAAP, and (3) judgments and estimates that must be made in applying a given principle.

Regulatory Requirements

Certain groups of companies are required to adhere to accounting principles that are not necessarily consistent with those required by the FASB. Public utilities and insurance companies follow rules prescribed by state regulatory agencies for regulatory purposes. In approving the financial statements of such entities, if the statements are not prepared in accordance with GAAP, the auditors' opinion says the statements are "consistent with practice followed in the industry," or words to that effect. When regulatory requirements differ from GAAP, most organizations prepare two sets of financial statements, one consistent with GAAP and the other consistent with the requirements of the regulatory agency.

Income Tax Principles

Principles governing the calculation of income for federal income tax purposes are basically the same as the principles of financial accounting. However, there are important differences, some of which are described here.

Under certain conditions, taxpayers may elect to disregard the accrual concept and to be taxed on the difference between cash receipts and cash expenditures. Many personal-services businesses do this.

The depletion allowance computed for tax purposes may bear little relation to the depletion principle of financial accounting. Tax accounting depletion may be based on cost or revenues; financial accounting depletion is based exclusively on costs.

In taxation, a distinction is made between ordinary income and capital gains, with different tax rates being applied to the two categories. In financial accounting, the distinction, although present, is not so important, because both ordinary income and capital gains usually enter into the measurement of net income.

The accrual basis of accounting is not completely followed in income tax accounting. For example, in income tax accounting, prepaid rent or subscriptions received by a cash-basis taxpayer are counted as revenue when the cash is received; but these prepayments are a liability, deferred (or unearned) revenue, in financial accounting.

Finally, as already pointed out, although the principles are basically the same, a company usually applies them differently in its tax accounting and its financial accounting. It does this primarily by changing the *timing,* rather than the *amount,* of revenues and expenses. For tax purposes, a company usually reports costs as early as it legitimately can and defers revenue until as late as it legitimately can so as to postpone cash outlays for taxes as long as possible. For financial accounting purposes, by contrast, it tends within the bounds of the matching concept to accelerate the recognition of income.

Latitude in Methods

Earlier chapters have listed some examples of topics on which alternative treatments are permitted within GAAP: Inventory can be recorded at LIFO, at FIFO, or at average cost, or some parts of inventory may be handled one way and some another; inventory cost may or may not include inward transportation, storage costs, handling costs, or cash discounts on purchases. Assets may be depreciated by any systematic and rational method.

In recent years, standards promulgated by the FASB have reduced the amount of latitude permitted. In some cases, such as the treatment of research and development costs, the FASB eliminated all but one alternative (software development costs expected to be recovered from future sales or used internally). In other cases, such as the treatment of certain leases, the FASB has carefully spelled out the circumstances under which each alternative practice must be used.

Basis of Choice

Given this latitude, how does the management of a company decide which one of two or more acceptable methods to use? In the case of companies whose common stock is traded on an exchange, a long-standing belief of many top managers has been that the stock price—and hence the shareholder value—will be maximized by choosing those methods that will maximize short-run reported earnings per share. This argument has been given by some companies in explaining why they have not changed from FIFO inventory accounting to LIFO, even when LIFO would improve their cash flows. (Recall that tax laws require a company to use LIFO for shareholder reporting in order to use it for income tax reporting.) Such companies seem to believe that the stock market values a company's stock by applying a price/earnings ratio to the earnings per share of companies in an industry, without regard to differences in accounting practices among those companies, and that it is therefore in a company's self-interest to report earnings as high as feasible.

In some cases, a company chooses its methods to conform with the methods of other companies in the same industry. In other instances, a company's loan agreements or bond indentures may contain minimum working capital or current ratio covenants, or ceilings on the debt/equity ratio. These may cause a company to retain a method if a change to an alternative would lower current assets or owners' equity, or they may cause the company to change to a method that would raise these items (e.g., a change from LIFO to FIFO).

Also, if the bonus of senior managers is calculated on the basis of reported earnings, then these managers may oppose a change that has the effect of reducing reported earnings. However, the board of directors should adjust the method of calculating the bonus in these circumstances.

On the other hand, a few companies have long believed that they can increase investor confidence and the market value of their stock by using the most "conservative" accounting principles (LIFO, accelerated depreciation, and so on) that tend to *minimize* short-run reported earnings. This "quality of earnings" philosophy assumes that investors are wary of companies that try to magnify their reported earnings by using "liberal" accounting principles. Some companies also may feel that the lower reported earnings, using conservative principles, will temper employee requests for higher wages or avoid media charges of profiteering.

Controversies over Principles

In many cases, an accounting requirement described matter of factly in this text has evolved only after years of controversy; in some instances, the requirement has not quelled the controversy. For example, the usefulness of reporting supplemental inflation-adjusted financial data was mentioned over 75 years ago by some academics. However, not until 1979 did the FASB require supplemental inflation-adjusted disclosures, and then only of large companies.[13] Controversy arose over whether the required constant-dollar amounts were very relevant and whether the replacement cost amounts were sufficiently objective. The FASB dropped the requirement in late 1986, during a period of very low inflation.[14] If at some point in the future annual inflation rates again exceed 10 percent, this controversy will arise again. In this matter, a clear consensus on what is "right" does not exist. In some instances, the business community is unable to reach such a consensus. In others, businesspeople may be in general agreement, but security analysts, accounting academics, or the chief accountant of the SEC may have differing views.

Efficient Markets Hypothesis

Many accounting academics and a few issuers and users of financial statements have been influenced in their views on accounting principles by research studies dealing with the **efficient markets hypothesis (EMH).** According to the EMH, a change in a company's accounting methods has no effect on the price of its stock; shareholders look behind the accounting change and recognize that there has been no actual change in the company's performance. Thus, a change in financial reporting depreciation methods (with the tax method left unchanged) is said to have no impact on the stock price because the price reflects real cash flows (which are unaffected since the method for income tax reporting was not changed) rather than "artificial" accounting numbers.

---

[13] "Financial Reporting and Changing Prices," *FASB Statement No. 33.*
[14] "Financial Reporting and Changing Prices," *FASB Statement No. 89.*

Other academics feel that studies whose results are used to support the EMH are inconclusive. They argue that the inability of the EMH research tools to *detect* an effect on stock prices is not the same as *proving* there has been no effect. Certainly, many nonacademics remain dubious about the EMH point of view. Evidence of this includes the great management uproar over the effect that proposed new accounting standards will have on reported earnings, even when corporate cash flows will not be affected by changing to the proposed method.

Example

The following quotes are taken from a leading business periodical's stories reporting on proposed FASB standards, none of which would have impacted a company's cash flows:

"If the FASB approves the new rule, reported income would be sharply pared, worsening [affected companies'] debt-to-equity ratios and making it tougher for them to borrow more money."

Moreover, why do many companies that could save taxes and thus improve cash flow by changing to LIFO continue to use FIFO? In many instances, management feels that markets are not efficient and that the lower reported earnings will diminish shareholder wealth. Similarly, there is evidence that *FASB 2,* which requires that R&D costs be expensed in the year incurred, has influenced managers not to authorize otherwise worthwhile R&D projects.[15]

In sum, rather than eliminating controversy, EMH research has added a new dimension to the ongoing controversies over accounting principles.

Signaling

A more recent line of academic accounting research is based on the belief that management's accounting choices (particularly those involving accounting changes) have information value to investors. The decisions signal management's view of the company's prospects and underlying economics. This research adds to our understanding about why particular accounting decisions are made. Like EMH research, it adds a new dimension to the ongoing controversy over accounting principles rather than eliminating controversy.

Implications of These Differences

The existence of diversity in accounting practice should not be considered as a reason for criticizing accountants or accounting. A business is a complex organism, and there is no conceivable way of prescribing a uniform set of rules for reducing the significant facts about that organism to a few pages of numbers any more than there is any way of formulating a standard set of rules for biographers. Standard procedures for listing physical characteristics, birth dates, marital status, and certain other information about a person can easily be specified, but these details do not really describe the person completely. The accuracy and usefulness of the picture of a person that emerges from a biography depends on the author's skill and judgment in the collection, analysis, and presentation of information about the subject. So it is with financial statements.

Nor should the existence of diversity lead to frustration on the part of the user. The consistency concept prevents diversity from becoming chaos. Although Company

---

[15] See Jean C. Cooper and Frank H. Selto, "An Experimental Examination of the Effects of SFAS No. 2 on R&D Investment Decisions," *Accounting Organizations and Society* 16, no. 3 (1991), pp. 227–42.

A may follow practices that differ from those of other companies, Company A ordinarily follows the same practices year after year; if it changes, the consistency concept requires that the change be disclosed. Thus, its statements are likely to be comparable with one another from year to year. Also, companies in a given industry tend to use the same methods in order to facilitate intercompany comparisons within the industry.

Inherent Limitations

In addition to the points noted above, it is important to remember that accounting has inherent limitations. The two most important—limitations that no foreseeable improvement in accounting practice can overcome—are that (1) accounting reports are necessarily monetary and (2) they are necessarily influenced by estimates of future events.

Accounting reports are limited to information that can be expressed in monetary terms. Nothing in the accounts explicitly describes the ability of the entity's personnel, the effectiveness of its organization, the impact of outside forces, or other nonmonetary information vital to the complete understanding of an entity.

Some accounting numbers are influenced by future events that cannot conceivably be foreseen, so these numbers are necessarily estimates. The depreciation expense of the current period, for example, depends partly on how long the assets will be used in the future. The real significance of accounts receivable and the related item of sales revenue cannot be assessed until the number of credit customers who will not pay their bills is known. The actual value of inventory depends on what the goods can be sold for in the future. The possible impacts of contingent future events—such as the results of pending litigation, retroactive agreements on wage rates, and redetermination of profits on contracts—are not shown in the financial statements, although if material they should appear in a note to the financial statements.

In accounting, one refers to the *measurement* of income rather than to the *determination* of income. According to the dictionary, to determine is "to fix conclusively and authoritatively," and accounting cannot do this. A measurement, on the other hand, is an approximation according to some agreed-on measuring stick. This is what accounting sets out to do.

Ethical Problems

In dealing with the issues mentioned above, the controller, or other accountant responsible for preparing the financial statements, may face ethical problems. Potential problems involve transactions that fall at different points along a spectrum of legality.

At one extreme, there are transactions that may be illegal under the Foreign Corrupt Practices Act, but that the accountant believes are in the best interests of the shareholders and society in general. For example, bribing a government official is illegal, but in some countries business cannot be readily conducted without greasing palms. It can be argued that deciding not to do business in such a country not only may deny shareholders profit opportunities but also may harm that country's citizens by denying access to worthwhile products or employment opportunities. What should the accountant do when she or he learns of such transactions?

Then there are transactions that management wants recorded in a way that does not "fairly present" the company's performance. For example, booking revenues before goods are delivered (perhaps in order to increase a year-end bonus or to meet a strongly held earnings-per-share expectation of influential security analysts) is clearly contrary to GAAP.

At the other end of the spectrum are management judgments about recording transactions that are neither illegal nor contrary to GAAP but that the accountant nevertheless feels are unsound. An example is reducing the percentage of the bad debt allowance in order to increase reported profit. Another example is the "big bath" phenomenon when a new senior management team writes off substantial amounts of assets (particularly intangibles) in the year it takes over, thereby reducing the amounts that will be charged off in future years and increasing the net income of those years. Such questionable transactions are collectively called *managing earnings*.

In all of these circumstances, ethical principles stated by professional organizations (e.g., the Institute of Management Accountants) require that the accountant take some action. If the matter is important and management is unwilling to change its opinion, then the accountant is required to notify the board of directors and, in some instances, the SEC. There are federal laws in place to protect these whistle-blowers from retribution.

The problem is that the accountant may not believe that the board or the courts will in fact provide this protection. Also, publicly challenging a superior's decision is, at a minimum, unsettling. Moreover, the accountant may fear being informally blacklisted, which makes finding alternative employment much more difficult. No book can state how these ethical problems should be resolved. Each individual needs to be sensitive to these issues so that, to the extent possible, such problems can be avoided and unpleasant personal dilemmas minimized.

Meaning of the Financial Statements

Preceding chapters have discussed in detail the treatment of specific items that are reported on the financial statements. With this discussion as background, we shall now attempt to summarize the meaning of each statement as a whole.

Income Statement

The income statement is the dominant financial statement in the sense that when it comes to a choice between a fair income statement presentation and a fair balance sheet presentation, the decision is usually made in favor of the former. For example, those who advocate the LIFO inventory method do so in the belief that in some circumstances it provides a better measure of income than does FIFO, although they know that it can result in unrealistically low inventory amounts on the balance sheet. Many balance sheet items are simply the offsetting debits or credits for entries that were designed to measure revenues or expenses properly on the income statement. The deferred income tax liability is the most notable example: Although recorded as a liability, it does not represent an obligation comparable with, say, a note payable.

The income statement measures the changes in retained earnings that have occurred for whatever reason during the accounting period, except for the payment of dividends. It does not necessarily reflect only the results of normal operations, since it also includes extraordinary transactions, the effect of accounting changes, the loss or gain on the disposal of assets, and even the loss or gain on the disposal of a major division.

In the majority of companies, the amount of net revenues realized from the sale of goods and services can be measured within fairly close tolerances. Adjustments to gross revenue are necessary to provide for uncollectible accounts, warranty costs, and similar items; but the proper amount of such adjustments often can be estimated within a narrow range. In some companies, such as those that sell on an installment basis or that perform long-term contracts on a fixed-price basis, the amount of net revenue that should be recognized is more difficult to estimate.

Usually, the appropriate amounts of expenses that should be deducted from revenues are more difficult to measure than are the revenue items. Judgments about these matters can have an important influence on net income.

**ILLUSTRATION
14–2**
**Effect on Income
of Alternative Cost
Practices**

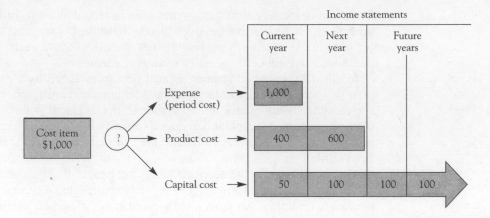

Capitalization

One important source of difficulty is the distinction between capital costs, product costs, and expenses. The effect on current income of expenditures made during the current period depends significantly on how these expenditures are classified. The difference is diagrammed in Illustration 14–2.

Consider the expenditure of $1,000 for labor services. If the labor cost is incurred for selling, general, or administrative activities, it is an expense, and the entire $1,000 affects income of the current period. If the labor cost is incurred in manufacturing a product, it is a product cost, and the $1,000 affects income only in the period in which the product is sold. (The diagram assumes a two-year period with 40 percent of these goods being sold in the current year.) If the labor cost is incurred in building a depreciable asset, it is capitalized as part of the cost of the asset, and it affects net income over a succession of future periods as the asset's cost is depreciated. Latitude exists as to which expenditures are to be capitalized and which are to be expensed. For those items that are capitalized, the amount to be charged as expense in a given period can vary widely, depending on the estimate of service life and the method of depreciation, depletion, or amortization that is used.

Quality of Earnings

The reliability of the income statement as a report of the company's performance differs widely among various types of companies. Analysts make judgments about the impact of these differences and refer to the *quality* of earnings as reported on a given income statement, as contrasted with the reported *amount* of earnings. The net income of a retail store that sells only for cash, has a high inventory turnover, and leases its building and equipment is of high quality because the reported amount is relatively uninfluenced by estimates. By contrast, an income statement is of lower quality if it contains large items that require estimates of future events (such as depreciation expense), significant nonrecurring gains or losses, or changes in accounting principles.

Balance Sheet

The balance sheet can be viewed as a statement of the resources controlled by an entity (assets) and of the sources of the funds used to acquire these resources (liabilities and owners' equity). No single overall characterization fits the individual balance sheet items. Rather, the balance sheet must be viewed as a collection of several types of items, with the amounts for each type being reported according to different concepts and the whole being tied together only in the mechanical sense that the sum of the debit balances equals the sum of the credit balances. The balance sheet is, therefore, literally a "sheet of balances." In terms of the method of measurement used, the principal types of balance sheet items are (1) monetary assets and liabilities, (2) unexpired costs, (3) inventories, (4) investments, and (5) other liabilities and owners' equity.

Monetary Items

These items include cash and other assets that represent a specific monetary claim against some external party, and liabilities that represent a specific monetary obligation to some external party. Accounts receivable are a monetary asset. The amount that each customer owes is definite, and it is usually possible to estimate the amount of uncollectible accounts within fairly close tolerances. Marketable securities are usually considered to be monetary assets. Monetary assets are reported at essentially their current cash equivalent, and monetary liabilities (which include most liabilities) are reported at the current cash equivalent of the obligation.

Unexpired Costs

Property, plant, and equipment; intangible assets; prepaid expenses; and deferred charges are initially recorded at acquisition cost and (except for land) are charged off as expenses in a succession of future accounting periods. Amounts reported on a given balance sheet, therefore, are amounts that have not yet been charged off. The balance sheet is the "temporary home" of these costs until the time comes for them to appear as expenses on an income statement.

Inventories

Inventories are reported at the lower of cost or market value. Except for the recognition of market value when it is below cost, inventories are reported in the same way as other unexpired costs.

Investments

Investments may be in securities owned in order to exercise control over another company. Special rules govern the way they are reported, as described in Chapter 8.

Other Liabilities and Owners' Equity

These include deferred income taxes, which arise as a consequence of the procedure that reflects the fact that most differences between a company's book and tax accounting practices are temporary and will reverse in some future period and which definitely are not a claim by the government against the business. Also, as described in Chapter 9, the precise borderline between liabilities and owners' equity is sometime unclear.

The amount reported in the owners' equity section does not show what the owners' stake in the company is worth, what the owners are entitled to, what can be paid to them as dividends, or what they will receive if the entity is liquidated. Basically, the paid-in capital amount is the amount of funds that the shareholders have "actively" furnished the company as new issues of stock have taken place, and retained earnings are the stockholders' "passive" investment of earnings that the company has not distributed to them as dividends.

Omissions

The balance sheet does not show all the valuable things that a business controls nor all of its obligations. It does not show the value of an entity's human resources, the value of new products or processes that result from research and development activities, or the value of future revenues that will result from current expenditures for advertising and sales promotion. The liabilities side obviously cannot report contingencies that the accountant does not know about, such as the costs involved in recalling a product subsequently found to be defective or the cost of complying with pollution-control regulations promulgated after a plant was built. In extreme cases, these unknowns can bankrupt a company when they come to light.

Statement of Cash Flows

The statement of cash flows is a derived statement in the sense that it is usually prepared from data originally collected for the balance sheet or income statement. It shows the sources of cash that the business obtained during the period and the uses of its cash. These sources and uses are categorized as being related to either operating activities, investing activities, or financing activities. The information on this statement is not affected as the income statement is by judgments about the capitalization of assets and the write-off of expenses. For example, the choices of depreciation method and service life can have a significant effect on net income, but they have no effect on the cash flow statement because the amount of depreciation charged is neither a source nor a use of cash. This is the principal reason that financial analysts like the cash flow statement. It is much more definite and is not influenced by the judgments and estimates that affect the other two financial statements. It does not, however, show how net income was earned. Since net income is the best overall measure of how well the business has performed during the period, a cash flow statement is therefore not a substitute for the income statement. Similarly, being a flow statement, the cash flow statement cannot provide the information on the financial position of the business that is given on the balance sheet, which is a status report.

Accounting Disclosures

Quality of Reporting and Disclosures: Going Beyond the Traditional Stakeholders

With more and more awareness growing in the society, firms are realizing that just reporting decent revenue growth with healthy margins will not be enough to sustain in today's world and that a firm needs to look beyond its traditional stakeholders, viz., shareholders, employees and lenders. The companies are also getting appraised from dimensions other than just financial performance. For example, shareholders are increasingly looking for a more rounded board composition, more voice and representation through independent directors, and a more vigilant and watchful auditors. And with society becoming more informed about their rights, firms can't take the "society at large" for a ride or ignore their concerns. Human right activists and environmental activists also put pressure on firms to behave nicely and responsibly with labour class and with mother earth, respectively. Even employees have started paying attention to issues like what does the firm do about the weaker and marginal sections of the society. They want to be identified with a company which "cares" and is hugely environment conscious. All these developments and many more have put so much pressure on the firm that the firms have started reporting about such issues in the Annual Report in detail. Although it makes the whole document a bit voluminous for shareholders to read, but these qualitative sections related to board structure, concern for the environment, etc. definitely improve the quality of reporting and firms report them as part of "good citizen" behaviour. Over a period of time, these add-ons are becoming unique differentiators between "good company' and "average company". In a nutshell, we can say that the companies are therefore presenting more than one "Report cards" to the shareholders. Financial performance report card is just not enough. We need your Corporate Governance Report Card, Sustainability Report Card and CSR report Card, too.

Corporate Governance Reporting

Corporate Governance is the set of systems, processes and principles through which a company is governed. These processes are actually executed by the Board of Directors (CEO is also a member of the Board) and various other board-level committees with a single most important objective of taking care of and protecting small shareholder's interests. The minority retail shareholders interest in the firm is best protected by the Board members and more particularly by the Independent Directors, who are expected to ask questions on behalf of the retail small shareholders to the management of the firm if they are not happy with a management proposal. Most good firms have half of the Directors in the board as Independent directors (one who doesn't have any financial interest in the firm).

In the Corporate Governance report section, a firm usually talks about the composition and size of the board, details about all the directors including independent directors, their experience, board seat fee being paid, number and detail of other firms where these individuals are directors, details related to the board level committees like Audit committee, Risk Management Committee, attendance records of the directors, their voting position on any resolution moved, etc. Through this section, the firm tries to convey to the markets that the decision-making process at the top in the firm is democratic, transparent and most decisions are taken on merit and not by personal choices or biases. By reading this section, shareholders can make an opinion about the level of corporate governance practice in the firm and can make a good understanding of the quality of top management which guides the future road map of the firm.

Sustainability Reporting

The concept of sustainability rests on the pillars of "Triple Bottom Line" which encompass profits, society and environment. Lord Nicolas Stern (2006) stated that "the cost of tackling climate change upfront is much smaller than confronting the consequences of climate change". Since then the aspect of sustainability from the financial perspective or financial sustainability has been a constant subject of deliberation among large corporates who don't want to be seen as only a profit-seeking firm. Socially responsible financial decision-making involves integrating environmental, social and corporate governance (known as "ESG") criteria, in a systematic and traceable manner (Illustration 14-3). There is a growing debate about what and how business leaders, managers and decision makers can genuinely contribute to a transition to an ecologically sustainable society. While concern for an ecologically sustainable society is not new, much of this debate has come to be dominated by international business, and its associations.

In order to survive and grow in an increasingly competitive and accountable business environment, firms are required to report not only on their financial performance, but also their nonfinancial performance. There is an increased call for transparency and accountability of the private sector in both developed and developing countries. Potential health and environmental risks posed by companies, and the goods and services they produce, are putting responsibility on firms to generate, assess and make information on their sustainability performance and impacts available to markets. Sustainability reporting represents a potential tool to generate data and measure progress and the contribution of companies towards objectives of global sustainable development. See Illustration 14-5, Section of Tata Motors CSR report highlighting their effort to preserve water. It can help companies and organizations measure their performance in all dimensions of sustainable development, set goals, and support the transition towards a low carbon, resource efficient and inclusive green economy. Ignoring sustainability, environmental, health and safety (EHS) and climate change risks and stakeholder concerns around these issues is no longer an option.

ILLUSTRATION 14–3 **Sample Template**

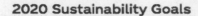

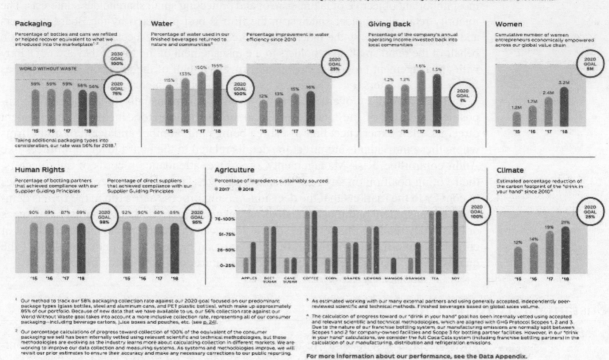

Source: Coca Cola Sustainability Reporting

Corporate Social Responsibility (CSR) Reporting

Any CSR activity, in itself, is a trend that appeals to change of business orientation from short-term to long-term goals and from maximum to optimum profit. A corporate social responsibility report is a periodical (usually annual) report published by firms to report their corporate social responsibility actions and results. It is a document that synthesizes and makes public all the information on the actions implemented by companies regarding their contribution to the principles of social responsibility. These are voluntary comprehensive reports involving not only economic data, but also information from environmental and social field. These reports communicate a firm's policy in respect to the environment, sustainability, and how they are directly focused on fulfilling the commitments made by the firm within the scope of social responsibility. CSR report of a firm provides a systematic approach to understand the management of socially responsible activities, identify future risks and opportunities and to better comprehend the possibility for long-term business venture.

CSR reports are generally used to achieve both internal and/or external goals. Illustration 14-4 Internally, CSR reports are important as they allow companies to estimate the impact of their activities on the environment, on society and on the economy. Through the detailed and meaningful data collected for the CSR report, companies have a chance to improve their internal operations and thereby reduce costs. Not only because they are empowered to optimize and reduce their energy consumption but also as they review their waste cycles and disposal, it will often leads to product innovation or circular economy opportunities. Also, since collecting this data will require collaborative efforts from various departments, employees will end up knowing that the company is focusing on CSR and sustainability, which may increase employee retention and decrease turnover (and its costs).

Externally, CSR and report can help firms to get into better engagement with their interested parties which may bring some benefits to the table. By letting their stakeholders know about the organization's short-, medium- and long-term projects decisions, firms can be better understood which may eventually have positive financial outputs. For instance, it can allow stakeholders to be aware that a specific firm which is contributing immensely to minimize the negative impacts of an environmental hazard or identify a firm which is only focused on growing profits for its managers and investors. Finally, consumers in the markets can decide whether they want to buy from a brand that promotes products made by weaker section of society by sourcing part of their produce to small scale industries run by women groups, investors can track whether their firms are aware of the consequences of climate change and what impact it will further have on their value chains and on business continuity. Similarly, journalists and media can share best case practices, NGOs and social activists can put pressure so that companies review their social security of employees' policy, etc.

Some of the common areas of CSR reporting identified are:

- Environmental Preservation
- Human Rights
- Employee Security
- Community participation
- Promoting better health standards
- Ethical Disclosures
- Social Impact disclosures

ILLUSTRATION 14–4 Sample CSR Report

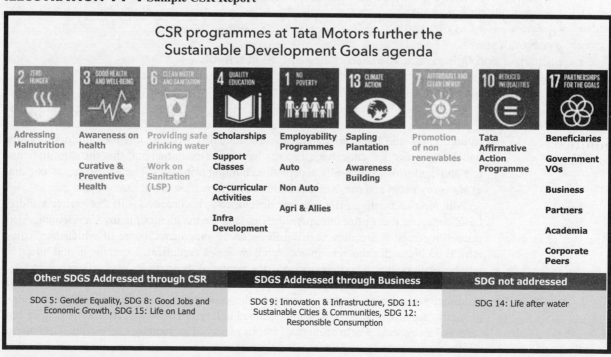

Source: Tata Motors CSR Report 2018

ILLUSTRATION 14–5

AMRUTDHARA

National drinking water programme through Summant Moolgaokar
Development Foundation (SMDF).

Why we do it ?

- 163 Million Indians lack access to safe drinking water (World Bank)
- 210 Million Indians lack access to improved sanitation
- 21% of communicable diseases are linked to unsafe water

Our Strategy

- Ensuring availability, accessibility and absorbability of water in water stressed villages
- Innovate context specific water solutions
- Instilling ownership and sustainability through community contribution

How do we fare ?

- Made water available to 2 lakh citizens spread across 413 villages
- Per capita availability is ~ 30 litres clean water/person/day (as per WHO standards)
- Distance saved to procure water is equivalent to 22 round trips from earth to moon
- Improved enrollment ratio and attendance of girls in schools

Source: Tata Motors CSR Report 2018

Summary

In addition to the financial statements, the annual report contains the auditors' opinion, which states that the underlying records have been examined and that the information is fair and conforms to generally accepted accounting principles. The annual report contains explanatory notes and may contain additional information about the company.

Although accounting principles are developed in accordance with three criteria and 11 basic concepts, these principles permit latitude in the treatment of many transactions. Also, accounting reports are necessarily influenced by judgments, some of which may cause ethical problems for the accountant. A business is a complicated organism, and no set of numbers can convey a completely accurate picture of its activities or its status.

The income statement reports revenues and expenses measured in accordance with accounting principles. It does not report the economic "well-offness" of the business, primarily because most expenses are measured in terms of historical cost rather than current cost. Balance sheet items are reported under a variety of measurement concepts. The balance sheet does not report many items at their actual value, nor are all things of value to the entity reported. The cash flow statement is not affected by estimates and a company's practices with respect to the matching and realization concepts as are the other two financial statements.

Problems

Problem 14–1.

You have been asked to prepare a brief presentation on the nature and purpose of the auditors' opinion for your investment club. The club members would like your presentation to answer these questions:

a. How is the "scope" of an audit determined? What role should the auditors' fee play in setting the scope?

b. How can the auditors examine the financial statements and related records of a company without reconstructing every financial transaction of the period under examination?

c. In the auditors' opinion, the auditors state whether or not the financial statements are presented "fairly." What, if anything, does this opinion of "fairness" have to do with accuracy of the statements?

d. If a company uses an accounting principle that is inconsistent with an FASB pronouncement, what must the auditors disclose?

e. What are the general reasons for issuing a qualified opinion?

How would you answer these questions?

Problem 14–2.

You are the chief financial officer of a small company. At a recent meeting of the directors, an appraisal report was circulated showing the current market value of the company's property, plant, and equipment was $3,500,000. The same assets were listed on the company's balance sheet at $1,750,000. This figure represents historical costs of 5 to 15 years ago less accumulated depreciation. During the meeting, a director addressed the following question to you: "It seems reasonable to value these assets for accounting purposes at the market price set by an independent appraiser; what justification is there for leaving these assets on the books at historical cost?"

Required:

a. Prepare an answer to the director's question.

b. If U.S. GAAP, like IFRS, allowed revaluation, how might you account for the revaluation? What would be the journal entries?

Problem 14–3.

What are some of the exceptions to the historical cost concept that generally accepted accounting principles require or allow?

Problem 14–4.

The income tax note shown in NMBT's 2010 annual report is reproduced below. NMBT is a Connecticut bank with $300 million in assets. Net income of $2,792,000 was reported in 2010 ($2,159,000 in 2009).

> The following table represents a reconciliation of the provision for income taxes as shown in the statements of operations with that which would be computed by applying the statutory federal income tax rate (34%) to income before income taxes:

Reconciliation of the Provision for Income Taxes			
	Years Ended December 31,		
Dollars in thousands	**2010**	**2009**	**2008**
Federal income tax provision at statutory rate	$1,078	$917	$571
Increase (decrease) in income taxes resulting from:			
State income taxes, net of federal tax effect	142	153	168

(continued)

Reconciliation of the Provision for Income Taxes			
	Years Ended December 31,		
Dollars in thousands	**2010**	**2009**	**2008**
Changes in valuation allowances and other deferred tax adjustments	(701)	(640)	(471)
Other	(140)	107	71
Actual provision for income taxes	$ 379	$537	$339
Current income tax expense:			
Federal	$431	$546	$572
State	215	232	238
	646	778	810
Deferred income tax benefit	(267)	(241)	(471)
Total provision for income taxes	$379	$537	$339

The tax effect of temporary differences giving rise to NMBT's deferred tax assets and liabilities at December 31, 2010 and 2009 are as follows:

Dollars in thousands	**2010**	**2009**
Deferred Tax Assets		
Allowance for loan losses	$ 771	$ 867
Deferred compensation	452	410
Capital loss carryforward	105	304
Deferred loan fees	(83)	156
Real estate owned	165	12
Other	(25)	75
Total deferred tax assets	1,385	1,824
Deferred Tax Liabilities		
Depreciation	—	(307)
Securities	(106)	(162)
Total deferred tax liabilities	(106)	(469)
Valuation allowance	(105)	(499)
Net deferred tax assets	$1,174	$ 856

NMBT will only recognize a deferred tax asset when, based on available evidence, realization is more likely than not. A valuation reserve is established for tax benefits available but for which realization is in doubt. In 2010, NMBT reduced the valuation allowance to approximately 6% of the deferred tax asset to recognize the remaining available Federal income tax benefits which NMBT expected to utilize, and other book/tax temporary differences. At December 31, 2010, NMBT recorded a valuation reserve against 100% of the State and Federal capital loss carryforwards which NMBT does not expect to utilize.

Required:

a. Explain the differences between the company's tax and book accounting. (Focus on the general explanation, not the specifics of the bank's accounts)

b. What information does this note contain that is relevant to a potential investor in NMBT's common stock?

c. What role did management judgment play in determining the company's provision for income taxes? (*Note:* The income tax note is one of the more complex and difficult notes to understand. Do not be discouraged if you do not understand all of its content. The purpose behind the problem is to illustrate the role of notes in financial reporting.)

Problem 14–5. Financial accounting statements are limited to information that can be expressed in monetary terms. What are some factors that are vitally important in evaluating the health and prospects of a company that do not appear in these statements?

CASES

Case 14–1

Quick Lunch*

In mid-2002, Mr. and Mrs. Richard Bingham decided to go into the restaurant business. Mr. Bingham was dissatisfied with his job as short-order cook in a small family-owned restaurant where he earned $9.75 an hour. During July 2002, the Binghams found a business that seemed to be what they wanted. This was the Quick Lunch, a lunch counter located in Fisher's Department Store downtown. The Quick Lunch was operated under a lease with the department store; only the equipment was actually the property of the operator of the lunchroom. The equipment was old, but Mr. Bingham thought that it was in fairly good condition.

The couple opened negotiations with the current lunchroom operator and quickly reached an agreement to take over the lease and equipment on September 1, and to pay the operator a price of $10,300. Of this price, Mr. Bingham estimated that $4,600 represented the fair value of the equipment. The lease expired on August 31, 2003, and was renewable for three years if

* Copyright © by the President and Fellows of Harvard College. Harvard Business School case 196-061.

Fisher's consented. Under the terms of the lease, Fisher's furnished space, heat, light, and water, and the operators (i.e., the Binghams) paid Fisher's 15 percent of gross receipts as rent.

The Binghams paid the $10,300 from their personal savings account and also transferred $5,150 to a checking account that they opened in the name of Quick Lunch.

Shortly after they started operations, the cooking range broke down. The Binghams thereupon sold the range for $400 (which was approximately its estimated value as a part of the $4,600) and purchased a new range for $4,000. It was installed immediately, and they paid $600 for its installation.

The coffee urn also broke down, but Mr. Bingham was able to repair it himself by working 16 hours one Sunday.

Early in 2003, the Binghams called in a firm that specialized in making out reports for small businesses and requested financial statements for Quick Lunch for the period ended December 31, 2002. From their cash register and checkbook, they had the following figures:

Cash receipts:	
Cash receipts from customers	$33,165
Sale of cooking range	400
Total cash receipts	$33,565
Cash disbursements:	
Food and supplies	$14,275
City restaurant license, valid September 1, 2002, to August 31, 2003	225

15% rent paid to Fisher's for September, October, and November	3,460
New cooking range	4,000
Installation of cooking range	600
Other operating expenses	90
Withdrawals for personal use	3,800
Total cash disbursements	$26,450

Before going home on December 31, the Binghams had estimated the value of food and supplies then on hand to be about $750 at cost. Early in January, they paid two bills, the December meat bill of $890 and the December rent of $1,515.

The Binghams also explained to the accountant that the cash receipts of $33,165 included $3,850 received from the sale of 140 "coupon books" at $27.50 each. Each book contained coupons with a face value of $30, which could be used to pay for meals. As of December 31, coupons with a face value of $2,700 had been used

to pay for meals; therefore, coupons with a face value of $1,500 were still outstanding.

Questions

1. Prepare a balance sheet as of December 31, 2002, and an income statement and cash flow statement for the four-month period ending December 31, 2002. Explain briefly your treatment of the coupon books and of anything else you believe needs comment.
2. Comment briefly on the significant information revealed by your financial statements.

Case 14–2
Accounting at MacCloud Winery*

Mike MacCloud has worked in the operations side of a winery for several years. Having built a strong knowledge of the art of making wine, he has decided to create his own wine label (i.e., brand). For his label, he planned to grow all of his own grapes. He has identified an ideal plot of five acres of land in Northern California that has most recently been used to grow soybeans. His initial plans are to lease a nearby building to use as a winery (i.e., a place for processing grapes, fermentation, and aging of his wine). However, Mike hopes some day to build his own winery and thus will only plant on four acres of land. Mike has agreed to lease the building for 10 years at $5,000 per year. It is estimated that the building is worth $32,000 and has a 30-year economic life. The lease contract Mike signed did not mention any bargain purchase option or that Mike might assume ownership of the leased building. The interest rate Mike receives on his personal bank account is 5 percent. When Mike started the business, he opened a checking and savings account for MacCloud Wines Inc. that

pays 6 percent annual interest. The annual interest rate the bank charges is 10 percent.

Mike purchased the five acres of land for $250,000. To finance the transaction, Mike borrowed $180,000 from the bank to be repaid $10,000 annually and a lump sum at the end of three years. In addition, Mike bought from Australia, special grapevines at a cost of $10,000 per acre of grapevine. The transportation costs totaled $2,500. Once Mike had in his possession the grapevines, he hired some extra help to plant the vines at a cost of $2,000 per acre.

While vines may produce a limited amount of grapes during the first five growing seasons of being planted (five years), the "young vine" grapes cannot be used for wine (or any other commercial purpose). Although Mike will not use these grapes, he will need to spend $1,000 per acre per year in each of the five years to fertilize and water the vines. If this is not done, the vines will not produce high-quality grapes in the future.

Beginning in the sixth growing season the vines will bear a full crop of high-quality grapes. Some vines continued to produce at this level as long as their 100th growing season. However, generally production

*Copyright © by the President and Fellows of Harvard College. Harvard Business School case 104-023.

begins to decline after the 75th growing season. Once production declines, the land will be replanted with a new set of vines. Interestingly, many experts believe that grapes from "old growth" vines (for the type of vines Mike is planting, a vine is "old growth" after it has been planted 50 or more growing seasons) make a higher quality wine. Once the vines begin to produce high-quality grapes, Mike will need to spend $1,500 per acre per year for fertilizing and water. If he does not provide these nutrients, the grapes produced that year will not be of high enough quality to produce wine. However, this will not affect the ability of the vines to produce high-quality grapes in the future.

Beginning with the first harvest, Mike planned to mature his wine in expensive oak barrels imported from France, which he believed were required for the production of above-average quality wine. Each barrel would be used for a period of up to five years to mature the better-quality wine. Thereafter, the barrel would be used on a one-year-cycle basis to mature the vineyard's lower-quality wines. At the end of 15 years, the barrel would be sold as a raw material to a manufacturer of charcoal chips for outdoor grills. Cheaper locally procured barrels with an average expected useful life of 10 years would be used to mature lower-quality wines. At the end of their useful life these barrels would also be sold to a charcoal chip manufacturer.

Questions

1. Should the leased building be accounted for as an asset? Should the agreement to pay lease rentals be recorded as a liability? Justify your answers. *Do not* refer to any FASB rules on this issue.

2. Record the journal entries to account for the bank loan for all three years. Assume the loan was made at the beginning of year 1 and repaid at the end of year 3. Assume all interest payments are made on an annual basis. The $10,000 per year payment is to reduce the loan's principal.

3. Applying the principles of accrual accounting, how should Mike treat the expenditures for the land, vines, vine planting, fertilizing, and water? Be specific regarding the treatment over time, including amounts, and the rationale for the treatments.

4. Without changing your answers to the above questions, consider the following facts:

   Mike's greatest concern is that his vines will contract Phylloxera disease, "Black Goo" syndrome or Pierce's disease. While these conditions do not kill the vines immediately, they reduce production of quality grapes by approximately 50 percent. Further, the vines generally die approximately 10 years after contracting the condition. While Mike will probably be able to avoid Phylloxera by planting genetically treated vines, incidents of Black Goo and Pierce disease have been increasing over the last several years and are most dangerous to vines that are less than three years old.

   How should the potential for vine disease be reflected in the financial statements if the vines have not been diagnosed with any of the diseases? Does this change if the vines are diagnosed with one of the diseases? Be specific regarding any mounts and the rationale for these treatments.

5. How should Mike account for the oak barrels?

6. How would the transactions in question 3 and the bank loan be recorded in the winery's indirect statement of cash flows.

Case 14–3

PolyMedica Corporation (A)*

On June 30, 2003, PolyMedica Corporation disclosed in its Form 10–K for the year ended March 31, 2003, that the company had been in discussions with the staff of the Securities and Exchange Commission (SEC) regarding its capitalization rather than expensing of direct-response diabetic and respiratory product advertising expenditures. The company was "eager to resolve this issue as quickly as possible."[1]

THE COMPANY

PolyMedica Corporation (ticker symbol PLMD) was a leading provider of direct-to-consumer medical products, conducting business through its Liberty Diabetes,

[1] PolyMedica Corporation Press Release, June 30, 2003.

Liberty Respiratory, and Pharmaceuticals segments. The Liberty Diabetes segment provided direct-to-consumer diabetes-testing supplies and related products primarily to Medicare-eligible customers suffering from diabetes and related chronic diseases. The Liberty Respiratory segment provided direct-to-consumer prescription respiratory medications and supplies primarily to Medicare-eligible customers suffering from chronic obstructive pulmonary disease (COPD). The Pharmaceuticals segment provided prescription oral medications not covered by Medicare directly to consumers and sold prescription urology and suppository products, over-the-counter female urinary discomfort products, and home-medical diagnostic kits.

As of March 31, 2003, PolyMedica had approximately 545,000 active diabetes customers, compared with approximately 440,000 as of March 31, 2002.[2] The company met the needs of customers suffering from diabetes by providing mail-order delivery of supplies directly to its customers' homes, billing Medicare and/or private insurance companies directly for supplies that were reimbursable, providing 24-hour telephone support to customers, and using sophisticated software and advanced order-fulfillment systems to provide products.

As of March 31, 2003, PolyMedica had approximately 63,000 active customers for its prescription respiratory medications and supplies, compared with approximately 46,000 as of March 31, 2002. The customers were serviced in a similar manner to the diabetic product customers.

BUSINESS STRATEGY

PolyMedica's principal strategy was to leverage its operating platform and compliance management to expand its business.

PolyMedica pursued continued growth in its direct-to-consumer businesses by expanding its customer base. Since 1996 the company had invested in an ongoing program of direct-response television advertising to reach a larger portion of the Medicare-eligible patient market. This campaign resulted in a significant increase in sales as the company expanded its active Medicare-eligible diabetes customers from approximately 17,000 in 1996 to approximately 545,000 in 2003.

As a result of the expansion of its customer base and its emerging ability to leverage the value of its customer base by marketing a range of products to its customers, PolyMedica was considering a number of new marketing initiatives. These initiatives included the use of broad-based advertising that might not qualify as direct-response advertising. The company was also considering expanding its customer base by purchasing businesses that provided products to consumers that complemented PolyMedica's existing products.

ACCOUNTING CONTROVERSY

In early 2003, the capitalization method used by PolyMedica to account for its approximately $50 million annual diabetic and respiratory products advertising campaign was questioned by several investors.

At the heart of the debate was the following question: Were direct-response advertising expenditures for diabetic and respiratory products an expense—a cost to be deducted from revenue as incurred? Or were they an asset, something that generated a future benefit for the company? (See Exhibit 1 for PolyMedica's policies regarding advertising expenditures.)

In 1993, the American Institute of Certified Public Accountants (AICPA), in Statement of Position (SOP) 93-7, ruled that most advertising should be treated as an expense and charged against revenue.[3] An exception was direct-response advertising, where it is possible to reasonably match expenses with the sales generated by each advertisement. In this case, the expenditure should be put on the balance sheet as an asset and written off over time. (See Exhibit 2 for a summary of SOP 93-7.)

To qualify for the direct-response exclusion, companies had to show proof that ads generated specific sales. Ads that only yielded leads, for which the company was required to expend additional marketing effort to create a sale, did not qualify for the special treatment. The exclusion was intended to be a narrow opening enabling companies to employ the asset-creation strategy only for specific ads that met a long list of conditions. "The criteria for getting into the box were intended to be tight," said Norman Strauss, the former national director of accounting for Ernst & Young. "The ad campaigns had to be narrowly targeted. You needed to set up systems for tracking responses."[4] Thereafter, to write off the capitalized advertising costs over a period longer than a year, the firm had to demonstrate that each sale generated a continuing stream of revenue.

---

[2] PolyMedica defined a person as an active customer if that person had placed an order and the company had shipped supplies to that person in the past 12 months.

[3] Jeffrey Krasner, "Woburn, Mass.-Based Blood Glucose Test Company Gets New Spokesman," *The Boston Globe,* January 22, 2003.

[4] Jeffrey Krasner, "Woburn, Mass.-Based Blood Glucose Test Company Gets New Spokesman," *The Boston Globe,* January 22, 2003.

EXHIBIT 1 PolyMedica Accounting Policies Regarding Advertising Expenditures

Advertising

Nondirect response advertising, promotional and marketing costs are charged to earnings in the period in which they are incurred.

Direct-Response Advertising

In accordance with Statement of Position 93-7 ("SOP 93-7"), direct-response advertising and associated costs for our diabetes supplies and related products, included in the Liberty Diabetes segment, for all periods presented are capitalized and amortized to selling, general and administrative expenses on an accelerated basis during the first two years of a four-year period. The amortization rate is such that 55 percent of such costs are expensed after two years from the date they are incurred, and the remaining 45 percent is expensed on a straight-line basis over the next two years. Management assesses the realizability of the amounts of direct-response advertising costs reported as assets at each balance sheet date by comparing the carrying amounts of such assets to the probable remaining future net cash flows expected to result directly from such advertising. We expense in the period advertising that does not meet the capitalization requirements of SOP 93-7.

Direct-response advertising and related costs for our respiratory supplies, included in the Liberty Respiratory segment, for all periods presented are capitalized and amortized to selling, general and administrative expenses on a straight-line basis over a two-year period.

In accordance with SOP 93-7, we recorded the following activity related to our direct-response advertising asset for the periods presented (in thousands):

	Fiscal Year Ended		
	March 31, 2003	March 31, 2002	March 31, 2001
Capitalized direct-response advertising	$48,409	$42,478	$31,466
Direct-response advertising amortization	36,460	30,306	19,604
Increase in direct-response advertising asset, net	$11,949	$12,172	$11,862
Beginning direct-response advertising asset, net	52,112	39,940	28,078
Ending direct-response advertising asset, net	$64,061	$52,112	$39,940

Source: PolyMedica Corporation, 10–K Filing with the Securities and Exchange Commission, March 2003.

PolyMedica ran hundreds of commercials directed at potential diabetic and respiratory product customers each year and tracked the results independently by giving each commercial its own toll-free number. "We have over 1,000 800 numbers," said Stephen C. Farrell, PolyMedica's chief financial officer.[5] "One of our challenges is getting good 800 numbers."[6] Thereafter, PolyMedica's business was based on taking the hassle out of buying the test strips, billing Medicare or insurers directly for payment, and filling out the paperwork. For each customer, the firm kept track of the prescription, doctor, and insurance carrier.

Typically, new customers responding to Poly-Medica's ads purchased a three-month supply of glu-cose test strips, worth about $120. When the 90-day supply was close to running out, customer service representatives called the customer's doctor, to ensure the prescription was still active and consistent with the patient's current test regimen, the insurance firm to arrange payment directly to PolyMedica, and the customer to confirm the additional sale in the event he or she had not returned the reorder card included with the first shipment. Some, such as the SEC and short sellers, questioned whether this work constituted significant additional marketing activity that would disqualify the initial ads from the special accounting treatment. At PolyMedica, though, such calls were considered administrative work, according to Farrell.[7] That enabled the company to claim that the initial sale generated the ongoing stream of income and hence to write off the advertising expense over a longer period.

[5] Jeffrey Krasner, "Woburn, Mass.-Based Blood Glucose Test Company Gets New Spokesman," *The Boston Globe*, January 22, 2003.
[6] Ibid.

[7] Ibid.

EXHIBIT 2 Summary of Statement of Position 93-7

The guidance in the SOP is based on the premise that most advertising may result in probable future economic benefits that meet the definition of an asset in FASB Concept Statement No. 6, Elements of Financial Statements. However, the American Institute of Certified Public Accountants' Accounting Standards Executive Committee (AcSEC) concluded that those assets (with the exception of assets resulting from certain direct-response advertising) would not meet the recognition criteria of reliability in FASB Concept Statement No. 5, Recognition and Measurement in Financial Statements of Business Enterprises. Under Concept Statement No. 5, to be reliable, the information must be representationally faithful, verifiable, and neutral. AcSEC concluded that for most advertising, the probable future economic benefits are not measurable with the degree of reliability required to report an asset in the financial statements. The exception is direct-response advertising that may result in probable future economic benefits that are measurable with the degree of reliability required to report an asset in the financial statements. The SOP requires the following.

Generally, the costs of all advertising should be expensed either in the periods in which those costs are incurred or the first time the advertising takes place.

The exception is direct-response advertising a) whose primary purpose is to elicit sales to customers who could be shown to have responded specifically to the advertising and b) that results in probable future economic benefits (future benefits).

The future benefits are probable future revenues the entity would not have without the advertising in excess of the costs to be incurred in realizing those revenues.

Demonstrating that direct-response advertising will result in future benefits requires persuasive evidence that its effects will be similar to the effects of responses to past direct-response advertising that resulted in future benefits.

Showing that a customer responded to direct-response advertising requires documentation linking the advertising to the sale, including a record that can identify the customer and the advertising that elicited the direct response. Such a record may include a file indicating the customer name and related direct-response advertisement; a coded order form, coupon, or response card included with an advertisement indicating the customer name; or a log of customers who have made phone calls to a number appearing in an advertisement.

Industry statistics would not be considered objective evidence that direct response advertising will result in future benefits.

The costs of advertising directed to all prospective customers, not only the portion of the costs attributable to individuals who become customers, should be used to report such assets initially. The costs eligible for capitalization include only incremental direct costs of the direct-response advertising.

The amounts of direct-response advertising reported as assets should be amortized over the estimated period of the benefits, based on the proportion of current period revenue from the advertisement to probable future revenue, subject to a net realizable value test. The realizability of amounts at which the future benefits of direct-response advertising are reported as assets should be evaluated at each reporting date.

Source: Andrew D. Finger, "Reporting on Advertising Costs," *The CPA Journal Online*, May 1994.

When questioned about the accounting treatment of advertising costs, PolyMedica officials said they had no choice but to capitalize direct advertising costs. "Our business is more akin to an insurance or annuity business than a traditional medical supplier. The formula of our business means we have to do it this way," said Samuel L. Shanaman, PolyMedica's CEO.[8] Moreover, Shanaman commented, "Investors who feel uncomfortable with the treatment can calculate an alternate income statement that removes the advertising from the balance sheet and treats it as an ordinary expense. However, given our business model, we believe that our current accounting is proper."[9] In fact, Poly-Medica's external auditors, Pricewaterhouse Coopers LLP, approved of the company's treatment of direct-response advertising expenditures.

As of June 9, 2003, 4.1 million shares of the company's stock had been sold by short sellers, who among other concerns about the company, such as a loss of brokerage research coverage and inquiries by the Department of Justice into the company's sales practices, believed that the company should be required to change its accounting policy for direct-response advertising to one of expensing as incurred.

[8] Ibid.

[9] Ibid.

EXHIBIT 3

POLYMEDICA CORPORATION Consolidated Balance Sheet		
For Period Ended March 31 (in thousands)	**2003**	**2002**
Current assets:		
Cash and cash equivalents	$ 27,162	$ 27,884
Investments	1,442	—
Accounts receivable (net of allowances of $22,556 and $15,539)[a]	61,168	44,059
Inventories	18,850	21,663
Deferred income taxes	13,960	10,622
Prepaid expenses and other current assets	3,438	1,727
Total current assets	$126,020	$105,955
Property, plant, and equipment, net	$ 53,304	$ 34,603
Goodwill	5,946	29,748
Intangible assets, net	108	698
Direct-response advertising, net	64,061	52,112
Other assets	1,530	1,276
Total assets	$250,969	$224,392
Current liabilities:		
Accounts payable	$ 12,576	$ 10,270
Accrued expenses	17,003	17,788
Current portion, capital lease obligations and note payable	2,310	742
Total current liabilities	$ 31,889	$ 28,800
Long-term note payable, capital lease, and other obligations	1,877	1,485
Deferred income taxes	20,528	20,524
Total liabilities	$ 54,294	$ 50,809
Shareholders' equity:		
Preferred stock, $.01 par value; 2,000,000 shares authorized		
Common stock, $.01 par value; 50,000,000 shares authorized; 13,314,982 and 13,300,477 shares issued as of March 31, 2003 and 2002, respectively	133	133
Treasury stock, at cost (1,029,393 and 1,143,158 shares as of March 31, 2003 and 2002, respectively)	(21,067)	(22,185)
Deferred compensation	(54)	—
Additional paid-in capital	119,375	119,891
Retained earnings	98,288	75,744
Total shareholders' equity	$196,675	$173,583
Total liabilities and shareholders' equity	$250,969	$224,392

[a] The majorities of PolyMedica's products provided are reimbursed by Medicare, a federally funded program that provides health insurance coverage for qualified persons age 65 or older and for some disabled persons, and are therefore subject to extensive regulation. Medicare reimbursement payments are sometimes lower than the reimbursement payments of other third-party payers, such as traditional indemnity insurance companies. Current Medicare reimbursement guidelines stipulate, among other things, that quarterly orders of diabetes supplies to existing customers be verified with the customers before shipment and that all doctor's orders for supplies be revalidated every 12 months prior to billing.

PolyMedica accepts assignment of Medicare claims, as well as claims with respect to other third-party payers, on behalf of our customers. It processes claims, accepts payments and assumes the risks of delay or nonpayment. The company also employs the administrative personnel necessary to transmit claims for product reimbursement directly to Medicare and private health insurance carriers. Medicare reimburses at 80% of the government-determined reimbursement prices for reimbursable supplies, and PolyMedica bills the remaining balance to either third-party payers or directly to customers.

The valuation of accounts receivable is based upon the creditworthiness of customers and third-party payers and the company's historical collection experience. Allowances are recorded as a selling, general, and administrative expense for estimated amounts expected to be uncollectible from third-party payers and customers. Estimates are based on historical collection and write-off experience, current trends, credit policy, and on PolyMedica's analysis of accounts receivable by aging category. Changes in judgment regarding these factors could affect the timing and amount of costs recognized.

Source: PolyMedica Corporation, 10–K Filing with the Securities and Exchange Commission, March 2003.

EXHIBIT 3 *(continued)*

POLYMEDICA CORPORATION Consolidated Statements of Income			
For Period Ended March 31 (in thousands)	**2003**	**2002**	**2001**
Net revenues	$ 356,185	$279,661	$220,046
Cost of sales	126,844	97,519	76,973
Gross margin	229,341	182,142	143,073
Selling, general, and administrative expenses	163,768	133,609	97,554
Income from operations	$ 65,573	$ 48,533	$ 45,519
Other income and expenses:			
Investment income	$ 247	$ 1,105	$ 2,867
Interest and other expense	(272)	(180)	(348)
Minority interest	—	(564)	(733)
	$ (25)	$ 361	$ 1,786
Income before income taxes	$ 65,548	$ 48,894	$ 47,305
Income tax provision	25,301	18,483	17,645
Income before cumulative effect of change in accounting principle	$ 40,247	$ 30,411	$ 29,660
Cumulative effect of change in accounting principle, net of taxes of $9,187 and $4,121[a]	($ 14,615)	—	$ (6,926)
Net income	$ 25,632	$ 30,411	$ 22,734
Income per weighted average share before cumulative effect of change in accounting principle:			
Basic	3.29	2.43	2.26
Diluted	3.21	2.38	2.18
Cumulative effect of change in accounting principle:			
Basic	(1.20)	—	(0.53)
Diluted	(1.17)	—	(0.51)
Net income per weighted average share:			
Basic	2.09	2.43	1.73
Diluted	2.04	2.38	1.67
Weighted average shares, basic	12,241	12,506	13,176
Weighted average shares, diluted	12,546	12,780	13,596

[a] During the third quarter of fiscal 2003, PolyMedica implemented Statement of Financial Accounting Standards No. 142, "Goodwill and Other Intangible Assets" ("SFAS No. 142"), retroactive to April 1, 2002. Effective April 1, 2002, the company recorded a goodwill impairment charge of $14.62 million, net of related taxes, or $1.17 per diluted weighted average share, as a cumulative effect of change in accounting principle for the adoption of SFAS No. 142. Net income for the fiscal year ended March 31, 2003 included this charge.

During the fourth quarter of fiscal year 2001, PolyMedica implemented Staff Accounting Bulletin 101 ("SAB 101"), "Revenue Recognition in Financial Statements," retroactive to April 1, 2000. Effective April 1, 2000, the company recorded a cumulative effect of change in accounting principle of $6.93 million, net of related taxes, or $0.51 per diluted weighted average share, for the adoption of SAB 101.

Source: PolyMedica Corporation, 10–K Filing with the Securities and Exchange Commission, March 2003.

EXHIBIT 3 *(concluded)*

POLYMEDICA CORPORATION Consolidated Statements of Cash Flows			
For Period Ended March 31 (in thousands)	**2003**	**2002**	**2001**
Cash flows from operating activities:			
Net income	$ 25,632	$ 30,411	$ 22,734
Adjustments to reconcile net income to net cash flows:			
Impairment of goodwill, net	14,615	—	—
Depreciation and amortization	6,250	5,733	5,214
Amortization of direct-response advertising	36,460	30,306	19,604
Direct-response advertising expenditures	(48,409)	(42,478)	(31,467)
Minority interest	—	564	662
Deferred income taxes	5,853	1,909	(1,533)
Tax benefit from stock options exercised	1,562	620	4,087
Provision for bad debts	25,901	21,000	15,530
Provision for sales allowances/returns	16,775	12,525	11,899
Stock-based compensation	267	—	—
Other	126	32	674
Changes in assets and liabilities:			
Accounts receivable	(59,785)	(45,615)	(19,635)
Inventories	2,813	1,128	(15,209)
Prepaid expenses and other assets	(1,553)	(997)	604
Accounts payable	2,306	(2,848)	(969)
Accrued expenses and other liabilities	636	10,609	2,429
Total adjustments	$ 3,817	$ (7,512)	$ (8,110)
Net cash flows from operating activities	$ 29,449	$ 22,899	$ 14,624
Cash flows from investing activities:			
Purchase of investments	$ (1,442)	$ (5,499)	$(20,300)
Proceeds from the sale of Investments	—	5,499	20,300
Proceeds from sale of certain assets	—	—	1,300
Investment in other assets	—	—	(200)
Purchase of property, plant, and equipment	(22,076)	(15,251)	(8,912)
Proceeds from sale of equipment	1	22	72
Net cash flows from investing activities	$(23,517)	$ (15,229)	$ (7,740)
Cash flows from financing activities:			
Proceeds from issuance of common stock	$ 2,282	$ 532	2,320
Repurchase of common stock	(3,563)	(18,002)	(6,641)
Contributions to deferred compensation plans	(1,384)	(1,125)	(1,768)
Payment of dividends declared on common stock	(3,088)	—	—
Payment of obligations under capital leases and note payable	(901)	(762)	(1,911)
Net cash flows from financing activities	$ (6,654)	$(19,357)	$ (8,000)
Net decrease in cash and cash equivalents	$ (722)	$(11,687)	$ (1,116)
Cash and cash equivalents at beginning of year	27,884	39,571	40,687
Cash and cash equivalents at end of year	$ 27,162	$ 27,884	$ 39,571

Source: PolyMedica Corporation, 10–K Filing with the Securities and Exchange Commission, March 2003.

Questions

1. Explain the difference between an asset and an expense.
2. Explain the role of advertising in the company's customer-acquisition strategy.
3. What are the arguments in favor of capitalizing the direct-response advertising expenditures? What are the arguments in favor of expensing the direct-response advertising expenditures as incurred? As a CEO of PolyMedica, would you favor capitalizing or expensing the direct-response advertising costs?
4. What would be the impact on the company's financial statement if PolyMedica had expensed the costs as incurred in 2003 and 2002? Calculate key balances that highlight any major differences.
5. As a CEO of PolyMedica, how might you respond to this direct-response advertising accounting issue raised by the SEC and short sellers?

Case 14–4

Tokyo AFM*

Prior to joining Tokyo Auto Fire and Marine (hereafter Tokyo AFM), a publicly traded Japanese casualty insurance company, in June 2001, Nobu Matsumoto had held various management positions in the insurance industry for twenty years, in Japan and overseas. He was appointed as Chief Executive Officer of Tokyo AFM after two financial service companies from the USA and Europe each acquired a 20% interest in Tokyo AFM. The intentions of these two new investors were to expand rapidly the operations of the company overseas.

Industry Background

Casualty insurance companies have two principal sources of revenue. The first source is insurance premiums, which are payments that clients (hereafter policyholders)—individual or businesses—make to insurance companies to provide protection against losses resulting from adverse events such as fire or natural catastrophes. Typically, these premiums are paid up front in cash for protection covering - to 5-year periods. The main costs associated with insurance contracts arise from the actual payment of losses subsequently incurred by policyholders and covered by the contracts.[1] Loss-related expenses are mainly divided between direct claim payments and indirect expenses related to processing claims. Typically, insurers also incur costs to acquire customers and set up policies. The main categories of acquisition costs consist of commissions paid to agents and salespeople, administrative policy issuance costs, advertising expenditures and agent recruitment and training.

The second source of revenue for insurance companies is investment income. Insurers invest their "float" in various financial instruments. In simple terms, the float is the amount of cash collected from policyholders and not yet paid out for claims or other expenses. Since casualty, particularly catastrophic, losses can occur at anytime, one of the challenges for insurers is to maintain an adequate level of liquidity in their portfolio so as to be ready to pay claims as they arise.

Brief Company History

Tokyo AFM was established in Tokyo in 1928 as Nippon Insurance Co., Ltd, which specialized in property fire damage insurance. Tokyo AFM gradually widened the range of its products over time to become a more comprehensive property-casualty insurance group. The company was listed on the Tokyo Stock Exchange in 1963. Over the years the company's profits had grown at a slow but steady pace until the casualty insurance industry was deregulated in the late 1990s. Soon after, the financial performance of Tokyo AFM deteriorated.

Despite Tokyo AFM's desire to remain an independent insurer, the industry's deregulation proved challenging. In early 2001, The American Banking Group acquired a 23.04% stake in Tokyo AFM and the German reinsurance group Bayern Re acquired 20.54% of the company's shares.

---

[1] An insurance contract is defined in economic terms by the International Accounting Standard Board (IASB) as "a contract under which one party (the insurer) accepts significant insurance risk from another party (the policyholder) by agreeing to compensate the policyholder if a specified un-certain future event (the insured event) adversely affects the policyholder."

Soon after his appointment as CEO, Matsumoto became concerned that certain Tokyo AFM's financial accounting policies did not reflect the economic reality of the underlying transactions, particularly those related to revenue recognition, contract acquisition costs, reserves for contingent future losses and investments in marketable securities. He has asked you to comment on the company's current accounting practices and to suggest any changes you might recommend along with your reasons. Be sure to identify the alternatives you rejected and the reasons for their rejection.[2] Do not dismiss an alternative or reach a decision on the grounds of "immateriality." If you make any assumptions, please state them.

Financial Accounting Concerns

Matsumoto was concerned about the following Tokyo AFM accounting policies and wanted your recommendation on each:

1. Premium revenue was recognized at the time the policyholder's upfront cash payment was received. The company's accountants argued that since the level of upfront payments received from policy-holders had been stable over the last few years, this method was an appropriate reflection of economic reality.

Example   Fuji Computers entered into a 5-year insurance contract with Tokyo AFM against earthquake damage to its headquarters building. As is customary, it paid the ¥100 million premium for the five-year coverage upfront in cash.

Question   How would you recognize revenues associated with this type of catastrophe insurance contract?

1. Incremental insurance contract acquisition costs related directly to the signing of the contract were expensed immediately. The company's accountants argued that this treatment was required to be consistent with the company's premium revenue recognition policy.

Example   On June 30, 2001, a policyholder paid an upfront ¥210,000 premium for a two-year property insurance contract for her Tokyo apartment. The contract was based on a product called "Home Umbrella."

It covered a variety of casualty losses and was sold by the company exclusively to individual residential customers.

The principal incremental contract acquisition costs were:

a. ¥50,000 commission fee paid to the agent who had worked directly with the policyholder. The fee was due to the agent upon the policyholder signing the contract, and was paid immediately upon signing.

b. ¥20,000 cost of marketing efforts incurred over the past six months to promote "Home Umbrella" through broad-based advertising (50%) and targeted phone calls (50%) to existing Tokyo AFM customers as part of a cross-selling strategy. The policyholder, who had just bought her apartment, was already using Tokyo AFM for her car liability insurance.

Question   Would you capitalize any of the above acquisition costs, or would you expense them immediately? If you were to capitalize the costs, over what period would you amortize them?

2. Broadly speaking, there two major types of insured events that could give rise to losses covered by insurance contracts:

- Events that actuarial analysis could assess and predict with a high level of accuracy across a large number of contracts (for example, events covered by automobile insurance).

- Catastrophes, which were generally adverse natural events such as earthquakes and hurricanes, but which could also be human-induced events such as terrorist attacks. Catastrophes were considered as "low probability high consequence" type of events. They were uncertain and very difficult to predict in terms of timing and extent of damage.

Exhibit 1 shows historical data on losses incurred by Tokyo AFM in automobile insurance and in catastrophe insurance.[3] For the coming year, the company had estimated that expected losses across all its automobile insurance contracts would amount to 70% of premiums. With respect to catastrophes, Matsumoto had come to the conclusion that the average expected losses would be 12% of premiums, but that any scenario between 4% and 20% was equally likely.[4]

---

[2] Please do not worry about the current level of acceptance of International Accounting Standards in Japan.

[3] Policyholders who wished that their property (including automobile) be covered for catastrophes had to purchase separate contracts.

EXHIBIT 1 Historical Loss Ratio[a] for Automobile Insurance and Catastrophe-related Damages for Takyo AFM

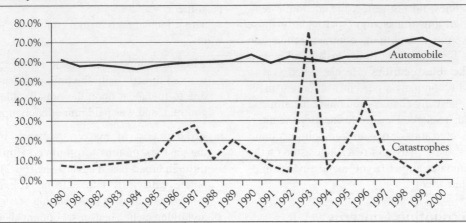

Source: Casewriter.

[a] The loss ratio is equal to total claims settled by insurance companies divided by total premiums collected from policyholders.

EXHIBIT 2 Market Price for Five-Year AAA Prime Credit Bond, Representative of Tokyo AFM's Holdings

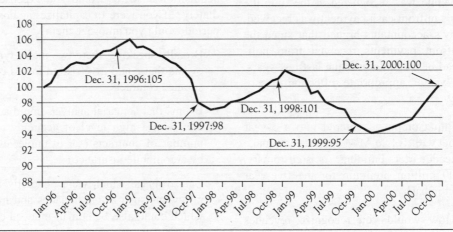

Source: Casewriter.

Question What accounting treatment would you choose for expected losses a) associated with automobile contracts and b) associated with catastrophes? From a shareholder's perspective, what concerns could arise with respect to the accounting treatment of expected losses?

3. Tokyo AFM accounted for its portfolio of investments in marketable securities at historical cost.

[4] Other scenarios were possible. In the event that a major catastrophe triggered losses that would be too large for the private insurance market to cover without going bankrupt, the government was expected to share reimbursement costs above a certain threshold.

The company invested primarily in long term liquid financial instruments (typically five-year bonds). Although a large portion of their portfolio was expected to be held until the bonds matured, the CEO wanted to set aside the remainder as ready to be sold at any point in time. Indeed, adverse events triggering losses could occur any day, and the company needed to maintain a certain level of liquidity to meet immediate cash needs.

Question How would you account for the company's marketable securities? See Exhibit 2 for price data on a ¥100,000-bond representative of Tokyo AFM's investments.

Appendix A
PRESENT VALUE OF $1 RECEIVED N YEARS HENCE

Years Hence	1%	2%	4%	6%	8%	10%	12%	14%	15%	16%	18%	20%	22%	24%	25%	26%	28%	30%	35%	40%	45%	50%
1	0.990	0.980	0.962	0.943	0.926	0.909	0.893	0.877	0.870	0.862	0.847	0.833	0.820	0.806	0.800	0.794	0.781	0.769	0.741	0.714	0.690	0.667
2	0.980	0.961	0.925	0.890	0.857	0.826	0.797	0.769	0.756	0.743	0.718	0.694	0.672	0.650	0.640	0.630	0.610	0.592	0.549	0.510	0.476	0.444
3	0.971	0.942	0.889	0.840	0.794	0.751	0.712	0.675	0.658	0.641	0.609	0.579	0.551	0.524	0.512	0.500	0.477	0.455	0.406	0.364	0.328	0.296
4	0.961	0.924	0.855	0.792	0.735	0.683	0.636	0.592	0.572	0.552	0.516	0.482	0.451	0.423	0.410	0.397	0.373	0.350	0.301	0.260	0.226	0.198
5	0.951	0.906	0.822	0.747	0.681	0.621	0.567	0.519	0.497	0.476	0.437	0.402	0.370	0.341	0.328	0.315	0.291	0.269	0.223	0.186	0.156	0.132
6	0.942	0.888	0.790	0.705	0.630	0.564	0.507	0.456	0.432	0.410	0.370	0.335	0.303	0.275	0.262	0.250	0.227	0.207	0.165	0.133	0.108	0.088
7	0.933	0.871	0.760	0.665	0.583	0.513	0.452	0.400	0.376	0.354	0.314	0.279	0.249	0.222	0.210	0.198	0.178	0.159	0.122	0.095	0.074	0.059
8	0.923	0.853	0.731	0.627	0.540	0.467	0.404	0.351	0.327	0.305	0.266	0.233	0.204	0.179	0.168	0.157	0.139	0.123	0.091	0.068	0.051	0.039
9	0.914	0.837	0.703	0.592	0.500	0.424	0.361	0.308	0.284	0.263	0.225	0.194	0.167	0.144	0.134	0.125	0.108	0.094	0.067	0.048	0.035	0.026
10	0.905	0.820	0.676	0.558	0.463	0.386	0.322	0.270	0.247	0.227	0.191	0.162	0.137	0.116	0.107	0.099	0.085	0.073	0.050	0.035	0.024	0.017
11	0.896	0.804	0.650	0.527	0.429	0.350	0.287	0.237	0.215	0.195	0.162	0.135	0.112	0.094	0.086	0.079	0.066	0.056	0.037	0.025	0.017	0.012
12	0.887	0.788	0.625	0.497	0.397	0.319	0.257	0.208	0.187	0.168	0.137	0.112	0.092	0.076	0.069	0.062	0.052	0.043	0.027	0.018	0.012	0.008
13	0.879	0.773	0.601	0.469	0.368	0.290	0.229	0.182	0.163	0.145	0.116	0.093	0.075	0.061	0.055	0.050	0.040	0.033	0.020	0.013	0.008	0.005
14	0.870	0.758	0.577	0.442	0.340	0.263	0.205	0.160	0.141	0.125	0.099	0.078	0.062	0.049	0.044	0.039	0.032	0.025	0.015	0.009	0.006	0.003
15	0.861	0.743	0.555	0.417	0.315	0.239	0.183	0.140	0.123	0.108	0.084	0.065	0.051	0.040	0.035	0.031	0.025	0.020	0.011	0.006	0.004	0.002
16	0.853	0.728	0.534	0.394	0.292	0.218	0.163	0.123	0.107	0.093	0.071	0.054	0.042	0.032	0.028	0.025	0.019	0.015	0.008	0.005	0.003	0.002
17	0.844	0.714	0.513	0.371	0.270	0.198	0.146	0.108	0.093	0.080	0.060	0.045	0.034	0.026	0.023	0.020	0.015	0.012	0.006	0.003	0.002	0.001
18	0.836	0.700	0.494	0.350	0.250	0.180	0.130	0.095	0.081	0.069	0.051	0.038	0.028	0.021	0.018	0.016	0.012	0.009	0.005	0.002	0.001	0.001
19	0.828	0.686	0.475	0.331	0.232	0.164	0.116	0.083	0.070	0.060	0.043	0.031	0.023	0.017	0.014	0.012	0.009	0.007	0.003	0.002	0.001	
20	0.820	0.673	0.456	0.312	0.215	0.149	0.104	0.073	0.061	0.051	0.037	0.026	0.019	0.014	0.012	0.010	0.007	0.005	0.002	0.001	0.001	
21	0.811	0.660	0.439	0.294	0.199	0.135	0.093	0.064	0.053	0.044	0.031	0.022	0.015	0.011	0.009	0.008	0.006	0.004	0.002	0.001		
22	0.803	0.647	0.422	0.278	0.184	0.123	0.083	0.056	0.046	0.038	0.026	0.018	0.013	0.009	0.007	0.006	0.004	0.003	0.001	0.001		
23	0.795	0.634	0.406	0.262	0.170	0.112	0.074	0.049	0.040	0.033	0.022	0.015	0.010	0.007	0.006	0.005	0.003	0.002	0.001			
24	0.788	0.622	0.390	0.247	0.158	0.102	0.066	0.043	0.035	0.028	0.019	0.013	0.008	0.006	0.005	0.004	0.003	0.002	0.001			
25	0.780	0.610	0.375	0.233	0.146	0.092	0.059	0.038	0.030	0.024	0.016	0.010	0.007	0.005	0.004	0.003	0.002	0.001	0.001			
26	0.772	0.598	0.361	0.220	0.135	0.084	0.053	0.033	0.026	0.021	0.014	0.009	0.006	0.004	0.003	0.002	0.002	0.001				
27	0.764	0.586	0.347	0.207	0.125	0.076	0.047	0.029	0.023	0.018	0.011	0.007	0.005	0.003	0.002	0.002	0.001	0.001				
28	0.757	0.574	0.333	0.196	0.116	0.069	0.042	0.026	0.020	0.016	0.010	0.006	0.004	0.002	0.002	0.001	0.001	0.001				
29	0.749	0.563	0.321	0.185	0.107	0.063	0.037	0.022	0.017	0.014	0.008	0.005	0.003	0.002	0.002	0.001	0.001	0.001				
30	0.742	0.552	0.308	0.174	0.099	0.057	0.033	0.020	0.015	0.012	0.007	0.004	0.003	0.001	0.001	0.001	0.001	0.001				
40	0.672	0.453	0.208	0.097	0.046	0.022	0.011	0.005	0.004	0.003	0.001	0.001										
50	0.608	0.372	0.141	0.054	0.021	0.009	0.003	0.001	0.001	0.001												

Appendix B
PRESENT VALUE OF $1 RECEIVED ANNUALLY FOR N YEARS

Years (N)	1%	2%	4%	6%	8%	10%	12%	14%	15%	16%	18%	20%	22%	24%	25%	26%	28%	30%	35%	40%	45%	50%
1	0.990	0.980	0.962	0.943	0.926	0.909	0.893	0.877	0.870	0.862	0.847	0.833	0.820	0.806	0.800	0.794	0.781	0.769	0.741	0.714	0.690	0.667
2	1.970	1.942	1.886	1.833	1.783	1.736	1.690	1.647	1.626	1.605	1.566	1.528	1.492	1.457	1.440	1.424	1.392	1.361	1.289	1.224	1.165	1.111
3	2.941	2.884	2.775	2.673	2.577	2.487	2.402	2.322	2.283	2.246	2.174	2.106	2.042	1.981	1.952	1.953	1.868	1.816	1.696	1.589	1.493	1.407
4	3.902	3.808	3.630	3.465	3.312	3.170	3.037	2.914	2.855	2.798	2.690	2.589	2.494	2.404	2.362	2.320	2.241	2.166	1.997	1.849	1.720	1.605
5	4.853	4.713	4.452	4.212	3.993	3.791	3.605	3.433	3.352	3.274	3.127	2.991	2.864	2.745	2.689	2.635	2.532	2.436	2.220	2.035	1.876	1.737
6	5.795	5.601	5.242	4.917	4.623	4.355	4.111	3.889	3.784	3.685	3.498	3.326	3.167	3.020	2.951	2.885	2.759	2.643	2.385	2.168	1.983	1.824
7	6.728	6.472	6.002	5.582	5.206	4.868	4.564	4.288	4.160	4.039	3.812	3.605	3.416	3.242	3.161	3.083	2.937	2.802	2.508	2.263	2.057	1.883
8	7.652	7.325	6.733	6.210	5.747	5.335	4.968	4.639	4.487	4.344	4.078	3.837	3.619	3.421	3.329	3.241	3.076	2.925	2.598	2.331	2.108	1.922
9	8.566	8.162	7.435	6.802	6.247	5.759	5.328	4.946	4.772	4.607	4.303	4.031	3.786	3.566	3.463	3.366	3.184	3.019	2.665	2.379	2.144	1.948
10	9.471	8.983	8.111	7.360	6.710	6.145	5.650	5.216	5.019	4.833	4.494	4.192	3.923	3.682	3.571	3.465	3.269	3.092	2.715	2.414	2.168	1.965
11	10.368	9.787	8.760	7.887	7.139	6.495	5.937	5.453	5.234	5.029	4.656	4.327	4.035	3.776	3.656	3.544	3.335	3.147	2.752	2.438	2.185	1.977
12	11.255	10.575	9.385	8.384	7.536	6.814	6.194	5.660	5.421	5.197	4.793	4.439	4.127	3.851	3.725	3.606	3.387	3.190	2.779	2.456	2.196	1.985
13	12.134	11.343	9.986	8.853	7.904	7.103	6.424	5.842	5.583	5.342	4.910	4.533	4.203	3.912	3.780	3.656	3.427	3.223	2.799	2.468	2.204	1.990
14	13.004	12.106	10.563	9.295	8.244	7.367	6.628	6.002	5.724	5.468	5.008	4.611	4.265	3.962	3.824	3.695	3.459	3.249	2.814	2.477	2.210	1.993
15	13.865	12.849	11.118	9.712	8.559	7.606	6.811	6.142	5.847	5.575	5.092	4.675	4.315	4.001	3.859	3.726	3.483	3.268	2.825	2.484	2.214	1.995
16	14.718	13.578	11.652	10.106	8.851	7.824	6.974	6.265	5.954	5.669	5.162	4.730	4.357	4.033	3.887	3.751	3.503	3.283	2.834	2.489	2.216	1.997
17	15.562	14.292	12.166	10.477	9.122	8.022	7.120	6.373	6.047	5.749	5.222	4.775	4.391	4.059	3.910	3.771	3.518	3.295	2.840	2.492	2.218	1.998
18	16.398	14.992	12.659	10.828	9.372	8.201	7.250	6.467	6.128	5.818	5.273	4.812	4.419	4.080	3.928	3.786	3.529	3.304	2.844	2.494	2.219	1.999
19	17.226	15.678	13.134	11.158	9.604	8.365	7.366	6.550	6.198	5.877	5.316	4.844	4.442	4.097	3.942	3.799	3.539	3.311	2.848	2.496	2.220	1.999
20	18.046	16.351	13.590	11.470	9.818	8.514	7.469	6.623	6.259	5.929	5.353	4.870	4.460	4.110	3.954	3.808	3.546	3.316	2.850	2.497	2.221	1.999
21	18.857	17.011	14.029	11.764	10.017	8.649	7.562	6.687	6.312	5.973	5.384	4.891	4.476	4.121	3.963	3.816	3.551	3.320	2.852	2.498	2.221	2.000
22	19.660	17.658	14.451	12.042	10.201	8.772	7.645	6.743	6.359	6.011	5.410	4.909	4.488	4.130	3.970	3.822	3.556	3.323	2.853	2.498	2.222	2.000
23	20.456	18.292	14.857	12.303	10.371	8.883	7.718	6.792	6.399	6.044	5.432	4.925	4.499	4.137	3.976	3.827	3.559	3.325	2.854	2.499	2.222	2.000
24	21.243	18.914	15.247	12.550	10.529	8.985	7.784	6.835	6.434	6.073	5.451	4.937	4.507	4.143	3.981	3.831	3.562	3.327	2.855	2.499	2.222	2.000
25	22.023	19.523	15.622	12.783	10.675	9.077	7.843	6.873	6.464	6.097	5.467	4.948	4.514	4.147	3.985	3.834	3.564	3.329	2.856	2.499	2.222	2.000
26	22.795	20.121	15.983	13.003	10.810	9.161	7.896	6.906	6.491	6.118	5.480	4.956	4.520	4.151	3.988	3.837	3.566	3.330	2.856	2.500	2.222	2.000
27	23.560	20.707	16.330	13.211	10.935	9.237	7.943	6.935	6.514	6.136	5.492	4.964	4.524	4.154	3.990	3.839	3.567	3.331	2.856	2.500	2.222	2.000
28	24.316	21.281	16.663	13.406	11.051	9.307	7.984	6.961	6.534	6.152	5.502	4.970	4.528	4.157	3.992	3.840	3.568	3.331	2.857	2.500	2.222	2.000
29	25.066	21.844	16.984	13.591	11.158	9.370	8.022	6.983	6.551	6.166	5.510	4.975	4.531	4.159	3.994	3.841	3.569	3.332	2.857	2.500	2.222	2.000
30	25.808	22.396	17.292	13.765	11.258	9.427	8.055	7.003	6.566	6.177	5.517	4.979	4.534	4.160	3.995	3.842	3.569	3.332	2.857	2.500	2.222	2.000
40	32.835	27.355	19.793	15.046	11.925	9.779	8.244	7.105	6.642	6.234	5.548	4.997	4.544	4.166	3.999	3.846	3.571	3.333	2.857	2.500	2.222	2.000
50	39.196	31.424	21.482	15.762	12.234	9.915	8.304	7.133	6.661	6.246	5.554	4.999	4.545	4.167	4.000	3.846	3.571	3.333	2.857	2.500	2.222	2.000

Author Index

Page numbers followed by n refer to notes.

Case Index

Subject Index

Page numbers followed by n refer to notes.